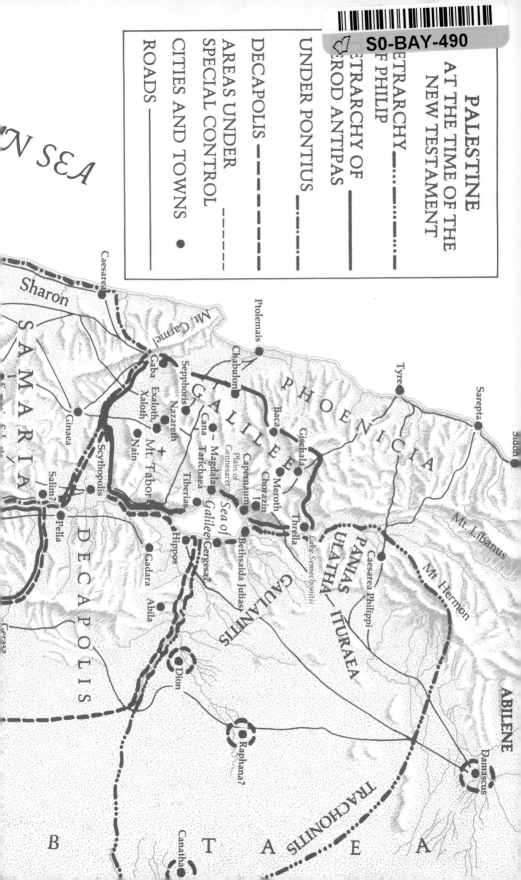

PALESTINE
AT THE TIME OF THE NEW TESTAMENT

ROADS ————
CITIES AND TOWNS •
AREAS UNDER
SPECIAL CONTROL ————
DECAPOLIS ————
UNDER PONTIUS ————
TETRARCHY OF
HEROD ANTIPAS ————
TETRARCHY
OF PHILIP ————

S0-BAY-490

MEDITERRANEAN SEA

Sharon
Caesarea
Mt. Carmel
Ptolemais
Tyre
Sarepta
Sidon

SAMARIA
Ginaea
Gaba
Exaloth
Xaloth
Sepphoris
Chabulon
Baca
Gischala
Meroth
PHOENICIA

Nazareth
Mt. Tabor
Nain
Cana
Magdala
Taricheae
Capernaum
Plain of
Gennesaret
Chorazin
Thrella
Lake Semechonitis
PANIAS
ULATHA
ITURAEA
Mt. Libanus
Mt. Hermon

Salim?
Scythopolis
Pella
Tiberias
Hippos
Sea of
Galilee
Bethsaida Julias
Gergesa?
Caesarea Philippi
GAULANITIS

DECAPOLIS
Gadara
Abila
ABILENE

Dion
Raphana?
Damascus

TRACHONITIS

Canatha

B   T   A   E   A

ANATOMY OF THE NEW TESTAMENT

ANATOMY
of the NEW
TESTAMENT
A Guide to Its
Structure and Meaning

THIRD EDITION

ROBERT A. SPIVEY
Randolph-Macon Woman's College

D. MOODY SMITH
The Divinity School, Duke University

Macmillan Publishing Co., Inc.
NEW YORK
Collier Macmillan Publishers
LONDON

Copyright © 1982, Macmillan Publishing Co., Inc.

Printed in the United States of America

Earlier editions, copyright © 1969 and 1974 by Macmillan Publishing Co., Inc.

Macmillan Publishing Co., Inc.
866 Third Avenue, New York, New York 10022

Collier Macmillan Canada, Ltd.

Library of Congress Cataloging in Publication Data

Spivey, Robert A., 1931–
   Anatomy of the New Testament.
   Bibliography: p. 510
   Includes indexes.
   1. Bible. N.T.—Introductions. I. Smith,
D. Moody (Dwight Moody). II. Title.
BS2330.2.S65 1982   225.6'1   81-11730
ISBN 0-02-415300-1   AACR2

Printing: 345678   Year: 23456789

ISBN   0-02-415300-1

To Martha and Jane

PREFACE

The third edition provides us with another opportunity to bring *Anatomy* up to date and otherwise improve it in light of criticisms and advice we have received from many colleagues who have used it in diverse academic situations. The basic plan and purpose remain the same, the reception accorded the earlier editions having confirmed a need for this sort of introduction to the New Testament. Nevertheless, some substantial changes have been made.

The book now begins with a brief prologue in which we make some statements about New Testament study and the purpose and nature of this book which we hope will be kept in mind as it is used. Chapter 1, the introduction, has been shortened considerably to focus at the outset only on the world of the New Testament, that is, the Jewish and Greco-Roman background. A summary account of the rise of early Christianity and the forces that led to the writing and selection of the books which make up the New Testament has been moved from the introductory section to a concluding chapter, where it has been augmented and lengthened. This material will be more intelligible to the student after study of the New Testament writings themselves. We have returned to a two-part organization of the book as a whole under the conviction that the major division of the New Testament is between the Gospels (focusing upon Jesus) and other writings (focusing upon the church). A major change, in line with this division, is the treatment of the Fourth Gospel (Chapter 5) alongside the Synoptic Gospels (Chapters 2, 3, 4) and before the historical reconstruction of Jesus (Chapter 6). In the previous two editions the Gospel of John was studied in a concluding chapter as reflective of the developing church. It is that, but the other Gospels are no less so. (The instructor who still wishes to reserve the treatment of the Fourth Gospel to the end with the Johannine Epistles and Revelation may do so with little or no disruption.) Summary sections now conclude Chapters 8 (Paul) and 10 (post-Pauline writings) as aids to the reader's comprehension. In the text, footnotes, and especially the bibliographical sections, we have taken account of significant works published since the last edition; more-

over, we have sought to keep footnotes to a minimum. Readers will
welcome the expansion of artwork as a helpful way of illustrating
the continuing delight and difficulty of interpretation. Finally, to aid
comprehension, we have tried to eliminate sexist language.

In study of the New Testament we have found that students
appreciate the two end maps of Palestine and the Mediterranean (see
the inside covers), the chronological chart (see p. xix), the indexes
of names and subjects and of biblical passages (see pp. 517–540), and
especially the Glossary (see pp. 500–509). Initial familiarity with and
frequent recourse to these aids to comprehension should make easier the task of understanding the New Testament.

We again wish to acknowledge the source *New Testament Illustrations: The Cambridge Bible Commentary on the New English Bible,* edited by Clifford M. Jones (New York: Cambridge University
Press, 1966), for the adaptation of the following figures: "Time
Chart of the New Testament," "Diagram of the Synoptic Problem,"
"Map of Galilee," "Diagram of the Temple," and "Diagram of Jerusalem." Adaptation of the "Diagram of the Formation of the Gospels" is courtesy of *Jesus in the Church's Gospels: Modern Scholarship and the Earliest Sources,* by John Reumann (Philadelphia:
Fortress, 1968). Adaptation of the end map of the Mediterranean
world is courtesy of *The Good News: The New Testament with
over 500 Illustrations and Maps* (New York: American Bible Society, 1953). Adaptation of the end map of Palestine is courtesy of *The
Westminster Historical Atlas to the Bible,* edited by George Ernest
Wright and Floyd Vivian Filson, revised (Copyright, 1945, by the
Westminster Press; 1956, by W. L. Jenkins. Adapted by permission.)
Several paragraphs from *Interpreting the Gospels for Preaching* by
D. Moody Smith (Philadelphia: Fortress, 1980) have been used with
the permission of the publisher.

We also wish to express gratitude and indebtedness to teachers
and colleagues and to students at Florida State, Randolph-Macon
Woman's College, and Duke for their stimulation in the present undertaking. We are grateful to those colleagues whose suggestions and
criticisms have contributed to this edition, particularly Professor
John H. Schütz of the University of North Carolina at Chapel Hill.
Finally, we again pay tribute to three scholars under whom we studied together at Yale—Paul Meyer, now of Princeton Theological
Seminary; Paul Minear, Winkley Professor of Biblical Theology,
emeritus; and the late Paul Schubert, Buckingham Professor of New
Testament Criticism and Interpretation.

We also wish to thank Kenneth J. Scott of Macmillan, editor in
the College and Professional Division, and his predecessors, John D.
Moore and Charles E. Smith, for their interest in this project. We
are grateful for the support of Randolph-Macon Woman's College

and of The Divinity School of Duke University. Father Dimitri Cozby, a graduate student at Duke, has kindly assisted us in several ways.

Our children—Hope, Lee, and Paul; Cynthia, Catherine, David, and Allen—have responded with good grace to the stringencies imposed by their fathers' aspirations. Our wives continue to tolerate our preoccupation with this project, which has now extended over the better part of two decades. The dedication of the book attests to our gratitude for their encouragement and significant help.

R.A.S.
D.M.S.

CONTENTS

List of Maps and Charts   xv
List of Illustrations   xvi
List of Abbreviations   xviii

Prologue: The Study of the New Testament   **1**

Introduction   **9**

1. The World of the New Testament   **13**

The Jewish Milieu   13
A Tragic History   *17*
A Persistent Obedience   *24*
  The Pharisees   *24*
  The Sadducees   *26*
  The Essenes   *28*
An Abiding Hope   *31*
The Greco-Roman World   34
Language and Culture   *35*
  Alexander the Great   *35*
  The Importance of the Greek Language   *36*
Government   *38*
Religion   *40*
  Traditional and Official Religion   *41*
  Popular Religion   *44*
  Diaspora Judaism   *51*

Part I: The Gospels and Jesus   **57**

**2. The Gospel According to Mark: Triumph Through
Suffering**   **61**

Prologue: The Spirit and Jesus in the World   67
The Gospel of Power: Jesus Opposes His Enemies   71

Encounter with Demons and Sickness   73
Debate with the Pharisees   76
The Power of Suffering: Jesus Wins His Disciples   80
Two Stages of Discipleship   83
Faith to Produce Healing   86
The Cross of Jesus   88
Epilogue: The Future Victory   92

3. The Gospel According to Matthew: A Radical Obedience   97

Introduction: The New Obedience   99
The Higher Righteousness   105
Fulfilling Righteousness   106
Teaching Righteousness   109
True Discipleship   112
The Kingdom of Heaven   114
The Forgiving Church   116
Peter as the Rock   117
Discipline in Community   119
Judgment: Doing God's Will   120
Believing Doers of the Law   122
Doing Mercy Without Calculation   122
Conclusion: Obedience and Resurrection   124
The Great Commission   125

4. The Gospel According to Luke: Witness to Jesus   133

Preface: A Time for True Remembering   135
Introduction: A Universal Story   137
Twofold Witness to Jesus   139
Initial Victory in the Temple   142
Gathering Witnesses in Galilee   143
The Offense of Jesus' Preaching   145
Sure Witness to the Word   148
Witness to the Word on the Journey to
    Jerusalem   150
Jesus' Word About the Present   151
Jesus' Word About the Future   154
The True Israel Through the Passion and
    Resurrection   154
The True Inheritors   157
Fulfilling the Scripture   158

5. The Gospel According to John: The Glory of Jesus   **166**

Introduction   169
   The Prologue: Jesus Christ as the Word   *169*
The Revelation of Christ's Glory Before the
    World   180
   The Healing of the Man Born Blind   *180*
The Revelation of Christ's Glory Before the
    Community   190
   Jesus' Last Will: The Prayer of Consecration   *190*

6. Jesus the Messiah: A Portrait   **202**

Introduction: The Tradition About Jesus   202
   Kerygma, Gospels, and Jesus of Nazareth   *205*
   The Basic Tradition of Jesus   *207*
The Healing Messiah   209
   Miracles in the First Century   *210*
   Miracles in the Synoptic Gospels   *211*
    The Eschatological Context   *212*
    Three Types of Miracles   *213*
    Miracles and Faith   *217*
   Miracles in the Twentieth Century   *218*
The Teaching Messiah   220
   The Proclamation of the Kingdom of God   *221*
    The Kingdom as Present and Future   *222*
    Jesus and Apocalypticism   *224*
    The Kingdom and the Parables   *226*
   The Radical Demand of the Kingdom   *231*
    The Demand of the Sermon on the Mount   *231*
    Jesus and the Law   *233*
   The Relationship of Jesus to His Message   *235*
    The Question of Jesus' Messianic
     Consciousness   *235*
    Jesus' Call to Discipleship   *244*
    The Authority of Jesus   *245*
The Suffering Messiah   247
   The Passion and Death of Jesus   *248*
    The Events of Jesus' Passion and Death   *250*
    The Passion Tradition   *254*
    Jesus' Death in the Tradition   *256*
   The Resurrection of Jesus of Nazareth   *258*
    The Resurrection Tradition   *259*
    The Resurrection Event   *263*

Part II: The Apostles and the Early Church   **271**

7. **The Acts of the Apostles: Witnessing to the World**   **275**

   Introduction: A New Beginning   277
   Jesus' Departure   277
   The Apostolic Witness   279
   Spirit, Gospel, and Church   281
   The Growth of the Church and Its Witness   288
   Stephen's Martyrdom   288
   Mission to the Gentiles   291
   Christianity's Triumphal March   295
   Paul's Speech at Pisidian Antioch   295
   Paul's Speech in Athens   298
   Jerusalem to Rome   304

8. **Paul: Apostle and Man of Faith**   **309**

   Paul and His Predecessors   311
   The Tradition of Moses   311
   Apostle by God's Revelation   313
   The Received Tradition   317
   The Word of the Lord   319
   The Freedom of the Gospel   322
   Hope   323
   Faith   326
   Love   332
   The Struggle of the Gospel   339
   Courage in Ministry   340
   Joy in Hardship   344
   Steadfastness Against Heresy   348

9. **Romans: The Gospel of Grace**   **357**

   Introduction: Righteousness by Faith   358
   God's Wrath: The Problem of Sin   360
   God's Righteousness and the Response of Faith   368
   Justification by Faith   369
   Abraham and the Promise to Faith   374
   God's Grace and Human Freedom   375
   The New Situation   375
   Freedom from Sin   378
   Freedom from the Law   379
   Life in the Spirit   382
   God's Faithfulness   384
   The Obedience of Faith   388

10. Post-Pauline Writings: The Development of the Church **395**

The Community as Institution   397
The Unity of the Church   *399*
Church Organization   *408*
A Community of Discipline and Doctrine   415
Faith and Action   *416*
Christ and Christians   *420*
The Suffering Servant   *422*
The Superior High Priest   *428*
A Community of Love and Hope   435
The Spirit of Jesus as Love   *436*
The Vision of the Prophet on Patmos   *443*

**11. Literature and Community: The New Testament and
Early Christianity**   **459**

The Emergence of Early Christianity   462
The Primitive Church and Jesus   *465*
The Crucifixion of Jesus   *466*
The Expectation of His Return   *468*
The Preservation of Jesus' Teaching   *469*
The Recounting of His Miracles   *471*
The Mission and Expansion of Christianity   *472*
The Preaching of the Gospel   *473*
The Success of the Gospel   *475*
Christianity's Identity   480
The Distinction of Orthodoxy and Heresy   *481*
Ordination, Creeds, Scripture   *482*
The Significance and Shape of the Canon   *488*

Epilogue: The Anatomy of the New Testament   **491**

Glossary   **500**

General Bibliography   **510**

Name and Subject Index   **517**

Biblical Index   **529**

List of Maps and Charts

Map of Palestine in the time of the New
    Testament   *Endpaper*
Time chart of the New Testament   xix

Diagram of the Synoptic problem   64
Diagram of the formation of the Gospels   66
Map of Galilee   72
Diagram of the Temple   143
Map of Judea   248
Diagram of Jerusalem   250
Map of Paul's missionary cities   296
Map of cities of Asia Minor   445
Map of the Mediterranean world in the time of the New
    Testament   *Endpaper*

List of Illustrations

Detail of Arch of Titus in Rome   12
The Jordan River   16
Antiochus Epiphanes   19
Roman theater in Amman, Jordan   21
Bar Kochba War coin   23
Jerusalem and the temple area   27
Cave of the Dead Sea Scrolls   29
Socrates   37
Temple of Zeus   42
Temple of Poseidon   44
Augustus   45
Dionysos   47
Mithras   48
Jesus carrying his cross   60
Nero   68
Crucifixion   81
Via Dolorosa   89
Crucifixion   91
Flight into Egypt   103
Bethlehem   104
"Calling of the Apostles"   108
Last Judgment   123
"The Resurrection"   126
"The Holy Family"   138
Jerusalem   139
Announcement of Jesus' birth to the shepherds   140
"The Adoration of the Shepherds"   141
Augustus and Tiberius   145
Nazareth   146
Synagogue at Capernaum   147
"The Return of the Prodigal Son"   153
Shepherd and sheep   155

"Supper at Emmaus"   161
Four evangelists   170
Pool of Siloam   182
"The Alba Madonna"   203
"Christ with the Sick Around Him, Receiving Little
    Children"   214
River Jordan and Sea of Galilee   216
Ploughing   227
Synagogue at Khirbet Shema   234
Entry into Jerusalem   237
Entry into Jerusalem   252
Garden of Gethsemane and Mount of Olives   255
"Crucifixion"   274
Christ giving the law to the apostles   279
Crucifixion   284
"The Conversion of Saint Paul"   290
Parthenon   301
St. Paul   314
"The Last Supper"   320
Hades carrying off Persephone   335
Temple of Apollo   336
Last Supper   338
"The Apostle Paul"   353
Colosseum   359
"The Fall of Man"   367
"Last Judgment"   368
Sacrifice of a bull   371
Wailing Wall   387
"Pieta"   405
Isaiah Scroll   411
Aphrodite   412
St. James   417
Mocking and flagellation of Christ   426
Menorah   434
Domitian   442
"Saint John the Evangelist on Patmos"   449
Jewish tomb   451
"The Vision of St. John the Divine"   455
"Christ in Glory"   460
Christ medallion   465
Roman Forum   475
"The Assumption of the Virgin"   483
Codex Sinaiticus   487

List of Abbreviations

Aufl.—edition (German; in bibliographical data).

EH—the *Ecclesiastical History* of Eusebius.

IB—*The Interpreter's Bible*, eds. George A. Buttrick et al., 12 vols. (Nashville, Tenn.: Abingdon, 1952–1957).

IDB—*The Interpreter's Dictionary of the Bible*, eds. George A. Buttrick et al., 4 vols. (Nashville, Tenn.: Abingdon, 1962). Supplementary Volume (1976).

KJV—the King James Version of the Bible.

LXX—the Septuagint (see the Glossary).

NEB—*The New English Bible*.

par., parr.—parallel or parallels (usually in the Gospels).

RSV—the Revised Standard Version of the Bible.

TDNT—*Theological Dictionary of the New Testament*, eds. G. Kittel et al. and trans. G. W. Bromiley, Vols. I–X (Grand Rapids, Mich.: Eerdmans, 1964–1976).

TIME-CHART OF THE NEW TESTAMENT*

Significant Pre-New Testament Dates
336-323 B.C.   Conquest and Rule of Alexander the Great
167-164 B.C.   The Maccabean Revolt
63 B.C.   Roman Rule of Palestine Begins

Date	Events	Herods	Governors of Judaea	Roman Emperors	New Testament Writings
		Herod the Great (37-4 BC)			
10				Augustus (27 BC-AD 14)	
BC	Birth of Jesus				
AD		Archelaus (4 BC-AD 6)			
10		Philip the Tetrarch (4 BC-AD 34)	Coponius (6-9) Marcus Ambivius (9-12) Annius Rufus (12-15)		
20		Herod Antipas (4 BC-AD 39)	Valerius Gratus (15-26)		
	Ministry of John the Baptist			Tiberius (14-37)	
30	Ministry of Jesus Crucifixion of Jesus		Pontius Pilate (26-36)		
40		Herod Agrippa I (37-44)	Marcellus (36-37) Marullus (37-41)	Caligula (37-41)	
	Paul's first missionary activity		Cuspius Fadus (44-46) Tiberius Alexander (46-48)	Claudius (41-54)	
50	Council of Jerusalem Paul in Corinth	Herod Agrippa II (50-100)	Cumanus (48-52)		1&2 Thessalonians
	Paul in Ephesus				Galatians
	Paul's journey to Jerusalem and arrest		Felix (52-58)		1&2 Corinthians Romans
60	Paul, prisoner to Rome		Festus (58-62)	Nero (54-68)	Philippians
	Paul, prisoner in Rome		Albinus (62-64)		Colossians
	Paul's martyrdom under Nero		Gessius Florus (64-66)		Philemon
70				Galba (68-69) Otho (69) Vitellius (69)	Mark
				Vespasian (69-79)	
80				Titus (79-81)	
				Domitian (81-96)	Matthew
90	Council of Jamnia				Luke Acts Revelation John
100	(Fall of Jerusalem A.D. 135)			Nerva (96) Trajan (98-117)	

*Chronology is only approximate, especially in regard to dating the books of the New Testament. The dates of the other twelve New Testament books are so uncertain that it is impossible to include them in the time chart.

Prologue: The Study of the New Testament

THE NEW TESTAMENT consists of twenty-seven early Christian writings which with the Old Testament, the Bible of Judaism, form the Christian Bible. Although the New Testament is thus comparable to the Old, there are significant differences. The Old Testament is more than three times the length of the New and was written down over a period of nearly a thousand years; the New Testament was written and composed in a mere fraction of that time. The Old Testament was written in Hebrew, the language of ancient Israel; the New Testament in Greek, the language of the Hellenistic world.

The four Gospel narratives stand at the beginning of the New Testament. They are followed by another narrative, the Acts of the Apostles, a history of the earliest church. Then come the epistles, twenty-one of them. Finally, Revelation, a book of apocalyptic visions, stands at the end of the collection. The twenty-one books styled epistles or letters are themselves of different types. A number of them are real letters (e.g., the Corinthian letters of Paul). Yet quite possibly many are not; at least they may not have been originally composed as letters (e.g., Hebrews, James, I Peter, and I John). They have characteristics more appropriate to treatises, sermons, or tracts.

The story of how and why these books were written and at length gathered into the collection we now call the New Testament is a long and complicated one. Each book originated within a particular historical situation. The individual books were preserved and brought together because they were deemed useful and authoritative in the church. By the end of the second century the Gospels, Acts, and the letters attributed to Paul were widely regarded as scripture. Not until the fourth century, however, did canonical lists appear containing exactly the twenty-seven books of our New Testament.

The study of the New Testament is a complex task that resists simplification. It has engaged the interests and talents of highly competent philologists, historians, textual critics, and exegetes, not to mention theologians, preachers of all sorts, believers, and many others. Such study has been undertaken with attitudes ranging from pious devotion to scholarly objectivity, skepticism, and even outright hostility.

Our purpose is not to instruct the reader in the manifold scholarly disciplines that inform New Testament study at the highest level. Nor is it to inculcate or encourage any particular attitude or religious disposition in approaching the text other than an openness to understand it. *Anatomy* will have served its purpose if it enables the reader or student better to appreciate the faith that gave rise to and is expressed in the New Testament writings, as well as the reasons those writings have been treasured for nearly two millennia in a believing community.

While many aspects of New Testament study are technical and quite difficult, it is not impossible for the layperson to read and understand the New Testament itself. Understanding, however, takes place at many levels and in many ways. Countless millions of people who have had little notion of the original setting or purpose of the New Testament, or the Bible generally, have read it with some kind or degree of understanding. It is easy enough for the scholarly exegete to dismiss such understanding as at best irrelevant and at worst a hindrance or a misunderstanding. The scholar forgets that this allegedly naïve reading of the text may in some of its dimensions or aspects be close to the origin and heart of New Testament faith. We do not seek to negate such understanding, but where possible to nurture and build upon it.

Historic Christianity, and particularly Protestant Christianity, has taken for granted that the narratives, beliefs, and moral implications of the New Testament are accessible to the serious reader. We agree in principle, but we wish to encourage and abet reading that takes seriously the nature of the various New Testament writings, their individual purposes, and the situations that called them forth. The pursuit of these matters will, we are convinced, refine and enhance understanding of the New Testament.

The very name "New Testament" bespeaks the existence of an Old Testament and thus of the Christian Bible. The New Testament should not be read as if the Old did not exist, if for no other reason than that the Old Testament was the sole Bible of the New Testament Christians and provided the presuppositions and much of the theological vocabulary of the new faith. There is a sense in which the authors of the Gospels, especially Matthew and Luke, regard their narratives as the continuation of the biblical story. The Christian Bible has continued to include the Old Testament, although there was some controversy about it during the second century. The affirmation of the Old Testament as scripture was, among other things, a way of making the New understandable, and of making sure how it was understood. Apart from its rootage in the Old, the New Testament is all too easily taken as treating of ethereal, spiritual, or otherworldly matters far removed from earthly realities. A course in Old Testament is a valuable preparation for the study of the New. Failing that, the serious reader will wish to read the Old Testament (especially the Pentateuch, I and II Samuel, I and II Kings, Psalms, and Isaiah) before, or along with, the New.

Anatomy intentionally emphasizes the content and interpretation of the New Testament. On the assumption that readers will want to know what the New Testament is about, what its authors intended to say, we have sought to direct attention to the text of the New Testament itself. To help readers come to a more than superficial or secondhand understanding, we have dealt extensively with representative texts from the various New Testament books. Working outward from these texts, we have then endeavored to display and illumine the character and movement of the different writings. What has resulted is certainly no comprehensive or even coverage of the New Testament, but a series of dissections designed to uncover the nature and structure of the New Testament books and of the collection as a whole. Thus our title, *Anatomy of the New Testament.*

Standard questions of introduction (authorship, date and place of composition, and so forth) have been dealt with in summary fashion. Sometimes these questions are not crucial for understanding the document in question; often they are insoluble. In the introductory notes at the beginnings of chapters or at other appropriate places, the readers' attention is directed to the existence of such questions. Where there is a consensus on a certain problem, it is stated. Where there is not, the authors briefly give their position and reasons for holding it. In any event, such questions are of little concern to readers until they have some knowledge of, and involvement in, the content of the New Testament itself. Thus, the sooner they can get to the text the better. Readers can always return to questions of introduction after they have become aware of their importance for the understanding of the text. Then they will be ready to consult more advanced works on the subject.

An initial and significant understanding of a New Testament text can be gained from an analysis of it in the context of the document of which it is a part. The religious and cultural background is not unimportant. Nevertheless, we believe that, where such matters are not directly and specifically related to the understanding of the text, their large-scale introduction will tend to confuse rather than inform the uninitiated reader. The same goes for the closely related matter of the meaning of the original Greek. Wherever possible we have simply begun from the text of the Revised Standard Version and have sought to explain it without recourse to questions of translation. Although such a course may lead to an imperfect understanding of the New Testament, we believe that it can engender an understanding that will serve the reader well as a beginning point for further study. The authors thus manifest their own belief that the subject matter of the New Testament does not lie beyond the grasp of the lay reader.

How then should one proceed in the study of the New Testament with the help of *Anatomy?* After familiarizing oneself with the important issues concerning the origin of the book in question

by reading the introductory notes, the reader should then look at the
brief outline of the entire biblical document to gain some prior conception of what it is about. Then read the New Testament book in
its entirety, preferably at one sitting. Only now is one adequately
prepared to dig into the representative texts with which the book
mainly deals. In doing this the reader should find the appropriate
section of *Anatomy* a guide and a help in understanding. It should
be emphasized that these interpretative sections, which constitute
the greater part of the book, will make little sense unless they are
read with the New Testament in hand.

The question of how to organize a general presentation and
study of the New Testament is an important one, and it will be
profitable to reflect upon it briefly before turning to the subject matter itself. It is not uncommon to begin with the Synoptic Gospels
and conclude with the Gospel of John or the Johannine literature.[1]
Such an organization creates some problems, however much one
may strive to offset them. It implies that the Synoptics are early and
present the historical Jesus and that John is late and does not. Alternatively, one could reasonably begin with the presentation of the
early church in Acts and deal next with the Pauline letters, which
are almost certainly the earliest Christian writings we possess. Such
a presentation would, however, seem to ignore the fact that Christianity began with Jesus, or with the Jesus movement, in early first-
century Palestine.

The organization of *Anatomy* is simple and is related to the
shape of the New Testament canon, the church's liturgical usage,
and the history of early Christianity. After an introductory chapter
which sets the stage, it falls into two major parts entitled, respectively, "The Gospels and Jesus" and "The Apostles and the Early
Church." The focus of the entire New Testament message is Jesus
and what God did through him. The perspective throughout is that
of the early church or churches, of Christians who believed in him.
It is erroneous to think that the Gospels and Jesus represent an earlier period and the letters and other writings a later, or that the Gospels have to do with Jesus and the letters and other writings with
the early church. The Gospels are products of the early church and
reflect its faith and practice over a period of more than a half-century (approximately A.D. 30 to 100). The development of the church
or churches can be studied by analyzing the Gospels. The other New
Testament writings, while they speak more or less directly of the
activities of Christians in the churches, nevertheless have to do
with the gospel about Jesus Christ. Some, the genuine Pauline letters, are earlier than the Gospels; a few (e.g., II Peter) are almost
certainly later. In studying the Gospels we shall be asking what is

[1] Cf. the earlier editions of *Anatomy* (New York: Macmillan, 1969, 1974).

said to the early church through the presentation of Jesus. In studying the other writings we shall typically be asking what is said about the gospel of Jesus through the discussion of many matters and issues relating to the early church.

It would have been theoretically possible and defensible to reverse the order of Parts I and II. The present arrangement, however, intentionally underscores the fact that Jesus of Nazareth is not only the focal point, but the historical beginning of the New Testament and Christianity. Each part concludes with an historical presentation, first of Jesus and then of the earliest church. It is no more possible to write a comprehensive history of the early church than it is to write a biography of Jesus, even if time and space allowed it. In both cases we must settle for characterizations. But such characterizations are not unimportant and the student is invited to ask whether they are accurate and adequate. Do they correspond to the evidence? That evidence is principally the New Testament itself, the careful study of which should precede, and provide a constant corrective to, any such characterization, whether in *Anatomy* or elsewhere. By first presenting the writings and encouraging their study we emphasize their priority.

Introduction

T HE FIRST-CENTURY Mediterranean world was dominated by the Roman Empire and by Hellenistic culture. Underneath the apparent unity and calm of a common language and a political hegemony, however, signs of forces that reflected widespread human longing and dissatisfaction were at work. The opening, introductory chapter focuses upon both the factors working for stability and those encouraging ferment. Out of this ambivalent environment the Christian faith originated and in it the New Testament writings were conceived, read, and eventually regarded as sacred.

Because of their roles in the development of the Christian faith, two crucial areas for study and reflection are (1) the religious and cultural heritage of the people of Israel, who chafed under Roman rule but who also expected that the God who had delivered them out of slavery in Egypt and exile in Babylon would not fail them, and (2) the intense religious crisis of the Hellenistic world under Roman rule, especially as seen in the dissolution of traditional Greek, Homeric religion and the rapid growth of mystery cults with their promise of meaningful life and individual immortality. This situation of change, frustration, fervor, and hope was the matrix for the emergence of a religious community centered around Jesus, a man of Israel; this community grew within two centuries into a religious movement of worldwide importance.

This scene from the Arch of Titus in the Roman Forum celebrates Titus'
capture of Jerusalem in A.D. 70. The victorious Romans bear triumphantly
the sacred objects of the Jerusalem temple, including the seven-branched
lampstand symbolizing the presence of God. (Courtesy of Jewish Museum.)

CHAPTER ONE

The World of the New Testament

The Jewish Milieu
  A Tragic History
  A Persistent Obedience
    The Pharisees
    The Sadducees
    The Essenes
  An Abiding Hope
The Greco-Roman World
  Language and Culture

Alexander the Great
The Importance of the Greek
  Language
Government
Religion
  Traditional and Official Religion
  Popular Religion
  Diaspora Judaism

The Jewish Milieu

Jesus was a Jew, and so were his first disciples. In fact, the earliest Christians did not think of themselves as members of a new religion separate from Judaism. Yet from the beginning Jesus and his disciples represented something new.

No new movement can be understood, however, apart from its historical antecedents and the factors that helped to produce it. The primary background of Jesus, early Christianity, and the New Testament was first-century Judaism. Judaism is, of course, one of the world's major religions, as it was in the first Christian century. A remarkable continuity or similarity exists between the Judaism of today and that of the first century, despite the changes that succeeding centuries have wrought. This continuity is in itself a clue to the character of that ancient faith.

Both Judaism and Christianity are historical religions. They share a faith in a God who deals with human beings, individually and collectively, in such a way that his will can be discerned in history. Crucial to both religions is the idea that God *reveals* or has revealed *Himself* in history. The holy scriptures of both religions are largely narratives of the past: legends, sagas, and historical accounts. Broadly speaking, they are testimonies to God's historical revelations. The Old Testament is a vast collection of legal, cultic, devotional, and narrative material set in a historical framework. It is the literary product of nearly a thousand years of Israel's history. Although the New Testament is much briefer and covers a much shorter period of time, it too tells of people and events in the conviction that God has wrought wondrous deeds in history that are of utmost importance for the future of humanity. Consciously and deliberately the New Testament writers take up the story of the Old Testament and bring it to a culmination.[1] Christianity's origin within Judaism in large measure determined its shape and fundamentally influenced the narrative form that is so important in the New Testament.

Judaism was a religion of revelation, history, and a book. As such, it was a religion steeped in tradition, but this tradition was not an end in itself. Rather it was a means by which Israel identified and understood itself as a distinct and chosen people, the people of the Lord. Moreover, much of the literature of the Old Testament and the oral and written traditions that developed from it were understood as divine directions intended to regulate Israel's response to the Lord's goodness. The most influential law code the Western world has known, the Ten Commandments, begins: "I am the Lord your God, who brought you out of the land of Egypt, out of the house of bondage. You shall have no other gods before me" (Exodus 20:2-3). The statement of what God has done leads to the statement of what the people ought to do in response, forming the basic structure of Old Testament law. The principal activity of many Jewish religious leaders in the time of Jesus was the interpretation and fulfillment of that law.

Revelation and history, tradition and law, although immensely important, were not the whole of Judaism. A part of obedience to the law was, in fact, the performance of worship worthy of God. The center of this worship was the temple in Jerusalem, and the heart of the temple was the sacrificial altar. Upon the altar the priests offered sacrifice to God, and thus provided a means of communica-

---

[1] The Old Testament had not actually been officially defined in the time of Jesus and earliest Christianity. Yet Jesus himself speaks of "the law and the prophets" (Matt. 5:17) and quotes from the Psalms (Mark 15:34; cf. Psalm 22:1) according to the New Testament. Thus he seems to have known the threefold division of sacred scripture—law, prophets, and writings—that is reflected generally in the New Testament. According to tradition, the Hebrew Old Testament canon was fixed by the rabbis at the Council of Jamnia in about A.D. 90.

tion. Until its destruction by the Romans in A.D. 70 the temple served as the focal point of Jewish worship. There sacrifices were offered daily and the festivals of the Jewish year, such as Passover, were celebrated. Jewish worship was not, however, confined to the temple even in the time of Jesus. In addition to private devotion, the service of the individual congregation or synagogue was the occasion of a nonsacrificial corporate and public worship. For most Jews even in Palestine the synagogue was the practical center of religious life, for there the reading and study of the law took place, and the observance of the law was the chief means of giving expression to their faith.

Another factor played a large role in first-century Judaism, namely, the land. The small piece of territory at the eastern end of the Mediterranean Sea, which is variously called the Holy Land, Palestine, or Israel, has been the occasion and cause of both hope and frustration for Jews for three thousands years. At least from the days of the Davidic monarchy the land was regarded as the promise and gift of God to his people. The promise was projected back into the days of the patriarchs Abraham, Isaac, and Jacob, who dwelt in and around the land but did not possess it. Yet Israel believed that God had promised the land to her, and in this faith they occupied and defended it. Israel could never rest easy in the land, however, for, subject to frequent threat and attack, she was only secure when the surrounding more powerful nations were momentarily weak or looking in other directions. In the late eighth century B.C. the territories of all the Israelite tribes except Judah were overrun by the Assyrians, and less than a century and a half later the Babylonians invaded Judea, laid siege to Jerusalem, and overthrew it. The Davidic kingship came to an end, and many of the people were deported into Babylonian captivity. The subsequent history of the land has been a troubled one. In fact, the modern state of Israel represents the first instance of Jewish control of the land since shortly before the time of Christ, and that control is still not uncontested. Since the Babylonian exile the land of Israel has been occupied or ruled by other peoples—Persians, Greeks, Romans, Christians, and Moslems. The question of the possession and rulership of the land was quite as important in Jesus' day, when the land was occupied by the Romans and ruled by puppet kings and imperial procurators, as it is today.[2]

[2] The definitive treatment of this subject is now W. D. Davies, *The Gospel and the Land: Early Christianity and Jewish Territorial Doctrine* (Berkeley: University of California Press, 1974).

The Jordan River coils southward from the Sea of Galilee through harsh hills. (Courtesy of National Geographic Society.)

A TRAGIC HISTORY

*How does the reality of Israel's history compare with her hope?

From the Babylonian conquest of Judea in 587 B.C. to the time of Jesus' death the Jews in Palestine lived mostly under foreign domination, relieved only by a century or so of relative independence under the Hasmonean dynasty just prior to the advent of the Romans in 63 B.C.[3] In the Babylonian conquest numbers of Jews were taken east by their captors to Mesopotamia. Others fled south to Egypt. The so-called diaspora, or dispersion of the Jews, began. From this time onward Jews in increasing numbers were to be found living outside their Palestinian homeland.

Shortly after the middle of the sixth century B.C. Babylonian overlordship was replaced by Persian. Jews were allowed to return to their homeland and to begin the restoration of the Jerusalem temple, which had been destroyed by the Babylonians. Although we have an incomplete picture of Jewish life under Persian rule, conditions were certainly much improved. More than two centuries of Persian domination came to an end late in the fourth century before Christ, when Alexander of Macedon and his armies moved east, sweeping everything before them. Alexander overran the Jewish homeland, and over the years he and his successors attempted to introduce Greek culture and customs there, as was their practice in all conquered territories. Alexander was as much a missionary of Greek culture as a conquering general. After his death in 323 B.C. his empire broke up as quickly as it had been formed. And although his successors could not preserve political unity, they were able to continue the process of Hellenization, that is, the spreading of Greek culture.

After the division of Alexander's empire, the Jews found themselves situated between two rival centers of power—the Seleucids, who controlled Mesopotamia and Syria, and the Ptolemies, who ruled Egypt. The geographical setting of Israel as a buffer zone between the two great powers of the Fertile Crescent made struggle over Palestine inevitable. By and large during the third century, Jewish Palestine was controlled by the Ptolemies with a minimum of

---

* The questions are meant to help the student read with interest and understanding. They are not meant to be exhaustive, but should rather stimulate reflection, enlarge perspectives, and sharpen focus on a major issue in the reading.

[3] The concerns of postexilic Israel are reflected in the later Old Testament books and treated directly in Ezra and Nehemiah. The Maccabean period is dealt with in I and II Maccabees. The *Jewish Antiquities*, a continuous history of the Jews to the Roman War by the first-century Jewish historian Josephus, is doubtless the most valuable single non-Biblical source. The Greek text and translation are available in The Loeb Classical Library in nine volumes, edited by Ralph Marcus and Allen Wikgren (Cambridge, Mass.: Harvard University Press, 1962–1963).

interference in Jewish internal affairs. After they defeated the Ptolemies in 198 B.C., a similar policy characterized the Seleucids' rule of Palestine. Following a period of changing rulers, however, Antiochus IV (called Epiphanes because he proclaimed himself to be "God manifest") ascended to the Syrian throne in 175 B.C., and the previous toleration disappeared under a forcible attempt to displace the religion of the Jewish people. Heathen altars were erected in the cities of Palestine and even in the temple at Jerusalem. Resistance was likely to mean death.[4]

In 167 B.C., martyrdom turned to revolution under the leadership of Mattathias, a village priest, and his five sons. The book of I Maccabees describes the outbreak of open revolt as follows:

> Then the king's officers who were enforcing the apostasy came to the city of Modein to make them offer sacrifice. Many from Israel came to them; and Mattathias and his sons were assembled. Then the king's officers spoke to Mattathias as follows: "You are a leader, honored and great in this city, and supported by sons and brothers. Now be the first to come and do what the king commands, as all the Gentiles and the men of Judah and those that are left in Jerusalem have done. Then you and your sons will be numbered among the friends of the king, and you and your sons will be honored with silver and gold and many gifts."
>
> But Mattathias answered and said in a loud voice: "Even if all the nations that live under the rule of the king obey him, and have chosen to do his commandments, departing each one from the religion of his fathers, yet I and my sons and my brothers will live by the covenant of our fathers. Far be it from us to desert the law and the ordinances. We will not obey the king's words by turning aside from our religion to the right hand or to the left."
>
> When he had finished speaking these words, a Jew came forward in the sight of all to offer sacrifice upon the altar in Modein, according to the king's command. When Mattathias saw it, he burned with zeal and his heart was stirred. He gave vent to righteous anger; he ran and killed him upon the altar. At the same time he killed the king's officer who was forcing them to sacrifice, and he tore down the altar. Thus he burned with zeal for the law, as Phinehas did against Zimri the son of Salu.
>
> Then Mattathias cried out in the city with a loud voice, saying: "Let every one who is zealous for the law and supports the covenant come out with me!" And he and his sons fled to the hills and left all that they had in the city. [I Maccabees 2:15–28]

---

[4]This attempt to suppress Jewish religious practice is to be distinguished from the process of Hellenization, i.e., the dissemination of Greek education and culture, which took place over a long period of years; M. Hengel, *Judaism and Hellenism: Studies in their Encounter in Palestine during the Hellenistic Period*, trans. J. Bowden (Philadelphia: Fortress, 1974), I, 58–106.

Antiochus IV (Epiphanes—"[God] Manifest") on a Greek coin. The reverse
side shows Apollo and bears the words: Basileōs Antiochou—"(coinage) of
King Antiochus." (Courtesy of American Numismatic Society.)

One of his sons, Judas, earned the nickname Maccabeus (Ham-
merer), and this name was applied to the finally successful Maccabean Revolt. In 165 B.C. Judas Maccabeus and his men seized the
temple and reclaimed it for Judaism. This victory has ever since
been celebrated in the feast of Hannukah (rededication). But it was
not until 142 B.C. that the last remnants of the Syrian Hellenizers
were driven from Jerusalem.

Although the Maccabean or Hasmonean dynasty was generally
welcomed as a blessed relief and the fulfillment of long-frustrated
expectations, its promise far outstripped its actuality. The propen-
sity of the later Hasmoneans to style themselves as kings and high
priests, as well as the internecine struggle among them, led to disillusionment. When the Romans arrived on the scene about a century after the Maccabean Revolt, their general, Pompey, supported
one Hasmonean claimant, Hyrcanus II, against the other, Aristobulus II. Although some supporters of Aristobulus offered fierce resistance, particularly at the temple, the Roman occupation of Palestine
and the Holy City could scarcely have been regarded as a disaster by
most Jews. For while Roman domination may have been inevitable,
the conduct of the later Hasmoneans made it seem initially less distasteful to Jews than it might otherwise have been. The Romans
allowed the weak Hasmonean Hyrcanus II to hold the office of high
priest and ethnarch. But Palestine was now in fact Roman territory,
and the power behind the throne was Antipater of Idumea, a master
of political intrigue who had helped engineer the Roman coup in the
first place.

Antipater brought his remarkable career to a culmination by having the Romans declare his son Herod king of the Jews. This Herod ruled effectively, if brutally, from 37 to 4 B.C. and figures prominently in Matthew's story of Jesus' infancy. He is commonly known as Herod the Great, in distinction from the lesser Herods who followed him. During his long and successful rule Herod accepted the necessity of appealing to Jewish religious zeal, at the same time devoting himself to the task of Hellenizing the culture and life of Palestine. He built cities according to the Hellenistic patterns, he constructed stadiums, gymnasiums, and theaters. Yet he also began to rebuild the temple in a more magnificent style. (Begun in 20 B.C., the reconstruction may not have actually been completed when the Roman War, which led to its destruction, broke out in A.D. 66.[5]) Despite his efforts, the Jews did not love or trust Herod. Nor did he trust them. He executed his Hasmonean wife Mariamne and eventually two of her sons, along with his ambitious and able son Antipater, who had married a Hasmonean princess. Antipater died only five days before Herod.

After the death of Herod, the kingdom was split into three parts and divided among three surviving sons. Philip became tetrarch of the region northeast of the Sea of Galilee, including Ituraea and Trachonitis, and reigned over that largely Gentile area from 4 B.C. until A.D. 34. Herod Antipas became ruler of Galilee and Perea and ruled from 4 B.C. until A.D. 39. Archelaus became ruler of Samaria, Judea, and Idumea, but was deposed after a short reign. Following the deposition of Archelaus in A.D. 6, a Roman procurator was installed as ruler of Judea. The procuratorship remained in effect continuously until the brief reign of Agrippa (37–44) and was resumed thereafter. Pontius Pilate (26–36) was the fifth of these procurators, surely one of the worst from the Jewish point of view. He took money from the temple treasury, brought military insignia with the emperor's image into Jerusalem, and ruthlessly destroyed a group of Samaritans who were watching a prophet perform a miracle. It is an understatement to say that he was not overly sensitive to Jewish religious sensibilities.

But Roman rule was not unremittingly brutal and oppressive. The procurator of Judea lived not in Jerusalem but in Caesarea. Although he had final responsibility, much authority was granted to the Sanhedrin, a group of about seventy distinguished Jewish elders—priests, scribes, and laymen. The high priest was the official head of this group and was, as he had been since the Babylonian exile, the most important Jewish governmental figure. In the vil-

---

[5] E. Mary Smallwood, *The Jews Under Roman Rule: From Pompey to Diocletian,* Studies in Judaism in Late Antiquity, 20 (Leiden: Brill, 1976), pp. 282–283, dates the completion of the temple ca. A.D. 64, followed almost immediately by extensive repair work on the foundations that was still underway when the war intervened.

Ancient Roman theater capable of seating more than 3,000 people. It stands in Amman, Jordan, on the site of the ancient (63 B.C.) Decapolis city of Philadelphia. (Courtesy of Pan American Airways.)

lages, synagogues served as law courts with scribes as authorities for interpreting and applying the law, or Torah.

Jesus was born during the reign of Herod the Great, lived in Galilee under Herod Antipas, and died in Jerusalem during the procuratorship of Pilate and the high priesthood of Caiaphas. Although Jesus was doubtless influenced by the political conditions of the times, there is little evidence that he made much impact upon them. Possibly he and his Palestinian followers opposed the group known as the Zealots, who were plotting military insurrection against Roman rule.[6] Although Jesus spoke frequently of the king-

[6]David M. Rhoads, *Israel in Revolution: 6—74 C.E.: A Political History Based on the Writings of Josephus* (Philadelphia: Fortress, 1976), pp. 52–59, points out that a party specifically called "Zealot" does not emerge until A.D. 66 (p. 53), although it is usually inferred from Josephus that Judas the Galilean founded the sect in A.D. 6. Cf. Smallwood, *The Jews Under Roman Rule*, p. 154.

dom of God and aroused hopes that he himself would become king, he evidently did not intend to lead a rebellion (cf. Luke 4:5–8; Matt. 4:7–10; John 6:15). For example, he allowed the payment of taxes to Caesar (Mark 12:13–17 parr.). Yet Jesus, like several others before him, was executed as a messianic pretender, a claimant to the throne of Israel, and thus a political rebel.

Be that as it may, the influence of the Zealots was increasing in the first half of the century. In Acts 5:35 ff. Gamaliel mentions Theudas, whom the procurator Fadus put to death, and Judas the Galilean, who had been put to death in A.D. 6, some three decades previously—despite the contrary statement of Acts. Gradually the tension between Roman and Jew heightened. What the Romans regarded as Jewish provocations led to retaliation, which in turn increased the tendency toward polarization of sentiment. More and more Jews became willing to fight and die, convinced that God would vindicate them in their righteous cause. Jewish Christians did not share the widespread enthusiasm for war, and when its outbreak seemed imminent those in Jerusalem fled for safety to Pella, across the Jordan river.[7] In A.D. 66 war broke out. Although the Jews fought bravely and enjoyed some initial success, they had little chance against Roman power. In A.D. 70 the Romans took Jerusalem after a long and grueling siege and laid it waste, destroying the temple. A few years later the last Jewish resistance at the fortress of Masada was overwhelmed. Even then the Jewish will to resist was not broken. When word circulated that Emperor Hadrian intended to rebuild Jerusalem as Aelia Capitolina and to erect a temple to Jupiter on the ruins of the Jewish temple, the Jews rallied around a leader called Bar Kochba ("Son of the Star"), whom the renowned Rabbi Akiba hailed as the Messiah of Israel.[8] Once more (A.D. 132–135) the Jews fought fiercely, but after a time were subdued. The Romans went ahead with their building plans and after the new city was complete forbade any Jew to enter it on pain of death. The trend of many centuries reached its logical end. Judaism had become a nation without a homeland.

Because the Jews believed that their land had been given them by the same God who had called them to be his chosen people, they chafed under foreign domination. Indeed, the character of Judaism during the time of Jesus and the early church was much affected by conditions in the Jewish homeland. The attitude of the Zealots, who regarded Roman rule as an affront against God to be removed by violent rebellion, has already been mentioned. During the period of Jesus' activity, however, theirs was not the only, or even the typical

---

[7] Eusebius, *Ecclesiastical History*, III, v. 3.

[8] Smallwood, *The Jews Under Roman Rule*, pp. 428–431, 437–438, argues that Hadrian probably also issued a ban prohibiting circumcision.

Coin of the Simon Bar Kochba War (A.D. 132–135). On the first side is a temple with four columns, within which there are a shrine and two scrolls of the law; the inscription reads, "Simon." On the other side are the lulab and ethrog, sacred objects. The inscription reads, "For the liberty of Jerusalem." (Courtesy of American Numismatic Society.)

expression of the spirit of Judaism. Although Jews generally looked for relief from foreign oppression and the restoration of the Davidic monarchy, many were content to wait upon God for the fulfillment of this hope, some thinking that it was near at hand. Certain other Jews had in effect already made their peace with Hellenistic culture and Roman rule and probably did not really yearn for their overthrow. Then, of course, there were large numbers of Jews living outside Palestine for whom political independence was not a burning issue. Indeed, rebellion in the homeland presented the grim and unwelcome possibility of retaliation against Jews elsewhere.

Moreover, it would be a mistake to view the Judaism of Jesus' time solely in terms of its reaction to an international political situation with unfortunate consequences for Jews. Many Jews continued to be primarily concerned with the right understanding of the law and the proper worship of God. The development of various schools of thought continued under Roman rule, and the Romans were willing to tolerate this so long as there was not overt dissension or violence.[9] Postexilic developments had already led to the formation of several schools of religious opinion among the Jews, making for a rather complex situation in the time of Jesus. We must now examine that situation more closely to understand why differing positions and parties existed and how their presence shaped the setting in which Christianity appeared.

[9]But in *ibid.*, pp. 256–272, the author points out that Judea suffered from uncharacteristically bad Roman government during the period leading up to the rebellion.

A PERSISTENT OBEDIENCE

Why was the law so important to Judaism?

If anything is central to Judaism it is the law (Hebrew, *torah*). Notwithstanding its human mediation through Moses, the Jew regarded the law as divine revelation. "The world and everything in it was created solely for the sake of the Law. . . ."[10] Strictly speaking, the law consists of the five books of Moses—the Pentateuch—which stand at the beginning of the Bible. Obedience to the Torah is, and has been, the paramount obligation of the Jew; it is the way to true righteousness. Because of its central position, practically every major religious group within Judaism can be categorized according to its attitude to the law.

> THE PHARISEES
>
> The Pharisees . . . are considered the most accurate interpreters of the laws, and hold the position of the leading sect. [Josephus, *The Jewish War*, II, 162]
>
> The scribes and Pharisees sit on Moses' seat; so practice and observe whatever they tell you, but not what they do; for they preach, but do not practice. [Matt. 23:2 f.]
>
> But when Paul perceived that one part were Sadducees and the other Pharisees, he cried out in the council, "Brethren, I am a Pharisee, a son of Pharisees; with respect to the hope and the resurrection of the dead I am on trial." [Acts 23:6]

Probably the single most influential and significant religious group within the Jewish community of New Testament times was the Pharisees. The Gospels make clear that they were important during the time of Jesus, and certainly they were predominant after the disastrous conclusion of the Jewish War (A.D. 70). After that war a rabbinic council assembled near the Mediterranean coast at Jamnia. The Council of Jamnia became a center for the study and interpretation of the law, and its influence proved far-reaching. Because it was dominated by Pharisees, it played an important role in the dissemination of the Pharisaic point of view throughout Judaism.

The history of the Pharisees and even the origin of their name is obscure. Very likely they stemmed from the Hasidim, or "pious ones," whose ferocious allegiance to the nation and the law gave impetus to the Maccabean revolt. The word *Pharisee* seems to be derived from a Hebrew verb meaning "to separate." If so, it would appropriately designate the Pharisees as those separated or chosen

---

[10] A saying attributed to Rabbi Benaiah, quoted by G. F. Moore, *Judaism in the First Centuries of the Christian Era, The Age of the Tannaim*, I (Cambridge, Mass.: Harvard University Press, 1927), p. 268.

by God for full obedience to the law. Yet Pharisees did not withdraw from society. Pharisaism was fundamentally a lay movement; Pharisees emphasized the necessity of obeying the laws of purity outside the temple precincts, particularly in their own homes and around their tables.[11] Because they understood Judaism primarily as interpretation of and obedience to the law, rather than in terms of nationalistic hopes or temple worship, the Pharisees were well situated to reconstitute and redefine Judaism in the aftermath of the destruction of the temple in the Roman War.

Two famous and important Pharisaic leaders were Hillel and Shammai. They were contemporaries and rivals who flourished in the latter part of the first century B.C. and the first decade of the following century. Around them gathered rival schools or houses of legal interpretation. Shammai's was known for its stricter, harsher interpretation of the law, whereas the interpretations of the house of Hillel were more liberal. Hillel's school eventually came to dominate. Some of the sayings attributed to Hillel closely parallel sayings ascribed to Jesus. Among these is the negative form of the Golden Rule: "What is hateful to yourself do not do to your neighbor. That is the entire Torah. All the rest is commentary. Now go forth and learn."[12]

In the New Testament the Pharisees are frequently spoken of together with the scribes, and the impression is created that they are closely allied, if not identical groups. The impression is not false, although it must be clarified. The scribes were authoritative custodians and interpreters of the law before the appearance of a distinct group called Pharisees.[13] Moreover, not all Pharisees were scribes. Yet it does not surprise us that the historic task of the scribes was largely taken up by the Pharisees, whose consuming interest was the interpretation and application of the law to every sphere of life. They continued and expanded the traditional interpretations of the law, the fruition of which is to be found in the so-called rabbinic literature, a large body of interpretative material from the earlier centuries of our era dealing with every phase of the law and with almost every aspect of religious and secular life.[14]

[11] See Jacob Neusner, *From Politics to Piety: The Emergence of Pharisaic Judaism* (Englewood Cliffs, N.J.: Prentice-Hall, 1973), p. 83. For a somewhat different, and incisively stated, interpretation of Pharisaic origins, see Ellis Rivkin, *A Hidden Revolution* (Nashville, Tenn.: Abingdon, 1978).

[12] Neusner, *From Politics to Piety*, p. 13. Cf. Matt. 7:12; Luke 6:31.

[13] Hengel, *Judaism and Hellenism*, I, 78–83, discusses the role of the scribes and scribal schools in preserving the integrity of Judaism in the Hellenistic period, while adopting new forms and conceptions.

[14] The basic document of the rabbinic literature, dating from the early third century, is *The Mishnah*, of which the standard English translation is that of H. Danby (London: Oxford University Press, 1933). *The Babylonian Talmud*, trans. I. Epstein, 35 vols. (London: Soncino Press, 1935–1952), includes, but is in the main a kind of

THE SADDUCEES

> The Sadducees hold that the soul perishes along with the body.
> They own no observance of any sort apart from the laws. . . .
> There are but few men to whom this doctrine has been made
> known, but these are men of the highest standing. [Josephus, *Jewish Antiquities*, XVIII, 16 f.]

> But the high priest rose up and all who were with him, that is, the
> party of the Sadducees, and filled with jealousy they arrested the
> apostles and put them in the common prison. [Acts 5:17 f.]

A second major group within Judaism, also mentioned in the
Gospels, is the Sadducees. As in the case of the Pharisees, their history and the derivation of their name is not entirely clear. Presumably the name is related to the proper name of Zadok, a high priest
appointed by Solomon. Whatever the history of the name and of the
group, by New Testament times the Sadducees were the priestly aristocracy. In Acts 5:17 the high priest and the Sadducees are linked
together and in 4:1 the priests, the captain of the temple, and the
Sadducees. The Sadducees seem to have stood in something of the
same relation to the priests as the Pharisees to the scribes. Pharisees
and Sadducees were thus religious brotherhoods centering upon the
authoritative interpretation of the law and the temple worship, respectively. As such they represented the chief foci of Jewish faith as
it existed prior to A.D. 70. Although the temple and its service of
worship had declined in practical importance as the majority of Jews
came to live outside the land of Israel, it was nevertheless the symbolic center of Judaism. On the altar sacrifices were offered to God
for God and his people to commune. Sins were covered and a right
relationship between God and his people restored and maintained.
Probably the most graphic example of this priestly function was the
yearly ritual of the Day of Atonement, when the high priest alone
entered the unapproachable Holy of Holies in the temple and there
came as the representative of the people, into the very presence of
the Holy One. On this day his action signified divine favor in that
he entered, met, and was not destroyed by the God of Israel.

As custodians of religious tradition and cultic ceremony the Sadducees were somewhat more conservative than the Pharisees. The
priests themselves held office by hereditary right. Moreover, the
Sadducees represented established wealth and position. With regard
to obedience to the law, they rejected all tradition and thus the ef-

---

learned commentary upon, the Mishnah. There is also a Palestinian Talmud. It is
shorter than the Babylonian Talmud and dates from the early fifth century, whereas
the latter dates from the late fifth century. A valuable introduction to the range of
rabbinic literature is the work of C. G. Montefiore and H. Loewe, *A Rabbinic Anthology* (New York: Meridian, n.d.).

Jerusalem and the temple area. The domed building is a Moslem shrine, the Dome of the Rock, which stands where the ancient Jerusalem temple was located. (Courtesy of Israel Government Tourist Office.)

fort of the Pharisees to extend the law's application to every situation in life in a binding way. They accepted only the word of scripture as authoritative. Politically, they were quietists and generally cooperated with the Romans. As members of the establishment it was in their interest to do so. They would have nothing to do with the relatively late doctrine of the resurrection of the dead, but rather adhered to the older and more typically Biblical (Old Testament) view that death is simply the end of significant conscious life. In this they differed from the Pharisees as well as from Jesus and the early Christians.

THE ESSENES

The Essenes have a reputation for cultivating peculiar sanctity. Of Jewish birth, they show a greater attachment to each other than do the other sects. They shun pleasures as a vice and regard temperance and the control of the passions as a special virtue. [Josephus, *The Jewish War*, II, 119 f.]

In addition to the Pharisees and Sadducees there existed at the time of Jesus a group called Essenes, whose exact identity and extent are not clear. Two important Jewish writers of the first century, the philosopher Philo and the historian Josephus, speak of them, although they are not mentioned by name in the New Testament. Since World War II, however, our knowledge of Essene or Essene-type groups has been immensely enlarged by the discovery of a monastery and an immense cache of documents at Qumran on the northwest shore of the Dead Sea.[15] The community existed there at the time of Jesus.

The Qumran movement, which began sometime during the second or early first century B.C., was characterized by a feeling of profound revulsion at the impurity of the temple worship and priesthood and the laxity in the observance of the law.[16] A figure called only the "teacher of righteousness" or the "righteous teacher" was apparently the founder of this group. Unlike the Pharisees and Sadducees, they withdrew from the mainstream of Jewish life, which they regarded as wholly corrupt, and often formed monastic communities. Even their festival calendar was different. Yet this withdrawal had a positive as well as negative side. It was not only a separation for the sake of the preservation of holiness, but a separation for a positive task and goal. First of all, the members of the community sought to carry out punctiliously the ritual and ethical requirements of the law and thus render a more acceptable obedience to God. This obedience was enforced under a strict discipline, and severe punishment was meted out for even minor infractions:

[15] The literature on the scrolls is voluminous, and scroll scholarship has become a major discipline within biblical study. Valuable still are Millar Burrows' two volumes, *The Dead Sea Scrolls* and *More Light on the Dead Sea Scrolls* (New York: Viking, 1955 and 1958, respectively). Both volumes contain translations of the major documents discovered up to the time of their publication. A handy collection of the important documents in translation has been made by G. Vermes, *The Dead Sea Scrolls in English* (Baltimore: Penguin, 1962). For other works relevant to the scrolls see the Suggestions for Further Reading at the end of this chapter.

[16] Hengel, *Judaism and Hellenism*, I, 251, traces the Essenes as well as the Pharisees to hasidic origins.

Cave near Qumran where some of the Dead Sea Scrolls were found. (Courtesy of Israel Information Services.)

One who walks before his neighbors naked when he does not have to do so shall be punished for six months. A man who spits into the midst of the session of the masters shall be punished thirty days. One who brings his hand from beneath his robe when it is torn, so that his nakedness is seen, shall be punished thirty days. One who laughs foolishly, making his voice heard, shall be punished thirty days. One who brings his left hand to gesticulate with it shall be punished ten days.[17]

In addition, they looked toward the future vindication of Israel, or at least of their own community as the remnant of the true Israel. This vindication was expected in the form of an apocalyptic drama, indeed, a conflict, in which the forces of light would overwhelm those of darkness.[18] The victory would never be in doubt, because God was to fight on the side of his elect. Such terms as *light, darkness,* and *elect* highlight the basic character of Qumran thought. Al-

[17] From the Manual of Discipline, following Burrow's translation, *Scrolls,* p. 380.
[18] Such an encounter is described in the community document designated The War of the Sons of Light with the Sons of Darkness (cf. Burrows, *Scrolls,* pp. 390 ff.; also Vermes, *The Dead Sea Scrolls in English,* pp. 122 ff.).

most everything was seen as a choice between black and white, with no compromise allowed.

> He has created man to govern the world, and has appointed for him two spirits in which to walk until the time of His visitation: the spirits of truth and falsehood. Those born of truth spring from a fountain of light, but those born of falsehood spring from a source of darkness. All the children of righteousness are ruled by the Prince of Light and walk in the ways of light: but all the children of falsehood are ruled by the Angel of Darkness and walk in the ways of darkness.[19]

This way of perceiving the world, often called *dualism,* was reflected in the group's extremely rigid attitude toward the law, in its implacable hostility toward those regarded as enemies, and in its view of the coming culmination of history. The triumph of the good people over the bad would result in the elimination of evil from the world.

The Qumraners, or Essenes, as they may be called, were not purely passive in their hopes and expectations. Rather, they saw themselves, and particularly their separatist existence in the desert, as the fulfillment of the prophecy of Isaiah 40:3 (cf. Manual of Discipline, VIII). They were in the wilderness preparing the way of the Lord. In this respect there is a striking similarity between the Qumran community and the New Testament church. In the New Testament the same Old Testament passage is found on the lips of John the Baptist, who views his task in a similar way. It is indicative of the fact that both the desert community and Jesus and his disciples lived in an atmosphere of apocalyptic or eschatological expectation. They looked forward to the coming of God. In fact, there were other similarities between the two groups. Both stood apart from prevailing forms of Jewish piety. Both looked to a central leader or founder, whether Jesus or the teacher of righteousness; in different ways both maintained a distinctive view of the law; both formed a community or sect of believers within Judaism. There has been a great deal of excitement over the Qumran discoveries; they have not only enlarged our view of ancient Judaism, but in several significant ways have brought us closer to the origins of Christianity.

Yet there are also significant differences. Christians insisted upon what they regarded as the essential meaning of the law rather than the letter. Jesus was denounced as a wine-bibber and a friend of publicans and sinners, and his disciples and the other early Christians continued to live among other men. They did not withdraw to themselves. Instead of savoring in advance their own salvation at

---

[19] From G. Vermes' translation of The Community Rule (or Manual of Discipline), in *The Dead Sea Scrolls in English,* pp. 75 f.

the expense of nearly everyone else, most Christians went out to preach their good news to humanity at large. Nevertheless, for the purpose of a historical understanding of Jesus, his disciples, and early Christianity, the Qumran documents are quite important. They reveal another Jewish sect of the same period that was engaged in alternately searching the scriptures and the heavens for signs of God's approaching kingdom. For the Christians these hopes and expectations found fulfillment, although not in the way anticipated. For the Qumran community and other Essenes there was apparently only disappointment in this world. The monastery was destroyed by the Romans in the war of A.D. 66–70, and the inhabitants hid their sacred scrolls in nearby caves, where they were accidentally discovered nearly two thousand years later.

AN ABIDING HOPE

What kind of Messiah were the Jews expecting?

Judaism in New Testament times was characterized not only by a memorable past and earnest efforts to obey the law of God in the present, but by its attitude toward the future. The Qumran discoveries are important evidence of this fact. As we have already noted, most Jews had definite ideas about the future, which were usually tied to the national destiny.

At one end of the spectrum stood those like the men of Qumran who looked for the dramatic intervention of God in history to destroy the wicked and establish forever the righteous Israelites. At the other stood the Sadducees, whose position of relative security and comfort in relation to the Roman authorities made them little disposed either to sedition or an apocalyptic outlook. The Sadducees looked for no cataclysmic end of history and no resurrection of the dead. In this respect they seem to have been in substantial agreement with the theology of the pre-exilic Israel. The Zealots sought to realize their hope by the recovery of national autonomy, under God, through armed rebellion (see pp. 13 f.). Apart from such extremes stood the Pharisees, who may have hoped for "the redemption of Israel" (Luke 24:21), but did not expect to initiate it by violent revolution.[20] Although differing in this respect from the Zealots, they were related to them both in their enthusiasm for the law and in their zeal for preservation of Jewish identity. Although the Pharisees abjured the kind of active cooperation with Roman authority in which the Sadducees engaged, they served along with

[20] According to Josephus (*The Jewish War*, II, xvii, 3), Pharisees were among the prominent men who attempted to dissuade the Zealots when they were in the process of launching the rebellion against Rome.

priests and Sadducees on the Sanhedrin, the highest Jewish court of
appeal under Roman rule. Moreover, they had a history of political
involvement during the Maccabean period. Unlike the Essenes, the
Pharisees were not monastically inclined.

It is difficult to say with certainty how the Pharisees expected
Israel's national destiny to be fulfilled. The rabbinic documents,
which generally express a Pharisaic point of view, do not look forward to an *imminent* apocalyptic drama whereby God would bring
ordinary history to an end and restore the fortunes of Israel. But the
rabbinic literature is not necessarily an accurate guide to Pharisaic
expectations during the period of Jesus and the writing of the New
Testament books. It reflects the attitude of Judaism after the Roman
War and the uprising of Bar Kochba, when disappointed Zealot and
revolutionary hopes made apocalyptic and messianic speculations
about such matters unattractive. Yet very probably the earlier Pharisees, like the Essenes, cherished such apocalyptic and messianic
hopes:

> Behold, O Lord, and raise up unto them their king, the son of
> David,
> > At the same time in which Thou seest, O God, that he may
> > reign over Israel Thy servant.
> And gird him with strength, that he may shatter unrighteous
> rulers,
> > And that he may purge Jerusalem from nations that trample
> > (her) down to destruction. . . .
> At his rebuke nations shall flee before him,
> > And he shall reprove sinners for the thoughts of their heart.[21]

In the intertestamental apocalyptic literature we find the expectation of a decisive culmination of history. The hope was widely
shared. This world or this age was to come to a conclusion with the
restoration of Israel's fortunes and the resurrection of her righteous
dead, marking the inauguration of the messianic age. After a period
of from several hundred to a thousand years, the general resurrection
(that is, of all the dead) would take place as a prelude to the final
judgment of God. Then God would usher in the "age to come," the
consummation toward which all history was moving. It is too much
to speak of a single plan or scheme, but the existence of similar
ideas and expectations, if in less systematized form, in the New Tes-

---

[21] The Psalm of Solomon 17, in the Pseudepigrapha, is usually regarded as typical
of Pharisaic messianic hope; vss. 23, 24, 27 are quoted. The passage is cited from
R. H. Charles, The *Apocrypha and Pseudepigrapha of the Old Testament,* II (Oxford:
Clarendon, 1913), p. 649. Psalm 17 is messianic without being clearly apocalyptic.
On the positive attitude of Pharisaism to apocalyptic during the New Testament pe-
riod, cf. W. D. Davies, "Apocalyptic and Pharisaism," *Christian Origins and Judaism*
(Philadelphia: Westminster, 1962), pp. 19–30.

tament shows that they were common currency in the Judaism of Jesus' day.

Apocalyptic and similar ideas were not espoused solely out of patriotic interests and hopes. The doctrine of the resurrection of the dead provided a lively individual hope and a means of justifying God's ways with men. If, as experience dictated, the righteous servants of God's law suffer in this life, they may expect better things when the dead are raised. The doctrine of the resurrection became the hallmark of the Pharisees (cf. Acts 23:6), so that in time a virtual anathema could be pronounced against those who disbelieved it. Belief in the resurrection appears rarely in the Old Testament, notably in Isaiah 26:19 and Daniel 12:2. Thus it is not surprising that the Sadducees did not feel obliged to share it. Nevertheless, the New Testament reports that Jesus (Mark 12:26 f.) as well as Paul (Acts 23:6) believed in the resurrection. In doing so they were following a Jewish tradition.

The whole complex of apocalyptic ideas, including the resurrection of the dead, the dualism of good and evil, the distinction between this age and the age to come, and the destruction of evil and the triumph of good in a cataclysmic cosmic upheaval and judgment, cannot be explained fully on the basis of the earlier, Old Testament tradition of Israel, whether historical, prophetic, or cultic. The apocalyptic frame of mind has marked affinities with Persian, particularly Zoroastrian, thought. This is especially true of the dualism, cosmic eschatology, and the last judgment. To what extent they may reflect direct borrowing or even more subtle influences is debatable, although such outside influences cannot simply be discounted, especially in view of the exposure of many Jews to foreign influences in the exile and the diaspora after the sixth century B.C. But the impotence and frustration of the Jews in their homeland doubtless provided the necessary seedbed and impetus for such ideas to develop. In due course this same kind of thinking provided the fertile ground out of which Christianity emerged. For John the Baptist came proclaiming the imminent judgment; Jesus announced the inbreaking of the kingdom of God in power (that is, the age to come); and the early Christians proclaimed that Jesus had risen from the dead and would come again in glory to render judgment (cf. also Daniel 7). Although Jesus surely felt himself to be a son of Abraham, as did the early Christians generally (cf. Gal. 3:29), and consciously stood in the tradition of the law and the prophets, he was the heir of ideas and perspectives that were unknown to the patriarchs, Moses, or Amos. Some of these were perhaps "foreign" in the sense of being non-Israelite. Yet the substance and framework of Jesus' message had deep roots in his prople's history and faith. Apart from the glory and the agony of that history Jesus can scarcely be fully understood. In his insistence on obedience to God's will in the present as the key to the future, Jesus exemplifies Israelite faith.[22] Jesus proposed a radical reinterpretation of both obedience and hope, but in the indissoluble linking of the two he was a true son of Abraham.

Judaism is history, law, tradition, worship, and the land. But perhaps more than anything else Judaism is and always has been a people—a people with a unique sense of identity and purpose, a chosen people, with all the distinctiveness, as well as liabilities, that such a concept implies. Our discussion of Judaism has naturally and perhaps inevitably focused upon the major religious groupings of the first century. But most Palestinians who considered themselves Jews were probably members of no definable religious group. To these people, or at least to the less conscientiously pious among them, the term *people of the land* (*am ha-aretz*) was applied. They were often looked down upon by those who were more scrupulous observers. Quite possibly Jesus himself was numbered among these humble folk (cf. John 7:15), certainly many of his followers were. In the Gospel of John they are described as ignorant of the law and accursed (7:49). But although frequently disparaged and even ridiculed, such folk were not necessarily unaware of their heritage and identity. This sense of belonging, together with resistance toward the claims of the religious establishment, is reflected in the attitude of Jesus himself. He was clearly aware of his identity as an Israelite, a Jew, yet he reacted sharply against claims of religious superiority. Like Jesus, the earliest Christians were Jews, and only gradually began to think of themselves in any other way.

The Greco-Roman World

Judaism provided the ingredients from which the new faith took shape. The pilgrimage and travail of Israel, its scriptures and its expectations, furnished the essential frame of reference for Jesus and his earliest followers. Yet Christian faith soon broke away from Judaism and spread rapidly among Gentiles throughout the Mediterranean world. In a sense, it became a universal form of Judaism. But how and why did this happen to the sect of Jesus' followers in particular? The answer to this is manifold, although it remains partly a mystery. But some valid reasons can be discerned by observing the conditions in the world into which Christianity spread.

[22] For a sensitive and sympathetic interpretation of Jesus as the embodiment of the Jewish understanding of faith, see Martin Buber, *Two Types of Faith*, trans. N. P. Goldhawk (New York: Macmillan, 1951).

LANGUAGE AND CULTURE
What is meant by Hellenistic culture?

Several hundred years before the beginning of the Christian era, in about the third century B.C., the Hebrew scriptures were translated into Greek. According to an ancient legend found in the Epistle of Aristeas (see the Glossary), the translation was done in Egypt for the royal library because of scholarly appreciation for the importance of the books. In all probability, however, the translation was made on the initiative and for the benefit of the Jews themselves, most of whom could read and understand Greek better than they could the ancestral Hebrew tongue.

ALEXANDER THE GREAT
The Jews had become widely scattered in Egypt and other places as a result of the Exile. They spoke Greek largely because of the remarkable influence of one man, Alexander of Macedon. Few individuals have had a greater impact upon the history, culture, and religion of the world than Alexander. Born in 356 B.C., he succeeded to the throne of his father, Philip of Macedon, in 334. Two years later he set out from his home in Macedonia to begin the conquest of the Persian Empire, which for years had menaced and invaded Greece. In eight years, he and his army swept as far south as Egypt and as far east as the Indus River at the westernmost reaches of India, where only the homesickness of is soldiers halted his advance. Although the Persian Empire and army proved ineffective against the more homogeneous and better disciplined army of Alexander, his military accomplishment cannot be minimized.

Of greater importance than military feats, however, was the cultural revolution that he accomplished. Alexander was not only a soldier but also a man of letters and a student of Aristotle. He was eager to establish Greek culture and language in the areas that he conquered, and his success in this respect was remarkable. Alexander seems to have envisioned a genuine cultural mixture throughout the ancient world, with the Hellenic (Greek) element as the common factor everywhere. The seriousness of his intention is exemplified in the fact that he and his soldiers took women of the East as wives. After his conquest he seemed content to remain there, and apparently regarded Babylon as his capital. There, quite unexpectedly, he died of a fever in 323 B.C. at the age of thirty-three, leaving no legal heir capable of succeeding him. His lieutenants struggled for control of his empire and soon managed to pull it apart. Thus the fruit of his military conquest, although immense, proved ephemeral, for his empire dissolved almost as quickly as it had emerged.

Although Alexander did not succeed in establishing a Macedonian empire that would survive his death, his efforts to spread Greek language and culture and to embed them in the life of the East proved highly successful, especially in the cities. He left as his heritage a string of Greek cities across the area of his conquest, outposts of Greek civilization. Probably the largest and most successful of these was the great Egyptian center of Alexandria, which appropriately bore his name. Here a large colony of Jews settled, and the first and most important translation of the Hebrew scriptures into Greek was made.

THE IMPORTANCE OF THE GREEK LANGUAGE

Alexander gave a particular form and character to the world into which Christianity was born. Nothing is more important for human history and culture than language, and nothing promotes communication and understanding like a common language. Among other things, Alexander bequeathed to the Mediterranean world a common language, Greek. It was not the Greek of Plato or Sophocles, but another newer and somewhat simpler dialect known as *koine,* or common, Greek. This Greek became the *lingua franca* of the ancient world three hundred years before the time of Christ.

People from widely separated areas and with vastly different backgrounds could talk to each other in Greek. Perhaps they could not construct complex Greek sentences with perfect syntax and inflection, but they could make themselves understood. Needless to say, this gift of common speech was of considerable importance in encouraging commerce and various sorts of interchange throughout the Alexandrian world. Indeed, in the centers of Greek culture established by Alexander, conscious attempts were made to promote and spread the manners and customs, especially the athletic games, of Hellenic civilization. The world that Alexander left was one world in a sense that it had never been before. Previously there had been great overarching empires such as the Assyrian, the Persian, and the Egyptian, and certainly different peoples and cultures had interacted; but never before had there been such an attempt to create a common world civilization as was actually and purposefully brought about by Alexander and his successors. This mixture of Hellenic (Greek) and Oriental elements is called Hellenistic civilization.

The importance of this universal Mediterranean civilization for Judaism and its offspring Christianity can scarcely be overestimated. For Judaism it was at once a threat and a benefit—a threat in that it tended to eliminate just those distinguishing features of life that characterized the Jewish community as such, but a benefit in that it made possible greater extension of the scope and influence of Judaism, especially Greek-speaking Judaism. For Christianity it was an immense boon. Without Alexander the rapid spread of Christianity through the Greco-Roman world might never have taken place. Certainly the Christian message had a power of its own, and its impact

The Greek philosopher Socrates, 470(?)–399 B.C. (Courtesy of the British Museum.)

cannot be attributed to favorable cultural factors alone. Nevertheless, it is a striking fact that the spread of Christianity in the first centuries occurred principally in those areas that fell under the sway of Alexander's, or at least of Greek, influence.

The New Testament itself was composed entirely in Greek, although the Gospels are in part based on earlier Aramaic sources, either written or oral. Except in Palestine and Syria, and perhaps to some extent even there, the preaching of the gospel was in Greek. In most places of any importance Greek was the language that was spoken and understood by both preacher and hearer. Even in Rome, to which Christianity spread at a very early time, and which we generally associate with the Latin language, Greek was generally spoken and understood. Yet despite the important role that Greek language and culture played in its spread, it would be incorrect simply to call Christianity a Greek religion. Viewed from the standpoint of its origin and original constituents, it is also Oriental and especially Jewish. It is not, therefore, the purely Greek element, but precisely this combination of Greek and Jewish, West and East, which was characteristic of Christianity in the Hellenistic world.

GOVERNMENT

What was the distinctive contribution of Rome to the birth of Christianity?

Alexander created a world but did not live to govern it. That task was ultimately performed by Rome. It is, of course, true that the limits of Alexander's conquests and those of the Roman Empire at its height were not the same. Alexander's conquests extended farther to the east, whereas the Roman Empire's orbit stretched far beyond Italy to the north and west. Yet in a sense the world of Alexandrian Hellenism and the world of Rome were one world.[23] Through her own conquest of Greece and wholesale appropriation of Greek culture in the second century b.c., Rome fell heir to the legacy of Greece just when she was emerging as the dominant military force and political power of the Western world. For a half-century before Christ and nearly half a millennium after, the Roman Empire gave to the Mediterranean world a political unity and stability. That unity, though not unbroken, was about as continuous and dependable as any so large and varied a segment of the world has known before or since. The marvel is not that the Roman Empire fell—crumbled is the better word—but that it stood so long. At the time of its greatest extent and vitality—that is, during the New Testament period—the Roman Empire stretched from Syria and Palestine to the British Isles. Of western Europe, only Germany and the Scandinavian countries remained outside the Roman orbit, and only Scandinavia completely outside. The southern and westernmost parts of Germany came under Roman domination, as did Austria as far north as the Danube.

[23] The great classical historian M. Rostovtzeff regarded the culture of the Roman Empire as basically Greek. In *A History of the Ancient World*, I: *The Orient and Greece*, trans. J. D. Duff (Oxford: Clarendon, n.d.), pp. 281 f., he writes, "The Latin culture of Italy and the West is one branch of the Greek culture of the third and later centuries—not a slavish copy, not an imitation, but an independent national development of Greek ideas, Greek art, and Greek literature in the Latin West, a participation by the West in the city-life of the Hellenic East with all its external characteristics."

The birth and development of Christianity as a world religion came about during the two centuries when Rome was at the zenith of its power (i.e., from 27 B.C., the accession date of Augustus Caesar, to A.D. 180, the year of the death of Marcus Aurelius, the philosopher emperor). This period, often referred to as the *pax romana* (peace of Rome), was a favorable time for the origin of a movement like Christianity. There was both absence of war and domestic order. Our present systems of law owe more directly to the Romans than to the Hebrews, and the *pax romana* was a time of lawfulness as well as peace. The Romans administered the empire with firmness, but with a certain sensitivity for the varieties of peoples and customs within their bounds. Local law enforcement and administration were left in the hands of local officials. Where local administration or law enforcement broke down, as in the case of Judea at the time of Jesus, the Romans intervened to make sure that anarchy did not reign. Roman officials were not universally good, as we have already noted. Pontius Pilate, for example, left a great deal to be desired. Yet the Romans themselves removed Pilate from power. Although it is true that Jesus died on a Roman cross and that Christians were persecuted by Romans, it is equally true, and probably just as important, that early Christianity benefited considerably from the peaceful and lawful conditions of Roman rule that accompanied its beginnings.

Early Christianity profited also from the network of roads and sea transportation that the Romans had developed and maintained, largely for military purposes. Again, policing of the roads was left to the various provinces and localities as long as they could do the job, but when and where conditions demanded, the Roman military intervened to keep roads open for travel and free of bandits and other potential harassments. It would certainly be wrong to imagine that travel in ancient times was as easy as it is today. Yet travel between virtually all parts of the empire was possible, and it was probably easier to go from Jerusalem to Rome in Paul's day than it was to travel from the East Coast to California in this country a little more than a hundred years ago.

Thus favorable conditions of language and culture as well as an orderly government and a workable transportation system favored the spread of the Christian gospel in the Greco-Roman world. They help to explain the rapid growth of the church and the ways in which the gospel found expression—not the least of which is the New Testament itself, a collection of books written in Greek, and in many cases written from one Christian or group of Christians to or for another. These documents attest not only a lively faith but also a sense of tangible relationship between one Christian church and another, which was made possible by the conditions of the time. Moreover, they display a concrete sense of mission concerning something called "the world" (Greek, *kosmos*), a concept not previously unknown, but given particular point and form by the vision and work of Alexander the Great and the political reality of the Roman Empire.

RELIGION

What were the major forms of religion in the Greco-Roman world?

According to the book of Acts, the apostle Paul began his famous speech to the Athenians by saying, "Men of Athens, I perceive that in every way you are very religious" (17:22). The world of New Testament times was a religious world. Christianity did not originate in a time of religious decline. Whatever may have been the general state of culture in the first century, religion did not lack vitality and vigorous manifestations.

A striking characteristic of the religious situation was its variety. This too is represented in Paul's speech, for he mentions the objects of their worship, among which is an altar inscribed to an unknown God, as if the Athenians were taking no chances on omitting, and therefore offending, any deity. People participated in various rites and ceremonies according to law, taste, or desire. The period was also marked by syncretism: various religious traditions merged together or were interpreted in terms of one another.

Such toleration did not mean that people by and large did not take religion seriously. If anything, just the opposite was the case. Only from the Christian or Jewish point of view could this toleration of, and participation in, a multiplicity of religious cults be taken as an indication of frivolity. The exclusivism of Judaism and Christianity was itself regarded as odd and even impious in ancient times, and the refusal of Christians and Jews to worship any god other than their own led their neighbors to brand them as atheists. This persistence in worshiping only one God was perhaps the factor that most clearly distinguished Christians and Jews in the ancient world, and it may have had something to do with the fact that of the religions of that civilization only Christianity and Judaism survive today. Yet elements of these religions have survived in Judaism and particularly in Christianity.[24]

The specific manifestations of piety in the Greco-Roman world are far too numerous to discuss here fully. Nevertheless, it will be helpful to notice several basic types of religion that were popular and significant. These include the religion of the Greco-Roman pan-

---

[24]For example, the date of Jesus' birth is unknown; Christmas is the Christianized version of an ancient Roman rite celebrating the winter solstice and return of the sun. Easter is a distinctly Christian holiday, but rabbits and eggs are pagan intrusions.

theon (a Greek word meaning a temple dedicated to "all the gods"), the worship of the ruler, mystery religions, Gnosticism, and Judaism. Against this background the emergence of early Christianity must be viewed.

TRADITIONAL AND OFFICIAL RELIGION

At the time of the emergence of Christianity and the writing of the New Testament books, the traditional religion of the Roman Empire was a complex and somewhat amorphous combination of both Greek and Roman elements. Prior to the Christian era there had been a distinctly Roman religious cult involving especially the gods of the hearth and the family, of which the public religion was an extension and enlargement. This state or city cult was presided over first by the king, and later by a pontifical college made up of several prominent men of the realm. Ancient Greek religion of the pre-Christian period seems to have consisted originally of a variety of local deities, each with a holy place. These were later submerged under, or incorporated into, the pantheon of very human gods known to us from Homer, who is the fountainhead of classical mythology. By the beginning of the Christian period an amalgamation of Greek and Roman deities had taken place. It was taken for granted that the Greek and Roman gods were for the most part actually the same gods, even if they had different names, and an equation of the various gods of the Homeric pantheon with Roman gods had been worked out. For example, the three very prominent Greek gods, Zeus, Hera, and Athena, were identified with the Roman Jupiter, Juno, and Minerva, respectively. Moreover, the purely Greek god Apollo was worshiped on the Palatine Hill in Rome.

By the beginning of the Christian era the traditional piety of Greece and Rome was facing competition from newer religions, especially those of Oriental origin, which were gaining enthusiastic adherents. Moreover, people of some education and intelligence had difficulty taking the myths and stories that were told about the gods seriously, at least insofar as they were understood as literal accounts of what actually took place or of the nature of divine reality. Folk of a philosophical bent, especially the Stoics, had been interpreting the myths in an allegorical way for some time.[25] That is, they took them to be narrative representations of philosophical truths, which really had nothing to do with the stories per se and could stand in-

---

[25] W. W. Tarn, *Hellenistic Civilization,* 3rd ed. rev. with G. T. Griffith (London: Arnold, 1952), p. 325, points out that Stoicism was the philosophy *par excellence* of the Hellenistic world. Other philosophies there surely were (e.g., Epicureanism, Platonism, Aristotelianism, Skepticism). Nevertheless, the Stoic outlook, especially the Stoic ethic with its responsibility toward the world as well as its inwardness, was predominant.

The magnificent ruins of a temple to Olympian Zeus in Athens. (Courtesy of Greek Press and Information Service.)

dependently of them. Thus the old gods got a new lease on life. For example, Zeus, the head of the Homeric pantheon, could be identified with "the general law, which is right reason, pervading everything . . . the Supreme Head of the universe" (Zeno, *Fragments*, 162, 152).[26] The Stoic monism, according to which God or the logos (Greek for "word" or "reason") pervades the universe much as the soul or animation pervades the body and gives it unity and purpose, was thereby reconciled with a mythology that had quite a different origin and meaning. Especially those stories of the gods consorting and cavorting with each other in ways that sober men came to regard as shameful were allegorized away, making room for the Stoic ethic, which centered in willing conformity with that reason or logos that governs the universe and the individual. The Stoics themselves, however, were not coldly rationalistic. Philosophy was for them a vital piety, and although this piety was grounded in a philosophical pantheism, its expression often took the form of hymns and prayers to a personal or quasipersonal God, as can be seen from a portion of Cleanthes' famous *Hymn to Zeus:*

[26] Cited from C. K. Barrett, *The New Testament Background: Selected Documents* (London: SPCK, 1957), p. 62.

Thou, O Zeus, art praised above all gods; many are thy names and
   thine is all power for ever.
The beginning of the world was from thee; and with law thou
   rulest over all things.
Unto thee may all flesh speak; for we are thy offspring.
Therefore will I raise a hymn unto thee: and will ever sing of thy
   power.
The whole order of the heavens obeyeth thy word: as it moveth
   around the earth:
With little and great lights mixed together: how great art thou,
   King above all for ever! [27]

The ancient Greco-Roman religion survived not merely in Stoic
reinterpretation but also in more naïve popular worship. As such, it
remained the traditional public religion of the Roman Empire, just
as its predecessors had been the official cults of old Rome and of the
Greek city-states. We find some indication of its survival in the
New Testament. According to Acts the people of Lystra, in what is
now Asia Minor, hailed Paul and Barnabas as Hermes and Zeus, respectively, upon their performance of a miracle. Moreover, a temple
of Zeus was located near that city (Acts 14:12 f.). There was in the
city of Ephesus a great temple of Artemis (cf. Acts 19:23 ff.), which
has been unearthed in modern times by archaeologists, as have
many other temples to the Greco-Roman deities. In addition, the
Roman emperor Augustus, who was ruling at the time Jesus was
born, made a serious effort to promote the traditional public cult,
especially the ancient Roman practices and ceremonies. Upon the
death of the high priest, he went so far as to assume that office
himself, reviving a custom long fallen into disuse, according to
which the kingship and high priesthood were united in one man.
   Beginning with Augustus' reign there was an increasing tendency to regard the emperor as a divine figure and to place him
among the pantheon of gods to whom worship was due. Although
Augustus coyly spurned divine honors during his lifetime, they were
accorded him upon his death. By the end of the first Christian century, it was no longer a question of ascribing divine honors and worship to deceased emperors. Now such veneration was deemed to be
due the living emperor as well. Not surprisingly, this led in due
course to a confrontation between the young Christian church and
Rome. For Rome insisted upon emperor worship as a pledge of allegiance—or devotion—to the emperor and thus to the empire. As
Pliny, governor of Bithynia, writes to the Emperor Trajan, "All who
denied that they were or had been Christians I considered should be
discharged, because they called upon the gods at my dictation and
did reverence, with incense and wine, to your image which I had

[27]*Ibid.*, p. 63.

Ruins of a fifth-century B.C. temple to Poseidon, Greek god of the sea, located at Cape Sounion near Athens. (Courtesy of Greek Press and Information Service.)

ordered to be brought forward for this purpose. . . ."[28] It was, in fact, a sort of loyalty oath, but one which Christians could not conscientiously take. Yet when emperor worship is seen against the background of the many gods and many lords of the ancient world (cf. I Cor. 8:5), and when the benefits accruing to humankind from the emperor's rule are recalled, we can understand why the authorities did not regard divine homage as too much to ask of any subject. Moreover, worship of the supreme ruler was not unknown in earlier times. The Romans were doubtless genuinely perplexed to find people who stubbornly refused to participate on religious grounds, as Jews and Christians did.

POPULAR RELIGION

Although the official religious rites of Greece and Rome were by no means dead at the beginning of the Christian era, they did not represent the principal form of personal piety. Their continued existence, and whatever vitality they had, was probably due largely to the role they played in expressing the political and cultural solidar-

[28] From Henry Bettenson, ed., *Documents of the Christian Church* (New York: Oxford University Press, 1947), p. 6.

ity of the Roman Empire and the Greco-Roman world. No sustained attempt was made to establish public religion to the exclusion of private practices and societies, however, and it is in the latter that the burgeoning variety and strength of religion in later antiquity can be most clearly seen.

Unfortunately, our knowledge of these practices and societies is quite limited, owing in no small measure to the aura of secrecy that surrounded many of them. This is especially true of the so-called *mystery religions*, which were gaining in prominence and popularity at the beginning of the Christian era. The vows of secrecy that the followers of these religions took were meticulously observed. Much of the ancient material on the mysteries comes to us at secondhand through Christian and Jewish sources. Consequently, we do not know in detail, or with a high degree of assurance, what they were like.

The most closely guarded secrets of the mystery religions were their rites of initiation, through which the novitiate first received the benefits that the cult deity bestowed. Apparently the candidate somehow reenacted or saw re-enacted the cult myth—that is, the

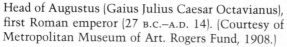

Head of Augustus (Gaius Julius Caesar Octavianus), first Roman emperor (27 B.C.–A.D. 14). (Courtesy of Metropolitan Museum of Art. Rogers Fund, 1908.)

story about the god or gods on which the cult was based—and thus participated in it. Through participation he received the salvation that was the very reason for the cult's being.

Perhaps the best account of the mystery ritual is found in Apuleius, *The Golden Ass* (xi, 22–26), from which the following description of an Isis initiation is taken:

> Then behold the day approached when as the sacrifice of dedication should be done; and when the sun declined and evening came, there arrived on every coast a great multitude of priests, who according to their ancient order offered me many presents and gifts. Then was all the laity and profane people commanded to depart, and when they had put on my back a new linen robe, the priest took my hand and brought me to the most secret and sacred place of the temple. Thou wouldest peradventure demand, thou studious reader, what was said and done there: verily I would tell thee if it were lawful for me to tell, thou wouldest know if it were convenient for thee to hear; but both thy ears and my tongue should incur the like pain of rash curiosity. Howbeit I will not long torment thy mind, which peradventure is somewhat religious and given to some devotion; listen therefore, and believe it to be true. Thou shalt understand that I approached near unto hell, even to the gates of Proserpine, and after that I was ravished throughout all the elements, I returned to my proper place: about midnight I saw the sun brightly shine, I saw likewise the gods celestial and the gods infernal, before whom I presented myself and worshipped them. Behold now have I told thee, which although thou hast heard, yet it is necessary that thou conceal it; wherefore this only will I tell, which may be declared without offence for the understanding of the profane.[29]

The myth of the cult naturally varied with the different mystery religions. Among others, there were the Eleusinian mysteries of Greece; the cult of Attis and Cybele, originating in Asia Minor; as well as that of Isis and Osiris, which had its origin in Egypt. Most of the cults were based originally upon fertility rites celebrating the return of the growing season. In time, however, the meaning of the cult myth was seen against the background of human life and death, so that through initiation into the mysteries one could assure oneself of a happy destiny beyond death. Scholars once confidently asserted that the common factor in the cult myths was the death and resurrection of a deity, in which the initiate participated vicariously through the rites and thus rose from the dead with the god (cf. Romans 6:1–11). This interpretation has been subject to dispute,[30] but it is probably not completely misleading.

[29] Cited from Barrett, *The New Testament Background*, pp. 98 f.

[30] Especially by Günter Wagner, *Pauline Baptism and the Pagan Mysteries*, trans. J. P. Smith (Edinburgh: Oliver & Boyd, 1967).

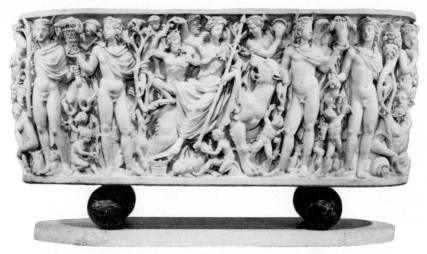

This Roman sarcophagus (*ca.* A.D. 220–230) shows Dionysos, the Olympian god who is the giver of the grape and therefore of wine, riding in triumph on a panther and surrounded by a host of figures including the Four Seasons. (Courtesy of Metropolitan Museum of Art. Purchase, 1955, Joseph Pulitzer Bequest.)

The traditional religions of Greece and Rome, like the religion of Israel, had focused primarily upon the ordering of life in this world, and did not promise the adherent a glorious life after death. The mysteries, however, appealed to human hopes and fears in the face of death and offered to those who became initiates the promise of eternal life. Membership in them presumed a belief in their efficacy and required a conscious act of the will, a decision. Thus the mystery religions had a character decidedly different from the traditional official religions and in some respects not unlike Christianity. They were private, they were oriented around hope and assurance for the future, and they were voluntary. Unlike Judaism and Christianity, however, they did not claim the exclusive loyalty of their adherents. A person might worship Zeus and the emperor and at the same time be an initiate of one or more mysteries. In fact, the official religions and the mysteries were complementary; they applied to different spheres of life, the one to public order and morality, the other to the need for emotional satisfaction and the assurance of the present and ultimate security of one's personal being and destiny.

At some time after the mystery religions moved into the center of the stage, there appeared another important spiritual phenomenon that was in some ways like them. We say "phenomenon" for it is not quite certain that *Gnosticism* should be called a religion. It was found in various places and in various forms. Until fairly recently most of our knowledge of Gnosticism came from Christian writers of the late second, third, and later centuries, all of whom

The god Mithras is kneeling on a prostrate bull, drawing back its head and stabbing it behind the shoulder with a short sword. A dog and a snake are springing up to drink the blood of the victim. A scorpion seizes the scrotum with its claws. Mithras was the Persian solar deity, whose worship became popular at the close of the Roman Republic. Many similar groups, all probably of the Roman period, have been found in different parts of the Roman Empire. 2nd Cent. A.D. (?). (Courtesy of the British Museum.)

portray Gnosticism as a Christian heresy in which a special knowledge (Greek *gnōsis*—hence the name Gnosticism) rather than faith is made the key to salvation. Gnosticism was regarded as the acute Hellenization of Christianity, a distorted translation of the Christian message into Greek ways of thinking and speaking. Yet recent research and discoveries have shown that Gnosticism is not simply derived from Christianity, and that it owes more to the East, to Syria, Persia, and Babylonia, and perhaps even to Judaism, than to classical Greek culture. (In this respect it is not unlike the mystery religions, many of which came from the Orient.) The exact nature and origin of Gnosticism are still obscure, however, and matters of controversy among historians of religion.

We can, however, get a fairly clear grasp of the thrust and meaning of Gnosticism. Wherever it appears, in whatever form, it is characterized by an extreme dualism of God and the world. In contrast to the Stoic monism, in which God and the world are essentially related and, indeed, indwell one another, Gnosticism takes God and the world to be separate and incompatible. Far from being the creation of the one God, as in orthodox Jewish and Christian thought, the world is at best an excrescence from the divine world, at worst the creation of an antigod. Its very existence is the antithesis of God's salvation. The mystery religions were primarily motivated by a desire to secure human existence in the face of death. Gnosticism also had this goal in view, but combined with it an abhorrence of evil, which was in general identified with this world and its history.

People live in the world, but at least some of them are not of it. For while human bodies are made of the same substance as the world, there is, or may be, hidden within each one a spark of the divine life. Salvation is then the rescuing of the divine spark from its imprisonment in the material world, and specifically in the flesh. The first and essential step is the recognition that one is not at home in this world, that one's essential being is related to the divine world and can find its way home.[31]

> Therefore if one has knowledge he is from above. If he is called, he hears, he answers, and he turns to him who is calling him, and ascends to him. And he knows in what manner he is called. Having knowledge, he does the will of the one who called him, he wishes to be pleasing to him, he receives rest.
>
> Each one's name comes to him. He who is to have knowledge in this manner knows where he comes from and where he is going. He knows as one who having become drunk has turned away from his drunkenness, [and] having returned to himself, has set right what are his own.[32]

Thus the process of salvation in Gnosticism involves, first of all, a sense of profound alienation from the world. One must find a way out of imprisonment in this world and into the world above. This can be done only by a special dispensation of knowledge by which the secrets of the way back to one's heavenly home are divulged. In Christian Gnostic systems Jesus is the heavenly revealer who awakens the adherents from their stupor in this world, reminds them of

[31] A similar point of view is found in a set of documents known as the Hermetic literature, or Hermetica. In their present form, these documents date from about the third century. They are not Christian, although they may have been influenced by Judaism. Whether they ought to be called Gnostic is a debated point. See Barrett, *The New Testament Background*, pp. 80–90, for examples from the Hermetica.

[32] Gospel of Truth, 22:3–20; from George MacRae's translation in *The Nag Hammadi Library in English*, ed. J. M. Robinson (San Francisco: Harper & Row, 1977), p. 40.

their heavenly home, reveals the secrets of the way, and also leads them back. The way back was often conceived as a rather long road, a tortuous climb back through the seven or more heavens, in each of which the Gnostics shed another part of the veil of flesh until the divine essence—the very quintessence of their being—arrives safely home.

This doctrine of salvation had its practical effects upon the life of the Gnostics, who felt themselves to be alien, and, in a sense, already withdrawn from the concerns of ordinary human life. This estrangement sometimes expressed itself in radical withdrawal from the world and its life, that is, asceticism. But it could also result in a free indulgence in sensual pleasure, for since the flesh and the physical world had no significance, what one did with them was of no importance. Whichever course was followed, the Gnostic refused any positive, constructive participation in this human life, which the poor deluded non-Gnostic held so important.

Early Christianity was deeply engaged with the Gnostic problem throughout the second century, and probably even earlier. We see traces of the conflict in the Johannine literature, Colossians, and the Pastoral Epistles, not to mention the extensive anti-Gnostic literature that appears from the time of Justin Martyr in the middle of the second century. In addition, a large collection of Gnostic literature going back to the second century (although the actual manuscripts are somewhat later) has recently been uncovered in Nag Hammadi in southern Egypt. It was obviously used by people who considered themselves Christians. Some of the books, such as the Gospel of Truth and the Gospel of Thomas, are apparently Gnostic interpretations of Christianity. Others have little explicit connection with anything we can identify with Christianity, except that they were apparently used by this Gnostic Christian church.

The discussion of Gnosticism raises the question of what influence it had on the formation of New Testament Christianity. It has been argued that Gnosticism came into being before the Christian faith arose and that when it came into contact with Christianity its doctrine already involved a myth about a redeemer who visited human beings in order to give them the knowledge of life. Some such doctrine is indeed found in the literature of Manichaeism, an Eastern religion post-Christian in origin (third century) and influenced by Christianity. It also appears in Mandaeism, the religion of a small Iranian sect that still exists and whose origin and antiquity is a matter of keen dispute. The sharpness and vigor of the modern debate is probably not unrelated to the fact that the Mandaean "redeemer myth" has real similarities to the Christian doctrine of Jesus as the Son of God whom the Father sent into the world, especially as it is set forth in the Gospel of John. Does the Christian doctrine recapitulate an earlier Gnostic myth? Certainly it is not just an imitation of such a myth, even if one existed. The canonical Gospels, which so clearly and intentionally portray the involvement of Jesus in this life and this world, are unprecedented in Gnostic literature. (The so-called Gnostic Gospels are quite different from the canonical documents.) Yet there is still the question of whether any sort of redeemer myth antedates Christianity. Here opinions divide sharply. Although the existence of a pre-Christian redeemer myth is controverted, the Gnostic perspective or attitude came into contact with Christianity at a very early time.[33]

There were, of course, other manifestations of belief and practice. These we can only note in passing. Many people in the ancient world were fascinated or oppressed by Fate (Greek, *heimarmenē*) or Fortune (Greek, *tychē*). Fortune came to be personalized and venerated as a goddess. The stars were thought to determine the course of people's lives, their fate. As a result, astrology, the "science" dealing with the influence of the stars on life, gained considerable popularity as the key to the secrets of human existence.[34] At the same time, some people relied on magic, invoking on occasion even the names of Yahweh and Jesus. There were also hero cults dedicated to those who had been elevated to the status of gods or demigods. Among these was the healing cult of Asclepius, who claimed many shrines and spas and thousands of devotees willing to ascribe to him miraculous cures no less amazing than those attributed to Jesus in the Gospels.

DIASPORA JUDAISM

In the complex religious picture of the Greco-Roman world, Judaism was a significant factor. Most Jews did not live in Palestine, but in other parts of that world. As noted previously, this diaspora or dispersion of Jews to the far corners of the world began as early as 587 B.C. with the conquest of Judah and the destruction of Jerusalem by the Babylonians. While conditions within the homeland became more difficult during the postexilic period and the number of Jews increased, the prospects of living outside of Palestine became increasingly attractive.

[33] Much of the research and scholarly discussion is published only in German. A good summary by a scholar avowedly skeptical of the existence of a pre-Christian Gnosticism which influenced the shape of early Christianity is Edwin M. Yamauchi, *Pre-Christian Gnosticism: A Survey of the Proposed Evidences* (Grand Rapids, Mich.: Eerdmans, 1973). On the redeemer myth specifically see Charles H. Talbert, "The Myth of a Descending-Ascending Redeemer in Mediterranean Antiquity," *New Testament Studies*, 22 (1976), 418–440. Talbert is also skeptical of claims of specifically Gnostic influence; he helpfully sets the whole discussion in the broader religious and cultural context of late antiquity and argues that the proximate background of the Christian descent-ascent motif is Jewish.

[34] See Hengel, *Judaism and Hellenism*, I, 238–241, who shows Jewish involvement in astrological speculation.

It is customary and useful to distinguish between the Judaism of
the land of Israel and that of the diaspora. Both shared in most of
the basic elements of Judaism mentioned at the beginning of this
chapter, yet outside Palestine significant changes had taken place,
most of which resulted from Hellenization. Hellenization, or accommodation to Greek culture, also took place in Palestine, as recent
research has made clear.[35] Outside Palestine, however, Judaism of
necessity began to take on some of the characteristics of a religion
as distinguished from a nation. Nevertheless, the Jews succeeded in
maintaining their ethnic identity and a certain separateness in their
ways and places of living. Yet Jews mingled to some extent with
Gentiles, were inevitably influenced by them, and vice versa. Ad-
justments to life in a predominantly Gentile world became necessary.

As has already been indicated, one of the most important adjust-
ments was in language. Judaism in the Greco-Roman world was
largely Greek-speaking. The fact that the Hebrew scriptures had
been translated into Greek and were read and interpreted in that
language doubtless influenced the way in which they were understood. Philo of Alexandria, a contemporary of Jesus and Paul, affords
a notable, if perhaps extreme, example of the kinds of changes that
could take place. A Jew who never once thought of surrendering that
hallmark of Judaism, the law, Philo nevertheless interpreted the Hebrew scriptures in terms of Hellenistic philosophy and piety by using the well-established Greek method of allegorizing. Thus he
could wring meanings from Biblical texts of which the original authors would have never dreamed. Eventually, Hellenistic Judaism
produced religious books containing ideas that were more Greek
than Jewish. For example, one reads in Wisdom of Solomon 3:1–9 of
the immortality of the souls of the righteous dead, a fundamentally
Greek idea, quite foreign to the Hebrew scriptures, although it has
since become rather common in Christian thought.

Another adjustment forced on the Jews by the dispersion involved their public worship. Up until the destruction of the temple
of Solomon at Jerusalem, the principal form of worship was sacrificial, officially performed at the Jerusalem temple, but sometimes
actually carried out elsewhere, much to the disgust of some prophets and other purists. After the fall of Jerusalem, the destruction of
the temple, the deportations, and the flight of refugees, another form
of worship began to gain pre-eminence, the worship of the synagogue, or individual congregation. The synagogue continues to be
the focal point of Jewish worship down to the present day. In New
Testament times synagogues were sprinkled around the Mediterranean world, as well as in Palestine. The Acts of the Apostles por-

[35] Ibid., esp. pp. 103–106.

trays Paul (and by implication other Christian missionaries) preaching the gospel in the local synagogue whenever he enters a new town.

The synagogues of the dispersion thus provided a ready-made platform for the early Christians, who, without necessarily ceasing to regard themselves as Jews, brought the good news of God's new salvation in Jesus the Messiah to the brethren and to others who might by chance listen. Inasmuch as new ideas and terms had already crept into the Hellenistic synagogue from the surrounding pagan culture, it need not surprise us to see these also in the New Testament. The New Testament writings, at least in their present form, were addressed to a church that had grown up in the midst of the Hellenistic culture of the Roman Empire. The importance of the Greek-speaking Judaism of the dispersion for early Christianity is epitomized in the fact that the New Testament is written in Greek. Moreover, the Old Testament, which is so frequently cited in the New, is more often than not quoted from the Greek version.

Diaspora Judaism also prepared the way for the universal emphasis of the Christian gospel. In fact, the existence of this kind of Judaism helps to explain how an historically exclusive community such as Judaism could have produced a missionary religion like Christianity. The Hellenistic synagogue itself did not disdain the missionary enterprise. There is some evidence of a sustained and serious effort to convert Gentiles to Judaism.[36] And not a few Gentiles were attracted by the antiquity and moral seriousness of the Jewish religion. The technical term for the conversion of Gentiles was proselytism and converts were called proselytes. Even where proselytism was not actively pursued, the situation of the Jews in the midst of an alien and potentially hostile culture demanded they look outward and have a decent respect for public opinion. One sees such an outward-looking perspective in Philo, but perhaps it is even more noticeable in the great first-century Jewish historian, Josephus. His extensive *Jewish Antiquities* is an elaborate exposition and explanation of the entire history and faith of his people for a literate Gentile audience. It is at once our best single source for the so-called intertestamental period and a monumental effort to make Jewish history intelligible to the wider world.

First-century diaspora Judaism was an important movement in and of itself, and it is of an extraordinary significance for the Christianity of New Testament times. For the modern student it illumines the path that Christianity traversed from its beginnings as a sect of Palestinian Judaism to the status of a world religion.

---

[36] As has been argued by Dieter Georgi, *Die Gegner des Paulus im 2. Korintherbrief: Studien zur religiösen Propaganda in der Spätantike* (Neukirchen-Vluyn: Neukirchener Verlag, 1964), esp. pp. 83–187.

In summary, the world into which Christianity came was one
world by virtue of the universal Hellenistic culture and Roman government, but the religious situation was complex and varied. Within
the variety, however, certain trends were developing: the waning of
the importance of the older gods and practices but their continued
existence alongside the more recently introduced emperor worship;
the emergence of popular philosophy on the one hand, and of religions of personal and otherworldly salvation on the other; and widespread disenchantment with the world.

In the midst of such a welter of religions and religious feeling,
Christianity must have seemed merely one more strange cult. Indeed, it was at first regarded as yet another manifestation of popular
superstition. The fact that its Jewish founder had been crucified as
a criminal did not escape the notice of the first Roman historian to
mention Christianity.[37] The Apostle Paul himself noted the humble
origins of most Christians (see I Cor. 1:26–29). Of all the religions
and religious movements of the ancient world few would have
seemed less likely to be the wave of the future than the Christian
church. Yet the church succeeded, for people were preoccupied with
the search for eternal life and yearned for regeneration, as well as for
a sure guide in ordering this life. Christianity's vibrant hope and
vigorous ethic spoke to their need. Moreover, the Christian community provided a source of identity and support in a world in
which old securities were disappearing.

Suggestions for Further Reading

Throughout the bibliographies subtitles and series titles have usually been
omitted to conserve space. Some works mentioned in notes are not repeated
in the bibliographies.

Primary Sources. The Old and New Testaments are cited according to
the Revised Standard Version, as is the Apocrypha of the Old Testament,
which is now bound with some editions of the RSV and other modern translations. Josephus' *Jewish Antiquities* and *Jewish War* are conveniently
available in original Greek and translation in The Loeb Classical Library
(Cambridge, Mass.: Harvard University Press), as are the works of Philo,
Eusebius' *Ecclesiastical History,* and the writings of the Apostolic Fathers.
Most of these writings are also available in other translations in paperback.

Jewish pseudepigraphal writings (writings under false names accepted
as canonical by no Christian or Jewish group) are available in the massive
translation and commentary of R. H. Charles, *The Apocrypha and Pseudepigrapha of the Old Testament,* 2 vols. (Oxford: Clarendon, 1913). A fresh
translation of the pseudepigrapha, including many additional writings, will
be made available by J. H. Charlesworth, *The Old Testament Pseudepigrapha* (scheduled for publication by Doubleday in 1982).

---

[37]Tacitus, *Annals,* XV, 44.

The Mishnah, which is the basic collection of material stemming from the earlier rabbis, has been translated and published by H. Danby (London: Oxford University Press, 1933). The Mishnaic tractate *Aboth* or *Pirke Aboth* ("fathers" or "chapters of the fathers") has been translated and published with a selection of ancient Talmudic commentary by J. Goldin, *The Living Talmud: The Wisdom of the Fathers* (New York: New American Library, 1957).

A reliable translation of the Qumran scrolls is G. Vermes, *The Dead Sea Scrolls in English,* rev. ed. (Baltimore: Penguin, 1970). One should, however, be alert to the fact that it does not contain more recently published documents such as the Temple Scroll. The most convenient compact collection of translated sources for Jewish religion is S. W. Baron and J. L. Blau (eds.), *Judaism: Postbiblical and Talmudic Period* (New York: Liberal Arts Press, 1954). For Hellenistic religions there is from the same press F. C. Grant (ed.), *Hellenistic Religions: The Age of Syncretism* (1953). For Gnostic sources see W. Foerster, *Gnosis: A Selection of Gnostic Texts,* trans. R. McL. Wilson (Oxford: Clarendon), I: *Patristic Evidence* (1972), II: *Coptic and Mandean Sources* (1974). A valuable collection of translations of sources relevant to the background of the New Testament is C. K. Barrett (ed.), *The New Testament Background: Selected Documents* (London: SPCK, 1957; Harper Torchbook).

Modern Works. R. Bultmann, *Primitive Christianity in Its Contemporary Setting,* trans. R. H. Fuller (New York: Meridian, 1956), is a classic brief survey of the religious and cultural milieu of early Christianity. A recent treatment of New Testament times is B. Reicke, *The New Testament Era: The World of the Bible from 500* B.C. *to* A.D. *100,* trans. D. E. Green (Philadelphia: Fortress, 1968). Still valuable on Judaism is G. F. Moore, *Judaism in the First Centuries of the Christian Era,* 3 vols. (Cambridge, Mass.: Harvard University Press, 1927–1930). There is also now E. Schürer, *The History of the Jewish People in the Age of Jesus Christ* (175 B.C.–A.D. 135), ed. G. Vermes, F. Millar, and M. Black, Vol. I (Edinburgh: Clark, 1973), a revision of a standard work. In addition, M. Hengel, *Judaism and Hellenism: Studies in their Encounter in Palestine during the Hellenistic Period,* trans. J. Bowden, 2 vols. (Philadelphia: Fortress, 1974), must be taken into account by serious students. A fresh and up-to-date introduction to important issues regarding the nexus of Judaism and Christianity in Palestine is E. M. Meyers and J. F. Strange, *Archaeology, Rabbis, and Early Christianity* (Nashville, Tenn.: Abingdon, 1981). S. Sandmel, *Judaism and Christian Beginnings* (New York: Oxford University Press, 1978), is a wide-ranging and useful survey of the history, sources, institutions, and ideas. Cambridge University Press will soon publish *The Cambridge History of Judaism* in four volumes, ed. W. D. Davies and L. Finkelstein, covering the period from the Exile to the codification of the Mishnah. On Judaism in the wider ancient Mediterranean world, V. Tcherikover, *Hellenistic Civilization and the Jews,* trans. S. Applebaum (Philadelphia: Jewish Publication Society, 1959), is still consulted; now there is also E. M. Smallwood, *The Jews Under Roman Rule* (Leiden: Brill, 1976), as well as D. M. Rhoads, *Israel in Revolution: 6–74* C.E. (Philadelphia: Fortress, 1976). D. S. Russell, *The Method and Message of Jewish Apocalyptic* (Philadelphia: Westminster, 1964), is a general survey of a mode of thought and literature closely related to early Christianity. Pharisaic Judaism before and during the period of Christian origins is treated by J. Neusner, *From Politics to Piety: The Emergence of Pharisaic Judaism* (Englewood Cliffs, N.J.: Prentice-Hall, 1973), a statement of that scholar's perspective and a summary of aspects of his compendious work; cf. also his *First-Century Judaism in Crisis: Yohanan ben Zakkai and the Renaissance of Torah* (Nashville, Tenn.: Abingdon, 1975). A different perspective on the origin of Pharisaism is found in E. Rivkin, *A Hidden Revolution* (Nashville, Tenn.: Abingdon, 1978). On the Qumran scrolls F. M. Cross, *The Ancient Library of Qumran and Modern Biblical Studies*, rev. ed. (Garden City, N.Y.: Doubleday, 1961), and M. Black, *The Scrolls and Christian Origins: Studies in the Jewish Background of the New Testament* (London: Nelson, 1961), remain reliable guides, but a more recent comprehensive treatment is G. Vermes, with P. Vermes, *The Dead Sea Scrolls* (Philadelphia: Fortress, 1978).

For the Hellenistic religious world, F. C. Grant, *Roman Hellenism and the New Testament* (New York: Scribner, 1962), is valuable, particularly for its extensive bibliography. On the mystery religions the best readily available work is still H. R. Willoughby, *Pagan Regeneration* (Chicago: University of Chicago Press, 1929). Traditional Greek and Roman religion is treated by H. R. Rose, *Religion in Greece and Rome* (New York: Harper & Row, 1959). Note also J. Ferguson, *The Religions of the Roman Empire* (Ithaca, N.Y.: Cornell University Press, 1970), which deals principally with the second and third centuries. For Gnosticism see H. Jonas, *The Gnostic Religion*, rev. ed. (Boston: Beacon, 1963), as well as R. McL. Wilson, *Gnosis and the New Testament* (Oxford: Blackwell, 1968), and E. M. Yamauchi, *Pre-Christian Gnosticism: A Survey of the Proposed Evidences* (Grand Rapids, Mich.: Eerdmans, 1973).

M. Rostovtzeff, *A History of the Ancient World*, 2 vols., trans. J. D. Duff (Oxford: Clarendon, 1926–1930), is available in paperback in volumes entitled *Greece* and *Rome*, from which some of the original material is omitted. Note also W. W. Tarn, *Hellenistic Civilization*, 3rd ed. rev. with G. T. Griffith (London: Arnold, 1952; paperback, Meridian), and F. E. Peters, *The Harvest of Hellenism: A History of the Near East from Alexander the Great to the Triumph of Christianity* (New York: Simon & Schuster, 1970), the latter notable for the effort to incorporate the religious and philosophical dimensions of history. *The Cambridge Ancient History*, 12 vols. (New York: Cambridge University Press, 1923–1939), is an invaluable reference tool.

For further readings on the early church and its canon, see Suggestions for Further Reading at the end of Chapter 11.

PART I

*The Gospels
and Jesus*

THE ORIGIN of the Christian faith was the career of Jesus of Nazareth, an event that could be understood only in the context of the history of the people of Israel and could be communicated only by means of literary and thought patterns of the first-century Mediterranean world. Yet the new religious faith grounded itself upon the story of a particular person, who lived and died in the land of Israel, as the revelation of God. Our study of the New Testament writings focuses in Part I upon this story of Jesus, first as portrayed in the Gospels (Chapters 2, 3, 4, 5) and then as portrayed by means of historical criticism (Chapter 6). Although the New Testament documents written earliest are the letters of Paul, the prior position of the Gospels in the New Testament collection accurately reflects the conviction of the early Christian community that the story of Jesus was the beginning of the faith.

It will be obvious that matters of life and death, both for individual Christians and for the churches, were filtered through the narrating of Jesus' actions and words. From without, the Christians faced problems connected with Jewish leaders in Israel, the Roman government in the Empire, and a Hellenistic culture that pervaded everyday Mediterranean life. From within, the churches struggled with the relation of the old and the new Israel, the nature of discipleship, the extent of the Christian mission, the place of miracles, the nature of power, order, and authority in the community, the relation between faith and ethics, and the delay of the end time. In speaking to these questions the early Christians acknowledged the authority of Jesus, while at the same time accepting the freedom to retell his story in the light of their changed situations.

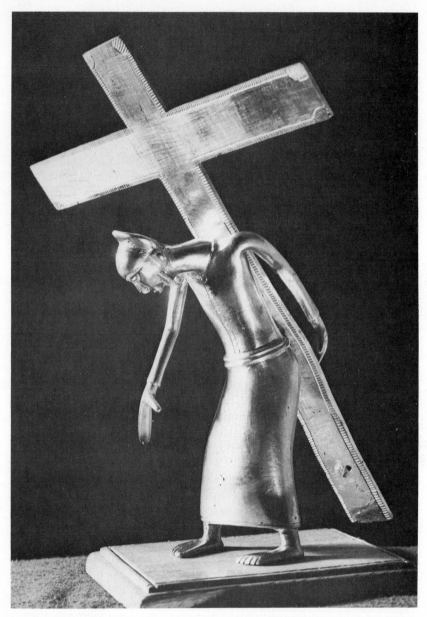

Statue of Jesus carrying the cross by Justin Accrombessi, contemporary artist from Ghana. (Courtesy of Spartaco Appetiti.)

CHAPTER TWO

The Gospel According to Mark: Triumph Through Suffering

NOTES ON THE NATURE OF A GOSPEL, GOSPEL CRITICISM,
AND THE GOSPEL OF MARK

Before turning to Mark's Gospel, we need to have in mind something of the nature of a Gospel. The Greek word for gospel, euangelion, *means "good news." This word had acquired religious significance in the Roman Empire, chiefly in the cult of the emperor, in which the appearance of the Roman emperor, his accession to the throne, and his decrees were known as glad tidings or gospels. Perhaps the New Testament usage was partly derived from the "good tidings" of freedom from bondage which Isaiah proclaimed to the people of Israel emerging from the Babylonian exile (see Isaiah 40:9; 52:7; 61:1). In the New Testament itself,* gospel *also signifies good news of salvation (see for example, Matt. 11:5; Rom. 1:1; I Cor. 15:1; Mark 1:1). Early usage of* euangelion *implied the oral nature of such news; however, with Mark, Matthew, Luke, John, and the apocryphal Gospels, the Gospel became a distinctive, literary category.* * *This literary type can best be defined negatively. The Gospels are not biographies in the modern sense, for they lack the usual interest in personal character and in the chronological order of Jesus' life. Neither are they myths, tales of the gods, because Jesus of Nazareth, the central figure of the Gospels, was a historical person. Yet elements of both biography (a story of a particular historical person) and myth (a tale of the divine action) are present in the Gospels. Basically the Gospels are religious proclamations based upon historical event.*

The writing of the first Gospel was no casual, accidental affair. Up until the time of Mark (or some unknown predecessor), the oral tradition about Jesus and the Hebrew scriptures were authoritative for the early

---

* To distinguish between Gospel as a book (e.g., Mark) and gospel as Christian preaching, we shall capitalize the former but not the latter.

church. Although Papias, a second-century Christian bishop, knew of writ-
ten Gospels, he still preferred the living tradition of the Lord to "the con-
tent of books" (Eusebius, EH, III, 39, 3 ff.). In early Christianity the Lord's
authority did not stop with his life and death. He was a living Lord; con-
sequently, the tradition was living and developing. When some Christians
took the step of writing down, and hence partially fixing, this tradition, it
was only because of pressing needs of the church.

One obvious reason for writing Gospels was the death of the apostles,
those who had been with Jesus. The church could not afford to lose the
tradition of Jesus. Mark probably originated in the mid-sixties when, ac-
cording to tradition, Paul and Peter, the two great apostles, were martyred.

Other motives were also at work in the writing down of the Gospels.
A church facing persecution needed to know the way in which Jesus him-
self had faced persecution. The early church, furthermore, had to struggle
to understand itself apart from the law, organization, rites, and customs of
Judaism. As the Christian mission expanded into the Gentile world, a fur-
ther crisis was posed by the problem of how a religion basically Jewish in
origin could appeal to the Hellenistic world without losing its identity and
distinctiveness. The church also had to face the problem posed by the de-
lay of the expected parousia (second coming of Jesus) and the end of the
world.

These, and more specific needs, were at work in the writing of Gospels.
Seemingly these problems could have been handled in some cases without
resorting to the Gospel form of literature. Yet the early church looked for
direction and guidance basically in the event of Jesus' life, death, and res-
urrection, so that the Gospel became the most appropriate vehicle for the
Christian message. Indeed, our first known Gospel (Mark) probably origi-
nated under the threat of persecution just as Jesus' ministry had taken
shape under the threat of danger and death.

The Gospel according to Mark is attributed by tradition to the John
Mark who was a companion of Paul and an associate of the other apostles.
Tradition connects him with Peter as well, but its reliability is disputed.[1]
Possibly all four canonical Gospels were first read by early Christian com-
munities as anonymous writings. For the sake of convenience, however,
we shall continue to use the customary names to identify the respective
Gospels.

Mark is generally thought to be the earliest Gospel. The evidence for
this view is derived from a comparison with the other two Gospels that
are quite similar, Matthew and Luke. These three Gospels are known as
the Synoptic Gospels. (Synoptic means that they see together; that is, they

---

[1] See the report by the Christian bishop and historian Eusebius (ca. A.D. 260–340) concerning the earlier tradition from another bishop, Papias (ca. A.D. 150), in *The Ecclesiastical History*, III, 39, 14. Papias or his predecessors may have inferred that Mark was the evangelist because of (1) Peter's role as the dominant disciple in the Gospel (fifteen references; see, for example, 1:16–20, 29–31, 35 f.; 3:13–19); (2) the absence of any tradition about direct Petrine authorship of a Gospel; and (3) the knowledge of an association of Mark with Peter in Rome (I Pet. 5:13; cf. Philemon 24; Col. 4:10; II Tim. 4:11).

present a common view of Jesus' ministry.) One can see and evaluate this evidence with the help of a synopsis of the Gospels, a volume in which the Synoptic Gospels are arranged in three parallel columns for easy comparison. Two striking facts emerge from such a study. (1) The order of events in the narratives of Matthew, Mark, and Luke is frequently the same. Where it is not, Matthew and Luke almost never agree with each other against Mark, although each alone may, and frequently does, agree with Mark against the other. (2) A similar observation can be made about the wording of the text in the narrative portions. Sometimes it is identical, but where it is not, Matthew and Luke only rarely have the same wording in disagreement with Mark. Thus in both cases, order of events and wording, one sees Mark and Matthew agreeing against Luke or Mark and Luke agreeing against Matthew rather frequently. The rarity of agreement of Matthew and Luke against Mark is very significant.

What does this mean? If one finds several factors occurring in the combinations, abc, ab, and bc, but never ac, one will observe that b is the common factor. Similarly, if one finds (a) Matthew, (b) Mark, and (c) Luke agreeing, or (a) Matthew and (b) Mark agreeing, or (b) Mark and (c) Luke agreeing, but seldom (a) Matthew and (c) Luke agreeing without (b) Mark, one will observe that (b) Mark is the common factor. If Mark is the common factor, without which Matthew and Luke rarely agree, then Mark must be the source of the other two, if it is not the result of the conflation (i.e., putting together) of those documents. But most scholars find it difficult, if not impossible, to understand Mark as the result of such a process of combination.

Mark is shorter, stylistically cruder, and more difficult to understand than is Matthew or Luke. It used to be thought that Mark had condensed the Gospel of Matthew, but Mark contains little of the teachings of Jesus found in Matthew. Would a condenser have omitted the most striking part of Matthew? Where Mark and Matthew report the same incidents, Mark's account is often actually longer and more detailed. Would a condenser have lengthened individual stories by adding various details? Such considerations support the view that Mark is our earliest Gospel, not a later condensation.[2]

There are many cases in which Matthew and Luke have similar or identical sayings of Jesus completely lacking in Mark. The different use and arrangement of this material in Matthew and Luke would seem to indicate that neither copied the other. Probably Matthew and Luke drew

[2]For more complete discussion see W. G. Kümmel, *Introduction to the New Testament*, trans. H. C. Kee, rev. ed. (Nashville, Tenn.: Abingdon, 1975), pp. 33–60. For a different solution, the priority of Matthew, see W. R. Farmer, *The Synoptic Problem: A Critical Analysis* (New York: Macmillan, 1964). For understanding the Synoptic problem a valuable aid is Burton H. Throckmorton, ed., *Gospel Parallels: A Synopsis of the First Three Gospels*, adapted from the Huck-Lietzmann Synopsis, 4th ed. (Nashville, Tenn.: Nelson, 1979). Such an arrangement of the Synoptic material is indispensable for study of the Gospels because it shows the remarkable similarities and differences within the Synoptic tradition which have brought forth the present most generally accepted hypothesis. Cf. also Reuben J. Swanson, ed., *The Horizontal Line Synopsis of the Gospels* (Dillsboro: Western North Carolina Press, 1975), which is particularly useful for minute comparisons.

upon a common source other than Mark. It no longer exists independently, but is usually called Q (German Quelle, meaning "source"). In addition Matthew and Luke both had access to special traditions either oral or written, which are sometimes referred to as M and L.

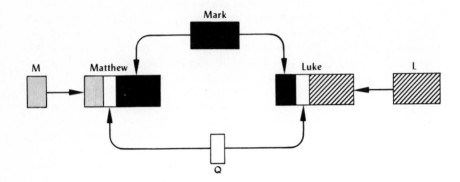

The insights of source criticism just described have been augmented by the results of form criticism, a discipline that goes behind the written sources to investigate the period of the oral tradition about Jesus. Form criticism as a discipline or method of biblical scholarship was developed in Germany, where it is known as Formgeschichte (form history). That name is more adequate than its customary English counterpart, for it makes clear that more is at stake than literary or traditional form. Form criticism is the study of the individual units of tradition—sayings, stories, parables, apocalyptic discourses—with a view to understanding how their form is related to their function and history in the primitive church. Form critics think that most of the tradition originally existed as individual units and that there was a stage at which these units of tradition, stories and sayings, were told and retold by word of mouth (cf. I Cor. 11:23); they assume that such traditional units were preserved and transmitted because they served a need and purpose in the church. Form criticism has proved credible insofar as it has been able to postulate settings, functions, and histories for units of tradition which shed light upon their meaning and interpretation. These self-contained units, "pearls" of tradition, were probably first strung together in a connected narrative by Mark. In the view of the earlier form critics (especially Bultmann), Mark was not so much an author as a redactor, a compiler of the tradition.

Redaction criticism, the analysis of the editorial work of the writers in relation to their sources, established that the writers used the tradition available to them in creative, constructive, and different ways. The basic insight of redaction criticism is that the evangelists were authors and theologians painting their own portraits of Jesus and addressing themselves to important theological issues in the church of the first century.

Redaction critics may have relatively high, or relatively low, estimates of the historical trustworthiness of the material conveyed in the Gospels. They bracket out the historical question to pursue the intention and meaning of the evangelists. "The question of what really happened," writes Willi

Marxsen, "is excluded from the outset. We inquire rather how the evangelists describe what happened."[3] Or, as Conzelmann put it in his work on Luke, "We must make it plain . . . that our aim is to elucidate Luke's work in its present form, not to inquire into possible sources or into the historical facts which provide the material."[4]

Redaction critics stress the insight that all the Gospels, especially the Synoptics, are based upon or arise out of three settings in life. First, there is the setting of Jesus' actual historical ministry. This setting was real, and its importance is not to be dismissed. In the case of most stories and sayings of Jesus, however, that Sitz im Leben is impossible to reconstruct except in a general way. Second, there is the setting in the life of the early church that preserved the Gospel tradition. Without doubt, tradition was preserved and transmitted because it performed a valued function in the religious community. This is the insight of form criticism, which deals with this period of oral, or informal, transmission. Third, we have the situation of the evangelists themselves. That situation in each case gave rise to the Gospels. The Gospels are not to be viewed as the products of that situation pure and simple; they are more than the last stage in the development of the tradition in the church. The evangelists sought to speak with relevance and power to their own situation, while being faithful to Jesus. The nature of their respective writings is the subject of the following four chapters.

Utilizing the insights of modern criticism as indicated, our method for determining the message of each Gospel consists of four simple steps: (1) Outlining the structure: *By determining the anatomy or basic outline (for example, its beginning, climax, and end), we can discern the intention and meaning of the Gospel. A detailed outline would involve classifying the separate sayings or episodes, known as pericopes.* (2) Enumerating frequent emphases: *These emphases become evident in examining the order and structure of the Gospel. The identification of such emphases serves to test any theory of the structure. Interpretation of a writing must take into account dominant emphases.* (3) Distinguishing tradition from redaction: *By seeing which earlier material is selected and how it has been shaped, we can arrive at probable conclusions about the intention of the author. This technique of criticism is more difficult to employ in the case of the Gospel of Mark because we do not have the sources of tradition which Mark used.* (4) Setting forth the historical context: *Some historical situation or combination of situations provided the impetus for the writing of each Gospel. On the basis of our knowledge of the history of early Christianity and the culture in which it lived, we seek an occasion that explains the origin of the Gospel in question. Our interpretation should fairly consistently fit some historical situation in the life of the first-century church.*

Of course, all four methodological steps mutually inform and correct each other. No neat, simple procedure alleviates the necessity for common sense and imagination as primary ingredients for understanding.

[3]Willi Marxsen, *Mark the Evangelist: Studies on the Redaction History of the Gospel,* trans. Roy A. Harrisville et al. (Philadelphia: Fortress, 1969), pp. 23–24.

[4]Hans Conzelmann, *The Theology of St. Luke,* trans. Geoffrey Buswell (New York: Harper & Row, 1960), p. 9.

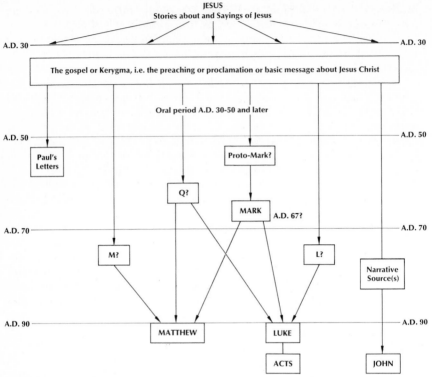

The formation of the Gospels.

We infer the date and place of Mark's origin from the Gospel itself. In Mark 13 (vss. 2, 14), the destruction of Jerusalem (A.D. 70) is either imminent or has just taken place. An early tradition about this Gospel testifies to its origin in Rome (see Eusebius, EH, VI, 14, 6). Mark was written to an audience which included Gentile Christians (see Mark 10:12—divorce by women was not possible in Jewish Palestine—and 5:41; 7:3 f., 11, 34; 15:22, where ignorance of Jewish practices is assumed). Furthermore, events in Rome during the mid-sixties admirably fit Mark's emphasis upon persecution. Such obvious emphases as the suffering of Jesus (8:31; 9:31; 10:33 f.), the centrality of the cross (chaps. 14 and 15), and the necessity for a suffering and serving discipleship (8·34–38; 9:33–50; 10:38–45; 13:9–13) frame Mark's urgent message to a persecuted community. Furthermore, Tacitus, the first-century Roman historian, describes persecution of Roman Christians in the mid-sixties by the emperor Nero, who evidently, in order to enlarge his palace complex, started a great fire that burned much of Rome:

> Therefore, to scotch the rumour, Nero substituted as culprits, and punished with the utmost refinements of cruelty, a class of men, loathed for their vices, whom the crowd styled Christians. . . . First, then, the confessed members of the sect were arrested; next, on their disclosures, vast numbers were convicted, not so much on

the count of arson as for hatred of the human race. And derision accompanied their end: they were covered with wild beasts' skins and torn to death by dogs; or they were fastened on crosses, and, when daylight failed were burned to serve as lamps by night. [*Annals*, XV, 44]

Mark's Gospel fits such a situation of persecution in Rome. It was likely written there shortly before the first destruction of Jerusalem by Titus in A.D. *70.*

Certainty in such matters is unattainable, but this view accommodates both the internal evidence (of the Gospel itself) and the earliest testimony. It also makes understandable why Mark should have been adopted and used as the principal narrative source independently by Matthew and Luke. Rome was at an early time an influential church (cf. Rom. 1:8), and its Gospel would have been regarded as authoritative.

Fuller interpretation of Mark awaits the exegetical sections in this chapter, but a few guidelines will help in reading. Mark is not simply biography or objective history, but rather religious proclamation with historical foundations. The Markan Gospel develops from a tradition about Jesus which circulated in the Christian community prior to the writing of the Gospel. Mark does not create this story afresh; at the same time this Gospel aims to strengthen first-century Christians in the face of persecution.

OUTLINE OF MARK:

Prologue: The Spirit and Jesus in the World (1:1–15)

The Gospel of Power: Jesus Opposes His Enemies (1:16–8:21)

  Encounter with Demons and Sickness (1:21–45)

  Debate with the Pharisees (2:1–3:6)

The Power of Suffering: Jesus Wins His Disciples (8:22–15:47)

  Two Stages of Discipleship (8:22–9:9)

  Faith to Produce Healing (9:14–32)

  The Cross of Jesus (15:33–47)

Epilogue: The Future Victory (16:1–8)

Prologue: The Spirit and Jesus in the World (1:1–15)

Why does Mark's Gospel begin with Jesus' baptism by John?

Mark's opening verse hardly sounds like an objective biography of Jesus of Nazareth. Neither an apology (as in Luke 1:1–4) nor a genealogy of Jesus (as in Matt. 1:1–17), the opening of Mark could scarcely attain a higher note of faith. Jesus Christ is named as though Christ were his last name. His name, however, was Jesus, and Christ is a bestowed title of honor, meaning "anointed one" or "messiah." Any lingering expectation of a neutral history is dispelled further by the final title, "Son of God." The significance of

Nero, emperor of Rome (A.D. 54–68), on a Roman coin. (Courtesy of American Numismatic Society.)

this designation for Mark becomes clearer at the climactic point of the story when Jesus is told by a voice from heaven that he is the "beloved Son" (vs. 11). The key introductory phrase of the opening verse, however, is probably "the beginning of the gospel." By the prologue's end (vs. 14) this phrase has become "preaching the gospel of God." Something has enabled "the beginning of the gospel" to become "preaching the gospel."

Mark starts, strangely, not at the beginning but in the middle of things. Mark begins with the baptism when Jesus was already an adult, instead of with Jesus' birth or childhood. Mark did know something about Jesus' earlier life, for later we are informed about Jesus' occupation and family (Mark 6:3). In Mark's view the baptism of Jesus is the crucial initiatory event for Jesus.

The Old Testament prophecy (1:2–3) points toward some kind of fulfillment. (Although Mark declares that the prophet Isaiah spoke these words, they are actually a combination of Malachi 3:1, Exodus 23:20, and Isaiah 40:3.) Something will happen. In fact, by the end of the prologue, the verb tense has shifted, "The time is *fulfilled*, and the kingdom of God *is at hand*" (1:15). Again, we apparently have an indication of the crucial importance of Jesus' baptism by John.

John the baptizer stands at the center of the next section (1:2–8). John is a wild man; he is in the wilderness, a preacher of judgment and repentance. He wears clothes of the wilderness, camel's hair and a leather girdle (cf. the description of Elijah in II Kings 1:8); he eats food of the wilderness, locusts and wild honey.[5] Although

---

[5] Although locusts were eaten during famines in the desert, the diet of John might also symbolize the double nature of the gospel, both judgment and comfort. In the Old Testament, locusts were invariably the agents of destruction and judgment (see, for example, Exodus 10:4; Psalm 105:34; Isaiah 33:4), whereas honey was traditionally the promise of peace and plenty (see, e.g., Exodus 3:8; Deuteronomy 6:3; Proverbs 24:13; Ezekiel 3:3).

nothing is said to identify John's ministry with that of Jesus, John nevertheless stands at the beginning of the gospel (cf. Acts 1:22; 10:37).

A striking feature of this section is its remarkable emphasis upon repentance for all the people of Judea and Jerusalem, as if a full-scale national repentance were taking place. John's decisive act is to baptize the people in the river Jordan. Through this rite of baptism, a cleansing or preparation takes place. Moreover, John declares that this baptism with water would be completed later by one who would baptize with the Spirit. Earlier we read a prophecy about John the baptizer (vss. 2, 3); now John himself prophesies (vss. 7, 8). Just this fact of his prophesying indicates that the Spirit is about to appear. In first-century Judaism the Spirit, which was the enabler of prophecy, was thought by many to have departed Israel with the last prophets (Haggai, Zechariah, and Malachi) and was expected only in the last days.[6] As John clearly points to the approach of another, Jesus, he also foreshadows an irruption of the end time, the time of the active Spirit.

A different mood pervades the next section (vss. 9–13). Whereas previously we had John the baptizer, the crowds, and baptism in the river, now Jesus alone appears. The heavens open, the Spirit descends, and a voice from heaven speaks. In other words, we have "cosmic language."[7] At his baptism, the Spirit descends upon Jesus and a voice says, "Thou art my beloved Son. With thee I am well pleased." This utterance combines portions of Psalm 2:7 and Isaiah 42:1. The Gospel of Mark is intent upon proclaiming the occurrence of a cosmic event in which the Son of God is designated. Does this mean that Jesus did not become Son of God until his baptism? Mark offers no opinion, for the text asserts simply that at this baptism God's Spirit rested upon Jesus, who was declared Son of God.

The title Son was used commonly as a designation for Israel in the Hebrew Scriptures (Exodus 4:22; cf. Jeremiah 31:9 and Hosea 11:1) and for those who especially represented the people of Israel, such as the king or high priest. It is most likely that "sonship" did not mean biological descent from God but signified special selection by God for a task. The appropriate response of "sonship," therefore, is obedience to the task. This Hebraic understanding of "sonship" suggests that the voice from heaven revealed to Jesus that God had chosen him for a task. In fact, the unexpected climax of Mark's introduction occurs when the Spirit drives Jesus into the wilderness

[6] See the coming of the Spirit in Acts 2:17–22, especially the prophecy from Joel 2:28–32. Also see G. F. Moore, *Judaism*, I (Cambridge, Mass.: Harvard University Press, 1958), p. 237.

[7] See J. M. Robinson, *The Problem of History in Mark* (Naperville, Ill.: Allenson, 1957), p. 26. In this chapter we are indebted to Robinson's analysis of the Gospel of Mark. Cf. U. W. Mauser, *Christ in the Wilderness* (Naperville, Ill.: Allenson, 1963), pp. 77 ff.

where he is tempted by Satan (vs. 12). The Spirit did not bring Jesus peace and contentment; instead the Spirit brought conflict with the power of evil, with Satan.

The importance of the Spirit's driving Jesus into the wilderness is underscored when we realize that Jesus was already in the wilderness at his baptism. Why does Mark want to emphasize the wilderness motif? Both Moses (Exodus 34:28) and Elijah (I Kings 19:8) spent forty days on Mount Sinai; moreover, the people of Israel wandered forty years in the wilderness before they could enter the Promised Land. Thus Jesus' sojourn in the wilderness may anticipate the founding of a new Israel.

The most striking feature of the Markan temptation story, especially in comparison with the temptation stories in Matthew (4:1–11) and Luke (4:1–13),[8] is its lack of narrative detail. In the Markan temptation story, Jesus' activity is overshadowed by the supernatural conflict between the Spirit and Satan. The outcome of this conflict, however, has already been anticipated in Jesus' baptism. By Jesus' act of submission to baptism the Spirit has come and with this coming Satan already is being defeated (see 3:23–29; cf. 10:38).

In these successive sections of Mark's introduction, the Spirit is the decisive factor. The Spirit is promised by John the Baptist and is already emerging in his prophecy (1:2–8). During Jesus' baptism (1:9–11) the Spirit descends upon him. In the temptation (1:12–13) the Spirit drives Jesus into conflict and victory over Satan. A likely clue to the meaning of Mark's introduction appears in the answer Jesus later gives to the accusation that he is in league with Satan: "But no one can enter a strong man's house and plunder his goods, unless he first binds the strong man; then indeed he may plunder his house" (Mark 3:27). Jesus' baptism and temptation manifest an initial conquest of Satan by the Spirit. Therefore, the way is cleared for Jesus' later conflicts with the demons, his religious opponents, and even his disciples. After Jesus' obedient submission to baptism, the Spirit drives him into a conflict that eventually will result in total victory.

The note of future victory resounds in the conclusion of Mark's introduction (vss. 14–15), where instead of "the beginning of the gospel" we now hear of "preaching the gospel of God." (Of course, *gospel* itself is good news and carries the notion of victory.[9]) After Jesus' baptism and temptation, the preaching of the good news of

---

[8] The closest verbal parallel to Mark's story occurs in the Jewish pseudepigraphal Testaments of the Twelve Patriarchs, probably written sometime between 140 and 110 B.C., "And the devil will flee away from you and the wild beasts will fear you, and the angels will come unto you" (Testament of Naphtali 8:4).

[9] For other Markan uses of *gospel*, see 1:1, 15; 8:35; 10:29; 13:10; 14:9. Also see the discussion of its central role in Mark by Leander Keck, "The Introduction to St. Mark's Gospel," *New Testament Studies*, 12 (1966), 352–370.

God can take place, because the Spirit has become active in Jesus' obedience. The crucial phrase, "the kingdom of God is at hand" (vs. 15), means neither that victory has fully arrived nor that triumph remains wholly future; rather, Mark proclaims that God's ruling presence is now nearer than it was before. This message, this gospel, rather than Jesus himself, is the object of belief (vs. 15). Therefore Mark concludes his introduction with Jesus' preaching the gospel of God which demands repentance and belief. The introduction has suggested to the reader that the gospel concerns a victory (the Spirit over Satan) to be won only through conflict (the wilderness) and obedience (the baptism of Jesus). The rest of Mark's Gospel narrates Jesus' triumph in conflict effected through his exorcisms, debates, and suffering.

The Gospel of Power: Jesus Opposes His Enemies (1:16–8:21)

Now that the Spirit has met Satan in the temptation of Jesus, the public action of Jesus can begin. Jesus came preaching that the kingdom of God is drawing near; this kingdom proclamation by its very nature aroused opposition. Forces are at work against the emergence of the kingdom, for the old order does not easily yield.

In the first half of the Gospel of Mark (1:16–8:21), opposition to Jesus comes in the main from two camps—the demons and the Pharisees. Jesus faces the opposition of the demons with exorcism and that of the Pharisees with debate. Thus this first half of Mark centers upon Jesus' miracles and teachings. Indeed, as we shall see, miracles and teachings are mingled within individual units of tradition because both are means for opposing his enemies. The two opposing forces differ in that the demons recognize Jesus yet do battle against him, whereas the Pharisees, though also utterly antagonistic to Jesus, do not recognize his true identity.

In the second half of Mark (8:22–15:47), the major opposition that Jesus faces is not that of enemies but rather of friends, his disciples. To be sure, the disciples did not put Jesus to death; the chief priests and scribes, along with the Roman authorities, were responsible for his crucifixion. Still, the disciples did oppose Jesus because they failed to understand why he had to suffer and die. Unless we keep in mind the disciples' misunderstanding opposition, the full meaning of Jesus' actions and teachings against the demons and the Pharisees will be missed. The Gospel of Mark shows that the opposition of enemies was met by direct action through exorcisms and debates; however, the opposition of friends required indirect persuasion, even apparent defeat in death.

This preference for persuading rather than compelling the disciples elucidates a major problem in the first half of Mark. After several disclosures of divine healing power, Jesus curiously asks to keep these miracles secret (1:43 f.; 3:12; 5:43). In effect, Mark seems to be saying that Jesus' power to make disciples had to be a hidden one. He won disciples not simply by naked, brute force, either of deeds or of arguments. Stark power did not convince, did not make a believer, did not get rid of fear. When demons had been exorcized and silenced in debate, the task of making true disciples still remained.

Nevertheless, in this first half of Mark miracles dominate. There

Galilee, Samaria, Syro-Phoenicia, and Syria

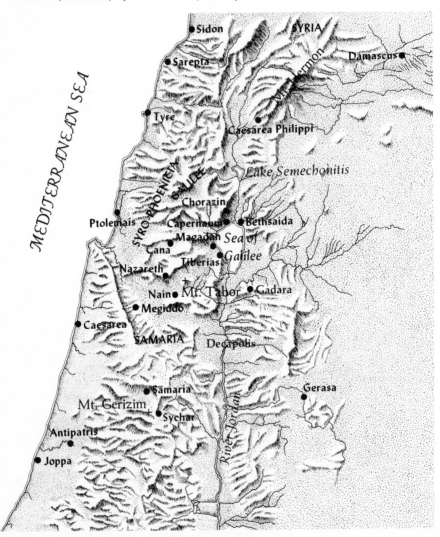

are nature miracles, such as stilling the storm (4:35–41; 6:45–52) and feeding the multitudes (6:30–44; 8:1–10); there are healing miracles, such as the healing of the leper (1:40–45) and the raising of the dead girl (5:35–43); and there are miracles of exorcism, the driving out of demons (1:21–28, 5:1–13; see also 1:34, 3:22). These last exorcisms provide a key to understanding the miracles in this Gospel. Mark summarizes the activity of Jesus in Galilee as that of preaching and casting out demons (1:39), and Jesus appoints the twelve to do the same tasks (3:14, 15; cf. 6:13). Evidently, for Mark, miracles are essentially the same as exorcisms. They do not constitute a separate class of acts or events.

A crucial question in regard to these actions is whether Jesus performs miracles by Satan or by God (3:20–30). For Mark Jesus performs exorcisms with the help of God; anyone who denies this source of Jesus' power (cf. 3:30) must be on the side of Satan. Now that the strong man, Satan, has been bound by the Spirit, Jesus is to plunder the house, to rid the world of demons (3:27). In demon exorcism we are to recognize a transcendent battle taking place in the life of Jesus and his contemporaries. Demons inhabit human beings; they are part of human history. Yet their power comes from beyond, from Satan. Similarly, Jesus exorcises demons, but he claims a power from beyond; for in Mark he is the Son of God, the one upon whom the Spirit descends.

ENCOUNTER WITH DEMONS AND SICKNESS (1:21–45)

Why does Jesus perform miracles?

The first exorcism in Mark (1:21–28) follows the calling of disciples and is set within the context of Jesus' teaching in the synagogue on the sabbath. Opposition between the teaching of the scribes and the authority of Jesus characterizes this scene. At first no one truly recognizes Jesus except the demon, who cries out, "I know who you are, the Holy One of God" (1:24; cf. 3:11; 5:7). Perhaps the demon spoke Jesus' true name to gain power over him. In the ancient world, knowledge and use of the name gave the speaker magic power.[10] More obviously the demon's recognition of Jesus

---

[10] A magic word, which automatically causes a desired effect, occurs occasionally in the exorcisms and healings that Jesus performs in Mark (see 5:9, 41; 7:34). Even this usage is, however, quite restrained when compared with the seemingly endless list of magic "names" used by other exorcists at the time of Jesus; see C. K. Barrett, *The New Testament Background: Selected Documents* (London: SPCK, 1957), pp. 31 ff. Two memorable Old Testament attempts to gain control through knowledge of the name are Jacob's wrestling with the angel (Genesis 32:29) and Moses at the burning bush (Exodus 3:13). Even today, "magical" use of the name persists in human relationships. For example, in some cultures to be on a first-name basis implies friendship and mutual trust, or to know a person's nickname is to know his "secret."

produces immediate opposition because the demon recognizes that an enemy has appeared ("Have you come to destroy us?"). The result of Jesus' appearance is heightened activity by the demon resulting in the man's convulsing and crying out. Jesus and the demon have absolutely no communion, only antagonism.

This exorcism implies a "before and after" motif, which occurs explicitly in other miracles of Jesus in Mark (see 6:45–52). Before the exorcism there is opposition, violence, crying out; afterward there is silence, victory, and the spread of Jesus' fame. Yet this particular exorcism does not end with a neat resolution of all difficulties. We are perplexed because the bystanders label the exorcism "a new teaching," instead of the expected powerful deed. Indeed the whole encounter seems both an exorcism of an unclean spirit and a debate about the question of authority (see 1:22, 27). Clearly for Mark, who as redactor is probably responsible for the emphasis upon authoritative teaching, Jesus' action and teaching are not finally separable. Moreover, the inconclusive ending of this episode (questioning among themselves) suggests that the exorcism had produced no final victory. Jesus still had to debate with the Pharisees. Thus this episode ends, perhaps ironically, on the note of the spread of Jesus' fame, a fame that will lead not to apparent success, but to death.

A brief healing episode (1:29–31) and two summary sections (1:32–34; 1:35–39) separate Jesus' first exorcism from the next major healing event (1:40–45). The healing of the disciple Simon's mother-in-law focuses attention upon the disciples who cannot heal. The disciples are impotent, even though she is one of their relatives. Moreover, Jesus' healing enables her to serve; the disciples also have to become servants, though in a different way (see 9:35; 10:35–45; 12:1–11). Therefore, even this brief episode points beyond itself to the necessity for disciples to perform service, a feat that becomes possible only after they allow themselves to be served by Jesus' death (10:45). A summary section of healing and exorcism follows (1:32–34). The people flock to a healer, the healings take place publicly; curiously, Jesus "would not permit the demons to speak, because they knew him."

In the following section (1:35–39) Jesus retires to a lonely place to pray. In response to the disciples' demands Jesus acknowledges only that he will go to preach in the next towns. The narrative mentions that he continued also "to cast out demons" (vs. 39). Evidently Jesus sees his primary mission as that of preaching (1:14) and the casting out of demons as secondary. This section concludes a connected series of episodes beginning with 1:21 and taking us through a day to the evening (1:32–34) and the following morning (1:35–39). Perhaps Mark places this series here because it presents typical acts of Jesus.

Jesus' key action here is praying. On three other occasions in

Mark, Jesus prays. Each time the motif of faithful discipleship is the common thread of the diverse incidents. After the feeding of the five thousand, Jesus prays (6:46); the immediate consequence is his calming appearance to the disciples terrified by the storm. At the healing of the epileptic boy Jesus tells the disciples that they are unable to heal because they have not prayed (9:29). Jesus also prays in the Garden of Gethsemane for strength to accept his impending death, while the disciples sleep (14:32–42). To become disciples, they will have to "watch and pray" (14:38). For Mark Jesus' mission is not primarily healing or exorcising demons; Jesus brings near the kingdom of God to effect *discipleship* rather than cures.

The subsequent episode tells of Jesus' healing of a leper (1:40–45). No demon appears in this healing miracle; the conversation takes place between Jesus and a man. Here for the first time Jesus is moved with pity, and when the man speaks to Jesus, there seems to be something like the element of faith: "If you will, you can make me clean." In distinction from the exorcism, this healing shows Jesus in touch with the person to be healed, moving more closely within the human realm and eliciting the response of faith. As in the case of the exorcism, the meeting with Jesus produces results; the victim is made well of leprosy and made fit for communion with others. Once again Jesus enjoins silence (cf. vs. 34), but this time he is not obeyed. Although this scene shows Jesus acting out of compassion and the man's incipient faith, something is still not right. Because the healed man goes "to spread the news," Jesus can no longer move about openly. Instead of righting everything, the healing seems to deter Jesus from his mission of preaching the gospel of God and making true disciples—that is, believers in the gospel (1:15).

In summary, the Markan exorcisms and healings depict one phase of the struggle that erupts with the mission of Jesus. The purely transcendent struggle between the Spirit and Satan foreshadowed in the temptation (1:12–13) now takes place at the transcendent-historical level of the "Holy One of God" versus the demons (1:24). As we shall see later, the conflict moves farther within history in the opposition between the rabbi Jesus and the Pharisees and finally between the suffering Son of Man and his disciples. Although the miracles, the most public deeds of Jesus, arouse the greatest reception (1:28), they also produce inconclusive results in the realization of Jesus' aim of gathering true disciples (cf. 1:16–20).

Jesus' demand for silence about the miracles requires an interpretation that makes sense of the Markan intent, for in understanding Mark the important question about Jesus' miracles is not whether he healed—undoubtedly he, as well as others, did—but rather what use the early Christians (in this case, Mark) made of this healing tradition. We have in Mark an apparent contradiction; the healing tradition does not convey the crucial aspect of Jesus' ministry, yet much of Mark's Gospel, especially the first half, consists of miracle tradition. Why then does Mark combine this miracle tradition with injunctions to be silent about the miracles (the so-called messianic secret)? Our answer to this question proceeds from the recognition that for Mark the basic meaning of Jesus' ministry consists in his suffering and death on the cross. For the winning of true disciples takes place only through the suffering death of Jesus. Mark neither doubts nor disdains the miracle tradition of Jesus; however, he sets that tradition within the special perspective of Jesus' death.

Mark's Christian contemporaries knew of divinely empowered miracle workers, whereas apocryphal stories of Jesus also emphasized his magical powers. In the infancy Gospel of Thomas the child Jesus is pictured as a great miracle worker: He makes sparrows of clay; he kills a lad who disturbs a pool he made; he destroys a child who strikes his arm; he stretches a short beam into a longer one to aid Joseph, his carpenter father; and so forth.[11] Such a popular, one-sided emphasis on Jesus as a divine miracle worker is rejected in the Gospel of Mark, not by ignoring that role, but by placing it within the context of Jesus' passion. Thus Mark suggests that the fundamental miracle of discipleship comes not through Jesus' miracle powers but, rather, through his death.

Miraculous signs, though not denied, are insufficient to turn followers of Jesus into genuine disciples. Later in Mark, Jesus replies to the Pharisees who come seeking a sign from heaven, "Why does this generation seek a sign? Truly, I say to you, no sign shall be given to this generation" (8:12). According to Mark, objective, public signs of power are not the basis of faith.

DEBATE WITH THE PHARISEES (2:1–3:6)

How are the miracles like the debates?

Communication takes place in many ways. Debate persuades by allowing the listener to hear both sides. Debate, therefore, commu-

---

[11]On the first-century Hellenistic miracle worker, see D. L. Tiede, *The Charismatic Figure as Miracle Worker* (Missoula, Mont.: Society of Biblical Literature, 1972); also J. M. Robinson, "The Problem of History in Mark, Reconsidered," *Union Seminary Quarterly Review*, 20 (January 1965), 136 f.; Carl H. Holladay, *Theios Aner in Hellenistic Judaism: A Critique of the Use of this Category in New Testament Christology*, SBL Dissertation Series, 40 (Missoula, Mont.: Scholars Press, 1977), has made questionable the use of "divine man" as a technical term for miracle worker. On the miracle-working Jesus in the Gospel of Thomas, see E. Hennecke, ed., *New Testament Apocrypha*, ed. W. Schneemelcher, trans. R. McL. Wilson et al., Vol. I, *Gospels and Related Writings* (London: Lutterworth, 1963), pp. 392–393, 396–397.

nicates in conflict, and the Gospel of Mark is an example of such communication by conflict. In Mark, Jesus' teaching takes place primarily in debate, with the Pharisees, with his enemies, or with the disciples, his friends. The debates with the Pharisees and the scribes have parallels with debates in the writings of the rabbis; however, the key for understanding the Markan debates is the exorcisms. Earlier we were puzzled by the people's astonishment at Jesus' *teaching* (1:22) when the story related the driving out of an unclean spirit. Mark seems deliberately to commingle healing action and teaching authority so that Jesus' conflicts (demons, Pharisees, and disciples) are all of a piece. The healing of the paralytic (2:1–12) demonstrates that healing action ("Rise, take up your pallet and walk") and authoritative teaching ("Your sins are forgiven") are inextricably interwoven and suggests implicitly that Jesus has to wrestle with the stubbornness of the Pharisees as well as crippling disease.

The prelude for our present section is once again the calling of disciples, in this case a tax collector named Levi (2:13 f.; cf. 1:16–20).[12] The closely related following episode shows Jesus' eating at table with sinners and tax collectors (2:15–17). Sinners presumably had in some obvious way broken the Mosaic law. Tax collectors were hired by those agents who purchased the right to collect taxes for the Roman government and in turn were allowed to extract heavy taxes from the Jewish people. Evidently the two groups were social outcasts, yet Jesus and his disciples ate at table with them. The scribes and the Pharisees object to the disciples about Jesus' conduct, not to Jesus himself. (Perhaps the involvement of the disciples at this point indicates that the issue was still a live one in the early church.) Even though not addressed directly, Jesus replies with an answer that silences everyone. He comes to the sick; that is the physician's duty. Jesus' opponents fail to grasp that a new society of disciples, those who follow Jesus, is being formed. The ancient rigid distinctions of clean and unclean, especially the procedure for forgiveness (see vs. 7), are being swept away in the new community that Jesus inaugurates.

The following section (2:18–22) concerning fasting probes this new society further. This time Mark distinguishes not only between Jesus and the Pharisees but also between Jesus' disciples and those of John the Baptist. Both the Pharisees and the disciples of John fast. But Jesus, as the bringer of good news, asserts the absurdity of fasting, for his disciples now experience a new reality ("the bridegroom").

The statement implying that they will fast after Jesus' death

---

[12] Curiously Levi does not appear in the later Markan list of the twelve disciples (3:16–19).

(2:19b–20) sounds less like a word of Jesus than a word of the early church justifying the later practice of fasting.[13] In the Markan context, however, fasting may refer to the suffering and persecution that the disciples will have to endure. In the second half of Mark, Jesus speaks unequivocally about the necessity of suffering. Indeed, Jesus' words (especially vs. 20) do not allow the reader to forget the impending death. The final words of the episode (2:21 f.) mark an end to the debate and an answer to the conflict over fasting. Everything stresses newness—the bridegroom is present, new cloth and new wine are available; fresh skins are needed, for the old cannot determine the new. The old order must make way for the new; real disciples know and act upon this "newness."

The first two episodes of this section stressed the breaking forth of a new society in connection with Jesus; the following two episodes hinge upon unorthodox sabbath activity. Even though the disciples violate the sabbath (2:23–28), the Pharisees now debate directly with Jesus. Jesus answers their charge by quoting scripture, citing the example of David (see I Samuel 21:1–6). His criterion, suggested by the David episode, is apparently that need takes precedence over law. Moreover, the first half of Jesus' final word ("The sabbath was made for man, not man for the sabbath"—vs. 27) also bears out this view, which in isolation sounds quite modern—that is, human considerations take precedence over legalistic ritual. Yet the final clause ("so the Son of man is lord even of the sabbath") indicates that we have in Jesus' saying something more than a general humanitarian principle. The appearance of the Son of Man signifies the beginning of the end time, the irruption of a new age (see pp. 238 ff.; cf. Daniel 7:13 and Mark 13:26). Jesus' disciples can now violate the sabbath because they are beginning to live out of the new time being ushered in with Jesus: the time for joy (vs. 19), the time for wine (vs. 22), and the time for forgiveness of sinners (vs. 17; cf. vs. 10).

The next episode places the debate with the Pharisees in the context of healing (3:1–6). In the synagogue, the stronghold of the Pharisees, Jesus is being watched—the Pharisees are not at first named. The atmosphere is that of a test of Jesus (cf. also 8:11; 10:2; 12:13; 15), similar to his time of testing in the wilderness. A comparison of this episode with the previous exorcism of the unclean spirit (1:21–28) illuminates how debate conflict is both similar to and yet also different from demon conflict. Jesus commanded the demon to be silent (1:25). Now, before the healing is performed, his opponents are silent before his question, "Is it lawful on the sabbath

---

[13] See Matthew 6:16–18. Rudolf Bultmann, *The History of the Synoptic Tradition,* trans. J. Marsh, rev. ed. (New York: Harper & Row, 1958), p. 151, classifies this word as a passion prediction added by the early church.

to do good or to do harm, to save life or to kill?" After the exorcism, even though there was questioning of his authority, Jesus' fame spread (1:27 f.). Now, after Jesus' sabbath healing his enemies plot to destroy him.

These enemies are labeled as Pharisees and Herodians. The Herodians may have been followers of Herod Antipas, tetrarch of Galilee and Perea (4 B.C.–A.D. 39) during the life of Jesus. They were probably royalists who hoped for restoration of a united monarchy, as in the time of Herod the Great (37–4 B.C.).[14] However the Herodians are identified, their presence at this point hints at Jesus' impending suffering and death. The only action specifically attributed to Herod Antipas in Mark is the beheading of John the Baptist (6:14–29; note vs. 29). Every Markan reference to the Herodians or to Herod explicitly points to a conflict ending in the death of Jesus (cf. 8:15 and 12:13 and 3:6 and 6:14 ff.). The new is upsetting to the old; the champions of sabbath observance cannot tolerate the presence of the Son of Man, who is lord even of the sabbath, and so they plot Jesus' death.

The remainder of the first half of Mark may be characterized as a development of what is already implied in the opening scenes of the Gospel. The old order's resistance to Jesus' message and action frees the good news to appeal to new multitudes, even those from Tyre and Sidon lying beyond Palestine (3:7–12). When rejected by the established religious authorities, Jesus forms the new Israel, founded upon the twelve disciples (3:13–19a). Whoever doubts the authenticity of this new community fails to see the clear manifestations of God's working through Jesus' casting out demons (3:28–30). Moreover, no one can rely upon a guaranteed privilege that reckoned physical descent as assurance of God's favor (3:31–35).

Nothing avails to eliminate the opposition to Jesus by the Jewish leaders. His parables about the breaking in of God's word are closed ciphers to all except the joyful few who really hear Jesus' word about a new society (4:1–20, esp. vss. 8 f. and vs. 20).

Even those who hear must receive further private instruction (see 4:33 f.), because Mark has in view the necessity for perseverance to the end (cf. 13:9–13). The hope for such endurance rests in the amazing power that accompanies Jesus ("Who then is this, that even wind and sea obey him?"—4:41). This power protects the disciples from the violent sea (4:35–41) and casts the fearsome unclean spirit Legion into the sea (5:1–13). Oddly, the people beg Jesus to leave their neighborhood because of his demon exorcism. Moreover, instead of the usual command to silence, Jesus urges the restored demoniac to tell his friends about the mercy God has shown (5:14–20).

[14] See F. C. Grant, "The Gospel According to Mark," *IB*, VII (Nashville, Tenn.: Abingdon, 1951), p. 683.

This injunction to speak about God's action contrasts all the more to the ending of the next episode (5:21–43), which explicitly enjoins silence. The preceding episode of the demon Legion (5:1–20) emphasizes, however, the destruction of the old and the people's fearsome response to that loss. In the present double episode of the raising of Jairus' daughter and the healing of the woman, we have references to two central themes of the second half of Mark: the necessity for faith (vs. 34) and the resurrection from the dead (vs. 41). The command to silence is appropriate to these themes. Although the people still figure in this narrative as they did in the exorcism, the center of attention is beginning to shift more clearly to the response of disciples (see vss. 31, 37, 40). This predominance of the disciples becomes more evident in the following stories: Jesus is rejected by his own people (6:1–6); he appoints the twelve disciples for a mission of healing and exorcism (6:7–13); John the baptizer is beheaded by Herod and his body is given to his disciples (6:14–29), perhaps in anticipation of the role for which Jesus is beginning to prepare his disciples. The disciples' return from the mission and the miraculous feeding of the multitudes (6:30–44) are to be viewed as a foreshadowing of the Lord's Supper and the death and resurrection of Jesus.

In summary, our brief journey through some of the remaining portions of the first half of Mark (up to 8:21) suggests that the debates with the Pharisees are matters of life and death (2:15–3:6). For Mark the new reality, especially the new society emerging in Jesus' disciples, represents a freedom toward the law that could not be tolerated within Pharisaism. Consequently, the religious leaders resist; they plan Jesus' death. In a certain sense Jesus opposed the demons more successfully and more easily than he did the Pharisees. Ironically, the reaction of the Pharisees to Jesus, their rejection and the plotting of his death, become the means for the accomplishment of Jesus' victory in making disciples (8:31; cf. 8:34). For even though the disciples remained close to Jesus throughout the first half of Mark, they had yet to learn the secret of Jesus' power. That came only with the death and resurrection.

The Power of Suffering: Jesus Wins His Disciples (8:22–15:47)

The second half of the Gospel of Mark centers upon the passion of Jesus. The passion story includes Jesus' decision to go to Jerusalem (10:32–34), the events of the last days in Jerusalem (11:1–14:72), and finally his death on the cross (15:1–47). Jesus' predictions of the passion begin in chapter 8. When we observe that the passion of Jesus thus embraces almost one half the Gospel, the characterization of

"The Small Crucifixion" by M. Grünewald (1460–1528). (Courtesy of National Gallery of Art, Washington, D.C. Samuel H. Kress Collection.)

Mark as a "passion story with an extended introduction" seems particularly apt.[15] In the first half of Mark, Jesus has dealt with his opponents, the demons and the Pharisees. In the second half, the human opponents will deal with Jesus. They put him to death by the

---

[15] See Martin Kähler, *The So-called Historical Jesus and the Historic Biblical Christ,* trans. C. E. Braaten (Philadelphia: Fortress, 1964), p. 80. Kähler made the remark about the Gospels; its force is most appropriate to Mark.

Roman form of capital punishment—crucifixion. Yet these last chapters do not dwell on the opponents of Jesus. Instead, the disciples and their understanding of Jesus become central.

At three crucial moments Jesus predicts the suffering he must undergo: "And he began to teach them that the Son of man must suffer many things, and be rejected by the elders and the chief priests and the scribes, and be killed, and after three days rise again" (8:31; cf. 9:31; 10:33 f.). The disciples' continuing misunderstanding or inability to accept this prediction becomes clear in the Garden of Gethsemane just before the arrest, trial, and crucifixion. They could not watch and pray while Jesus was going through temptation (14:38–41). The terse, seemingly final, verdict on the disciples is pronounced immediately after Jesus' arrest, "And they all forsook him, and fled" (14:50). Indeed, even the closest disciple, Peter, denied Jesus not once, but three times (14:66–72).

The disciples' denial and flight occur because of their unwillingness to acknowledge that their own discipleship must share the same quality as Jesus' suffering. Mark's Gospel speaks not only about the nature of Jesus' messiahship, but also about the nature of discipleship; the second half of Mark implies that there is no victory except through suffering and conflict.

Structural considerations show that Mark 8:22–10:52 is the central, pivotal part of the Gospel, introducing its second half. This long section begins with the story of the blind man who at first sees men like trees walking. It ends with the gift of sight to blind Bartimaeus, who then chooses to follow Jesus. Before this point in the Gospel is reached Jesus' miracles are recounted in great numbers and much detail. His teaching is frequently mentioned but not extensively given or described, except in controversial scenes such as Mark 7:1–23, when Jesus denounces the Pharisees and the tradition of the elders. Mark contains a number of controversy scenes and stories. We have noted how these are related to the demon exorcisms, which are characterized by struggle between the demons and Jesus. With 8:22–26 decisive new factors suddenly enter the picture. First, in response to Jesus' question Peter confesses Jesus as Messiah (8:27–30). Then Jesus repeatedly predicts his approaching suffering and death as the Son of Man. Jesus appears transfigured before his disciples (9:2–8), but they are far from understanding the meaning of this and other things that are transpiring. Indeed, the whole section mirrors and emphasizes the disciples' lack of understanding, both of Jesus and of themselves. This is nowhere more evident than in those instances in which Jesus instructs them in the meaning of discipleship (8:31–38; 9:33–37; 10:35–45). When the disciples, or James and John, seek preferment, Jesus admonishes them by his own example: "Whoever would be great among you must be your servant, and whoever would be first among you must be slave of all. For the Son of man came also not to be served but to serve, and to give his life as a ransom for many" (10:43–45).

Immediately afterward Jesus enters Jerusalem (11:1–11) and the passion week is already beginning. We are clearly now in a new episode of the Gospel. The structure, the arrangement of the material, and the emphases that emerge in the narrative show that a distinctive teaching about messiahship and discipleship is being set forth and emphasized in Mark 8:22–10:52. The theme of the true character of Jesus' messiahship leads to the reiterated and heavily emphasized teaching about discipleship. This section is a fitting introduction to the second half of the Gospel, which presents Jesus' death. We learn at the outset what that death implies for Jesus' messiahship and for true discipleship.

TWO STAGES OF DISCIPLESHIP (8:22–9:9)

What is Jesus' response to Peter's confession?

The point of transition from the first portion of Mark to the second can be located in the incident at Caesarea Philippi, where Peter confesses Jesus as the Christ (the Messiah) and Jesus answers by declaring that his mission is one of suffering (8:27–33). The preceding episode, the healing of the blind man at Bethsaida (8:22–26), dramatically symbolizes what follows. This story stands out as the only two-stage healing in the Gospels. When Jesus first heals, the man sees only dimly and men look like trees walking; then Jesus heals again and the blind man sees everything clearly. The unique manner of this healing seems to prefigure the "seeing" of the disciple Peter in the next episode. Peter sees that Jesus is the Christ; however, he does not yet understand the suffering nature of Jesus' messiahship (vs. 32). Peter, like the other disciples, must go through a second stage of "healing" before he can become a true disciple (cf. 8:34 ff.).

Peter's confession occurs on the way to the villages of Caesarea Philippi, located at the far northern end of Palestine where Hellenistic influence was most prevalent. The location suggests that underneath Jesus' query about his identity may lie the question of whether his ministry should extend beyond the borders of Israel. At any rate, the answers of others (John the Baptist, Elijah, a prophet) are inadequate (cf. 6:14 f.). When Jesus turns the question to the disciples, Peter, speaking for them, answers, "You are the Christ." Jesus then charges them not to tell anyone who he is (8:30). Previous commands of silence concerned his exorcisms and healings; now Jesus commands silence about his identity.

This passage serves as the focal point for what has become known in New Testament research as the problem of the "messianic secret," a term that includes Jesus' commands to keep silent about his miracles (1:34, 44; 3:12; 5:43; 7:36) and his identity (8:27–30; 9:9), his private instructions to the disciples (7:17 f.; 9:39 f.; 10:10), and his private interpretation of parables (4:10 ff., 33 f.).[16] The two most frequent proposals for understanding the "messianic secret" are (1) that Jesus commanded silence to keep the uninstructed multitudes from learning about and perverting his nonpolitical messiahship into a political one or (2) that Jesus actually did not understand himself to be the Messiah. In the latter case, the secrecy motif is an attempt to explain, from the standpoint of the early church's faith that Jesus was the Messiah, why Jesus was not publicly recognized as such and why the tradition was relatively devoid of messianic claims. Both these solutions betray a modern preoccupation with the question of whether Jesus thought that he was the Messiah. But Mark was not interested in this as an historical problem. In the Gospel the question is not whether Jesus was Messiah, but why he was the kind of Messiah he was.

Within the Gospel itself the "messianic secret" focuses the reader's attention on the question of the nature of Jesus' messiahship and consequently upon the nature of Christian discipleship. The disciples, including Peter, misunderstood the role of Jesus as the Christ. As the Son of Man (the apocalyptic, heavenly figure) Jesus must suffer many things and be killed, and after three days rise (8:31). Peter's rebuke of Jesus leads to Jesus' rebuke of Peter (vss. 32 f.). The disciples' expectation of a miracle-working Messiah who delivers his followers from all unpleasantness into great reward (cf. 10:32–45) is rejected. The "messianic secret" restrains and tones down the miracle tradition of Jesus precisely because the reader is being forced to acknowledge and accept Jesus' suffering.[17]

The subsequent section on discipleship (8:34–9:1), spoken not only to the disciples but also to the multitudes, characterizes following Jesus as fellowship in service and suffering. The character of Jesus' messiahship determines what discipleship must be. The disciples, in becoming followers of Jesus, have taken the first step; however, they have not yet realized the full implications of discipleship. Victory can be realized only in conflict. Just as the Spirit

---

[16] For a succinct discussion of the "messianic secret" literature, see Kümmel, *Introduction to the New Testament*, pp. 90–92. The classic treatment is still that of William Wrede, *The Messianic Secret*, trans. by J. C. G. Greig (Cambridge: Clarke, 1971).

[17] See Hans Conzelmann, *Jesus*, trans. J. R. Lord (Philadelphia: Fortress, 1973), pp. 48 f. N. Perrin, "Towards an Interpretation of the Gospel of Mark," *Christology and a Modern Pilgrimage* (Claremont, Calif.: New Testament Colloquium, 1971), pp. 1–78, observes a thrice-repeated pattern of Jesus' prediction of his suffering, misunderstanding by the disciples, and Jesus' enunciation of true discipleship (Mark 8, 9, and 10). This pattern and the message it conveys—the true disciple follows Jesus and shares his suffering—are central to the structure and meaning of Mark.

fought Satan, and just as Jesus opposed demons and Pharisees, so too the disciples must continue to struggle until the end. That, according to Mark, cannot be far off: "There are some standing here who will not taste death before they see the kingdom of God come with power" (9:1, cf. Mark 13:24–37). Nowhere, however, does Jesus himself connect the coming kingdom with his title, Christ. In Mark at least, Jesus is not to be understood primarily as the political messiah, the expected restorer of Israel.[18] The most frequent Markan designation for Jesus is the Son of Man. As Son of Man he exercises freedom over the law (2:10, 28), goes to his suffering and death (8:31 and passim), and will come again as eschatological judge (8:38; 13:26; 14:62).

This section (8:34–9:1) focuses upon the nature of discipleship rather than on the identity of the one whom the disciples follow. Not until the following episode, the transfiguration scene (9:2–9), does Mark return to the question of Jesus' identity. There Jesus, with three disciples, climbs a high mountain where he is transfigured. His clothes become glistening white, like those of the angels; moreover, even Moses and Elijah appear to speak with him. According to Israel's tradition, Moses gave the law from a mountain (Exodus 19:16 ff.) and Elijah prophesied from a mountain (I Kings 19:9 ff). Thus Jesus converses with the two men representing Israel's heritage of the law and the prophets. Again the disciples misunderstand (vs. 6), not realizing that the coming of Jesus in some way fulfills the law and the prophets, for Jesus alone remains (vs. 8).

The climactic statement of the transfiguration scene, made by the voice from the cloud ("This is my beloved Son; listen to him"— vs. 7), alludes to the kingly tradition of Israel (cf. Psalm 2:7). If any other Old Testament figure were worthy of this distinguished company on the mountain, it would be David, the king of ancient Israel (cf. 2:25; 10:47 f.; 12:35 ff.). Possibly his exclusion prevents any political misunderstanding about the role of Jesus. At any rate, the voice announces to the disciples that Jesus is the eschatological king of Israel, the true final king. Jesus is Son of God with kingly power. At another crucial revelation of Jesus' identity in Mark, similar words are spoken (1:11). Mark's opening, "The beginning of the gospel of Jesus Christ, the *Son of God*" (1:1), has already coupled this designation with Jesus.

Such kingly power has to be viewed, however, in the context of the injunction "listen to him" (vs. 7). In the following section (9:9–13), Jesus not only charges the disciples to be silent, but explicitly links his power with both John's suffering ("Elijah has come"—vs. 13) and his own (vs. 12). The final Markan designation of Jesus as

---

[18] See 8:29; 13:21 f.; 14:61; 15:32. Mark of course does not deny the appropriateness of this title when properly used (cf. 1:1; 9:41; 12:35–37).

Son of God occurs at the cross (15:39). Jesus' kingly power fulfills
the law and the prophets by enduring suffering. A definite scheme
thus appears: at the baptism, Jesus is declared Son of God by a voice
from heaven. At the transfiguration, Jesus is announced as Son of
God by a voice from the cloud to the three major disciples. At the
cross, Jesus is proclaimed Son of God by a Gentile centurion. By
implication, the kingdom comes with power (9:1) when the Son of
God's suffering is acknowledged and accepted by Jesus' disciples.

FAITH TO PRODUCE HEALING (9:14–32)

Why is the attitude of the father better than that of the disciples?

From this point to the end of the Gospel, the disciples are often
in the foreground (see esp. 9:33–41; 10:23–31; 13:1 ff.) and always in
the background. In 9:14–32, the healing of an epileptic boy, Mark
combines two stories, the one showing how a father's faith enables
his son to be healed and the other drawing a contrast between the
master's ability and the disciples' inability to heal,[19] in order to present an example of genuine faith for the disciples. They are unable
to heal because they do not yet understand the nature of true belief
(cf. 9:32).

The argumentative disciples form a contrast with the beseeching
father. He cries out, "I believe; help my unbelief!" (vs. 24), thereby
demonstrating that all things are possible to the believer (vs. 23).
The disciples cannot heal because they do not pray (vs. 29). Prayer
is characteristic of Jesus' life-style (1:35; 6:46). Later the ability to
pray seems almost equivalent to the act of faith: "Therefore I tell
you, whatever you ask in prayer, believe that you receive it, and you
will" (11:24; cf. 11:22–26). The necessity for prayer becomes evident
in the major Markan prayer episode, Jesus in the Garden of Gethsemane (14:32–42). The disciples are to wait while Jesus prays (vs.
32), but they are also warned to pray (vs. 38). Jesus prays that suffering (the cup) might pass from him; however, he asks that God's will,
not his own, be done. The disciples cannot heal, because they neither pray nor believe; they do not accept Jesus' death. The necessity
for such an acceptance is made explicit at the close of this healing
episode (9:30–32). Again, Jesus predicts future conflict, but the disciples "did not understand the saying, and they were afraid to ask
him" (vs. 32).

In fact, fear dominates the disciples (cf. 4:40; 5:15; 9:6, 32;

---

[19]Note that the boy's condition is described twice (9:17, 21 f.) and that the con-
vulsions take place twice (9:20, 26). Cf. Vincent Taylor, *The Gospel According to St.
Mark* (New York: Macmillan, 1955), pp. 395 f., and Bultmann, *History of the Synoptic Tradition,* pp. 211 f.

10:32; 16:8). Perhaps this indicates that Mark's Gospel was written to a church undergoing persecution, as was suggested earlier. According to Mark, this fear can be overcome by faith (vs. 23). The worst the disciples had to fear from persecution was death. In the healing of the epileptic boy, however, even the verdict, "He is dead" (vs. 26), proves false because of the father's faith. Moreover, although Jesus, as the Son of Man, will be killed, "after three days he will rise" (vs. 31). If the disciples truly follow Jesus, then they too will go through persecution into victory.

For the time being, however, the disciples are afraid. Out of their fear and lack of faith they dispute about greatness (9:34), deter non-disciples from casting out demons (vs. 38), and in general unsuccessfully try to avoid persecution (vs. 50). They have still to understand that Jesus' messiahship rejects bread and circuses and demands discipleship of service (vs. 41) to one another (vs. 50).

As Jesus goes into Judea (10:1) and enters Jerusalem (11:1), he moves inevitably toward his death. The narrative of the events leading up to and including Jesus' death is in Mark dominated by four separate but interrelated themes: fulfillment of the old, desertion by the disciples, victory through failure, and the necessity of Jesus' death. While they are characteristic of Mark, each is also traditional in the sense that it was shared by other Christians.

Fulfillment of the Old. The Pharisees try to trap Jesus by raising the question of divorce (10:2–12), but Jesus declares that the will of God is communicated through the scripture rather than being identical with the scripture. A man who obeys the law goes away sorrowful because his allegiance rests finally with himself rather than with God (10:17–22). Jesus triumphantly enters Jerusalem, the holy city of Israel, but only to cleanse the holy temple (11:1–19). Indeed, Jesus cannot accept the crowd's accolades ("Blessed be the kingdom of our father David that is coming!"—11:9) because Christ is not the Son of David (12:35–37) in a political sense. The kingdom that Jesus announces brings the end of history (chap. 13) rather than the restoration of Israel's kingdom. The religious leaders of Israel reject this new society and its leader to their damnation (12:1–12) because they quibble about taxes (12:13–17) and resurrection (12:18–27) and ignore God's coming near. In the narration of the passion itself, there are many allusions to the Old Testament. Scripture is fulfilled, but in ways that could hardly have been anticipated.

Desertion by the Disciples. The disciples continue to follow Jesus; however, they question his "hard" sayings (10:23–31) and they follow only in fear (10:32). Just before Jesus' trial they all flee (14:50). Moreover, Mark underscores that fact with the little tale of the young follower of Jesus who flees away naked (14:51–52). The most crushing rejection of Jesus occurs in Peter's denial (14:66–72), especially tragic when viewed against Jesus' prediction and Peter's protest (14:26–31).

Victory Through Failure. The disciples are, however, the closest followers of Jesus, and in spite of their desertion, Jesus will still come to them in Galilee after his death. In fact, the Last Supper anticipates such a reunion (14:12–28). The disciples may confidently look forward to it. Their confidence has several grounds: Jesus shows mercy even to little children (10:13–16); the God who can do all things is at work (10:23–31); the one thing necessary is a recognition of need (10:46–52; cf. 9:23) and a letting go of self (12:41–44)—that is, a response of faith (11:20–26).

Necessity of Jesus' Death. The disciples' paralyzing fear in the face of persecution (see 13:9, 19) cannot be taken as final, for Jesus' death by crucifixion is the way in which God's victory will be achieved for them (10:32–45). This death not only is predicted by Jesus, but it also is prepared for by the anointing with costly ointment (14:1–9) and is celebrated in the Last Supper (14:12–25). It occurs at the instigation of one of the disciples (14:10 f.). Although Jesus himself prays that his death may be avoided, he accepts the cross as God's will (14:32–42). In the scenes immediately before and during the crucifixion Jesus' innocence is apparent (14:53–65, 15:1–15) and his behavior is exemplary (15:16–32). Thereby Mark shows the injustice of the human agents in Jesus' death and the perfect submission of Jesus to a death that ultimately triumphs through God's will.

Significantly, the context in which the reader of Mark views Jesus' suffering in his trial and death (chaps. 14–15) is the prediction of the suffering and future triumph of the church of Jesus (chap. 13). This address by Jesus, known as the "little apocalypse," maintains a tension between the imminence of the end (vss. 14, 26, 29, 30, 35) and the recognition that the time of its coming is unknown; not even Jesus knows exactly when it will come (vss. 7, 21, 32). Mark's apocalyptic look into the future is an explicit warning to the church against understanding Christian existence as present power, even in miraculous acts (see vss. 6–8, 21–27). The present consists of suffering which, because it is acknowledged, accepted, and not avoided, will eventually lead to triumph.

THE CROSS OF JESUS (15:33–47)

What is the meaning of Jesus' last words?

The Markan account of the crucifixion itself seemingly depicts an action accomplished by Jesus' opponents. Jesus remains passive. Pilate's question as to whether he is the king of the Jews is answered enigmatically (15:1–5). Jesus makes no plea for his life before the

Part of the Via Dolorosa, the traditional way through which Jesus carried his cross to Golgotha. (Courtesy of Israel Government Tourist Office.)

crowd when Barabbas is released (15:6–15). He does not protest the scourging (15:16–20). Someone else carries his cross. Furthermore, he does not even acknowledge those who mock his helplessness on the cross (15:21–32). The one action of Jesus upon which Mark centers is the loud cry from the cross in his native Aramaic language: "My God, my God, why hast thou forsaken me?" (15:34; cf. Psalm 22:1). The meaning of this cry can only be understood from the context. The setting for Jesus' death is somber. At noon darkness comes over the whole land for three hours before he dies (vs. 33). Although normally it took at least twelve hours for someone to die by crucifixion, Jesus died after only six. At the critical moment, Jesus shouts this cry of apparent despair. Someone rushes to give him vinegar while others mockingly ask whether Elijah will come to help. Then he "uttered a loud cry, and breathed his last" (vs. 37). In reading the text, we observe that Jesus gave two loud cries just before his death. Perhaps "My God, why hast thou forsaken me?" was a later addition spelling out what the "loud cry" was.[20] If so, then Mark, or the tradition lying behind Mark, added these words for a specific reason. Whatever the answer to the question of the cry's origin, clearly this shout is the Markan key to Jesus' death.

Traditionally these words (vs. 34) have been considered the "cry of dereliction," the cry of despair at abandonment by God. Yet these words may be a cry of victory, for they are the opening words of Psalm 22, which begins in despair but ends on a note of triumph: "All the ends of the earth shall remember and turn to the Lord; and all the families of the nations shall worship before him. For dominion belongs to the Lord, and he rules over the nations" (Psalm 22:27 f.). Perhaps so, but such reasoning should not remove the element of despair and real suffering. Clearly the Psalmist suffers, and Jesus suffers; Mark intends for the reader to perceive Jesus' sense of despair, even to the point of apparently being abandoned by God. Thus Jesus' last fearful word in Mark maintains tension to the very end. No premature miracle rescues Jesus from this final struggle with God himself (cf. 14:36).

The preceding scene at the cross (15:29–32) stresses the Markan perception of the necessity of suffering. Here Jesus is mocked because he cannot save himself, although he has claimed to save others. The mockers ironically make Mark's point. Suffering cannot be avoided for Jesus, the disciples, and Mark's persecuted church, because thereby others can be saved.

In addition, Mark claims for Jesus and the church victory in suffering. The mockery over his boast of destroying and rebuilding the temple in three days (15:29 f.) is answered by the tearing apart of the temple curtain at Jesus' death (vs. 38). A curtain that limits access to God is rent asunder, for Jesus' death extends God's relation with Israel to all men. Fittingly the Gentile centurion confesses Jesus as "Son of God" (vs. 39). The extension of God's salvation to everyone answers the mocking of those waiting for Elijah to take Jesus down. God has come down to open the temple. The principal actor in the passion is neither Jesus nor the people and officials, but God. In Jesus' suffering, God is acting to effect triumph. We might have anticipated this conclusion. Even when Jesus cried out in despair (vs. 34),

---

[20] See Bultmann, *History of the Synoptic Tradition,* p. 313, but cf. Taylor, *The Gospel According to St. Mark,* p. 594.

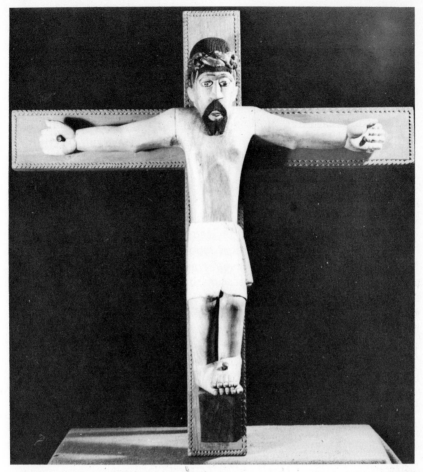

Jesus' crucifixion by a contemporary African sculptor, E. G. Isacco. (Courtesy of Spartaco Appetiti.)

his cry was addressed to God; he was praying. In Mark, prayer or faith makes all things possible, even victory in the face of apparent defeat (cf. 14:34 f.; 9:29; 11:24).

Mark depicts three responses to Jesus' death: those of the centurion (vs. 39), the women (vss. 40 f.), and Joseph of Arimathea (vss. 42–47). The most important of these is that of the centurion (cf. 1:1, 11; 9:7). Unlike the disciples who were earlier afraid (4:40; 6:50; 10:32), the centurion boldly confesses Jesus as the Son of God. This affirmation occurs directly after Jesus' death. Possibly the centurion was impressed with the manner in which Jesus died, but the Markan text mentions no such impression. What we do know is that "Son of God" is a key Markan designation of Jesus (1:1). At the baptism such sonship involved obedience to God (1:11); at the transfiguration such sonship announced the kingly power of Jesus (9:7); and now at the crucifixion the centurion proclaims Jesus as God's Son precisely at his death. Thereby Mark manifests Jesus' suffering messiahship as the key to discipleship.

The women confirm that Jesus is dead, for the disciples have all fled and they are the only ones left. In addition, however, the Galilean women make peculiarly good Markan witnesses of Jesus' death. We are told that they "followed him, and ministered to him" (vs. 41). Of course, "following" is another way of saying discipleship (cf. esp. 1:17), and their "ministering" picks up Jesus' emphasis upon "service" (the same Greek word): "For the Son of man also came not to be *served* but to *serve,* and to give his life as a ransom of many" (10:45). Furthermore, Jesus charged his disciples, "If anyone would be first, he must be last of all and *servant* of all" (9:35). These women are the first followers of Jesus to see his death, witness his burial, and hear the resurrection report. They were apparently also the first followers to accept Jesus' way of service. The way of discipleship receives further explication in the action of Joseph of Arimathea, a respected member of the Jewish council (vs. 43). In contrast to the "real" disciples, he has courage (cf. 14:50). Furthermore, he seeks the kingdom of God, whereas the disciples appear to be seeking their own welfare (cf. 10:35–45).

The passion story ends with conclusive evidence of the death of Jesus. Pilate learns from the centurion that Jesus has died quickly (15:44). The body is laid and sealed in the tomb. Yet already in the centurion, the women, and Joseph of Arimathea, something new is being born.

Epilogue: The Future Victory (16:1–8)

Did the empty tomb prove the resurrection for the women?

After Jesus' death the Christian reader expects a happy ending: resurrection and glorious triumph. The note of victory is in fact present in Mark's epilogue, but it is restrained. Among the Gospels, only Mark fails to record an appearance of Jesus to the women or disciples.[21] The Gospel ends with verse 8 rather than the spurious ending, verses 9–20. The only evidence contradicting the natural assumption that the death is final is the empty tomb story, which in itself is ambiguous. The absence of Jesus' body does not necessarily prove his resurrection (cf. Matt. 28:13–15).

---

[21] Our interpretation of Mark's ending omits Mark 16:9–20 because this passage is doubtless a later addition to the text. See Taylor, *The Gospel According to St. Mark,* p. 610. Although most textual critics agree that 16:9–20 is not the original ending, some would claim that the original has been lost.

These opening verses (1–4) set the atmosphere for the incident. The women are going to perform a pious deed, to anoint the body of Jesus. Evidently burial was hasty and they could not anoint the body on the holy sabbath. At the first opportunity ("early in the morning") they go to the tomb. They have come to honor the dead Jesus, but their plans are upset. Mark portrays a young man sitting in the open tomb, who, from his apparel, must be an angel, a messenger from God. Naturally the women are quite amazed, but the angel chides them for their perplexity (vs. 6a). Earlier encounters with Jesus evoked similar awe and amazement from the crowds (1:27; 9:15), the Pharisees (12:17), and the disciples (10:24). This response, however, falls short of the required act of faith. Amazement and awe at Jesus' numinous, divine quality are not enough. Neither is the reaction of fear (16:8) an adequate response to Jesus, whether on the part of Jesus' opponents (11:18) or his disciples (4:40; 9:6, 32). Amazement and fear are already linked at the first explicit reference to Jesus' unalterable movement toward Jerusalem: "And they were on the road, going up to Jerusalem, and Jesus was walking ahead of them; and they were amazed, and those who followed were afraid" (10:32). True discipleship consists of more than awe at the numinous or fear at the realities of human finitude. Something more, a response of faith, a victory through suffering, is meant by Mark (cf. 4:40; 10:52; 11:22).

The women, disciples, and Peter are promised that something more will occur. Jesus will go before them into Galilee (16:7). Of course, they have no guarantee other than the angel's word (cf. 14:28) that he will appear in Galilee. The precise reason for the choice of Galilee is not certain. Perhaps the disciples are to meet Jesus in Galilee, rather than Jerusalem, to gather forces for the Gentile mission. The precise meaning of the promise is also unclear. Perhaps the disciples are to await the second coming of Christ, the parousia, when God's kingdom will fully come (cf. chap. 13).[22] More likely, they will await a resurrection appearance of Jesus ("there you will see him"; cf. 14:28). Whatever the exact meaning, the promise stresses the future. Everything has not yet happened; a future victory awaits. The Markan story of Jesus does not promise to deliver the church from persecution, even though in Jesus' life and death a first victory has been won. Satan was bound, demons were exorcized, opponents were defeated in debate, disciples were gathered. Moreover, the future promises a second, complete victory. But the future can still only be assured through faith. In the present the church faces strife and persecution.

---

[22] See the Galilee hypothesis of Willi Marxsen, *Mark the Evangelist: Studies on the Redaction History of the Gospel*, trans. James Boyce et al. (Nashville, Tenn.: Abingdon, 1969), who also sees the Markan situation as one of persecution.

Mark's concluding words ("for they were afraid") corroborate this interpretation. Some scholars challenge this ending, even though manuscript evidence decisively supports it, because it sounds like a half sentence.[23] Nevertheless, the present ending of Mark fits the Gospel. The women are left with fear, the normal and ever-present fear of a church undergoing persecution in the mid-sixties at Rome. Of course, Mark wishes to encourage endurance, faith, and prayer in spite of fear, but the Gospel does not command faith at the last instance. Instead, Mark's whole Gospel implies the need for faith in a final victory, because an initial triumph through suffering has occurred in Jesus. Mark is realistic enough to acknowledge fear and Christian enough to proclaim the breaking of fear's power through faith in a future victory promised by the suffering and resurrected Jesus.

In summary of our Markan interpretation, let us briefly review the results of our four-step methodology:

In *structure* this Gospel presents a series of conflicts between Jesus, allied with God's Spirit (1:1–15), and opponents at various levels: Satan, demons, Pharisees, and finally disciples. The major Markan watershed is Peter's confession at Caesarea Philippi (8:22 ff.); from this point attention shifts to Jesus' relationship with his disciples. The first half of Mark shows Jesus' victorious movement toward apparent success both in miracle and debate, whereas in the second half he moves toward apparent failure in death and the disciples' misunderstanding.

We have found five *emphases* that are basic: the miracles of Jesus, his passion, the "messianic secret," the call to discipleship, and the confession of Jesus as Son of God. Our interpretation reconciles the apparent contradiction of the first two emphases (the "strong Jesus" of miracles versus the "weak Jesus" of death) through the third emphasis, which calls attention also to Jesus' use of persuasion in making true disciples (the fourth emphasis). Mark took over the miracle tradition of Jesus and set it within the perspective of Jesus' passion, for the creation of the disciples' faith could occur only if Jesus abandoned miracles at his death to allow God to work.

The "messianic secret" motif occurs precisely at those points where the tradition was most likely to be understood to represent Jesus as a divine man with power to avoid any difficulty. In effect, Mark opposed such an attitude about Jesus and the life of discipleship. The fifth and final Markan emphasis supports this reading of

[23]In addition, the end of a manuscript, especially a papyrus scroll, could easily be lost. Although inferior manuscripts provide what was deemed a more satisfying ending to Mark (cf. 16:9–20), Matthew and Luke appear to know only our version, which ends at 16:8. Their respective resurrection appearance stories do not parallel Mark's longer ending (16:9–20). Cf. note 21.

Mark: The declaration of Jesus' sonship at the baptism and at the transfiguration is finally affirmed at Jesus' death.[24] Jesus is Son of God in death, but not because of any miracle-working power.

Although we do not have the Markan sources of tradition from which to study his *redaction* of that material, we can see that such motifs as the "messianic secret" and the predictions of Jesus' suffering death and resurrection either occur in Mark's transitional sections or otherwise give evidence of the evangelist's hand. Moreover, we may safely assume that Mark selected and arranged the tradition in order to accomplish his purposes; notice the dominance of miracle tradition in the first half and the passion story in the second half. In comparison to Matthew and Luke, Mark used little teaching material of Jesus. Mark obviously wished to stress the passion.

The Markan *situation* requires the bolstering of the church undergoing persecution, probably at Rome in the mid-sixties. Jesus Christ, the Son of God, had himself gone through persecution and no escape had been offered him. Jesus triumphed through his suffering and the same victory is promised to the faithful disciple, "For whoever would save his life will lose it; and whoever loses his life for my sake and the gospel's will save it" (8:35).

Suggestions for Further Reading

The Synoptic Gospels. Probably the classic work on the problem of Synoptic relations and sources is B. H. Streeter, *The Four Gospels: A Study of Origins*, rev. ed. (London: Macmillan, 1930). The arguments for the priority of Mark, its use by Matthew and Luke, their use of a common sayings source, Q, and their use of distinctive sources M and L are all stated here. A discussion of further advances in the study of Gospel origins, especially form criticism, is V. Taylor, *The Formation of the Gospel Tradition*, 2nd ed. (London: Macmillan, 1935). Also useful is F. C. Grant (ed.), *Form Criticism* (New York: Harper & Row, 1962), containing essays by R. Bultmann and K. Kundsin. Both pioneering studies in form criticism are available in English: Bultmann, *History of the Synoptic Tradition*, trans. J. Marsh (New York: Harper & Row, 1968), and M. Dibelius, *From Tradition to Gospel*, trans. B. L. Woolf (New York: Scribner, 1934). J. Rohde, *Rediscovering the Teaching of the Evangelists*, trans. D. M. Barton (Philadelphia: Westminster, 1968), provides a comprehensive survey of redaction-critical research on the Synoptic Gospels and Acts. The Biblical Commission's *Instruction concerning the historical truth of the Gospels*, published in 1964 with papal approval, constitutes a guarded Roman Catholic endorsement of form criticism explicitly (V) and redaction criticism implicitly (VI. 2; IX); for the text see Augustin Cardinal Bea, *The Study of the Synoptic Gospels*, ed. J. A. Fitzmyer (New York: Harper & Row, 1965), pp. 79–89. An excellent recent

---

[24] Note how the occurrences of "Son of God" confirm the Markan structure: 1:1, 11; 9:7; and 15:39.

book dealing with the Gospels generally is H. C. Kee, *Jesus in History: An Approach to the Study of the Gospels,* 2nd ed. (New York: Harcourt, 1977). J. L. Mays (ed.), *Interpreting the Gospels* (Philadelphia: Fortress, 1981), is a valuable collection of articles from the journal *Interpretation.* F. W. Beare, *The Earliest Records of Jesus* (Nashville, Tenn.: Abingdon, 1962), affords useful commentary on the Synoptic Gospels, following Huck-Lietzmann, which in turn is followed by the RSV *Gospel Parallels,* ed. B. H. Throckmorton, 4th ed. (Nashville, Tenn.: Abingdon, 1979). A valuable aid for study of the Gospels is D. R. Cartlidge and D. L. Dungan (eds.), *Documents for the Study of the Gospels* (Philadelphia: Fortress, 1980).

   The Gospel According to Mark. Commentaries in series named in the General Bibliography, III, are not all mentioned individually at the ends of chapters. As a rule, commentaries on the Greek text are not listed.

   Among the more helpful recent commentaries are the following: D. E. Nineham, *The Gospel of St. Mark* (Baltimore: Penguin, 1963); E. Schweizer, *The Good News According to Mark,* trans. D. H. Madvig (Richmond, Va.: John Knox, 1970); and H. Anderson, *The Gospel of Mark* (London: Oliphants, 1976). An extensive and fully responsible commentary written from a somewhat more conservative viewpoint is W. L. Lane, *The Gospel According to Mark* (Grand Rapids, Mich.: Eerdmans, 1974). A number of important works treating themes or aspects of Mark have appeared over the past twenty-five years. These include J. M. Robinson, *The Problem of History in Mark* (Naperville, Ill.: Allenson, 1957); T. A. Burkill, *Mysterious Revelation: An Examination of the Philosophy of St. Mark's Gospel* (Ithaca, N.Y.: Cornell University Press, 1963); E. Best, *The Temptation and the Passion: The Markan Soteriology* (New York: Cambridge University Press, 1965); W. Marxsen, *Mark the Evangelist: Studies on the Redaction History of the Gospel,* trans. R. A. Harrisville et al. (Nashville, Tenn.: Abingdon, 1969); and H. C. Kee, *Community of the New Age* (Philadelphia: Westminster, 1977), a ground-breaking effort to move beyond form and redaction criticism in undertaking literary and sociological analysis of Mark. The extremely influential work of W. Wrede, which deals principally with Mark, is now available in English translation: *The Messianic Secret,* trans. J. C. G. Greig (Cambridge: Clarke, 1971). There is a statement of the late N. Perrin's approach to Mark, "Towards an Interpretation of the Gospel of Mark," in H. D. Betz, ed., *Christology and a Modern Pilgrimage: A Discussion with Norman Perrin* (Claremont, Calif.: New Testament Colloquium, 1971), pp. 1–78. P. J. Achtemeier, *Mark,* Proclamation Commentaries (Philadelphia: Fortress, 1975), provides a helpful, brief treatment of the Gospel in light of recent scholarship.

CHAPTER THREE

The Gospel According to Matthew: A Radical Obedience

NOTES ON THE GOSPEL OF MATTHEW

Like the Gospel of Mark, Matthew contains no direct reference to its author and place of origin. The earliest possible reference to the Gospel of Matthew is a report from Papias (ca. A.D. 130):

> Matthew compiled the reports in the Hebrew language, and each one interpreted them as best he could (Eusebius, *EH*, III, 39, 16).[1]

This information is, however, unclear and of dubious value. In fact, it does not seem to be a reference to our Matthew, which was written in Greek. Because our Gospel is based upon Mark and the Q sayings source, it is unlikely that it was written by Matthew, a disciple and eyewitness (cf. Mark 3:18 parr.).

The Gospel was probably at first anonymous. Authorship may have been attributed to Matthew, one of the twelve disciples, because only this Gospel distinguishes Matthew as a tax collector (10:3; cf. Mark 3:18), making the incident of the calling of a tax collector (who is Levi in Mark 2:14) a story about Matthew (Matt. 9:9). We do not know the reason for this other than to give some prominence to Matthew.

The author was familiar with Jewish Christianity and wrote to a Greek-speaking audience. Possibly he was a Christian scribe, similar to the

---

[1]See W. G. Kümmel, *Introduction to the New Testament*, rev. ed., trans. H.C. Kee (Nashville, Tenn.: Abingdon, 1975), pp. 53–55. Eusebius also earlier wrote, "Matthew, having first preached to the Hebrews, when he was about to go to others, compensated for the loss of his presence . . . by delivering to them in writing his Gospel in their native language" (*EH*, III, 24, 6).

Jewish scribes of the law (see 13:52).[2] *He took over and expanded the Markan framework by adding two types of material, sayings common also to Luke (Q source) and special Matthean tradition, which came from oral tradition or from a written source or sources. Matthew used so much sayings material that narrative tends to be dominated by discourse. The Jesus of Matthew is at least as much a teacher as an actor. Our five-part outline of Matthew (excluding the Introduction, 1:1–2:23, and Conclusion, 26:2–28:20) reflects the evangelist's own intention. The end of each major discourse section is clearly marked by an editorial conclusion (see 7:28 f.; 11:1; 13:53; 19:1 f.; 26:1 f.).*

The place of origin of Matthew's Gospel is generally thought to be Syria, probably the city of Antioch. The oldest witness to this Gospel may be Ignatius, bishop of Antioch. Although he does not cite it by name, his letters (A.D. 110–115) contain bits of Matthean material. In all probability, Matthew was written after A.D. 70, for its addition to the parable of the marriage feast ("The king was angry, and he sent his troops and destroyed those murderers and burned their city"—22:7; cf. Luke 14:21) apparently refers to the destruction of Jerusalem in that year. Because Mark was probably composed shortly before Jerusalem's fall, some time would likely have elapsed before Mark's authority became sufficient for the anonymous author of Matthew to use it as a primary source. Consequently, a date of about A.D. 80–100 seems likely. Indeed, the obvious tension between the Christianity of Matthew and the Judaism of the Pharisees (cf. Matt. 23) also suggests a date after the Roman annihilation of the temple in A.D. 70. At this time Judaism retrenched in the face of the threat of possible extinction and began to develop a rabbinic, Pharisaic uniformity heretofore unknown. Sectarian movements within Judaism, such as Jewish Christianity, became suspect and eventually may have been read out of the developing normative Judaism.[3]

Clearly this Gospel is more systematically and intricately organized than is that of Mark. It emphasizes fulfillment of prophecy, Jesus as teacher, and the place of the law and final judgment within the Christian congregation. These broad interests suggest a churchly Gospel written to give direction to the community as it faced problems pertaining to organization, separation from Judaism, and disappointed eschatological hopes. Matthew serves the church, and probably for that reason the church placed it first in the New Testament canon. Because it is written to give guidance to the church, Matthew may be compared with a roughly contemporary document, the Manual of Discipline of the Qumran community. The method of Old Testament interpretation in Matthew also bears some re-

[2] See Krister Stendahl, *The School of St. Matthew and Its Use of the Old Testament* (Philadelphia: Fortress, 1968); cf. Gottfried Schille, "Das Evangelium des Matthäus als Katechismus," *New Testament Studies,* 4 (1957–1958), 101–114.

[3] See W. D. Davies, *The Sermon on the Mount* (New York: Cambridge University Press, 1966), pp. 83–90. G. D. Kilpatrick, *The Origins of the Gospel According to St. Matthew* (Oxford: Clarendon, 1946), p. 109, cites the Birkath ha-Minim, a Pharisaic benediction from ca. A.D. 85, which he reads as follows: "For the excommunicate let there be no hope and the arrogant government do thou swiftly uproot in our days; and may the Christians and the heretics suddenly be laid low and not be inscribed with the righteous. Blessed art thou, O Lord, who humblest the arrogant."

semblance to that found at Qumran, particularly in the Habbakuk Commentary.[4]

OUTLINE OF MATTHEW:

Introduction: The New Obedience (1:1–2:23)

The Higher Righteousness (3:1–7:29)

Fulfilling Righteousness (3:13–17)

Teaching Righteousness (5:17–20)

True Discipleship (8:1–11:1)

The Kingdom of Heaven (11:2–13:52)

The Forgiving Church (13:53–19:2)

Peter as the Rock (16:13–23)

Discipline in Community (18:15–22)

Judgment: Doing God's Will (19:3–26:1)

Believing Doers of the Law (21:28–46)

Doing Mercy Without Calculation (25:31–46)

Conclusion: Obedience and Resurrection (26:2–28:20)

The Great Commission (28:16–20)

Introduction: The New Obedience (1:1–2:23)

Matthew's Gospel begins with his special tradition. This tradition appears to be largely legendary: a genealogical list of Jesus' ancestors; a story of Jesus' birth; exotic wise men from the East, their encounter with Herod and worship of the baby Jesus; the flight to Egypt; the slaying of the innocent children; and the return to Nazareth. These matters may seem preliminary to the real work of Jesus, which for Mark began at Jesus' baptism and ended at the crucifixion. But these "Christmas stories" bear the heart of Matthew's message, his good news.[5]

The genealogy (1:1ff.) helps in understanding the birth story (1:18–25). At first glance, this list of Jesus' ancestors looks rather unpromising for determining Matthew's intent and purpose. We notice that the genealogy is divided into three sets of generations of fourteen each—from Abraham to David, from David to the Babylonian deportation, and from Babylon to the Christ (vs. 17). Abraham is the father of the Jewish people, for Israel's God is the God of Abraham, Isaac, and Jacob (see Genesis 12:1–3; cf. Matt. 3:9; 22:32). The Christ who climaxes this genealogy fulfills the hope of Israel; therefore, the age of fulfillment is dawning with the birth of the expected Messiah. This Christ is also descended from David, the great king

---

[4] See Stendahl, *School of St. Matthew*, pp. 183 ff.

[5] The fullest treatment of the Matthean (and Lukan) infancy narratives is Raymond E. Brown, *The Birth of the Messiah: A Commentary on the Infancy Narratives in Matthew and Luke* (Garden City, N.Y.: Doubleday, 1977), distinguished for its wealth of historical information as well as its sensitivity to the theological dimensions of the subject.

in Israel's history. (Only in Matthew is Jesus' Davidic descent traced through the royal line.) Indeed, the Lord promised through the prophet Nathan that David's offspring would be established in a kingdom forever (II Samuel 7:12–17). Thus Jesus Christ will fulfill Israel's hopes prefigured in Abraham and David (see 1:1). Yet the Babylonian exile, the next major division in the genealogy, meant disaster for Israel's hope of establishing a political kingdom in which God's rule would triumph. Perhaps for Matthew the deportation raises the question of whether fulfillment of Israel's hopes will take a form other than that of a Davidic political kingdom.

The inclusion of women in the genealogy suggests a possibility of the unexpected; the Christ who comes may not correspond to the image of the Messiah for whom Israel was waiting. In the ancient world, descent was traced through the male; yet five women intrude into the genealogy: Tamar (vs. 3), Rahab and Ruth (vs. 5), the wife of Uriah (vs. 6), and Mary (vs. 16).[6] Moreover, these are quite unusual women. Tamar disguised herself as a harlot to seduce her father-in-law Judah so that she could bear children, Perez and Zerah (Genesis 38). Rahab, the harlot of Jericho, saved Joshua's two spies and consequently preserved her own life when the walls of Jericho fell (Joshua 2, 6). Ruth, the Moabitess who was loyal to her Hebrew mother-in-law, gained her future husband Boaz one night during the grain festival (Ruth 3). And the wife of Uriah is none other than that Bathsheba who bathed in the right place during "the spring of the year" and thus became the wife of David (II Samuel 11–12). Likely each of these women was a foreigner. Yet in spite of this and their questionable moral actions, God acted through each of them.

Within this setting, Matthew's story of Jesus' birth takes place, with the genealogy strongly suggesting that Jesus' ancestry includes not only the men (especially Abraham and David) but also the women, Tamar, Rahab, Ruth, Bathsheba, and finally Mary. Clearly our story (vss. 18–25) centers on Joseph's response to the pregnancy of his betrothed Mary. Although Matthew explicitly talks about a virgin birth (vss. 18, 20, 23, 25), the story focuses not upon wonder at the virgin Mary but, rather, on how Joseph will react to the dilemma posed by the question of whether she is pregnant from unfaithfulness or the power of God.[7] Not only is the question posed

---

[6] According to one view, Matthew's genealogy serves to prove that Jesus was the Messiah because he was descended from Abraham and especially David. Yet Joseph does not, according to the following verses, father Jesus, even though the genealogy would have to be traced through him to function as proof. This tradition might have originally (apart from 1:18–25) proved the Davidic descent of Jesus and therefore his messiahship, but in the Matthean context, descent from David through Joseph cannot be maintained. Cf. Sherman Johnson, "The Gospel According to St. Matthew," *IB*, VII (Nashville, Tenn.: Abingdon, 1951), pp. 252 f.

[7] H. J. Held, "Matthew as Interpreter of the Miracle Stories," *Tradition and Interpretation in Matthew*, trans. P. Scott (Philadelphia: Westminster, 1963), pp. 238 f., maintains that this story is the composition of the evangelist himself and

within the birth story itself but also by the preceding section. Inclusion of the women in Matthew's genealogy raises the question of how God works to achieve his purposes, and at the culmination of the birth story Joseph must decide whether Mary's pregnancy is God's action.

Joseph at first thinks that he has been wronged by Mary. "Being a just man" he decides to divorce her quietly (vs. 19). According to Jewish law, a man could do one of two things. He could bring his betrothed to public trial where conviction of infidelity might carry the penalty of death by stoning, or he could divorce his betrothed privately. Engagement, like marriage, could only be severed by divorce. Joseph generously opts for the latter course. At this moment, however, the angel intrudes and through a dream Joseph learns about a higher righteousness (see, for example, 3:15; 5:20; 5:33). He hears that this conception is from the Holy Spirit, the agent of God's activity on earth; furthermore, this son of Mary will "save the people from their sins" (vs. 21)—people like Tamar, Rahab, Ruth, and Bathsheba (cf. 9:1–13; 26:28).

The theme of Jesus as the savior of his people is developed in the following quotation from Isaiah 7:14 (vss. 22 f.). Whether these words are from the angel or the narrator, the birth of Jesus fulfills the Old Testament and signifies Emmanuel ("God is with us"). This linking of Jesus as savior from sins and Jesus as a sign of God's presence also occurs near the opening of the Matthean miracle section (8:1 ff.). There another quotation from the prophet Isaiah ("He took our infirmities and bore our diseases"—53:4; Matt. 8:17) affirms Jesus as the bringer of forgiveness and the presence of God (cf. Matt. 9:1–7). Still another, subsequent statement of Jesus sounds like a promise of Emmanuel, "For where two or three are gathered in my name, there am I in the midst of them" (18:20). It is immediately followed by Jesus' declaration of the necessity for limitless forgiveness (18:21 f.), for Matthew understands Jesus' coming as bringing both forgiveness and God's presence (see Mark 2:7).

This good news does not imply that Matthew understands the Christian gospel to be the end of human responsibility, for the heart of this story is Joseph's response. Joseph forgives; Joseph accepts the presence of God, when it draws near to him in a dream. The text simply states that when he "woke from sleep, he did as the angel of the Lord commanded him; he took his wife" (vs. 24). Joseph obeyed; he practiced a higher righteousness.

Throughout Matthew, beginning in this opening scene and ending with the last words of Jesus to the disciples (28:20), the theme of obedience recurs (see 5:17–20; 7:15–27; 21:28–32). Such obedi-

---

suggests that the usage of catch phrases, such as taking a wife (1:20, 24), bearing a son (1:21, 23, 25), and calling his name (1:21, 23, 25), are evidences of the evangelist's work.

ence is not, however, a meritorious work. Radical obedience occurs in God's forgiveness and presence (again, see 28:20). Therefore, Joseph is no hero but rather one who responds to God's initiative in Jesus' birth.

The second chapter of Matthew's introduction has little direct connection with the first. The first half of chapter 2 is dominated by the "wise men from the East," and the entire chapter is organized around a series of geographical places: the East, Jerusalem, Bethlehem, Egypt, and finally Nazareth.[8]

The wise men and their reaction to the birth of Jesus compose the initial scene (vss. 1–18). Perhaps they are Zoroastrian priests or Babylonian astrologers, but without doubt they are Gentiles. Whereas Joseph showed the reaction of a loyal, just Jew to the birth of Jesus, now we see the response of wise Gentiles (28:19). They have come to worship him as they would a king or a god (2:2, 8, 11; cf. 14:33; 28:17). Their reaction to Jesus' birth contrasts with that of Herod, the political king, who can think of Jesus only as a threat to his rule. And with some reason, for the unusual star's appearance serves as a sign of a crucial event: the old age, typified by Herod's kingdom, yields to the new, manifested in the birth of Jesus. At the midpoint of this chapter a small unit of tradition (vss. 13–15) discloses Matthew's intent. After the wise men have left, an angel of the Lord again appears to Joseph. This time he is told to flee to Egypt, and again Joseph obeys (vs. 14). By his response to the dream revelations the story moves forward.

All this occurred in order "to fulfill what the Lord had spoken by the prophet, 'Out of Egypt have I called my son'" (vs. 15; cf. Hosea 11:1). Originally this verse recalled Israel's being brought out of Egypt. Now "my son" refers not to Israel, but to Jesus. Chapter 2, furthermore, contains tradition suggesting that Jesus is to be understood as a new Moses. Moses lived in Egypt before leading the people to the promised land; Jesus also fled to Egypt before coming to Nazareth. The Hebrew male children were killed at the birth of Moses; the Bethlehem male children were killed at the birth of Jesus (2:16–19; cf. Exodus 1:15–2:10). Yet the text seems to imply something more than a Moses-Jesus typology. Jesus is not a new Moses, but a new Israel. The Old Testament equated God's Son with the people, not Moses (Exodus 4:22). The Moses analogy is present within Matthew;[9] however, the text primarily proclaims the for-

---

[8] See Krister Stendahl, "Quis et unde? An Analysis of Matt. 1–2," *Judentum, Urchristentum, Kirche: Festschrift für Joachim Jeremias,* 2d ed. (Berlin: Töpelmann, 1964), pp. 97 ff.

[9] The "forty days and nights" of fasting in the wilderness temptation (4:2) picks up the "forty days and nights" Moses also fasted when he wrote the commandments from God (Exodus 34:28). In the six antitheses (5:21–48) Jesus elaborates the commandments of Moses; indeed, the entire Sermon is from the Mount (cf. Exodus

The flight into Egypt of Joseph and Mary with the baby Jesus as portrayed by a contemporary Chinese artist, Hua Hsiao Kuan. (Courtesy of Spartaco Appetiti.)

The present-day city of Bethlehem. (Courtesy of Pan American Airways.)

mation of a new Israel. In Judaism Moses never occupied the exalted position of Jesus. Whereas Moses was honored and respected, Jesus is worshipped (2:11; 28:17).

In his own demonic way Herod recognizes the breaking in of a new era. He tries without success to kill the new "king" (vss. 16 ff.). Fittingly, the chapter ends with Jesus in Nazareth (vs. 23). From this

---

19:2 f.). Finally, the five-part structure of Matthew (see the initial outline) parallels the Pentateuch, the five books of Moses. See B. W. Bacon, *Studies in Matthew* (New York: Holt, 1930). On the other hand, it is striking that in the first two chapters the Exodus texts dealing with the birth and childhood of Moses are not cited. W. D. Davies, *The Setting of the Sermon on the Mount* (New York: Cambridge University Press, 1966), pp. 14–25, examines Bacon's view of Matthew's structure and stops just short of being persuaded. Jack Dean Kingsbury, *Matthew: Structure, Christology, Kingdom* (Philadelphia: Fortress, 1975), pp. 1–25, argues that the two basic divisions of Matthew are 4:17–16:20 and 16:21–28:20. John P. Meier, *The Vision of Matthew: Christ, Church and Morality in the First Gospel* (New York: Paulist Press, 1979), in discussion with Kingsbury adopts a structure similar to the one we follow.

point, the focus of the narrative narrows, and a particular history replaces the prophetic, eschatological overview of the introduction. Whether the first two Matthean chapters contain history in the sense of observed and reported events is debatable. A comparison with the Lukan infancy narratives discloses agreement on certain nodal points (e.g., the virginity of Mary) but otherwise wide-ranging divergencies and differences. The stories do, however, proclaim Matthew's understanding of the new Christian way. This way of radical obedience becomes possible with the appearance of Jesus, who both is and brings into existence the new Israel.

The Higher Righteousness (3:1–7:29)

This section, like the four other major Matthean sections, consists of narrative and discourse. The narrative includes the baptism, temptation, preaching, and calling of disciples by Jesus (3:1–4:25). The discourse is the Sermon on the Mount (5:1–7:29). By this arrangement, Matthew uses the discourse of Jesus to interpret the narrative, which he has basically taken over from Mark. Our interpretation of this overall section, as a depiction of "higher righteousness," is borne out by a comparison of treatments of John the Baptist.

Both Matthew and Luke record John the Baptist's reaction to some people who come out to be baptized by him (3:7–10; cf. Luke 3:7–9—Q source). According to Luke, John's scathing attack is directed against the multitudes because they are not bearing fruit that befits repentance. Matthew characteristically has John the Baptist assault the Pharisees and Sadducees, although in the time of Jesus they were the groups most likely to show obedience. Thus through his presentation of the incident, Matthew stresses that even the Pharisees are not bearing good fruit. Therefore, they are liable to judgment, and their claim to descent from Abraham will be of no avail against final judgment (vss. 9 f.). A higher righteousness is demanded.

This discussion of the necessity of bearing fruit receives further explanation in the discourse of the Sermon on the Mount: "So, every sound tree bears good fruit, but the bad tree bears evil fruit" (7:17; cf. 7:18–20). Matthew prefaces this statement with an attack upon false prophets who appear in sheep's clothing, pretending to be righteous (7:15 f.). These false prophets rely upon their record of prophesying and casting out demons in the face of God's judgment (7:21–23). But such activity is of no avail unless they produce fruits—that is, deeds of righteousness, such as loving the enemy (5:44), not being angry with one's brother (5:22), praying without hypocrisy (6:5), not judging (7:1), and so on. Although the Matthean words of Jesus clearly define the higher righteousness (5:20) that Jesus demands, hearing is not enough; doing is indispensable (7:24). Therefore, Matthew moves from an emphasis on redefining righteousness to the necessity for practicing it. Higher righteousness is more than knowledge; it consists also of doing.

FULFILLING RIGHTEOUSNESS (3:13–17)

Why does Jesus accept baptism by John the Baptist?

Jesus' first act in the Gospel of Matthew occurs in connection with his baptism. In Mark, Jesus did not really act at the baptism; rather he was acted upon by John the Baptist. Matthew, by way of contrast, shows Jesus acting during this baptism by John. In comparing this baptism story (Matt. 3:13–17) with that of Mark (Mark 1:9–11), we note four distinct Matthean characteristics that illumine his intention: (1) the preaching of John the Baptist and Jesus are identical; (2) Jesus explicitly decides to be baptized; (3) his baptism fulfills all righteousness; and (4) the voice from heaven does not speak to Jesus but apparently to John the Baptist.

According to Matthew, both John the Baptist and Jesus proclaim "Repent, for the kingdom of heaven is at hand" (3:2; 4:17).[10] Such identical messages show clearly that Matthew does not reject the close relationship of John and Jesus. Yet Matthew also makes clear that John the Baptist's message is prophecy, "Prepare the way of the Lord, make his paths straight" (3:3; Isaiah 40:3), whereas Jesus' coming is fulfillment, "The people who sat in darkness have seen a great light, and for those who sat in the region and shadow of death light has dawned" (4:16; Isaiah 9:1 f.). There is no polemic against John the Baptist. We have already seen that John the Baptist's injunction to bear good fruit (3:10) is supported and elaborated by Jesus at the close of the Sermon on the Mount (7:16). Moreover, Matthew's Jesus, unlike Mark's, decides to leave Galilee to be baptized by John (vs. 13). What happened without explanation in Mark (1:9) occurs in Matthew because of Jesus' decision and action (cf. vs. 14).

In Matthew, John's protest about the inappropriateness of his baptizing Jesus is answered by the first words of Jesus, "Let it be so now; for thus it is fitting for us to fulfill all righteousness" (vs. 15). This answer, appearing only in Matthew, explains why the sinless Jesus needed a baptism for repentance. Such an apologetic motif oc-

---

[10] Matthew's preference for "kingdom of heaven" rather than "kingdom of God" probably reflects his reluctance to use the name God. Such reluctance is characteristic of Judaism and may further support the Jewish-Christian origin of Matthew. Cf. the opening preaching of Jesus in Mark, "The time is fulfilled, and the kingdom of God is at hand; repent and believe in the gospel" (1:15).

curs in accounts of Jesus' baptism in noncanonical Gospels.[11] Jesus' reply may also be understood as his acceptance of a requirement for the whole nation, to establish an identity between himself and his people. Both explanations make Jesus' baptism into a routine of going through the motions. But in Matthew Jesus himself initiates the action and says that this baptism is "to fulfill all righteousness" (cf. 5:17), a central Matthean theme. Consequently, we need to look more carefully into Jesus' reply.

In the first place, Matthew uniformly uses "righteousness" to mean that conduct that is in agreement with God's will and well pleasing to him. It is rightness of life before God.[12] This term will be considered more fully in the following section. In anticipation, however, we may say that Matthew does not speak about righteousness as a preliminary step toward the kingdom of heaven but, rather, as the very substance of this kingdom (see 5:6, 10, 20; 6:33).

Second, the fulfilling of all righteousness should be understood in the context of the preceding verses (3:11 f.), where John declared that he himself only baptized with water for repentance, but that after him would come one who would baptize with "the Holy Spirit and with fire." The Holy Spirit, of course, signifies the presence of God (see 1:18), and fire depicts judgment, as the context implies ("unquenchable fire"). The coming of Jesus, then, is the sign both of God's presence (cf. 1:23) and his judgment. The relationship between the two was already anticipated in John the Baptist's previous speech (3:7–10). Judgment comes to whoever does not bear fruit. But, as this passage makes clear (3:13–17), God's presence now makes it possible to bear fruit because the Holy Spirit has come with Jesus. Jesus willingly undergoes baptism, for because of the Spirit's presence he can now be obedient (bear fruit) and fulfill all righteousness, being well pleasing to God (vs. 17).

The unexpected plural in Jesus' answer to John, "thus it is fitting for *us* to fulfill all righteousness," must in this context refer to Jesus and John the Baptist. John the Baptist also is obedient ("he consented"—vs. 15). Jesus obeyed in his decision to come from Galilee to be baptized and John the Baptist acted to complete Jesus' obedience. With their fulfillment of all righteousness, the Spirit of

---

[11] In the Gospel of the Ebionites, John asked Jesus to baptize him *after* the voice spoke from heaven. The Gospel according to the Hebrews reports the following dialogue, "Behold, the mother of the Lord and his brethren said to him: 'John the Baptist baptizes unto the remission of sins, let us go and be baptized by him.' But he [Jesus] said to them: 'Wherein have I sinned that I should go and be baptized by him? Unless what I have said is ignorance (a sin of ignorance)." Hennecke, *New Testament Apocrypha*, I, 157 and 146–147 resp.

[12] G. Barth, "Matthew's Understanding of the Law," in *Tradition and Interpretation in Matthew*, pp. 138 f.

"The Calling of the Apostles Peter and Andrew" by Duccio di Buoninsegna (1228–1319). (Courtesy of National Gallery of Art, Washington, D.C. Samuel H. Kress Collection.)

God appears visually to Jesus and aurally to John the Baptist (in Mark 1:11 the voice spoke to Jesus).

This interpretation of the story of Jesus' baptism is supported by the following temptation story (4:1–11). The beloved Son of God, announced in the baptism, now acts as the Son in response to each temptation. "If you are the Son of God" (vss. 3, 6) does not really imply that Jesus might not be the Son of God. The baptism (3:17) left no doubt that Jesus was the Son of God. The only doubt concerns the nature of the sonship, whether Jesus will act in obedience to God or on his own authority. Just as obedience characterized his baptism, so the temptations show the Son of God acting in accordance with the will of God (vss. 4, 7, 10).

After the temptation, Jesus first goes to territory close to the Gentiles (4:12–16) where he begins to preach (vs. 17) and immediately calls disciples (vss. 18–22). These disciples respond by following him (vss. 20, 22). A brief summary section of healings (vss. 23–25; cf. Mark 1:21–3:11) shows how he attracts crowds from everywhere and leads into the first discourse, the Sermon on the Mount.

TEACHING RIGHTEOUSNESS (5:17–20)

What is the righteousness which exceeds that of the scribes and Pharisees?

The Sermon on the Mount (chaps. 5–7) has been acclaimed as the heart and center of Christian faith. In Matthew, this is the first and most important discourse of the Gospel. In all probability, the Sermon was not spoken by Jesus on one occasion, for much of the same material is scattered throughout the Gospel of Luke (see, for example, the Sermon on the Plain, Luke 6:17–49, but also 12:22–34). Hence the arrangement of the tradition probably reflects Matthean interests and concerns.

The significance of the Sermon on the Mount for Matthew is illustrated by the fact that his passion story picks up motifs already prepared for in the Sermon. For example, in Gethsemane Jesus prays word for word the third petition of the Lord's Prayer (26:42; cf. 6:10). Jesus also advocates peace in the confrontation at his arrest (26:52; cf. 5:39). Moreover, Jesus never relaxes the commandments; he is innocent and righteous (27:4, 19, 24; cf. 5:19). Jesus refuses to reply to the high priests' request for an oath (26:63; cf. 5:34). All these instances are Matthean additions not found in the Markan text.

Two preliminary observations about the staging will serve to characterize this discourse. First, Jesus appears as a rabbi, a teacher (5:2). This initial depiction of Jesus contrasts with that of Mark where Jesus initially appeared as a miracle worker and healer (Mark 1:21 ff.). Second, the Sermon is delivered from the Mount. Two other crucial events, the transfiguration scene (17:1 ff.) and the final word to the disciples (28:16 ff.), occur on a mountain in the Gospel of Matthew. The delivery of the Sermon from the mountain is deliberately reminiscent of Moses' receiving the law on the mountain in the wilderness (Exodus 19). According to Matthew, a new teaching comes from the mountain—a righteousness higher than that delivered by Moses.

In addition, two further observations about the content of the Sermon show its intention and meaning. First, it begins with a series of nine beatitudes or blessings (5:3–12), which describe the condition of those for whom Jesus' message is good news—"the poor in spirit," "those who mourn," and "the meek" (5:3–5).[13] These conditions are not requirements, for Matthew declares the unmerited grace of God in present blessing and promises future participation in the kingdom of heaven to those who have need. Even the last six "beatitudes" (5:6–12), which might be taken as ethical requirements, are still within the setting of unconditional blessing. Any "merit" goes back to the astonishing generosity of God. Thus the opening of the Sermon on the Mount stresses God's favor rather

---

[13] See Barth, *Tradition and Interpretation in Matthew,* pp. 144–146.

than his demand. Second, the Sermon on the Mount ends with a clear call to obedience (7:15–29): "You will know them by their fruits" (7:16). Entrance into the kingdom of heaven will reward whoever "does the will of my Father who is in heaven" (7:21); the wise man hears Jesus' words and does them (7:24). Hence the grace of God does not make obedience unnecessary.

We now turn to the word of Jesus about the law and prophets (5:17–20), which appears only in Matthew. In the first three verses Jesus declares his complete acceptance of the law and the prophets. Nothing will pass away from the law until all is accomplished. No one may relax one of these commandments or teach anyone else to do so. This complete acceptance of the law is difficult to understand in view of later criticism of the law. The final verse demanding a "higher righteousness" (vs. 20) already hints at criticism, but other passages are more explicit. John the Baptist is identified with the law and the prophets, yet he who is least in the kingdom of heaven is greater than he (11:11–15). Matthew follows Mark in Jesus' criticism of the law's distinction between clean and unclean: "Hear and understand: not what goes into the mouth defiles a man, but what comes out of the mouth, this defiles a man" (15:10; cf. Mark 7:14 f.). Nevertheless, Jesus' first words on the law (vss. 17–19) make clear that Jesus is no antinomian (that is, one who disavows the law). He expects nothing less than fulfillment of the law. Although Matthew does contain a torrid diatribe against the scribes and Pharisees (chap. 23), this criticism is directed toward their failure to practice and observe the law (23:3) and their hypocrisy (23:13. 23, 25, and so on).

In another passage, however (22:34–40; cf. Mark 12:28–34), Jesus discusses the nature of the law and the prophets and generalizes that the first and great commandment is love of God, and the second love of neighbor. *All* the law and the prophets depend on these commandments (vs. 40). This conclusion, which appears only in Matthew, suggests that the "higher righteousness" that Jesus teaches consists of a primary relation with God and a secondary relation with other people. This view of higher righteousness helps to explain the castigation of the scribes and Pharisees that follows (chap. 23). As we noted, they are chastised because they do not observe the law and are hypocrites. Yet by any "normal" measure the scribes and Pharisees were the most observant group within Israel, during both the time of Jesus and of Matthew. Only by the extraordinary norm of the love of God and the love of neighbor which nevertheless is derived from the law and the prophets, could they be denounced.

We have already encountered the verb "to fulfill" in Matthew. At the baptism Jesus and John the Baptist fulfilled all righteousness (3:15), primarily by their respective acts of obedience. Here in the Sermon, "he who does them and teaches them shall be called great in the kingdom of heaven" (vs. 19b). Jesus fulfills the law and the prophets not only in deed, but also in teaching. Matthew understands the congregation of followers of Christ as founded not only upon Jesus' action but also upon his teaching. Jesus' closing words in the Gospel reiterate this theme, "Go therefore and make disciples of all nations . . . teaching them to observe all that I have commanded you" (28:19 f.).

The key to Jesus' teaching about fulfillment of the law and the prophets lies, of course, in the enigmatic last verse of this passage (vs. 5:20), where Jesus calls for more righteousness than that of the scribes and Pharisees. The rest of the Sermon seeks to teach this higher righteousness, which first becomes explicit in the "antitheses" of the Sermon on the Mount.[14]

The six antitheses (5:21–48) are so designated because of the antithetical form in which they are cast, "You have heard it said . . . but I say to you." These antitheses seem to indicate that Jesus pays attention to a person's intention as well as to the actual deed. His words would therefore advise the hearer to root out evil thoughts so that evil actions will not follow. We might observe that such good advice is easier to hear than to heed. It is sometimes difficult to refrain from killing, committing adultery, and hating one's neighbor; it is almost impossible to keep from anger, lust, and hate of one's enemy. These words are not, however, a counsel of despair, for the extremely radical nature of their demand elicits from the hearer the recognition that these are more than human commands. The antitheses set forth the will and presence of God. The commandments are transparent so that God shines through them. Indeed the Sermon's opening beatitudes already indicated the present blessings of God. Moreover, Jesus' following teaching emphasizes the availability of God in prayer (6:5–15) and everyday life (6:25–34). Therefore, the final, seemingly impossible requirement, "You, therefore, must be perfect as your heavenly Father is perfect" (5:48), is Jesus' call to align oneself with the perfection or righteousness of God, which God not only requires but also manifests. With the demand for the higher righteousness comes the gift of God's grace.

Matthew develops the entire Sermon under the implied rubrics of love of God and love of neighbor as the fulfillment of the law and the prophets (cf. 7:11 f.). The antitheses call for an unlimited concern for the neighbor (vss. 21–48; see also 7:1–5), whereas the remaining sections of the Sermon point to the one gracious source of life. What is impossible apart from God becomes a promise in his presence (6:33). The Sermon on the Mount begins with the promise

---

[14]On the intrinsic connection of the concept of "righteousness" in 5:20 and the following antitheses, see R. S. McConnell, *Law and Prophecy in Matthew's Gospel: The Authority and Use of the Old Testament in the Gospel of St. Matthew* (Basel: Reinhardt, 1969), pp. 34 ff.

of blessings (5:1–12) and ends with the demand for obedience (7:24–27). This tension characterizes the Jewish Christianity of Matthew and is actually typical of the New Testament as a whole. God's grace enables people to obey; it does not nullify human responsibility.

True Discipleship (8:1–11:1)

In the first major section of the Gospel, Jesus appeared as Messiah of the word (chaps. 3–7), but in the second major section he appears as Messiah of the deed. Matthew has brought together ten miracle narratives (chaps. 8–9), accounts of Jesus' deeds, which lead naturally into the missionary discourse (chaps. 10) that describes the deeds required in discipleship (10:42).

This movement from Jesus' miracles to the disciples' working is reflected in Matthew's threefold division of the miracle section. The first part (8:2–17) portrays Jesus as bearing the infirmities and diseases of all people—the leper, the centurion's servant, the disciple's mother-in-law. By his healings Jesus fulfills the prophet Isaiah's word, "He took our infirmities and bore our diseases" (8:17; cf. Isaiah 53:4). The middle and dominant division (8:18–9:17) places the disciples at the center of action. The initial episode (8:18–22) shows a concern about "following." Next the plight of the perishing disciples (8:23–27) is overcome in the power of Jesus' exorcism of the two demoniacs (8:28–34) and the healing forgiveness of the paralytic (9:1–8). After these miracles Jesus immediately calls the disciple Matthew, who is a tax collector, for Jesus has come not to call the righteous, but the sinners (9:9–13). Therefore, Jesus' disciples rejoice rather than fast as John's disciples do (9:14–17). In distinction from the previous division's emphasis on the disciples, the third and final part of the miracle section (9:18–38) concerns faith. Indeed, Matthew has reduced the narration about the raising of the daughter and the healing of the woman with the hemorrhage (9:18–26) to a bare minimum to emphasize the essential point of the father's faith. The same is true of Matthew's treatment of the healing of the two blind men (9:27–31); moreover, faith is implicitly the subject of the final healing of the dumb demoniac (9:32–34). Without faith there is no miracle.

Matthew's miracle section portrays a compassionate healer, drawing out disciples who believe in working with God rather than the prince of demons (9:34). Thus Jesus draws out faithful disciples who will continue his own work. In other words, he calls for faithful disciples to join with him in the labor of sharing the suffering of people.[15] Confirmation of our view that Matthew intends to define

[15] See Held, *Tradition and Interpretation in Matthew*, pp. 165 ff.

discipleship in this section (chaps. 8–10) is found in the transistional sentences. Only Matthew says, "When he came down from the mountain, great crowds *followed* him" (8:1; cf. Mark 1:39 f.). "Following"—that is, discipleship—is actually the theme of the Matthean miracle section.

The missionary discourse (chap. 10), which immediately follows the miracles, links the twelve *disciples* directly with the acts that Jesus has just performed: "And he called to him his twelve disciples and gave them authority over unclean spirits, to cast them out, and to heal every disease and every infirmity" (10:1; 8:16–17). Finally, the closing transitional sentence of this section reads, "And when Jesus had finished instructing his *twelve disciples,* he went on from there to teach and preach in their cities" (11:1).

The composition and character of Matthew's missionary discourse (chap. 10) suggest that this tradition is more than simply the report of Jesus' instructions to his twelve disciples. This discourse concerning the nature of true discipleship is primarily intended for the disciples in the congregation of Matthew's time. This is evident in the changes Matthew has made in his Markan tradition (cf. Mark 6:7–13). First, Matthew has no report of Jesus' disciples' actually carrying out the mission that he gave them. Although his Markan source contained the statement that "they went out and preached that men should repent . . . ," Matthew lacks even that (Mark 6:12 f.; cf. Matt. 10:14 f.). For Matthew, this missionary task was delivered to the church that came into existence with the death and resurrection of Jesus (28:19 f.). Second, Matthew inserts a passage from Jesus' apocalyptic discourse concerning the future end of the world (Mark 13:9–13) into Jesus' missionary discourse (Matt. 10:17–25), which is intended to instruct the church for its present task. According to Matthew these words are spoken by Jesus to the church for application to the time between Jesus' resurrection and his parousia; thus Matthew changes an apocalyptic warning into churchly instructions.

Matthew's editing or redaction does not mean that he has no regard for tradition, that he changes it at will or creates it anew. Indeed, his respect for the tradition extends to inclusion of two sayings with which he does not agree; the disciples are to go only to the lost sheep of Israel (10:5), and they "will not have gone through all the towns of Israel before the Son of man comes" (10:23). These words clearly reflect an earlier stage of the tradition that Matthew has included in order to frame them within his more comprehensive understanding of discipleship, which extends to both Israel and the Gentiles.[16]

---

[16]Note how Matthew adds the phrase, "and the Gentiles" (10:18; cf. Mark 13:9). Also note emphasis upon Gentiles in 2:1 ff.; 8:5–18; 12:18–21; 15:22–28; 24:14; and 28:19.

In this treatment of discipleship Matthew has shown Jesus as the Messiah in deed, whose miracles alleviate suffering humanity (8:16 f.). In turn, the disciples are to respond with obedient deeds. They realize true discipleship insofar as they acknowledge Jesus' lordship and follow him, performing acts of mercy toward others (10:42).

The Kingdom of Heaven (11:2–13:52)

Were Matthew presenting an historical narrative in the usual sense, we might expect information in this section about what happened to the disciples after they responded to Jesus' missionary imperative (chap. 10). Instead, this section details further activity of Jesus and the reaction, both positive and negative, which he elicits. First, a series of passages deals with the relationship of John the Baptist and Jesus (11:2–19); next, the cities that rejected Jesus are chastised (11:20–24); blessing is then pronounced upon those who accept the yoke of Jesus (11:25–30); and controversy with the Pharisees involving a series of miracles follows (chap. 12). The section ends with a series of parables initially addressed to the crowds, but adapted by Matthew for the disciples (chap. 13).

The key to this section lies not so much in the order of events as in the way in which Matthew has brought his own special interests to them. Four emphases stand out:

1. The section is devoted overall to the question of the nature of the kingdom of heaven. The opening incident raises the Christological question, "Are you he who is to come, or shall we look for another?" (11:3). However, Jesus' answer and the ensuing discussion transform the Christological question into an eschatological one, the nature of the kingdom of heaven. Although John the Baptist is greater than anybody else born of woman, "yet he who is least in the kingdom of heaven is greater than he" (11:11). Moreover, in a later debate with the Pharisees about whether Jesus casts out demons by God or Beelzebul, the climactic answer again focuses on the kingdom: "But if it is by the Spirit of God that I cast out demons, then the kingdom of God has come upon you" (12:28). Finally, the discourse of this section unveils the "secrets of the kingdom of heaven" (13:11). The seven kingdom parables with which this section ends show that, for Matthew, understanding of Jesus as the Christ comes through understanding Jesus' proclamation about the kingdom of heaven.[17]

---

[17] For a discussion of the place of these parables in the theology of Matthew, see Jack D. Kingsbury, *The Parables of Jesus in Matthew 13* (Richmond, Va.: John Knox, 1969).

2. This kingdom of heaven is a kingdom of mercy. Jesus answers John the Baptist's disciples by enumerating his deeds of mercy (11:5; cf. Luke 7:22). Furthermore, Jesus' demand for discipleship is a yoke that is gentle and restful, because Jesus himself is gentle and lowly in heart (11:28–30, only in Matthew). Sabbath observance is understood within the context of mercy (12:7 f.; cf. 9:13 and Hosea 6:6). Indeed, Jesus' parable of the sower proclaims God's abundant mercy; the sower generously sows seed everywhere without distinction, and the seed on good soil bears grain prodigiously (13:3–8).

3. The kingdom of heaven is, however, not mercy only; judgment also occurs. Chorazin, Bethsaida, and Capernaum will be brought down on the day of judgment because they rejected the words of mercy (11:20–24). Jesus' opponents, especially the Pharisees, will be brought to account on the day of judgment because they have not borne the good fruit—that is, acts of mercy (12:33–37). Indeed, this present generation is an evil one (12:45, only in Matthew). Finally, at the close of the age "all causes of sin and all evildoers" will be gathered out of the kingdom and thrown "into the furnace of fire; there men will weep and gnash their teeth" (13:42; cf. 8:12; 13:50; 22:13; and so on).

4. Jesus' disciples are the ones who will realize the true nature of the kingdom of heaven. Those who have been gathered to Jesus learn that the kingdom is both mercy and judgment. They are the "babes" who learn that this yoke is easy (11:25–29). They are the true family of Jesus. Matthew alone records Jesus' saying that the disciples are his mother and brothers (12:49; cf. Mark 3:34). Matthew also directs the final six kingdom parables to the disciples, for they are the ones who know the secrets of the kingdom (13:10–17). Indeed, Matthew omits Mark's castigation of the disciples, "Do you not understand this parable? How then will you understand all the parables?" (Mark 4:13). In Matthew the opposite point is true—the disciples do understand; therefore, when Jesus asks them, "Have you understood all this?" (13:51), the only possible answer is "Yes." Matthew then concludes, "Therefore every scribe who has been trained for the kingdom of heaven is like a householder who brings out of his treasure what is new and what is old" (vs. 52). The new refers to the kingdom of mercy, new in comparison with Pharisaic insistence on strict sabbath observance (cf. 12:12b); the old refers to the kingdom of judgment, the old expectation of judgment under the criterion of obedience to the will of God (cf. 12:50). Therefore, the scribe trains for the kingdom by accepting the new mercy and by carrying out the old obedience. Matthew speaks to the church in the time between the resurrection and the parousia, a time of mercy and judgment. The disciples have no security other than the gracious presence of Christ (cf. 10:40; 28:20). They are to work between the times so that at the future judgment they will be found merciful.

Matthew thus prepares for the subject matter of his next section, the church.

The Forgiving Church (13:53–19:2)

In Matthew's preceding section, the kingdom of heaven was characterized as an eschatological reality, already present in mercy and expected in judgment. In this section, stress falls upon the church, the community of disciples existing between the resurrection and the parousia, those who are closely identified with the mercy motif of the kingdom of heaven.

As in every other section of Matthew, here also narrative is dominated by discourse. What Jesus teaches controls his own actions and those of his opponents and disciples. The concluding discourse (17:22–19:1) centers upon the nature and authority of the church. Fittingly, then, the climactic action of the narrative (13:53–17:21) is Jesus' establishment of Peter as the rock upon which the church is built (16:17–19). We receive clues as to the intention of this section simply by observing the heightened role of Peter. For example, Matthew takes over Mark's story of Jesus' walking on the water (14:22–33; Mark 6:45–52) and, instead of using it as an occasion to illustrate the disciples' misunderstanding (Mark 6:51 f.), shows Peter's amazing, albeit faltering, courage in trying to walk on the water. When he sinks from fear, Peter cries out with a Christological confession, "Lord, save me" (14:30). Partly because of Peter's action, at the end of the story the other disciples worship Jesus and confess, "Truly, you are the Son of God" (14:33). Matthew's stress on the Christological foundation of the church is evident in the exalted titles for Jesus in this part of the Gospel: "Lord" (15:22; 16:22; 17:4, 15), "Son of God" (14:33; 16:16), "Son of man" (16:13, 27 f.), and "Son of David" (15:22). All are Matthew's additions.[18]

The increased emphasis upon Peter is matched by a more prominent role for the disciples throughout this section. Perhaps the clearest evidence is Matthew's treatment of the two feedings of the multitudes. In the feeding of the five thousand (14:13–21; cf. Mark 6:30–44), Matthew omits the question in which the disciples misunderstand Jesus (Mark 6:37). In Matthew the disciples immediately understand, but they doubt their ability to supply bread for the multitudes: "We have only five loaves here and two fish" (14:17). Moreover, in Matthew the disciples actually fetch the food (14:18). Finally only Matthew depicts the disciples' duplication of Jesus' action in distributing the loaves to the crowds (vs. 19b; cf. Mark 6:41). Similarly, in the feeding of the four thousand (15:32–39; cf. Mark

---

[18] Cf. Kingsbury, *Matthew: Structure, Christology, Kingdom,* esp. pp. 96–127.

8:1–10), the disciples again immediately understand their task; they are concerned only about their ability to accomplish it (vs. 33; cf. Mark 8:4). Once more the disciples actually give the bread to the people in imitation of Jesus (vs. 36; cf. Mark 8:6). Matthew also omits distribution of the fish to the crowds (Mark 8:7), thereby bringing his account closer to the actual celebration of the Lord's Supper in the church's life. By implication, the disciples are ministers of the church. Through Matthew's use of the tradition, these events in the life of Jesus are in the process of becoming events in the life of the church.

The conclusion is inescapable. By using the framework of Mark (Mark 6:14–9:32), by abbreviating it and adding other material, especially that not found in other Gospels, Matthew has turned this section into a discussion about the church. On the surface we have here a series of incidents: the death of John the Baptist, the two feedings, the healing of the Canaanite woman, controversy with the Pharisees and the Sadducees, the confession by Peter, the transfiguration, and an extended teaching section. But such a surface view does not do justice to the careful way in which Matthew illuminates the nature of the community brought into being by the life, death, and resurrection of Jesus and charged to act with disciplined forgiveness until his coming again.

PETER AS THE ROCK (16:13–23)

Why does Matthew's account of Peter's confession differ from Mark's?

Only in Matthew does Jesus explicitly accept Peter's confession at Caesarea Philippi (cf. Mark 8:27–33; see pp. 83 ff.). Indeed the source of Peter's insight is said by Jesus to be none other than "my Father who is in heaven" (16:17). Furthermore, Peter has the keys to the kingdom: whatever he binds and looses (that is, his solemn decisions in matters of discipline) will be upheld on the judgment day (vs. 19; cf. 18:18).[19]

[19]Our interpretation of this celebrated passage stresses the founding of the church through Peter rather than the founding of the episcopacy through Peter. Without going into the much debated question of the authenticity of 16:17–19, we contend that Matthew speaks here not so much of the primacy of Peter as of the primacy of the church (cf. esp. 18:17–18). Peter represents the disciples and the disciples in turn represent the church. Further exegesis of the passage supports this contention. For a brief valuable discussion of the question of authenticity, see F. W. Beare, *The Earliest Records of Jesus* (Nashville, Tenn.: Abingdon, 1962), pp. 137–139. See also K. L. Schmidt, "The Church," *Bible Key Words*, ed. and trans. J. R. Coates (New York: Harper & Row, 1951), pp. 35–50, and Oscar Cullmann, *Peter: Disciple-Apostle-Martyr*, trans. F. V. Filson, 2nd ed., (Philadelphia: Westminster, 1962), pp. 161–242. A summary of the discussion from a Roman Catholic point of view may be found in

In spite of this seeming praise of Peter, after Jesus' announcement that he must suffer (vs. 21), Peter and Jesus engage in controversy (vss. 22 f.). Perhaps Matthew is simply following Mark so that Peter's difficulty with Jesus should be overlooked; however, this explanation is not sustained by closer scrutiny of the text. Matthew could have omitted the rebuke by Peter and the retort of Jesus as Luke did (Luke 9:18–22). Moreover, Matthew not only includes the rebuke by Peter, but he increases Peter's opposition to Jesus' suffering by adding Peter's words, "God forbid, Lord! This shall never happen to you" (vs. 22). At one moment in Matthew Peter is literally praised to the heavens and the next moment he is thrust into the company of Satan (vs. 23).

Matthew's tension between praise and blame for Peter is deliberate. He wishes to say that, although the church has accepted Jesus as the Lord and the Son of the living God and has thereby been granted the authority to bind and loose on earth, individual Christians, like the disciple Peter, have to accept Jesus' suffering. Even the disciple Peter is not spared suffering. Christians must imitate Christ. Even though the church has the authority to bind and to loose, disciples cannot avoid Christ's way. Thus Matthew's earlier identification of Christ with the role of the suffering servant (12:18–21) takes on new meaning, for the disciples must also become suffering servants (cf. 5:10–12).

The inescapability of suffering as a disciple is now depicted in Jesus' definition of discipleship as taking up one's cross and following him (16:24–28). To his Markan source (cf. Mark 8:34–9:1) Matthew adds that, when the Son of Man comes in glory, "he will repay every man for what he has done" (vs. 27). Matthew's emphasis on obedience implies that, although the church exists between the resurrection and the second coming, with great power to bind and to loose, every disciple is still accountable to the Judge for what he has done. Peter is pronounced blessed, but his blessedness, along with that of all disciples, will have to endure and be judged.

To sum up this episode, confession of Christ leads to the founding of a church whose authority is binding. The disciples, however, must not be complacent or self-righteous, but must do the will of God to prepare for the future judgment. The nature of the church that has been founded becomes transparent in the following discourse.

A. Robert and A. Feuillet, *Introduction to the New Testament*, trans. P. W. Skehan et al. (New York: Desclee, 1965), pp. 787 ff. See Raymond E. Brown, Karl P. Donfried, John Reumann, et al., *Peter in the New Testament: A Collaborative Assessment by Protestant and Roman Catholic Scholars* (Minneapolis and New York: Augsburg and Paulist Press, 1973), for a discussion of Peter as an object of exegetical investigation and theological reflection.

DISCIPLINE IN COMMUNITY (18:15–22)

Does discipline mean life based on law?

Just as Peter's confession of the Christ was not simply an occasion for praise and rejoicing, so too Matthew's depiction of the disciples' liberation from the Pharisaic law (15:1–20; 16:1–2) does not mean the creation of a community without discipline. Matthew's concluding discourse for the church (17:22–19:2) asserts that the Christian disciple comes under discipline of the churchly community. The incident of the temple tax (17:24–27), which serves as a transition to the discourse, illustrates the point. In this distinctively Matthean scene that follows a prediction of suffering (17:22), Jesus and Simon Peter discuss whether the temple tax should be paid. Although "the sons are free" (17:26), Jesus orders the paying of the tax in order not to give offense (17:24–27). The members of the church possess freedom, yet freedom is restricted by the necessities of a community (cf. I Cor. 10:23 f.).

Our present passage (18:15–22), in agreement with what precedes, indicates that it may be necessary for the church to exclude people in exercising its authority to bind on earth (18:18). But this power of excommunication does not exist for the purpose of condemning people, for the church acts under rules (vss. 15 f.) and always in forgiveness (vss. 21 f.). This concern for the individual Christian is indicated by the talk about "children" (18:3) and "little ones" (18:5, 10, 14). These "little ones" are to be received, not because they are actual children but, rather, because they are the disciples, the members of the congregation.[20] Just as Matthew characterized the disciples by "little faith" (see 8:23–27; 14:31; 16:8; 17:20), so the "little ones" are Christian disciples who journey from the privilege of forgiveness (18:10–14) to deeds of obedience (18:5–9). Indeed, these same little ones are blessed in the beatitudes. They are poor in spirit, mourning, meek (5:3–5); they yearn after righteousness, mercy, purity in heart, peace, knowing that they are blessed (5:6–12).[21] Matthew sets the discipline of the church in the context of God's grace. Even the community that exercises discipline consists of "little ones" who are in constant need of mercy (18:14).

Finally, the passage containing the most rigorous word of discipline in Matthew ("Let him be to you as a Gentile and tax collector"—vs. 17b) closes with the most definite promise of Christ's presence ("For where two or three are gathered in my name, there am I

---

[20] Cf. Eduard Schweizer, "Observance of the Law and Charismatic Activity in Matthew," *New Testament Studies*, 16 (1970), 213–230, esp. 229; also Schweizer's note, *New Testament Studies*, 20 (1974), 216.

[21] See Barth, *Tradition and Interpretation in Matthew*, pp. 121–125.

in the midst of them"—vs. 20). The church exists, then, not only with authority to bind and to loose, but also in the authority of the gracious presence of Christ. Consequently the church's most characteristic activity is that of worship (2:2, 8, 11; 8:2; 9:18; 14:33; 20:20; 28:9, 17). Such worship, adoration of the Lord, allows the church to bind or loose in a distinctively Christian way, the way of forgiveness. Therefore, Matthew concludes his exhortation for discipline in the church community with a word of Jesus about the radical necessity to forgive (18:21 f.) and with a long parable (only in Matthew) about the necessity to punish the wicked servant who does not forgive (18:23–35).[22]

The church community is founded upon the confession of Jesus as the Christ. In its exercise of authority for judgment and discipline the constant limiting factor is Jesus' demand for forgiveness (cf. 6:14 f.). Matthew's congregation of believers is the forgiving church.

Judgment: Doing God's Will (19:3–26:1)

Matthew's discussion of the church as the forgiving community leads into this section: the church facing the last judgment. The judgment theme is found in Jesus' apocalyptic pronouncement (chap. 24), especially the command of watchfulness for the coming end (24:36–51), and the parables of the wise and foolish maidens, the talents, and the great judgment (chap. 25). The church, which exists in the blessedness of forgiveness, also has to live under the threat of judgment. In the light of this judgment, the disciples are called to do God's will.

Although again Matthew is dependent upon Mark's framework (Mark 10–13), his use of Q and his special M tradition and his shaping of all the material have made this section into a manual on how the church meets judgment by doing the will of God. For example, the opening unit of tradition, the debate with the Pharisees about divorce (19:3–12; cf. Mark 10:1–12), places a discussion about doing the will of God in the proper Jewish-Christian context of the law. Several other episodes also concern interpretation of the law: the rich young man (19:16–30), paying taxes to Caesar (22:15–22), the resurrection question (22:23–33), the great commandment question (22:34–40), and the "woes" against the scribes and Pharisees (chap. 23, esp. 23:23 f.).

---

[22]In regard to the connection between binding and loosing in 18:18 and 16:19, G. Bornkamm maintains that 18:18 refers to the disciplinary authority of the congregation and 16:19 to the teaching authority of Peter. See "The Authority to 'bind' and 'loose' in the Church in Matthew's Gospel: The Problem of Sources in Matthew's Gospel," *Jesus and Man's Hope*, I, ed. D. G. Miller and D. Y. Hadidian (Pittsburgh, Pa.: Pittsburgh Theological Seminary, 1970), pp. 37–50.

According to Matthew, to do the will of God one must properly understand the nature of the law. Matthew is concerned about discerning the will of God in the law and, most important, obeying it. In Jesus' divorce discussion with the Pharisees, Matthew has apparently softened the radical prohibition against divorce (cf. Mark 10:10–12) by allowing divorce on the grounds of unchastity (19:9, cf. 5:32). Yet in the very next episode Matthew shows a demand for obedience to the law more stringent than that of his Markan source, for the young man must be perfect (19:21; cf. Mark 10:21).[23] The will of God cannot be equated either with a stricter or more lenient interpretation of the Jewish law. The one thing necessary for the doing of God's will is the very presence of God, "With men this is impossible, but *with God* all things are possible" (19:26).

Matthew's concept of reward for doing God's will is different from the idea of reward as so much merit accumulated through following the formula of the law. Instead, Matthew proclaims that there are no degrees of reward; the only and final reward (25:41–46) is God's presence, already anticipated in the doing of God's will. For example, Jesus answers the disciples' question about reward (19:27–30) with the parable of the laborers in the vineyard (20:1–16; only in Matthew), which teaches that no one grumbles in the joy of God's generosity (see vs. 15). Moreover, those who reject Jesus' authority, notably the Pharisees (see esp. chaps. 21 and 22), do not bear fruit (21:19) or, if they do, they keep it for themselves (21:33–44); therefore, they cannot escape judgment. The narrative portion of this entire section (19:3–23:39) ends then appropriately with the chastisement of the Pharisees. Their discernment of the law and their obedience were for their own justification instead of the doing of God's will. Thus at the judgment they will be condemned.

A final indication of the preoccupation with judgment in this section of the Gospel is the narrative setting in the territory of Judea and the city of Jerusalem (see 19:1; 21:1, 10; 24:1). At Jerusalem the condemnation of Jesus takes place, but that judgment ultimately turns against Jesus' enemies and for his disciples if they continue to do God's will. Jesus' second coming as the Son of Man will determine whether disciples are sheep or goats, accepted or rejected (25:31 ff.). The test for discipleship is the same one Jesus had to pass: the doing of God's will, not one's own (26:39). The passages selected for further examination confirm this understanding of Matthew's view of judgment.

[23] The suggestion that Matthew commends two levels of morality, one for real Christians and another for halfway Christians, is not defensible. In the Sermon on the Mount the injunction to "be perfect" (5:48) is for all disciples—that is, all Christians. See Barth, *Tradition and Interpretation in Matthew*, p. 99, and cf. W. D. Davies, *The Setting of the Sermon on the Mount* (New York: Cambridge University Press, 1964), pp. 95, 209–215.

BELIEVING DOERS OF THE LAW (21:28–46)

Is promising to do the law enough?

The parable of the two sons (21:28–32) has to do with the authority of Jesus and, in the last analysis, the authority of the church. The preceding incident (21:23–27) closed with Jesus' saying that he would not tell the chief priests and elders by what authority he was acting. Note how this parable is related to the previous episode by the reintroduction of John the Baptist (vs. 32; cf. vs. 25).

In the parable itself the son who first said he would not go, but then went, actually did the will of the father. This means that mere words claiming obedience (cf. vs. 30) are without value. Jesus' authority can only be understood in terms of whether association with him produces actual obedience. Further, Jesus' opponents, the chief priests and elders, who turn out to be Pharisees (21:45), are condemned because even though they saw John's righteousness they did not believe him (vs. 32). This "higher righteousness" requires both an actual obedience and belief. The nature of such belief becomes clearer in the following parable.

In the parable of the wicked tenants (21:33–46; cf. Mark 12:1–12), the owner sends his servants and his son "to get his fruit" (vs. 34), all to no avail, because the tenants kill the emissaries from the owner. The climax of the parable is reached when the owner returns, puts the tenants to death, and delivers the vineyard to other tenants "who will give him the fruits in their seasons" (vs. 41; cf. Mark 12:9). Matthew's conclusion to the parable, which is not in his Markan source, states that the kingdom "will be taken away from you and given to a nation producing the fruits of it" (vs. 43; cf. Mark 12:11). The trouble with the wicked tenants was not their failure to produce fruit (cf. 21:19), but their refusal to acknowledge the rightful owner of the fruit. The Pharisees do not believe; they try to justify themselves by their obedience rather than acknowledging the gracious God. According to Matthew, the Pharisees recognize that this parable is directed against them (see 21:45 f.). We note that Matthew underscores the necessity for obedience, but additionally asserts the need for belief in the giver of all obedience—God through Christ (cf. 21:42). Only thereby will the church be delivered from self-righteous, possessive obedience.

DOING MERCY WITHOUT CALCULATION (25:31–46)

What happens unexpectedly in the parable?

Matthew's understanding of judgment and the end time is contained in the final discourse (chap. 25), which comments upon the apocalyptic disclosures that precede (chap. 24; cf. Mark 13). The par-

The Last Judgment with Christ separating the sheep from the goats. Part of an early fourth-century Christian sarcophagus. (Courtesy of Metropolitan Museum of Art. Rogers Fund, 1924.)

able of the ten maidens (25:1–13; only in Matthew) and the parable of the talents (25:14–30; cf. Luke 19:12–27) give a framework for viewing judgment. The prospect of judgment may be wrongly met in one of two ways—either in relaxed carelessness about the future as seen in the five foolish maidens or in paralysis caused by anxiety over the severity of the judge as seen in the wicked and slothful servant.

The judgment itself is depicted in the final parable (25:31–46; only in Matthew), which tells about the shepherd who will separate the sheep from the goats. The standard of separation is simply whether the one judged has performed acts of mercy for a fellow human being (25:35 f.). The element of surprise of this parable is that neither the righteous nor the unrighteous realized that their deeds of mercy were acts performed (or not performed) for the Lord (vss. 37 ff.). The climactic word of Jesus, "Truly, I say to you, as you did it to one of the least of these my brethren, you did it to me" (vs. 40), alludes to the fact that mercy for the neighbor, and service to others, is service to Christ (cf. 7:21–23). Therefore, the true disciple shows mercy to others without calculation, without thinking that his deed will somehow cause God's judgment upon him to be more favorable. Such noncalculation grows out of a relation with Christ in which anxiety is diminished and the disciple responds to whatever human need is at hand, especially to the neighbor (10:40–42).

Those who show mercy act without calculation, without thought that thereby they will ensure their future blessedness. They are merciful because they have been shown mercy; moreover, their deeds for the neighbor are deeds for Christ, who is present in the least of the brethren. Thus Matthew pictures the church in the time between the first and second comings. The church's role of obedience in that time has been most clearly anticipated in the final death and resurrection of Jesus, Lord of the congregation, who serves as the paradigm for the Christian life.

Conclusion: Obedience and Resurrection (26:2–28:20)

At the outset of this concluding section Matthew gives clear indication that Jesus' passion occurs at the bidding of God. The passive voice ("will be delivered up to be crucified," 26:2; see also 26:18) represents the divine action. The action of both Jesus and the other characters is determined by a power not their own. For example, the woman who anoints Jesus' head with the expensive ointment (26:6–13) prepares his body for burial even though her action would ordinarily be understood as the expression of a mere sentiment or as an anointing of kingship (see 27:11, 29, 37, 42). Ironically, however, her anointing for death is also an anointing of the future Lord of the congregation. Moreover, Matthew hints at the victory of the resurrection by reminding the reader that Jesus is the Son of God (27:40, 43; only Matthew). The power of resurrection over death is also evident in the supernatural events surrounding Jesus' death: the earth shook, rocks were split, saints were raised from the dead and appeared to many in the holy city (27:51–54; cf. Mark 15:38 f.).

Matthew subtly transforms the Markan passion story so that the element of Jesus' suffering, which cannot be removed completely, is modified by Jesus' obedience and becomes a paradigm for disciples. Insofar as Jesus acts or speaks in the passion, he voluntarily accepts his death; he obeys God's will. He could have called legions of angels, but "how then should the scriptures be fulfilled?' (26:54, 56; cf. Mark 14:48–50). Matthew adds to Mark's account of Jesus' accepting the cross ("nevertheless, not as I will, but as thou wilt"—26:39, cf. Mark 14:36) a reinforcing word of obedience, "My Father, if this cannot pass unless I drink it, thy will be done" (26:42). Thereby, Matthew shows that in his passion Jesus fulfills the "higher righteousness" he set forth in the Sermon on the Mount (6:20; cf. 7:24); Jesus acts as the one who fulfills "all righteousness" (3:15).[24] The Jesus of Matthew not only demands obedience, he enacts obedience. His resurrection and establishment as Lord of the congregation are based upon faithful obedience to God.

[24] Barth, *Tradition and Interpretation in Matthew*, pp. 143 ff., also points out how Jesus' silence (esp. 26:63) is interpreted by Matthew as fulfillment of Jesus' word against swearing in the Sermon on the Mount (5:33–37). In Matthew, therefore, the "swearing" denial of Peter (26:69–75) becomes all the more telling as a sign of disobedience.

THE GREAT COMMISSION (28:16–20)

What are Jesus' final words to the disciples?

In the final words of Matthew (28:16–20) the resurrected Jesus charges the disciples—that is, the Christian congregation—with the task of teaching all nations to observe what he has commanded (28:20). Such observance is now possible because Jesus has obeyed: at death the bruised reed did not break; he brought judgment to victory (12:20).

Matthew follows Mark in depicting the burial of Jesus and the subsequent discovery of the empty tomb by the women. To this he adds the appearance of Jesus to the women (28:9 f.) and an account of the efforts of the Jewish leaders to make it appear that the body was stolen (28:11–15; cf. 27:62–66). The second and final appearance of the risen Jesus is obviously of greatest importance for Matthew. It occurs in Galilee (26:32; 28:7) at a mountain (5:1; 15:29; 17:1). The disciples' reaction to this climactic moment is described briefly: "They worshiped him (see 2:2; 18:26; 28:9); but some doubted" (vs. 17). This report of doubt strikes the reader as inappropriate, especially since the disciples have just worshiped Jesus. In other resurrection appearances doubt also occurs, but in those instances some further action of Jesus overcomes the doubt (Luke 24:41; Mark 16:14; John 20:25). Here the expression of doubt is simply followed by the word of Jesus. As the disciples make no further response, we can only conclude that Jesus' word overcomes the doubt. We shall discover in looking more closely at this passage that doubt is finally to be vanquished in the disciples' obedience to Jesus' subsequent command.

Before exhorting the disciples to action, the resurrected Jesus declares, "All authority in heaven and on earth has been given to me" (vs. 18). Jesus' authoritative announcement has an implicit reference to the cosmic enthronement of the apocalyptic Son of Man depicted in Daniel: "And to him was given dominion and glory and kingdom, that all peoples, nations and languages should serve him; his dominion is an everlasting dominion, which shall not pass away, and his kingdom one that shall not be destroyed" (7:14). The combination of authority, dominion, and extension to all nations makes this passage relevant to Jesus' word.[25] Jesus' authority in heaven and on earth exists until "the close of the age," that is, while the church exists. Previously, Matthew dealt with the subject of authority as an aspect of Jesus' earthly activity: he taught with authority (7:28 f.), he healed with authority (8:9), he forgave with authority (9:6, 8). Now the resurrected Jesus is put in touch with this world; his authority is expressed precisely through the disciples' earthly task of

---

[25] G. Barth, *Tradition and Interpretation in Matthew*, p. 133.

"The Resurrection" (*ca.* 1509–15) painted by M. Grünewald as one wing of the Isenheim Altarpiece. (Courtesy of Marburg Art Reference Bureau.)

making obedient disciples. The new thing about this authority is that with Jesus' resurrection it is extended to include all the nations.[26]

Matthew, furthermore, does not allow the resurrected Jesus to become a heavenly Lord issuing new revelations that will inevitably split the church between the specially blessed recipients of a new, more authoritative heavenly message (cf. II Cor. 12:1 ff.) and the unblessed rank and file. Such a possibility is excluded by the resurrected Jesus' word to the disciples: "teaching them to observe all things that I *have commanded* you" (vs. 20a; cf. 24:34 f.). The resurrected Lord's words are rooted not in heavenly visions or revelations, but in words already spoken by the earthly Jesus. Yet Matthew does not allow the authority of the resurrected Jesus to rest simply with Jesus' activity on earth. The disciples, in the presence of the Resurrected One, will extend his authority to all nations. Consequently, the church's mission extends beyond those who claim election simply because of membership in the chosen people Israel (3:9; 21:33–43; cf. II Cor. 11:15–29).

Matthew's distillation of the resurrected Jesus' authority to the simple command to make disciples, baptize, and teach obedience (28:19, 20a) may contain another subtle warning in addition to those against the notions of a chosen people or a continuing revelation. In the spurious ending of Mark's resurrection account (16:9–20), Jesus gave a commission to his disciples that included preaching, baptizing, and performing charismatic acts of healing, exorcism, and speaking in tongues.[27] On the surface, these phenomena seem much more impressive as evidence for the authority of Jesus and his disciples than Matthew's simple obedience. However, Matthew has already prepared the reader for this more austere concept of authority, for he had denied that such manifestations were proof of faith and obedience (7:21–23). True discipleship will be demonstrated not in ecstatic, marvelous activity, but, rather, in obedience. More than ever the disciples are called to obey the words Jesus commanded. What at first appeared to be simply a call to missionary endeavor, on closer inspection turns out to be a call for discipleship that embraces obedience.

Looking now more directly at the imperative from the resurrected Jesus (vss. 19, 20a), we find that the task is divided into three stages: making disciples, baptizing them, and teaching them to ob-

[26]G. Bornkamm, "Der Auferstandene und der Irdische," *Zeit und Geschichte,* ed. E. Dinkler (Tübingen: J. C. B. Mohr, 1964), pp. 174 f. If worldwide mission begins only after Jesus' death and resurrection, this may account for Matthew's omission of the report about the sending out of the twelve, even though Jesus does give them instructions for their missionary journey (10:1–11:1).

[27]Although Mark 16:9–20 is a spurious ending (see p. 92), it may well represent tendencies at work in early tradition of the church.

serve all that Jesus has commanded. Matthew definitely emphasizes the first and the third, for he sees the church as the community of discipleship (13:52; 16:13–20; 27:57), which consists of lowliness, readiness for suffering, and above all obedience (10:40–42; 16:24–27; 18:1–6; 22:11–14). The esteem in which Matthew holds discipleship is illustrated by the fact that he recognizes only one level of church membership. In first-century Judaism the ambitious disciple hoped one day to become the teacher or rabbi. But in Matthew, Jesus says to his disciples, "But you are not to be called rabbi, for you have one teacher, and you are all brethren" (23:8; only in Matthew). Although Matthew never has the disciples address Jesus with the title teacher or rabbi (instead their more customary form of address is "Lord"), there can be little doubt that the final words to the disciples establish once and for all that the Lord of the congregation is, in the last analysis, the only Rabbi or Teacher.[28]

The Gospel according to Matthew has thus come full circle. The initial emphasis on the radical obedience of Joseph (1:24) has now been expanded through the body of the Gospel to spell out the way of righteousness (3:15; 5:6, 20; 6:33) that is fulfilled in obedience (7:21; 21:28–32; 25:31–46). The disciples are to observe all that Jesus has commanded. Yet this radical demand becomes possible because in Jesus, his mission and message, God has come near (1:23; 18:20).[29] Above all, the way of righteousness was fulfilled by the action of Jesus, particularly his obedient submission to death (20:26–28). Therefore, the final word of the resurrected Jesus assures the disciples that the Lord of the congregation both is and will be with them until the close of the age. The continuing presence of Jesus with the congregation means that these final words are not a farewell from Jesus. As long as the congregation continues, the resurrected Jesus lives and abides in the obedience of his disciples to his teaching.

In summary, our investigations show that the Gospel of Matthew is an interpretation of the tradition of Jesus based upon Mark's Gospel, the Q collection of sayings, and the oral tradition. Matthew's interpretive procedure does not, however, mean that he did not stand in the service of the tradition of Jesus which he received.

[28] Bornkamm, *Zeit und Geschichte*, pp. 182 f.
[29] This view of Matthew's Christology would seem to find support in the work of M. J. Suggs, *Wisdom, Christology, and Law in Matthew's Gospel* (Cambridge, Mass.: Harvard University Press, 1970), p. 130: "In relation to the law, Jesus transcended familiar categories: as he was the incarnation of wisdom, so was he the embodiment of Torah. Therefore, Matthew's Jesus is fully entitled to issue the invitation: 'Come to me, all who labor and are heavy-laden, and I will give you rest. Take my yoke upon you, and learn from me; for I am gentle and lowly in heart, and you will find rest for your souls. For my yoke is easy and my burden is light.'"

He remains faithful to it. Both Matthew and Luke combine the predominantly narrative Gospel of Mark with the predominantly discourse collection of Jesus' sayings known as Q. Thereby these Gospels serve as a check against any inclination within the early Hellenistic Christian community toward making the Christian faith into a kind of mystery religion dominated by the pattern of a dying and rising god. In effect, Matthew and Luke are saying that Christian faith involves a particular teaching.

This protection of the Christian faith is especially clear in Matthew. This Gospel's stress on the words that Jesus spoke binds the Christian revelation to the historical Jesus, one whose past words and actions demand and promise obedience. The Christian congregation, therefore, knows its unity and origin in the historical Jesus. Even though Matthew may contain words of Jesus that were never spoken by him during his ministry (ironically 28:18–20 probably belong in this category),[30] its principal function in bringing together the narrative and the discourse traditions is to limit in principle the revelation of Christian faith to Jesus of Nazareth. Matthew and the other canonical Gospels thereby preserved the peculiar glory and offense of Christian faith, the "scandal of particularity." A particular person at a particular time and place is claimed as the revelation of the creating and judging God of the universe.

We can now review generally our use of four approaches in understanding Matthew's Gospel:

The *structure* of Matthew is clear-cut. The Introduction (1:1–2:23; see the outline at the beginning of the chapter) sets the tone for the main body of Matthew. The coming of Jesus establishes a new and more radical obedience (Joseph); moreover, this obedience takes place within the "new Israel," where Jew and Gentile (wise men) worship together. Matthew then sets forth the Gospel in five major sections consisting of narrative-discourse, reminiscent of the five authoritative books of Moses. Book One (3:1–7:29) depicts the "higher righteousness" both effected (the baptism) and demanded (Sermon on the Mount) by Jesus. Book Two (8:1–11:1) previews the life of discipleship by showing that the miraculous deeds of Jesus call for deeds of love and service in the mission of the disciples. Book Three (11:2–13:52) puts earthly activity into the perspective of the kingdom of heaven. Present mercy stands within the context of future judgment; the followers of Christ are to train for this future event. Book Four (13:53–19:2) sets this present mercy into the context of the forgiving church, where the basis for discipline and exclu-

---

[30] See F. W. Beare, "Sayings of the Risen Jesus in the Synoptic Tradition: An Inquiry into Their Origin and Significance," *Christian History and Interpretation: Studies Presented to John Knox*, ed. W. R. Farmer, C. F. D. Moule, and R. R. Niebuhr (New York: Cambridge University Press, 1967), pp. 161–166.

sion becomes the unwillingness to practice forgiveness. Book Five (19:3–26:1) appropriately concludes with the expectation of future judgment on the basis of deeds, not promises. Furthermore, the doers of mercy are those who live in faith without thought of reward. The Conclusion (26:2–28:20) reports Jesus' obedient submission to death and God's response, which is the resurrection. Finally, the Risen Lord commissions the disciples, both Jew and Gentile, to obey and to teach obedience, knowing that he abides with them till the close of the age.

Matthew's carefully worked out structure already indicates this Gospel's *major emphases.* We may now bring them together under three headings: the new obedience, its source, and its community. Matthew advocates a higher righteousness, which is a new obedience. This higher righteousness enables and requires radical obedience, and the spelling out of this obedience becomes clearer in Matthew's treatment of the law. Nowhere does he claim that the law has been abolished; on the contrary, the law is affirmed. Yet Matthew emphasizes the love of God and the love of all peoples, which must not be neglected through preoccupation with carrying out details of the law. Thereby Matthew seeks to make the will of God present and alive.

The second major emphasis is upon the source of higher righteousness, the Lord Jesus Christ. In one sense the Jesus of Matthew is a more majestic figure than is the Jesus of Mark. Matthew tends to abbreviate Mark's miracle stories and consequently to make them even more inexplicable as human events. Yet this abbreviation is the primary means for expressing the dominance of Jesus' teaching. Even in the miraculous acts, Jesus is a teacher, an extraordinary first-century rabbi. This teaching makes Jesus an authoritative, majestic figure. The Jesus of Matthew, however, is also a lowly and obedient figure. He fulfills the scripture by becoming the suffering servant who not only teaches obedience to disciples, but actually performs it. The mighty Lord goes to his death in obedient lowliness, thereby fulfilling the way of higher righteousness.

The third and final emphasis follows from the preceding ones: the higher righteousness fulfilled in Christ must be realized in the congregation. This community of Christ-followers learns that the present is determined by the mercy of God's presence, even for the sinner. The beatitudes proclaim God's love for the poor in spirit, the meek. The congregation knows itself as the "little ones," who obediently await the final judgment in the presence of Christ.

Our total interpretation has depended upon observation of Matthew's *redaction* of the tradition. Among other things, redaction criticism shows that Matthew's treatment of the disciples is significantly less harsh than is that of his predecessor Mark. Yet our study suggests that Matthew has a more realistic view of the disciples' actual behavior than has Mark. Matthew recognizes that the disciples do "understand" Jesus; after all, they followed him. Nevertheless, they were still of "little faith" because they had not yet acted in obedience. According to Matthew, they could not obey until Jesus completed his own obedience through death and resurrection.

The general *situation* that produced the Gospel of Matthew is in many ways implicit in the document itself. Matthew's Gospel arises out of Judaism and Jewish Christianity, but it has passed beyond both. This insight explains the tension between obvious Judaistic tradition (e.g., 5:18 f.; 10:6) and the universal scope of the Gospel (e.g., 28:16 ff.). In the first place, Matthew does not reflect a church that observes the Jewish law and still stands within Judaism. Although the law is kept, such observance is motivated by consideration for Jewish Christians who still have scruples for the minutiae of the law (cf. 17:26 f.). Here Matthew and Paul stand together, for Paul memorably formulates a similar position. " 'All things are lawful for me,' but not all things are helpful" (I Cor. 6:12; 10:23). Freedom is not license. Moreover, the congregation of Matthew already understands itself as opposed to Judaism (not to Israel and the Old Testament), for Judaism in Matthew's understanding has already become Pharisaism (see 3:7; 5:20; 9:34; chap. 23).

Second, the eschatology of Matthew cannot be classified as "apocalyptic." Matthew's church did not cherish the belief that the end of the world was just around the corner and that people should gird themselves by extreme piety and ethical effort for the imminent encounter with God. True, Matthew emphasized the coming of the final day (chap. 24; cf. also 4:17; 26:28), yet he also spoke about a time of waiting for the church. For Matthew the church's time was truly significant (see 24:6, 36 ff., 42 ff.). Indeed, the close of Matthew (28:16–20) would make no sense if the evangelist expected the end to come immediately.

Matthew strikes out in more than one direction. On the one hand, as we have seen, he attacked Pharisaic Judaism's misleading interpretation of the law. On the other, Matthew attacked a Christianity that was developing without regard for its roots in Israel and the Old Testament into an unrestrained and undisciplined spiritualism. Matthew understood Christian faith to be firmly rooted in the historical Jesus. While rejecting Pharisaism, he used the teaching of Jesus to oppose any lack of moral responsibility. Matthew called his congregation to the obedience that Jesus had both commanded in his teaching and fulfilled in his passion.

It is evident from Matthew that his church is a community with Jewish roots. Standing within this community Matthew maintains the Jewish themes of righteousness and obedience to the law; but he sets them within the context of faith in Jesus Christ, in whom they are fulfilled. Because of God's action through Christ and his continuing presence with the congregation, the end of Christian faith is not at all unlike the way. Thus, the kingdom of heaven is both present and future. Therefore, Matthew's Gospel mirrors not only the "life of Christ," but also the life of the Christian community as he envisioned it should be.

Suggestions for Further Reading

Reliable commentaries include J. C. Fenton, *The Gospel of St. Matthew* (Baltimore: Penguin, 1963); D. Hill, *The Gospel of Matthew* (London: Oliphants, 1972); and E. Schweizer, *The Good News According to Matthew*, trans. D. E. Green (Richmond, Va.: John Knox, 1975).

Some other worthwhile and recent books are G. D. Kilpatrick, *The Origins of the Gospel According to St. Matthew* (Oxford: Clarendon, 1946); K. Stendahl, *The School of St. Matthew and Its Use of the Old Testament*, reissue (Philadelphia: Fortress, 1968); G. Bornkamm, G. Barth, and H. J. Held, *Tradition and Interpretation in Matthew*, trans. P. Scott (Philadelphia: Westminster, 1963); W. D. Davies, *The Sermon on the Mount* (New York: Cambridge University Press, 1966), an abridgment of the author's longer and more technical work, *The Setting of the Sermon on the Mount*, published by the same press in 1964; M. J. Suggs, *Wisdom, Christology, and Law in Matthew's Gospel* (Cambridge, Mass.: Harvard University Press, 1970); and J. D. Kingsbury, *Matthew: Structure, Christology, Kingdom* (Philadelphia: Fortress, 1975). Kingsbury's *Matthew*, Proclamation Commentaries (Philadelphia: Fortress, 1977), is a valuable brief, up-to-date survey of the interpretation of Matthew. J. P. Meier, *The Vision of Matthew: Christ, Church, and Morality in the First Gospel* (New York: Paulist Press, 1979) enters into discussion with Kingsbury from a critical Catholic perspective.

CHAPTER FOUR

The Gospel According to Luke: Witness to Jesus

NOTES ON THE GOSPEL OF LUKE

An early tradition about the Gospel of Luke, from the Muratorian Canon,[1] states that both the Gospel According to Luke and the Acts of the Apostles were written by the same author. This view is supported by the opening verses of each book, which in both cases contain dedications to a certain Theophilus, and by Acts' reference to a "first book" (1:1). The two books definitely display a kinship in style and emphasis. Yet neither Luke nor Acts makes a direct claim about the author's identity. Luke-Acts is an anonymous two-volume work.

To be accepted by the church at the end of the second century, a Gospel needed a claim to apostolic authority. According to tradition, Mark rests upon the authority of one great apostle, Peter; similarly, Luke rests upon the authority of another, Paul. In his letters, Paul mentions as a companion, "Luke, the beloved physician" (Col. 4:14; Philemon 24; II Tim. 4:11). Furthermore, Luke may have accompanied Paul on some of Paul's missionary journeys as the occasional use of "we" in Acts (e.g., 16:10 ff.) suggests.

Some doubt attaches to the relationship to Paul, but a few things may be said with some certainty about the author of the Gospel According to Luke. He was more consciously an author than were the writers of either Mark or Matthew. The preface (1:1–4) makes explicit the literary aim of the Gospel: it is dedicated to Theophilus and speaks knowingly of previous works. Probably the author of Luke was a Gentile Christian. He spoke Greek as his native tongue and, in general, minimized the controversy with the Pharisees that so dominates Matthew and, in part, Mark.

---

[1]A catalogue of New Testament writings originating in Rome about A.D. 200. For the text see Edgar Hennecke, *New Testament Apocrypha*, I, ed. W. Schneemelcher and trans. R. McL. Wilson (Philadelphia: Westminster, 1963), pp. 43–44.

134   *The Gospels and Jesus*

Luke is not, however, an example of modern historical writing. It is a Gospel, religious writing. Although Luke used the Gospel of Mark, as did Matthew, he used his source more critically. Whereas Matthew took over practically all of Mark, Luke used about half. Like Matthew, Luke used the sayings source Q. In addition, there is a considerable body of tradition, found only in Luke.

As in the case of the other Synoptic Gospels, the dating of Luke is difficult and precarious. Like Matthew, Luke seems to know about the actual destruction of Jerusalem (cf. Luke 21:20 and 19:43 f.). The earliest date for Luke would therefore be sometime after Jerusalem's fall in A.D. 70. Because the introduction of Acts alludes to the Gospel (1:1), Luke was presumably written before the final version of Acts. The letters of Paul were written in the middle of the first century but were not assembled before the end of that century. It is unlikely that the author of Luke-Acts knew the Pauline letters. At least he does not mention them. Therefore, a date sometime before the end of the first century is suggested. According to the preface (1:1–4), Luke apparently belongs to the third stage of the Christian tradition; he speaks of eyewitnesses, collectors, and his own composition. If so, then a date only shortly before the turn of the century would be appropriate. Luke-Acts was likely written sometime between A.D. 80 and 100. Little can be said about the geographical origin of Luke other than it probably did not originate in Palestine. Although the occasion of the writing of Luke is unknown, the evangelist's general purpose may be inferred from the fact that his is the only Gospel with a sequel, an Acts of the Apostles. The rest of this chapter and Chapter 7 will examine this purpose more closely. We may, however, anticipate our study by suggesting that Luke presents a view of the history of salvation extending from the time of Israel through the life of Jesus and continuing in the history of the church.[2] The good news for Israel is extended through Jesus to all people.

OUTLINE OF LUKE

Preface: A Time for True Remembering (1:1–4)
Introduction: A Universal Story (1:5–2:52)
Twofold Witness to Jesus (2:22–40)
Initial Victory in the Temple (2:41–52)
Gathering Witnesses in Galilee (3:1–9:50)
The Offense of Jesus' Preaching (4:16–30)
Sure Witness to the Word (8:1–21)

Witness to the Word on the Journey to Jerusalem (9:51–19:27)
Jesus' Word About the Present (15:1–32)
Jesus' Word About the Future (19:11–27)
The True Israel Through the Passion and Resurrection (19:28–24:53)
The True Inheritors (20:9–19)
Fulfilling the Scripture (24:13–35)

[2] See Hans Conzelmann, *The Theology of St. Luke,* trans. G. Buswell (New York: Harper & Row, 1960).

Preface: A Time for True Remembering (1:1–4)

Did Luke intend to write history or biography?

In the first four verses Luke makes the reader conscious of the predecessors of his own account, using a literary device not found in the other Gospels, yet common in the writings of antiquity. That the style of the preface was a literary convention can be seen from a comparison of the opening sentences of Luke and Acts with the prefaces of the first-century Jewish historian Josephus. His *Against Apion*, Book I, opens:

> In my history of our Antiquities, most excellent Epaphroditus, I have, I think, made sufficiently clear to any who may peruse that work the extreme antiquity of our Jewish race, the purity of the original stock and the manner in which it established itself in the country which we occupy today. . . . Since, however, I observe that a considerable number of persons . . . discredit the statements in my history concerning our antiquity, . . . I consider it my duty to devote a brief treatise to all these points, in order at once to convict our detractors of malignity and deliberate falsehood, to correct the ignorance of others, and to instruct all who desire to know the truth concerning the antiquity of our race.

Book II begins in this way:

> In the first volume of this work, my most esteemed Epaphroditus, I demonstrated the antiquity of our race, corroborating my statements by the writings of the Phoenicians, Chaldeans, and Egyptians. . . . I also challenged the statements of Manetho, Chaeremon, and some others. I shall now proceed to refute the rest of the authors who have attacked us.[3]

The very fact that Luke followed the prevailing literary fashion of his day indicates part of his purpose—to make his Gospel acceptable to the literate individual. Yet the preface suggests an intent more definite and a more wide-ranging purpose.

With the statement that many others have undertaken to compile a narrative about the things that he will relate, Luke obviously gives up any claim to originality. Nor does he claim a divine revelation superseding all other previous accounts. Still, the opening verses unmistakably give the impression that he means to set things right in this Gospel. Although there have been other compilers and eyewitnesses and ministers of the word, Luke purposes to write a

---

[3] Cited according to H. St. J. Thackeray's translation, *Josephus*, Vol. I (Cambridge, Mass.: Harvard University Press, *The Loeb Classical Library*, 1926), pp. 163–165, 293.

better, truer Gospel than anything yet presented. This prefatory statement alone excludes the notion that each writer worked independently of all preceding tradition. In all probability among Luke's many sources are Mark, the Q source, and special Lukan tradition.

Luke's historical situation emerges in the statement of his relation to his predecessors (vs. 2). In all, there are three stages of the gospel tradition. The first stage of eyewitnesses consists of those who have been with Jesus most intimately; for example, the twelve apostles (6:12 f.; cf. Mark 3:13 f.). Later we learn that apostles are those eyewitnesses who were with Jesus from the baptism to the ascension (cf. Acts. 1:21–26). The second group, ministers of the word, pass on the eyewitness tradition by preaching. Although in Acts ministers of the word are first of all the apostles themselves, there are other ministers, such as Stephen and Philip, who preach the word. The final stage, in which Luke himself stands, is that of the compilers of the tradition. With the advantage of hindsight the compiler is able to see what is most important and worthy of being preserved. Although Luke stands within that third phase, he intends to surpass all the rest. By "following all things closely" (vs. 3), he expects to give both an orderly and truthful account of the life, death, and resurrection of Jesus (vs. 4). Not only does Luke consider his compilation of the tradition more adequate than that of his predecessors, but also he considers this third stage the most advantageous perspective. In some ways it offers a more comprehensive and truthful perspective than that even of eyewitnesses, although the latter are certainly indispensable.

Luke stresses that he is going to write an "orderly account" (vs. 3). This cannot mean that he is going to arrange his account differently, for Luke generally follows Mark's order. Probably Luke refers to his general scheme for placing Jesus within the history of salvation so that Jesus fulfills the story of Israel and initiates the story of the church. He emerges as an author who is quite aware of what he is doing. Perhaps the "Theophilus" to whom he addresses his work (vs. 3) is an actual person: an esteemed Roman official or an eminent citizen; or perhaps the name "friend of God," which is what the name means, stands for the religious reader who as a "God-fearer" is interested in Christianity. Whoever Theophilus may have been, he was certainly someone who had a preliminary knowledge of the Christian faith and was willing to read both the story of Jesus and that of the early church. He represents all who wished to know the truth about these things (literally, "words"—vs. 4).

Luke's preface suggests his purpose. He seeks to write a Gospel of Jesus that will serve as the foundation for the church. Luke understands himself as living at a time in which true remembering needs to take place; he wishes to recover and reformulate the roots of Christian faith so that the certainty and continuity of Christian faith from the beginning up to the present can be established: from Israel through Jesus to the church. Implied within this positive purpose is Luke's intention that the reader be guarded from error or heresy—which is another way of saying the reader must hear the whole Christian tradition, not just part of it.

Introduction: A Universal Story (1:5–2:52)

The first two chapters of the Gospel according to Luke are concerned primarily with the birth stories of John the Baptist and Jesus of Nazareth. This tradition is not contained in the other Synoptic Gospels, although another infancy narrative is, of course, found in Matthew. Although most persons and incidents in these chapters are not mentioned later in the Gospel, the motifs found here are consistent with the rest of the Gospel and help to illuminate its intention. A sustained look at two passages from this section will support this contention.[4] At this point we can do no more than hint at some motifs that emerge in the introduction.

This Gospel opens with a priest named Zechariah, who will be father of the Baptist, in the temple at Jerusalem (1:5 ff.), a city important to Luke. Like none of the other Gospels, Luke's begins in Jerusalem. In the central journey section Jerusalem is the destination (9:51). There in his last days Jesus takes over the temple (19:47; 21:37 f.; 24:53). Jesus' resurrection appearances occur in Jerusalem and its vicinity rather than in Galilee as in the other Synoptics (24:6; cf. 24:13, 18, 33). Finally, the disciples wait in Jerusalem until the Holy Spirit manifests itself so that they may witness to the rest of the world (see Acts 1:4, 8).

A prominent emphasis of Luke's opening chapter is the twofold nature of witness.[5] The birth of Jesus is coupled with the birth of John. A revelation occurs to Mary, the mother of Jesus; a revelation is also given to Zechariah, husband of Elizabeth, mother of John the Baptist. John is the forerunner, Jesus is the fulfillment (1:45). The babe in Elizabeth's womb leaps at the meeting with Mary, mother of Jesus (1:39–45). John is "prophet of the Most High" (1:76); Jesus is the "Son of the Most High" (1:32). The two are not, however, set against one another but are in continuity. John the Baptist belongs to the time of Jesus as a witness and a prophet (cf. 1:80 with 2:40, 52; also see 3:4 ff.).

---

[4] See P. S. Minear, "Luke's Use of the Birth Stories," *Studies in Luke-Acts,* ed. L. E. Keck, and J. L. Martyn (Nashville, Tenn.: Abingdon, 1966), p. 127; and W. B. Tatum, "The Epoch of Israel: Luke i–ii and the Theological Plan of Luke-Acts," *New Testament Studies,* 13 (1966–1967), 184–195.

[5] The element of twofoldness in Luke is emphasized by H. Flender, *St. Luke: Theologian of Redemptive History,* trans. R. H. and I. Fuller (Philadelphia: Fortress, 1967).

"The Holy Family" by El Greco (1541–1614). (Courtesy of National Gallery of Art, Washington, D.C. Samuel H. Kress Collection.)

View of present-day Jerusalem. (Courtesy of Israel Government Tourist Office.)

As we shall see, both Simeon (2:22 ff.) and the prophetess Anna (2:36 ff.) also testify to Jesus.

Luke carefully sets the story within the context of world history: "In the days of Herod" (1:5), "In the sixth month" (1:26), "In those days a decree went out from Caesar Augustus" (2:1; cf. 3:1). Yet Luke emphasizes the role of women and the humble: Elizabeth and Mary are in the foreground; the shepherds come and worship Jesus (2:8 ff.; cf. 1:53; 6:20; 7:22). A romantic idyllic quality pervades this section where salvation emerges among humble folk, women exult in childbirth, and shepherds come to worship a babe born in a manger.

TWOFOLD WITNESS TO JESUS (2:22–40)

Why do Simeon and Anna receive Jesus in the temple?

The Simeon episode (2:22–35) portrays Jesus' parents as law-abiding adherents of the Jewish faith (cf. 2:39). After Jesus' circumcision on the eighth day (2:21), attention turns to the purification of the mother, which according to Jewish law took place on the thirty-third day after circumcision or the fortieth day after birth (see Levit-

icus 12:2–8). Strangely, this story depicts the parents as bringing the
child Jesus "to do for him according to the custom of the law" (vs.
27). But purification is for the mother, not the child. Perhaps Luke
is unfamiliar with Jewish practices, or it may be that we have in the
Gospel of Luke something more than simply an historical account
of Jesus' life. Even when the mother's purification is taking place,
attention remains on Jesus.

As the scene begins it presents a contrast between the old man
Simeon, who has been patiently waiting for the consolation of Israel,
and the child Jesus. Upon seeing Jesus, he exclaims, "Lord, now let-
test thou thy servant depart in peace" (2:29–32). The astonishment
of Jesus' father and mother at Simeon's words (2:33) is itself surprising, for they already knew that Jesus was to be a messianic figure
(cf. 1:32 ff.; 2:13 ff.). But Simeon's speech does contain one new
item, for Jesus' coming is "a light for revelation to the Gentiles" (vs.
32). Jewish parents would understandably be surprised, especially
since the news comes from a devout fellow Israelite (cf. vss. 34 f.).
Even this point is not entirely novel, however, for Simeon's speech

The announcement of Jesus' birth to the shepherds, by a contemporary
Chinese artist, Lu Hung Nien. (Courtesy of Spartaco Appetiti.)

"The Adoration of the Shepherds" by Giorgione (1477–1510). (Courtesy of National Gallery of Art, Washington, D.C. Samuel H. Kress Collection.)

goes back to Isaiah the prophet (cf. 52:10; 42:6; 49:6). Still the principal point of this episode, and of the entire introduction, is that Jesus is for all people, even Gentiles.[6] He is meant for old and young, for women like Mary and Elizabeth, and for priests and shepherds.

In the final part of this episode the old prophetess Anna appears (2:36–38). Again we have Luke's twofold witness: An old man and an old woman praise Jesus. Anna's piety is also exemplary (vs. 37). Her actions are similar to those of the early Christians who also went to the temple in order to worship and pray (cf. Acts 2:46–3:1). Furthermore, what she anticipates—"the redemption of Jerusalem" (vs. 38)—is effected in the early church by the life of Jesus (cf. 19:28–24:53, especially 24:21). Antiquity, represented by the old woman and the old man, prophesies the new salvation and calls attention to that redemption's ancient roots in Israel.

[6] Appropriately, the message about Gentiles occurs in the temple, where symbols of exclusion abound. Its outer court allowed the presence of Gentiles and women, but the inner court was reserved only for male Jews in good standing. The Holy of Holies within the temple could be entered only once a year and then only by the high priest. See William Stinespring, "Temple, Jerusalem," *IDB*, IV (Nashville, Tenn.: Abingdon, 1962), pp. 534–560.

INITIAL VICTORY IN THE TEMPLE (2:41–52)

What is the impression given by Jesus' first action in Luke?

The one boyhood story of Jesus contained in any of the canonical Gospels places Jesus in the temple.[7] This Lukan emphasis was already apparent in the initial scene with Zechariah and the preceding encounters with Simeon and Anna. After Jesus' first action, a triumphant demonstration before the rabbis in the temple, his parents question him and he replies, "Did you not know that I must be in my Father's house?" (2:49). The temple is Jesus' inheritance because he fulfills the hope of Israel.

This conversation takes place with Jesus' mother (2:48) rather than with his father. Throughout the introduction, Mary rather than Joseph has the lead. In the purification episode, Simeon speaks to Mary (2:34). In fact, Mary is mentioned twelve times in the opening two chapters. And, finally, "his mother kept all these things in her heart" (2:51). Yet in the rest of the Gospel she is not particularly important and is even rebuked (8:19 ff). The fact that her womb bore Jesus and that her breasts were sucked by him is declared insignificant in comparison with those "who hear the word of God and keep it" (11:27 f.; only in Luke). Luke's emphasis upon Mary does not particularly stress the virgin birth; the passages themselves concentrate on a series of wonders rather than one particular miracle.[8] The consistent flow of marvels underlines the fact that "with God, nothing will be impossible" (1:37).

The essential point of the birth stories, around which Luke's introduction is built, is the stress on the overwhelming power of God. Luke uses the miraculous birth of Jesus (Luke 1–2) to introduce Jesus' life in the same way as he uses the miraculous birth of the church (Acts 1–2) to introduce the church's mission. The outpouring of the Spirit upon various people at Jesus' birth is matched in Acts by the Spirit's descending upon apostles and disciples. The close of the introduction anticipates further developments (2:52). This verse duplicates an earlier one (2:40). Further manifestations of God through the Spirit are thereby foreshadowed, for what was begun by the Spirit (cf. 1:15, 35, 41, 67; 2:25, 26) is now to be accomplished in the ministry of Jesus. The characters function passively to receive the Spirit. God's power acts in Jesus' birth. Only with the final episode, Jesus in the temple, does a person act with authority. And this action serves as the transition to Luke's first major section, in which Jesus gathers witnesses in Galilee for the journey to Jerusalem and the temple.

[7] The apocryphal Gospels contain numerous stories of the infancy of Jesus, sometimes grotesque and occasionally distasteful; see Hennecke-Schneemelcher, *New Testament Apocrypha*, I, pp. 363–417.

[8] See Minear, *Studies in Luke-Acts*, p. 129.

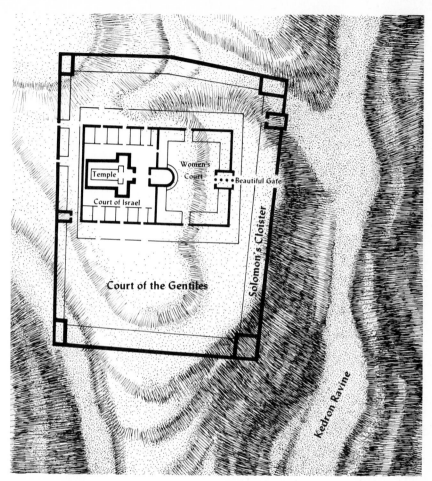

Herod's temple and its precincts.

Gathering Witnesses in Galilee (3:1–9:50)

Thus far the source of Luke's material has been his special tradition, but at this point (3:1) the major source becomes the Gospel of Mark. A segment of Luke, found also in Matthew but not in Mark, is probably derived from the Q source. We would be on relatively uncertain ground in trying to deduce the aims and purposes of Luke from his use of this source, simply because we do not possess Q. We shall therefore largely confine our distinguishing of tradition and redaction to Luke's use of the Markan source. In addition, we shall continue to assume that the special Lukan material reveals something of the purpose of this Gospel.

Luke locates the beginning of Jesus' ministry in two spheres, that of world history (3:1; see also 2:1) and that of God's word. This word is first preached by John, the son of Zechariah (Luke 3:2 ff.). Curiously, John the Baptist seems to be handled rather carelessly by Luke. For example, whereas Matthew carefully showed that Jesus was baptized by John to fulfill righteousness (Matt. 3:13 ff.), Luke does not make clear to the reader that Jesus was even baptized by John (cf. 3:20 f.). That could be Luke's way of minimizing his role, although John the Baptist preaches exactly the same message of repentance and forgiveness (3:3) which becomes the heart of Jesus' own proclamation (see Luke 15; 24:47 and pp. 151 ff.). As the opening birth stories already indicated, this Gospel shows a high regard for John (cf. 7:28). Yet the Baptist still belongs to the old Israel (16:16), though he is the one who points ahead to the new time of Jesus (3:16).[9] Only Luke shows John in prison before Jesus is baptized or begins his ministry (3:18–21), perhaps because in his view the Baptist belongs to the time of Israel.

Characteristic Lukan emphases abound in this first major section. Jesus is a universal savior: the genealogy goes from Jesus back to Adam, the first man (3:38), not to Abraham (Matt. 1:1 f.). Jesus is an example of piety: whenever a crisis arises, he is at prayer (5:16; 6:12; 9:18, 28 f.). Moreover, the Spirit descends upon Jesus while he is praying almost as if the Spirit were summoned by prayer rather than by the baptism (3:21; cf. Mark 1:9 f.). The Gospel of Luke apparently seeks to establish the practice of prayer as a basis for the continuing life of the church. Emphasis upon the church's contemporary situation may be reflected in Luke's omission of Mark's summary of Jesus' preaching, "The time is fulfilled, and the kingdom of God is at hand; repent, and believe in the gospel" (Mark 1:15). Although Luke also mentions the kingdom in this section, Jesus rarely preaches the kingdom as if it were imminent (see 4:43 and 8:1; cf. 9:27). This loss of a sense for the imminent coming of the kingdom is related to his greater emphasis on the church.

This section narrates Jesus' gathering of disciples in Galilee. Many people flock to him (4:15, 42; 5:1, 15); some are in opposition (5:30; 6:2) and remain only in the crowd (6:17; 7:11); but he gathers the disciples (5:1–11). Indeed, from the disciples, he calls the twelve together whom he "named apostles" (6:13; cf. Mark 3:14). Here in Jesus' own territory there is the gathering of those who will be witnesses to carry on his work after his death. (At Jesus' ascension, two men address the disciples as "men of Galilee"—Acts 1:11.) The continuing importance of women is shown by their inclusion alongside the twelve as part of Jesus' retinue (8:2 f.). Later, they too, along with the twelve, will be witnesses. "The women who had come with him *from Galilee* followed, and saw the tomb, and how his body was laid; then they returned, and prepared spices and oint-

[9] See Conzelmann, *The Theology of St. Luke,* pp. 20 ff.

Caesar Augustus (27 B.C.–A.D. 14) and Tiberius Caesar (A.D. 14–37) on Roman coins. (Courtesy of American Numismatic Society.)

ments" (23:55 f.; see 23:49). Luke seeks to establish certainty of witness: someone had accompanied Jesus all the time, from his baptism until the day when he was taken up (see Acts 1:21 f.).

THE OFFENSE OF JESUS' PREACHING (4:16–30)

Do the people of Nazareth have reason to become angry with Jesus?

In Mark, Jesus' first public act is to exorcize a demon (1:21–28); in Matthew it is to deliver the Sermon on the Mount (chaps. 5–7); in Luke it is to preach in his home synagogue at Nazareth. This episode's special importance is indicated not only by its position at the beginning of Jesus' public ministry, but also by Luke's uncharacteristic departure from the Markan order (cf. Mark 6:1–6).

Jesus appears as a pious Jew: "He went to the synagogue, as his custom was, on the sabbath day" (vs. 16). He there reads from the prophet Isaiah,[10] whose message from the Old Testament (Isaiah 61:1–2; 58:6) proclaims the end time; the Spirit acts, good news is preached to the poor, and a new age has dawned. After finishing, Jesus says, "Today, this scripture has been fulfilled in your hearing" (vs. 21; only in Luke). In other words, salvation has appeared with Jesus. He has come to preach good news to the poor, to release the captive, and to proclaim the arrival of the good news. The kingdom is not merely imminent; it has also in some sense arrived.

The reception accorded Jesus by the people of Nazareth is rather surprising. They at first accept him as the one who brings salvation

---

[10]Worship in a Palestinian synagogue consisted of the recitation of the Shema, a prayer, a fixed lection or reading of the law, a free lection from the prophets, an explanation, an application of one or both scriptural passages, and a blessing by the priest, or a prayer by a layman; see Gilmour, *IB*, VIII, p. 89.

(vs. 22). In Luke's source (Mark 6:1–6), the people immediately took offense at Jesus' claim to authority. In Luke, "Is not this Joseph's son?" (vs. 22), seems to proceed from surprise rather than from anger (cf. Mark 6:3). But in Luke also Jesus is finally rejected, not because he claims authority, but because he extends salvation to the wrong people.

Clearly, Jesus thinks he will be expected to perform miracles as he has in Capernaum (vs. 23; although Luke has not yet reported any miracles). Jesus rejects their request, speaking of the miracles in the Old Testament that the prophets Elijah and Elisha performed not for the people of Israel, but for foreigners. Immediately, the audience's anger is aroused. Jesus' proclamation is going beyond Israel to the Gentiles. They drive him out of the city and almost kill him, but he escapes (vss. 29 f.). We might now expect Jesus to leave Palestine to preach to Gentiles. Luke, however, stands under the authority of tradition, and there is no record in the Synoptic tradition of Jesus' more than briefly going outside Israel. For Luke the matter is resolved as Jesus' saying finds fulfillment in the church's mission. Acts makes clear that the Gentiles do hear the word (cf. Acts 11:18; 22:21; 28:28).

View of present-day Nazareth. (Courtesy of Israel Government Tourist Office.)

Ruins of ancient synagogue at Capernaum, built in the second or third century on the site of one Jesus visited. (Courtesy of National Geographic Society.)

Incidents following this opening scene further reveal Luke's intention. What Jesus has done in Nazareth, he now proceeds to do in Capernaum (4:31 ff.). He refused to perform a miracle at Nazareth, but in this synagogue and on this sabbath, he heals. The point may be to show Jesus' sovereignty (cf. 4:31 f., 41); more likely Jesus now heals because he is on his way toward his goal. When the people try to hold him, he says, "I must preach the good news of the kingdom of God to the other cities also; for I was sent for this purpose" (4:43). Precisely because this preaching to other cities cannot be done by Jesus alone, the necessary conclusion to the opening Nazareth scene is the calling of disciples. When Jesus' ministry has concluded, these disciples will be the instruments for spreading the message beyond Israel to the cities of the Gentiles.

A comparison between the calling of disciples in Luke (5:1–11) and in Mark (1:16–20) shows that the stories are quite different. Luke alone includes a miracle, that of the great catch of fish. Stress is laid, however, upon the consequence of the miracle, Simon Peter's confession of sin, "Depart from me, for I am a sinful man, O Lord" (vs. 8). After this repentance, Simon Peter and those with him become fishers of men or true disciples. But the Pharisees and their scribes upbraid them for eating with "tax collectors and sinners" (5:30). Jesus defends his disciples' behavior, however: "I have not come to call the righteous, but sinners to repentance" (5:32).

Another example of the Lukan repentance motif is contained in the story of the woman "who was a sinner" (7:36–50). Although this story has some affinities with Mark (14:3–9; cf. John 12:1–8), its present form has a distinctly Lukan cast. In Luke, the sinful woman who shows great love to Jesus serves as the occasion for a parable of Jesus which stresses that someone who has been forgiven then loves (7:43). Yet the actual incident first mentions the woman's love, then Jesus' forgiveness (cf. 7:47 f.). That her love is an expression of repentance is clear from the story: she is a sinner, she weeps, she kisses the feet of Jesus. Perhaps the ambiguity about which comes first, repentance or forgiveness, is intentional. Repentance and forgiveness are both necessary and cannot readily be distinguished by a logical or chronological priority (see 3:3). Repentance, the response of individuals, occurs with forgiveness, the action of God. The essential point, however, has to do with quantity, not sequence, for her great love and God's great forgiveness contrast with the petty formality of the Pharisees.

Jesus' presence elicits two kinds of response, either rejection by those who cling to the old righteousness or repentance by those who accept his promise of salvation. Those who repent become witnessing disciples to the forgiveness that Jesus brings.

SURE WITNESS TO THE WORD (8:1–21)

How does the parable of the sower relate to the work of the church?

In the introduction of this passage, a number of witnesses are gathered around Jesus, the twelve, and the women (8:1–3). At its close, the mother and brothers of Jesus, who come to see him, are told, "My mother and my brothers are those who hear the word of God and do it" (8:21). This sequence is designed by Luke to demonstrate that true disciples not only hear Jesus' word, but also go out to become preachers of this word (cf. 8:15; see 1:2; Acts 6:1–7).

In comparing this section with its parallels in Mark (4:1–34; 3:31–35), two major differences are evident: first, Luke shifts the position of the discussion about the true mother and brothers of Jesus so that it now follows, instead of precedes, the parable of the sower; second, Luke has only one parable (Luke 8:4; cf. Mark 4:2). Both changes reflect Luke's concentration upon the theme of the word of God. For example, in Luke's interpretation of the parable of the sower Jesus says, "Now the parable is this: The seed is the word of God . . ." (8:11; cf. Mark 4:13 f.).

Luke's version of the parable of the sower (8:4–8) unfolds much as in Mark (4:1–9) except that Mark emphasized response to Jesus' teaching in parables, whereas Luke stresses response to Jesus' message of the word of God. By a series of slight changes Luke transforms the passage into an exhortation for careful and sure witness. Such phrases as "the seed is the word of God" (8:11; cf. Mark 4:13), "then the devil comes and takes away the word from their hearts that they may not believe and be saved" (8:12b; cf. Mark 4:15), and "they are those who, hearing the word, hold it fast in an honest and good heart, and bring forth fruit with patience" (8:15; cf. Mark 4:20) show Luke's intention to depict the importance of hearing and holding to the word of God.

Further emphasis upon the time of the church may be suggested by Luke's inclusion of "the devil" in Jesus' interpretation (8:12b; cf. Mark 4:15). According to Luke's temptation story, the devil left Jesus to return at an opportune time (4:13; cf. Mark 1:13; Matt. 4:11). In Luke this satanic figure does not begin to act again until Jesus' last days (22:3, 31) and he continues during the early days of the church (Acts 5:3; 10:38; 13:10; 26:18). The time between Jesus' temptation and passion is for Luke an ideal time of the kingdom of God (cf. 10:18; 11:20). In that idyllic period a foundation was laid so that in later conflict disciples who had truly heard would continue steadfastly preaching the word. Consequently, the saying about not hiding the lamp (8:16) refers in Luke to those who hear the word and patiently bring forth fruitful witness (8:15; cf. Mark 4:20). Gathering sure disciples in Galilee assures the faithful continuation of the word of God into the time of the church.

The next episodes in Luke, basically following the order of Mark, are a series of miracles: the miracle of calming the waves (8:22–25); the driving out of the demons at Gerasa (8:26–39); the healing of the woman with the flow of blood (8:43–48); and the raising of the dead daughter (8:40–42, 49–56). This series culminates when Jesus "called the twelve together and gave them power and authority over all demons and to cure diseases, and he sent them out to preach the kingdom of God and to heal" (9:1–2). The witnesses are gathered, are convinced, and even Herod begins to wonder (9:7–9). The crowds are filled, for after the feeding of the five thousand "twelve baskets of broken pieces" are left over (9:10–17). Only then are the disciples asked to affirm that Jesus is the Christ of God (9:18–20).

The conclusion of the first part of Luke, "the gathering of witnesses in Galilee," begins a discussion of Jesus' identity, and especially of the necessity of his suffering (9:21–27, 43b–45). At the close of this first major section instead of Mark's "he that is not against *us* is for *us*" (Mark 9:40), Luke's Jesus says, "he that is not against *you* is for *you*" (9:50). These are clearly instructions for the early church. Luke anticipates the separation of Jesus from his disciples in the postresurrection period after Jesus has ascended into heaven (cf. Acts 1:9–11).

Witness to the Word on the Journey to Jerusalem (9:51–19:27)

The Galilean witnesses gathered by Jesus must journey with him to Jerusalem. Luke's second major section, which narrates the journey, seems much longer than the short distance (about sixty miles) and the brief time (about three days) that it would take to travel from Galilee to Jerusalem. Although Jesus is on the way to Jerusalem all this time, he seems to make little physical progress (see 9:51; 10:1, 38; 13:22, 33; 17:11; 19:11).

Luke's reason for such an extensive account of the journey is not simply an interest in geographical matters, for it is difficult to answer questions about Jesus' itinerary from Galilee to Jerusalem on the basis of the information in the text. For example, we are uncertain whether he went through Samaria, which separates Galilee from Jerusalem (cf. 9:53). Luke does make clear, as the journey progresses, that certain people are present with Jesus throughout the trip. Continuity in witness to the work and word of Jesus is thereby assured (cf. 23:49).

The opening verse is a key for this section, "When the days drew near for him to be received up, he set his face to go to Jerusalem" (9:51; only in Luke). Jesus goes to Jerusalem because, "I must go on my way today and tomorrow and the day following; for it cannot be that a prophet should perish away from Jerusalem" (13:33; only in Luke). As prophet to Israel, Jesus goes to die at Jerusalem, the capital of Israel. The journey turns out to be instruction in the purpose and meaning of Jesus' death.

A comparison of the structure of Luke's Gospel with that of the Acts of the Apostles reveals a striking similarity that helps to illuminate the reason for the journey. In Acts the order is: first, the Spirit's appearance in Jerusalem; second, journeys of missionaries, especially Paul; third, Paul's arrest and trial ending in Rome. In Luke the order is: first, gathering of witnesses in Galilee; second, the journey to Jerusalem accompanied by preaching the word; third, Jesus' arrest, trial, crucifixion, and resurrection in Jerusalem. Together Luke-Acts shows a continuity of witness stretching from Galilee to Rome; the journey motif emphasizes an orderly, gradual development of the new faith.

Luke throughout this section stresses the theme of witness, and in two senses: (1) a witness *observes* something; (2) a witness *testifies* to something. These senses correspond to his distinction between "eyewitnesses and ministers of the word" (1:2). The first two episodes (9:51–56 and 9:57–62; mainly special Lukan material) indicate the necessity of following Jesus closely—that is, of observing. The mission of the seventy (10:1–17) implies that the twelve remained with Jesus even during the sending out of the seventy (10:1;

note "others"); moreover, the disciples are singled out, "Then turning to the disciples he said privately, 'Blessed are the eyes which see what you see!' " (10:23; cf. Matt. 13:16). Other passages point out that disciples are always with Jesus so that his journey has been faithfully observed (11:1; 12:1, 22, 41; 16:1; 17:1, 5, 22; 19:28–40). By and large, these passages belong to the editorial work of Luke. By the end of this section the emphasis includes not only faithful observation but also faithful testifying to what has been observed (cf. 19:11–27).

This entire section (9:51–19:27) is a depiction of Jesus' telling the disciples about the word of God. They are shown that women matter, especially the one who sits attentively at Jesus' feet. (See also the story of Mary and Martha, 10:38–42.) Prayer is part of Jesus' life and those with him (11:1 ff.). The kingdom of God becomes present whenever Jesus casts out demons (11:20). Physical closeness to Jesus guarantees nothing by itself; the blessed are "those who hear the word of God and keep it" (11:27 f.). True disciples cannot be satisfied with the old rules of piety (11:37–12:3). Riches are clearly a barrier to hearing the word that Jesus proclaims (12:13–34; cf. 14:33; 16:11, 14, 19–31; 18:22–30; 19:1–10). Watchfulness and faithfulness are demanded over a long period of time (12:41–49) and repentance is necessary now (13:1–9). Jesus' ministry must continue for a considerable time (13:10–35); furthermore, the end of the world is not in sight (17:20 ff.). The messianic banquet with Jesus will include great multitudes, the unexpected (14:13), the Gentiles (14:23; cf. 17:18 and 10:33); but not all will enter (14:25–35). The following special Lukan material from the journey gives the heart of Jesus' instructions: repentance and forgiveness.[11]

JESUS' WORD ABOUT THE PRESENT (15:1–32)

What is the common emphasis of all three parables?

Jesus' words, "He who has ears to hear, let him hear" (14:35), are a transition to the statement: "Now the tax collectors and sinners were all drawing near to him" (15:1). In the center of the journey section, Luke inserts three parables, of which only the parable of the lost sheep occurs outside Luke (cf. Matt. 18:12–14). They clarify and extend Jesus' word, which the disciples are to transmit to others. The Pharisees and the scribes are irritated by Jesus' association with sinners (vs. 2). In contrast, the parables emphasize joy and openness to all (cf. 15:7, 10, 32), a prominent motif throughout Luke (cf., for example, 1:14, 44; 2:10; 6:23).

[11]Further elaboration of the repentance-forgiveness motif is given in these distinctively Lukan sayings: the word from the cross (23:34), the word to the criminal on the cross (23:39–43), and the charge to resurrection witnesses (24:47).

The first two parables pose a problem of interpretation for the general conclusions of each speak of a sinner's repenting (15:7, 10), yet such repentance is hardly exemplified in the parables themselves. A lost sheep or a lost coin does not repent. The usual explanation is that the general conclusions anticipate and more properly belong to the third parable, that of the prodigal son. Moreover, this last parable contains the key passage concerning repentance, for the prodigal son repented—"when he came to himself . . ." (15:17).

An opposite conclusion could be drawn, however: Luke's very purpose in using the two introductory parables is to *prevent* an incorrect reading of the parable of the prodigal son in terms of repentance. The first two parables unmistakably emphasize the initiative of the one who seeks out the lost. Whether this is Jesus or God is not crucial—probably both are intended—for the decisive announcement is that salvation is present (see 4:21; 10:9; 11; 11:20; 17:20; 18:30; 19:9). Luke is addressing the charge made against Jesus that he eats with sinners (vs. 2), and he claims that precisely the avowed sinner recognizes what is happening and, unlike the Pharisees and scribes, receives the forgiveness of God.

A more appropriate title for the familiar parable of the prodigal son would be the parable of the prodigal's father. The parable runs smoothly and understandably through the son's realization that he would be better off as one of his father's hired servants (vss. 17 f.), at which point he returns home confessing himself a sinner. The surprise of the story is the way in which the father receives him. Instead of greeting him with self-righteousness ("I told you so") and a demand that he demonstrate his "repentance," the father runs out to embrace him and gives orders to bring the best robe, the ring, shoes, and the fatted calf. He will have a feast for his son. There is joy and merriment for one who was lost and is now found (vs. 24).[12]

To prevent our missing the point, the elder son is introduced. He is angry; he cannot understand his father's joyful reception, much as the Pharisees and scribes cannot understand Jesus' action. But the father exclaims, "Son, you are always with me, and all that is mine is yours. It was fitting to make merry and be glad, for this your brother was dead, and is alive; he was lost, and is found" (vs. 32). The elder brother fails to recognize the joy and salvation that is already present. He needs to repent and to accept the good news of God's forgiveness (15:7, 10, 25–32). Only then is God's word truly heard.

These same themes of forgiveness and repentance recur in the

---

[12] In Buddhist literature there is a similar parable which speaks of a son who also wastes his inheritance and returns home. This father, however, makes the son do penance for a number of years to prove that he is truly repentant and worthy of being received back as his son. See R. Otto, *India's Religion of Grace and Christianity*, trans. J. H. Foster (London: SCM, 1930), pp. 136 ff.

"The Return of the Prodigal Son" by Murillo (1617–82). (Courtesy of National Gallery of Art, Washington, D.C. Avalan Foundation.)

remaining portions of the journey. The rich man tries too late to repent (16:19 ff.), and the poor man Lazarus cannot help him. Unexpectedly, some do repent because the kingdom is in their midst (17:11–21). He who hears Jesus' word is one who impetuously keeps knocking at the door (18:1 ff.) and admits that he is a sinner in need of God's mercy (18:9 ff.). Things are unhappy for those who are self-satisfied (18:18–23), yet whoever calls on the mercy of Jesus will see (18:35–43). Even a rich chief tax collector will be saved because he sees himself as a sinner (19:1–10). The word Jesus proclaims during this journey effects salvation; those who are close to him will testify to what they have heard and seen, "Today salvation has come to this house, since he also is a son of Abraham" (19:9).

At times, Luke seems to be saying that salvation has arrived. But Luke knows that there is more to come: the long history of the church will be unfolded by those acting under the Spirit of God. Although Jesus' final days in Jerusalem are coming, Luke does not think that nothing else remains to be done. Hence he closes this journey section with the parable of the pounds.

JESUS' WORD ABOUT THE FUTURE (19:11-27)

Who is the nobleman in this parable?

In Jesus salvation is present (see 10:18; 11:20; 17:20). Yet how does the presence of salvation in him relate to the coming kingdom of God? The opening of the parable of the pounds does not suggest the expectation of an imminent kingdom (19:11; cf. 21:8 and Acts 1:6 ff.). Seemingly, present salvation and future kingdom are distinguished in the thought of Luke, and the kingdom is in the indefinite future.[13]

In the parable of the pounds, the nobleman goes into a *far country* to receive kingly power (cf. Matt. 25:14–30), a hint that in Luke's eschatology the king will return again only after a long journey. Some citizens do not want him to be king; they resist by sending an embassy to oppose him. The surprise of the parable is that when he returns, he condemns the one who in fear of him as a severe judge had simply hidden the gift away. But concentration upon God's future severity misses the point. Although the king does deal severely with his enemies at the end (vs. 27), the one who makes use of the gift of salvation (that is, continues his witness to a forgiving God over a long period of time) need not fear.

Throughout this section Jesus' word brings forgiveness for whoever will receive it—sinners, people in the highways and hedges, a prodigal son, or foreigners. But if they do not see and testify to it, then judgment will come. A joyful present and a threatening future have been proclaimed as they journeyed to Jerusalem. Now Luke brings Jesus into the city where he must die and be resurrected.

The True Israel Through the Passion and Resurrection (19:28–24:53)

In the third and final section of the Gospel of Luke, two distinctive motifs emerge: first, Jesus' triumph in the temple; second, Jesus'

---

[13]One famous passage suggests, however, that the kingdom is already present, "Behold, the kingdom of God is in the midst of you" (17:20 f.; only in Luke). Evidently Luke means that the key to the future kingdom is already present in the word and action of Jesus, which bring forgiveness and effect repentance. The kingdom itself will not come until the disciples shall have gone throughout the world with this word of forgiveness and repentance (24:47). Indeed, Luke follows this kingdom saying (17:20 f.) with a caution against assuming that the kingdom's Son of Man has already come (17:22 ff.). Conzelmann, *The Theology of St. Luke*, pp. 120–125, sees the distinctive Lukan eschatology as directed to the problem of the delay of the parousia in early Christianity. C. H. Talbert, "The Redaction Critical Quest for Luke the Theologian," *Jesus and Man's Hope*, I, ed. D. G. Miller and D. Y. Hadidian (Pittsburgh, Pa.: Pittsburgh Theological Seminary, 1970), pp. 171 ff., sees Luke combating those Christians who believe the kingdom has already come with the final events in Jerusalem.

Shepherd and sheep in the Judean hills near Jerusalem. (Courtesy of Pan American Airways.)

innocence. The temple motif is not new in Luke.[14] Now, however, he reiterates his emphasis more insistently. Jesus is teaching daily in the temple (19:47; 20:1; 21:37 ff.; 22:53); even after the resurrection the disciples return to the temple to bless God continually (24:53). Moreover, the apocalyptic discourse takes place in the temple rather than on the Mount of Olives as in Mark and Matthew (21:5–28; cf. Mark 13:1 ff. and Matt. 24:1 ff.). Why then does Luke so emphasize Jesus' frequenting the temple?

In the Acts of the Apostles the earliest church is also centered in the temple (cf. Acts 2:46; 3:1 ff.; 5:20). Apparently Jesus establishes himself in the temple in order that the early church may also operate from this base. Thereby Luke seeks to show how the new

---

[14]See the introductory section, esp. 2:41–52. The order of temptations in the Gospel of Luke may reflect Luke's temple emphasis. In Luke 4:1–13, Jesus' temptation to throw himself off the temple's pinnacle is the last temptation (unlike the parallel in Matthew 4:1–11), perhaps to signal the temple scene as the climactic one.

faith in Jesus is the true Israel and the authentic extension of the dominant religious institution of Israel. Luke's apology consequently assures both Jewish and Gentile believers of the antiquity and continuity of the new faith. The disciples, who return to the temple immediately after the resurrection appearances to bless God and to await the power of the Spirit (24:53), are neither a band of fanatics expecting the end of the world nor political revolutionaries against the Roman Empire. This latter emphasis becomes most explicit in the book of Acts (see pp. 307 f.), but already in the Gospel the truth and validity of Christian faith are demonstrated.

The second major motif of this passion and resurrection section is the trial and death of the *innocent* Jesus. A special Lukan detail illustrates this emphasis: at Jesus' trial before Pilate, the elders of the people accuse Jesus of having forbidden the giving of tribute to Caesar (23:1–5; cf. Mark 15:1–5), but an earlier debate about Jesus' authority absolutely established the falsity of this charge (20:19–26). In Mark, Pilate, the Roman procurator, finds Jesus not guilty on only one occasion (15:14), but in Luke this verdict of innocence occurs three times (cf. 23:4, 14–16, 22). Luke alone records the incident of Herod's declaring Jesus innocent (23:6 ff.). Furthermore, in Luke the centurion at the cross says, "Certainly, this man was innocent" (23:47); whereas in Mark he said, "Truly this man was the Son of God" (15:39; cf. Matt. 27:54). The subtle way in which Luke opposes Jesus to Barabbas suggests that Jesus was not an insurrectionist like Barabbas (cf. Luke 23:19, 25 with Mark 15:7). Jesus' climactic word from the cross establishes his innocence, "Father, forgive them for they know not what they do" (23:34; only in Luke). Luke further underlines Jesus' innocence as one of the thieves from the cross says, "We are receiving the due reward of our deeds; but this man has done nothing wrong" (23:41; only in Luke). This major theme receives further and unqualified substantiation in Acts, "This Jesus . . . you crucified and killed by the hands of *lawless* men" (Acts 2:23; cf. Acts 8:32 ff. and 17:30).

The innocent Jesus is falsely accused, tried, and executed. Instead of concentrating upon the guilt of those responsible for this miscarriage of justice, Luke focuses upon Jesus' triumph even under adversity. At the cross Jesus' general word of forgiveness (23:34) and his forgiveness of the repentant thief (23:39–43) show that guilt need not be overwhelming. Moreover, this passion is the working out of God's plan for the true Israel. ("This Jesus, delivered up according to the definite plan and foreknowledge of God"—Acts 2:23; cf. 3:18 and Luke 22:22.) Jesus dies a martyr's death prefiguring the martyrdom of others in the early church, especially Stephen and James (cf. Acts 7:54–8:3; 9:1; 12:1 ff.). But through all these events God's word of "repentance and forgiveness of sins" is being preached to all nations (24:47), and his plan is thus fulfilled.

THE TRUE INHERITORS (20:9–19)

To whom will the vineyard be given!

In focusing intently upon the passion events up to and including Jesus' death and resurrection, Luke is obviously in company with the other Synoptic Gospels. In the parable of the wicked tenants Luke shows his understanding of the reason for Jesus' death and resurrection.

In the preceding passage (19:47–20:8), Jesus' authority for teaching daily in the temple has been challenged by the chief priests and the scribes. Comparing the opening of the parable with its Markan source (Luke 20:9; cf. Mark 12:1; Matt. 21:33), we are struck by Luke's distinction between the people *to* whom this parable is spoken and the chief priests and the scribes *against* whom it is spoken (cf. 20:19). In Mark's version (12:1–12), the parable is clearly a polemic against the chief priests, scribes, and elders because they have rejected God's servants, the prophets and even the "beloved son" (Mark 12:6, see pp. 69 f.). The identity of the Markan "others" who will receive the vineyard is indefinite, although the reader may surmise that they are the Gentiles (Mark 13:10; cf. also Matt. 21:43).[15]

In Luke, however, this parable is addressed not to Jesus' opponents, but to the people, who "hung upon his words" (19:48). Furthermore, the people protest strongly the destruction of the former tenants and the giving of the vineyard to others: "When they heard this, they said, 'God forbid!' " (20:16b; only in Luke). This protest serves, however, to allow Jesus to restate his conclusion (vss. 17 f.) and to imply that the people do finally accept Jesus' word, for the leaders acknowledge that the people are on Jesus' side (vs. 19) although they themselves are not.

Throughout this section Luke consistently portrays the people as being sympathetic to Jesus. They are the ones who praise God (18:43); they listen in the temple (19:48, 21:38); they observe Jesus' defeat of the authorities (20:26). They stand by watching at the crucifixion; it is the rulers who scoff (23:35). Within Jewish tradition reference to "the people" carries with it the connotation of God's chosen people, the people of Israel.[16] Consequently the alignment of the people with Jesus implies that Jesus' word is finally accepted by Israel.

In the Book of Acts, Luke clarifies the identity of the "others" (Luke 20:16). They are the true inheritors, for they are "the men of

---

[15] Joachim Jeremias, *The Parables of Jesus*, trans. S. H. Hooke, rev. ed. (New York: Scribner, 1963), p. 76, suggests that "others" refers to the "poor." The leaders of the people reject the gospel; therefore, Jesus offers it to the poor.

[16] See *"laos"* in Kittel, *TDNT*, IV, pp. 29–57, and esp. Luke 2:32 and Acts 26:17, 23. Cf. Acts 4:10; 28:26 f.

Israel" and the Gentiles who hear the preaching (cf. Acts 2:22; 3:12; 13:16, 46–48). The last speech of Paul, at the conclusion of Acts, confirms that the Gentiles have become the true people of God, because the old Israel has rejected the preaching (Acts 28:26–28). However, Luke clearly shows in the parable that the people are on Jesus' side so that "others," the inheritors, include both Jew and Gentile. In Luke, a parable concerning the rejection of Jesus becomes also a parable stressing the true inheritors, those who *hear.*

Luke nonetheless emphasizes rejection in this parable, and in his own special way. Jesus' explanation of the reason for the tenants' destruction reads as follows in Mark:

> Have you not read this scripture:
> > The very stone which the builders rejected
> > > has become the head of the corner;
> > this was the Lord's doing,
> > > and it is marvelous in our eyes?
> > > > [Mark 12:10 f.; cf. Psalm 118:22 f.]

In Luke the element of praise (last two lines) is omitted and another condemnation is added (20:18; cf. Isaiah 8:14 f.). Thereby Luke emphasizes the judgment that occurs for those who do not truly understand or interpret the scripture. They cannot tell the true from the false Israel. This necessity for rightly interpreting the scripture is the subject of our final Lukan passage.

FULFILLING THE SCRIPTURE (24:13–35)

Why is the risen Jesus not recognized immediately?

Before turning to this climactic event on the road to Emmaus, we need to observe the way in which Luke prepares for this scene. Throughout the passion, especially after the parable of the wicked tenants, two themes mutually reinforce each other: (1) these events necessarily happened; (2) they were closely and surely witnessed.

Definite things must happen before the end can come (Luke 21:12) to fulfill scripture (21:22; 22:37; esp. 24:25–27, 32). These things are done at the bidding of God, who alone is in command of the situation (see 21:18, a Lukan addition picking up 12:7). God's direction of the events is implicitly claimed by the assurance that these things happen to fulfill scripture: "Was it not necessary that the Christ should suffer these things and enter into his glory?" (24:26; cf. 22:15 f.).

Not only must these things happen, but they also have to be observed by the disciples, especially the apostles. For after Jesus is gone, "this will be a time for you to bear testimony" (21:13; cf.

Mark 13:10; see esp. Luke 24:48). To ensure this witness the apostles, disciples, and women of Galilee are constant companions of Jesus. It is especially important for the apostles to be with Jesus (22:14; cf. Mark 14:17). We learn in Acts that an apostle is one who "beginning from the baptism of John until the day when he was taken up from us" was constantly with Jesus (Acts 1:21–26). The apostles continue with Jesus in his trials (22:28); they follow Jesus to the Mount of Olives (22:39; cf. Mark 14:26), and even when they fall asleep, it is "for sorrow" (22:45; cf. Mark 14:37). Luke omits Mark's statement, "And they all forsook him and fled" (14:50). At the crucifixion, "all his acquaintances and the women who had followed him from Galilee stood at a distance and saw these things" (23:49; cf. Mark 15:40 f.). Luke insists that ministers of the word based their testimony on eyewitness reports. They observed in order that the truth about these things might be known (see Luke 1:1–4).

The story of the empty tomb, which precedes the road to Emmaus story, bears out these preliminary observations (24:1–12; cf. Mark 16:1–8). Two men greet the women instead of a single young man (cf. Mark 16:5). This twofold witness guarantees authenticity (see pp. 139 ff.). Luke also subtly changes what had been a prediction of Jesus' future appearances in Galilee into a statement about what Jesus said while he was in Galilee (24:6; cf. Mark 16:7). This change brings his text into harmony with Luke's view that the resurrection appearances were in Jerusalem (cf. Matt. 28:16). Luke's Gospel shows a clear, straightforward development: beginning in Galilee, extending to Jerusalem, and from there to the rest of the world (24:47). Moreover, Luke's story of the empty tomb points ahead to the confirmatory appearances to the disciples, for when the apostles hear the report from the women, "these words seemed to them an idle tale, and they did not believe them" (24:11). Luke's stress upon both continuity and certainty required more than an account by excited women. Full recognition of the resurrected Jesus occurs only when his followers meet him on the road to Emmaus (24:13 ff.). That this meeting takes place "on the road" is in keeping with the journey motif of Luke. Furthermore, we hear twice in this episode about "the things that have happened" (24:14, 18); indeed, Jesus asks, "What things?" (24:19). These lines recall the Gospel's introduction, for this was to be a narrative about "the things which have been accomplished among us" (1:1; cf. 1:4).

The puzzle of this story is the initial nonrecognition of Jesus by the men. Perhaps they were kept from recognizing him because God willed it thus (vs. 16). Yet why should God want to keep them from recognizing Jesus? Probably they failed to recognize him because of their preoccupation with the tragic events of the preceding days (vss. 19–21). Jesus proceeds to interpret the scriptures to show that the Christ did have to suffer to enter into his glory (vss. 26 f.). Jesus' role in God's plan was that of a suffering servant (see 22:37; Isaiah 53:12). Even this disclosure, however, does not enable them to recognize Jesus, although later they recall, "Did not our hearts burn within us while he talked to us on the road, while he opened to us the scriptures?" (vs. 32).

The crucial moment of recognition comes only during the meal: "Their eyes were opened and they recognized him; and he vanished out of their sight" (vs. 31). Later their report confirms that the decisive act was "the breaking of the bread" (vs. 35). There are at least two immediate possibilities for understanding the significance of the "breaking of bread": (1) Jesus performed a familiar act which they had often observed; therefore, they recognized him. (2) The "breaking of bread" was a sacramental communal act of worship in the early church (Acts 2:42, 46), and Luke thereby implies that the believer knows the resurrected Jesus primarily in the sacrament of the church. Neither view is wholly satisfying. The first does not take account of the fact that Jesus must have done other familiar things on the way; and the second presupposes a strong sacramental emphasis not otherwise present in Luke.

A different interpretation also takes its cue from the act of eating. In the following story (24:36–43), even though Jesus appears directly to the disciples and tells them to look at his hands and feet, they still "disbelieved for joy" (vs. 41). Only after he has eaten does he speak his farewell address. Again, eating seems to be crucial for full recognition. The closest previous reference to eating was during the Last Supper with the apostles (22:14–19), at which Jesus said, "I have earnestly desired to eat this passover with you before I suffer; for I tell you I shall not eat it until it is fulfilled in the kingdom of God" (vss. 15 f.; only in Luke). Evidently, Jesus will not eat until suffering is accomplished. That he now eats with the disciples indicates that his suffering has been completed and that he is now raised to glory. Therefore, in Luke the scripture interpretation emphasizes the necessity for suffering (24:26 f.), and the eating with the disciples (24:30, 35, 42 f.) emphasizes that the suffering is accomplished and the glory of Jesus has begun. With that sure foundation, the church can now receive its charge from the risen Christ.

Jesus' final words to the disciples suggest the plausibility of this interpretation (24:44–49). The redemption of Israel is effected by Jesus' suffering, which fulfills scripture (vss. 45 f.). Repentance and forgiveness of sins are to be preached beginning from Jerusalem and extending to all the world (vs. 47). The witnesses who have observed and who will now testify await only the coming of the Spirit (vss. 48 f.; cf. Acts 1:8). Because Jesus' word and deed are now accomplished and because his followers can continue the witness, the new Israel returns to the temple with joy and with Jesus' blessing (24:50–53).

"Supper at Emmaus" by Rembrandt (1606–1669). (Courtesy of Alinari Art Reference Bureau.)

In summary, the purpose of the Gospel of Luke, like that of Mark and Matthew, is religious proclamation and reflection, not simply historical reporting. This characterization does not mean that there is no history recorded in Luke. Of all the Gospel writers Luke is the most consciously interested in preserving the truth about the life of Jesus. But for him, as for most historians in the first century, truth is not simply equated with historical data. Luke intended for his reader to see the life of Jesus through a proper perspective, that of the third generation. He wrote so that careful observation and a comprehensive outlook would be available to the church of his day. As a convenient means of bringing together results, we shall now review this presentation in light of our four approaches to understanding a Gospel:

The *structure* of Luke is distinctive. Only Luke follows his Gospel about Jesus with a second volume on the early church. In itself this structure indicates Luke's interest not only in Jesus, but also in the church which he originated. A long-range perspective on the life of Jesus is also suggested by the preface, where Luke writes of three stages of the tradition: eyewitnesses, ministers of the word, and writing of the Gospel.

In Luke's introduction Simeon, a man of Israel who has long awaited salvation, is finally rewarded by Jesus' appearance to him in the temple. Toward the close of his life Jesus frequents the temple and, in effect, triumphs in this central religious institution of Israel. After Jesus' death and resurrection the disciples return to the temple to wait for the coming of the Spirit, which will empower their preaching of repentance and forgiveness to all people. Their testimony to Jesus' message is certain because they have observed its beginning from Galilee to Jerusalem.

This overall view of Luke is confirmed by the threefold division of the Gospel itself: gathering witnesses in Galilee (3:1–9:50), witness to the word on the journey to Jerusalem (9:51–19:27), and the establishment of the true Israel through the passion and resurrection (19:28–24:53). These main divisions show how the old is incorporated into the new. Israel is on a journey through the Old Testament culminating in the life of Jesus and moving into the early church. Luke's structure is devised to ensure that the journey has been recorded closely and presented in the correct order.

The frequent *emphases* of Luke confirm our proposed structure for the Gospel. A classification of emphases, though somewhat artificial, does help to clarify Luke's major points of interest. These include the new faith as the true Israel, the history of salvation's expansion to include world history, and the necessity for accurate and continuous witness.

Luke affirms that the new religion is the true Israel. What happened to Jesus occurred according to the word of God, known through the Old Testament. Thus Jesus' first public act was to preach fulfillment of the prophet Isaiah in the synagogue at Nazareth (4:16 ff.). Moreover, at the resurrection appearances Jesus interpreted his suffering as a fulfillment of scriptures (24:27, 44). These things are presented as sure because all were predicted and foretold in the scriptures. The witness of Jesus began and ended with correct interpretation of the scripture. A further emphasis supporting the theme of "the true Israel" is the centrality accorded the temple and Jerusalem. The Gospel opens with Zechariah in the temple in Jerusalem; at the introduction's close, Jesus is placed in Jerusalem in the temple. The journey section of the Gospel moves toward Jerusalem, "he set his face to go to Jerusalem" (9:51; cf. 13:33). The passion centers primarily on Jesus' teaching in the temple (19:47 f.). In addition, the Gospel closes with the disciples' return to the temple in Jerusalem (24:52 f.). This elaborate picture of Jesus in the temple and in Jerusalem implies that Jesus embodies the true Israel and that his followers are the authentic people of God.

The character of this New Israel as the nonsubversive, legitimate extension of the old receives confirmation in the elaborate detail showing Jesus' innocence of any wrongdoing. Jesus did not forbid the paying of tribute to Rome (20:19–26). Rome, both Pilate and the centurion, proclaimed the innocence of Jesus (23:4, 14 ff., 22, 47); the repentant thief declared Jesus free of any wrongdoing (23:41). This theme of innocence is extended and enlarged in Acts, particularly in Luke's portrayal of the favorable disposition of Rome to the new religious movement. Paul is declared thoroughly and completely innocent (Acts 25:25; 26:31 f.). Indeed, Luke-Acts may be viewed in part as an apology to Christians on behalf of Rome (contrast Revelation's view of Rome as the beast). Certainly any educated Roman reader would conclude that Christianity and Rome were not at cross-purposes.

The second major emphasis of Luke is that the true Israel aims to embrace the whole world. For Luke, the world outside Israel is not an adversary, but a mission field: Luke-Acts progresses from Galilee to Jerusalem and on to Rome. Furthermore, Luke records traces of world history (2:1; 3:1; also Acts 24:27) to keep this final goal in mind. Involvement with the world occurs by God's acting in the Spirit through the person of Jesus (Luke) and eyewitnesses and ministers of the word (Acts) to bring "truth" to all people (Luke 24:47 and Acts 2:38 f.). Luke's Christianity is universalistic: Simeon speaks about salvation "to the Gentiles" (2:32); Jesus' genealogy goes back to Adam (3:38); and Jesus' opening preaching speaks favorably of Gentiles (4:24–29). Of course, the second volume shows the extension of the new religion beyond the confines of the old Israel (Acts 10:1–11:18).

The final major Lukan emphasis is witness (1:2), which consists of accurate observation (eyewitnesses) and truthful testifying (ministers of the word). Apostles, disciples, and women accompanied Jesus throughout his ministry; they in turn became, or were followed by, preachers who declared Jesus' own themes of repentance and forgiveness (Luke 15; 24:47; Acts 2:38). Forgiveness begins with the divine initiative, irrespective of human action; Jesus' actions embody this forgiveness in the present (7:48). Yet forgiveness elicts a human response of repentance. Whoever receives the forgiveness or mercy of God acts without anxiety for the future coming of God's judgment (cf. 19:1–10). In Jesus salvation becomes available (4:21; cf. 23:43); therefore, the ministers and preachers of the early church testify to what God has done in Jesus and continues to do. As witnesses they preach the "good news" (2:10; 3:18; 4:18; 7:22; 16:16) of forgiveness and repentance.

Luke's *redaction* of the tradition has been used consistently as a key in the establishment of Luke's emphases. Luke's shaping of Mark—for example, in the parables of the sower (8:4–21) and the wicked tenants (20:9–18)—disclosed his emphasis on the word of God (8:11) and the true Israel (20:9).

There have been many attempts to identify precisely the *histor-*

ical situation of Luke, none of them unexceptionable. Our interpretation, instead of precisely locating the historical situation in which Luke was written, views the Gospel generally as an apology. It was not designed primarily to convert the unbeliever, but speaks principally to Christians and "almost" Christians, showing the continuity and certainty of the Christian faith. According to Luke, the journey of Christian faith is made in joy and victory. The life and work of the church of Luke's time is authentic, according to the scriptures, because the true Israel is emerging and because the world is slowly and surely being Christianized. The forgiving Jesus is presented as standing both as the fulfillment of the old and the sure originator of the new. The witnesses have not been arbitrarily chosen; they were prepared for their task, and their present successes show the sweep and power of the new way.

Luke's Gospel has something of the romance about it. There are women, there are journeys and quests, there are successful adventures. At the end of the Gospel the disciples are in the temple blessing God and waiting for the Spirit's coming with power for the mission. At the end of Acts of the Apostles Paul is preaching in Rome and things will turn out well. Luke idealizes the story, perhaps, but he thereby testifies to the faith and history of Jesus and the early church. What was founded by Jesus, observed by the apostles, and proclaimed by them will continue without faltering until all have come into the kingdom of God and the fellowship of the Lord Jesus Christ "quite openly and unhindered" (Acts 28:31).

Suggestions for Further Reading

Worthwhile commentaries include A. R. C. Leaney, *A Commentary on the Gospel According to St. Luke* (New York: Harper & Row, 1958); G. B. Caird, *The Gospel of St. Luke* (Baltimore: Penguin, 1963); and E. E. Ellis, *The Gospel of Luke* (London: Nelson, 1966).

The most important single study of the theology of Luke-Acts is H. Conzelmann, *The Theology of St. Luke,* trans. G. Buswell (London: Faber & Faber, 1960). I. H. Marshall, *Luke: Historian and Theologian* (Grand Rapids, Mich.: Zondervan, 1971), and E. Franklin, *Christ the Lord: A Study in the Purpose and Theology of Luke-Acts* (Philadelphia: Westminster, 1975), take up from Conzelmann the task of attempting to understand Luke theologically, but wish nevertheless to qualify his approach in significant ways. C. H. Talbert, *Literary Patterns, Theological Themes, and the Genre of Luke-Acts* (Missoula, Montana: Scholars Press, 1974), undertakes a literary analysis of Luke on the basis of classical models. F. W. Danker, *Luke,* Proclamation Commentaries (Philadelphia: Fortress, 1976), represents a fresh approach to Luke in a Hellenistic setting. A valuable summary of scholarship is C. K. Barrett, *Luke the Historian in Recent Study* (London: Epworth, 1961). An important collection of articles on Luke, L. E. Keck and J. L. Martyn (eds.), *Studies in Luke-Acts* (Nashville, Tenn.: Abingdon, 1966), honors Professor Paul Schubert. Old, but still pertinent, H. J. Cadbury, *The Making of Luke-Acts* (New York: Macmillan, 1927), marked out the direction that the following generation of scholarship would take. See also Suggestions for Further Reading at the end of Chapter 7.

CHAPTER FIVE

The Gospel According to John: The Glory of Jesus

Of all the books of the New Testament, John's Gospel is perhaps the most intriguing and perplexing. It is intriguing because of its contents and the questions it raises, perplexing because of the seemingly insoluble nature of some of these same questions. We shall here deal briefly with only the most important problems.

1. The most obvious problem is the relation of John to the Synoptics. The Gospel of John differs widely from the other Gospels in a number of very specific ways. In John the geographical locus of Jesus' ministry is mainly Judea rather than Galilee; Jesus travels to Jerusalem more frequently; his ministry apparently takes place over a longer period; there are fewer, but more impressive miracle stories; and Jesus speaks in long discourses about himself and his mission. In addition, many events of the Synoptic accounts are missing in John. The omissions include Jesus' temptation, the messianic confession of Peter, the institution of the Lord's Supper, and the agony in Gethsemane. Conversely, much of what is found in John does not appear in the other Gospels—for example, the wine miracle at Cana, the long controversies with the Jews, the raising of Lazarus, and the extended farewell discourse and prayer with the disciples. In reading John after having studied the Synoptics one can quickly grasp the extent and nature of these differences and discover others. How are they to be explained? Did John know the other Gospels and attempt to supplement, correct, or replace them with his own? Or did he not know them, either because he lived in a remote place or because he wrote before the other evangelists—at least before he was able to see and digest their works?

2. Scholars once assumed that John, as the latest Gospel, must be explained on the assumption that the author knew the Synoptics and was in some way influenced by them. It is entirely possible, however, that both the differences and similarities of the material in John and the Synoptics may result in part from John's use of sources other than the Synoptics. Complex theories of John's sources have been advanced by modern scholars.[1] *Such theories, however, tend to collapse of their own weight and for lack of support external to the Gospel itself. Nevertheless, intensive research makes John's use of a narrative source or sources appear highly probable. Almost certainly he had a passion narrative other than Mark and drew upon a miracle tradition (perhaps a written source) different from, although related to, that found in the Synoptics. Whether he possessed a primitive narrative source which included not only Jesus' (miraculous) acts but also his passion is still a much debated question.*[2] *But sources cannot account for all John's differences from the Synoptics. For example, his language and style are much closer to the three Johannine Epistles (cf. pp. 435–441) than to the other Gospels. These writings must be the product of a common author or school.*

3. The most discussed questions in the history of modern Johannine research have to do with the identity of the evangelist and the date and place of composition.[3] *According to the ancient and generally accepted tradition of the church, the Fourth Gospel, as well as the Johannine Epistles and Revelation, are the work of the apostle John (presumably the son of Zebedee, although this is not always clearly stated in the early sources), who lived to a ripe old age in the city of Ephesus and composed the Gospel while residing there. But there are reasons for taking a skeptical attitude toward this tradition, and even in antiquity the Johannine authorship of Revelation was subject to doubt. First, our earliest sources are silent about any Ephesian residence of the apostle John. For example, in writing to the Ephesians at the beginning of the second century, Ignatius makes a great deal of Paul's connection with Ephesus, but says nothing about John's having lived there. Yet if the tradition is right, John lived in Ephesus much longer and later than did Paul, and the memory of him should have been much fresher. Second, John is not widely quoted by orthodox Christian writers until the end of the second century. This fact suggests that the acceptance of John's Gospel as scripture on a par with the other Gospels was not immediate. Moreover, we know that the Fourth Gospel was rejected completely in some quarters of the church. In the third place, traces of evidence indicate that John, the son of Zebedee, may have been martyred, perhaps at the same time as his brother James (Acts 12:2). How seriously one takes this evidence is likely to depend on whether one under-*

[1] The best known of which is R. Bultmann's, set forth in the course of exegesis in *The Gospel of John: A Commentary,* trans. G. R. Beasley-Murray et al. (Philadelphia: Westminster, 1971).

[2] The case for a primitive Gospel has been most carefully and forcefully argued by R. T. Fortna, *The Gospel of Signs: A Reconstruction of the Narrative Source Underlying the Fourth Gospel* (New York: Cambridge University Press, 1970).

[3] For a full discussion of these matters and a presentation of the relevant evidence, see C. K. Barrett, *The Gospel According to St. John: An Introduction with Commentary and Notes on the Greek Text,* 2nd ed. (Philadelphia: Westminster, 1978), pp. 100–134; also Raymond E. Brown, *The Gospel According to John (I–XII): Introduction, Translation, and Notes,* The Anchor Bible, 29 (Garden City, N.Y.: Doubleday, 1966), pp. lxxxvii–civ.

stands Mark 10:39 as a positive indication of the martyrdom of John as well as James. It is argued, with some force, that this saying of Jesus would not have been preserved had it not been fulfilled by the death of both James and John. Fourth and finally, the Gospel of John itself does not name the son of Zebedee as its author. It is often argued that the Gospel points unerringly in this direction. If, however, the ancient tradition of the church did not name John as the author, it is doubtful that one would think of him in connection with this Gospel. Some would say that John presents himself under the guise of the Beloved Disciple. But if this is so he presents himself incognito, for nowhere is the Beloved Disciple identified with John, not even in 21:24, where he is named the author of the Gospel. Furthermore, at least this verse, and probably all of chapter 21, is judged by many scholars as a later editorial addition to the original Gospel.

Although the date and place of composition must remain uncertain, especially if the tradition of Johannine authorship is doubtful, we are not completely at a loss in fixing the origin of the Gospel. The earliest certain evidence of its use (that is, commentaries, papyrus fragments, and the like) stems from Egypt, but in that dry climate such evidence had the best chance to survive. Those scholars who do not accept the traditional locus of Ephesus tend to favor a Near-Eastern, especially Syrian, rather than Egyptian origin. Although it can no longer be assumed that the Fourth Gospel is dependent on one or all of the other three, and is thus necessarily later, the situation of the church and the development of Christian thought that it reflects combine to indicate a date no earlier than about the last decade of the first century.[4]

4. Over and above the reasons for questioning the traditional view of Johannine authorship, there is the further question posed by the character of the Gospel itself. Does it represent an eyewitness report of Jesus' ministry? Probably not. If we take the Synoptic Gospels, especially the Synoptic tradition of Jesus' preaching, as a reliable guide to the way in which Jesus spoke and taught, then it is difficult to accept the Johannine picture of Jesus as historical in the strictest sense. The words of John's Jesus have a different aura about them. Thus even those who defend Johannine authorship usually acknowledge that the evangelist has by no means presented a verbatim account of Jesus' words and deeds, but has exercised a free hand in reinterpreting what Jesus actually said and did.[5]

5. Another problem that further complicates the picture is the religious and cultural background of the Fourth Gospel. From what milieu does it stem and to what sort of audience is it addressed? If the Gospel stems directly or indirectly from John, the son of Zebedee, a Palestinian background must be presupposed. The many differences from the Synoptics and the apparently Hellenistic language and thought of the Fourth Gospel once made a Palestinian origin appear impossible. The discovery of the

---

[4]Brown, *The Gospel According to John*, pp. lxxx–lxxxvi, esp. lxxxv. Cf. Barrett, *The Gospel According to St. John*, pp. 127–128. On the other hand, John A. T. Robinson argues for a date prior to A.D. 70, contending that the Jewish-Roman War and the destruction of the temple are not mentioned or presupposed; see *Redating the New Testament* (Philadelphia: Westminister, 1976), pp. 254–311.

[5]Ibid., pp. xcix–c.

Dead Sea Scrolls and the recognition that Palestinian Judaism of the first century took several forms and was not simply the prototype of rabbinic Judaism have meant that a Palestinian origin of the Johannine tradition no longer appears out of the question. At present the problem of the origin and background of the Fourth Gospel is vigorously debated, although there is increasingly a tendency to see John against some sort of Jewish background.

6. Uncertainty exists as to whether the canonical text of John has been partially rearranged and edited. Probably at least chapter 21 is a later addition. It may well be that chapters 5 and 6 once stood in reverse order, for reversing them eliminates a strange and unexplained alteration of Jesus' locale from Galilee (4:43 ff.) to Jerusalem (chap. 5) and back to Galilee (chap. 6). Moreover, 6:1 presupposes that Jesus has been in Galilee just previously. Nevertheless, we shall take as a starting point the Gospel in the form in which it lies before us in all Greek manuscripts and versions. The basic organization is rather simple:

OUTLINE OF JOHN

Introduction (1:1–51)
    The Prologue: Jesus Christ as the Word (1:1–18)
    The Revelation of Christ's Glory Before the World (2:1–12:50)
    The Healing of the Man Born Blind (9:1–41)
    The Revelation of Christ's Glory Before the Community (13:1–21:25)
    Jesus' Last Will: The Prayer of Consecration (17:1–26)

Introduction (1:1–51)

The Gospel of John falls into several rather well-defined parts. The first chapter stands apart from the body of the Gospel as a kind of introduction. It in turn falls into two major parts, the prologue, which is treated in some detail in the following paragraphs, and the witness of the Baptist to Jesus. Jesus receives the first disciples from John, who directs them to him. As they come, they quickly recognize or are told who Jesus is. The chapter ends on a note of expectation concerning the revelation of God in Jesus that will take place during his ministry. The prologue sets the stage for this revelation.

THE PROLOGUE: JESUS CHRIST AS THE WORD (1:1–18)

How does it help to explain Jesus to say that he is "the Word"?

The prologue of John is the traditional Gospel reading for Christmas Day, for the church has discerned that it expresses even more fully than the birth stories of Matthew and Luke the import of the coming of the Christ into the world.

Plaque from a tenth-century German or north Italian book cover. Agnus Dei displayed on a cross between emblems of the four evangelists—Matthew, the man; Mark, the lion; Luke, the ox; and John, the eagle. (Courtesy of Metropolitan Museum of Art. Gift of J. Pierpont Morgan, 1917.)

The rhythmic, almost poetic character of the prologue is easily perceived. There is, for example, a peculiar chainlike progression in the repetition of key words in verses 1–5 and 9–12. A recent translation admirably preserves both the strophic form and this chainlike sequence:

> In the beginning was the *Word;* the *Word* was in God's presence, and the *Word* was *God.*
> He was present with *God* in the beginning.
> Through him all things *came into being,* and apart from him not a thing *came to be.*
> That which had *come to be* in him was *life,* and this *life* was the *light* of men.
> The *light* shines on in the *darkness,* for the *darkness* did not overcome it.[6]

Although the sequence is not perfect, it is too pronounced to be coincidental and unintentional. This structure of the prologue is, however, broken by 1:6–8 and 15 (set off in RSV by a separate paragraph in the one case and by parentheses in the other), which refer not to the Word, the subject of the rest of the prologue, but to John the Baptist. In addition, several other verses (13, 17–18) do not seem to be a part of the basic structure. Quite likely we are here dealing with an early Christian hymn that the evangelist has annotated and incorporated into his Gospel. (Cf. Phil. 2:6–11; Col. 1:15–20; and I Tim. 3:16 for other such hymns.) The hymn might possibly be pre-Christian, but more likely the evangelist adopted a Christian hymn used by his own church. When the probable additions and annotations are stripped away, its language, style, and theology are nevertheless still "Johannine"; the basic hymn and the Gospel appear to share a common perspective and vocabulary.[7]

The RSV paragraphing offers an initial clue to the character and content of the prologue. As we can see, verses 1–5 are a literary unit, the first part of the prologue or hymn; verses 6–8 are a prosaic interlude. Then comes the second section of the hymn, verses 9–12(13), followed by the third and concluding section, verses 14–18 (less vs. 15, another prosaic interpolation). These divisions correspond

---

[6]Brown, *The Gospel According to John,* p. 3.

[7]Quite aside from its importance in the Gospel, this hymn is significant for another reason. Along with other similar passages in the New Testament, it shows that the earliest church had a lively and enthusiastic service of worship in prayer and song. On the analysis and background of New Testament hymns see Jack T. Sanders, *The New Testament Christological Hymns: Their Historical Religious Background* (New York: Cambridge University Press, 1971). While there is considerable agreement on the existence of a hymn behind the Johannine prologue, C. K. Barrett, *New Testament Essays* (London: SPCK, 1972), pp. 27–48, sees no compelling reason to postulate it.

roughly to the thematic divisions of the prologue. In verses 1–5 the theme is God, creation, and the Word; in verses 6–8, John the Baptist; in verses 9–13, the Word in the world; and in verses 14–18, the community's confession of the Word.

This structure, however, only raises the basic questions of the meaning of the prologue and its relation to the rest of the Gospel. An answer to these questions has to proceed initially by way of an analysis of the key term *Word* (Greek, *logos*). Who or what is the Word? In the first place, the Word is Jesus Christ. When this is said, however, several related questions are cast into sharp relief. In verses 1–5 does the author intend to speak of the man Jesus of Nazareth? He can hardly mean that Jesus of Nazareth was with God before all creation and that he was the mediator of all creation. Where, moreover, does this concept of the Word originate? It is perhaps to be understood against the background of Greek philosophy, in which the term and concept of *logos* were quite important. Or it might be seen against the background of the Old Testament and Jewish concept of the word of the Lord. It is clear that the Word *denotes* Jesus Christ; what more it means remains to be determined.

The Greek philosophical meaning of *logos* is not related directly to John's use of the term. The Stoic understanding of *logos* as the world principle has little or nothing to do with the Word which is Jesus Christ. Nevertheless, the fact that the Greek term *logos* comprehends such varied meanings as explanation, argument, principle, thought or reason, language, speech, and divine utterance is relevant. So is the use of the term in late Jewish and pagan religious texts to designate God's agent in creation and world government. This last usage occurs especially in Jewish texts influenced by Greek thought, where word is sometimes identified with wisdom (Greek, *sophia*) as God's agency of communication with the world. It is clear enough that the *logos* of John is God's speech, his self-disclosure to the world, and, as the text makes plain, the means through which God creates. This range of meaning is the background of the author's usage.

In regard to the Old Testament and Jewish concept of the word of God, the idea that the word which God spoke through the prophets was now incarnate in Jesus Christ is a proposition to which John would doubtless have assented. But nothing in the text indicates that precisely this thought was at the center of his attention. Still, the most obvious and immediate background of the concept of the Word is the creation story of Genesis 1, which also opens with the phrase "in the beginning." Like Genesis, John speaks of the creation. Although Genesis does not say that God created all things by the Word, it does portray each stage of creation as resulting from God's speaking. "And God said, 'Let there be light'; and there was light" (Genesis 1:3). The fact that in Genesis God first creates light is paralleled by John's emphasis on light throughout the prologue. Moreover, the motifs of darkness and light appear together in both places. In Genesis God speaks and there is light where darkness had heretofore prevailed; and God separates the light from the darkness (1:3–5). This then leads to an account of the beginning of night and day. In John's prologue, however, the distinction between light and darkness develops into a sharply defined dualism, which is characteristic of the Gospel as a whole. That is, a sharp distinction is drawn between the forces of light and darkness, truth and falsehood, God and Satan, and so on. Such a dualism was common not only to Zoroastrianism, Gnosticism, and late Platonism, but also to certain forms of Judaism. That such a dualistic world view could arise even within the bounds of first-century Palestinian Judaism has been shown by the discovery of the Qumran scrolls in which a dualistic view of the world, men, and events very similar to that of the Gospel of John is presented. The similarity between John and Genesis reveals the common ground on which they stand. But the strikingly different dualism of John is equally significant, for it shows that John belongs in the first-century religious world.

Nevertheless, it would be wrong to leave the impression that understanding the prologue first requires understanding the Greek use of *logos*, the Old Testament creation story, or first-century sectarian Judaism. All these are helpful, but John speaks clearly and directly apart from those contexts. After all, John has always been a popular Gospel for Christians, most of whom have not had the faintest conception of its historical background.

The major reason John speaks plainly is that he intends to speak only about Jesus Christ. His choice of terminology and the use of motifs from the Genesis creation story turn upon his purpose of setting forth the meaning and significance of Jesus. This holds true even though the name Jesus does not occur until the end (vs. 17). Of course, a Christian reader would know that the Word was Jesus Christ before he read further in the Gospel. Yet the name of Jesus is not called until the prologue has moved from the cosmic or the metaphysical plane to the historical.

The movement from the rather abstract, if dramatic and impressive, talk about the *logos* to the level of historical events takes place by stages. Verses 1 and 2 deal with the relation of the Word to God, which is defined in the closest possible terms without John's saying that *logos* and God are simply equivalents. The statement, "And the Word was God," is immediately qualified by "He was in the beginning with God." In addition, the Greek of the former statement lacks the definite article (*ho* = "*the*") before "God," which indicates something less than a total identification of the word with God.[8]

[8] The key phrase is translated variously: "the Word was God" (Douay, Jerusalem, KJV, RSV); "what God was, the Word was" (NEB); "the Logos was divine" (Moffatt); and "the Word was divine" (Goodspeed).

Still, in verses 3 and 4 the most exalted status and functions are attributed to the Word.

At this point we can scarcely avoid asking whether the evangelist actually thought that Jesus created the world. That the *man* Jesus was the agent by whom God created the world is a strange idea. For New Testament faith, however, Jesus Christ is not simply to be equated with the historical man Jesus of Nazareth (cf. I Cor. 8:6; Phil. 2:6 f.; Col. 1:15 f.; Heb. 1:2 f.), although he is inseparable from him. He is the Son of God, the Word of God, the Christ, the Son of Man. In him God reveals himself to and acts on behalf of humankind in a decisive way. The terms and categories that we find appropriate to describe historical persons and events can no longer quite comprehend him. In him the God who creates the world now saves it from its evil and folly. God's action in creation and redemption are one. Over against any purely otherworldly spirituality John affirms that the Word by which God creates the world is the same Word by which he redeems it. This Word can be identified with a special historical person and event, Jesus, whom John will name before the prologue is complete. The God who creates through his Word also reveals himself and saves through the same Word. Since the coming of Jesus Christ, this Word cannot be conceived apart from him.

Whether verse 5 refers to the Word as it was already present in creation at the beginning and throughout history or to the Word revealed in Jesus is the next question.[9] Interpreters have never agreed. Probably John intends the statement to apply to Jesus Christ as the Word become flesh. Yet the prologue could be read down to verse 14 under the assumption that the author is speaking of God's activity through his Word first in creation (vss. 1–4) and then in revelation— that is, the word of the Lord to the Old Testament prophets and seers. In verses 10–13, however, it becomes increasingly clear that the evangelist must have had Jesus Christ already in view, although the non-Christian reader of the Gospel might not have realized this. This contention is supported by the position of the passage dealing with the Baptist (vss. 6–8). The Baptist comes before Jesus, preparing his way. Thus it would be natural to suppose that the mention of the Baptist leads directly to the first explicit reference to Jesus' coming (vss. 9 ff.), or, conversely, that the first suggestion of Jesus' presence in the world, if that is to be found in verse 5, evokes the recollection of John the Baptist.

The treatment of John (vss. 6–8) is most interesting. He is a man

---

[9] It is possible that the Greek *katelaben* (RSV, "overcome") in verse 5 should be translated "comprehended," in the sense of "understood." This would make the verse closely parallel to verses 10 and 11. It is not impossible that the author realizes the ambiguity of the term and intentionally uses it to convey both meanings.

sent from God and a witness sent beforehand that all people, or at least all Israel, might believe. The place of John as forerunner is already fixed by the earlier tradition, and it is here accepted in principle. Yet the evangelist also finds it necessary to say that the Baptist is not the light (vs. 8), probably indicating that already (vs. 5) he understands the light to be Jesus himself. This and subsequent negative statements about the Baptist in which he denies he is the Christ may represent a subtle polemic against certain of John's disciples. That there were disciples of the Baptist is clear enough from the Gospels (cf. also Acts 18:25). John's Gospel affords the most tangible evidence that there was an actual rivalry between the early church and the Baptist sect,[10] but otherwise the New Testament evidence permits few firm conclusions as to the nature of the Baptist sect or of that rivalry. In any event, the evangelist wishes to emphasize the singular importance of Jesus by asserting his superiority to any possible rival. The witness of John the Baptist appears again in verse 15 (cf. vs. 30). The fact that John should be introduced somewhat awkwardly at this point to make his witness suggests that verse 15, like verses 6–8, is an interpolation. Moreover, we observe the same polemical interest at work here. John bears witness as much against himself as for Jesus.

At verse 9, John shifts back into the poetic style and returns to the themes of the first five verses, as he thinks of the coming of Jesus Christ into the world (vss. 9–13). In verse 10, the "world" is used in two different senses: divine creation ("the world was made through him") and the world of men apart from God ("the world knew him not"). Of the two the second is characteristic of the Fourth Gospel and I John, where it implies the world in alienation from God. His own people is Israel, the Jews (vs. 11). The ways in which they reject him are put forth in the first half of the Gospel (chaps. 2–12), especially the closing verses of chapter 12. By their rejection of Jesus, the Jews become the prime representatives of the world in the negative sense. In the last half of the Gospel, this world, whether Jew or Gentile, forms the hostile background against which Jesus gathers together his community of disciples, the church. Although "the world" sums up human opposition to Jesus in John, there is another sense in which the world is the object of

---

[10] Such a rivalry may also be implied by such passages as Luke 7:18–35 and 11:1, although their tone is by no means so clearly polemical as John's. Followers of John the Baptist continued as a sect within Judaism throughout the first Christian centuries. Acts reports that Paul encountered some disciples of John at Ephesus, who were distinguished from Jesus' followers in that their baptism did not include the gift of the Holy Spirit (Acts 19:1–7). The Mandaean religious movement, which still exists in Iran, holds John the Baptist in high esteem and may have originated from a Baptist sect. See C. H. Dodd, *The Interpretation of the Fourth Gospel* (New York: Cambridge University Press, 1953), pp. 115–130.

God's love in sending Jesus (3:16). Thus overcoming the world (16:33) is not only defeating it, but ultimately saving it.

Now (vss. 12 f.) the evangelist speaks of those who receive Jesus—that is, "believe in his name." As in the Old Testament "name" is more than just the verbal designation. It signifies the reality and importance of the person as an individual. To believe in Jesus' name is, therefore, not merely to confess him verbally, but to have faith in who and what he is. To all who so believe, Jesus gives power or authority (Greek, *exousia*) to become children of God. Such children of God are born through no human agency, but through the will of God (see chap. 3). In John those who are begotten by God are begotten by faith.

After John 3:16, 1:14 is probably the most cited passage in the Fourth Gospel. In the history of theology, it has proven to be extremely suggestive. It is the prime scriptural basis for belief in the Incarnation, the Christian doctrine that in Jesus God became man. Against any Gnostic or docetic watering down of the full humanity of the Word, John 1:14 stands as an impregnable bulwark. In contrast to the modern state of mind that looks with skepticism upon any claims of manifestations of God in human life and history, ancient peoples were, by and large, willing and able to entertain a variety of such claims. Thus the idea that God had in some form dwelt among the people was not so likely to give offense. What would be novel and potentially offensive both to Jew and to Greek was the claim that God, or at least the Word, had become flesh—that is, a real, mortal man. Therefore the claim that the one who fully reveals God is nevertheless a man whose origins can be accounted for quite naturally (cf. 1:45 f; 7:15, 41, 52; 8:48) is a constant source of consternation and offense throughout the first half of the Fourth Gospel. John's statement that the Word became flesh is unique in the New Testament. Nevertheless, it does not stand out as a strange or foreign body. If anything, the reverse is true; John 1:14 has been taken to be a kind of summation of the New Testament view of Christ. The interpretation of the meaning and significance of Jesus as presented in the whole range of New Testament teaching is aptly epitomized in John's statement that the Word became flesh.

The Word not only became flesh or human, Jesus as a man was "full of grace and truth." Here a distinctively Pauline term, *grace* is combined with the distinctively Johannine *truth*. By the time John wrote, *grace* was probably a part of the standard Christian vocabulary, a brief but meaningful way of referring to all God had done in Jesus. Although the word *truth* was certainly not strange to Christian ears, John is noteworthy for the way in which he applies the term to Jesus himself. It becomes a virtual synonym for Jesus in his solemn manifestation as the Christ. "I am the way, the truth, and the life," says Jesus to Thomas and the other disciples in the farewell discourses (14:6). Jesus is truth. In John this does not mean he is the right in contrast to the wrong, or the correct in contrast to the erroneous, not even the true in contrast to the false in the usual sense. Rather, he is the real, even the divine reality, in contrast to everybody and everything that is false and deceptive.[11] In short, he is the one upon whom all people can depend, and who will not let them down, in contrast to all the false supports and securities of life.

Preoccupation with the doctrine of the Incarnation has nevertheless meant that the rest of this verse (vs. 14) has not received the attention it deserves. The fact of Jesus Christ's coming is not introduced, but summarized, in the statement that the Word became flesh. Although the significance of this statement as a concise summation of Christian belief about Jesus is clear, the latter half of the verse is important in the development of the Gospel. Not only has this gracious and true man dwelt among the people, but they—or at least some of them—have really seen him. That is, they have seen him for who he is. Thus, *"We* have beheld his glory. . . ." (Note the change to the first person plural, signifying the witnessing and believing community.) His glory is the presence and activity of God in him. In Judaism *glory* is the shining radiance of God's presence, once thought to dwell in the temple. The verb *dwell* in this same verse has the more specific meaning of "to pitch a tent," "to tabernacle." According to Jewish tradition God dwelt in his temple as in a tabernacle or tent. Indeed, the ancient predecessor of the Jerusalem temple was a tabernacle or tent, and according to the Old Testament, God's glory, name, or presence dwelt there. Thus the dwelling of the Word among us and the beholding of the glory are ideas with a prior relationship in Jewish thought. Against this background the thrust of the evangelist's statements becomes even clearer. Jesus is the new temple or tabernacle, the new place where God manifests himself to man, where his glory is beheld (cf. 2:19–22). The description of this glory, "as of the only Son from the Father," is typically Johannine. In John, Jesus is the Son and God is his father in a special sense.

Where or how is this glory to be manifest? Only the Gospel proper can answer this question. The first half of the Gospel provides a partial answer. The glory is manifest in the word and deeds of Jesus, which in John are called signs. Chapters 2–12 relate these manifestations of the glory (cf. 2:11). The use of miracles as signs of Jesus' glory in John seemingly sets that Gospel in sharp contrast to the Synoptics, for in the latter Jesus refuses to do miracles as signs in this sense. Yet Jesus' glory is not simply his miraculous power. The supreme manifestation of his glory is his death on the cross (cf. esp. 12:23 ff.).

When John writes, "We have beheld his glory," he refers to the

---

[11] See R. Bultmann's article on *alētheia,* etc., in G. Kittel, *TDNT,* I, pp. 245 ff.

apostolic *we* (cf. I John 1:1 ff.). The authoritative witness in the
church attests the glory of Christ. The "we have beheld" is founded
upon the apostolic eyewitness of Jesus Christ, but is not limited to
it. The physical seeing of Jesus is not disparaged by the author, but
in itself it is of no particular advantage. Faith has direct access to
Jesus. At the end of the Gospel, Jesus says to "doubting Thomas,"
who has just received physical evidence of his resurrection, "Have
you believed because you have seen me? Blessed are those who have
not seen and yet believe" (20:29). Moreover, genuine seeing is not
confined to physical sight, but involves true perception of the nature
of a person or thing (cf. chaps. 9 and 14). "We have beheld his glory,"
therefore, does not simply vouch for the apostolicity or authenticity
of an eyewitness standing behind the Gospel. The "we" who speak
are not necessarily first-generation Christians or the disciples of the
historical Jesus, but all those who have rightly perceived the Word
of God in Jesus Christ and have thereby beheld his glory.

After the Baptist interpolation (vs. 15), the theme of the incarnate glory is again taken up (vs. 16). The fact that here the *we* so
obviously means the Christian community implies that the whole
church is also included in the *we* of verse 14. The fullness (vs. 16) is
presumably the fullness of grace and truth in the Word become flesh
(vs. 14). This is confirmed by the concluding phrase "grace upon
grace," which probably ought to be understood in the sense of "grace
abounding." Jesus and Moses are then set over against one another
in almost Pauline fashion, with Moses representing the law and
grace and truth again associated with Jesus Christ (vs. 17). Only now
is Jesus actually named, and his identity with the Word put beyond
question. In a skillful way the prologue leads the reader up to the
point at which Jesus' name is called, although almost from the beginning the Christian reader would have recognized who was in
view. The dramatic sense, manifest throughout the Gospel, appears
at the outset as the evangelist builds toward the climax of the prologue. Although the polarity between Moses as lawgiver and Jesus
as the source of grace and truth occupies an important place in the
prologue, it is not prominent in the rest of the Gospel. The central
problem for Paul, the relation of law and grace, has apparently become for John a thing of the past. Later he calls the law "your law,"
implying that the law as such is now considered only an aspect or
institution of the Jewish religion (8:17). Yet there is in the Fourth
Gospel a recurring juxtaposition of Jesus and Moses, in which Jesus
emerges as the superior.[12]

The concluding verse (18) presents a textual problem because all

[12] W. A. Meeks, *The Prophet-King: Moses Traditions and the Johannine Christology* (Leiden: Brill, 1967), provides a very rich and helpful investigation of Jewish
traditions about Moses which may have influenced the Fourth Gospel.

the ancient manuscripts do not agree. Probably the reading *God* (RSV, footnote) is to be preferred over *Son*, even though *only Son* accords somewhat better with John's usage elsewhere.[13] Then we would have to read "only begotten God," or the like. Jesus as only begotten God would not, however, be an impossible concept for John, particularly in view of his understanding of him as the creating and revealing Word. The point is clear enough. That no one had ever seen God would have been a commonplace to the educated Jew or the sophisticated Greek, and it is surely not the author's principal purpose to enlighten the reader on this point. Instead he points once again to the definitive character of the revelation of God in Christ: "he has made him known." In a real sense, verse 18 reiterates the burden of the message of verses 14–17. The glory of God is manifest for the salvation of all people in Jesus. Possibly it is significant that the evangelist maintains that no one has seen God and does not claim that now in Jesus he is seen. Jesus does later say, "He who has seen me has seen the Father" (14:9); however, this statement occurs after extensive exposition on the theme of the subordinate relation of Christ to God. It is made to the disciples and presupposes the Johannine notion of seeing as truly perceiving. Moreover, it is clear from the immediate context that it does not imply a one-to-one identity of Jesus and the Father.

As verse 14 points forward to the revelation of the glory in Jesus' public ministry and finally his death, verses 16–18 point to the revelation of the glory of God in a fuller, more immediate way to the Christian church, the community of Jesus' disciples. For if the end of Jesus' public ministry is his rejection (12:37–43) and death, the end of his more intimate concluding revelations to his disciples is their believing, seeing, and knowing (chap. 17). Yet John knows that this fuller knowledge did not actually occur during Jesus' earthly life. Both the farewell discourses and certain sayings in the first part of the Gospel (2:22; 7:39; 12:16) point forward to Jesus' death and the period thereafter. The time of the resurrection, the Spirit, and the church is the time when the meaning and significance of his life and death is to be understood and appreciated more fully by his own followers.

[13]Both the manuscript evidence and the logic of textual criticism ("Prefer the harder reading or the one which best explains the others") argue in favor of this reading. Its existence in a very early papyrus manuscript (p 66) indicates that it could not have been introduced to combat the later Arian heresy.

The Revelation of Christ's Glory Before the World (2:1–12:50)

The public ministry of Jesus in the Fourth Gospel is characterized by signs and controversy. Both are found in the other Gospels, but in John the signs are principally revelatory miracles. Parables and other forms of public teaching, familiar from the Synoptics, are notable for their absence from John. Jesus does not teach a hostile world, but confronts it with his astonishing deeds and lofty claims. The account of the healing of the man born blind in chapter 9 typifies these characteristics of the Fourth Gospel.

THE HEALING OF THE MAN BORN BLIND (9:1–41)

How do the miracle stories of the Fourth Gospel present its message?

The miracle stories of the Fourth Gospel are distinctive. They are significantly fewer than in the Synoptic Gospels, but nevertheless more important, for they are signs manifesting Jesus' glory. The sheerly miraculous element seems heightened in John, yet the acts themselves are no more sensational than they are in the other Gospels. John, however, develops each story more fully by showing Jesus talking with bystanders and opponents about the implications of the miracle. This Johannine emphasis upon the explanatory discourses of Jesus reflects his concentration on the miracles as "signs"—pointers to the nature and mission of Jesus (see 6:26 ff. and cf. 20:30 f.).

The Fourth Gospel also employs a somewhat different set of miracle stories. The transformation of water into wine at Cana (2:1–12) has no parallel in the Synoptics; nor do the stories of the Samaritan woman (chap. 4—Jesus' knowledge of her past is miraculous), the man at the sheep gate pool (chap. 5), the man born blind (chap. 9), and the raising of Lazarus (chap. 11). Jesus' foreknowledge of Nathanael (1:45–51) may also be miraculous; in any case it also has no parallel. On the other hand, the bread miracle (6:1–14), the walking on the water (6:16–21), and the healing of the ruler's son (4:46–54) have definite Synoptic parallels (cf. Mark 6:32–44; 6:45–51; and Matt. 8:5–10, respectively). Other incidents—including the passion—have clear Synoptic parallels but are not miraculous (cf. 2:13–22; 12:1–11; 12:12–19; 13:21–30). Of the miracle stories found only in John, those of chapters 5 and 9 are similar to several Synoptic stories. The changing of water into wine, however, is a feat unparalleled in the Synoptics, where Jesus' miracles are characteristically healings or demon exorcisms. Of the latter there is not one in John. Although Jesus raises the dead in the Synoptics, there is nothing like the elaborate story of the raising of Lazarus anywhere else in the New Testament.

Some significance has to be attached to the arrangement of the miracle stories in John. Although there is no systematic progression from one to another, most are especially suited for their positions in the Gospel. The miracle of the new wine symbolically introduces Jesus' public ministry. The story of Jesus' revelation to the Samaritan woman (chap. 4) stands directly over against the inability of Nicodemus, the teacher of Israel, to grasp his meaning (chap. 3). The miracles of chapters 5 and 6 are integrally related to the long dialogues that follow them. The most artfully constructed and theologically pregnant of the miracle stories (chaps. 9 and 11) appear last. In the one, Jesus restores the gift of sight (light), and in the other, life. The raising of Lazarus from the dead (chap. 11) gives concreteness to Jesus' claim that "as the Father raises the dead and gives them life, so also the Son gives life to whom he will" (5:21). Thus this miracle graphically portrays the character of his mission and work. Moreover, it leads directly to Jesus' own death, which, paradoxically, is the source of life to all who believe.

Because of its distinctly Johannine character, the story of the restoration of sight to the blind man (chap. 9) merits further attention. In both style and content it is typical of the Fourth Gospel. The first paragraph (9:1–12) is in many respects similar to the Synoptic miracle stories. The story is introduced with only the vaguest kind of connection with the preceding scene. Such an introduction is common in the Synoptics. The idea that sickness or deformity is punishment for sin (vss. 2 f.; cf. vs. 34) is an ancient one, and dies hard (cf. Luke 13:1–5). Although Jesus rejects it (vs. 3), his own interpretation of the man's blindness is scarcely more acceptable to modern humanitarianism. Here we have one of two remarkable parallels to chapter 11, where the sickness of Lazarus is said to be for the glory of God and of the Son (11:4). The point, however, is not that God deforms people to show his own power, but that in and through such misfortune the power of God vindicates itself (cf. Genesis 50:20). The second parallel (vss. 4 f.) corresponds to 11:9 f. Here, and probably also in 11:9 f., we are dealing with a subtle allusion to the coming death of Jesus. Already its inevitability has been indicated by passing references of the evangelist (2:22; 7:39) and by the attitude of the Jews in controversy with Jesus (5:18; 8:37, 40, 59). Now as the public ministry draws toward its close, Jesus' last acts of healing are placed under the shadow of the cross. That Jesus says, "I am the light of the world" (vs. 5), shows the close connection between the prologue and the Gospel proper. This statement of Jesus belongs to a group of "I am" sayings which are distinctive of the Fourth Gospel (6:35; 10:11; 11:25; 14:6; 15:1). These sayings express the Johannine view that Jesus proclaims himself and his dignity. By contrast, in the Synoptics Jesus proclaims not himself, but the kingdom of God, and such "I am" statements are seldom if ever found.

The miracle itself is described briefly and with restraint (vss. 6 f.). In Mark also Jesus is said to heal with spittle (8:23); once in Luke (17:12–15) the healing likewise takes place after Jesus has sent the persons involved away. The pool of Siloam, where Jesus sent the man, has actually been located in modern times. For the evangelist,

The pool of Siloam of Jesus' time is still in use in Jerusalem today. (Courtesy of Arab Information Center.)

however, the significant thing about the pool was the meaning of its name, "sent." Throughout the Gospel Jesus is described as the one sent by God (e.g., 3:17). The man's obedience to Jesus and the results are described as succinctly as possible. In fact, the basic miracle story is much less elaborate and detailed than are many similar stories in the Synoptic tradition. This may indicate that John possessed a primitive miracle story in simple form. At least it shows that in this instance he was not interested in the details of the miracle (contrast 11:38–44).

We have already seen (vss. 4 f.; possibly vs. 3) examples of the evangelist's own additions to this simple story. From verse 8 onward we lose track of the older story almost completely. There is now a dialogue, mostly in Johannine style and principally concerned with questions fundamental to Johannine theology. At most, the Synoptic miracle stories concisely report the reaction to Jesus' miracles. By contrast, John's main interest is quite obviously in the theological issues that arise as a consequence of the miracle. His emphasis is reflected in the literary form; a traditional story forms the basis of, and affords the springboard for, a developed dialogue. The dialogue, unlike anything in the Synoptics, is quite typical of John. Much the same pattern of event plus interpretation may be observed in Chapters 5 and 6, and a variation upon it in chapter 11, where a traditional miracle story has apparently been interlaced with Johannine dialogue and discourse. In fact, something of the same style appears also in chapters 3 (Nicodemus) and 4 (the Samaritan woman). In both instances a meeting between Jesus and another person leads into a dialogue or a dialogue and discourse, and in each case the conversation develops just those themes that the evangelist wishes to emphasize. On a smaller scale this occurs in connection with the cleansing of the temple (2:13–22). On a considerably larger scale chapters 13 through 17 may be interpreted as conforming to this pattern. There the events of the Last Supper, especially the washing of the disciples' feet and the identification of Judas as the betrayer of Jesus, lead into an extensive dialogue and discourse. Something of the same phenomenon occurs in the trial scene, where the arraignment before Pilate, recounted in the Synoptics, provides the occasion for a uniquely Johannine account of the conversation between Jesus and the Roman procurator. Even in the resurrection story (chap. 20) the evangelist does not end the Gospel with an account of the empty tomb (Mark) or a vision of the risen Lord and a commission (Matthew and Luke). Instead, the risen Jesus engages in dialogue with Thomas, and his last word—virtually the last word of the Gospel—is his response to him (20:29). Even in the appendix (chap. 21) the same pattern appears, with Peter and Jesus engaged in conversation and Jesus' final word addressed to him. The emphases of the Synoptic Gospels are usually implicit in the choice, structure, and editing of the material. In John, however, such points become explicit and even tend to occupy the center of the stage. The evangelist makes the issues clear and at the same time shows that they are rooted in the words and work of the historical Jesus.

After the account of the healing, there are several interrogations of the blind man (9:8–12, 13–17, 18–23, 24–34). First the man's neighbors question him (vss. 8 ff.), then the Pharisees (vss. 13–17). Then the man's parents are questioned by the Jews (vss. 18–23). Finally, the Jews return to question the man himself a second time (vss. 24–34). Probably no distinction is to be drawn between Pharisees and Jews in this instance. John's characteristic designation of those who oppose Jesus and his work is simply "the Jews." When he does mention a particular sect of Judaism it is the Pharisees. The reason for this is not obvious. If, however, John was written after the Roman war (A.D. 70), the main Jewish opponents of Christianity would have been Pharisees. The other principal sects, Sadducees, Zealots, and Essenes, had been either dissolved or sharply reduced in size and influence as a result of that conflict. Therefore, John's reference to the Pharisees is probably an indication that they were the group most actively competing with or opposing Christianity at the end of the first century. We shall see some indication that this is the case before the end of this chapter. By contrast, the Synoptic material still views Jesus' ministry from the standpoint of Palestinian Judaism before the destruction of the temple, although the evangelists themselves may reflect a later time and other places.

A brief narrative (vss. 8–12) reports more of the healed man's background and conveys the astonishment and even disbelief of his neighbors (vss. 8 f.). The man calmly and certainly identifies himself as the blind beggar whom they have known, and describes how and by whom he has been healed. As the story progresses, this man's modest but unwavering certainty is noteworthy. Here, as elsewhere, he possesses no theoretical or other knowledge about his benefactor. He knows only that the man called Jesus has healed him.

When brought before the Pharisees (vss. 13–17), the man's certainty and simplicity are impressive (vs. 15). For the first time we learn that the healing had been performed on the day of the sabbath (vs. 14), a common feature of the Synoptic tradition, where Jesus is more than once accused of illegally performing healings—and therefore working—on the sabbath (cf. also John 5). The division among the Pharisees (vs. 16) is typical of the division that Jesus causes. Some people reject him out of hand, because he violates their preconceptions of what a holy or righteous man must be: "He does not keep the sabbath." Others are at least open to the testimony of his works, to see them as "signs," signifying who Jesus is. The question is then put to the blind man: "What do you say about him, since he has opened your eyes?" Earlier the man has simply spoken of "the man called Jesus." Now he says that he is a prophet. Probably the significance of the term *prophet* is to indicate that Jesus is not a sinner, as his detractors contend, but a man sent from God.

The Jews' mounting opposition to Jesus next takes the form of refusal to believe that the man had actually been born blind (vs. 18), so his parents are called to testify (vss. 18–23). The parents are obviously not anxious to involve themselves, but they do give a minimally truthful testimony. The man who claims to have been healed by Jesus the prophet is, in fact, their son who was born blind (vs. 20). This, however, is as far as they are willing to go. For all questions about how or by whom he was healed, the parents refer the questioners back to their son (vs. 21). The evangelist now interjects an explanation of the reticence of the parents (vss. 22 f.). This explanation does not really fit the time of Jesus, but rather the end of the first Christian century. Only after the destruction of Jerusalem and the formation of the Council of Jamnia, would people have actually been forced to leave the synagogue for professing Christ.[14] The theme of being cast out of the synagogue occurs more than once in John (12:42; 16:2; cf. Luke 6:22) and is probably a reflection of that situation. Despite the parents' timidity, the attempt to discredit the claims of the man, and indirectly to discredit Jesus, comes to grief on the hard fact that a change has occurred in him. He was born blind, but is so no longer.

The same hearing continues and the man is called a second time (vss. 24 ff.). Despite the lack of conclusive evidence against Jesus, the opposition to him has now hardened (vs. 24). The serenity of the man healed contrasts with the obviously hostile jury (vs. 25). Rather than debating his questioners, he simply recites what he knows on the basis of what he has experienced. This most effective and infuriating response (especially in view of the failure to show that the man was not blind in the first place) drives the questioners now to take a new tack (vs. 26). This apparent attempt to get at the facts may hide a suspicion that Jesus has used spittle in the act of healing and is therefore guilty of adopting the tricks of an illegal sorcerer. At this point the man shows the first signs of irritation (vs. 27). His reply is intentionally cutting and draws a bitter retort (vss. 28 f.). Of course, the Jews' claim to be the true disciples of Moses would not have been accepted by the evangelist (5:45–47). That the man is Jesus' disciple has not heretofore been suggested. Nevertheless, before the end it turns out to be true.

In verse 29, as throughout chapters 2–12, rejection of Jesus is based upon a religious certainty that refuses to question itself, a

---

[14] See J. L. Martyn, *History and Theology in the Fourth Gospel*, rev. ed. (Nashville, Tenn.: Abingdon, 1979), esp. pp. 24–62. Cf. Brown, *The Gospel According to John*, pp. lxxxv, 374, 379 f.

harking back to an earlier revelation that is now viewed as immutable law, admitting of no further clarification, alteration, or argument. That the Jews or Jesus' opponents do not know the origin of Jesus is altogether typical of John's thought. To know Jesus' true origin is to know that he is sent by God. The Jews ironically do not know the tragic truth of their observation that they are ignorant of Jesus' origin.[15] The man's response to the statement of the Jews, who have set themselves up as religious authorities (vs. 30), is a classic reflection upon the capacity of the self-styled judges to judge Jesus. The didactic elaboration of the brusque retort (vss. 31–33) strikes home, because it is based on presuppositions that the questioners turned accusers also share. The response of the man healed is so devastating that the Jews can only lash out in frustrated anger and vent their rage upon him. They cast him out—possibly out of the hearing room, but more probably out of the synagogue or the Jewish community (cf. vss. 22 f.).

The latter interpretation is in accord with the remainder of the account (vss. 35 ff.). After the man healed has been ejected from the Jewish community because of his refusal to repudiate Jesus, Jesus himself returns to him. At this point the man still has no special theological knowledge about Jesus. In verse 35 we find one of the fairly numerous instances of the term *Son of Man* in John's Gospel. As in the Synoptics it appears on the lips of Jesus himself, presumably as a self-designation. Although in John it has lost much of its apocalyptic coloration (cf. Daniel 7), it is still a term of dignity, not of humiliation. The man's answer to Jesus' question is typically guileless (vs. 36). Only now does Jesus reveal his full and true identity (vs. 37). The man's response (vs. 38) indicates that he understands Son of Man to be a messianic title. How we should understand *Lord* in verse 38 is a question. In the Synoptics the word can appear as only a polite form of address, *Milord*, or *Sir*, but here the meaning almost certainly goes beyond that. "Lord, I believe" is a Christological confession, as is made plain by the statement that at this point the man worshiped Jesus. The final words of Jesus (vss. 39 ff.), now addressed not so much to the man as to the total situation, are a commentary on his whole mission.[16]

---

[15] On the motif of Jesus' origin and background in the Fourth Gospel, note several earlier passages: 1:46; 3:31 ff.; 6:42; 7:15, 27, 41 f., 52; 8:23, 41 f., 57 f.

[16] There is an apparent anomaly in this statement of Jesus. For elsewhere it is explicitly said that he does not come in order to judge (3:17 f., where the word *condemn* translates the same Greek word *krinō*, "to judge"; also 12:47). From 5:22 ff., however, it is clear that the son does judge. The difficulty is resolved if we see that the ultimate purpose of Jesus' coming is not judgment but salvation (3:16 ff.). Yet from this, judgment inevitably results, because some reject with great hostility the salvation that is offered and persist in evil (3:19 ff.). This negative statement of Jesus' purpose is doubtless influenced by the context, as it follows a narrative in which hostility toward Jesus and his work has been vigorously expressed.

What are we to make of the strange statement that Jesus has come in order that those who do not see may see and in order that those who see may become blind (vs. 39)? The traces of Jewish-Christian polemic at the end of the first century already noted in this chapter lead us to suspect that the same situation is in view here. Those who do not see are not the physically blind, or the import of Jesus' statement would be that as he goes about giving sight to the blind, so he also puts out the eyes of those who see. This is obviously absurd. The blindness and sight referred to here are of a different order. Jesus said at the first of this story (vs. 5) that he is the light of the world (cf. also 1:4 ff; 8:12; 12:46). He gives sight to those in darkness, but those who try to walk by their own light are blinded. To receive sight, to see the true light, one must recognize his condition of blindness. The Jews who insist upon their prior revelatory knowledge ("we see") and their right to judge Jesus become blind because of this pretension. Their rejection of Jesus proves their blindness, whereas their insistence that they see confirms their guilt (9:41). From here it is only a step—perhaps the evangelist has already taken that step, but at least he lays the basis for it—to the application of this principle to humankind at large. The pretension that one already sees prevents that self-knowledge and recognition of one's true condition that is the first step to genuine sight. So the effect of Jesus' appearance is to blind such people (vs. 39), at least until they are ready to recognize their actual state.

On the basis of these observations we are in a position to make some generalizations about this chapter and its relation to the Gospel as a whole. The chapter is a kind of paradigm of Jesus' public ministry, portraying in dramatic form the statement of the prologue (vs. 5) that the light shines in darkness and the darkness has not comprehended (or "overcome") it. Moreover, verses 9–13 of the prologue take on concreteness in the light of this story. At the same time it represents a movement or progression in Jesus' ministry. The hostility that has become evident already (cf. chaps. 7 and 8) could not be made plainer than here. Also, this portrayal of Jesus as the giver of sight and, by implication, of light, prepares the way for the final manifestation of Jesus as the giver of life (chap. 11). The principal point of the story does not lie in its contribution to historical knowledge of Jesus' ministry. The questions addressed arise not out of Jesus' own time, but out of encounters between Christianity and Judaism or Christianity and the world. That this is no "spiritualizing" interpretation of the text, but represents the genuine intention of the author, seems clear from the concluding word of Jesus (vss. 39 ff.); in the terms of the narrative he succinctly characterizes his whole mission.

In the background of this chapter stands John's distinctive view of Jesus as the light and life of humankind. The miracle itself is indispensable in that it manifests the fact that Jesus really changes people. The stubborn insistence of the healed man upon the fact of his healing bears eloquent testimony to this. He grounds his relation to Jesus on what has actually happened to him, even though he cannot give this experience adequate expression until Jesus reveals himself to him, and he acknowledges and worships the Christ whose reality and activity on his behalf he has already felt. Although the Johannine Christology is here in evidence, it is more or less in the background. In the foreground is soteriology (the concept of salvation and its effect)—not so much who Jesus is, but what he does. In fact, who he is becomes known through, and is grounded upon, what he does. As Jesus here manifests himself as the light of the world by giving sight to the blind, so in chapter 11 he appears as the resurrection and the life by raising the dead.

The fact that the specific doctrine of Christ and Jesus himself remain somewhat in the background suggests another observation. There is a sense in which the real hero of the story is the nameless man who is healed. This is true of this particular miracle story as of no other in John. Certainly neither the restored man of chapter 5 nor Lazarus in chapter 11 emerges as a hero. The ruler of 4:46–54 comes off well, as in the Synoptic parallels, but his character is not displayed and developed in the same way. However, if Jesus did not reappear at the end of chapter 9 to confirm the man in his newly found faith and to pronounce a final interpretative word over the whole affair, we would have to say that after the brief account of the miracle Jesus simply fades out of the picture, except as he is present in his embryonic disciple.

Although there is no exact parallel to this feature in a Johannine miracle story, the account does bring to light an important Johannine characteristic—namely, the author's interest in the various types of people who confront Jesus. Whatever one thinks about the historical basis of the stories of John, clearly many of the characters who encounter Jesus are typical and perhaps symbolic. There is Nathanael, the true Israelite in whom there is no guile (1:47 ff.). There is Nicodemus, the teacher of Israel, who at first cannot comprehend Jesus and yet later defends him and finally returns to help bury him (3:1 ff.; 7:50; 19:39). In some contrast to Nicodemus is the nameless Samaritan woman, the representative of a heterodox Judaism (4:7 ff.). Yet if the characters are symbolic, they are also lifelike. In chapter 11 Mary and Martha, along with the wily Caiaphas, stand out as real people. And even Pontius Pilate shows a touch of humanity in the passion narrative (18:28 ff.). Although the disciples do not appear in the farewell discourse except to ask questions, their questions are understandable in view of the total picture that John has painted. Thus Thomas' question (14:5) contributes to the traditional portrayal of him as "doubting Thomas." With the exception of Peter, and perhaps James and John, the other disciples are shadowy characters in the Synoptics. By contrast, in John some of these other disciples play significant roles (for example, Philip, Thomas, Lazarus, and Nathanael), but James and John are not mentioned by name.

Pre-eminent among the disciples in the Fourth Gospel is, of course, the unnamed Beloved Disciple, certainly an exemplary figure among Jesus' circle of disciples, along with Peter. We have seen that there is no firm basis in the Gospel for the traditional identification of this disciple with John, the son of Zebedee. Alternatively, the Beloved Disciple has been identified with Lazarus by some interpreters, whereas others have insisted that he is a composite, ideal figure, and not any single historical person. The objection that John would not have invented such a person is met by the rejoinder that we cannot prove that John did not invent any number of the characters in the Gospel, about whom we know nothing either from the Synoptics or from any other source. Here, as at so many points, John alternately mystifies and tantalizes the reader and defies the historical investigator.

The story of the healing of the blind man mirrors both the characteristics and the perplexities of the Fourth Gospel. We find here a true-to-life picture of how people react when older orthodoxies are confronted by new claims and a remarkably lifelike and sympathetic picture of the man whom Jesus healed. In and behind this scene there appears John's understanding of the nature and work of Jesus Christ. Yet for all that the portrait of Jesus lacks the humanity of the other characters. This is all the more surprising in view of the intensely human—if authoritative—Jesus who emerges at many points in the Synoptic account. The Johannine Jesus, however, behaves strangely by human standards (2:4; 7:2–10; 11:6). This state of affairs is enough to set us on our guard against reading John as simply an historical report. It is finally less so than any of the other Gospels. John's portrayal of Jesus is not designed to represent his humanity for the benefit of our curiosity and to make him personally more familiar. Rather, as in the prologue he speaks of Jesus as the Word or revelation of God, so in the body of the Gospel he speaks of the Word of God under the form of Jesus of Nazareth. Although he does not deny that Jesus was really man, his primary interest and emphasis are focused upon his conviction that through him God is speaking to man. The single-mindedness of this theological concept is etched sharply against the background of John's perceptive presentation of humanity in all its color and concreteness. At this he is a master, and it is nowhere more apparent than in the story of the man blind from birth.

The Revelation of Christ's Glory Before the Community (13:1–21:25)

In the Gospel of John, Jesus' glory is revealed throughout his public ministry, but the world cannot perceive it for what it is. The disciples see and believe, but their understanding is necessarily limited before Jesus' death and resurrection. During the final period of his ministry Jesus reveals himself directly and explicitly to his disciples. Still their perception is limited, but ultimately they witness the risen Jesus and come to fully adequate faith.

JESUS' LAST WILL: THE PRAYER OF CONSECRATION (17:1–26)

Is this final utterance of Jesus primarily a prayer or a proclamation?

From the end of the first half of the Gospel when he withdraws from the world (chap. 12) until the moment of his arrest (18:1 ff.), Jesus is continually with his disciples.[17] In this period fall the Last Supper (chap. 13), the farewell discourses (chaps. 14–16), and the prayer of consecration (chap. 17). There is a certain rough conformity with the Synoptics, although there Jesus first gives his eschatological discourse (Mark 13) and only afterward eats the Last Supper with his disciples (Mark 14:12–25). Then, after they have all gone out from the supper, he prays (Mark 14:32–42).[18] The basic character of the various events is, however, different. In the Synoptic account the supper is a Passover meal, at which Jesus institutes the sacrament of the Lord's Supper. In John the meal is not a Passover celebration and Jesus, instead of instituting the sacrament of the Lord's Supper, washes the disciples' feet. The Johannine discourses have to do with Jesus' death and reunion with his disciples, the Synoptic with the cataclysmic events leading up to the end of the world. Jesus' last prayer in John is a carefully wrought exposition of his legacy to his disciples. His own death is mentioned, but in its peculiarly Johannine significance as the glorification and consecration of the Son of God. In the Synoptics Jesus prays in Gethsemane, "Abba, Father, all things are possible to thee; remove this cup from me; yet not what I will, but what thou wilt" (Mark 14:36; cf. John 12:27 f.).

---

[17] The disciples have usually been taken to mean the twelve, although this is nowhere made explicit in the text. In 6:66 ff. all the disciples except the twelve seem to be drawing back from Jesus. Yet immediately thereafter (7:3) it appears that Jesus has disciples other than the twelve. Therefore one ought not to assume that *disciples* (after 6:66) always implies the twelve.

[18] Also, in both John and the Synoptics, Jesus concludes the meal on the solemn note of the disciples' desertion and Judas' betrayal. Mark 14:26–31 is paralleled by John 13:36–38 (at the end of the supper proper) and 16:32 (at the end of the discourses).

The Synoptic account is probably closer to the actual historical situation of Jesus than are the more abstractly theological, polished petitions of the Johannine prayer. Yet the Johannine prayer is important in illuminating the Fourth Gospel.

The first verse establishes the fact that this is, in form at least, a prayer; the simple, direct way of addressing God is typical of Jesus (Mark 14:36; cf. Luke 11:2). With the announcement that the hour has come (17:1; cf. 12:23), Jesus signals the imminence of the crucifixion, which is also the hour of his glorification. The glorifying of the Son is now to take place in his death and exaltation to heaven. Especially in John, crucifixion, resurrection, and exaltation are tied closely together. God glorifies Jesus by turning his death into victory, and the glory that Jesus thereby shares is nothing less than the glory of God, his imposing power and nature as he makes it known to all peoples. Already the Word's becoming flesh and dwelling among humankind has been subtly compared with God's glory dwelling in the temple (1:14; cf. 2:19 ff. and 4:20 ff.). Now the close connection between the Father and Jesus allows the evangelist to assert that Jesus shares in the Father's glory (cf. especially vs. 5).

Because Jesus' authority or power to give eternal life (vs. 2) can be fully exercised only as he is glorified, he calls upon the Father to glorify him (vs. 1). At this point John's emphasis on predestination comes to light (cf. vs. 6). That is, Jesus has authority over all flesh (all people), but gives life only to those God gives him (vs. 2). Like Paul, John stresses the security of the elect in God (those God has given Jesus), not the exclusion of others. The fundamental Johannine theological premise is that God loves the world and sent the Son to save it (3:16 ff.; 12:47; 17:20 ff.). Jesus has been given authority over all humanity. He is not related only to the elect. Whatever else it may be, John's concept of election is a way of explaining how Christ could be sent to save humankind, although not all are saved (cf. 12:37–43). Their loss could not occur apart from the divine will and purpose. Neither God nor Christ could fail. The predestination may also be a product of the Johannine dualism of which we have already spoken. Where such dualism occurs in either Gnosticism or apocalypticism, different as they may be, the idea of predestination often appears also. Still, John's unwillingness to be bound by such a dualistic world view is reflected in his insistence that God loves the world and that the Word became flesh in Jesus. At best there is an unresolved tension.

The definition of eternal life (vs. 3) shows the distance between John and any apocalyptic world view. Eternal life is an eschatological concept, and in chapter 3 it appears in conjunction with the term *kingdom of God,* so familiar from the Synoptic Gospels. The phrase *eternal life* also occurs in the Synoptics themselves (cf. Mark 10:17; "Good Teacher, what must I do to inherit eternal life?"). There it is understood to refer to the life of the age to come (Mark 10:30). Although in John eternal life is not robbed of its future dimension (14:1–7; 17:24), the evangelist emphasizes its present reality (vs. 3).

The Son glorifies the Father—that is, renders the praise and service due him—by obediently doing his work (vs. 4). Now he prays, "Father, glorify thou me" (vs. 5; cf. vs. 1). The new element in this petition is the reference to Christ's pre-existence, his being with the Father before creation. There is thus a close connection between this passage and the prologue (1:1; see pp. 169 ff.). The meaning of God's glorifying Jesus is that he fully affirms and accepts his work.

Because verse 5 harks back to verse 1 and brings to a conclusion the theme of the glory of Christ, we may regard verses 1–5 as the introduction of the prayer (cf. RSV paragraphing). The remainder and greater part of the chapter contains Jesus' petition for the church, although the term *church* itself is never used. This longer section falls into three parts (vss. 6–19, 20–23, 24–26), but the division between them is not sharp. There is some justification for viewing verses 6–8 as the continuation of the first part, or as a transitional section, because in these verses (as perhaps in vss. 12 and 14) the ministry of the earthly Jesus as it touches upon the disciples is still in view. One might suggest that verse 4 refers to Jesus' ministry before the world (chaps. 2–12), whereas verses 6–8 (cf. vss. 12, 14) focus upon his special work among his disciples.

The name of God (vs. 6), an Old Testament expression, indicates the very reality of God himself, and Jesus reveals nothing less to his disciples. "Thy word" is simply another way of referring to God's self-disclosure in Jesus, approximately the equivalent of "thy name." Alongside mortals Jesus stands out as the man in whom God is incarnate; however, over against the Father he is not a rival or second God. His subordination to the Father is emphasized throughout the Gospel (e.g., 5:19–24, 30–46 passim) and is reflected in the fact that those who believe in him have been given him by the Father (vss. 2, 6). They are not his personally, but his insofar as they are God's. Both verses 7 and 8 underscore Jesus' subordination to the Father. Jesus says nothing of his own accord (vs. 7). His word is the word of God, and insofar as he says anything about himself he says that he is from God, the one whom God has sent. To believe in Jesus is first of all to believe that God has sent him.

It is somewhat strange that Jesus speaks of himself in verses 1–5 in the third person and even refers to himself as "Jesus Christ" (vs. 3), a name that never appears on his lips in the Synoptic Gospels. In fact, through verse 8 the prayer contains no genuine petitions, with the possible exceptions of verses 1 and 5. Instead, Jesus tells the Father what he has done (vs. 4), what authority he has (vs. 2), and the nature of eternal life (vs. 3). The author of the Gospel has the reader in mind in this prayer. Thus in the opening verses he provides the proper setting and gives the reader a clear orientation by having Jesus expound the character and meaning of his ministry. As the hour tolls and he goes to the cross (vs. 1), he does so in the full knowledge that in both life and death he glorifies God by accomplishing his work. The success of that work can be seen in the faithful disciples, whom he has called out of the world and instructed in the most intimate communion with himself (chaps. 13–16). The prayer occurs only after the Last Supper and Jesus' extensive discourses and conversations with the disciples. Only then is the groundwork laid for such statements about the disciples as we find in this prayer. Having now secured the disciples to himself, Jesus turns with them to God.

Yet throughout the farewell discourses the disciples remain full of misunderstandings and uncertainties. Jesus' own piercing retort (16:31 f.) reveals the inadequacy of their final solemn affirmation (16:29 f.). The evangelist knows well that the disciples' awareness of Jesus and his work remains incomplete until after his death (cf. 2:22; 7:39; 12:16; 13:7; 16:7–15; 16:31 f.). In the discourses Jesus tells his disciples things they cannot fully understand until he has departed from them. Jesus has guarded them and they have kept his word, although in his own lifetime they have not understood it. With his departure, however, his word and work take on new meaning. In the prayer Jesus already views his disciples as if they had moved into this deeper understanding. In fact, one might say that in the farewell discourses the Christ speaks to his earthly disciples from the perspective of his resurrection, whereas their perspective is limited because they stand on this side of Jesus' departure and return. In the prayer the postresurrection church comes into view, and the statements of Jesus about his disciples are now made not on the basis of their behavior during his earthly ministry, but their postresurrection faith, which is about to become a reality.

In verse 10 the unity of the Father and the Son is again the theme. The glory of the Son manifests itself in this world in Jesus' disciples: "and I am glorified in them." But the situation of the disciples in the world is contrasted with that of Jesus, who now returns to the Father (vs. 11). As he returns to his heavenly glory, he prays for his disciples: "Keep them in thy name." This means "keep them in closest communion with thee." For the first time in the prayer the motif of the unity of the disciples emerges (vs. 11); it will be developed further (vss. 20 ff.). Those who are given to Jesus come into closest unity with him and thereby with God and also with each other. In praying the Father to keep the disciples in his name, Jesus only asks that the work that he had done be continued (cf. vs. 12). He has already promised his disciples (cf. chaps. 14–16) that it will be. The only one lost is Judas, and his loss is in fulfillment of scripture (cf. Matt. 27:9 f.; Acts 1:15–26).

The somewhat repetitive style of the prayer and of the Johannine discourses in general now becomes apparent (vs. 13). The last part of verse 13 is of interest for two reasons. First, Jesus now indicates that his words are not primarily for the benefit of the Father, but of the disciples, who are listening ("these things I speak in the world . . ."). The author probably has in view not only the disciples of the historical Jesus, but any Christian who may read this book. If so, this says something about the purpose and character of this chapter. It is more a "last will and testament" than a prayer in the usual sense. Second, the theme of the disciples' rejoicing, which has already come into prominence in the farewell discourses (15:11; esp. 16:20, 24; cf. also 16:33), is introduced here for the first time. A fundamental characteristic of the disciples' existence in the world is joy. This joy does not include the assurance of peace, security, and worldly pleasure, for the disciples will experience tension and hostility vis-à-vis the world (vs. 14). Far from being comfortably at home in the world, they are not of the world. So their peace and joy is of another order, as Jesus himself has already said (14:27; cf. 16:33); it is the quality of their life in fellowship with God through Christ.

Despite their alienation from the world (vss. 14 and 16), Jesus does not ask that his disciples be taken out of the world (vs. 15; cf. I Cor. 5:9 ff.). This important petition, occurring in the midst of repeated assertions that the disciples, like Jesus, are not of this world, excludes any Gnostic or otherworldly piety that rejects the world. The Johannine position is not otherworldly or Gnostic. In fact, it may be explicitly and pointedly anti-Gnostic. *World* here is the world that people create in alienation from God. Therefore, rejection of this world is not the rejection of the created order or of things material. Moreover, God loves the world, even in its alienation from him. This petition (vs. 15) means that the Christian is not to be prematurely removed even from this sinful world. His separation from the world is separation from the world's sin. He is protected from the Evil One, that is, Satan. He is therefore sanctified (made holy) in or by the truth (vs. 17). As the one who reveals the only true God (17:3), Jesus is the personification of truth. He signifies what is finally real, dependable, and trustworthy, over against all that is only appearance or sham. So the Christian is made holy in the truth which is Jesus, consecrated to God, and separated from the world. Yet even as the disciples are inwardly separate from the world, they are also sent out into the world. They are sent as Jesus himself was sent. "Thus the community's holiness is not just something negative, but involves a positive task as well. . . . As the sending of the Son is not only his destiny but his task, so also is the sending of the community through the Son."[19] The church is not a community living in seclusion, for it lives for the world.

[19]Bultmann, *The Gospel of John*, p. 409.

As Jesus makes his disciples holy, so also he makes himself holy (vs. 19; the same Greek word, *hagiadzo*, is translated in vs. 17 as "sanctify" and in vs. 19 as "consecrate") for their sake. Jesus' consecration of himself culminates in his death. Taken out of context this statement would not necessarily imply a reference to Jesus' death; however, the long discussion of his death and its meaning in the farewell discourses warrants such an interpretation. The prayer is a culmination and capstone of these discourses. Furthermore, it stands immediately before the passion narrative and in a real sense introduces it. The evangelist does not wish to tell the traditional passion story until he has made clear to his reader exactly who is dying, what is to be accomplished by his death, and for whom it is being accomplished.

After the long petition for the disciples (vss. 6–19, or at least 9–19), Jesus prays for "those who are to believe in me through their word" (vss. 20 ff.). This can only be the later church. We should not think, however, that now Jesus ceases to pray for his disciples and begins to pray for the church. Instead John extends the scope of the entire prayer to include not only those who believe through actual contact with Jesus, but also those who believe the apostolic witness. The latter have equal access to the truth of Jesus Christ (20:29).

Jesus prays for the unity of the church (vs. 21; cf. vs. 11). But in what does this unity consist? It is grounded upon the unity of Jesus and the Father. It is an incorporation of the believers into that unity ("that they may be in us"). The unity of the church is therefore no purely social or organizational phenomenon. Neither is it a matter of agreement on doctrinal or other matters. Unity involves a union of the many beings in the One Being. Yet John has to be interpreted carefully on this point. He does not speak of the absorption of souls into the One Soul or of the obliteration of individuals. Individual personal identity is maintained within this union. And except for 10:34, an Old Testament proof text used in a debate about messiahship, there is no talk of the deification of believers in John. Nevertheless, in this union the Christian attains a new status, if not a new being.

The end in view is not, however, the self-glorification of the disciple. Jesus is glorified in accomplishing his mission in the world and among men. His glory is manifest in the crucifixion. The follower of Jesus is sent into the world on the same mission (vs. 18). The unity of the church serves the purpose of that mission (vs. 21). The church's glory in this world is the accomplishment of that mission—that the world may know. Thus Jesus can say (vs. 22) that he gives to the disciples the glory that God has given him. Such glory is no heavenly radiance having nothing to do with this world or its needs; it is given only in conjunction with the fulfillment of God's work in the world. Unity in glory means unity in mission. Through the sharing of this glory the church becomes one with itself—an integral unity—and one with its Lord. Such unity is also unity with God (vs. 23). Again, the purpose of this unity is said to be "that the world may know." In verse 23 this knowledge has to do not only with God's sending of the Son, and therefore the Son's status and mission, but with the practical meaning of that sending. In it God's love for Christ, and also for his disciples, is made manifest. The unity of the church thus bears witness to God's sending of the Son and to the right interpretation of that sending as the expression of his love.

To speak abstractly of the union of God, Christ, and the believers, and of the believers with one another, leaves unanswered the question of how this unity achieves tangible form. Such visible expression is found in the love of the brethren for one another. The one explicit command of Jesus (13:34 f.) is that his disciples love one another. This is the indispensable outward mark of discipleship. In the long allegory of the vine (15:1 ff.) it became apparent that the key to abiding in the vine is obedience to the love commandment (cf. 15:6–17). The crucial importance of the commandment to love is also underscored by I John (cf. 3:11 ff.). The argument of the First Letter that God in Christ has shown his love toward the community, and that the brethren ought therefore to love one another (especially 4:7–21), or otherwise their religious confession is a delusion, is mirrored in the Gospel. If we take with proper seriousness the repeated statement of I John that God is love (4:8, 16), and give due weight to the assertion that the coming of the Son is the expression of God's love (3:16 ff.; I John 4:9 f.), we are not surprised to learn that the unity of the church is a unity of love. Nor should we make a rigid distinction between a religious unity of the believers in God and Christ and a practical unity in love. God's being as he reveals it to all peoples is his being favorable toward humanity, that is, his love. The church's unity in love is the communal expression of the reality of God's love. At the same time this love is no illusion, nor is it some sort of invisible spiritual reality that no one can touch or see. Just as I John insists on the tangible expression of love (3:15–18), the Gospel defines love as the willingness to wash the guests' feet (13:1–17) or to lay down one's life for one's friends (15:13; cf. 10:11–18). Jesus himself exemplifies this love by his death on the cross.

The prayer now ends (vss. 24–26). Jesus looks beyond the disciples' present existence in this world to the heavenly glory (vs. 24). This glory is not their own, however, but a beholding of Christ's original heavenly glory (cf. vs. 5). Thus heaven is where Christ is; and, insofar as it can be conceived at all, it is the beholding of Christ. In a concluding summary certain motifs of the whole prayer are taken up and reiterated (vss. 25 f.). The world's rejection of God is contrasted with Jesus' and his church's acknowledgment of him (vs. 25). Jesus then bids farewell with a promise (vs. 26). Pointing to his earlier revelation of God's name (vss. 6, 12), he promises to continue to make it known to his people, to the end that God's love for him, and Jesus himself, may be in them. The prayer thus concludes on a note that calls attention to the distinction between church and world. Christ and his church stand over against the world, yet not for the sake of the world's condemnation but for its salvation. A positive outlook on the world's possibility of salvation is basic to Johnnine thought (3:16 f.).

That the Gospel does not end after this magnificent prayer is a sure indication that for the evangelist Christianity is life and event as well as meditation and prayer. The death that we have been prepared to witness and to understand must now take place. So Jesus moves into the garden, where Judas betrays him, and thence to the court of the high priest, to Pilate's judgment seat, and to Calvary. Christ does not ascend from the cross, as in some Gnostic accounts, leaving Jesus behind. Jesus dies a real death and is buried, and, according to John's firm conviction, is really raised from the dead.

Yet the risen Christ does not add anything essentially new to the historical Jesus as John portrayed him in the Gospel. For in a sense that Jesus already is the risen Christ, the exalted one. But until his hour arrives he cannot be recognized as such. Not even his disciples, who believe in him, can comprehend the full import of his mission and message. Only in the light of his death and exaltation does his true nature become manifest to his own disciples, who are then able to see the real meaning and import of his earthly ministry. Whoever the author of the Gospel may have been, he was certainly such a disciple, and his portrayal of Jesus takes into account the fuller knowledge of him that is only possible after his death.

The *historical circumstances* under which the Fourth Gospel was written are not known with certainty. As we observed earlier, scholarship has tended to place the origin of the Gospel in Jewish or Jewish-Christian circles. Although tradition and earlier generations of Gospel criticism viewed Asia Minor, particularly Ephesus, as the Gospel's home, more recent scholarship favors Syria. There a confluence of Jewish sectarian and Gnostic or similar influences would be conceivable. The Qumran Scrolls offer many affinities with John, which say something about its provenance. Even though the Scrolls do not prove that the Gospel in its present form is Palestinian, a Palestinian origin of the Johannine tradition seems more likely now than a generation ago. Certain of the Scrolls manifest a dualistic way of thinking that is strongly reminiscent of John.[20] Although it

---

[20] For essays on the relation of John to Qumran in contemporary research, see J. H. Charlesworth, ed., *John and Qumran* (London: Geoffrey Chapman, 1972); especially helpful is Charlesworth's article, "A Critical Comparison of the Dualism in 1QS 3:13–4:26 and the 'Dualism' Contained in the Gospel of John," pp. 76–106.

may be too much to argue on the basis of the Scrolls, or for other reasons, that the Fourth Gospel is relatively early (before A.D. 70 or the end of the Jewish-Roman war), the Johannine tradition may well reach back to a much earlier period than the Gospel. The development of Christian thought and the sharp hostility to Judaism manifested in the Gospel make a date toward the end of the first century probable.

Distinguishing *tradition* from *redaction* is much more difficult in John than in the Synoptics, where Mark is a source of the other Gospels and Q may be inferred from the common sayings material of Matthew and Luke. Yet some redaction-critical judgments are possible. In the exegesis of the prologue a poetic pattern was observed which suggested the use of an earlier hymn or source. In the interpretation of chapter 9 it was apparent that the evangelist employed a miracle story similar to those in the Synoptics and developed it extensively by the use of conversations involving Jesus, the man healed, his parents, and the Jews. Precisely in the dialogue and discourse portions of this and other Johannine episodes the major themes of distinctively Johannine theology are set forth. Although the evangelist doubtless intended his work to be read and understood as a whole, a knowledge of his manner of composition helps in grasping his procedure of composition and therefore his purpose.

As to the *structure*, the Fourth Evangelist tells the story of Jesus' ministry, and although his version is quite different from the Synoptics it is recognizably the same story. The prologue, unique to John, identifies Jesus in relation to the creative and redemptive activities of God. Then follows an account of the Baptist and of the calling of Jesus' disciples. This is in turn followed by a narrative of Jesus' public ministry, at least part of which is in Galilee. Finally, Jesus enters Jerusalem to face his opponents and his ultimate fate. After having instructed his disciples and eaten a last meal with them, he is arrested, put on trial, and executed. The broad outline of the Gospel is similar to the Synoptics.

Nevertheless, there are peculiarly Johannine features of this outline that cannot be dismissed as mere minor differences. Jesus' public ministry is even more sharply distinguished from his last days in Jerusalem than in the Synoptics. After the conclusion of the public ministry (chap. 12), Jesus has nothing more to do with the Jews or this world. To be sure, he goes to his death at their hands, but they are only agents of the divine plan, of which he seems to be fully aware. This sharp division in the structure of the Fourth Gospel corresponds to the Johannine dualism, in which the forces aligned with evil are drawn up against those aligned with Christ. Indeed, the division is reflected in the prologue's statements regarding the reception of Jesus' mission (1:10-12). As in the other Gospels, the crucifixion is a public event, but its real significance is only understood by the faithful, who view it in the light of the glorification.

The character of Jesus' public ministry differs markedly from the Synoptics, in which the setting is Galilee. In John, Jesus goes repeatedly to Jerusalem, and most of the action takes place there. He appears at Jewish festivals, where he can be contrasted with the sources of revelation in the old Israel and where he can engage the Jewish authorities in debate. Moreover, the patterns of his speech and action differ in ways we have already noted.

The *emphases* of the evangelist are mirrored in the structure of his Gospel. Jesus reveals himself to the world through signs and words (chaps. 2–12), after which he reveals himself fully to his disciples in a most intimate interchange in seclusion from that world (chaps. 13–17). What he reveals is God. We often read of the glory or the glorifying of Christ in the Fourth Gospel. This glory is not a personal quality, but Jesus' transparency to the will and work of God. Jesus glorifies God in that he lets God's glory shine through him by doing the work—that is, carrying out the mission that God has given him (John 5:36; 9:4; 17:4). God glorifies Jesus by revealing himself as God in and through his works. God's glory is already seen in Jesus' public ministry in a preliminary way. His miracles are signs of the glory. But finally and most importantly the glory is seen in the crucifixion (12:23), which is the culmination and completion of the manifestation of the glory. According to John, the last word of Jesus is, "It is finished" (19:30). His work has been accomplished.

In his death Jesus transcends the limitations of his earthly existence so that the glory of God in him becomes visible to all who will believe, whether or not they have seen or known him (20:29). The resurrection for John can then only be the divine Yes to what is already present in Jesus' life and death. Jesus performs preliminary signs indicating who he is, but in his self-giving death he becomes a model or symbol of God's self-giving love (13:34 f.).

Quite obviously John's emphasis falls heavily upon the questions of who Jesus is and what his appearance means, not only in the signs and passion narratives but in the words of Jesus himself. In the Fourth Gospel Jesus talks at length about himself and his mission. He talks about Christology. This way of talking stands in contrast to the Synoptic Gospels, where the Christological question is more implicit than explicit. For John, however, it was imperative that Christology be put on Jesus' own lips, for he maintains that the Christian affirmations about Jesus of Nazareth are inseparable from the historical figure, and, conversely, that such affirmations are the only adequate explanations of who he really was and is.

In many ways the Gospel represents the most advanced development of New Testament thought. In all probability, Christianity was born amidst enthusiastic expectation of the imminent return of Jesus and the establishment of God's kingdom. Doubtless there was at first little thought of such things as ecclesiastical organization and the theological expression of the faith, of institutional self-preservation and self-explanation. Although in Paul the church had its first, and in some ways its greatest, seminal theological mind, his insights were left largely undeveloped for a generation after him. Meanwhile, the Gospels were composed as the church felt the need for ordering its life in accord with Jesus' way of life and explaining its own existence by reference to his. Certain authors developed particular theological and practical themes as the needs arose. It remained, however, for John to reinterpret definitively the primitive faith at a time when eschatological expectation had waned and the church was growing as an institution. Significantly, he wrote not a church history, not a manual of discipline, not an apocalypse, not a treatise, but a Gospel narrative. Thus, with considerable literary skill and theological acumen he reminded his readers that faith is not finally a matter of future expectation or contemporary institutional life, whether conceived sacramentally or hierarchically. Faith is knowing Jesus and being sustained by the food and drink that he gives to those who hunger and thirst. It is walking by the light of Christ. It is dependence on the source of life, the only true God and Jesus Christ whom he has sent. According to John, the fundamental question to which faith must answer is the question posed by Jesus Christ. Who is he? It is the measure of John's importance that he identified this question and out of his own conviction gave a decisive theological answer. In both respects he helped determine the direction and shape of Christian thought for many centuries to come.

Suggestions for Further Reading

Commentaries on John are numerous. The work of R. E. Brown, *The Gospel According to John*, 2 vols. (Garden City, N.Y.: Doubleday, 1966, 1970), is the best all-around commentary for the student who does not use Greek. Inability to read Greek will inhibit the use of Bultmann's famous work, *The Gospel of John: A Commentary*, trans. G. R. Beasley-Murray (Philadelphia: Westminster, 1971), as well as Barrett's valuable commentary, *The Gospel According to St. John*, 2nd ed. (Philadelphia: Westminster, 1978). The first two volumes of R. Schnackenburg, *The Gospel According to St. John*, trans. K. Smyth et al. (New York: Seabury, 1968, 1980), are available in English, taking the commentary through chapter 12 of the Gospel. There is also B. Lindars, *The Gospel of John* (London: Oliphants, 1972), quite a useful commentary of reasonable scope.

Other noteworthy works on John include the following: C. H. Dodd, *The Interpretation of the Fourth Gospel* (New York: Cambridge University Press, 1953) and *Historical Tradition in the Fourth Gospel* (New York: Cambridge University Press, 1963); E. Käsemann, *The Testament of Jesus: A Study of the Gospel in the Light of Chapter 17*, trans. G. Krodel (Philadelphia: Fortress, 1968); O. Cullmann, *The Johannine Circle*, trans. J. Bowden (Philadelphia: Westminster, 1976); J. L. Martyn, *History and Theology in the Fourth Gospel,* rev. ed. (Nashville, Tenn.: Abingdon, 1979). R. T. Fortna, *The Gospel of Signs: A Reconstruction of the Narrative Source Underlying the Fourth Gospel* (New York: Cambridge University Press, 1970), is a most thorough effort to reconstruct a narrative source behind John. R. Kysar, *The Fourth Evangelist and his Gospel* (Minneapolis: Augsburg, 1975), is an extensive and careful survey of the state of research. D. M. Smith, *John* (Philadelphia: Fortress, 1976), like other Proclamation Commentaries, sets out an interpretation based on contemporary scholarship. R. E. Brown, *The Community of the Beloved Disciple* (New York: Paulist Press, 1979), suggests a reconstruction of the history and character of the Christian circles that produced the Gospel and Letters of John.

CHAPTER SIX

Jesus the Messiah: A Portrait

Introduction: The Tradition About Jesus
  Kerygma, Gospels, and Jesus of Nazareth
  The Basic Tradition of Jesus
The Healing Messiah
  Miracles in the First Century
  Miracles in the Synoptic Gospels
  The Eschatological Context
  Three Types of Miracles
  Miracles and Faith
  Miracles in the Twentieth Century
The Teaching Messiah
  The Proclamation of the Kingdom of God
  The Kingdom as Present and Future
  Jesus and Apocalypticism
  The Kingdom and the Parables

The Radical Demand of the Kingdom
  The Demand of the Sermon on the Mount
  Jesus and the Law
  The Relationship of Jesus to His Message
  The Question of Jesus' Messianic Consciousness
  Jesus' Call to Discipleship
  The Authority of Jesus
The Suffering Messiah
  The Passion and Death of Jesus
  The Events of Jesus' Passion and Death
  The Passion Tradition
  Jesus' Death in the Tradition
  The Resurrection of Jesus of Nazareth
  The Resurrection Tradition
  The Resurrection Event

Introduction: The Tradition About Jesus

To write a "life of Jesus" is impossible. We cannot accurately understand or portray Jesus' chronological and psychological development. The nature of the sources does not permit this kind of historical reconstruction. Indeed, sources for the historical Jesus outside the Gospels are meager. Although the Gospel of John provides some historical traditions, as well as chronological and topographical data,

"The Alba Madonna" by Raphael (1483–1520). (Courtesy of National Gallery of Art, Washington, D.C. Andrew W. Mellon Collection.)

its portrait of Jesus is so colored by the hues of later Christological reflection that it is difficult to use as a source for the historical Jesus.[1] Far more than in the other Gospels the very stuff (or traditions) of John has been permeated by its distinct theological perspective. The Synoptics are therefore our chief sources.

We learn nothing new about Jesus from contemporary secular and Jewish sources. Perhaps the most important attestation of Christianity, and therefore of Jesus, in Roman historical writings is found in the *Annals* of Tacitus (early second century), who reports the false accusation by Nero that Christians were responsible for the

---

[1] Cf. Barrett, *The Gospel According to St. John: An Introduction with Commentary and Notes on the Greek Text*, 2nd ed. (Philadelphia: Westminster, 1978), p. viii: "I do not believe that John intended to supply us with historically verifiable information regarding the life and teaching of Jesus, and that historical traditions of great worth can be disentangled from his interpretative comments."

disastrous fire in Rome (A.D. 64). The first-century Jewish historian Josephus recounted Jewish history during the period of Jesus' life, and although he described the Essenes and John the Baptist in some detail, he barely mentioned Jesus. When the likely Christian embellishments of the text are discounted, it is certain only that Josephus refers to "James, the brother of Jesus who was called the Christ" (*Jewish Antiquities*, IX, 1). Polemical references in the Jewish Talmud contain little independent tradition about Jesus.[2] Although no early non-Christian source questions the historical existence of Jesus, at the same time the literature takes little notice of him.

The extant apocryphal Gospels appear to be more extensive sources for the historical Jesus. These Gospels, which did not become part of the Christian New Testament canon, can be divided into two basic types. Later, popular Gospels provide additional stories about Jesus, especially his hidden childhood. Much of this material, like the infancy Gospel of Thomas and the Gospel of Peter, helped to satisfy pious curiosity and served to entertain the faithful. Gnostic Gospels, like the Gospel of Philip and the Nag Hammadi Gospel of Thomas, present a secret teaching of Jesus which elaborates a way higher than that given in the common Gospel tradition.[3] (The Gospel of Thomas does contain a number of sayings of Jesus that are probably authentic, but most are found also in the canonical Gospels in somewhat different form.) Although the apocryphal Gospels purport to offer much additional teaching and narrative material, they are fundamentally insignificant for reconstructing the historical Jesus. The later, popular Gospels are characterized by a grotesque appeal to vulgar taste and are obviously fictitious. The Gnostic Gospels are marked by an esoteric wisdom that renders Jesus' message and mission unintelligible save to the initiated few.

Another source for the historical Jesus is the so-called *agrapha*,

[2]For a listing and discussion of these references, see Maurice Goguel, *Jesus and the Origins of Christianity*, I, trans. Olive Wyon (New York: Harper & Row, 1960), pp. 70–104, and Joseph Klausner, *Jesus of Nazareth*, trans. Herbert Danby (New York: Macmillan, 1926), pp. 17–62. Note also Morris Goldstein, *Jesus in the Jewish Tradition* (New York: Macmillan, 1950). Samuel Sandmel, *Judaism and Christian Beginnings* (New York: Oxford University Press, 1978), p. 397, has summed up the situation aptly: "Accordingly, though Jesus was a Jew, there are no Jewish sources of any value about him."

[3]For texts and discussions of apocryphal Gospels, see E. Hennecke, *New Testament Apocrypha*, I, ed. W. Schneemelcher and trans. R. McL. Wilson (Philadelphia: Westminster, 1963). For a complete translation of the Nag Hammadi corpus, including Gnostic Gospels and many other writings, see James M. Robinson, *The Nag Hammadi Library in English* (San Francisco: Harper & Row, 1977). See Elaine Pagels, *The Gnostic Gospels* (New York: Random House, 1979), for an interpretation of the significance of the Gnostic Gospels in the internal struggles of early Christianity. David R. Cartlidge and David L. Dungan, *Documents for the Study of the Gospels* (Philadelphia: Fortress, 1980), is an extremely useful collection of material from the apocryphal Gospels and other writings relevant to an understanding of the New Testament Gospels.

sayings attributed to Jesus and preserved outside the canonical Gospels—for example, the word of Jesus handed down by Acts, "It is more blessed to give than to receive" (20:35).[4] Although some of these sayings may be authentic, they are relatively few and do not greatly affect understanding of the historical Jesus.

Astonishingly little tradition about Jesus is found in the literature of the New Testament apart from the Gospels. On several occasions Paul refers to the tradition of the Lord that he had received (I Cor. 11:23–26; 15:3 f.; cf. 7:10, 12, 25). Probably Paul knew more Jesus tradition than he cites. Nevertheless, the rarity of Paul's citation of Jesus' words or deeds proves the rule: little tradition of Jesus can be identified with certainty in the latter half of the New Testament.

Thus the principal sources for knowing the historical Jesus are the Synoptics, but they do not include the information necessary for a biography. In previous chapters we have learned that the Gospels have only secondarily any chronological, psychological, or factual interests. With the exception of the infancy narratives of Matthew and Luke, they tell us nothing of Jesus' life before the beginning of his brief ministry. Still, their concern for proclamation of good news took the form of telling the story of Jesus. Although we cannot know every detail about his life, the Gospels do give sufficient material to portray the historical Jesus with some assurance.

In this chapter we shall attempt to reconstruct one portrait of Jesus of Nazareth that emerges out of the Gospel portraits. Our justification for this procedure lies not only in contemporary historical interest in Jesus, but also in the inclusion of not one but four Gospel portraits in the New Testament. The Gospels invite an encounter once again with the historical Jesus of Nazareth.

KERYGMA, GOSPELS, AND JESUS OF NAZARETH

The Christian church was founded upon belief in the resurrection of the crucified Jesus; his apparently ignominious death was seen as the decisive act of God for the salvation of humankind (I Cor. 15:3). This faith was generally held in anticipation of his imminent return in glory to judge and to rule. From the beginning Christians felt impelled to announce to others the good news (gospel) of what God had done in Jesus. This proclamation or *kerygma* (see the Glossary) was based upon what God had done through Jesus rather than what Jesus himself had done.[5] Its power did not rest in new knowledge or

---

[4] See Joachim Jeremias, *The Unknown Sayings of Jesus*, trans. R. H. Fuller (London: SPCK, 1957).

[5] See C. H. Dodd's *The Apostolic Preaching and Its Developments* (New York: Harper & Row, 1951), esp. pp. 7–35; Oscar Cullmann, *Christ and Time: The Primitive Christian Conception of Time and History*, trans. F. V. Filson (Philadelphia: Westminster, 1950), especially pp. 124–130; Rudolf Bultmann, *Theology of the New Testament*, I, trans. K. Grobel (New York: Scribner, 1951), esp. pp. 42–53.

wisdom but rather in an event—the death and resurrection of Jesus.

The kerygma's concentration upon that event is the seed from which the Gospels ultimately grew. The Gospels presuppose, and to a remarkable extent are based upon, this early Christian preaching. The words with which the Fourth Gospel closes are also applicable to the others: "These (things) are written that you may believe that Jesus is the Christ, the Son of God, and that believing you may have life in his name" (John 20:31). This also was the purpose of the kerygma, the proclamation of the gospel. Even the traditions of Jesus that came to the Gospel writers from oral tradition and written sources were already, down to individual units, shaped by the interests of the church. In fact, early Christians remembered the tradition of Jesus only because they were convinced that God had acted for them in this man, especially in his death and resurrection.

Yet no matter how much the Gospels may have been indebted to the kerygma, they were also history.[6] The Gospels show that Christian faith is not based upon myth. The early Christians believed that the source of life and faith within their community was ultimately God, but the means of God's action was Jesus of Nazareth. From our reading of the canonical Gospels, it has become evident that the writers, even the Fourth Evangelist, show loyalty to the tradition of Jesus, at the same time exercising freedom toward it. This freedom was a natural corollary of the early community's conviction that Jesus was not dead but had been raised to live and speak as their Lord. Their loyalty to the tradition reflected their conviction that the risen Christ was always also the historical Jesus.

In studying the Gospels, however, it is essential always to remember the history of Christian faith and experience that they presuppose. In earlier generations Christian readers have more or less shared this faith. They have thus read the Gospels with the proper major premise in view. Yet preconceptions and prejudices have often distorted such reading. Whether or not modern readers share the faith of those early Christians, they are in a position to understand what it was and how it influenced the telling of the story. One must bear in mind also that the Gospels in their present form are not, for the most part, the product of the earliest witnesses, but appeared only as, or after, they passed from the scene (John 21:20–24; Luke 1:2). They are the legacy of that primal witness as it was bequeathed to the church.

---

[6]Charles H. Talbert, *What Is a Gospel? The Genre of the Canonical Gospels* (Philadelphia: Fortress, 1977), has recently shown a relationship between the Gospels and ancient religiously motivated biography, thus reversing a dominant emphasis of twentieth-century scholarship.

THE BASIC TRADITION OF JESUS

Although the Gospels do not always record the exact deeds and words of Jesus, they do portray the historical Jesus as well as the Christ of faith. In our treatment of the tradition of Jesus, we will make use of several criteria or procedures in trying to identify the historical materials: (1) A solid *core* of authentic tradition about Jesus can be identified "when there are no grounds either for deriving a tradition from Judaism or for ascribing it to primitive Christianity, and especially when Jewish Christianity has mitigated or modified the received tradition, as . . . too bold for its taste."[7] Of course, such a core does not set the outer limits of material that may stem from Jesus. Undoubtedly some traditions with Jewish or early Christian parallels originated with him. In a less rigorous way, we can also identify a core with historical probability if the tradition of Jesus contains facts that are awkward for early Christianity, for example, Jesus' death by crucifixion, the Roman form of capital punishment.

(2) We can work also with broad *cross sections* of the tradition. This may mean examining different types of materials such as Jesus' teaching about the kingdom, his interpretation of the law, his miraculous deeds, crucifixion, and so on.[8] But we must also pay attention to different sources of materials such as Mark, the Q tradition, and special traditions of Matthew, Luke, and John. We can thereby confirm the historical probability of motifs, saying, and actions that appear in more than one strand of tradition, for example, Jesus' association with sinners and his nonobservance of the sabbath.[9]

(3) With the establishment of a factual core derived from elements of the tradition that reflect both discontinuity with Jesus' environment (1, preceding) and continuity among themselves (2, preceding), the historical reconstruction is guided also by the criterion of *coherence*. For example, the portrayal of Jesus as one who breaks the sabbath coheres with the instances in which on other grounds he clashes with the authority of scribes, tradition, or even scripture. Thus, we seek to portray with even greater detail the one coherent, historical figure who stimulated the varied tradition.

A coherent portrait is neither a collection of facts about Jesus nor an interpretation of him. We are neither so empirical that we

[7]Ernst Käsemann, "The Problem of the Historical Jesus," *Essays on New Testament Themes*, trans. W. J. Montague (Naperville, Ill.: Allenson, 1964), p. 37.

[8]See N. A. Dahl, "The Problem of the Historical Jesus," *Kerygma and History*, trans. and ed. C. E. Braaten and R. A. Harrisville (Nashville, Tenn.: Abingdon, 1962), pp. 138–171, esp. 153 f.

[9]Such multiple attestation may be an important criterion in cases where an item of tradition appears in several independent strata (Mark, Q, M, L). Occurrence in all three Synoptic Gospels may not, however, be very significant, because it may only result from the other Gospels' use of Mark.

want only the facts nor so idealistic that we want only the meaning of Jesus. Yet we acknowledge that the basic tradition of Jesus does contain facts. Not all the facts we might desire are included; we possess no details of Jesus' physical appearance, educational background, home environment, and so on. The narratives of Jesus' birth are not intended to answer to such human interests, but rather to convey certain important theological ideas.[10] Basically, they show that Jesus' coming is the result of God's purpose rather than human intention. Yet these stories have also aroused among Christians and others the most intensely human feelings about Jesus. While the Matthean and Lukan stories are quite different and cannot be combined, they share certain theological points. For example, according to both Matthew and Luke, Jesus was conceived of the Holy Spirit, born of the Virgin Mary, and yet descended from David through Joseph. In neither Matthew nor Luke is there any hint or indication that knowledge of this miraculous birth played a role in Jesus' ministry. Nor is it mentioned elsewhere in the New Testament. The birth narratives are not really exceptions to the rule that we know very few personal details of Jesus' life.

What we possess in considerable quantity are traditional materials, basic to the Synoptic Gospels, that have to do with the *miracles* of Jesus, his *teaching*, and his *death*. The existence of these three separate strands of the basic tradition raises the question of their interrelationship. To some extent these strands represent the interests of different groups of Christians. A coherent picture of Jesus must somehow show how the three major tradition areas unite in one historical figure. How, for example, does the powerful Jesus who performs miracles relate to the Jesus who is powerless to prevent his own death? This particular problem is already seen and dealt with by the authors of the Gospels.

The basic tradition of Jesus includes not only facts, but meaning. The early Christians did not feel free to read any meaning into Jesus. They saw his deeds, words, and death in the light of the commonly held conviction that he was the Messiah. Therefore, in our presentation we speak of the healing Messiah, the teaching Messiah, and the suffering Messiah.[11] The Gospels, even John, unanimously and unequivocally see all three main aspects of Jesus' mission and message as messianic, and our reconstruction takes this into account. The reconstruction of such a portrait does not, however, prove that

[10] Cf. Raymond E. Brown, *The Birth of the Messiah* (Garden City, N.Y.: Doubleday, 1977), p. 8: "It is the central contention of this volume that the infancy narratives are worthy vehicles of the Gospel message; indeed, each is the essential Gospel story in miniature."

[11] For this typology we are indebted to Professor Paul Meyer, who suggested it in lectures at Yale Divinity School some years ago. He is not, of course, responsible for our elaboration.

Jesus was the Messiah; it only makes this messianic claim comprehensible in terms of tradition.

In this chapter we must depend upon the portraits of Jesus that appear in the Gospels. They in turn complement rather than contradict one another, for each evangelist looked at Jesus from a different perspective. They were concerned less about exactness in detail than about being true to their basic conceptions of Jesus. Something of the same freedom and loyalty should accompany our study of the tradition of Jesus.

The Healing Messiah

Doubtless to some early Christians Jesus' miracles were crucially important. The most characteristic miracles in the Synoptics are Jesus' healings, especially the exorcism of demons, which Mark emphasizes. After reporting three healings by Jesus, Matthew summarizes the meaning of Jesus' miracles as follows, "This was to fulfill what was spoken by the prophet Isaiah, 'He took our infirmities and bore our diseases'" (Matt. 8:17; cf. Isaiah 53:4). Similarly, when John the Baptist's disciples ask Jesus whether he is the one to come or whether they should look for another, Jesus replies, "Go and tell John what you have seen and heard: the blind receive their sight, the lame walk, lepers are cleansed, and the deaf hear, the dead are raised up, the poor have good news preached to them. And blessed is he who takes no offense at me" (Luke 7:22 f.; see Matt. 11:4–6; cf. Isaiah 29:18 f.; 35:5 f.; 61:1). The miracles are done by Jesus to heal, to bring health. Therefore, in our presentation of the miracles Jesus is designated as the healing Messiah. He both ministers to the needs of people and in the evangelists' view fulfills the Old Testament's expectation of messianic activity.

Miracle stories comprise a large part of each of the Gospels. Nearly one third of the Gospel of Mark is devoted to healings. Matthew and Luke report practically all the Markan miracles and add others. Depending on how one counts, between thirty and forty miracles are reported in all the Gospels. In Peter's first speech to the Gentiles, no mention is made of Jesus' teaching, but the good news includes "how God anointed Jesus of Nazareth with the Holy Spirit and with power; how he went about doing good and healing all that were oppressed by the devil" (Acts 10:38). Even the Talmud (see the Glossary) acknowledges that Jesus healed, but dismisses his work as that of a sorcerer.[12] Contemporary stress on Jesus' teachings has to reckon with the unequivocal Gospel evidence that one of Jesus' principal activities was healing.

[12] See Klausner, *Jesus of Nazareth*, pp. 27 f.

In the Synoptic Gospels, however, Jesus' miracles are not used as powerful signs to prove his messiahship; in fact, Mark seems deliberately to combat this tendency within the tradition (see pp. 83 ff.). When the crowds gathered around Jesus after many healings, his friends "went out to seize him, for they said, 'He is beside himself.' And the scribes who came down from Jerusalem said, 'He is possessed by Beelzebub, and by the prince of demons he casts out demons' " (Mark 3:21 f.). Thus healing miracles could be the work of God or of the devil; they do not prove messiahship. Indeed, according to one major New Testament strain Jesus' power is not in mighty works, but in his crucifixion and death. Christ crucified is "to those who are called, both Jews and Greeks . . . the *power* of God and the wisdom of God" (I Cor. 1:24). Moreover, to desire miracles as proof of Jesus' messiahship would be to seek after signs (cf. I Cor. 1:22). When the Pharisees come to Jesus asking for a sign, he replies, "An evil and adulterous generation seeks for a sign; but no sign shall be given to it except the sign of the prophet Jonah" (Matt. 12:39; see Mark 8:12). Despite such reservations about signs in the Synoptics and Paul, miracles do function as signs of who Jesus is in the Gospel of John. This is only one of the many differences that exist between the Fourth Gospel and the others. In all probability the Synoptics are closer to Jesus' own view, while in John later controversy about Jesus' identity has led to the use of the miracle tradition in this polemical way.

Before looking more closely at miracles in the Gospels, we need to understand the first century's view of miracles so that the miracle tradition is set within its environment. This, in turn, will set the stage for our final section when we look at miracles from the modern perspective.

MIRACLES IN THE FIRST CENTURY

Were miracles common in the ancient world?

In the first century, indeed in the New Testament itself, Jesus is not the only miracle worker. Simon the Magician is said to have done great wonders and amazed people by his magic. Moreover, he tried to buy the Spirit from the apostles and was refused because according to Peter the gift of God could not be obtained with money (Acts 8:9–24). Simon desired the Spirit because the disciples performed signs and great miracles (Acts 5:12). The apostle Paul himself performed wonders (II Cor. 12:12). Even the rabbis, who were known primarily as teachers, performed miracles. Onias, the Circlemaker, a rabbi in the first century B.C., is reported to have made it rain for Israel neither too fiercely nor too gently, but in moderation. A famous miracle worker in Greek literature was Apollonius of

Tyana, a Pythagorean philosopher who lived during most of the first Christian century.[13] He is reported to have miraculously exorcised a demon from a young man who later became a philosopher and a miracle worker himself.

Within this context the miracles of Jesus are not quite so unusual. In fact, some early Christians felt constrained to enlarge the miracle activity of Jesus beyond what is reported in the Gospels. Consequently, in the apocryphal Gospels bigger and better miracles are attributed to Jesus. According to the infancy Gospel of Thomas, Jesus fetches water for his mother with a garment instead of a pitcher. When the carpenter Joseph discovers that one of the boards for a bed is too short, his son Jesus corrects the situation by stretching the board to the proper length. Also in the same Gospel, Jesus makes twelve clay birds that become real birds after he claps his hands. When a young boy disturbs a pool of water in which Jesus is playing, Jesus withers him as if he were a tree.[14] Under the influence of popular piety Jesus became a real magician. Miracle stories served both to entertain the pious and to support their belief that Jesus was the Christ, the Son of God.

This brief glance at miracles in the ancient world makes us aware of the different "miracle world" of the Gospels. We might inquire, however, whether the tendency to make Jesus a bigger and better miracle worker was not already at work in the oral tradition that circulated before the Gospels were written. Therefore, we will be interested to see whether the Gospels, especially the Synoptics, have furthered or checked the tendency toward the miraculous in the tradition.

MIRACLES IN THE SYNOPTIC GOSPELS

Did the miracles reported in the Gospels all actually happen?

The Gospels do not contain the word *miracle*. Miracle is a modern term that, according to Webster, describes an occurrence contrary to known scientific laws. Because the evangelists wrote at a time in which there was no commonly accepted concept of "known scientific laws," they understood miracles as powers, wonders, mighty works, signs. These strange, remarkable happenings caused people to be amazed and terrified, and to wonder whether these occurrences were the power of God (the good) or of Satan (the evil).

[13]C. K. Barrett; *The New Testament Background: Selected Documents* (London: SPCK, 1957), pp. 150 f., 76–79. See Cartlidge and Dungan, *Documents for the Study of the Gospels,* pp. 205–242, where extensive portions of Philostratus' *Life of Apollonios of Tyana* are reproduced.

[14]See Hennecke, *New Testament Apocrypha,* I, 392–399.

Remembering this, we may nevertheless, for convenience's sake, speak about miracles in the Gospels. The term corresponds roughly to the reported events.

To understand miracles in Jesus' ministry, we must first take account of the view of the world and history in which they are set, then attempt to classify the miracles according to type, and finally explore the relation of miracles to faith. We deal primarily with the Synoptics rather than with John because in all probability they are closer to Jesus' own position in their estimate of miracles.

THE ESCHATOLOGICAL CONTEXT

The proclamation of the kingdom of God dominates the preaching and teaching of Jesus. We have already noted that John the Baptist's disciples inquired of Jesus whether he was the expected one (Luke 7:18–23; Matt. 11:2–6). This scene implies a question about whether the kingdom of God is already present or approaching, for the kingdom and the Messiah were closely related in Jewish apocalyptic thought. In fact, Jesus answers the implied question about the kingdom rather than the direct messianic one, as he points to what is happening in miracles, healings, and the preaching of good news to the poor (Luke 7:22 f.). These occurrences fulfill the Old Testament prophecy (Isaiah 29:18 f.; 35:5 f.; 61:1), as Luke makes quite clear. When Jesus speaks at the Nazareth synagogue, he proclaims that the promises of the scriptures—release of the captives, sight to the blind, good news to the poor, release for the oppressed—are fulfilled that day in him (Luke 4:16–21). In short, Jesus' miracles are signs that the eschatological kingdom of God is breaking in.

This linking of Jesus' activity and the present irruption of the kingdom is found elsewhere in the Synoptic Gospels. According to some first-century Jewish thought, the activity of the Spirit of God ceased with the close of prophecy and would reappear on earth only at the end time.[15] Now, through the teaching and healing of Jesus, the Spirit of God is said to be manifested. Jesus says, "But if it is by the Spirit of God that I cast out demons, then the kingdom of God has come upon you" (Matt. 12:28; cf. Luke 11:20). When the seventy are sent on a mission, their healing of the sick is to be accompanied by the words, "The kingdom of God has come near to you" (Luke 10:9). When Jesus and his disciples heal, the defeat of Satan and the reign of God begin.[16]

The breaking in of the kingdom of God in the miracle activity

---

[15] See G. W. H. Lampe, "Holy Spirit," *IDB*, II, pp. 626–638; cf. also Acts 2:17–21 and Joel 2:28–32.

[16] A. Fridrichsen, *The Problem of Miracle in Primitive Christianity*, trans. Roy A. Harrisville and J. S. Hanson (Minneapolis: Augsburg, 1972), pp. 74 f., also stresses the eschatological context of Jesus' miracle-working activity.

of Jesus is not, however, the kingdom's final realization.[17] The miracles signify an inaugurated kingdom, not a completed one. This setting of Jesus' miracles within the context of "inaugurated eschatology" has at least three implications: (1) The nature of the irrupting kingdom defines the meaning of the miracles rather than the reverse; the kingdom's promise includes and extends beyond physical healing, as the exorcisms already suggest. (2) The miracles point to the working of God rather than to the status of Jesus. God's kingdom, not the rule of Jesus, is inaugurated. (3) From the standpoint of Jesus' opponents these miracles or wonders are ambiguous and can be viewed as the work of Satan as well as of God.

This view of Jesus' intention receives further support from the Synoptic tradition. Jesus refuses to use the miracles as signs to validate himself (Mark 8:11 f.; Matt. 12:39). Similarly, the temptation stories show Jesus' declining to elicit support by the performance of miracles or spectacular feats (Matt. 4:1–11; Luke 4:1–13). The healings bear witness to the kingdom's appearance, and this extraordinary presence of God Jesus consistently and continually proclaims in his message.

THREE TYPES OF MIRACLES

Now that we have discerned the framework of the proclamation of the kingdom in which the miracles occur, we turn for a closer look at the actual miracle stories themselves. The Synoptic Gospels contain basically four types: exorcisms, healings, resuscitations, and nature miracles. All except exorcism are found also in John. The first three have to do with changes in human subjects; the fourth involves changes in inanimate matter. Generally speaking, the exorcisms pertain to what we would call mental disorders and the healings to physical diseases; for our purposes they both can be treated under one heading—healings.[18] Therefore, we are left with three major types of miracles: healings, nature miracles, and resuscitations.

An example of *healings*—the healing of the leper (Mark 1:40–45; cf. Matt. 8:1–4 and Luke 5:12–16)—illustrates why both exorcisms and physical healings belong together. Jesus' anger (1:43) is directed neither against the physical disease nor against the leper (note Jesus' compassion, vs. 41), but toward the demon that inhabits him. We

[17]Cf the proponent of "realized eschatology," C. H. Dodd, "Miracles in the Gospel," *Expository Times*, 44 (1932–1933), 504–509; Dodd, *The Parables of the Kingdom*, rev. ed. (New York: Scribner, 1961); and Norman Perrin, *The Kingdom of God in the Teaching of Jesus* (Philadelphia: Westminster, 1963), pp. 58–74.

[18]Stories of miraculous cures tend to display a remarkably similar form. They are often characterized by (1) a statement briefly setting the scene, (2) a description of the illness, (3) an account of the healing itself, (4) some indication or proof of the reality or validity of the healing, (5) the reaction of onlookers.

"Christ with the Sick Around Him, Receiving Little Children" by Rembrandt (1606–1669). (Courtesy of Metropolitan Museum of Art. Bequest of Mrs. H. O. Havemeyer, 1929.)

may make several generalizations on the basis of this story. First of all, although the initiative for the healing comes partly from the leper himself, Jesus' presence breaks down fateful resignation to his illness (cf. Mark 2:4 f.; 10:51; John 5:6 f.). A new power is breaking through the old barrier dividing the clean from the unclean (cf. Leviticus 13:45). Second, this healing does not prove Jesus' messiahship, for Jesus acts simply out of compassion. Moreover, Jesus uses the ordinary channels for certification of a healing, sending the man to the priest. This is apparently done not to establish the miraculous deed but, rather, to emphasize the new "clean" existence God offers him. Third, Jesus commands the healed man to silence about the miracle. Whether this command originates with Mark or Jesus himself, its effect is to subordinate the role of Jesus' healing to his primary proclamation of the nearness of the kingdom of God. As best we can tell, this order of priorities goes back to Jesus himself.

The question of whether the miracle occurred may be illumined by the fact that the "leprosy" spoken of need not have been the incurable disease called by that name. Moreover, similar miracles have been attributed to others.[19] Nevertheless, such considerations

---

[19] See R. Bultmann, *History of the Synoptic Tradition,* trans. J. Marsh (New York: Harper & Row, 1968), pp. 218–244. Also F. W. Beare, *The Earliest Records of Jesus* (Nashville, Tenn.: Abingdon, 1972), pp. 72–74.

are not decisive. There is an overall impression of authenticity that stems from the fact that the miracle does not call attention to itself. The restraint in detail bespeaks its probable historicity. It is pointless, though, to offer scientific or psychological explanations of what happened; for although these are not ruled out in principle, they are purely speculation in light of the silence of the text about most matters of detail.

Two examples of *nature miracles* are the feeding of the five thousand (Mark 6:30–44; cf. Matt. 14:13–21; Luke 9:10–17 and John 6:1–14) and the stilling of the storm (Mark 4:35–41; cf. Matt. 8:18–27 and Luke 8:22–25). In comparing the Gospels' accounts of the feeding of the five thousand, we note that the evangelists have exercised freedom in detail regarding the occasion of the miracle. They agree, however, that Jesus is surrounded by hungry throngs at a place where food is not accessible. We cannot find a setting for an earlier, nonmiraculous version of the story; the central point is that of a miraculous feeding, possibly with eucharistic overtones. It is beside the point to explain this story as some kind of picnic in which Jesus and his disciples encourage the people to generosity. Yet when this is said, the question of whether such an incredible miracle took place remains still unanswered. The form of this story clearly reflects the eucharistic practice of the early church (see Mark 6:41). Therefore, the miracle may be a postresurrection story, based upon the Christians' experience in the Lord's Supper that the living Christ feeds the hungry multitudes.[20] Such a conjecture is supported by the fact that this nature miracle concentrates more upon the person and action of Jesus than do most other miracle stories. This kind of emphasis on Jesus may reflect a concern of the early church more than the attitude of the historical Jesus and is characteristic of the Fourth Gospel (see 6:15 ff.). But again, the compassion upon the multitudes is what we would expect of Jesus of Nazareth. The essence of the story agrees with our evolving picture of the historical Jesus. The form, however, reflects the interests of the early church. The historical critic is justified in questioning the historical probability of this miraculous feeding even apart from considerations of whether the event could have happened. This does not necessarily mean, however, that no event lies at the root of this story.

The stilling of the storm on the Sea of Galilee also belongs in the category of nature miracles (Mark 4:35–41 parr.). Its present form may obscure an earlier story about the exorcism of a storm demon (4:39; cf. 1:25). As it now reads, however, it demonstrates Jesus' authority over nature and challenges the disciples' lack of faith (4:40 f.). Moreover, this action by Jesus seems to embody that salvation ascribed to God in the Old Testament: "Who dost still the roaring of the seas, the roaring of their waves, the tumult of the

[20]See Bultmann, *History of the Synoptic Tradition*, p. 230; cf. II Kings 4:42–44.

The Jordan River flowing into the Sea of Galilee, from the north. (Courtesy of Israel Government Tourist Office.)

people" (Psalm 65:7; cf. 89:9).[21] The entire miracle story makes Jesus the object of religious awe. Probably we have here a Christological confession, occasioned not by an incident out of Jesus' life but by the total impact of Jesus, particularly his death and resurrection. Again this conclusion does not mean that no actual historical event lies at the root of this story.

An example of *resuscitations* is the story of the raising of Jairus' daughter (Mark 5:21–43; cf. Matt. 9:18–26 and Luke 8:40–56).[22] It is strangely interrupted by an account of the healing of the woman with the hemorrhage (Mark 5:25–34 parr.). Yet this break in the story of the resuscitation is not accidental, for the interlude illustrates the power of believing (cf. 5:36). The striking thing about the healing of the woman with the hemorrhage is its occurrence without Jesus' being aware of her presence. Consequently, Jesus did not intend the miracle (see 5:28–30). If the miracle happens without Je-

[21] See Beare, *The Earliest Records of Jesus*, p. 121; cf. also Psalm 106:9, 107:23–32. Bultmann, *History of the Synoptic Tradition*, pp. 234 f., denies the relevance of the psalm parallels.

[22] Only two other resuscitations are reported by the Gospels, the raising of the widow of Nain's son (Luke 7:11–17) and of Lazarus (John 11:1–44). For parallels, see Bultmann, *History of the Synoptic Tradition*, pp. 233 f.

sus' intent, then in a sense the miracle happened to Jesus as well as the woman. This healing of the woman makes the implicit point that belief in Jesus is actually faith in the power that works through Jesus rather than in Jesus himself (5:30, 34).

This understanding of belief is then taken up in the raising of Jairus' daughter (5:36). Jesus' raising of the dead girl might rest upon an actual incident in which he aroused a girl who was in a coma (cf. vss. 35 f., 39). As it now stands, however, it raises the question of whether belief in God goes so far as to affirm the victory of Jesus over death. Thus the story of Jesus' raising of Jairus' daughter uses an actual incident of healing to affirm a central matter of faith, God's power to raise the dead. Such faith becomes the center of attention in the Fourth Gospel. There Jesus first claims the God-given power to raise the dead (5:25–29), then most dramatically exercises that power as he restores Lazarus to life, calling him forth from the grave (11:43).

MIRACLES AND FAITH

A consistent theme of all three types of miracle story is the response of faith. But what is the relation between faith and miracles? In the Gospel of Mark faith appears only in connection with miracles, but at the same time no one truly believes until after Jesus' death (14:50 cf. 15:39). One possible answer to the question of why the miracles did not produce lasting faith is that they were not miraculous enough; enduring faith could only result after the great miracle of Jesus resurrection. Yet this suggestion does not take account of the obvious fact that many people believed Jesus' life ended with his death; not everyone believed in the resurrection. Moreover, the resurrection is not portrayed as a public event of the same order as the miracles.

Another view of the relation between faith and miracles maintains that faith is the triggering mechanism that produces miracles. God is always ready to perform miracles; consequently, if a person has faith, miracles occur. Support from the Gospels for this understanding is found especially in such statements as, "And he (Jesus) could do no mighty work there, except that he laid his hands upon a few sick people and healed them. And he marveled because of their unbelief" (Mark 6:5 f.; cf. Matt. 13:58). Furthermore, Jesus replies to the woman with the hemorrhage, "Daughter, your faith has made you well; go in peace and be healed of your disease" (Mark 5:34 parr.). The disciples' astonishment at the withered fig tree prompts Jesus to say, "Have faith in God. Truly, I say to you, whoever says to this mountain, 'Be taken up and cast into the sea,' and does not doubt in his heart, but believes that what he says will come to pass, it will be done for him" (Mark 11:22 f. and Matt. 21:21; cf. I Cor. 13:2). In John, of course, it is the other way around.

Miracles as signs lead to faith, although they sometimes meet resistance (John 9; cf. 2:23–25). But traces of the other view of the relation of miracles and faith appear even there (4:48–50; 5:6; cf. 14:13 f.).

Yet before we conclude that according to Jesus faith produces whatever the believer wishes, we should remember that in the Gospels even Jesus did not have his own way. The temptation stories set the tempo for Jesus' entire life in that he denies his natural impulses. Moreover, in Gethsemane Jesus prays, "Abba, Father, all things are possible to thee, remove this cup from me; yet not what I will, but what thou wilt" (Mark 14:36 parr.). Because the cup was not removed, we can only conclude that faith is not an automatic device for accomplishing the will of Jesus or of the believer. Faith's ultimate object is God and His will. In the Gospels, faith means that man trusts, accepts, and responds affirmatively to the coming of God. If in some instances faith appears as the condition for a miracle, or vice versa, the reader ought not to conclude that this represents the fundamental understanding of faith in the Gospels or in the ministry of Jesus. The faith that Jesus demands is belief in the good news of his announcement of the coming of God and His kingdom. Everything else depends on such faith (Mark 1:15; 8:34–38; Matt. 12:28; and so on).

Undoubtedly Jesus did perform "miracles": demons were cast out, the sick were healed, the people were terrified and amazed at his actions (see Mark 1:27; 2:12; 9:15). Yet these extraordinary acts were ambiguous and did not prove that Jesus was the Messiah. Some people saw this as the work of the devil; others saw and did not believe (cf. Mark 3:22). These events, like many at that time and many since, aroused temporary wonder, amazement, and faith. But in themselves, the miracles did not produce that faith which changed "sinners" into persons who radically obeyed, trusted God instead of themselves, forgave their enemies, and lived out of the assurance of God's favor.

MIRACLES IN THE TWENTIETH CENTURY

Do miracles still happen? Did they ever?

To understand miracles we need a clearer view about the nature of miracle language.[23] Miracle language describes events that are awesomely significant for the people to whom these events occur. In fact, they are so significant that these people are usually willing to commit themselves to a changed understanding of life, them-

---

[23] See I. T. Ramsey, *Religious Language* (New York: Macmillan, 1957), pp. 167–174.

selves, and other people. We have all seen or heard about such people who have been "miraculously" saved from a disease or an accident and consequently began to live quite differently. The fact that the religious media often produce exaggerated claims about such "miracles" does not mean they are not experienced.

What happens in miracles is that the impersonal world comes alive; something happens that is extraordinarily significant and could not have been expected under normal conditions. No doubt scientific language can be used to describe a miracle. For example, a man survives a severe heart attack that normally would have been fatal. The personal background of this man, the work of the physicians, and his psychological desire to live can be described with accuracy; however, for him and possibly for others, this scientific language does not suffice. Some mysterious "more" was at work for which his only appropriate language is that of a miracle. The full story is not told by the impersonal language of scientific law.

To express this extraordinary event, many people speak about miracle as a "breach of scientific, natural law." Taken literally, however, such language can be misleading, because scientific laws are statements about cause and effect based upon empirical observation. Out of observation and experiment a law is formed, then with more testing it is found to be inadequate, so the law is reformulated; then it is again found to be inadequate, reformulated again, and so forth. We need to keep in mind that scientists themselves realize that the models or laws that the scientific process constructs are only aids toward understanding reality. They are impersonal oversimplifications that are useful in a pragmatic way but are not determinative of reality. To mistake these "scientific, natural laws" for reality itself pushes the observer into a flat "scientific" (actually unscientific) view of the world in which all complexity and mystery are abolished for the sake of certain solutions.

Turning back to the New Testament miracles, we find that an adequate understanding of miracle language does not fit with the explanation that the feeding of the five thousand was a display of generosity. Such an interpretation reduces the miracle to scientifically comprehensible language. But such language does not tell the full story. Miracle stories convey mystery; they speak about extraordinary events, situations in which things are more than they seem. Miracle stories claim that a power is at work which is personal concern—that is, the will of God, which declares itself personal at a point where it is not expected. The point of miracle stories is not scientific explanation; their point is beyond all such explanation.

It has been thought possible to reconcile biblical miracles with a modern view of the world by assigning them to those areas of experience that have not yet been explored or explained by science. Thus all conflict with the sciences is avoided. But the increase of scientific knowledge threatens radically to reduce such areas, and thus the scope of the miraculous activity of God. Conversely, it is possible to regard all events as miraculous because they stem from God. This notion is usually associated with pantheism (from the Greek words *pan*, "all," and *theos*, "God"; God is all). The first option views miracle as an event contrary to nature and reduces God's activity to peripheral, occasional interventions. The second option, pantheism, asserts God's activity in every event and hence renders human activity insignificant. Yet neither of these viewpoints corresponds with the Biblical perspective, and each threatens to dissolve miracles either into remote and barely conceivable possibilities or into everyday occurrences.

According to the Gospels, Jesus' miracles were real, specific, and discernible events. Yet they occurred in an atmosphere of eschatological expectation and faith. When wrenched from this context, they look like the works of a magician or a sorcerer. In his own time and in the earliest church the question of miracle could not be separated from faith in Jesus' preaching and power, both of which had to do with the dawning kingdom of God. Faith could not, and cannot, prove the miracles happened; faith provides the context in which their meaning can be discussed. Apart from their eschatological context, Jesus' miracles, if they are not rejected outright, must be viewed as occult phenomena with certain parallels in ancient and modern times. If, however, one believes that the new age was really dawning in Jesus, a basis is provided for understanding the miracles.

Did the miracles then occur? Do miracles occur? A book such as this can give no final answer. No empirical evidence exists to prove faith or that miracles did and do happen. Faith involves an interpretation of the evidence. Christian faith interprets the evidence in favor of God's action in personal lives and in the course of history, at the same time admitting that the evidence in both arenas may be ambiguous, and usually is.

The Teaching Messiah

Before the Gospels were written there were collections of Jesus' saying, his teachings. For some popular Christianity Jesus has always been the teacher. Ernest Renan, who wrote a popular life of Jesus, depicts him as a young rabbi whose "sweet theology of love won him all hearts. His preaching was gentle and mild, full of nature and the fragrance of the country. . . . [He was] a winsome teacher who offered forgiveness to all on the sole condition of loving him."[24]

---

[24] A. Schweitzer, *The Quest of the Historical Jesus*, p. 185, trans. W. Montgomery (New York: Macmillan, 1954), paraphrases and quotes from Renan's *The Life of Jesus* (New York: Albert & Charles Boni, 1936).

This sentimental Jesus, the teacher of goodness and love, has won over people down through the ages. Yet the partial distortion of this portrayal was evident even to Renan, who was forced by the tradition of Jesus to maintain that at a later stage in his life Jesus became a transcendent revolutionary; his simple love was unable to convince the hard hearts of the Jewish leaders. One aspect of Renan's theory is as unlikely as the other, and the sweet appeal of the loving, tender Jesus pales against the power, compassion, and awe that accompany the actual teaching of Jesus.

Our portrait of the healing Messiah has already pointed to the urgency with which Jesus taught and acted. He proclaimed the irruption of the kingdom of God. Tributes to Jesus as the greatest teacher the world has ever known and characterizations of his message as "one of the most wonderful collections of ethical teaching in the world"[25] miss the major point. Even the important ideas of the fatherhood of God and the brotherhood of man[26] do not take account of the eschatological core of Jesus' teaching. Since Schweitzer's monumental *The Quest of the Historical Jesus* no one can talk about the teaching of Jesus without dealing first with the center of Jesus' teaching, his eschatological preaching of the kingdom. Of course, that eschatology, insofar as it involves the expectation of an imminent end of this world, as part and parcel of the establishment of God's rule, raises problems for the modern mind. For example, can Jesus' teachings still be valid today in view of the fact that the end did not come immediately? If Jesus were wrong about one thing, he could be wrong about many things. Our efforts to understand the teaching of Jesus cannot be governed, however, by a desire to assure the immediate relevancy of his words.

THE PROCLAMATION OF THE KINGDOM OF GOD

Did Jesus proclaim the immediate end of the world and the coming of God's kingdom?

In the Synoptic Gospels the message of Jesus centers upon the kingdom of God, "Now after John was arrested, Jesus came into Galilee, preaching the gospel of God, and saying, 'The time is fulfilled, and the kingdom of God is at hand; repent, and believe in the gospel' " (Mark 1:14 f.; the formulation may be Mark's, but it accurately summarizes Jesus' message). After the scribe applauds Jesus' summary of the law in the twin commandments of love of God and neighbors, Jesus says to him, "You are not far from the kingdom of

[25]Klausner, *Jesus of Nazareth*, p. 381; cf. T. W. Manson, *The Teaching of Jesus* (New York: Cambridge University Press, 1955), p 285.
[26]Cf. Adolf Harnack, *What Is Christianity?* trans. T. B. Saunders (New York: Harper & Rowe, 1957), p. 68.

God" (Mark 12:34). In the beatitudes Jesus says, "Blessed are you poor, for yours is the kingdom of God" (Luke 6:20; Matt. 5:3). Concerning John the Baptist, Jesus says, "Truly, I say to you, among those born of women there has risen no one greater than John the Baptist; yet he who is least in the kingdom of heaven is greater than he" (Matt. 11:11; Luke 7:28). In one petition of the Lord's Prayer Jesus prays, "Thy kingdom come. Thy will be done, on earth as it is in heaven" (Matt. 6:10; cf. Luke 11:2). Jesus' exorcisms suggest the coming of the kingdom, "But if it is by the Spirit of God that I cast out demons, then the kingdom of God has come upon you" (Matt. 12:28; Luke 11:20). Obviously, Jesus' proclamation is pregnant with the kingdom of God. Yet the meaning of Jesus' kingdom proclamation is debatable.

Two major questions concerning Jesus' concept of the kingdom have been debated by scholarship in this century. First, did Jesus stress the present kingdom, the future kingdom, or some combination of the two? Second, was Jesus' teaching oriented toward an apocalyptic kingdom to be brought about by God or an ethical kingdom to be realized by human response? The debate was started by Schweitzer's contention that the kingdom was imminent in time and apocalyptic in character. Although the questions are related, we shall reserve the latter for treatment under Jesus' radical demand. In considering the former question, we shall group the varied sayings according to present or future orientation to reach tentative conclusions about Jesus' temporal emphasis. As a check upon our findings, we shall briefly investigate seven kingdom parables (Matthew 13). Then we shall be able to say more precisely how Jesus' kingdom proclamation is oriented to the present and future.[27]

THE KINGDOM AS PRESENT AND FUTURE

Altogether the three Synoptic Gospels contain approximately 114 references to the kingdom of God. This contrasts with 34 references in the rest of the New Testament, including the Gospel of John, where the kingdom is not a prominent element of Jesus' teaching. As we would expect, the Gospels of Matthew and Luke, which embody the bulk of Jesus' teachings, contain more references than does Mark (54 in Matthew, 41 in Luke, 19 in Mark).

The kingdom of God is said to be already present in some sense

---

[27]For valuable, discussions of Jesus' proclamation of the kingdom of God, see Perrin, *The Kingdom of God in the Teaching of Jesus;* and Gösta Lundström, *The Kingdom of God in the Teaching of Jesus,* trans. J. Bulman (Richmond, Va.: John Knox, 1963); also R. H. Hiers, *The Kingdom of God in the Synoptic Tradition* (Gainsville: University of Florida Press, 1970), esp. pp. 93 ff. For Perrin's final reflections upon, and revisions of, his earlier views see *Jesus and the Language of the Kingdom: Symbol and Metaphor in New Testament Interpretation* (Philadelphia: Fortress, 1976), esp. pp. 1–88, 194–204.

in Jesus' mission and message. Several passages refer to Jesus' activity as indicative of the kingdom's presence. Jesus says that his exorcisms by the Spirit of God show that "the kingdom of God has come upon you" (Matt. 12:28; cf. Luke 11:20). As we can be reasonably certain that Jesus did perform exorcisms (see pp. 213 f.), it is highly probable that he himself is responsible for relating the exorcisms to the kingdom's presence. On another occasion in which Jesus is asked by the Pharisees when the kingdom is coming, he replies, "The kingdom of God is not coming with signs to be observed; nor will they say, 'Lo, here it is!' or 'There!' for behold, the kingdom of God is in the midst of you" (Luke 17:20 f.).[28] Evidently the present already contains what the Pharisees seek in the future. After the seventy go out upon their mission and find that they also can conquer demons, Jesus says to them, "I saw Satan fall like lightning from heaven" (Luke 10:18). Satan's defeat marks the beginning of the end time (cf. Rev. 20:1–3).

These passages raise questions of translation or interpretation. Moreover, there are relatively few instances in which the presence of the kingdom seems to be unequivocally stated. The presence of the kingdom is also placed in question by sayings of Jesus in which the kingdom is clearly in the future. For example, according to the summary of Jesus' teaching which was quoted initially (Mark 1:14 f. par.), the kingdom is "at hand"—that is, has not yet arrived. It is nearer than before (around the corner) but not yet present. In spite of these sayings, however, Jesus' kingdom message is not oriented only to the future. This point is confirmed by the parables (see pp. 226 ff.); Jesus' exorcism of demons and his miracle-working power suffice to indicate the present irruption of the kingdom.[29]

The kingdom of God in the message of Jesus is also future, however, and the evidence for this futuristic emphasis is quite overwhelming. The previously cited summary statements of Jesus' preaching (Mark 1:14 f.; Matt. 4:17) declare the kingdom to be future, though imminent. The prayer Jesus gives to his disciples contains a petition for the future coming of the kingdom (Matt. 6:10; Luke 11:2). After the confession of Peter at Caesarea Philippi, Jesus instructs the disciples, "Truly, I say to you, there are some standing here who will not taste death before they see the kingdom of God come with power" (Mark 9:1; Matt. 16:28; Luke 9:27). At the Last Supper, Jesus says to the disciples, "Truly, I say to you, I shall not drink again of the fruit of the vine until that day when I drink it

[28] The final phrase "in the midst of you" may be translated "within you." See W. G. Kümmel, *Promise and Fulfillment*, trans. D. M. Barton (London: SCM, 1957), pp. 33 f., and Perrin, *The Kingdom of God in the Teaching of Jesus*, pp. 174–178.

[29] See Kümmel, *Promise and Fulfillment*, pp. 105–40, for a summary of evidence that Jesus understands the kingdom as already present; cf. also Perrin, *The Kingdom of God in the Teaching of Jesus*, pp. 74–78.

new in the kingdom of God" (Mark 14:25; Matt. 26:29; Luke 22:18).
Jesus speaks frequently about entering and receiving the kingdom of
God. Such sayings also fit the concept of a future or coming king-
dom (Matt. 5:20; 7:21; 18:3; 19:23; 25:34; Mark 9:47; 10:15; 15:43;
Luke 9:62; 12:32; 18:17).

If, as seems reasonable, we can associate with the kingdom other
references to the coming of the end time, such as the coming of the
Son of Man, the tribulations of the last day, the coming of the judgment, then we have an abundance of indirect evidence that Jesus
understood the kingdom as future. The apocalyptic discourse (Mark
13; cf. Matt. 24 and Luke 21) speaks again and again of the impending future tribulation that ushers in the rule of God. Although it
contains much material that probably did not originate with Jesus,
it would scarcely have obtained its present form had he not proclaimed the future, coming kingdom of God.

One surprising thing about the apocalyptic discourse, however,
is the near neglect of the concept of the kingdom. It is mentioned
only once in Mark, and only twice in the other Synoptics. One saying does deal explicitly with the imminent coming of the kingdom,
"When you see these things taking place, you know that the kingdom of God is near" (Luke 21:31). Here, however, Luke has evidently modified a word of Jesus which was originally spoken about
the Son of Man (cf. Mark 13:29). The other saying does not necessarily support the idea of a future coming of the kingdom: "And this
gospel of the kingdom will be preached throughout the whole world,
as a testimony to all nations; and then the end will come" (Matt.
24:14). In this saying the kingdom is identified with the gospel and
partly disassociated from the end. If this were a genuine word from
Jesus, then Jesus would have preached the kingdom as a preparation
for the end and therefore a present possibility. Yet Mark's silence at
this point and the neat way in which this saying fits into Matthew's
program for the disciples (Matt. 28:16–20) render it suspect. We can
only conclude on the basis of individual sayings and related apocalyptic references in the teaching of Jesus that he himself proclaimed
the kingdom as future.[30] But this conclusion has to be coupled with
Jesus' message of the kingdom as also present. There is a tension
between present and future in the Gospels that goes back to Jesus
himself.

JESUS AND APOCALYPTICISM

In the tradition of the Synoptic Gospels Jesus proclaims the
kingdom as both present and future. It is frequently said, and rightly

[30] For evidence supporting the idea of the future kingdom, see Perrin, *The Kingdom of God in the Teaching of Jesus*, pp. 79–84; also Hiers, *The Kingdom of God in
the Synoptic Tradition*, pp. 93 ff. For a different categorization of the kingdom sayings
see J. L. Price, *Interpreting the New Testament* (New York: Holt, 1971), pp. 251–260.

so, that Jesus must be understood against the background of Jewish apocalyptic thought. Yet Jesus is no ordinary apocalyptic thinker. Two marks characterize apocalyptic teaching, but only the first of them is fully shared by Jesus. First, apocalypticism looks toward a future consummation of history which God will command. Second, this event is set in a dualistic framework and occurs as the final climax of an overall "plan" for history. Jewish apocalyptic literature, which developed during the period between the Maccabean uprising and the final destruction of Jerusalem (167 B.C. to A.D. 135), embodied the fundamental hope that "the succession of world powers, Babylonian, Median, Persian, Seleucid Greek, [and Roman] would be brought to an end by an act of God in history whereby God himself will take the dominion into his own hands."[31] This view reflects pessimism about any possibility of people's extricating themselves from the present evil situation. The powers of Satan, represented by the foreign powers dominating the Jewish people, had won the upper hand. The only hope was the advent of God's new age, in which the old powers would be annihilated and his reign established. This world view deals in dualistic contrasts: good and bad, new and old, God and Satan. In its perspective on history and God's plan it presumes that the world has become progressively more evil, descending from an initial paradise to the present hell on earth. This evil, instigated by humankind and God's adversary Satan, is especially rampant against God's elect in the last days.[32] But God's plan, visible only to the discerning elect, calls for a final intervention in which everything will be reversed, so that the oppressed will triumph and the rulers will be destroyed. Therefore, apocalypticism calls for repentance in face of the terrible judgment of the imminent end.

Jesus is related to this apocalyptic world view, but not closely enough to warrant labeling him an apocalypticist. John the Baptist, the angry preacher of judgment (see Matt. 3:1–12), deserves that title more than Jesus does, and the book of Revelation with its fantastic imagery of the end time has quite appropriately been called the Apocalypse (see Rev. 21:1–8). Jesus is an eschatological teacher who proclaims the imminent end (Mark 1:15 par.; Matt. 8:11 f. par.). Yet Jesus proclaims neither knowledge of the plan of God nor a pessimistic, dualistic rejection of this world. Jesus rejects the favorite apocalyptic sport of looking for signs and speculating about the exact time for the end (Mark 8:12; cf. Matt. 16:1; Luke 11:29). Even in the so-called apocalyptic discourse, which to some degree is the

[31]Perrin, *The Kingdom of God in the Teaching of Jesus*, p. 53, is presenting the view of F. C. Burkitt.
[32]See Daniel 7:2–8, the book of Revelation, and the War of the Children of Light Against the Children of Darkness, which depicts the final eschatological battle. Cf. T. H. Gaster, *The Dead Sea Scriptures* (Garden City, N.Y.: Doubleday, 1956), pp. 275–306.

product of a later time, Jesus refuses to speculate (Mark 13:32). When the Pharisees ask Jesus about the time of the kingdom's coming, Jesus replies that the kingdom is not coming "with signs to be observed," for it is already in their midst (Luke 17:20 f.). John the Baptist's disciples inquire whether Jesus is the sign that the apocalyptic end time has arrived (Matt. 11:2–6; Luke 7:18–23). Jesus' only answer is to describe what he is doing. Even though his acts of preaching and healing are good news, they are hardly the dreadful, cataclysmic signs of the end of the world.

Jesus claims that the kingdom is inaugurated in his ministry. It is in the process of being realized, but it has not yet fully come, for its completion is still future. That was the secret of Jesus' message about the kingdom, and his parables bear this out.

THE KINGDOM AND THE PARABLES

In our discussion of Jesus' proclamation of the kingdom we have thus far deliberately ignored the numerous kingdom parables. The parables are usually linked to Jesus' message about the kingdom by the introductory phrase, "the kingdom is like," or its equivalent. The connection of the parables and the kingdom message becomes further established when we recognize that they were spoken to concrete, historical situations in the life of Jesus and are not intended to convey general truths.[33] It is not too much to say that if Jesus taught anything, he proclaimed the irruption of the kingdom of God and that if he taught in any form, he spoke in parables.

Before looking at a group of kingdom parables in Matthew 13,[34] we need to understand something of the nature of the parable. To begin with, the parables of Jesus have accumulated redactional additions during the course of their oral and written transmission. This material was added to make the parables meaningful to later situations. One way in which the early church made Jesus' parables applicable was by allegorizing, giving them new meaning by making each point of the parable refer to some Christian truth.[35] In Matthew the interpretations of the parables of the sower (13:18–23) and of the weeds in the field (13:36–43) are examples of such allegoriza-

---

[33] J. Jeremias, *The Parables of Jesus*, rev. ed., trans. S. H. Hooke (New York: Scribner, 1963), esp. pp. 115 ff., ably supports this view of the parables. A most perceptive view of the relation of the parables and the kingdom message is elaborated by D. O. Via, Jr.: "The parables offer some help in interpreting Jesus' eschatology at the conceptual level, but more importantly, they are an independent and richer expression of the *intention* of his explicit eschatology" (*The Parables: Their Literary and Existential Dimension*, Philadelphia; Fortress, 1967, p. 205).

[34] This block of parables which Matthew has conveniently grouped together provides a representative sample of Jesus' teaching about the kingdom. See B. Gerhardsson, "The 7 Parables in Matthew XIII," *New Testament Studies*, 19 (1972), 16–37.

[35] See the discussion of allegory and parable in Via, *The Parables*, pp. 4–10.

Present-day ploughing in Galilee, not unlike that in the time of Jesus. (Courtesy of Israel Government Tourist Office.)

tion. But this sort of interpretation is not true to the original intent of the parables. Jesus was not a Christian, and Jesus' parables were not designed to fit already established patterns of meaning. Jesus spoke parables to drive home a specific point by way of an analogy drawn from the everyday world. The parables are not stories told to illustrate general truths; they are sharp words with implied directives for concrete situations.[36] Our use of religious language to interpret the parables must not lose sight of the fact that parables seldom mention God or use religious language. In the parables Jesus talks about eschatology and God in everyday language, implying that the meeting with the unexpected, with God, occurs within the world.

In the Gospel of Mark, parables are spoken in order that the "mystery" of the kingdom of God may be hidden from those outside, but later revealed to the disciples (Mark 4:10–13). To suggest, however, that Jesus spoke in parables so that his hearers would not understand and in another way to his disciples so that they would understand seriously distorts the intent both of the tradition and of Jesus. Still, this interpretation does contain an element of truth

[36] Cf. A. Jülicher's position as described in Jeremias, *The Parables of Jesus*, p. 19.

about Jesus' parables, for the hearer who resists does indeed find the parables enigmatic and puzzling. The parables, in other words, are self-evident only to the eyes of faith.

The parables include the everyday but also the unexpected. In the parables attention is focused not upon the particulars, but upon the total impact of the story. By contrast, allegory allows the particulars to dominate by referring each element to some previously known framework of meaning. But the many elements of the parable are a whole, and it is impossible to translate the parable into other terms. Any generalization about a parable is always secondary. Consequently in our interpretation of certain parables we need to keep in mind that genuine understanding occurs simply in reading and hearing the parables. The directive, the stimulus to action or to repentance, that they imply is clear enough in most parables. We need here ask only about the view of the kingdom that they imply or assume.

The parable of the sower (Matt. 13:3–8; cf. Mark 4:3–8 and Luke 8:5–8) requires some knowledge of Jesus' time and place to be understood. First, the harvest image was already connected with the eschatological notion of the end of the world; the end time was the harvest time (cf. Isaiah 9:3; Psalm 126:6). Second, the yield of grain (13:8) was excessively large; a tenfold yield would have been a good harvest, and a yield of seven and a half an average one.[37]

Assuming that this parable was spoken by Jesus, we may dispense with the interpretation (13:18–23), for it is quite difficult to imagine that this allegory tells what the parable meant to the first hearers. For example, the identification of the birds with "the evil one" is artificial and would have been unlikely to occur to Jesus' listeners. The parable points quite simply to activity taking place in the present: seed being sown, but much seed being lost. Jesus speaks this parable about the sower not to encourage endurance from people already committed to him (cf. vs. 21), but to declare what is happening in their midst. The unexpected element of the parable is the size of the harvest—verse 8. A good yield would be tenfold; these results are incredible. Even now the sowing is taking place; moreover, the future harvest will be beyond imagination. Undoubtedly the parable's movement portrays in everyday, yet unexpected, language Jesus' proclamation of the kingdom. The present is for Jesus the time of the hidden coming of the kingdom; the future will witness an unbelievable consummation of that kingdom. Salvation is not only future but already present in a hidden way.[38]

The parable of the weeds in the field (Matt. 12:24–30) also has

[37] See Jeremias, *The Parables of Jesus*, p. 150.
[38] Ibid., pp. 77–79, 149–151; Jeremias classifies this under Jesus' preaching of "great assurance" of salvation.

an allegorical interpretation which is clearly secondary and does not belong to Jesus' message (13:36–43). According to the interpretation, Jesus warns against false security by depicting vividly the punishment and reward of the last judgment. But this interpretation obscures the surprising point of the story.

Again we have a parable of the harvest. This time, instead of announcing a magnificent future yield and thereby claiming hidden significance for the present sowing, the parable depicts the future as a time of judgment, a process of separation (vs. 30). But the present is a time when judgment cannot be exercised (vs. 29). Actually the weight of the parable falls on the latter point. Final judgment belongs to God, not to humanity (cf. Matt. 7:1 and Luke 15). Any attempt to bring judgment into the present misses the point of Jesus' proclaiming the kingdom as inaugurated (cf. Matt. 13:44 ff. and Mark 2:18 ff.), but not realized.

The following twin parables, the parable of the mustard seed (Matt. 13:31 f.; cf. Mark 4:30–32 and Luke 13:18 f.) and the parable of the leaven (Matt. 13:33; cf. Luke 13:20 f.) also speak about present and future. Note that exaggeration has occurred in the Matthean and Lukan accounts, for in actuality the mustard seed only becomes a large shrub, about nine feet in height, rather than a tree.[39] Also the specified measures of meal is a huge quantity of flour for a housewife, approximately fifty pounds (cf. Gen. 18:6). Many modern interpreters have viewed these parables as depicting the growth of the kingdom of God, which starts small but through the course of years grows through human effort until it encompasses the whole world. But this interpretation misses both the eschatological urgency of Jesus' message and the thrust of the images themselves. Jesus uses the tiny and insignificant mustard seed and leaven to surprise the hearer with the tremendous results: the tree that shelters the birds and enough dough for a housewife to feed 150 people. These are parables not of growth, but of contrast. Jesus contrasts the small, present beginning with the great result to come in the future. The process of growth is nowhere mentioned so that the "how" of this great result remains a mystery.

The twin parables of the treasure (Matt. 13:44) and the pearl (Matt. 13:45 f.) further elaborate humankind's present response to the kingdom.[40] No calculation is involved; the finder of the treasure and the finder of the pearl have only one thing on their minds—the grace of the find that overshadows everything else. The finders do not understand themselves as surrendering everything but as gaining the one essential thing, the treasure or the pearl. In one instance,

---

[39] Jeremias, *The Parables of Jesus*, p. 31, suggests that the tree imagery heightens the eschatological flavor of the parable and reflects Daniel 4:17.

[40] See Jeremias, *The Parables of Jesus*, pp. 32 f., 198 ff.

the treasure is found accidentally by a laborer in the field; in the other, the merchant finds the pearl after a great search. But in both cases, everything is forgotten in the joy of finding the treasure and the pearl.

These two parables, which deal with present response to the kingdom, are followed by the parable of the net and the fish, a parable relating to the future (Matt. 13:47–50). Jesus' original parable probably consisted simply of the image of throwing the net and gathering and sorting the good and bad fish (vss. 47–48), but Matthew's redactional addition (vss. 49–50; cf. Matt. 8:12; 13:42; 22:13) correctly interprets this parable in light of the final judgment. The future orientation becomes evident when this parable is seen together with the parable of the weeds and the wheat (13:24–30); for the latter's secondary point was that judgment could and would take place in the future.

In summary, Jesus' parables, like his kingdom message, stress both the present and the future: a small beginning now is to be consummated fully in the future. This present beginning is a time for great joy. Whoever seeks to control the future by immediate judgment loses the future reward. Whoever discerns the present activity of God will be astonished at the final results.

We may now make certain negative conclusions about the kingdom of God in the proclamation of Jesus. First, Jesus did not mean by the kingdom of God primarily a political territory or social order under God's rule.[41] In Jesus' message God's "kingship" (a possible translation of the Aramaic and the Greek) was of an order different from society's normal structures of government. Second, Jesus did not engage in apocalyptic speculation. His proclamation of the kingdom was not marked by the usual imagery and extravagances of apocalyptic. The refusal of signs, the lack of description about the future kingdom of God, the absence of a strict dualism, and the omission of any complex plan of God meant that Jesus' kingdom message was not apocalyptic in any conventional sense. Third and finally, Jesus never viewed the kingdom of God as a slowly evolving movement within history which could be brought about by humankind's adhering to the principles of his own ethics.

To these negative conclusions, we may now add certain positive comments about Jesus' kingdom teaching. God's activity, not human effort, was foremost in his conception of the coming kingdom. When in John's Gospel Jesus says that his kingdom is not of this world (18:36), the Synoptic teaching is transposed to a Johannine

[41] S. G. F. Brandon, *Jesus and the Zealots* (Manchester: University Press, 1967), *does* see a political interest in Jesus, but his view is not widely accepted. See Martin Hengel, *Was Jesus a Revolutionist?* trans. W. Klassen (Philadelphia: Fortress; 1971), and the same author's *Victory over Violence: Jesus and the Revolutionists,* trans. David E. Green (Philadelphia: Fortress, 1973).

key, but not falsified. The kingdom was both present and future, yet its futurity was not described in lurid apocalyptic imagery any more than its presence was conceived as a purely inner or spiritual reality. The kingdom involved both the action of God and the response of the people. The present hidden reality of the kingdom challenged the disciple to accept it now, and thus enabled him joyfully to anticipate the future. God was the primary actor: divine initiative came forth in the history of Jesus and would encompass the world at the future consummation. Jesus' eschatological message proclaimed an "already" and a "not yet." Already in Jesus' activity the kingdom is inaugurated, but it has not yet fully come.

Three major questions about Jesus' kingdom proclamation yet remain. What is the relationship between the eschatological and the ethical messages of Jesus? Is the kingdom's inauguration to be located in the word or deed of Jesus? How does Jesus' death relate to his proclaiming of the kingdom? The last two questions carry us beyond the eschatological teaching of Jesus into the question of his "messianic consciousness" and his role as "suffering Messiah"; however, we need to keep them in mind to get a full picture of Jesus' kingdom message and to recognize that no part of the historical Jesus remains untouched by the kingdom proclamation.

THE RADICAL DEMAND OF THE KINGDOM

How is Jesus' kingdom proclamation related to his demand for obedience to God?

Scholarly debate has focused on whether the kingdom was future or present. Much of this discussion, however, boils down to the rather simple question of whether Jesus was primarily an apocalyptic prophet or an ethical teacher. As long as the question is framed as a simple alternative, the modern mind would most often favor the ethical teacher. But if one or the other must be chosen, Jesus was actually closer to being an apocalyptic prophet. As we have seen, however, the heart of Jesus' message was an eschatological proclamation of a kingdom *both* present *and* future. It included God's action and the necessity for man's response. Yet how does the good news of the inauguration of God's kingdom relate to the ethical demand of Jesus? Is the urgency of the demand undercut by the proclamation of God's presence? We will now deal directly with these important questions.

THE DEMAND OF THE SERMON ON THE MOUNT

The most concentrated expression of Jesus' radical statement of the will of God occurs in the Sermon on the Mount (Matt. 5–7). The higher righteousness (5:20) is defined by prohibitions against anger

(5:22), the lustful look (5:28), divorce (5:32), and swearing (5:34). Jesus also commands nonresistance to evil (5:39) and love for one's enemies (5:44). All this reaches a stunning climax: "You, therefore, must be perfect, as your heavenly Father is perfect" (5:48).

These words of Jesus (5:21–48), called the "antitheses" because they are set over against the law of Moses, are so radical that they could hardly be inventions of the early church. Further words, such as the prohibitions against anxiety (6:25), the command not to judge (7:1), and the injunction to do the will of the Father (7:21), strike the reader as extraordinarily demanding. Basically, they must be from Jesus. Their radical character can hardly be ascribed to Matthew or to the transmission of his tradition because this Gospel and its tradition show a conservative, and at times almost Judaizing, treatment of the tradition: Jesus fulfills the law and the prophets (5:17).[42] Consequently, we are concerned not with the authenticity of Jesus' words of radical demand but with their meaning, especially their relation to his kingdom proclamation. Is Jesus' radical demand a call for righteousness *for* the kingdom or *of* the kingdom? Does this call for obedience to the will of God lay down conditions *for* entrance into the kingdom or does it show those deeds which signify the presence *of* the kingdom? If the former, then the kingdom truly is future; if the latter, then the kingdom may be both present and future.

There have been a number of proposed solutions to the problem of the relation of Jesus' teaching in the Sermon to his preaching about the coming kingdom. Most emphasize ethics at the expense of eschatology, or vice versa. In some cases eschatology has been virtually ignored, and Jesus' teaching interpreted as a counsel of perfection for an elite group (e.g., a monastic order). A popular Protestant interpretation has viewed the ethical injunctions as impossible to fulfill and therefore really intended to evoke despair and repentance.

Our basic understanding of the Sermon has already been set forth in the treatment of Matthew (see pp. 109 ff.). Although some material in Matthew 5–7 may come from the evangelist or his tradition, rather than from Jesus, the Sermon taken as a whole does not misrepresent him. Two conclusions are unavoidable. On the one hand, no hint at all is given in the Sermon that anything less is required than obedience to the demands of Jesus. On the other hand, we do not read that this obedience is to take place through the unaided effort of the hearer of Jesus' words. The validity of these observations may be elaborated from several perspectives. First, the opening beatitudes, are to be understood to mean that God loves

---

[42] See W. D. Davies, *The Setting of the Sermon on the Mount* (New York: Cambridge University Press, 1963), esp. pp. 105–108, 412–414; cf. Käsemann, *Essays on New Testament Themes*, pp. 37 f.

those who eagerly receive what is graciously occurring in the present. In addition, the blessing of God as present eschatological action effects higher righteousness, greater obedience. Second, although this new reality means a deeper regard for the life of one person with another (Matt. 5:21–48), still this new life, according to Jesus, is built on the relationship that the Father has already established with humanity (5:48). Third, barriers to the relationship with God—hypocrisy, prayer for show, anxiety about one's own destiny—have to be eradicated (see Matt. 6). Seeking first the kingdom and righteousness of the Father enables one to find freedom and enjoyment in the present. Fourth, the future belongs to God (7:1; cf. 7:7). God's grace accompanies Jesus' command, yet whoever encounters the grace of God must still bear good fruit (7:19) and face God in the future judgment (7:24–27).

Matthew correctly understands the relation of eschatology and ethics in Jesus' teachings: reward is not just some future prize for good deeds accomplished in the present; reward belongs already to the right relationship with God. Present blessings and obedience simply become expanded and enlarged in the future. Jesus' proclamation of the kingdom seeks to bring a response from his hearers, a response defined as doing the will of God. Thus the righteousness that Jesus demands is no righteousness *for* the kingdom, not even the proper attitude with which to unlock the kingdom. Instead Jesus demands the righteousness *of* the kingdom. To be sure, this kingdom is only partially present, inaugurated, but the power of the kingdom is already at work. A close reading of the Sermon reveals that Jesus speaks as one convinced that the kingdom is breaking into the present and will be consummated both as the act of God and the response of man in the future.

JESUS AND THE LAW

Indirect support for the unity of Jesus' kingdom preaching and ethical teaching may be seen in the fact that Jesus' words, especially in the Sermon on the Mount, express a freedom toward the law only possible for one convinced that the eschatological time was beginning. In the antitheses Jesus opposes his understanding of the law to that of Moses, even though no ordinary rabbi would dare assume that kind of authority. His "but *I* say unto you" implies that for him the present is a time of radical reinterpretation of the old law. This reinterpretation, characterized by the command to love one's enemies and by prohibitions against lust, anger, and swearing, is rooted in the dawning of the kingdom of God. Nowhere else does Jesus' daring become more evident than in his abolition of the law's crucial distinction between clean and unclean: "Hear me, all of you, and understand: there is nothing outside a man which by going into him can defile him; but the things which come out of a man are

The late Roman synagogue at Khirbet Shema in Galilee. Note the *Bema* (podium) facing Jerusalem in far wall and the *Beth Ha-Midrash* (House of Study) in upper right. (Courtesy of Eric M. Meyers.)

what defile him" (Mark 7:14 f.; cf. Matt. 15:1–20). With God's coming near, distinctions of the sacred and the profane, the clean and the unclean, are no longer valid. Jesus' message urges his hearers to seek and to do the will of God in the law—in view of the coming kingdom—rather than to quibble over insignificant minutiae (cf. Matt. 23:23 f.).[43]

The solution, therefore, to the problem of eschatology and ethics in Jesus' message entails a recognition that the kingdom is both present and future. The kingdom is present in blessing; therefore, no one can afford to spend time in calculating the end of time. God is present; therefore, people have to respond, to hear, and to obey today. Yet the kingdom is also future. Final judgment can be exercised by no one other than God. The urgency of Jesus' demand derives not from the law as a thing of the past, but from the onset of the kingdom or rule of God, a prospect that dominates the future.

[43] The question of the exact status of the law in the messianic age in the thinking of Jesus' Jewish contemporaries is discussed by W. D. Davies, *Torah in the Messianic Age and/or the Age to Come* (Philadelphia: Society of Biblical Literature Monograph Series, 1952).

THE RELATIONSHIP OF JESUS TO HIS MESSAGE

If Jesus thought of himself as Messiah, what would "Messiah" have meant to him?

The center of Jesus' message is the proclamation of the inaugurated kingdom of God. The person of Jesus does not stand at the center of his message. Jesus points to God, not himself, for he speaks not about his own person, but about God's rule. The Synoptic Gospels show little interest in Jesus' personality or self-consciousness, for they are concerned with his mission and message. Yet it would be a mistake to infer that the question of Jesus' identity is of little or no importance. The relationship of Jesus to his proclamation of the kingdom is an important question raised by the tradition itself.

The New Testament unequivocally maintains that the identity of Jesus is related to his work.[44] In other words, the question, "Who was he?" leads to another question, "What did he do?" At least in the Synoptics eschatology, rather than Christology, is the center of Jesus' proclamation. In his message Jesus proclaims God's kingdom, whereas in his deeds he manifests its power. Thus Jesus appears as the crucial figure in the history of God's dealing with humanity.

THE QUESTION OF JESUS' MESSIANIC CONSCIOUSNESS

A logical beginning place for understanding Jesus' view of himself is the various Christological titles used by either Jesus or his contemporaries. The major titles are Son of God, Savior, Lord, Messiah or Christ, Son of Man, and prophet. Of these the first three are not used by Jesus in the Synoptic tradition. Only rarely do they appear in the Synoptic Gospels. Son, in the sense of Son of God, is common in the Fourth Gospel although Savior and Lord are not. Of course, the Johannine Jesus proclaims himself, his messianic dignity and sonship, whereas in the other Gospels he does not. But John's presentation can no longer be taken at its face value as historical. One may possibly contend that John supplements the other Gospels or traditions and provides another perspective on Jesus. Although this is in some sense true, it is not a consideration that supports the historicity of the Johannine view alongside the others. That the distinctive and characteristic traits of the Johannine portrayal of Jesus should be regarded as having the same, or greater, historical value, then the Synoptics is scarcely credible. For had Jesus actually spoken in the terms he employs in the Fourth Gospel, it is impossible to understand why the other Gospels and traditions should so little reflect this fact, inasmuch as the faith they too affirm is enunciated by the Johannine Jesus. Therefore, our study of Jesus' self-conscious-

[44] See Oscar Cullmann, *The Christology of the New Testament*, trans. S. C. Guthrie and C. A. M. Hall (Philadelphia: Westminster, 1959), pp. 3 ff.

ness must begin with the Synoptics, and the last three titles, Messiah or Christ, Son of Man, and prophet, are the most important ones for this investigation.

The basic messianic hope of first-century Israel was the hope for a political Messiah, usually expected to be an heir of King David, and perhaps Son of God (see Psalm 2:7). He was to overthrow the political enemies of Israel, establish the chosen people in a new and perfect reign of David, and inaugurate the kingdom of God.[45] Of Jesus' actions the entry into Jerusalem (Mark 11:1–10 par.) and the subsequent overthrow of the money changers in the temple (Mark 11:11–19 parr.) are most susceptible to political interpretation. Although Jesus here appears in the role of political revolutionary, at least at one point the tradition apparently denies his linkage with David, "How can the scribes say that the Christ is the son of David?" (Mark 12:35, but cf. Rom. 1:3). Significant evidence for Jesus' political messiahship is the fact that he was undoubtedly executed as a messianic pretender, a political threat to the Roman government and the status quo (John 11:47–50). At the trial Pilate asks him, "Are you the king of the Jews?" (Mark 15:2), and the inscription over the cross describing the charge against him read "King of the Jews" (Mark 15:26; cf. 15:18, 32). Nevertheless, the total impression of the tradition works against viewing Jesus as a messianic political figure.[46] At the temptation the devil is rebuked when he offers Jesus political power (Matt. 4:8–10 par.); moreover, Jesus not only denies that he is seeking to establish an earthly kingdom (Mark 10:42–44), but offers no resistance at his arrest, trial, and death (Mark 14:48 f.). If Jesus was arrested and executed as a politically subversive messianic pretender, this only shows how thoroughly his opponents misunderstood or misused him (see especially the discussion of Mark, pp. 87 ff.).

An important alternative type of first-century Jewish expectation was apocalyptic. It looked forward to an end of history in which God would effect the perfect, supernatural kingdom without any human aid. As we have already seen, Jesus' eschatological message fits more comfortably into this world view than that of political messi-

[45]Not all hopes for the restoration of Israel were tied to the figure of the Messiah. For example, the Messiahs of the Qumran community were apparently not expected to play the major role in the redemption and restoration of the fortunes of the true Israel. In some Jewish eschatological hopes and schemes the Messiah apparently played no role.

[46]Brandon, *Jesus and the Zealots*, sees Jesus as a politically oriented messianic figure sympathetic with the Zealots. But to make his case he must argue or imply that a major part of the Jesus tradition, along with the impression that it has created, is the work of the early church, which was deliberately erasing the political dimension from Jesus' ministry. The chief criterion for this radical dealing with the tradition sometimes seems to be Brandon's own historical hypothesis about Jesus. Therefore, his thesis, although in some respects attractive, is finally not persuasive.

Entry of Jesus into Jerusalem by the contemporary Chinese
artist Luca Cheng. (Courtesy of Spartaco Appetiti.)

anism. Of the many messianic titles of the New Testament, the "prophet" and "Son of Man" are most at home within this atmosphere of urgent expectation of God's final, cataclysmic act. No doubt John the Baptist functions as a prophet announcing the imminent approach of the last days (Matt. 11:9; Mark 1:2–8), and Jesus was named prophet by some of his contemporaries (Matt. 14:5; 21:11). Yet Jesus seldom uses the designation "prophet" of himself (Mark 6:4 parr. and Luke 13:33), and then only to quote a proverbial saying.

The situation is quite different with the "Son of Man" title, which appears frequently in Jesus' speech as a self-designation. Moreover, according to the Synoptics no one else used this title as a designation for Jesus. In fact, it is rarely used by anyone else in the entire New Testament. Consequently, "Son of Man" appears to be the title by which Jesus designated and understood himself. Yet this seemingly obvious conclusion requires further scrutiny in the light of the background of the term and its varied uses in the Synoptic tradition.

The term *son of man* (*bar nash* or *bar nasha*) was apparently not uncommon in the Aramaic speech of Jesus' time, although it is an oddity in Greek. It seems to have served as an indefinite pronoun meaning "anyone" or "a man." Perhaps it could also stand as the personal pronoun, I, although this is still disputed among experts in the Aramaic language.[47] In any event, this term clearly could have been used by Aramaic-speaking contemporaries of Jesus, and thus by Jesus himself.

Son of Man also appears as a title in late Jewish apocalypticism. There the Son of Man is a mythical, transcendent, supernatural figure associated with the final cataclysmic end of the world. He was to come with clouds of heaven and to be given everlasting kingdom and dominion over all people (cf. Dan. 7:13 f). Although in Daniel the Son of Man was probably identified with the remnant people of Israel, he later became a definite messianic figure.[48] In certain apocalyptic literature of late Judaism (Enoch 48:2 ff.; 72; IV Ezra 13) the coming of the Son of Man signifies the demise of the old era and the

---

[47]Geza Vermes, in an appendix to the third edition of Matthew Black's *An Aramaic Approach to the Gospels and Acts* (Oxford: Clarendon, 1967), pp. 310–328, argues strongly for the first-person pronominal use on the basis of a wide survey of nearly contemporary Aramaic documents. From his evidence it is at least clear that "son of man" could be used by a speaker in an oblique reference to himself, although Vermes may press the evidence too far in maintaining that it is the exact equivalent of the first-personal pronoun.

[48]In Ezekiel (2:1, passim) and the Psalms (8:4; 80:17), *Son of Man* is used more as a form of address than as a title; see Cullmann, *Christology of the New Testament*, p. 138.

beginning of the new. He was to be the judge of the world who would gather his elect around him. (This view is reflected in John 5:27, where it is said that authority to hold judgment is given Jesus because he is the Son of Man, as well as in Matt. 25:31–46, the so-called Parable of the Last Judgment; in the latter case Jesus is not explicitly named.) Such a figure corresponds to the concept of the Son of Man reflected in many sayings attributed to Jesus.

The Son of Man sayings in the Synoptic Gospels can be classified under three types: (1) those that speak of a future, glorious Son of Man; (2) those that speak of the present, suffering Son of Man; and (3) those that speak of an earthly Son of Man. By and large, they do not overlap. The types of Son of Man language already mentioned would be most closely related to (3) and (1), respectively.

Mark records that after Peter's confession at Caesarea Philippi, Jesus says, "For whoever is ashamed of me and of my words in this adulterous and sinful generation, of him will the Son of man also be ashamed, when he comes in the glory of his Father with the holy angels" (8:38; cf. Luke 9:26 and Matt. 16:27). Here is the *future, glorious Son of Man.* The apocalyptic discourse of Mark 13 (parr., in Matt. and Luke) brings out details of the Son of Man's coming—how he will "send out the angels, and gather his elect from the four winds, from the ends of the earth to the ends of heaven" (Mark 13:26 parr.).[49] The nature of the relationship between Jesus and this Son of Man remains unclear, although the fact of a relationship is clearly asserted: "And I tell you, every one who acknowledges me before men, the Son of man also will acknowledge before the angels of God" (Luke 12:8 f; cf. Matt. 10:32 f.). In the apocalyptic Son of Man sayings Jesus never explicitly says that he is the Son of Man, nor is that a necessary inference. Because references to the apocalyptic Son of Man appear in all strata of the Synoptic tradition (Mark, Q, and the material distinctive to Matthew and Luke) as well as in John, the case for the authenticity of these sayings appears to be strong. Moreover, the criterion of discontinuity, when applied to these sayings, tends to vindicate them. Although the figure of the Son of Man appears in Judaism, it is in the Gospels distinctively related to the earthly ministry of Jesus. Precedent for such usage is hard to find. The fact that the term appears as a rule only on the lips of Jesus implies that it was not taken up, or created by, the Christology of the later church. Yet the authenticity of the apocalyptic Son of Man sayings has recently been seriously challenged on the basis of the fact that *Son of Man* does not appear alongside, or in association with, the eschatological concept of Kingdom of God

---

[49] For other apocalyptic Son of Man sayings, cf. Luke 12:40; 17:22–30; 18:8; 21:36; Matt. 13:41–43; 19:28; 24:29–44; 25:31 ff.

in the tradition, and only rarely in the editorial work of the evangelists.[50] But this view, although plausible, must nevertheless confront
the fact of the clear limitation of this usage to the sayings of Jesus
in the tradition. Furthermore, it is precisely the apocalyptic type of
Son of Man sayings that are most strongly attested.

The sayings concerning the *present, suffering Son of Man* are
more stereotyped and less varied than are those in the first category.
They teach "that the Son of man must suffer many things, and be
rejected by the elders and the chief priests and the scribes, and be
killed, and after three days rise again" (Mark 8:31 parr.).[51] The most
crucial saying of this type speaks explicitly of Jesus' redemptive mission, "For the Son of Man also came not to be served but to serve,
and to give his life as a ransom for many" (Mark 10:45 par.; cf. Luke
22:27).

A less clearly defined type deals with the *earthly activity of Jesus as Son of Man*, apart from his suffering. In this role Jesus has
authority to forgive sins (Mark 2:10 parr.) and is lord of the sabbath
(Mark 2:27 f. parr.). The earthly Son of Man is accused of being a
glutton, a drunkard, a friend of tax collectors and sinners (Matt.
11:18 f.; Luke 7:33 f.); and, as Son of Man, Jesus has nowhere to lay
his head (Matt. 8:20, Luke 9:58).[52]

How then are we to understand the Son of Man sayings and the
relationship among the three types of sayings? Are they all authentic
words of Jesus, or have some sayings originated in the early church?
How is it possible to relate the suffering Son of Man and the future
glorious Son of Man, especially when Jesus talks of the latter as if
he were someone other than himself?

One basic understanding of the relationship of the three types of
Son of Man sayings takes it clue from the saying, "For the Son of

[50] This view was advanced originally by Ph. Vielhauer, "Gottesreich und
Menschensohn in der Verkündigung Jesu," *Festschrift für Günther Dehn*, ed. W.
Schneemelcher (Neukirchen: Verlag der Buchhandlung des Erziehungsvereins Neu-
kirchen, 1957), pp. 51–79. Since then it has been adopted by a number of scholars;
see the excellent summary in Norman Perrin, *Rediscovering the Teaching of Jesus*
(New York: Harper & Row, 1967), pp. 185 ff., 259 f. Perrin's book appeared too late
to mention the massive study by Frederick Borsch, *The Son of Man in Myth and
History* (Philadelphia: Westminster, 1967), which supports the conclusion that the
apocalyptic type of Son of Man sayings is authentic. See also H. E. Tödt, *The Son of
Man in the Synoptic Tradition*, trans. D. M. Barton (Philadelphia: Westminster,
1965), who offers an extended critique of Vielhauer's position (pp. 328–347). That the
Son of Man was actually a conception or a figure in pre-Christian Jewish apocalyptic
has recently been challenged by Perrin, *Rediscovering the Teaching of Jesus*, pp.
164 ff., and R. Lievestad, "Exit the Apocalyptic Son of Man," *New Testament
Studies*, 18 (1972), 243–267. The scholarly discussion of the Son of Man sayings remains very much in the forefront of research into Christian origins.

[51] See also Mark 9:9 par.; Mark 9:31; cf. Matt. 17:22 f. and Luke 9:44; Mark 10:
33 f. parr.; Mark 14:21 par.; Mark 14:41; cf. Matt. 26:45 and Luke 22:48.

[52] Cf. also Luke 11:29 f. (Matt. 12:40); Matt. 13:36 ff.; and Luke 19:10.

Man also came not to be served but to serve, and to give his life as
a ransom for many" (Mark 10:45; Matt. 20:28). The future, glorious
Son of Man has to act in the present as the suffering servant (see
Isaiah 53). Jesus realizes that his suffering and death are necessary
to bring forgiveness for humankind. Otherwise the future, glorious
coming in power and judgment as Son of Man would only bring condemnation. Thus Jesus' messianic consciousness uniquely combines
two originally separate and distinct messianic expectations, the suffering servant and the Son of Man.[53]

This interpretation of Jesus' messianic consciousness finds a
place for all three strands of the Son of Man tradition: Jesus understands his first earthly activity as that of announcing the kingdom
and enacting suffering for redemption of sins, and his future activity
of glory will follow upon its successful completion. This explanation, however, is called into question by the difficult fact that the
expression *servant of God* occurs only once in the Gospels (Matt.
12:18), and that instance is likely Matthean redaction (cf. 12:18 ff.).
Another possible implicit reference to the suffering servant occurs
again in the Matthean editorial conclusion of a group of miracle stories (Matt. 8:17). Had Jesus understood himself as God's suffering
servant, it would be remarkable that this fact made no stronger
impression upon the tradition. Although the early church undoubtedly read Jesus' death in light of the suffering servant of Isaiah (see
Mark 10:45 par. "his life as a ransom for many," and Mark 14:24
par. "blood poured out for many"), the evidence that Jesus saw his
role as that of the suffering servant is at best ambiguous.[54] If Jesus
saw himself under any messianic title, it was Son of Man. It is therefore a questionable procedure to interpret this title in the light of
suffering servant when it is not at all obvious that Jesus thought of
himself as the servant.

The interpretation of Jesus' use of the Son of Man title can be
clarified by three critical observations: First, in the apocalyptic Son
of Man sayings Jesus speaks of the Son of Man as someone other
than himself. Second, the suffering Son of Man sayings, with their
stereotypical form and very explicit reference to Jesus' having to suffer, die, and be raised on the third day, seem to be the early church's
confession put into Jesus' mouth. (We have to reckon with the cre-

[53] See Cullmann, *Christology of the New Testament*, pp. 51–82, 164, and 317 f.
Other numerous supporters of this understanding of Jesus' consciousness include
William Manson, *Jesus the Messiah* (Philadelphia: Westminster, 1946); Vincent Tay-
lor, *Jesus and His Sacrifice* (New York: St. Martin's, 1953); J. Jeremias and W. Zim-
merli, *The Servant of God*, trans. H. Knight (London: SCM, 1961); and J. W. Bowman,
The Intention of Jesus (Philadelphia: Westminster, 1943).

[54] See also Acts 3:13, 26; 4:25–30; Rom. 4:25; I Peter 2:21–25. Cf. M. D. Hooker,
Jesus and the Servant (London: SPCK, 1959); and Eduard Schweizer, *Lordship and
Discipleship* (London: SCM, 1960), pp. 50 f.

ative handling of the tradition by the early church.) Third, the miscellaneous type of saying reflects the early church's assumption that Jesus referred to himself as the Son of Man. Under that assumption the reporters of the Jesus tradition quite naturally and easily substituted *Son of Man* for an original *I* (for example, Matt. 10:32 f.; cf. Luke 12:8 and Mark 8:38 par.).[55]

As we have noticed (p. 239), the apocalyptic Son of Man sayings commend themselves as the words of the historical Jesus. Despite the fact that they belong to separate strands of the tradition, the proclamation of a coming Son of Man also fits well into Jesus' conception of the coming kingdom. Moreover, if only this type were original with Jesus, then it is possible to understand how the other two types of Son of Man sayings arose. The early church identified the expected Son of Man with Jesus. Therefore, it felt no compunction about both substituting *Son of Man* in sayings of Jesus which originally had the simple *I* (the third type) and creating sayings that explained the central mission of Jesus, his death and resurrection (the second type), as the destiny of the Son of Man.

Earlier we maintained that Jesus' eschatological message was both present and future oriented. Accordingly, the Son of Man sayings stress the future glorious coming and the significance of the present, "And I tell you, every one who acknowledges me before men, the Son of man also will acknowledge before the angels of God; but he who denies me before men will be denied before the angels of God" (Luke 12:8 f.; cf. Matt. 10:32 f.).[56] This and similar apocalyptic Son of Man sayings confirm what we have already discovered about the message of the historical Jesus: (1) although pointing to an eschatological future, wild apocalyptic detail is noticeably lacking. (2) Warning and promise (tension of present and future) are characteristically combined. (3) The sayings call for a response to Jesus, his message and his action. (4) This response does not, however, center on Jesus' understanding of himself but, rather, on the crisis of salvation and new life for his hearers. Those who respond to Jesus in the present are preparing salvation for the future. Jesus understood his present activity of proclaiming the kingdom and calling for radical obedience to the will of God as decisive for the future consummation of the kingdom.

---

[55] Cf. also Matt. 16:13 and Mark 8:27. It is not impossible that Jesus used the term *Son of Man* to refer to himself without regarding it as a title in the usual sense of the term; this is the position of Leivestad, "Exit the Apocalyptic Son of Man." On the other hand, the sayings on which such a view would have to be based are more heterogeneous than the apocalyptic sayings and less strongly attested by tradition-historical standards.

[56] See also Mark 8:38 (Luke 9:26); Matt. 24:44 (Luke 12:40; Luke 17:22 f; Matt. 24:26 f.); Matt. 24:37–39 (Luke 17:26 f.); Luke 11:30 (Matt. 12:40). Tödt, *The Son of Man in the Synoptic Tradition*, p. 344, carefully argues for the authenticity of these Son of Man sayings.

Do we then imply that Jesus did not claim to be the Son of Man and therefore made no messianic claim? If so, we seem to be running counter to the explicit evidence of the New Testament. In this regard three passages found in the Synoptic Gospels—the confession of Peter at Caesarea Philippi, John the Baptist's question to Jesus, and Jesus' answer to the high priest at the trial—must be examined.

Although each of these incidents is often taken to mean that Jesus claimed to be the Messiah, close examination shows that this is not necessarily the case. In the Markan account of the confession at Caesarea Philippi (8:27–33), Peter does say that Jesus is the Messiah; however, Jesus does not accept the title without qualification.[57] When John the Baptist sends emissaries to Jesus to determine whether he is the One to come, the Messiah, Jesus does not give a direct answer. Although Jesus' response is usually taken as affirmative, Jesus points only to his activity and does not claim or accept any title (Matt. 11:2–6). In the trial scene Jesus answers the high priest's question about messiahship positively (Mark 14:62), but the historicity of this exchange is at least questionable. Moreover, the Matthean and Lukan versions of the incident do not contain this clear, affirmative answer, and it is possible that the original text of Mark did not.[58] In view of the unanimous testimony of the New Testament writers that Jesus was the Christ, it is quite striking that the Synoptic writers so seldom portray him as making, or even accepting, messianic claims. Whether Jesus thought of himself in explicitly messianic terms is a difficult question to decide. It is clear enough, however, that he did not measure the response to his message and action by the titles that hearers might confer upon him. Rather the true response came about when people saw in his mission and message the advent of God's kingdom. Allegiance to Jesus or honoring him with messianic titles meant nothing unless a new reality, a new way of life, resulted for those whom Jesus encountered.

What, then, was Jesus' understanding of himself? Although he offered no Christological blueprint, he must certainly have reflected upon his own role in the mission upon which he embarked. The crucial aspect of Jesus' self-concept becomes clear in his reply to the inquiry of John the Baptist's disciples, "And blessed is he who takes no offense at me" (Matt. 11:6; Luke 7:23). In context, Jesus says that he asks nothing more than acknowledgment of the miracles that are occurring and the good news that is being proclaimed. In other words, the center of Jesus' message is the eschatological salvation

[57] See R. H. Fuller, *The Mission and Achievement of Jesus* (London: SCM, 1963), pp. 109 f.; and Cullmann, *The Christology of the New Testament*, pp. 120–125. Milan Machoveč, *A Marxist Looks at Jesus* (Philadelphia: Fortress, 1976), believes that the scene represents Jesus' honest quest for his proper role (esp. pp. 127–129).

[58] See Bultmann, *History of the Synoptic Tradition*, pp. 269–271; also Borsch, *The Son of Man in Myth and History*, pp. 391–394.

being offered the hearer.[59] Although Jesus did not announce himself or proclaim his own messianic dignity, his message and actions were based upon convictions about his unique mission and calling. Thus, to question Jesus' so-called messianic self-consciousness is not necessarily to take the position that the question of his identity, role, and importance in the history of God's dealing with his people were unimportant to him. The following observations speak to the character and strength of Jesus' self-consciousness.

JESUS' CALL TO DISCIPLESHIP

Jesus' authoritative self-consciousness is implicit in his call to discipleship. Jesus gathered disciples (Mark 1:16–20), crying out, "Follow *me* and *I* will make you become fishers of men" (Mark 1:17; Matt. 4:19; cf. Luke 5:10). He summoned Levi, the tax collector, with a curt, "Follow me" (Mark 2:14; Luke 5:27 f.; cf. Matt. 9:9). Jesus speaks, people drop what they are doing and follow then or not at all (cf. Luke 9:59–62).

The Gospels report that the Pharisees had disciples (Matt. 22:16), as did the later rabbis and John the Baptist (cf. Mark 2:18 parr. and John 1:35). Yet despite certain analogies with other leaders and teachers, Jesus stands out as one who called disciples with an unprecedented authority. Indeed such authority already implies something like a messianic claim: "Nothing like this is to be found except in connection with the would-be messiahs, Judas and Theudas, and with John the Baptist, who was however regarded by his disciples as a messianic figure."[60] Our assessment of the evidence has made us hesitate until now to speak of any direct, explicit messianic claim by Jesus. We are not, however, thereby committed to the position that Jesus retreated from any assumption of authority. That there ever existed a gentle Jesus, meek and mild, is highly improbable. To form a coherent portrait we must bear in mind the authoritative claim that is at least implicit in Jesus' teaching, healing, and suffering. Probably this claim comes to clearest expression in Jesus' calling of disciples.

Jesus called disciples to a close, personal relationship with himself (Mark 1:17; 2:14). The source of that authoritative action lay in Jesus' proclamation of the dawning of the kingdom (Mark 1:15), for this sense of God's immediate presence gave impetus to the call. Henceforth, the disciples had a new allegiance; the old had to be left behind, whether vocation (fishing, tax collecting), possessions (Mark

---

[59] This point receives support in Mark 8:38, where instead of enjoining a positive "acknowledgment," Jesus commands a negative "not being ashamed"; and in Matthew's parable of the great judgment (25:31–46), where the meeting with the Son of Man evokes a judgment based not upon confession of Jesus, but rather upon whether the disciple loves the neighbor. In addition, Jesus nowhere identifies himself with the Son of Man in this parable.

[60] Schweizer, *Lordship and Discipleship*, p.14.

10:17–31 parr.), or sacred obligations (Matt. 8:22 par.). Discipleship promised no easy way. The disciples were called to proclaim the kingdom and heal the sick (Mark 6:7–13; cf. Matt. 10:1–11:1; Luke 9:1–6; 10:1–12) and to follow Jesus in service and suffering (Mark 10:32–45 parr.). Nevertheless, the relation to Jesus promised a blessed future for whoever, without shame, remained close to him (Mark 8:38; cf. Matt. 16:27 and Luke 9:26).

Jesus' call to discipleship was not an autonomous act on his part. Rather it resulted from his proclamation of the inbreaking kingdom of God, and the understanding of God's radical demand which that message involved. Jesus rejected the temptations of worldly security symbolized by the miracle of bread, the possession of the temple, and the rulership of all kingdoms (Matt. 4:1–11; Luke 4:1–13). Similarly Jesus called disciples away from their security to the business of following him. Only those who followed would truly know Jesus and recognize that his confidence rested not in himself but in the God who beckoned him to proclaim the kingdom, heal the sick, and risk his life in Jerusalem.

THE AUTHORITY OF JESUS

For the sake of clarity the evidence for Jesus' implicit authority may be divided into four groupings:

1. That Jesus *acted* with authority in the exorcisms and healings as well as in the calling of disciples has already become apparent. Of first importance is the fact that these acts were all the more authoritative by virtue of their having been done in the context of Jesus' proclamation about the dawning kingdom of God.

2. Jesus indirectly *claimed* an unprecedented immediate relationship with God. An indication of this close relationship was Jesus' use of *abba*, the child's intimate, everyday word for father, to address God. This way of speaking to God was so daring that the Synoptics record only one instance of it, in the Garden of Gethsemane, where Jesus prayed, "Abba, Father, all things are possible to thee; remove this cup from me; yet not what I will, but what thou wilt" (Mark 14:36; cf. Rom. 8:15; Gal. 4:6). No parallel for such intimate familiarity with God is known from first-century Judaism.[61] A second indication of such an intimate relationship was Jesus' remarkable use of *amen* to introduce a pronouncement. Ordinarily *amen*, meaning "so be it," was a liturgical response. In Jesus' usage, however, it is a solemn assurance, like the swearing of an oath.[62] Thus in effect, Jesus' style of teaching claimed an authority unprecedented among first-century rabbis and teachers.

3. Jesus authoritatively grants *forgiveness* to all sorts of people.

---

[61] See R. Kittel, "*Abba, TDNT*, I, pp. 3 f.

[62] The RSV translates the Greek *amēn* with "truly." See Matt. 5:18; Mark 3:28; Luke 23:43; and Käsemann, *Essays on New Testament Themes*, pp. 41 f.

The forgiveness of God was, of course, nothing new to Judaism, but Jesus proclaimed a more radical forgiveness. For him all men were basically in need of forgiveness because no one could merit God's favor. But beyond this, Jesus is reported to have himself spoken a word of forgiveness over sinners (Mark 2:5; Luke 7:48; 23:34). In so doing he assumed a unique position of authority (Mark 2:7). Although proclaiming the kingdom of God, both in terms of judgment and forgiveness, Jesus spoke primarily in terms of the latter, "I came not to call the righteous, but sinners" (Mark 2:17 parr.; Luke 7:36–50; 18:9–14).

4. The final evidence for Jesus' assumption of authority is his *radical interpretation of the law*. Jesus was and remained a Jew in his obedience to the law, as the Gospel tradition attests. Yet Jesus radically reinterpreted the law in at least three particular respects: First, he denied that impurity could invade an individual from external sources (Mark 7:1–23 par.). Such an extreme qualification of the ancient world's distinction between clean and unclean constituted an attack upon the law's cultic structure, whether or not Jesus acknowledged it. Second, Jesus set his own authority over against that of Moses, especially in the antitheses of the Sermon on the Mount (Matt. 5:21–48). The antitheses ("But I say to you . . .") followed traditional rabbinic form. But a rabbi opposed his teaching to other rabbis whereas Jesus opposed his teaching to that of Moses. This authoritative claim exceeded the bounds of piety. Third, Jesus set scripture over against scripture and by so doing assumed authority over the written word of scripture (Mark 10:2–12; cf. Matt. 19:3–12). Although scribes developed oral interpretation of the scriptures, their interpretation did not set one passage over against another and claim that one scripture was less authoritative because it represented a concession to human weakness.

How could Jesus assume such authority? The probable explanation proceeds from the central proclamation of Jesus concerning the irruption of the kingdom of God. This emergent rule of God rendered all other authority provisional and transitory. The preaching of the inaugurated kingdom gave to Jesus' message a fresh, revolutionary quality that inevitably offended those who respected traditional authority.

Healings were occurring; disciples were being called; forgiveness was being offered; a new community of "forgiven sinners" was being formed; and the law was being radically reinterpreted. Something new was appearing in many forms. But Jesus' treatment of the law was very likely the primary cause for opposition to him. Jesus had touched the nerve of first-century Judaism. Eventually the separation of his followers ("Christians") from the old religious community resulted. Understandably, the leaders of Judaism rejected Jesus and his authority; opposition led ultimately to his being handed over to be crucified by the Roman government as a politically dangerous revolutionary. To this last dramatic chapter of Jesus' ministry we now turn.

The Suffering Messiah

Our efforts to reconstruct the historical Jesus have been guided by the principle of coherence. According to the tradition, Jesus of Nazareth was a man who healed, taught, and suffered a criminal's death. Our portrait of him must include these three elements in a coherent, understandable way or else historical criticism is unable to make sense of the tradition. The necessity for coherence becomes a problem when we now turn to the final element in the historical Jesus tradition, the death of Jesus. Why was Jesus crucified? Was his death simply the tragic end of a man who had gone about doing good, both in deed and word? How was it possible that one who had performed miracles could die in such weakness? How could one who evidently attracted such crowds of followers have been completely deserted at the last days? Such questions were potentially embarrassing. Yet the early Christians did not conceal Jesus' death; they proclaimed it.

Already some indications of answers to these questions have become apparent. The Teaching Messiah turned out to be something more than an instructor in good works, piety, and universal kindness. At the center of Jesus' teaching was the kingdom proclamation. As herald of the kingdom, Jesus claimed an authority which startled and astounded some and threatened others. The challenge of Jesus' authoritative message and activity met resistance that finally culminated in his death.

We have already observed that the healing Messiah possessed authority. But without faith in the power of God, healing did not take place. Moreover, the healings that Jesus effected demonstrated not his rulership but his service to God and others. The Gospel of Matthew aptly and succinctly characterized the miraculous healing power of Jesus with the passage from Isaiah, "He took our infirmities and bore our diseases" (Matt. 8:17). Surprisingly, just that passage could be applied to the death of Jesus (Matt. 26:28; cf. Rom. 5:8 and John 3:16). Perhaps the powerful miracle-working Jesus and the crucified Jesus complement, rather than contradict, each other.

We have also come to recognize Jesus' limited use of power by the way in which the miracle tradition is treated in both Mark and Matthew. The heightened miracle tradition in the first half of Mark did not succeed in producing true discipleship. The disciples became truly faithful only after Jesus' death and resurrection. In Matthew, condensation of the Markan miracle tradition focused attention

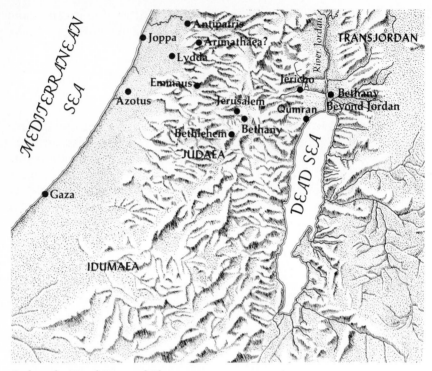

Judea, the Dead Sea, and Idumea.

upon the word of Jesus rather than upon his miracle power. Each Gospel affirms that Jesus worked miracles, yet each Gospel sets the miraculous within the framework of a ministry that concludes with Jesus' crucifixion. Jesus' power did not deliver him from that apparently ignominious end. Jesus' words and works led unerringly to his death. In this sense it is correct to say that the Gospels are "passion narratives with extended introductions."

THE PASSION AND DEATH OF JESUS

Why did Jesus go to his death in Jerusalem?

Before looking more closely at the passion narrative, we need to reckon with possible reasons for Jesus' final fatal journey to Jerusalem. Although the Fourth Gospel records several trips to Jerusalem, the Synoptic Gospels give the impression that Jesus journeyed from Galilee to Jerusalem only at the close of his ministry.[63] This journey

[63] Our interpretation of Mark has already shown the difficulty of accepting the Markan outline as a reliable chronological guide to Jesus' ministry. The movement between Galilee and Judea in the Fourth Gospel is, however, very likely governed by

occupies a central place in the Gospels. As we discovered, Luke made that journey the crucial middle section of his Gospel (Luke 9:51–19:29). Mark's tradition describes the journey to Jerusalem as a decisive and awesome step, "And they were on the road, going up to Jerusalem, and Jesus was walking ahead of them; and they were amazed, and those who followed were afraid" (Mark 10:32; cf. Matt. 20:17 and Luke 18:31).

Some New Testament interpreters take at face value the Markan view that Jesus went to Jerusalem to die. For example, it is maintained that a new conviction dawned upon Jesus at Caesarea Philippi: "The [apocalyptic] tribulation, so far as Jesus is concerned, is now connected with an historic event: he will go to Jerusalem, there to suffer death at the hands of the authorities. He must suffer for others . . . that the kingdom might come."[64] This hypothesis not only takes Mark (8:31) at face value, but assumes that Jesus had an apocalyptic mind-set. As we have seen, both aspects of the hypothesis are subject to serious question. Moreover, so far as we can tell from the Synoptic Gospels themselves, Jesus did not act in Jerusalem as if he were carrying out a preconceived plan to die. The hypothesis rests in part upon the view that Jesus took upon himself the role of the suffering servant of Isaiah 53: "For the Son of man also came not to be served but to serve, and to give his life as a ransom for many" (Mark 10:45). We previously suggested that this saying more likely reflects the faith of the early church than the consciousness of Jesus.

The reasons for Jesus' journey to Jerusalem can be discussed when we look at the incidents that reportedly took place in Jerusalem. As an alternative working hypothesis we suggest that Jesus went to Jerusalem to preach the coming kingdom of God, for no person who had a message for Israel could fail to take it to the capital city. In Jerusalem Jesus sought a final decision about the irrupting kingdom.[65] In the carrying out of this mission Jesus could hardly have been blind to the possibility that his own death might result (cf. Luke 13:33). That he consciously sought his death, however, is improbable. Jesus' kingdom proclamation does not center upon his own role, and the traditions of the kingdom and the coming Son of Man say nothing explicitly about his intention to die. Moreover, the view that Jesus sought to bring in the kingdom through his suffering lacks support of the Gospels themselves.

---

literary and theological factors rather than a desire to remain faithful to history. We can be certain of little more than that Jesus' mission began with his baptism and ended with his crucifixion. See Kümmel, *Introduction to the New Testament*, pp. 63 f.

[64] Schweitzer, *The Quest of the Historical Jesus*, pp. 386 f.

[65] See Bornkamm, *Jesus of Nazareth*, pp. 154 f.

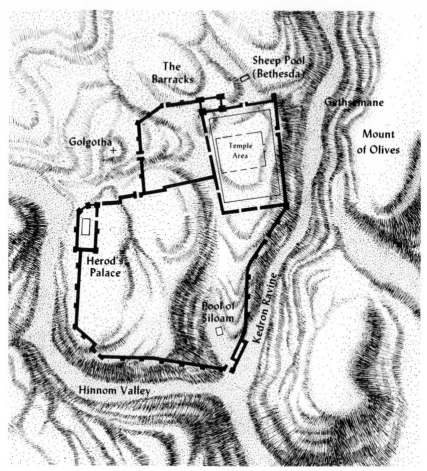

Jerusalem.

THE EVENTS OF JESUS' PASSION AND DEATH

Unlike other traditions in the Synoptics, the passion story, beginning with the entry into Jerusalem (Mark 11:1; Matt. 21:1; Luke 19:28), constitutes a full, detailed narrative covering a period of days. Moreover, we get the impression that we are being told the facts without obvious embellishment or the intrusion of faith considerations. The opponents of Jesus have the upper hand, and Jesus dies. The impression of accuracy is heightened by the remarkable agreement of the Synoptic Gospels in sequence of events and in details, an agreement considerably greater than in the earlier portions of the Gospels. This becomes even more pronounced with the arrest, trial, and crucifixion of Jesus. Moreover, the Fourth Gospel (John 18–19) seems but another voice in the Synoptic chorus. Nowhere else does it agree so closely with them.

The major episodes of the passion story in their general order are the triumphal entry into Jerusalem (Mark 11:1–10); the cleansing of the temple (Mark 11:15–19); the controveries about authority (Mark 11:27–33, 12:1–12, 13–17, 18–27, 28–34); the apocalyptic discourse (Mark 13); the anointing of Jesus (Mark 14:3–9); the Last Supper (Mark 14:12–25); Jesus in the Garden of Gethsemane (Mark 14:32–42); Jesus' arrest and trial (Mark 14:43–65); the release of Barabbas (Mark 15:6–15); and finally the crucifixion and burial of Jesus (Mark 15:16–47). The narrative follows a sequence that is broadly historical. Manifestly several of the crucial events must have occurred in the order in which they are presented: entry into Jerusalem, temple cleansing, the subsequent question about authority, the Last Supper, Gethsemane, Jesus' arrest, the crucifixion and burial. Thus we may proceed with some confidence to the following reconstruction of Jesus' activity and reception in Jerusalem.

Jesus' triumphal entry into Jerusalem was open to dangerous misinterpretation. The acclamation of the crowds, "Blessed is the kingdom of our father David that is coming!" (Mark 11:10; cf. Matt. 21:9; Luke 19:38), designated him as a political king who would restore the fortunes of Israel by leading a revolution to overthrow Roman domination. With respect to these hopes Jesus' first action upon entering Jerusalem was ambiguous; he went into the temple and drove out the traders and money changers (Mark 11:15–19). Ordinarily the Court of the Gentiles, where this event must have taken place, would have been well policed, with a Roman garrison stationed nearby. How Jesus was able to get away with such an act is a major and unresolved historical question. The question is particularly difficult if Jesus' act is viewed as an armed assault. Nevertheless, the view that Jesus had an armed force with him and was actually bent upon armed revolution has occasionally been advanced.[66] Aside from the fact that the whole Jesus tradition scarcely supports this position, it is by no means clear what Jesus would have hoped to gain for an armed revolt by the expulsion of money changers and vendors from the temple precincts. If, however, the central focus of Jesus' mission and message was proclamation and inauguration of the kingdom of God, it is reasonable to suppose that he would have gone to the Holy City, and to the holiest place in the city, to announce the coming of that kingdom (Malachi 3:1).

---

[66] This is the view of Brandon, *Jesus and the Zealots*, pp. 330 ff. Although the "attack" upon the temple was, in our view, not motivated by political, revolutionary aims, it might well have been construed as a subversive and ominous act by the Romans as well as the Jewish temple authorities. It is noteworthy that Jesus is said to have predicted the destruction of the temple (Mark 13:2); this prophecy was hurled back at him by opponents (Mark 14:58; 15;29). If these opponents took Jesus to be a revolutionary or Zealot, they were mistaken. But if they saw in him a threat to the status quo, they were not misled.

Entry of Jesus into Jerusalem. Sculpture from a lintel over a doorway near Massa Carrara, Italy (*ca.* 1175). (Courtesy of Metropolitan Museum of Art. Purchase, 1962. The Cloisters Collection.)

The temple's corruption then provoked him to hostility against its custodians. Understandably, the religious leaders reacted violently to this action (Mark 11:18); at the trial they accused him of having come to destroy the temple (Mark 14:57 f.; cf. 13:2).

Accordingly, the passion story centers more upon the question of what authority Jesus possessed to do these things than upon the specifically messianic question (Mark 11:28). The opponents of Jesus tried to fit him into the category of a political revolutionary (cf. Mark 12:13–17) and to engage him in theological disputes (cf. the resurrection question in Mark 12:18–27 and the query about the First Commandment in Mark 12:28–34). But Jesus continued to threaten their security by proclaiming the immediacy of God's rule (Mark 12:17, 27, 34), which demanded the response of the whole person (cf. the poor widow in Mark 12:41–44). Jesus preached the dawning kingship of God rather than a political, spiritual, or moral ideology. That emphasis becomes most evident in the passion story's apocalyptic discourse; for the final days are unmistakably to be the triumphant coming of God's kingly rule and the world's judgment (note especially Mark 13:24–26 and 32 f.). Even though the apocalyptic discourse is in part not from Jesus, its position in the passion story authentically elaborates the eschatological aspect of his last message.

It is uncertain whether the Last Supper that Jesus shared with his disciples was a Jewish Passover meal.[67] In any event, the setting makes clear that the meal was eschatological, "Truly, I say to you, I shall not drink again of the fruit of the vine until that day when I drink it new in the kingdom of God" (Mark 14:25). This word of Jesus[68] indicates that by this time he knew that his death was im-

---

[67] See Dibelius, *Jesus*, pp. 128–132. Also cf. J. Jeremias, *The Eucharistic Words of Jesus*, trans. A. Ehrhardt (Oxford: Basil Blackwell, 1955), esp. pp. 1–60.

[68] Bornkamm, *Jesus of Nazareth*, p. 160, argues that it is authentic.

minent. His overwhelming conviction about the immediacy of the reign of God elicited followers but also aroused opponents who now sought his death. The proleptic anointing of Jesus' body for burial (Mark 14:3–9) and his betrayal by Judas (Mark 14:10–21) point to the impending death. Ordinary piety had been offended. Moreover, Jesus' kingdom proclamation made him vulnerable to misunderstanding or misrepresentation as a political revolutionary. Ironically, the very reason for Judas' betrayal may have been his disappointed realization that Jesus was not going to lead an armed revolt against Rome. But about Judas' motivation one can only speculate; the texts are silent.

In the Garden of Gethsemane Jesus prayed that he might escape death if he would not thereby betray God's rule and will (Mark 14:36; cf. 8:35). After Gethsemane Jesus was alone, deserted even by his closest disciples (Mark 14:37, 40; see esp. Peter's denial, 14:66–72). The Gethsemane story may not be the report of an eyewitness—who was there?—yet it makes sense of the last hours of Jesus. In substance if not in detail, it is an accurate portrait. Jesus' feelings are intensely human.

The trial scene raises some difficult historical questions;[69] our subsequent conclusions, therefore, must remain conjectural. Although the authorities, including the Jewish high priest, condemned Jesus because he claimed to be the Messiah, no other record exists of any Jewish court ever condemning anyone as a messianic pretender. In view of the fact that Jesus was undoubtedly killed, not by the Jewish form of capital punishment, stoning (cf. Acts 5:26; 7:58 f.), but by Roman crucifixion, it has been suggested that the trial before the Sanhedrin was invented by the early church as anti-Jewish polemic. Probably Jesus was only arraigned before Jewish authorities and then delivered to the Romans who executed him as a messianic pretender. Although Jesus' radical view of obedience and his seeming disregard for tradition doubtless aroused opposition among Pharisees, even as the Gospels report, the Markan account of the trial and death of Jesus—indeed, of the Passion Week—indicates little or no opposition on their part. Since the Pharisees were the ancestors of the Judaism which emerged from the Roman War, this fact should have some bearing on Christian-Jewish relations, and especially the question of responsibility for Jesus' death.

According to the Markan account Jesus died rather quickly (15:44) and with a loud cry (15:37). At his death his body was re-

---

[69] See Bornkamm, *Jesus of Nazareth*, p. 163. For a different account, cf. Paul Winter, *On the Trial of Jesus* (Berlin: Walter de Gruyter, 1961). John R. Donahue, *Are You the Christ? The Trial Narrative in the Gospel of Mark*, SBL Dissertation Series, 10 (Missoula, Montana: Scholars Press, 1973), finds evidence that the Markan trial narrative is, at least in its present form, mainly the composition of the evangelist from traditional materials.

quested by Joseph of Arimathea, whom Mark identifies as a member
of the Sanhedrin (15:43). Pilate granted his request and Jesus' body
was taken down on the evening of the crucifixion. Joseph then buried Jesus, according to Matthew (27:60) in his own new tomb. In all
probability the story of the burial is based upon a kernel of historical
fact. It is simple, brief, and direct. The principal character, Joseph of
Arimathea, is mentioned in all the Gospel accounts, including John.
He is unknown from other sources, but just this fact leads us to
trust the reports. Otherwise it would be difficult to account for the
introduction of this person to perform the important task of burial.

THE PASSION TRADITION

At this point we may profitably reflect about the overall nature
of the passion tradition. This series of connected incidents makes
sense, and the events absorb our interest purely as story. Few pious
or theological interpretations interrupt the flow of the action. Later
Christian doctrines on the death of Jesus are not the specific focus
of attention. Yet the passion story cannot be read simply as a neutral
detached account of the last days of Jesus in Jerusalem. The faith of
the church is at work to interpret the meaning of Jesus' passion and
death.

In the study of the Gospels we have already become aware of
some disagreement about details in the passion story. For example,
Jesus' word of forgiveness from the cross in Luke (23:34) leaves quite
a different impression from his final agonizing cry in Mark (15:34;
Matt. 27:46). In John Jesus remains in control until the very last
when he announces, "It is finished," and expires (19:30). Yet obviously the various passion stories tell of the same event, the death
of a Jewish religious figure in first-century Palestine, and they tell
the story in much the same terms. But in all the accounts another
dimension is visible. The conviction that somehow God is at work
in the very death of Jesus governs the telling of the story. The reader
does not look away from the incidents to grasp this dimension and
understand their meaning. Rather the events contain their own
meaning, their own depth dimension, which is conveyed within the
story but is not identical with it. Jesus died and his death clarified
who he was.

Two further observations about the passion story support our
contention that it seeks to communicate the divine action in terms
of history. First, the major events are seen as the fulfillment of sacred scripture. This is especially evident in the crucifixion scene
where parts of the narrative correspond closely to Psalm 22 (Mark
15:24, 29, 34; cf. Psalm 22:18, 7, 1, respectively).[70] In earlier scenes

[70] See also Mark 15:36 (Psalm 69:21); Mark 15:19 (Isaiah 50:6); Mark 15:28, note
relegation to alternate reading in RSV (Isaiah 53:12); Mark 15:43 ff. (Isaiah 53:9), and
so forth.

View of Jerusalem with the Garden of Gethsemane in the center and the Mount of Olives in the background. (Courtesy of Pan American Airways.)

allusions to the Old Testament are also numerous. When Jesus enters Jerusalem, he apparently fulfills the prophecy of Zechariah 9:9: "Rejoice greatly, O daughter of Zion: Shout aloud, O daughter of Jerusalem: Lo, your king comes to you; triumphant and victorious is he, humble and riding on an ass, on a colt the foal of an ass" (cf. Mark 11:1–10). The cleansing of the temple fulfills the prophecies of Isaiah 56:7 and of Jeremiah 7:11 (cf. Mark 11:11–18). These Old Testament allusions are not intended to prove that Jesus was the Messiah so much as to confirm the belief that within these events God was at work in extraordinary ways.

Second, the Synoptic Gospels do not dwell on the physical suffering of Jesus in the crucifixion. Although the reader is made aware that this form of execution was terrifying (cf. the scourging, Mark 15:15; the striking, 15:19; the offering of the drug, 15:23; the loud cry, 15:34, 37), the enormous possibilities for exploiting detailed description of torture in order to win human sympathy are not real-

ized. The Roman author Cicero (106–43 B.C.) called crucifixion "that
cruel and disgusting penalty."[71] Because death by crucifixion represented one of the highest achievements of the torturer's art, we
might surmise that the lack of emphasis on physical suffering in the
Gospels was due to pious considerations or delicate concern for
readers, but the point probably lies elsewhere. The purely human
sphere of torturous agony and sympathetic response is minimized
because Jesus' crucifixion was regarded primarily as the saving activity of God rather than the ordeal of a righteous martyr. Jesus is not
portrayed, except in Luke, as a hero or martyr in the modern, or
ancient, sense.

JESUS' DEATH IN THE TRADITION

In the death of Jesus the passion story reaches its climax. Our
conclusions concerning the earliest Christian convictions about the
nature of that death may be gathered up in four pointed statements:
(1) The real actor in the passion story was God. (2) God willed the
death of Jesus. (3) That death was willed in order that men might be
set free. (4) Jesus willed his own death by his life. These motifs are
formative and important, not only for the passion narratives of the
Gospels, but for the tradition lying behind them. We see them at
work already in the earliest creeds (I Cor. 15:3) and liturgies (I Cor.
11:23 ff.), as well as in certain crucially important formulations in
Paul's theological arguments (Rom. 5:6 ff.; II Cor. 8:9; Phil. 2:8). It
is likely that at a stage between these early statements and the passion narratives of the Gospels there existed more rudimentary passion narratives, in whose composition these motifs had already been
at work.

Although the death of Jesus occurred because of the enmity of
conventional piety and political complicity, the *real actor in the
passion was God*, not human beings. During the course of events
the will of the characters was subject to the will of God. This is
reflected in Mark's emphasis upon the necessity of Jesus' death and
the events associated with it (cf. Mark 8:31; 14:31). Further confirmation of the "divine necessity" for Jesus' death comes from one of
the primary verbs used in the passion story, *paradidōmi* (see Mark
13:9, 11, 12; 14:10; 15:1, 10, 15). This Greek verb can be translated
"to betray," "to hand over," or "to deliver." In Mark, Jesus predicted, "Behold, we are going up to Jerusalem; and the Son of Man
will be *delivered* to the chief priests and the scribes, and they will
condemn him to death, and *deliver* him to the Gentiles; and they
will mock him, and spit upon him, and scourge him, and kill him;
and after three days he will rise" (10:33 f). Next Judas (representing
the disciples?) delivered Jesus into the hands of the Jewish authori-

---

[71]*Against Verres V*, 64. Cf. the further description quoted by Goguel in *Jesus
and the Origins of Christianity*, II, pp. 534 f.

ties (Mark 14:10 f., 18, 21, 41 f.) and the Jewish authorities in turn delivered Jesus into the hands of Pilate (Mark 15:1, 10). Finally Pilate delivered Jesus to be crucified (Mark 15:15). In the passion story, this inexorable deliverance of Jesus to death is a token of the power of God at work behind the events.

The action that God willed was the death of Jesus. God did not directly reveal this information to Jesus' contemporaries. This statement reflects the conviction of faith that the death of Jesus was, under the circumstances, the will of God. In the two direct Old Testament quotes that refer to the impending death, Jesus says to his opponents, "Have you not read this scripture, 'The very stone which the builders rejected has become the head of the corner; this was the Lord's doing, and it is marvelous in our eyes'?" (Mark 12:10 f.; cf. Psalm 118:22 f.) and to the disciples, "You will all fall away; for it is written, 'I will strike the shepherd, and the sheep will be scattered.' But after I am raised up, I will go before you to Galilee" (Mark 14:27 f.; cf. Zechariah 13:7). Both quotations are intended to imply that the death of Jesus occurred at God's bidding. Moreover, in the Gethsemane prayer Jesus asked that the cup of suffering be taken away from him *unless* his death were God's will (Mark 14:36).

The reason that God wills Jesus' death has nothing to do with divine wrath; quite the opposite, for *Jesus died in order that the guilty might go free.* This is aptly illustrated in the Barabbas episode (Mark 15:6–15). At this point in the story all notion of a trial has been abandoned, and the one amnesty possible at the festival is the center of attention. When the crowd demands the death of Jesus instead of Barabbas, the revolutionary and murderer, Pilate asks, "Why, what evil has he done?" (vs. 14) The same question dominates the reader, for Jesus had done nothing to deserve their enmity. Barabbas was guilty; Jesus was innocent. The crowd's verdict was completely wrong. Why, then, should God assent to injustice and will the death of Jesus? Jesus, who was finally crucified by the Romans as an insurrectionist, dies in order that the real revolutionary might go free. This is the meaning of Jesus' death; the death of the innocent one allows the guilty to go free. Ironically, this point becomes explicit at the crucifixion in the scoffing of the bystanders and the chief priests as they demand that Jesus miraculously descend from the cross (Mark 15:29 f.): "He saved others; he cannot save himself" (Mark 15:31). Of course, Jesus could not come down from the cross because he would thereby disobey the will of God and annul his mission and message, the bringing of life and freedom to sinners (cf. Mark 2:17 and 14:41). Jesus could do no miracle precisely because the miracle of God's coming near in forgiveness rather than judgment was taking place. Within the event of a Roman execution occurred the salvation of humankind—so the New Testament faith claims (Rom. 5:8; cf. John 3:16; Mark 10:45; I Peter 3:18; and the like).

Jesus willed his own death by his life. We have already observed the historical improbability that Jesus saw himself as the suffering servant of Isaiah, whose death was a means of reconciling God with man. Probably Jesus did not enter Jerusalem with the express intention of dying, but rather to proclaim the coming kingdom of God. But if Jesus' death were not understandable as the outcome of his life, then there would be no reason why the Christian faith should be tied to this historical person's death. Why not anyone's death? Or, why any death at all?

The statement, Jesus willed his own death by his life, is deliberate. In effect, we are saying that Jesus' death climaxed and actualized his proclamation of the irruption of the kingdom of God. Jesus' radical sense of the nearness of God, his consequent break with the usual standards of righteousness, his association with sinners, and his radical criticism of tradition aroused a reaction that eventuated in his death. To be sure, Jesus did not go about his mission in Jerusalem blindly. He knew that his message and action had set in motion forces that might cause his death, but he did not seek it.

Jesus does express his intention to die in sayings ascribed to him in the Gospels, but these are likely the church's later interpretation of the meaning of his death as God's act. The interpretation is made definitive by putting it on Jesus' lips. Although it is difficult to regard such sayings as historically authentic, they nevertheless portray faithfully the way in which Jesus' death is related to his life. It makes a difference to historical interpretation and to Christian faith that Jesus was not accidentally run down by a chariot. He died during a Jewish Passover on a Roman cross.

Although we have so far concentrated upon his death, Jesus' full identity was only seen in the light of the resurrection. But our reading of the Gospels confirms that the resurrection cannot be separated from the death. For Christian faith, the passion and resurrection are one story. Whether the early Christians were right, whether the story was true, still remains a matter of faith. Certainly Jesus died on a cross, that much is virtually indisputable. Yet whether that cross was really the salvation event depends upon whether the resurrection report is believed. Without the cross the resurrection is meaningless, but without the resurrection the cross remains only a tragedy.

THE RESURRECTION OF JESUS OF NAZARETH

What was the resurrection of Jesus? An event? A belief? A hope?

According to the New Testament, the resurrection is central for faith: "If Christ has not been raised, then our preaching is in vain and your faith is in vain" (I Cor. 15:14; cf. 15:17). Without the resurrection there would have been no Gospels, no history of the apostles, no letters, no vision of the future, and no church. The origin of New Testament faith is the victory over death realized in Jesus of Nazareth.

When we talk about the resurrection of Jesus we cannot lose sight of the obvious fact that death and resurrection belong together in the New Testament tradition. Who Jesus was is answered by what he did in his life and death and by what was done for him in his being raised from the dead—"Was it not necessary that the Christ should suffer these things and enter into his glory?" (Luke 24:26).

Although the modern mind might find congenial the view that the resurrection stories are simply interpretations of Jesus' true identity as the one sent by God and have nothing to do with an actual event, the nature of the resurrection tradition will not allow this easy conclusion. This tradition does not read like a mythological tale. Its realistic quality allows for and demands historical investigation. To maintain that the event of Jesus' resurrection is removed from historical investigation denies the factual claim of the early Christian faith. On the other hand, to maintain that historical investigation can decide about the resurrection denies the uniqueness and mystery of the event. Whether the resurrection of Jesus occurred is a question "for the answering of which evidence is relevant, but the evidence might all be believed without the question itself being answered in the affirmative."[72]

Keeping in mind, then, the centrality of the resurrection in the New Testament tradition, its inseparable relation to Jesus' death, and the important, but not decisive, role of historical criticism in investigating the resurrection, we turn to the nature of the resurrection tradition. In due course, we shall return to the problem of the nature of the resurrection itself.

THE RESURRECTION TRADITION

The major New Testament sources of the resurrection tradition are I Corinthians 15:3–8, Mark 16:1–8, Matthew 28:1–20, Luke 24:1–53, and John 20:1–21:25. They present a bewildering array of material. The variety of the resurrection tradition itself poses a problem. Our first task is to understand the discrepancies and similarities within the resurrection tradition. Next we will look at the two major types of resurrection tradition—the empty tomb reports and the accounts of resurrection appearances. Only then can we classify the traditions as to their various emphases and attempt a preliminary understanding of the nature of the resurrection.

---

[72]Ramsey, *Religious Language*, p. 149. Cf. Bornkamm, *Jesus of Nazareth*, p. 180, and P. M. Van Buren, *The Secular Meaning of the Gospels: Based on an Analysis of Its Language* (New York: Macmillan, 1963), p. 128.

Discrepancies within the New Testament resurrection traditions are obvious. According to Paul's tradition (I Cor. 15: 3–8) the
first appearance is to Peter, then to the twelve, and so on. In the
Synoptic Gospels no appearance to Peter is directly reported (cf.
Luke 24:34 and John 21). In Mark and Matthew, only the women
visit the tomb of Jesus. Luke adds that Peter then follows alone. In
John's Gospel, Mary visits the tomb; then Peter and the beloved disciples follow. In Mark and Matthew, Jesus appears to the disciples
in Galilee; in Luke and John he appears in Jerusalem. Paul's tradition reports resurrection appearances to the five hundred and to
James; the Gospels make no mention of any such event. Mark and
Matthew do not report Jesus' eating with his disciples; Luke and
John do. According to Luke, Jesus vanishes from the sight of two
disciples on the road to Emmaus. Moreover, both Luke and John
hand on the tradition that Jesus passed through closed doors. Such
obvious discrepancies and variety raise questions about the nature
of the resurrection tradition. Does a substantial historical core exist,
or are these reports flights of the Christian imagination?

Paul's resurrection tradition (I Cor. 15:3–8) lists a number of
eyewitnesses to the appearances of the resurrected Christ. This tradition does not claim that the witnesses saw the resurrection
itself—that is, the emergence of Jesus from the tomb or his resuscitation, but rather that they saw the resurrected Christ. Paul, however, admits that he was untimely born (vs. 8); that is, his resurrection appearance was unusually late. Paul's tradition places the
initiative for the appearances not with those to whom the risen
Christ appeared, but with the Resurrected One himself. Moreover,
the resurrection is said to have taken place "on the third day" (vs.
4). Although this time reference was probably not meant to be exact,
it stresses that the resurrection occurred shortly after Jesus died.[73]
The phrase "in accordance with the scripture" (vs. 3) declares that
what happened in Jesus was not the death and resurrection of just
any man but of one who fulfilled the promise of God to Israel. The
tradition also makes it quite explicit that he who was raised and
appeared to his followers and Paul is the same Jesus who died and
was buried. The Christ of faith is linked by this resurrection tradition to the historical Jesus.

In Mark (16:1–8) no resurrection appearance is reported. Instead
there is only the story of the empty tomb, in which the young man
announces that Jesus has risen and will appear to the disciples in
Galilee. Again, the initiative is with Jesus. This resurrection tradi-

---

[73] See Hugh Anderson, *Jesus and Christian Origins: A Commentary on Modern
Viewpoints* (New York: Oxford University Press, 1964), p. 214. We are indebted in
this discussion of the resurrection tradition to his analysis (ibid., pp. 211–237). For
another, more extensive analysis of the resurrection materials see R. H. Fuller, *The
Formation of the Resurrection Narratives*, rev. ed. (New York: Macmillan, 1980).

tion is characterized by the women's awe at finding the tomb empty (vss. 5, 6, 8). They came piously to pay homage to the dead body, but the crucified Jesus departed ahead of them.

Matthew's tradition (28:1–20) enlarges that of Mark. His story of the empty tomb includes a resurrection appearance to the women (vs. 9), which is followed by an appearance to the disciples in Galilee (vss. 16–20). Here the dominant mood is one of joy and worship. In contrast to this response, we read that the Jews have made elaborate precautions to prevent the theft of Jesus' body (27:62–66; 28:11–15). The resurrected Jesus speaks to his disciples about their future tasks and affirms his identity with the historical Jesus (". . . teaching them to observe all that I have commanded you" vs. 20; see pp. 125 ff.).

Luke (24:1–53) contains the most elaborate tradition of the resurrection in the Synoptic Gospels. The empty tomb is subordinated to the resurrection appearances, for, as Luke puts it, "these words seemed to them an idle tale, and they did not believe them" (vs. 11). In the road to Emmanus story (vss. 13–35), the two disciples do not recognize Jesus by his physical appearance. They only know him when he, taking the initiative, explains the scriptural basis for his death and resurrection and performs the familiar act of blessing, breaking, and giving the bread. "Then they told what had happened on the road, and how he was known to them in the breaking of the bread" (vs. 35). Jesus then eats with his disciples to show that he is not a disembodied spirit (vss. 36–43), even though he has just been reported to have vanished and appeared again in the same context (cf. vss. 31 and 36). Like Matthew, Luke includes Jesus' final instruction to his disciples, which reiterates Luke's message of Jesus: "Repentance and forgiveness of sins should be preached in his name to all nations, beginning from Jerusalem" (vs. 47). Luke's resurrection account ends with Jesus' departure (vss. 50–53; cf. Acts 1:9–11). In Luke as in the other accounts, something happens because of the Resurrected One's initiative. Furthermore, it is again made clear that the risen Jesus could not be known apart from his historical life and death. More directly than in Matthew the task of the church is explained and handed over to the disciples. In fact, they must now perform that task without the aid of the resurrected Jesus.

In John's Gospel's account (John 20:1–21:25) Mary Magdalene comes alone to the tomb; Peter and the other disciples follow later. Then Mary receives an appearance of the risen Christ whom she recognizes only after he speaks her name. Curiously, she is told not to hold him (vs. 17), for he has still to ascend to the Father. Before departing to the Father Jesus gives the disciples the Holy Spirit (20:22), after having demonstrated that he is the same Jesus who has been crucified. This point is underscored in the appearance of Christ to Thomas. The first Johannine resurrection appearances, like those of Luke, are reported to have occurred in Jerusalem. The appendix of John, however, consists of an appearance in Galilee (chap. 21; cf. Matt. 28:16–20) in which Jesus directs his disciples so that they are able to make a catch of fish on the lake. Then he eats with them in a scene that is faintly eucharistic. Finally, there follows an encounter in which the risen Jesus three times questions Peter about his love for him. The effect seems to be to restore the fallen Peter who denied Jesus before his death.

The traditions we have surveyed present two problems centering about the relation between the empty tomb stories and the appearance narratives and the character of the resurrection appearance themselves.

The empty tomb story appears in all four Gospels, although it is not mentioned by Paul in the earliest report of the resurrection appearances. Quite possibly the empty tomb story circulated later than the reports of appearances. This conclusion rests in part upon evidence within the resurrection stories themselves that the tradition of the empty tomb was not initially known (e.g., Luke 24:34; cf. John 21:3). Its inclusion in the Synoptic Gospels can be attributed to their dependence on Mark, although its appearance in John may be due to a separate tradition. There are also parallels to the empty tomb story in the history of religions.[74] Moreover, we need to keep in mind that the empty tomb was an ambiguous witness to the resurrection. It attests the absence of the body, but not necessarily the reality or presence of the risen Jesus. Not illogically the Talmud reports that the body of Jesus was stolen. Apparently against just such a rumor Matthew elaborated a defense (28:11–15). Probably the empty tomb story reflects the deliberation of faith about what actually happened to Jesus' body, for according to the best New Testament evidence the early disciples were convinced of Jesus' resurrection, not by the empty tomb, but by the appearances.[75] These appearances of the risen Christ attest most accurately the nature of the resurrection tradition. In effect the disciples exclaimed, "He appeared to me!" Their faith had been broken by Jesus' death and they had fled. Yet something had happened at the resurrection, something not of their own initiative, but of the One who acted through the crucified Jesus—the God who raised him from the dead.

The problem of the character of the resurrection appearances is summed up in the question of whether they were physical or spiritual. The traditions seem to say that the resurrection was both physical and spiritual. Jesus ate with the disciples, they could see

---

[74] See E. Bickermann, "Das leere Grab," *Zeitschrift für die Neutestamentliche Wissenschaft,* 23 (1924), 281–292.

[75] For a positive evaluation of the historicity of the empty tomb, see H. von Campenhausen, "The Events of Easter and the Empty Tomb," *Tradition and Life in the Church,* trans. A. V. Littledale (London: Collins, 1968), pp. 42–89.

and touch the marks of the nails; but he could go through closed doors and vanish out of their sight. Paul claimed that the appearance to him was of the same nature as the appearances to Peter, the twelve, and so on (see Acts 9:1–9; 22:4–11; 26:9–18), but how could that be a physical appearance? Indeed, in the same chapter of I Corinthians, he describes the resurrected body as a spiritual, not a physical, body and says that flesh and blood (that is, a physical resurrection) cannot inherit the kingdom of God (I Cor. 15:50; cf. 15:35–58). Like the evangelists, Paul knew that he was talking about a mystery which no "either . . . or," either physical or spiritual, could solve. The decisive emphasis in all accounts is that the one who appeared was the same Jesus who had also died and been buried. Faith believed that the risen Jesus was no figment of the imagination; the historical Jesus had been raised from the dead. Therefore, the disciples knew that death had been conquered. Exactly how it was conquered remained a mystery, but that it was conquered Paul was as certain as the evangelists: "Thanks be to God, who gives us the victory through our Lord Jesus Christ" (I Cor. 15:57).

In summary, the varied resurrection traditions point to some basic assumptions about the resurrection. The death of Jesus had left the disciples in confusion (Luke 24:4) or fear for their lives (Mark 14:50). At Jesus' death, he was completely alone, forsaken by all of them (cf. John 16:32). But at the resurrection, the disciples were changed and made new. This transformation is implicit in the various traditions. It was not of their own doing; they attributed it to the resurrected Jesus who had appeared to them. Jesus' resurrection was not a product of faith. Rather, the resurrection had forced itself upon them, sometimes unwanted and always unexpected. And the resurrected One who appeared was always that Jesus whom they had known in his life and death.

THE RESURRECTION EVENT

Although differences exist among the resurrection traditions, the accounts unanimously agree that the one who died and was buried was also raised and appeared to a number of eyewitnesses. One can be reasonably certain that something happened, but the historian is less certain exactly what happened. As even our sources acknowledge that the resurrection is a unique event, analogous occurrences cannot be adduced to support its actuality.

If the resurrection was a historical occurrence, it was, according to the New Testament, one that could be separated neither from Jesus' death nor from the act of faith. The resurrection was not a separate event beside the death of Jesus. It preserved, and was based upon, knowledge of that event. We have already noted that the tradition continually stressed that the resurrection had fully occurred only when the risen one was identified and recognized as the crucified Jesus of Nazareth. Furthermore, resurrection faith pointed to something new. Easter was the beginning of Christian faith. Not until Easter did the disciples have the Spirit and power, for not until Easter was the identity of Jesus as the reigning Christ manifest. Yet Easter was rooted in Jesus' life and death. Thus with some justification the Christian era is dated from the birth, rather than from the resurrection, of Jesus.

What precisely did the resurrection mean for the earliest Christians? It meant, in summary, that despite appearances, even Jesus' crucifixion, God had not abandoned him. Moreover, the message of Jesus, which had centered on the proclamation of the kingdom, could now be presented in a new form in which the action of God was seen to have taken place already. A new dimension was added to Jesus' proclamation. The message about the irrupting presence of God became concrete in his death and resurrection. In new faith and confidence the disciples were able to recommit themselves and remain disciples. The resurrection was an answer to death, for the resurrection cannot be viewed otherwise than from the perspective of death. In the Gospels resurrection occurred only after the agony and seeming finality of Jesus' passion and death. Yet for the disciples Jesus' resurrection anticipated and overcame the threat represented by their own deaths (cf. Rom. 6).

What the resurrection is and what it means cannot be confirmed by historical investigation, even if that investigation could vindicate all the apparent factual claims that the New Testament makes. At stake is the truth of the Christian faith's claim that God was in Christ. To believe in the resurrection is to believe that this is in a unique sense true. Not to believe in the resurrection is to reject that claim, even if one honors Jesus as a very great religious leader and martyr. The New Testament witnesses insist that the resurrection was real and not an illusion. Yet they never separate resurrection and faith, as if the resurrection could have been experienced and analyzed apart from faith. Faith accompanies every resurrection report of which we have any record.

The recurrent interest in the Turin Shroud (so named because it has for the last four centuries been preserved in the Cathedral of St. John the Baptist in Turin, Italy) raises in an interesting way the question of the relationship between resurrection faith and historical evidence.[76] The shroud, venerated as the burial shroud of Jesus, shows faintly but unmistakably the front and back images of the body of a crucified man. Apparent bloodstains and other marks of injury on the wrists, feet, side, back, and brow suggest the wounds

---

[76] For a good report of recent investigation and opinion concerning the shroud, see Virginia Bortin, "Science and the Shroud of Turin," *Biblical Archaeologist*, 43 (1980), 109–117.

inflicted upon Jesus before and during his execution. Scientific tests so far conducted seem to indicate that, whatever the origin of the image, it was not produced by painting. Carbon testing, which would date the shroud within a century or two, has not yet been carried out. At present it is uncertain whether the shroud is closer to four hundred or two thousand years old. But given the state of scientific knowledge, it cannot be categorically denied that this is the burial shroud of Jesus. On the other hand, that is far from proven. Even if the shroud dates from the first century, and even if it could be proven that the image resulted from a flash of light, a quasi-photographic process (as some suggest), that would not prove it to be the burial shroud of Jesus. And if it were, his resurrection would not thereby be demonstrated. At most we are confronted with a remarkable phenomenon, with striking correspondences to the Gospel descriptions of Jesus' suffering and death. Even the empty tomb did not lead directly to resurrection faith. Resurrection faith has always been based on testimony to a living reality.

For Christians after the first generation, believing in the resurrection has meant believing the reports and records of the witnesses. Yet Christians have not usually been content to think that faith in the resurrection, faith in Christ, is nothing other than the ability or willingness to believe what one is told. New Testament writers addressed readers who had not seen the resurrected Lord and by and large did not expect to see him. For them and others the preaching of the good news, worship in the church, and the presence of the Holy Spirit in the community and with the individual surrounded and supported the word of the witnesses. Although the report of the witnesses was considered necessary, the believer in the church gained his own access to Christ through other means as well. Thus in the Gospel of John the resurrected Jesus blesses those who have not seen and yet believe, immediately after having demonstrated to Thomas the reality of his risen body (John 20:26–29). Thereby he assures later Christians that their faith may be as surely grounded as that of the first witnesses. Jesus proclaimed the coming of God's new world, the kingdom of God. In the resurrection the earliest Christians perceived that this reality of which he spoke was actually coming to be. In the church they found a new community to receive this reality and proclaim it to the whole world. In the Spirit they found confirmation that their faith was based neither on illusion nor on an isolated occult phenomenon, but upon the will and action of God.

Our fundamental working assumptions in this chapter have been two: (1) Although the Gospels are kerygmatic documents, they have not deliberately perverted or falsified the object of their attention, Jesus of Nazareth. (2) By working with three major areas of the tradition of Jesus—the healing, teaching, and suffering material—it is possible to understand the nature of each and their unity in the one historical figure Jesus. Thus the criterion of coherence was crucial for our portrait of Jesus. We have sought to represent the mystery of Jesus of Nazareth, a unique historical person. In the consequent portrait, we have consistently attempted to understand the continuity, rather than identity, between the mission and message of Jesus and the church's message about Jesus.

Jesus performed miracles of healing, out of compassion rather than for power. Jesus proclaimed the irrupting rule of God, without claiming to know the future or making humankind's response insignificant. Jesus demanded forgiveness of enemies, fellowship with sinners, radical obedience to the heart of the law, and announced God's blessing to the poor, the repentant, the believing, and the merciful. Jesus called disciples and followers, without promise of immediate reward but with a command to service. Jesus went to Jerusalem to proclaim the kingdom, and neither sought nor rejected the death that came. Jesus spoke, acted, and died. According to the faith of the church, God raised him from the dead.

Suggestions for Further Reading

Many popular books about Jesus, especially lives of Jesus, are really historical novels that rely upon the imaginations—more or less disciplined—of the authors. Almost all the reliable information about Jesus that survives is found in the canonical Gospels. The apocryphal Gospels add little to what we already know. The best source for these is E. Hennecke, *New Testament Apocrypha*, ed. W. Schneemelcher, trans. R. McL. Wilson (Philadelphia: Westminster, 1963), I. (Vol. II contains other early writings.) References to Jesus in ancient Jewish sources are collected and treated by Morris Goldstein, *Jesus in the Jewish Tradition* (New York: Macmillan, 1950). A good summary treatment of the extrabiblical sources pertaining to Jesus may be found in H. C. Kee, *Jesus in History: An Approach to the Study of the Gospels*, 2nd ed. (New York: Harcourt, 1977), pp. 40–75. Translations of the more important of these have now been published by F. F. Bruce (ed.), *Jesus and Christian Origins Outside the New Testament* (Grand Rapids, Mich.: Eerdmans, 1974), in a volume of convenient size and scope.

The history of nineteenth-century attempts to write a life of Jesus is brilliantly recounted and criticized by A. Schweitzer, *The Quest of the Historical Jesus*, trans. W. Montgomery with a new introduction by J. M. Robinson (New York: Macmillan, 1968), who was among the first to establish the eschatological character of Jesus' teaching. A history of more recent discussion of this problem is provided by N. Perrin, *The Kingdom of God in the Teaching of Jesus* (Philadelphia: Westminster, 1963). A ground-breaking book on Jesus' eschatology, now available in English, is J. Weiss, *Jesus' Proclamation of the Kingdom of God*, trans. R. H. Hiers and D. L. Holland (Philadelphia: Fortress, 1971). Weiss' book (first published, 1892) actually antedates the original publication of Schweitzer (1906). Critical efforts to recover the Jesus of history subsequent to Schweitzer are assessed by J. M. Robinson, *A New Quest of the Historical Jesus* (Naperville, Ill.: Allenson, 1959), and H. Anderson, *Jesus and Christian Origins* (New York: Oxford University Press, 1964).

Among other important modern works on Jesus are the following: R. Bultmann, *Jesus and the Word*, trans. L. P. Smith and E. H. Lantero (New York: Scribner, 1934), M. Dibelius, *Jesus*, trans. C. B. Hedrick and F. C. Grant (Philadelphia: Westminster, 1949); M. Goguel, *The Life of Jesus*, trans. O. Wyon (New York: Macmillan, 1933); and G. Bornkamm, *Jesus of Nazareth*, trans. I. and F. McLuskey with J. M. Robinson (New York: Harper & Row, 1960). The volume by Bultmann embodies the results of that scholar's form-critical methodology. Somewhat more conservative historically is the form-critical approach of Dibelius and his interpretation of Jesus. Written from a more liberal theological point of view, Goguel's work is nevertheless more conservative in its historical results. Bornkamm's book is the fruit of the so-called new quest. A number of the most important works on Jesus from the past two centuries have been republished in a Lives of Jesus Series edited by L. E. Keck (Philadelphia: Fortress).

G. Vermes, *Jesus the Jew* (Philadelphia: Fortress, 1973), attempts to see Jesus afresh against the background of Judaism. Cf. J. Klausner, *Jesus of Nazareth* (New York: Macmillan, 1926). J. Bowker, *Jesus and the Pharisees* (New York: Cambridge University Press, 1973), sets Jesus over against the Pharisees and presents the relevant sources in translation. Important for general background are J. Jeremias, *Jerusalem in the Time of Jesus*, trans. F. H. and C. H. Cave (Philadelphia: Fortress, 1969), and J. Wilkinson, *Jerusalem as Jesus Knew It* (London: Thames and Hudson, 1978); the latter contains excellent photographs as well as a wealth of information. See also works on Judaism mentioned at the end of Chapter 1.

On the teaching of Jesus, one may still consult with profit T. W. Manson, *The Teaching of Jesus*, 2nd ed. (New York: Cambridge University Press, 1935), and the more recent work of N. Perrin, *Rediscovering the Teaching of Jesus* (New York: Harper & Row, 1967). A bracing rejoinder to some of the perspectives of the latter is P. S. Minear, *Commands of Christ* (Nashville, Tenn.: Abingdon, 1972). A most important recent scholarly treatment of Jesus' message is J. Jeremias, *New Testament Theology, I: The Proclamation of Jesus*, trans. J. Bowden (London: SCM, 1971), the culmination of a lifetime of study of the Palestinian and Jewish background of the Gospels and the Jesus tradition. Jeremias has also produced basic works on *The Parables of Jesus*, trans. S. H. Hooke, rev. ed. (New York: Scribner, 1966), and *The Eucharistic Words of Jesus*, trans. N. Perrin (New York: Scribner, 1966). (The former is available in a simplified version for students who do not use Greek in *Rediscovering the Parables*, New York: Scribner, 1966.) The character of Jesus' language and forms of speech as represented in the Synoptics has been a subject of recent interest; for example, Amos Wilder, *The Language of the Gospel: Early Christian Rhetoric*, rev. ed. (Cambridge, Mass.: Harvard University Press, 1971); D. O. Via, *The Parables: Their Literary and Existential Dimension* (Philadelphia: Fortress, 1967); and R. C. Tannehill, *The Sword of his Mouth* (Philadelphia: Fortress, 1975).

On the question of Jesus' own understanding of his role, there is a va-

riety of scholarly opinion. Schweitzer forcefully argued that Jesus thought
of himself as the coming Messiah and that every major move of his ministry
was dictated by his concept of his role in the eschatological drama. He was
in part reacting to the view of W. Wrede, who thought that Jesus did not
regard himself as the Messiah (*The Messianic Secret,* see p. 84). Bultmann
in several works, especially *Theology of the New Testament,* I, trans. K.
Grobel (New York: Scribner, 1951), pp. 26 ff., strongly espoused Wrede's
view. More conservative is W. Manson, *Jesus the Messiah* (London: Hodder
& Stroughton, 1943). In support of Bultmann's view that Jesus also did not
identify himself explicitly as the Son of Man is H. Tödt, *The Son of Man in
the Synoptic Tradition,* trans. D. M. Barton (Philadelphia: Westminster,
1965). There is doubt in some quarters that Jesus even spoke of the coming
Son of Man at all; cf. Perrin, *Rediscovering the Teaching of Jesus,* p. 198.
Somewhat more positive in his appraisal of the authenticity of the Son of
Man sayings, F. H. Borsch, *The Son of Man in Myth and History* (Philadelphia: Westminster, 1967), draws upon a wide-ranging investigation of the
history of the concept.

The relationship of Jesus to political activity in Palestine is explored by
M. Hengel in two small books: *Was Jesus a Revolutionist?* trans. W. Klassen
(Philadelphia: Fortress, 1971), and *Victory over Violence: Jesus and the Revolutionists,* trans. D. E. Green (Philadelphia: Fortress, 1973). On the social
context and consequences of Jesus' ministry, G. Theissen, *A Sociology of
Early Palestinian Christianity,* trans. J. Bowden (Philadelphia: Fortress,
1978), yields important insights and implications.

The miracles of Jesus are treated by R. H. Fuller, *Interpreting the Miracles* (Philadelphia: Westminster, 1963). An older study, A. J. Fridrichsen,
The Problem of Miracle in Primitive Christianity, trans. R. A. Harrisville
and J. S. Hanson (Minneapolis: Augsburg, 1972), published originally in
1925, is nevertheless remarkably up to date in terms of perspective and
questions raised. Helpful discussions of the problem of miracles per se appear in C. F. D. Moule (ed.), *Miracles: Cambridge Studies in their Philosophy and History* (London: Mowbray, 1965), and in T. A. Burkill, *Mysterious
Revelation* (Ithaca, N.Y.: Cornell University Press, 1963), pp. 41–61. For a
historical survey of the subject, see S. J. Case, *Experience with the Supernatural in Early Christian Times* (New York: Century, 1929); also R. M.
Grant, *Miracle and Natural Law in Greco-Roman and Early Christian
Thought* (Amsterdam: North-Holland, 1952).

P. Winter, *On the Trial of Jesus,* eds. T. A. Burkill and G. Vermes, rev.
ed. (Berlin: Walter de Gruyter, 1973), emphasizes the literary and historical
problems surrounding the trial and finds that the Gospels have overplayed
the Jewish role. A similar view is taken by W. R. Wilson, *The Execution of
Jesus: A Judicial, Literary and Historical Investigation* (New York: Scribner, 1970). The Roman role is emphasized by Brandon in *Jesus and the Zealots* (Manchester: Manchester University Press, 1967) and in *The Trial of
Jesus* (London: Batsford, 1968). On the other hand, the basic correctness of
the Gospel accounts of this matter is supported by J. Blinzler, *The Trial of
Jesus,* trans. I. and F. McHugh (Westminster, Md.: Newman, 1959). E. Bammel has edited a valuable collection of essays, *The Trial of Jesus: Cambridge Studies in Honour of C. F. D. Moule* (London: SCM, 1970), mostly
in agreement with the viewpoint of Blinzler. D. R. Catchpole, *The Trial of*

Jesus: A Study in the Gospels and Jewish Historiography From 1770 to the Present Day (Leiden: Brill, 1971), and G. S. Sloyan, *Jesus on Trial: The Development of the Passion Narratives and Their Historical and Ecumenical Implications* (Philadelphia: Fortress, 1973), provide rich bibliographical and other resources.

R. H. Fuller has recently revised his comprehensive study of the resurrection traditions, *The Formation of the Resurrection Narratives*, rev. ed. (New York: Macmillan, 1980). Note also the collection of essays edited by C. F. D. Moule, *The Significance of the Message of the Resurrection for Faith in Jesus Christ* (London: SCM, 1968). On the birth narratives the commentary of R. E. Brown, *The Birth of the Messiah* (Garden City, N.Y.: Doubleday, 1977), is the basic work.

A theological assessment of the quest of the historical Jesus has been made by L. E. Keck, *A Future for the Historical Jesus: The Place of Jesus in Preaching and Theology* (Nashville, Tenn.: Abingdon, 1971). The problem of method in Gospel investigation and Jesus research is attacked by R. S. Barbour, *Traditio-Historical Criticism of the Gospels* (London: SPCK, 1972), who makes sharp criticisms of some currently accepted procedures and assumptions. Fully informed about Gospel research is the stimulating book of M. Machoveč, *A Marxist Looks at Jesus* (Philadelphia: Fortress, 1976). The monumental work of the Roman Catholic theologian, E. Schillebeeckx, *Jesus: An Experiment in Christology*, trans. H. Hoskyns (New York: Seabury, 1979), is eloquent testimony to the possibility of integrating exegetical research and theological reflection, as well as to the fact that exegetical-theological perspectives and problems now look very much the same from Protestant and Catholic sides.

PART II

*The Apostles and
the Early Church*

T HE CRITICAL MOMENT for the origin of Christian faith is bound up with the question, "How did the proclaimer become the proclaimed?" That is, how did Jesus, who proclaimed the irrupting kingdom of God, become himself the subject of proclamation in the apostles' preaching? Jesus announced the kingdom, but the early church appeared. How did this come about? In studying the Acts of the Apostles (Chapter 7) and the Pauline letters (Chapters 8 and 9), we have an opportunity to reflect both about the historical development of this religious community and the theological grounding of the Christian church upon Jesus who was proclaimed as Christ.

In one sense, the writing of Acts, and its subsequent acceptance into the Christian canon, represents a decisive step in the formation of the early church. Acts provides a continuing stress on history (cf. Luke) and a new emphasis on the importance of the church alongside Jesus Christ. The New Testament is concerned not only with getting right with God through Jesus Christ but also with getting right with fellow believers in the Christian community. We shall be interested to see how Acts wrestles with such questions as the relation of the church to Judaism, the Christians' attitude toward the Roman state, the connection between the power of the Spirit and the church's apostolic authority. Moreover, we shall be especially concerned to see how Paul, the first great Christian theologian, develops these and such related questions as the human condition and the nature of sin, the work of Christ in bringing God and humanity together, the marks of Christian community, and the tension between present life in Christ and the future end of history.

In studying the post-Pauline writings (Chapter 10), it becomes evident that the movement from the apostles to the later church is characterized by its overall preoccupation with giving the community institutional form as Christians gird themselves for a long period of existence in the world. In these writings we see a tightening of discipline and doctrine, the development of orthodoxy over against heresy. The affirmation of the goodness of creation, the demand for action as well as belief, insistence upon the indispensability of the scriptures of Israel, the subordination of extreme religious behavior for the common good, the distinction between clergy and laity, the right ordering of family relations, the Christians' respect for and fear of the state, the inspiring figure of Jesus, as suffering servant and as the one victoriously seated in the heavens, the call for brotherly love, and the dramatic call for faith in the final victory of God—all these reflect the range and depth of the coming of age of the church under the leadership of the apostles' successors.

"Crucifixion" by the German painter M. Grünewald (completed 1511) is a panel of the Isenheim Altarpiece. The figures, other than Jesus, are Mary, the disciple John, Mary Magdalene, and John the Baptist. The latter repeats John 3:30; the letters INRI above the cross are the initial Latin letters of the inscription, "Jesus of Nazareth, King of the Jews." (Courtesy of Marburg Art Reference Bureau.)

CHAPTER SEVEN
The Acts of the Apostles: Witnessing to the World

NOTES ON THE ACTS OF THE APOSTLES

Acts was written by Luke, the author of the Gospel, probably within the last two decades of the first century. The book ends with Paul's debating and preaching while under arrest in Rome. We are not told about his ultimate fate. But there are strong hints (cf. Acts 20:22–25, 38) that Luke actually knew of Paul's death, even though he did not report it. Paul arrived in Rome about A.D. 59 and, according to the last statement of Acts (28:30 f.), remained there two years. Presumably he died in the early sixties during the reign of the Emperor Nero nearly a decade before the liquidation of the Jewish rebellion. Luke wrote his Gospel after that rebellion and the Book of Acts was composed subsequently (Acts 1:1). Luke used Mark as a source for his own Gospel and Mark itself was not composed until about A.D. 65 or later (see pp. 66 f. and 134).

By his own account (1:1–3) Luke used sources in composing his narrative of the ministry of Jesus, and he may have had sources for the Book of Acts. The detailed account of Paul's journeys in chapters 13–28 is probably based on some record of Paul's travels. In addition to this itinerary, Luke knew traditional stories from the earliest days of the church (e.g., 3:1–10; 5:1–11). Whether he had any traditions or records of the speeches he records is another question that will have to be considered as we examine some of the speeches. Judging from the practice of ancient historians, he likely wrote these speeches with considerable freedom, impressing them with his own literary style and thought. Particularly in chapters 1–2, Luke has skillfully tied the narrative together with summary statements (e.g., 2:43–47), in which he speaks in general terms of the activities of the early church.

Like the Gospels, Acts is a narrative, a story, and it may profitably be read as such. Yet Acts is more than just a story, even as the Gospels are.

In and through the story the author's understanding of the meaning and truth of the subject matter can be perceived. Within a schematic presentation Luke gives us a great deal of information about the early church. A comparison with Paul reveals that, although Acts may contain some inaccuracies, it is in touch with actual historical events.[1] Still, Luke apparently did not know a great many things about the origin of Christianity which we may infer from other documents, and he seems to have omitted deliberately some things that did not accord with his understanding of the essence of apostolic Christianity.

For example, Luke does not tell how Christianity reached Rome, although Christians are already there in Rome when Paul arrives (Acts 28: 14 ff.). Paul's letter to the Romans also makes it clear that Christians were there before him.[2] After chapter 12 all activity is centered about Paul and those associated with him, for Luke uses Paul to personify the entire Gentile mission. Doubtless Paul was a very important apostolic figure. Yet the present-day estimate of his importance as the apostle to the Gentiles may be somewhat exaggerated as a result of his pre-eminence in Luke's narrative.

The prominence given Paul should be seen over against the fact that Acts relates little about the activities of the twelve. With the exception of Peter they are all shadowy figures. True, John accompanies Peter in the early chapters, but he is at best a silent partner. The report about James in chapter 12 includes neither the reasons for his martyrdom nor the conditions under which it took place. There is, of course, a list of the eleven apostles (Acts 1:13), but little is said about what happened to the group individually or as a whole.[3] Probably Luke concentrates on Paul at least partly because he has information about him and lacks reports about the twelve. But in certain cases other factors may have been at work in the selection of material.

Paul's letters indicate that there was considerable disagreement and even hostility toward his Gentile mission on the part of some of the more

[1] That Acts has a solid historical foundation in the times that it portrays is shown by H. J. Cadbury, *The Book of Acts in History* (New York: Harper & Row, 1955).

[2] Presumably Christianity also reached Egypt at a rather early date, but we learn nothing about this from Acts. Nor do we learn anything about any expansion of Christianity to the East. In fact, we are told nothing very specific of the founding of the church in Antioch (11:9), probably the most important early Christian center outside Jerusalem.

[3] Later legend connects individual apostles with Christianity in various lands; for example, John with Ephesus and Thomas with India. Although it cannot be said that all these legends lack any factual basis, it is impossible to establish a case for their historicity because of the uncertain origin of the tradition on which they are based. As much as we might like to know what happened to these followers of Jesus, we search Acts in vain for any substantial traces of their whereabouts and activity. The ancient Roman Catholic tradition maintains that Peter was the founder and the first bishop of the church at Rome, although this claim has been widely disputed by Protestant scholars. Recently, O. Cullmann, in his book *Peter: Disciple–Apostle–Martyr*, trans. F. V. Filson, 2nd ed. (Philadelphia: Westminster, 1962), has accepted as probable the claim that Peter was at least martyred in Rome.

conservative members of the Jerusalem community, who believed that Judaism was, so to speak, the prerequisite for Christianity. Luke does not avoid reporting this fact. As we have noticed, the question of the gospel and the Gentiles is raised throughout the Book of Acts, although the sharp edge of the controversy is consistently dulled. In every instance (cf. chaps. 11, 15, 21) the problem is amicably settled without harsh words or bitterness. Yet it keeps recurring. How much Luke knew of the extent of these controversies is hard to say.[4] Surely he should have known a great deal had he been Paul's companion (see p. 133). In any case, he portrayed the life of the early church and the development of the Christian mission as more harmonious and free of disagreement and friction than they actually were.

OUTLINE OF ACTS

Introduction: A New Beginning (1:1–2:47)
Jesus' Departure (1:1–11)
The Apostolic Witness (1:12–26)
Spirit, Gospel, and Church (2:1–47)
The Growth of the Church and Its Witness (3:1–12:25)
Stephen's Martyrdom (6:1–7:60)

Mission to the Gentiles (10:1–11:18)
Christianity's Triumphal March (13:1–21:14)
Paul's Speech at Pisidian Antioch (13:17–41)
Paul's Speech in Athens (17:16–34)
Jerusalem to Rome (21:15–28:31)

Introduction: A New Beginning (1:1–2:47)

The first two chapters of Acts lay out and define the themes and principal concerns that are fundamental to the rest of the work. For this reason they must be examined carefully. Numerous questions may be raised as one studies these chapters, all of which are refinements of the basic question about what Luke, the author, was trying to say or to accomplish.

JESUS' DEPARTURE (1:1–11)

What task does the departing Jesus give the disciples?

The first two verses of the Acts of the Apostles hark back to Luke's earlier work, which is also addressed to Theophilus. There can be little doubt that by "the first book," the author means the Gospel of Luke. The brief description, "all that Jesus began to do and teach, until the day when he was taken up," corresponds to the content of the Gospel. The "many proofs" of the resurrected Christ (vs. 3) are found in the final chapter of Luke (24:36 ff.; perhaps in

[4]See Philipp Vielhauer, "On the 'Paulinism' of Acts," *Studies in Luke–Acts*, ed. L. E. Keck and J. L. Martyn (Nashville, Tenn.: Abingdon, 1966), pp. 33–50.

24:44 ff.). Even without such clear indications, however, there would be strong reasons for supposing that the two books are by the same author, for they are written in the same style and from the same general point of view. The story that began with Jesus will now be continued. The Gospels anticipate and presuppose a continuation of the story. The reader will now be told what form that continuation took.

Despite the obvious points of contact, there are apparent discrepancies and inconsistencies between the resurrection accounts of Luke 24 and the content of Acts 1. Nothing is said about forty days of resurrection appearances in the Gospel, nor is there any mention of the kingdom of God in all of Luke 24 (cf. Acts 1:3). The command to stay in Jerusalem (vs. 4) appears also in Luke 24:49, but the word of Jesus about the baptism of John and baptism by the Holy Spirit (vss. 4 f.) is found neither in Luke 24 nor anywhere else in the Gospel. Is Luke simply careless? Probably the explanation lies rather in a difference of emphasis and purpose.

Luke's own purposes and interests come to light in the next section (vss. 6–11, esp. 6–8). The hope that the two disciples on the road to Emmaus had already voiced (Luke 24:21) is now put in the form of a question: "Lord, will you at this time restore the kingdom to Israel?" The disciples seem to be asking whether Jesus will now fulfill the traditional hopes of the Jewish nation with the inauguration of the kingdom of God on earth. Jesus does not answer directly. Instead he replies that it is not for them to know the times and seasons that the Father has fixed by his own authority (cf. Mark 13:32). In other words, these matters must not be their primary concern. Such hopes as they have will be fulfilled in God's own way at the time of His choosing. Thus the disciples' expectations are effectively put off.

The reason for this delay is given in the very next verse: "But you shall receive power when the Holy Spirit has come upon you; and you shall be my witnesses in Jerusalem and in Judea and Samaria and to the end of the earth." The time of the kingdom is not yet, because the gospel must first be preached throughout the world. The witnesses to Jesus have a mission to perform. The coming of the Spirit has already been mentioned (vs. 5); now its specifically missionary function is spelled out. The Spirit empowers the disciples for their mission, which is described in stages: Jerusalem, Judea, Samaria, and the end of the earth (vs. 8). These stages correspond to the plan of the Book of Acts, in which the mission of the church unfolds by degrees: first in Jerusalem and the environs, then Samaria, then Syria, Asia Minor, Greece, and finally Rome. With Paul's preaching of the gospel in Rome the book of Acts comes to an end. This commissioning of the disciples for a worldwide mission is in close agreement with Luke 24:47, where the risen Jesus tells

Christ giving the law to the apostles. A relief marble fragment from the second half of the fourth century. (Courtesy of Metropolitan Museum of Art. Beata M. Brummer, 1948, in memory of Joseph Brummer.)

them that repentance and forgiveness are to be preached in his name to all nations, beginning from Jerusalem.

Luke's description of the ascension of Jesus (vss. 9–11) has become the model for its conception and artistic representation in the church. But the ascension is portrayed in this way only in Acts. Even in the Gospel of Luke it is described much more enigmatically (24:51). Here Luke carefully reconstructs the scene to drive home a point. The ascension is now viewed not from the standpoint of Jesus, but of the waiting disciples. Jesus indeed ascends to heaven and will return in like manner. The disciples ("men of Galilee"), however, are not to stand looking up into heaven in expectation of him, for they have already been given a task. They can perform it with the assurance that their ultimate hopes and expectations will not be disappointed, for Jesus will return in God's good time. But the interval gains a special significance; it is the period of the church and its mission. To that work the disciples' and the reader's attention is directed.

THE APOSTOLIC WITNESS (1:12–26)

Why does Acts record the selection of a twelfth apostle to replace Judas?

The disciples returned from the Mount of Olives, where the ascension apparently took place,[5] and gathered in an upper room in Jerusalem (vss. 12–14). The list of disciples present agrees with that found in Luke 6:14–16 with one notable exception. Judas Iscariot,

[5] According to Luke 24:50 f. the ascension took place at or near Bethany. The seeming contradiction suggests that Luke may have mistakenly taken Olivet and Bethany to be the same place; cf. K. Lake and H. J. Cadbury, eds., *The Beginnings of Christianity, V, Additional Notes to the Commentary* (New York: Macmillan, 1933), p. 475.

the betrayer of Jesus, is missing (cf. vss. 16–22).[6] What became of him? It is strange that Peter should have to answer this question for his fellow disciples and companions. Presumably they were in as good position as he to know what had occurred. Moreover, these folk would have surely known who Judas was, so why was it necessary for Peter to identify him so thoroughly? Verses 18 and 19 underscore the difficulty, for here Peter translates *Akeldama*, which would certainly not have been necessary for his Aramaic-speaking hearers, and refers to "their language," as if his hearers spoke a language different from that of the inhabitants of Jerusalem. This cannot have been the case. Verses 18 and 19 have to be understood as a notation addressed to the reader, and for this reason these verses appear in parentheses in the RSV. In the Greek text, however, the words were not set apart; the author evidently felt no obligation to distinguish clearly between Peter's words to his hearers and his own message for his readers. Probably he would not have considered such a distinction nearly so important as we would. Thus, as one reads Luke's account, he may well ask to whom the speeches of the chief characters are directed and to what extent they are means by which Luke sets before his *reader* the meaning of the events that are unfolding. To understand the speeches one must always ask what role they play in the unfolding of the book of Acts.

The Old Testament quotations (vs. 20; cf. Psalms 69:25 and 109:8) form not only the culmination of the first half of Peter's speech, but also the transition to the second part (vss. 21–22) in which he sets forth a course of action. A replacement for the disqualified and defunct Judas must be chosen: "His office let another take." Furthermore, the replacement must have a specific qualification; he must have accompanied Jesus and his disciples during his ministry up to the time of his ascension. He may then become a witness, with the apostles, to the resurrection. In the selection of the new apostle (vss. 23–26), two men are put forward by the group, but the widest latitude is left for God (or Jesus, depending on whom is here meant by "Lord") to make the final choice. The new man is to be no less an apostolic figure than the eleven original disciples.

Luke is careful to show that the number of the original twelve apostles was again filled out before the beginning of the church's missionary activity. (The word *apostle* comes from the Greek *apostolos*, which is in turn related to the verb *apostellein*, "to send out"; the apostles are literally "men sent out.") The concept of *twelve* apostles probably originates with the *twelve* tribes of Israel (cf. the

---

[6]Notice that the Acts' description of Judas' death differs from that given in Matthew 27:3–10, except that in both cases the name of the place where he died is the Field of Blood. Perhaps the fact that Luke preserves the Aramaic name whereas Matthew's version appears to be based upon the Old Testament quotation indicates that Luke's version is the older. (Matthew purports to quote Jeremiah, but the exact passage cannot be found; cf. Zechariah 11:12–13.)

saying of Jesus in Matt. 19:28 and Luke 22:30). Perhaps Luke was aware of this connection with the Old Testament and the Israelite nation, because for him the church, led by the apostles, was the new Israel. Yet Luke, like Paul, seems more interested in the close relation between apostleship and the resurrection of Jesus (Acts 1:22; cf. I Cor. 9:1: "Am I not an apostle? Have I not seen Jesus our Lord?"; also 15:8, where Paul explicitly relates the appearance of the risen Jesus and his apostleship). Unlike Luke, however, Paul did not believe that having been a disciple of Jesus was an indispensable qualification of an apostle. Paul himself had not been and he distinguishes between the twelve and the apostles in I Corinthians 15:5, 7. He evidently regarded the twelve as apostles, but did not limit apostleship to them. Nevertheless, precisely this identification of apostles with the twelve disciples of Jesus has informed the Christian understanding of "apostle" and "apostleship" down through the centuries. The church has come to share Luke's view that there can be, and is, no doubt about the existence and competence of a complete and fully qualified group of twelve apostles identical with the inner circle of Jesus' disciples.

After Matthias is selected he plays no role in the story—nor do many of the twelve. In fact, the twelve were not the only early witnesses to the gospel of Jesus Christ. Not even in Acts do they play the predominant role in preaching the gospel. For only Peter appears as a real flesh and blood figure. But Luke, who has written to Theophilus in the first place so that he may know the truth of the things of which he has been informed (Luke 1:4), uses the concept of the twelve to assure the reader of the legitimacy, historical accuracy, and therefore the truth of the Christian message.

In chapter 1 Luke has done two principal things. First, he has explained the meaning of Jesus' departure and of the indefinite period before his return. Second, through his treatment of the reconstitution of the twelve apostles, he has shown that real contact still exists between Jesus and his disciples on earth. The apostles guarantee this, for they have firm connections with Jesus of Nazareth, of whose resurrection and life they are witnesses. Luke can now turn his attention to the description and exposition of the earliest missionary preaching of the Christian church. The missionary preachers will now tell about Jesus. But how and to what end?

SPIRIT, GOSPEL, AND CHURCH (2:1-47)

What is the relation of the coming of the Spirit to Peter's proclamation?

Chapter 2 falls into two main parts, verses 1–13, a depiction of the descent of the Holy Spirit upon the disciples and the reaction of the bystanders, and verses 14–43, an account of the earliest missionary preaching by Peter. The remainder of the chapter (vss. 43–47) gives a brief general description of the life of the Jerusalem church.

The day of Pentecost comes on the fiftieth day after the sabbath of the Passover, according to the Jewish calendar. This would be the forty-ninth day after the resurrection and, according to the Lukan chronology, a little over a week after the ascension of Jesus.[7] (Jesus' resurrection appearances continued over a period of forty days.) In the Gospel of John, however, the Holy Spirit comes, not at Pentecost and after the ascension of Jesus, but directly from the risen Jesus himself (John 20:21–23). Indeed, the ascension is not described at all in John. Luke evidently separates into chronological sequence events or experiences that were not so divided in the memories of other early Christians (i.e., the resurrection of Jesus, the ascension, and the bestowal of the Holy Spirit).

Luke regarded the coming of the Holy Spirit (cf. vss. 1–4) as a miraculous event. Yet we should not assume that Luke attached primary importance to such signs as the wind and fire. For him the most marvelous thing was the inspiration of the apostles and their speaking in tongues. Only highly unusual accompanying circumstances could do justice to this remarkable event. The rushing of the wind and the tongues "as of fire" are subordinate to the main miracle of inspired speech.

That Luke is describing a genuine experience of early Christianity need not be doubted. We learn also from Paul that the gift of the Spirit was associated with speaking in tongues (I Cor. 14). Be that as it may, Paul assumes that without interpretation this speaking in tongues (glossolalia) is unintelligible to the hearer, as indeed it generally is when practiced by pentecostal Christians today. Precisely the authentic note of the first part of the story calls into question the interpretation of the nature of glossolalia (cf. vss. 6–8), where it is understood as a speaking in the various native languages of the people who are gathered in Jerusalem. In Luke's view, a miracle of translation has occurred.[8] That, however, is not what speaking in tongues was in early Christianity according to the Pauline account.

The description of the circumstances under which the multitude came together and the course of events as a whole show Luke's own perspectives and interests. When the disciples are gathered in one place, the Spirit descends and they immediately begin proclaiming "the mighty works of God" (vs. 11) in all the languages of those Jews who have come from far and wide to dwell in Jerusalem, pre-

---

[7] According to Acts 1:3 Jesus continued to appear to his disciples for forty days after the resurrection. Note the close connection of the Christian celebrations of Good Friday, Easter, and Pentecost with the Jewish feasts of Passover and Pentecost.

[8] From ancient times commentators have seen in the miracle of understanding at Pentecost the resolution of the confusion of tongues at the Tower of Babel (Genesis 11:1–9). At most we have an allusion. No explicit connection is made.

sumably for the feast of Pentecost. These people hear the commotion and come together. Some inquire sincerely as to what all this means (vs. 12). Others understandably attribute the uproar to new wine (vs. 13). Luke provides as auspicious an occasion and hearing as possible for Peter's sermon or speech. Accordingly, the audience, although Jewish, is thoroughly cosmopolitan and representative of the eastern half of the Mediterranean world, the mission field of early Christianity (vss. 8–11). To this great congregation Peter addresses himself, standing with the eleven (vs. 14) to emphasize the authoritative character of his speech. The speech is not only Spirit-inspired but also apostolic. Indeed, the evangelical preaching is represented initially and definitively in the speech of Peter (2:14–42), the first Christian missionary sermon.

After Peter first explains that the Christians are not drunk (vss. 14–16), he declares that their speaking fulfills what was spoken by the Old Testament prophet Joel. There then follows the long quotation from the book of Joel (2:28–32), which is a description and prediction of what will happen in the days when God restores the fortunes of Judah and Jerusalem (Joel 3:1). Not only will there be the standard apocalyptic signs (vss. 19–20), but also the pouring out of God's Spirit (vss. 17—18), which results in visions, dreams, and especially prophecy. Apparently Luke understands the speaking in tongues of the apostles and their companions as the prophecy of which Joel spoke.

This first Christian preaching begins with an appeal to the Old Testament. This connection is typical of the New Testament as a whole, for the Christian gospel is understood as the fulfillment of an ancient promise. Jesus Christ is the culmination of what God has been doing from creation on in the history of Israel. So even the gift of the Spirit and the speaking in tongues are set forth as fulfillment of Old Testament prophecy. The Christians, as this very text states, believed themselves to be possessed of prophetic power and authority. Thus they were able to perceive and declare the fulfillment of the prophetic words that the men of the Old Testament, so to speak, cast out ahead of them. The early Christian preachers, therefore, claimed implicitly a better understanding of Old Testament texts than their human authors could have had.

The prophetic word (vss. 17–21) was doubtless understood to concern both the present manifestation of the Spirit and the forthcoming signs of the end, as well as the appeal of the Christian preaching for conversion in the light of these startling occurrences (vs. 21). Before this appeal could be made, however, its specifically Christian basis had to be set forth, for Peter has so far only said that the time for fulfillment of the Old Testament prophecies and of God's promises to his people has come. The distinctly Christian proclamation appears in verses 22–24. Most surprising is the brevity

Crucifixion of Jesus by a contemporary Brazilian sculptor, A. Solimoes. (Courtesy of Spartaco Appetiti.)

of the reference to Jesus' ministry (vs. 22). Jesus himself is not presented as the acting subject. Rather he is the means or agent through whom God acts. This is true even of his miracles. The divine purpose at work in the crucifixion is made quite clear (vs. 23), and the same purpose is also discerned in the resurrection (vs. 24) as the Old Testament proof from prophecy (vss. 25–28) shows. The author recognizes that the words of the Psalm (16:8–11) were generally believed to have been spoken by David about himself, but he maintains (vss. 29–31) that they were actually meant to apply to Jesus.

Only after the Old Testament proof is the disciples' witness to the resurrection mentioned (vs. 32), but even then it is passed over rather briefly. Emphasis falls rather upon the ascension of Christ to heaven (vs. 33), again confirmed by the Old Testament (vss. 34 f.; from Psalm 110:1), and upon the gift of the Spirit. Apparently, Peter does not draw a sharp distinction between the raising of Jesus from the dead and his ascension (or exaltation) to heaven. In Luke's own mind, however, the distinction is very clear. Jesus is first raised from the dead; then after forty days he ascends into heaven. Luke's view probably represents a later development in relation to what is attributed to Peter.

The speech reaches its pinnacle and conclusion in verse 36. Once again God is the subject who acts upon Jesus. Jesus becomes, or at least is recognized as, "Lord and Christ" only with the resurrection and exaltation. This point of view is rather uncommon in the New Testament, for Jesus is usually regarded as having been the Messiah during his earthly ministry. Yet just because this verse does not conform to the common conception, and because it would scarcely have been set forth at a time when that conception was widespread, it may well present a primitive point of view. Certainly the crucifixion and resurrection were pivotal points in primitive Christian experience and faith.

Peter's appeal for conversion and repentance follows naturally (vss. 37–42). As he has already indicated ("Let all the house of Israel therefore know . . ."—vs. 36) and as the situation demands, it is still addressed to Jews. Yet there is already a hint that it will not be limited to them (see vs. 39). The hearers are called upon to repent and to be baptized, and the gift of the Spirit is promised. No explanation is given here or anywhere else in the New Testament of why believers had to be baptized. According to every indication, baptism was practiced from the very beginning, yet we do not know precisely why or how it became the ritual of initiation into the Christian community.[9]

Whereas the practice of baptism was universal, the call to repentance has a particularly Lukan ring. Of course, Luke was not the first to set forth a relation between baptism and repentance or to describe conversion in terms of repentance. The understanding of repentance as the essential element of Christian conversion is, however, quite characteristic of Luke (see pp. 151–153). Although re-

[9] Paul, whose letters are the earliest New Testament writings, simply mentions baptism as a matter of course, as if it were a long-accepted practice. In Matthew 28:19 Jesus commands it. But Paul did not know Matthew, and that command very likely reflects early Christian practice. At best there is no explanation of why baptism should be commanded. Acts mentions some disciples, presumably Christians, who knew only the baptism of John the Baptist and had not received the Holy Spirit (19:1–7). In the Gospels and the missionary speeches of Acts, John's baptism marks the beginning of Jesus' own ministry, and John's baptism in water is contrasted with Christ's baptism in the Holy Spirit. All of this suggests that Christian baptism is somehow rooted in the baptism of John. Yet baptism may have been practiced by Christians quite apart from the influence of John, inasmuch as the Jewish community baptized new converts, as well as circumcising them. The Qumran community also practiced baptism or lustrations (washings), but their rite was repeatable, whereas early Christian baptism—or at least the form with which we are familiar—was a once-for-all ceremony. But cf. M. Black, *The Scrolls and Christian Origins* (New York: T. Nelson, 1961), pp. 91 ff. On baptism see O. Cullmann, *Baptism in the New Testament*, trans. J. K. S. Reid (London: SCM, 1950), and G. R. Beasley-Murray, *Baptism in the New Testament* (New York: St. Martin's, 1962).

pentance and forgiveness were already possible for the Jew (cf. Psalm 51), Luke believed that God's forgiveness and the possibility of repentance were made known in an unprecedented way in the coming of Jesus. Baptism "in the name of Jesus Christ" (2:38) was the symbolic expression of repentance and the acceptance of God's forgiveness. The act itself implies a washing away of sin.

Peter's Pentecost sermon is the first of a number of speeches in the book of Acts. Ancient historians sometimes used a speech by a leading figure as a literary device to convey something to their readers which they thought was important for an understanding of persons or situations. Such a procedure was understood by the reader and not considered dishonest or fraudulent. Luke's composition and use of speeches, seems to follow this ancient practice, although he may have drawn upon earlier traditions or sources.[10]

At the end of Peter's speech and the account of the conversions, Luke presents a glimpse of the life of the early Jerusalem church. Such general summaries were probably composed by Luke. They recur frequently in Acts and usually reflect such knowledge of the early church as could be gathered by the author from the traditional stories that he narrates. For example, the reference to common ownership (vss. 44 f.) is probably a generalization based upon the stories of Barnabas and Ananias and Sapphira (4:36 f.; 5:1–6). The signs and wonders, as well as the "fear" (vs. 43), are exemplified in such miracle stories as 3:1–10, 9:32–35, and 9:36–43. The general favor that the Christians found among the people (2:47) is also mentioned in 4:21 and 5:33–39, quite possibly traditional material. Such matters as the great number of converts, the breaking of bread, and attendance in the temple are included in the summary without the direct support of traditional stories. This is not to say that Luke simply manufactured them, but he may have believed he had a right to describe these activities and attribute them to the early church on the basis of what he knew of Jesus and the disciples, and of what he knew of the church of his own day. Of course, we cannot be sure that Luke did not possess more detailed information from earlier days which did not come to him in the form of traditional narra-

---

[10]M. Dibelius, "The Speeches in Acts and Ancient Historiography," *Studies in the Acts of the Apostles,* ed. H. Greeven and trans. M. Ling (London: SCM, 1956), pp. 138–191, esp. 138–140, and H. J. Cadbury, *The Making of Luke–Acts* (New York: Macmillan, 1927), pp. 184–193. The existence of Semitisms in the Acts speeches may betray older traditions behind them; see Max Wilcox, *The Semitisms of Acts* (Oxford: Clarendon, 1965), esp. pp. 49, 180 ff. Traditional materials and perspectives may be more prominent in some speeches than in others. R. F. Zehnle, *Peter's Pentecost Discourse: Tradition and Lukan Reinterpretation in Peter's Speeches of Acts 2 and 3* (Nashville, Tenn.: Abingdon, 1971), finds considerable evidence for tradition in Acts 3, whereas he maintains that the Pentecost speech of Acts 2 is mainly a Lukan composition.

tives. Yet we have already noted that Luke did not hesitate to set forth the ascension in distinct and different ways, in the Gospel and Acts, apparently supplying details as needed.

Nevertheless, Luke has some basis for these details. That large numbers of people were converted at the beginning would have seemed only natural to him in view of the size and influence of the Jerusalem church, which, however, disappeared before the destruction of Jerusalem (A.D. 70) and perhaps twenty years before Luke wrote. The common meals might have been suggested not only by the sacrament of the Lord's Supper and the story of the Last Supper (Luke 22:14–27), but also by the traditions about the resurrection of Jesus in which he eats with his disciples (Luke 24:35, 42 f.; John 21:1–14). Attendance in the temple could have been deduced from the location of the miracle story of 3:1–10 or from the account of the vow that Paul took (21:17–26). It is, moreover, still probable that Luke mentions some things simply because they are important to his story. The immediate success of the Christian witness at the very heart of Judaism, the constant presence of Christians around the temple, the table fellowship and piety of Christians, all represent typical Lukan motifs. Especially significant is the emphasis on Christianity's acceptance and prominence in the Holy City of Judaism, for in Luke's view the church is the new, and true, Israel.

Thus Luke's conception of the piety and life of the early Christian church appears in 2:42–47. The rich resources of his Gospel afforded relatively little information that he was able to sort out and use in Acts. For the early chapters he had only a collection of various stories and anecdotes, which he was able to weave together into a surprisingly smooth and coherent narrative. Yet there is a sense in which Luke knew enough to tell the story that he wanted to tell and to achieve his own goals. The opening chapters of Acts are a good example of this fact. Here Luke accounts for the departure of the risen Jesus from his disciples, the reason that he has not yet returned, the existence and mission of the church, and the foundation of that church upon the apostolic witness. Then he proceeds to report the bestowal of the Spirit upon the disciples and to give an extended example of the preaching of the apostolic church, followed by a brief characterization of its life. This preaching (i.e., Peter's speech) contains the elements characteristic of Christian preaching in subsequent ages: the announcement and demonstration of the fulfillment of scripture, the centrality of the crucifixion and resurrection, a characterization of the historic ministry of Jesus, the announcement of the coming of the Spirit, and an appeal for repentance and conversion, which naturally includes the offer of forgiveness.

The Growth of the Church and Its Witness (3:1–12:25)

Our initial insights into the way the author of Acts works, as well as his interests and goals, must be tested for their adequacy in illuminating the rest of the book. Attention now turns to the first major section (chaps. 3–12), which depicts the gradual extension of the church beyond the confines of Judaism and Palestine.

STEPHEN'S MARTYRDOM (6:1–7:60)

What is the historic importance of the stoning of Stephen for Luke?

The power manifest in the preaching and healing activity of the apostles in Jerusalem is portrayed in chapters 3–5. The stories found there are not told simply for their own sake; they show important aspects of the church's life and mission about which Luke wants his readers to know. They depict the Christians' preaching and healing in Jerusalem, especially in the vicinity of the temple, the center of the Jewish religion. The location is significant, for Luke wants his reader to understand that Christianity emerged out of the very heart of Judaism and is the true expression of the ancient faith. The refusal of the apostles to be silent, even when officials warned or punished them (4:19 and 5:29), shows how strong was the sense of mission in the very earliest Christian congregation. Yet in chapters 3–5 the mission is confined to Judaism and indeed to the city of Jerusalem.

In chapters 6–7, however, the basis is laid for the extension of the witness. Chapter 6 describes the "murmuring" of the Hellenists against the Hebrews because their widows had been overlooked in the daily distribution, which must have been the church's way of looking out for its poor and disadvantaged (6:1). Who are these Hellenists and Hebrews? It is clear that they are Christians. Beyond that, absolute certainty is not possible. Probably by "Hebrews" is meant Aramaic-speaking Christians. In that case "Hellenists" means Greek-speaking Christians (note the Greek names, vs. 5), although, as soon becomes apparent, they are distinguished by factors other than language. Apparently the seven Hellenists who were appointed to serve tables and to see that their widows were not slighted did not stick strictly to their jobs. Luke's narrative makes this fact clear, although he himself does not remark upon it.

Stephen first appears not as a waiter, or even an administrator, but as a wonder worker and especially a debater, incurring the hostility of the Jews (6:8–15). The charges made against him (vss. 11, 13 f.) indicate a sharp break on the part of some Christians with the institutions of Judaism. The accusation about destroying the temple (vs. 14) has a familiar ring, for according to Mark 14:58 it was first leveled at Jesus himself (cf. Mark 13:2; 15:29; John 2:19). Insofar as Stephen questioned the validity of the law (6:13), he stood with the apostle Paul and later Hellenistic Christianity against Judaism and the Jewish or Judaizing Christians. Whatever Stephen's views, he held them with great tenacity. If anyone had hoped that Stephen's appearance before the council (the Jewish Sanhedrin) would exonerate him of the suspicions and charges against him, his hopes would certainly have been cruelly dashed by the speech that Stephen chose to make.

The speech (7:1–53) is in its present form the composition of Luke himself. It does not answer the question of the high priest (7:1), and the council probably would not have endured such a long, largely superfluous, and, from their point of view, defamatory speech in answer to so simple a question. The speech contains an extensive statement of the theological position of Stephen, which is by implication that of the Hellenists. Although it does not deal with the charges made against Stephen, it sheds some light on how such charges may have arisen, for Stephen denounces the past disobedience of the Israelite people, questions the necessity of the temple (vss. 47 ff.), and concludes with a strong denunciation of the betrayal and murder of Jesus. The final reference to the law (vs. 53) is almost an afterthought.

The reaction of Stephen's hearers to such a speech was predictable. The account of his subsequent death, traditionally the first Christian martyrdom, includes an additional bit of information about a young man named Saul, who held the coats of those who were stoning him (vss. 58 ff.). This Saul is the man who, under his Roman name of Paul, became the great Christian apostle to the Gentiles. Around him the latter half of the Book of Acts revolves. We know from Paul's own letters (especially Gal. 1:11–24) that he was a persecutor of the church before he himself became a Christian, and it is certainly not impossible that he was in Jerusalem and present on this occasion. According to Acts, Stephen, the first Christian critic of Judaism, was martyred in the presence of the one who was to become the decisive figure in Christianity's separation from Judaism. History has witnessed stranger ironies.

The bulk of chapter 8 describes the missionary harvest reaped as a result of the persecution that broke out on the heels of Stephen's martyrdom. Philip makes converts in Samaria (cf. Acts 1:8), and on the road south from Jerusalem to Gaza he converts an Ethiopian eunuch to Christianity and baptizes him on the spot. Others also went out from Jerusalem preaching the word (8:4), but Luke tells us only of the instances involving Philip. His statement of 8:4 (cf. 11:19–21) very likely conveys exactly what happened in this first

"The Conversion of St. Paul" by Tintoretto (1518–94). (Courtesy of National Gallery of Art, Washington, D.C. Samuel H. Kress Collection.)

demonstration of the maxim that the blood of the martyrs is the seed of the church.

Because, according to Luke's account, the gospel has now spread outside Jerusalem into Judea, Samaria, and Galilee, the territory of ancient Israel, we are prepared for the next step, the evangelization of the Gentiles. Now then the apostle to the Gentiles must appear at the center of the stage. So we are next told of Paul's conversion (chap. 9). Probably this is the best attested event in the entire New Testament. There are no less than three accounts in the Book of Acts (cf. also chaps. 22 and 26). In addition, there is the account from Paul's own hand in Galatians (1:11–17), as well as other allusions to the event in his letters (e.g., I Cor. 9:1; 15:8).

With the appearance of Paul, we reach a point in the narrative at which it is possible to check the accuracy of the Acts account and also to learn something more about the methods and intentions of Luke as an author. The comparison of Acts with the evidence of Paul's letters is a complex and difficult task, and one that we shall not undertake in detail. Nevertheless, the consensus of scholarship allows us to adopt the general principle that, where Acts contradicts or cannot be made to fit what Paul says, the critical reader must prefer Paul. He provides firsthand information, whereas Acts is secondary.

Luke's primary purpose in writing, moreover, was not that of a contemporary historian or journalist. He was not much interested in the variety and complexity of events and phenomena that constituted early Christianity. Reporting accurately everything that happened would not have accomplished his purpose. He wished to tell the story of how Christianity spread in such a way that it would not only inform the reader, but also edify the church and bring it to a better understanding of the ways in which God had accomplished his purpose in its history. Hence, in describing the expansion of Christianity, Luke concentrates on Paul, the imposing missionary figure of the previous generation about whom he has some information and concerning whom he can presuppose familiarity on the part of at least the Christian reader. Thus in the last portion of Acts, which sees Paul move from Antioch to Rome, many details and whole areas of the mission and expansion of Christianity are necessarily ignored.

MISSION TO THE GENTILES (10:1–11:18)

Why is Cornelius' conversion described at such length?

Peter is portrayed by Luke as the founder of the mission to the Gentiles and the representative of the "liberal" position that the gospel can be preached to those outside the bounds of organized Judaism, presumably without their first becoming members of the Jewish congregation. Thus, Peter's position is close to that of the apostle Paul, who struggled so valiantly for the principle that Peter establishes with relative ease. If Peter actually secured so large a victory at the outset, however, we might wonder why Paul had so much difficulty. In fact, Paul himself had something less than admiration for Peter, whose tolerant conduct among Gentiles was at first what we would expect on the basis of the Acts passage, but who later seems to have reversed his field (cf. Gal. 2:11 ff.). In the light of Paul's struggle and his description of Peter's conduct in Galatians (following, pp. 326–328), we might ask whether Peter actually won a victory as a result of this incident, or whether he himself was as fully committed to the mission to the Gentiles as the Acts passage would lead us to believe. The Book of Acts itself indicates that the question about the status and obligations of Gentile converts did not die easily. It is the chief subject matter of chapter 15, and in chapter 21 Paul is arrested for the last time in an incident growing out of this question and controversy.

Acts gives a lengthy account of the conversion of Cornelius and the subsequent discussion of its meaning. This grouping of narrative and discourse materials is quite complicated. The complexity stems in some measure from the editorial work of Luke, who has woven together older traditional material. The long account can, of course, simply be read as an interesting story, without asking what purpose

Luke might have had in incorporating it at this point in his narrative. But such an approach would ignore the most important question. Furthermore, one should ask why so much of the story, especially the reports of visions, is repetitious.

The vision of Cornelius at Caesarea instructs him to summon Peter from Joppa (10:1–8). Even while his emissaries are on the way, Peter in turn has a vision (10:9–16). Cornelius' men then explain to Peter the purpose of their mission and bring him with them to Caesarea (10:17–19). After Cornelius has explained the details of his vision (10:30–33), Peter delivers what amounts to a missionary sermon; the Holy Spirit descends upon those standing about, and Peter commands that they be baptized. When Peter returns to Jerusalem he is criticized by the circumcision party for going to uncircumcised men and eating with them. So Peter, to justify his actions, recounts the entire course of events (11:1–18). Upon hearing this, his critics' mouths are stopped. Indeed, they glorify God and fall into line with the position that Peter has espoused.

Although the vision (10:1–8) does not require detailed explanation, it is worth observing that Cornelius was a Roman officer and thus a representative of the power and prestige of the Empire. He is also described as "a devout man who feared God" (vs. 2), which may mean that he was a Gentile associate of a Jewish synagogue, who had not formally become a Jew. That he was still a Gentile is clear from the subsequent narrative and discussion of his conversion to Christianity.

Cornelius' approach to Peter is made at the direction of an angel. The angel comes at the ninth hour (3:00 P.M.) while Cornelius is at prayer, and Cornelius sees him clearly. There can be no mistaking the divine origin of the instruction to be delivered. Of the character or appearance of the angel we are told nothing; this is of no importance to Luke; he is interested only in the origin and authority of the message, symbolized by the angel. In Acts several such messages are delivered in visions—also an indication of divine authorization. For example, in the next stage of the narrative Peter sees another vision while standing on the housetop at midday, as the emissaries from Cornelius approach the city of Joppa.

The meaning of Peter's vision (10:9–16) is not so obvious as that of Cornelius. In fact, Peter is said to be puzzled about it (vs. 17). In itself the vision seems to indicate that all animals may be eaten without regard for Jewish custom and law. There is little reason for Peter to be perplexed about this, except in view of the approaching mission from Cornelius, about which, of course, he as yet knows nothing. Luke and the reader know about it, however. Therefore, the perplexity at this point is really more appropriate to the reader than to Peter—a sure sign that Luke has his reader in mind. Peter's perplexity disappears by the time he reaches Cornelius at Caesarea (vss.

28 f.). In the meantime the Spirit has instructed him to go with the three men who have come from Cornelius, for the Spirit has sent them. Peter goes with them to the house of Cornelius, who has already gathered his close friends and family for what he obviously expects will be an important occasion. This is underscored by the way in which he greets Peter (vs. 25). Peter's response is like that of Paul and Barnabas in a similar situation (14:15). Only at this point do we discover that Peter has now understood the meaning of this vision on the rooftop at Joppa: "God has shown me that I should not call any man common or unclean" (vs. 28). The vision evidently had to do primarily with the status of human beings rather than of animals. This interpretation of the vision becomes possible only in the light of the events that follow it. A new meaning is given to the vision different from the one that had seemed obvious, but had left Peter "perplexed." Its real meaning is that God is no respecter of persons.

This point is not, however, immediately developed. Instead, we hear Cornelius describe his vision to Peter (10:30–33). So, Peter first tells Cornelius his vision, or at least its meaning; then Cornelius tells Peter his. Luke would not have recounted all this had it not suited his purpose; for even if his report is strictly historical, there must have been some reason for him to give such an overly complete account. He could have simply reported that Cornelius recounted to Peter his vision and all that had happened in connection with it. Probably the clue to Luke's procedure is found in verse 33: "Now therefore we are all here present in the sight of God, to hear *all that you have been commanded by the Lord.*" Luke is concerned to show that the initiator of all these events is not humankind, but God. No one acts until he is moved to do so by the divine initiative and Cornelius anticipates nothing else from Peter but what he has been commanded of God. The abundance of visions and reports of visions emphasizes that what is taking place is something other than the natural course of events or the working out of a human scheme to evangelize the Gentiles. Thus the break with the past in the offering of the gospel to the Gentiles comes about by the will and action of God who gives explicit guidance and direction to the major participants in this drama.

Now that all has been properly prepared, Peter delivers his sermon (10:34–43). It has a great deal in common with the other missionary speeches of Acts. The initial statement, however, applies specifically to the present unprecedented situation (34 f.), making clear that God is favorably disposed toward what is about to happen. In addition, the tenor of the speech sets it somewhat apart from similar pronouncements. Peter, after his opening remarks, introduces the main body of his speech, the Christian kerygma, with the phrase "you know," thus making his presentation of the gospel a kind of review of matters with which his audience is already familiar. Apparently they have not been converted up to this point because the time has not been right. In the latter part of the speech (vss. 39 ff.) emphasis falls on the crucifixion and resurrection of Jesus and on the authority of the witnesses and their obligation to proclaim the gospel of forgiveness of sins in Jesus' name to all (vs. 42). This implies that Peter's own proclamation to these Gentiles is fully justified.

Before Peter can make the characteristic appeal for repentance and conversion (cf. 2:37–42), the Holy Spirit descends upon his hearers (vs. 44), who promptly begin speaking in tongues (vs. 46). All this is witnessed by Jewish Christians (vs. 45), who are amazed that God should give his Spirit even to Gentiles. That these people, Gentiles though they may be, should be baptized is now a foregone conclusion (vss. 47 f.). The Jewish Christians are in no position to object, inasmuch as they themselves have observed the manifestation of the Spirit. That the Spirit should be given before baptism could only be taken as an unmistakable sign of the will of God in the matter.

Peter now returns to Jerusalem, where he encounters the criticism of the circumcision party (11:1 ff.) and in response to them explains fully what happened. Again Luke is not content simply to say that Peter gave an explanation, but gives a full account of it. We now get the second rendition of Peter's vision (vss. 4–10) and the third of Cornelius' (vss. 13–15). Thus Luke drives home the significance of the events he is recounting. In fact, the whole point of Luke's narrative really comes to focus in Peter's somewhat repetitious response to his critics. Only here does the sense of the preceding narrative finally become entirely clear: God wills the conversion of worthy Gentiles to Christianity. Although it is not obvious from the question (vs. 3) that this is what the Jewish Christians are challenging, their final concession (vs. 18) indicates that for Luke precisely this question is settled by the conversion of Cornelius.

A closer examination of certain details of the text confirms this observation. In 11:14 Cornelius' account of his vision is expanded to include as its central point the expectation that Peter will preach the gospel to him and his household. This expectation was not expressed in the earlier accounts (cf. 10:33 and 10:3–6). In Peter's report of his own sermon (11:15), the Holy Spirit no longer falls upon the Gentiles toward the conclusion of his speech, but at the beginning—a further indication of the divine initiative. The descent of the Spirit is then likened to Pentecost (chap. 2). This is a new dispensation of the Spirit of God in fulfillment of Jesus' own promise (11:16; cf. 1:5), and Peter draws its full implications for the missionary practice of the church: "If then God gave the same gift to them as he gave to us when we believed in the Lord Jesus Christ, who was I that I could withstand God?" (vs. 17). Peter had no idea of preaching to Gentiles. Rather the Gentile mission originated in an epoch-making revelation by God of his purposes for the church and the gospel. This interpretation of the meaning and significance of the conversion of Cornelius and its aftermath is borne out in Luke's report of the Jerusalem Council, where Peter defends the Gentile mission on the basis of the Cornelius incident (see Acts 15:7–9).

Christianity's Triumphal March (13:1–21:14)

In the next section of Acts Luke narrates the movement of Christianity from the East to the West, from Antioch in Syria to Greece, making the transition from Jerusalem to the West seem natural and normal. He skillfully dovetails these two major parts of his account so that the coming mission to the Gentiles is prefigured by the conversions of Cornelius and Paul and by the speech of Stephen. In fact, the descent of the Spirit and the preaching of Peter at Pentecost before the representatives of many lands already points ahead to the wider missionary effort. After the scene shifts away from Jerusalem, we are kept aware of the authority and vitality of the Jerusalem church, and of the contact between it and the Gentile mission (15:1–35). The church's work and geographical distribution may become diverse, but its origin, loyalty, mission, and purpose are one. This conviction Luke shares with other New Testament writers, but he expresses it in a unique way.

This portion of the Gentile mission falls into several sections defined by Paul's various activities:

1. First missionary journey: Cyprus and Asia Minor (13:1–14:28).
2. Jerusalem Council (15:1–35).
3. Second missionary journey: entry into Greece (15:36–18:22).
4. Third missionary journey: Ephesus and Greece (18:23–21:14).

Note how this part of Acts shows the progress of gospel witness across the world. The concentration on Paul's missionary journeys in Acts typifies the perspective of the author. The gospel is on the move.

PAUL'S SPEECH AT PISIDIAN ANTIOCH (13:17–41)
Why does Paul here preach to the Gentiles?

In chapters 13 and 14 we find the first description of missionary activity beyond Palestine and Syria. (This was not the first such effort, however; cf. 11:19–20.) Paul and Barnabas are commissioned,

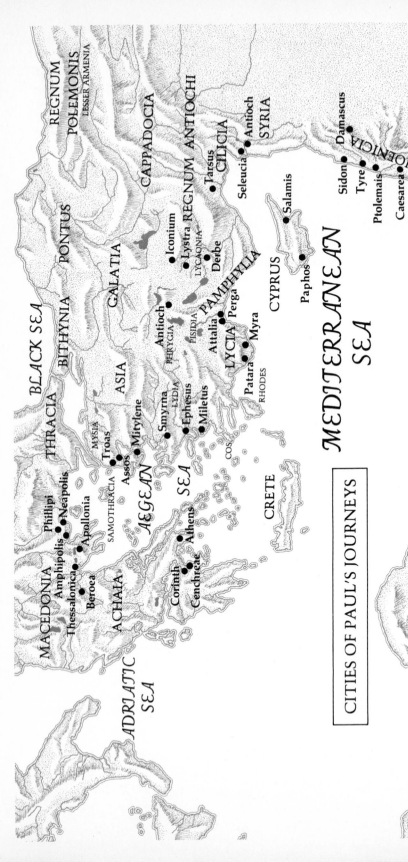

CITIES OF PAUL'S JOURNEYS

not by the Jerusalem church, but by the church at Antioch (13:1–3), and sent off under its auspices. This church had been founded by those fleeing Jerusalem during the persecution of the Hellenists. It is perhaps understandable that the Jerusalem church may have had some reservations about its activities and that the Antiochene Christians may have harbored some resentment toward the mother church. After all, the Jewish Christians had been able to remain in Jerusalem after the founders of the Antioch church had been driven out, presumably because of their radical views about their ancestral traditions.

The most important incident of chapter 13 is the sermon of Paul (13:17–41) in the synagogue at Pisidian Antioch. Throughout Acts and until the end of his missionary labors in Rome, Paul is portrayed as appealing first to the Jews in every city he visits. Although such a procedure fits almost too well with Luke's conviction about the relation of Christianity to Israel, the Hellenistic Jewish synagogue doubtless provided an almost indispensable foothold for the earliest Christian preaching. In keeping with the setting, Paul's sermon is an address by an Israelite to Israelites, although some Gentile God-fearers are also present (vs. 16). It is designed to portray Jesus, the son of David, as the culmination of their history of salvation, the One promised by God. In proof of this Paul calls upon the Old Testament to show how the ancient prophecies are now fulfilled in him, especially in his resurrection. Many of the Jews believe (vs. 43), but some do not, and, characteristically, the nonbelievers work systematically to undermine him (vs. 45). This resistance moves Paul and Barnabas to condemn these recalcitrant Jews and to turn forthwith to the Gentiles, still quoting the Old Testament (Isaiah 49:6) to justify their action (13:44–47).

In 14:15–18 Paul and Barnabas are at Lystra making their first address to a purely pagan audience. This speech has less in common with the sermon of chapter 13 and the earlier missionary speeches than with Paul's address to the Athenians (see pp. 301 f.). At the end of chapter 14 Paul and Barnabas return to Antioch. The question of whether non-Jewish converts to Christianity had to be circumcised in accordance with Jewish law was not raised in the Cornelius incident (10:1–11:18), although we were left with the impression that they were not. Now at the beginning of chapter 15 a group of Christians from Judea who insist upon circumcision arrives in Antioch. Their appearance provides the occasion for the resolution of this and related questions in favor of Paul and Barnabas at the Jerusalem Council.[11] Circumcision is not required. Yet a similar or related question is again raised against Paul in chapter 21.

[11] The relation of the council of chapter 15 to the meeting between Paul and the leaders of the Jerusalem church described in the second chapter of Paul's letter to the Galatians is a problem that has long tantalized and puzzled scholars. Cf. Kümmel, *Introduction to the New Testament*, pp. 301–304.

At the end of the Jerusalem Council (chap. 15) and after a sharp dispute over John Mark, Paul and Barnabas separate. Paul returns to the scene of their earlier missionary activity, taking Silas with him (15:36–41). Thence he heads west and, reaching Troas, sees the vision of the man from Macedonia (16:9) that leads him to extend his missionary effort to Europe. Europe here means Macedonia and Greece, which was henceforth, with Ephesus, the main focus of his missionary activity until his imprisonment and subsequent journey to Rome. His chief missionary accomplishments were in the Greek cities of Philippi (chap. 16), Thessalonica (17:1–9), and Corinth (chap. 18) and in the Asian city of Ephesus (chap. 19). Luke, however, gives an extended account of the relatively brief visit of Paul to Athens.

PAUL'S SPEECH IN ATHENS (17:16–34)

How does Paul's preaching take advantage of pagan piety?

As a mission field Athens is certainly not typical—Paul's efforts there seem to have borne little fruit. However, Luke's account of his visit occupies a prominent place and includes the longest rendition in Acts of a sermon before an entirely Gentile audience. Obviously, Luke regards Paul's stay in Athens as an important event. Therefore, we need to understand its significance for him.

Luke's brief description of the character of Athens and the Athenians shows that he has some awareness of the nature as well as of the importance of the city.[12] Yet he reports that Paul was not at all impressed by Athens, and was shocked by the profusion of idols he found there (vs. 16). His displeasure led him to engage in debate, not only in the synagogue, as had previously been his custom, but even in the public marketplace (vs. 17). Although Luke does not indicate it this is presumably the same marketplace where centuries before Socrates engaged his fellow Athenians in discussions. Perhaps Luke is aware of a certain parallel here, even though he does not mention Socrates' name, for we read that Paul is accused of preaching "foreign divinities" (vs. 18). The Greek *xenōn daimoniōn* could as well be translated "of strange demons" and thus corresponds closely to that *diamōn* which led Socrates to raise those simple, pointed, and troublesome questions that at length roused the ire of his fellow Athenians and led to his execution as an atheist.[13]

---

[12] The Athens of Paul's time was not large even by ancient standards. E. Haenchen, *The Acts of the Apostles: A Commentary*, trans. H. Anderson et al. (Philadelphia: Westminster, 1971), p. 517, puts the total number of citizens (not total population) at about five thousand.

[13] *Daimōn* has the meaning "good spirit" rather than "demon" as the latter is usually understood. The accusation against Socrates was twofold: (1) corruption of the young and (2) neglect of the traditional gods and the recognition of new and strange deities (*daimonia*).

Paul's lack of appreciation of Athenian culture is no greater than the Athenians' misunderstanding of him, as his encounter with the Stoic and Epicurean philosophers shows (vs. 18). The epithet that some of them apply to him, babbler, means literally "cock-sparrow." It was a term of derision for a person who, without real understanding, picks up ideas from here and there, as the sparrow picks up seed, and passes them off as his own. That this estimate of Paul is an offhand judgment based on no genuine understanding of him may be inferred from the fact that the philosophers take Jesus and the resurrection to be two gods. (This is not quite as absurd a misunderstanding as it may seem, for the Greek word *anastasis*, resurrection, is feminine in gender, and pagan gods frequently had goddesses as consorts.) In the light of this beginning, the Athenians' desire to hear Paul's teaching in greater detail is difficult to understand. Luke insists that it only stems from their insatiable curiosity about anything new (vss. 20 f.).

Paul was taken to the Areopagus (vs. 19) by the Athenians, and there he made his speech. At the time of Paul a court was held on the Areopagus—the name means Mars Hill—which is a small promontory west of the more famous Acropolis. Although it has sometimes been suggested that Paul was himself taken there to be tried, this is nowhere explicitly stated (although the verb *took hold of* in vs. 19 could imply arrest). Moreover, the whole affair does not read like a legal proceeding. Rather, Paul is put on display, almost as if he were some kind of freak, by a crowd of intellectual dilettantes.

Paul's initial remark (vs. 22) is probably not to be taken in a negative or sarcastic sense. Rather, as the following verses show, it is the point of contact with the pagan audience that Paul hopes to follow up and develop in his delivery of the Christian message. This becomes clear in vs. 23, where Paul concedes that this "unknown god" is worshiped in a valid, if inadequate, way by the Athenians. The time has now come, however, for the unknown God to be revealed in the Christian preaching. A right understanding of this God will mean the recognition of the erroneous character of the pagan worship that has heretofore been offered (vss. 24 f.). This point of view is not, of course, unique to Christianity. It is also Jewish, and this part of Paul's speech may owe something to earlier Jewish missionary propaganda. Furthermore, although the idolatry and polytheism described here may have been practiced and taken seriously by many people in the ancient world, the cultured Greek would have also shared something of Paul's attitude. In fact, verses 24 ff. may owe as much to Stoic philosophy as to Judaism and the Old Testament.

The concepts (vss. 26 ff. esp.) actually fit better into the Stoic view of the cosmos than into the biblical-Jewish conception of the history of salvation. For verse 26 has to do with the characteristic Stoic ideas of the providence of God and verses 27 and 28 with his immanence or presence in the world. Moreover, just at the point at which we might have expected a quotation from the Old Testament, Paul quotes the Greek poet Aratus (vs. 28).[14] Thus does Paul accommodate his message to what is familiar and acceptable to his Greek hearers. When seen in the light of verse 29, verses 26–28 support the assertions of verses 24 and 25 and thus drive home the argument against idolatry. Although verses 26–28 are now frequently cited as biblical proof of the brotherhood of all peoples under God, in this context they are probably not intended primarily to set forth that idea. Rather, they are an argument from the evidence of the existence of God in human beings and nature to a conclusion concerning the nature of God and the proper knowledge and worship of him. God orders the world and humanity (vs. 26) in such a way that they should be disposed to seek him (vs. 27), and he so indwells his creation that this seeking is by no means vain (vss. 27 f.). Indeed, as the quotation from Aratus shows, the idea of immanence is understood to imply that humankind already has a close relationship to God: "For we are indeed his offspring." Probably Luke takes this to mean that humanity is God's creature in line with the Old Testament and Hebraic point of view and not in the sense of kinship which the poet originally intended. Nevertheless, creaturehood here already implies the possibility of knowing God and having access to him.

Only in verses 30 and 31 does Paul turn from these arguments about natural theology, which many Hellenistic Jews or even pagans might have found perfectly congenial, to the distinctly Christian message. The whole history of paganism down to the moment in which Paul speaks is described simply as "times of ignorance" that God has overlooked (vs. 30). The pagan world will presumably incur no guilt as a result, provided that it now repents. No mention at all is made of the ministry and crucifixion of Jesus in this preaching of repentance; only the coming judgment is invoked, and only in connection with it is Jesus mentioned. Even then Paul does not explicitly name him, but only alludes to him as the man whom God has appointed to judge the world, giving assurance of this "to all men by raising him from the dead." At the mention of the resurrection of the dead, Paul is interrupted; some hearers become contemptuous— the late Jewish and Christian notion of resurrection is foreign to them—but others remain curious (vs. 32). Paul departs (vs. 33), and although we have the impression that his preaching to the Athenians was something less than a success, he does succeed in making a few converts to the faith (vs. 34).

---

[14]*Phaenomena*, 5; cf. Cleanthes, *Hymn to Zeus*, 4. Only the last of the two quotations marked in the RSV has been positively identified. "In him we live and move and have our being" has sometimes been attributed to Epimenides, but it may not be a quotation at all.

The Parthenon, celebrated temple of Athena, built in the fifth-century B.C. on the Acropolis at Athens. (Courtesy of Greek Press and Information Service.)

The speech is notable on several counts. First, it differs from the missionary speeches of chapters 1–13 in its total lack of reference to the Old Testament and the history of Israel. Second, it is in important respects remarkably dissimilar to the thought of the genuine letters of Paul. Third, it has certain affinities, as we shall see, with the speech ascribed to Paul and Barnabas in 14:15–18. In fact, this is one of the rare places in the New Testament in which a positive, though highly qualified, estimate of pagan piety and culture is expressed or implied and a natural theology is set forth. Each of these points demands further comment.

We have already noticed that at just the point we would have expected Paul to refer to the Hebrew scriptures (Old Testament) he quotes a pagan poet. The Old Testament would have been of little use in confirming the truth of the Christian message before a non-Jewish audience who did not accept its authority in the first place. The appeal to this purely Gentile audience had to be made on the basis of arguments from Hellenistic natural theology and Greek literature. This does not mean that the use of the Hebrew scriptures in Christian preaching was regarded either by Paul or Luke as a purely apologetic device. There is ample reason to suppose that both regarded it as revelation in and of itself. Yet the non-Jewish hearer might be brought to assent on other grounds. In the other instance of a missionary sermon before a non-Jewish audience, the brief speech of Paul and Barnabas (14:15–18), there is no reference or allusion to the Hebrew scriptures or the narrative of salvation history. It may be that in recounting the speeches to Gentile audiences in this way Luke is following a common procedure, or is influenced by a common practice of the Hellenistic Christian mission in his own day.[15] As far as we know, Paul did not limit his use of the scriptures to situations in which he was addressing Christians of Jewish background only.

This observation leads directly to our second point. The first three chapters of the Epistle to the Romans suggest that Paul's attitude toward the pagan world was not that portrayed in the Areopagus speech. Whereas in his speech pagan piety and the possibility of a natural theology are the point of contact and, in fact, the basis of his preaching, in Romans practically the reverse is true (see pp. 360–368). In Romans, the knowledge of God is indeed possible because of creation and the natural order, but the possibility of such knowledge is not the basis of Christian preaching. Rather it is grounds for condemnation because it does not lead to a proper response to God (1:18–23). In Acts the hearers are credited with worshiping God without knowing him; in Romans mankind is charged with knowing God but not worshiping him. Whereas in Acts 17:30 the past prior to the preaching of the gospel is simply a period of ignorance for which no blame is placed, in Romans human history is the history of sin. Further, when the salvation event is announced in Acts 17:31, Paul speaks primarily of the coming judgment, with a backward look at the resurrection. In Romans 3:21 ff. the salvation event is described in terms of the cross. Admittedly Paul's speech is interrupted, but we have the impression that with the mention of the resurrection and judgment he has said all he meant to say. Thus in almost every important respect Paul's Areopagus speech seems to be the antithesis of the theology of Paul in Romans. This naturally raises the question of whether this speech is Paul's or whether Luke has put into Paul's mouth what he considers to be an appropriate and typical missionary sermon to Gentiles. In order to ascribe the

---

[15] Ulrich Wilckens, *Die Missionsreden der Apostelgeschichte: Form- und traditions-geschichtliche Untersuchungen*, (Neukirchen: Neukirchener Verlag, 1961), p. 99, suggests that Luke employed a pattern of heathen missionary preaching attested by I Thess. 1:9–10 and Heb. 5:11–6:2. B. Gärtner, *The Areopagus Speech and Natural Revelation*, trans. C. H. King (Lund: Gleerup, 1955), argues, however, for the basically Pauline character of the speech.

speech to Paul, one may surmise that after this occasion Paul gave up this apologetic approach. That is, after an unsuccessful attempt to make contact with pagan culture in the preaching of the gospel, he took a more hostile stance toward the world. Yet there is little indication in all the genuine Pauline letters that the apostle himself ever espoused such a theological position as we find in the Acts speech. It is much easier historically to understand the Areopagus speech as the composition of Luke. This, of course, does not mean that Paul did not visit Athens and preach there (cf. I Thess. 3:1).

Thus Luke seems to be presenting what he considers a typical missionary sermon to Gentiles. This observation can be supported further by our third point, namely, that the Areopagus speech has its closest affinities with the speech of Paul and Barnabas to a pagan audience at Lystra (14:15–18). The Lystra speech manifests certain specific points of agreement with the Areopagus address. Especially striking are the concept of divine creation (vs. 15), the notion that God has tolerated the idolatry of the Gentiles in times past (vss. 15 f.), and the belief that the beneficent natural processes attest a divine author (vs. 17). Except for the lack of direct reference to Christ, the Lystra speech is quite similar to the one at Athens. And like the latter, it is dissimilar to the speeches of chapters 1–13 and unlike the theology of the Pauline epistles.

Actually both the Athens speech and the Lystra speech are most unlike the Pauline theology and the rest of the New Testament in their ascription of a positive and significant role to a natural knowledge of God, a knowledge both possible and extant apart from the Jewish and Christian traditions. They are also unique in regarding the history of humanity prior to the coming of Christ and the preaching of the gospel as ignorance rather than sin. The revelation in Christ is not, first of all, the revelation of God's wrath (cf. Rom. 1:18) and of human sinfulness, but of a coming judgment and the necessity of repentance (Acts 17:30 f.) and forgiveness. Thus, for Luke the human predicament is not quite so desperate as for Paul, and pagan culture and piety are allowed to play a positive preparatory role for the appearance of the gospel.

The idea of a valid general revelation apart from Israel and the Old Testament, although rare in the New Testament, was taken up and developed by Christian apologists and theologians of the second and third centuries and has persisted among Christians down to the present. For Luke, the entire world and its history provide the scope for the Christian mission and message. Its roots are to be found not only in the history of Israel, but also in general human history and culture. Luke's Gospel traces the genealogy of Christ back to Adam, and in Acts the necessary presuppositions of Christian preaching are found in a popular philosophic view of God and the world, as well as in the Old Testament.

Jerusalem to Rome (21:15–28:31)

What is the end result of Paul's arrest and trials?

The final major section of Acts, chapters 21–28, is devoted entirely to the fortunes of Paul from his last visit to Jerusalem until his arrival as a prisoner in Rome. According to Luke, Paul was taken into custody by the Romans to save him from an angry Jerusalem mob. They accused him of "teaching men everywhere against the people and the law and this place," as well as defiling the temple by bringing Greeks into it (21:28). From the point at which Paul is arrested near the temple in Jerusalem (21:33) to the end of the book he is a Roman prisoner. (Probably he, like Jesus, died at the hands of the Romans, although Luke does not tell us.) Paul is at first held for a couple of days in Jerusalem. Then he is transferred to Caesarea, the site of the Roman governor's headquarters (chaps. 24–26), and finally, on the basis of his own appeal as a Roman citizen to trial by Caesar, he is sent to Rome (chaps. 27–28). At each stage Paul's innocence is affirmed (23:29; 25:25; 26:31 f.). There the story simply ends, with Paul a prisoner in Rome, albeit with certain freedoms and privileges. As we take leave of him he is still "preaching the kingdom of God and teaching about the Lord Jesus Christ quite openly and unhindered" (28:31).

The larger part of chapters 22–28, with the exception of the sea voyage to Rome (chap. 27), is devoted to extensive descriptions of Paul's defense of himself before the representatives of Judaism and Rome. It is as if the prophecy of 9:15 were being literally fulfilled: "He is a chosen instrument of mine to carry my name before the Gentiles and kings and the sons of Israel." Luke describes Paul's hearings and speeches in considerable detail. Paul's conversion, reported in full in chapter 9, is repeated with some variations in chapters 22 and 26. In the course of many scenes and speeches several themes are often reiterated. Paul has not betrayed Judaism; rather, he understands his whole mission to pertain directly to the fulfillment of the hope of Israel. Paul's mission to the Gentiles is not simply his own idea, but the direct result of divine causation and directive. Thus Paul's conversion is always closely linked to his commission to preach to the Gentiles—as it is by Paul himself (Gal. 1:15 ff.). Paul's innocence of any crime is established with certainty. The various hints, statements, and indications tending to exonerate Paul are well summarized in the conversation between Agrippa and Festus reported at the end of chapter 26, where it is agreed that Paul could have been released had not he appealed to Caesar. Yet the fact that he must stand before Caesar (27:24) is not finally a tragedy, although it has tragic overtones (e.g., 20:22–25, 38), but the culmination of the triumphant spread of Christianity across the known world and the high point of Acts. Although Paul's imprisonment and journey to Rome might be regarded by some as the result of the work of evil men or the quirk of a cruel fate, for Luke they are nothing other than the fulfillment of the will of God.

The *structure* of the Acts of the Apostles must be considered in connection with the Gospel. At the same time the division between Gospel and Acts is more than a convenient literary device. It marks a major division in Luke's theology and perception of history. Luke envisages a drama of three distinct phases: the period of Israel and her prophetic message; the fulfillment of this prophecy in the earthly mission of Jesus; and the mission of the church, likewise a fulfillment of ancient prophecy. His threefold division of the history of salvation can be discerned from the shape and structure of his writing. The Old Testament (cf. Luke 1:5–2:51 esp.) constitutes the first part of a story of salvation that finds its culmination in the coming of Jesus as the Christ (Gospel). But this fulfillment was not limited to the historic appearance of Jesus of Nazareth; it embraced also the existence and mission of his church (Acts).

The basic structure of Acts itself is quite simple. After the ascension, the election of Matthias, and the inaugural preaching of the gospel by Peter, which take place in or around Jerusalem, there are three principal divisions. The first deals with the establishment and growth of the church within Palestine (chaps. 3–12), the second with the expansion of the church to the Gentile world (chaps. 13–21), and the third with Paul's victory against opposition (chaps. 22–28). Even as the journey of Jesus to Jerusalem forms the central part of the Gospel, so the missionary journeys of Paul are the central portion of Acts. Just as the last part of the Gospel deals with the arrest, trial, and death of Jesus, so the last seven chapters of Acts narrate the arrest of Paul, his trials, and the eventual journey to Rome. The motifs of journeying and witnessing thus predominate in Acts as in Luke's Gospel.

The *emphases* of Acts are intricately bound to its structure, and intimately related to those of the Gospel. In fact, the same emphases—Christianity as the new Israel, worldwide expansion, and the importance of witnessing—are developed somewhat further in Acts. In the Gospel, Luke is tied to the tradition of Jesus, which he cannot radically change, but in Acts he can with a relatively free hand tell the story of the church's advance so as to bring out its meaning and truth.

Luke was deeply convinced that Judaism should have become Christianity, and, as it had not, that the promises to Israel were being fulfilled through Christ in the church. Thus the new faith is the proper and genuine continuation and fulfillment of the old. The many quotations from, and allusions and references to, the Old Testament clearly convey this emphasis.

In fact, the culmination of Paul's ministry in Rome (recounted in chap. 28) is his application of the famous Isaiah 6:9–10 passage to those Jews who had not believed his preaching (vss. 25–28). A large part of Israel has forfeited its inheritance to the Gentiles by rejecting the gospel, and the young Christian church has now become the true Israel.[16]

Acts is often called "the first church history," and in a sense it is. Yet insofar as it is a history at all, it is history of a very special kind. It has been written from a definite theological perspective with certain purposes in view. When all allowances are made for Luke's motivations and interests, however, it is apparent that a major part of his purpose in Acts is to tell an interesting and, for the most part, happy story. He describes the establishment of Christianity and its progress across the Greco-Roman world during the apostolic age. The scope of the gospel is universal, and it will not be denied. Although we hear of persecutions and martyrdoms in the course of this story, the storyteller's attitude remains confident and optimistic throughout, and the narrative is brought to an end on a positive note (28:30 f.). The gospel knows no obstacle too great and no enemy too powerful to stand in the way of its successful march from Jerusalem to Rome. The universal emphasis, which is subtly conveyed in Luke's Gospel, becomes the principal subject matter of Acts.

The centrality of Luke's emphasis upon the universality of the Gospel implies an emphasis on witnessing. Again, what is handled somewhat indirectly in the Gospel becomes a major theme of Acts. In Acts 1 Luke's first concern was to show that in the apostolic group, the twelve, a firm basis for the witness to Jesus had been established. Matthias, who was elected to the twelve to replace Judas, qualified by virtue of intimate and long-time knowledge of Jesus. Having been a witness of Jesus he was qualified to bear witness. If Luke emphasizes the universality of the gospel, he does so by telling of the apostles and others witnessing. Their witnessing encounters persecution, as we had already been led to expect by the Gospel. Indeed, the witness (Greek, *martyr*) may even become a martyr, as in the case of Stephen, not to mention Peter, Paul, and others who are arrested and otherwise harassed.[17] Although Luke takes full account of such dangers, he does not dwell upon them, for he is fully convinced that such opposition fails utterly to impede the spread of the gospel and the growth of the church.

[16] This fact is also reflected in his Gospel, 4:16–30. Jesus begins his ministry with a clear indication that he is to be rejected by the Jews and accepted by Gentiles.

[17] The tradition of Paul's martyrdom is found only in extracanonical documents: I Clement v, 7; Acts of Paul, x; Eusebius, *EH*, ii, 22. The supposed site of Paul's martyrdom is commemorated by the ancient church St. Paul Outside the Walls in Rome. The present structure was rebuilt in modern times after fire destroyed the fourth-century building. According to tradition, Peter also was martyred at Rome (see note 3).

The method of *redaction criticism,* which can be so profitably applied to the Gospel, yields less fruit in Acts because, although we can identify the major sources of the Gospel (Mark and Q) with some certainty, it is quite difficult to separate tradition from redaction in Acts. Nevertheless, the assumption that sources and traditions of some sort lie behind Acts is probably warranted. Evidence of the author's editing can surely be found in the summary reports and transitions and especially in the overall structure. It is also likely that the speeches in their present form are largely his composition. The material of Acts is well permeated with Luke's own point of view, which can usually be identified with some confidence.

As to the *historical occasion* or *situation* of Acts, the author probably writes for the general reader, but the needs and purposes of the church are nevertheless in the forefront of his attention. No doubt he expected the work to be useful to the church for apologetic or missionary purposes. As an apologist, Luke wants to show that Christianity is not a subversive movement. In the Gospel he went out of his way to prove that Jesus was innocent of any crime (Luke 23:47; see p. 156). A similar motif appears in the statement about Paul which Agrippa made to Festus, the Roman procurator: "This man could have been set free if he had not appealed to Caesar" (26:32). Christians are arrested not because the authorities have seen them commit a crime, but because they have become involved in some incident as a result of the accusations or actions of either Jews or Gentiles. The only Christian martyrs mentioned in Acts are victims of the Jews. That Luke should have had some interest in showing Christians innocent of any crimes against the state is thoroughly understandable. After all, Jesus had been crucified by the Roman authorities, whatever role the Jewish leaders may have played, and this fact was apparently widely known. Thus, from the outset Christianity stood under the suspicion of being a subversive movement, and this suspicion could only have been heightened by the refusal of Christians to participate in the worship of the Roman emperor. Luke intends to show that the suspicion is groundless.

Luke's literary aspirations, reflected in the formal prefaces and in the style and tone of his work, make it very difficult to pin down a definite time and place of origin within early Christianity. Because of his apologetic concern to show Jesus and the church politically innocent in relation to the Roman Empire, a Roman origin has sometimes been suggested. This suggestion is plausible and possible, if not compelling. But the same literary style and historical interests that make Luke difficult to locate within the first century contribute to our understanding of his general situation. The character and quality of his writing suggest a Christianity well on its way to becoming an established world religion. Indeed, history confirmed the worldwide vision of Luke-Acts, for the new faith became the official religion of the Roman Empire within less than three centuries.

Suggestions for Further Reading

The best commentary on Acts, understood as a theological document, is E. Haenchen, *The Acts of the Apostles: A Commentary*, trans. H. Anderson, R. McL. Wilson, et al. (Philadelphia: Westminster, 1971). More conservative on historical issues is F. F. Bruce, *Commentary on the Book of Acts* (Grand Rapids, Mich.: Eerdmans, 1954). A worthwhile shorter commentary on Acts is that of C. S. C. Williams, *A Commentary on the Acts of the Apostles* (New York: Harper & Row, 1957). For works on the history of earliest Christianity, see the Suggestions for Further Reading, Chapter 11; for works on Luke-Acts, Chapter 4.

In addition, the following books deal principally with Acts. M. Dibelius, *Studies in the Acts of the Apostles*, ed. H. Greeven and trans. M. Ling (New York: Scribner, 1956), is a collection of pioneering essays on the literary analysis and interpretation of Acts written over a period of decades by the well-known German scholar. On the historical basis of Acts, H. Cadbury, *The Book of Acts in History* (New York: Harper & Row, 1955); the same author's *The Making of Luke-Acts* (New York: Macmillan, 1927), is still valuable. F. J. Foakes-Jackson and K. Lake (eds.), *The Beginnings of Christianity*, 5 vols. (London: Macmillan, 1920–1933), is a landmark of scholarship; the work has now been reissued (Grand Rapids, Mich.: Baker Book House). J. C. O'Neill, *The Theology of Acts in Its Historical Setting*, 2nd ed. (London: SPCK, 1970), links Acts to second-century Christianity and the Apologists. J. Jervell, *Luke and the People of God* (Minneapolis: Augsburg, 1972), is a collection of significant essays dealing mainly with Acts. The most extensive history of research, W. W. Gasque, *A History of the Criticism of the Acts of the Apostles* (Grand Rapids, Mich.: Eerdmans, 1975), is avowedly conservative in perspective.

CHAPTER EIGHT

Paul: Apostle
and Man of Faith

Paul and His Predecessors [1]
  The Tradition of Moses (*II Cor-
    inthians 3:12–18*)
  Apostle by God's Revelation
    (*Galatians 1:1–2:10*)
  The Received Tradition (*I Cor-
    inthians 15:1–8*)
  The Word of the Lord (*I Corin-
    thians 7:10 f.; 9:14; and
    11:23–26*)
  The Freedom of the Gospel

  Hope (*I Thessalonians 4:13–5:11*)
  Faith (*Galatians 2:11–21*)
  Love (*I Corinthians 8:1–13*)
The Struggle of the Gospel
  Courage in Ministry (*II Corin-
    thians 4:1–15*)
  Joy in Hardship (*Philippians
    1:12–26*)
  Steadfastness Against Heresy
    (*Colossians 2:8–15*)

NOTES ON PAUL'S CAREER

*The Acts of the Apostles gives a clear picture of the nature and scope of
Paul's missionary career. Nevertheless, some difficulties arise when one
attempts to reconcile Acts' description of Paul and his message with Paul's
own letters. It is possible, however, to make an approximate correlation of
the Acts account of Paul's career with the letters, to bring his life and work
into relation with the main events of the epoch in which he lived, and thus
to construct a tentative Pauline chronology. On the basis of an ancient
inscription found at Delphi in Greece, Gallio's proconsulship in Corinth
can be dated about A.D. 51–52. According to the Acts report, while Paul
was in Corinth for eighteen months on his second missionary journey
(15:36–18:21) he was arrested and brought before this same Gallio
(18:12 ff.). Thus we can arrive at an approximate date for Paul's first visit
to Corinth; this is the surest fixed point of Pauline chronology. We may
confidently place Paul's career in the middle third of the first century.*

---

[1] This heading is suggested by the book of the same title by Archibald Hunter,
rev. ed. (Philadelphia: Westminster, 1961).

Probably he was converted in the early thirties and died in the early six-ties. Within this period there is less certainty about the exact dating of events. (For an approximate chronology of Paul and the Pauline letters, see the chart on p. xix.[2])

More of the New Testament has been ascribed to Paul than to any other author. The Pauline authorship of Hebrews is universally rejected among critical scholars, however, and that of the Pastorals (I and II Tim-othy and Titus) generally so, with Colossians and II Thessalonians as well as Ephesians sometimes considered doubtful. Therefore, Luke would seem to have been the most prolific New Testament author. Yet slightly more than one half of Luke's total work is about Jesus and therefore embodies much pre-Lukan tradition. Of the rest more than one half is about Paul. That so much later literature was ascribed to Paul and that his chief rival for literary productivity devoted a great part of his second work to a de-scription of his career are accurate indications of the significance of the man. Paul was not only the most important missionary of the first Chris-tian generation; he was also its most productive literary figure. Moreover, he was a notable organizer, man of affairs, and thinker. We would know a good deal about him if we had only the Book of Acts, in which he plays so large a role. Fortunately, we also have at least some of his letters, which reflect not only his activities and thought, but also his own personality.

The purpose of this chapter is threefold. First, passages from Galatians and the Corinthian letters will be examined to show how Paul was related to those who were apostles before him (Gal. 1:17) and to the tradition of Christian preaching and teaching that was already forming ("Paul and His Predecessors"). Second, we shall discuss the typical emphases of Paul's gos-pel ("Hope," "Love," "Faith;" cf. I Cor. 13:13) and attempt to see how they were related to actual situations and problems in the churches in which he worked ("The Freedom of the Gospel"). In this case the churches in question were in Thessalonica, Galatia, Antioch, and Corinth. Third, and finally, a study of texts from II Corinthians, Philippians, and Colossians will illustrate the problems that beset Paul as he sought to fulfill his ap-ostolic calling ("The Struggle of the Gospel"). From this treatment should emerge an idea of Paul's place and role in the primitive church, a sense of the content of his gospel in its relation to human problems and life, and a feeling for the struggles he faced and his motivation for enduring them. It should be noted that the texts treated under the first section, "Paul and His Predecessors," are not the earliest ones written, nor are they presented in the order in which they were written. They were chosen because they afford us valuable insights about Paul's earlier career, and his antecedents. The remaining texts are arranged in their approximate order of composition

---

[2]Something like the chronology reflected in our table (following the contents) has been widely accepted, but there is by no means universal agreement. The most recent thorough treatment in English, which comes to somewhat different conclu-sions, is that of Robert Jewett, *A Chronology of Paul's Life* (Philadelphia: Fortress, 1979). The problem of Pauline chronology has recently become the subject of intense investigation. Cf. also Gerd Lüdemann, *Paulus der Heidenapostel, Band I: Studien zur Chronologie,* (Göttingen: Vandenhoeck & Ruprecht, 1980), whose interest was stim-ulated by the earlier work of the American scholars John Knox and D. W. Riddle.

(*I Thessalonians, Galatians, I Corinthians, II Corinthians, Philippians, Colossians*) *and at the same time deal with central themes of Paul's preaching and ministry.*

Paul and His Predecessors

Probably Paul was the most important and creative figure in the history of early Christianity and the development of its thought. Yet he already stood within and relied upon a tradition. As a Jew Paul read the Hebrew scriptures and regarded them as authoritative. As a convert to faith in Jesus as the Messiah, Paul referred back both to his own experience and to primitive creedal formulations held by other Christians as well. As a member of a community of disciples reaching back to Jesus, Paul was able to call upon at least a limited number of sayings of the Lord.

THE TRADITION OF MOSES (II Cor. 3:12–18)[3]

Do Jews and Christians read the Old Testament in the same way?

II Corinthians 3, although interesting and important in several ways, is crucial for understanding what Paul thinks about scripture, that is, the Old Testament. Of course, for Paul what later Christians have called the Old Testament was simply the Bible, as it is for Judaism today. For Paul, however, scripture points to Christ and can only be understood in light of him.

Chapter 3 is part of Paul's long, digressive defense of his apostleship, which extends over several chapters and interrupts an account of his meeting Titus in Macedonia just before writing the letter (cf. 2:13; 7:5). So sharp is the break away from, and back to, this account that Paul's apostolic defense has even been regarded as belonging to another letter, inserted here by a later editor.[4] However that may be, it is apparent that what Paul says about scripture takes the form of a shorter digression within the longer excursus on apostleship.

In the text Paul probably mentions "letters of recommendation" (3:1) because his opponents, rival apostles who have come to Corinth since his departure (11:5), have brought such letters from other

---

[3] Outlines and Notes on the Corinthian correspondence and Galatians appear in the subsequent sections, where portions of these books are dealt with for their own sake. In this section the relevant passages are to be read for the light they shed on Paul's personal history and attitudes.

[4] This view is rather common in Europe, especially among the students of Rudolf Bultmann. See W. Marxsen, *Introduction to the New Testament*, trans. G. Buswell (Philadelphia: Fortress, 1968), pp. 77–91, for an account of this partition theory of II Corinthians. Marxsen thinks that the apostolic defense (2:14–7:4) was written between the writing of I Corinthians and Paul's second visit to Corinth (see p. 340).

authorities in the church. "You yourselves," says Paul to the Corinthians, "are our letter of recommendation" (3:2). This metaphor then leads Paul to a comparison of letters of Christ written by the Spirit upon human hearts with letters written on tablets of stone (3:3). By the latter he means the law of Moses.

Paul's real point is not to compare the Corinthian Christians with the law of Moses, but to contrast his apostolic letters of recommendation, that is, the Corinthians themselves, to the letters of his opponents. But Paul is so captivated by his language that he begins to digress. First, however, he issues a ringing affirmation of the sufficiency and legitimacy of his own apostolic ministry (3:4–6). Yet even in this affirmation he cannot resist taking up the comparison "written in human hearts" and "written on stone" (vs. 6), which he has made in connection with the letters (vs. 3), to describe his own ministry in similar terms. He has been made minister of a new covenant, not in a written code but in the Spirit (3:6): to translate literally, "the letter (of the code) kills, but the spirit gives life." Here Paul refers not only to his personal ministry, but to the ministry of Christ, properly understood.

In the following paragraph (vss. 7–11) Paul makes a comparison, or contrast, between two dispensations (Greek, "ministry"), the dispensation of death and that of the Spirit. He has in mind, on the one hand, the giving of the law of Israel at Sinai (cf. Exodus 34:29–35), and on the other, the giving of the Spirit to the church through Christ. Although Paul speaks quite negatively, if not disparagingly, of the law, we learn elsewhere (Rom. 3:31; 7:7–12) that he did not consider it to be evil. The contrast in this section (vss. 7–11) is between the God-given law, which in itself cannot give life, and the life-giving Spirit of Christ. The problem is not, in fact, with the law per se. Its glory may be inferior and by itself it does not bring life. But the law is not therefore invalid. There is a proper reading of the law and an improper reading. Israelites do not truly understand the law. Moses' veil, put over his face so that the Israelites could not look upon its fading splendor (vss. 7–13), symbolizes the problem (cf. Exodus 34:29–35). At first (vs. 14), the reader imagines that the veil on Moses' face implies a veil over the law (law = Moses). But in fact that veil is really over the minds of the hearers (vs. 15). Why and how the switch has taken place is not obvious. Probably it is because of the use of the Septuagint of Exodus 34:33, 35 in verse 16: "but whenever he (RSV, "a man") turns to the Lord, the veil is removed." In the Old Testament text this statement applies to Moses, but Paul wishes to use it of the person who is converted ("turns to the Lord"). It is that person who, like Moses, has the veil over his face. When that one, like Moses, turns to the Lord (in conversion), the veil is removed. Thus Paul's application of the passage about Moses to the believer accounts for his moving the veil from Moses to the minds of the disbelievers. Just this use of the passage affords an example of the kind of reading of the law he is talking about. The Exodus passage in question does not obviously have the meaning Paul desires. Only from his Christian perspective can this meaning be assigned to it. Notice that the Lord (Greek, *kyrios*) is now no longer Yahweh, but the Lord Jesus Christ. This Lord is the Spirit, and the Spirit gives freedom (vs. 17). Paul leaves the reader with a picture of Christians with faces unveiled beholding the glory of the Lord (not the fading, secondary glory of Moses' face) and "being changed into his likeness, from one degree of glory to another" (vs. 18).

What Paul says here about the way the law is read in the synagogue and the way it is read by Christians provides some indication and justification for his own way of reading the Old Testament. He shares this perspective with many other Christians, and it is rather widely reflected in his own letters and in the rest of the New Testament. The struggle between Jews and Christians over the sacred scriptures is beginning. Paul speaks of the law, by which he may mean only the Pentateuch, although he once refers to the Old Covenant (vs. 14) or, as it could just as easily be rendered, the Old Testament. Whether Paul has in mind all scripture or only the five books of the Pentateuch is not a crucial question, for the Pentateuch was certainly the heart of scripture for Israel, and scripture was above all else law.

Behind this entire section is the tension between letter and spirit. Paul first speaks of letters (*epistolai*) of recommendation. This suggests writing (*graphein*), and that in turn suggests what is written (*gramma*, or letter in that sense). Of course, the law is written upon tablets of stone and administered through Moses, who received it from God on Mount Sinai. The spirit on the other hand affects the human heart directly (vs. 3) and is administered through Christ, or by means of Paul, his minister. For Paul the actual functioning of the Spirit and the Lord Jesus Christ are indistinguishable, so that he can say that the Lord *is* the Spirit (vss. 17 f.). The Spirit is therefore the Spirit of Christ. Thus for Paul the Hebrew scriptures are authoritative in so far as interpretation is guided by the Spirit of Christ. This new standard marks a sharp break from Jewish interpretation.

APOSTLE BY GOD'S REVELATION (Gal. 1:1–2:10)

Why does Paul seek to establish his independence of all human authority?

In this section of Galatians Paul speaks of two meetings with other apostles in Jerusalem (1:18; 2:1). Such meetings are also mentioned in the Book of Acts. (In fact, Acts mentions five visits to Jerusalem, while Paul himself speaks of only three.) At this point

Saint Paul, a plaque from thirteenth-century France. (Courtesy of Bulloz Art Reference Bureau.)

identification of the precise occasion of these meetings is not important. Instead, we want to understand Paul's own attitude toward his Christian predecessors and his estimate of where he stood in relation to them. Fundamental to Paul's perspective is the aside at the beginning of Galatians. He is an apostle, "not from men nor through man, but through Jesus Christ and God the Father, who raised him from the dead" (1:1). Clearly and unequivocally Paul grounds his apostleship, and therefore his right to preach to the Gentiles, upon the call of God in Jesus Christ. It is not finally or fundamentally dependent on any human approval. He is not an apostle because some other apostles have instituted or ordained him as such. Therefore, he is not dependent for the source and authority of his gospel upon any human institution or agency.

Paul's theological grounds for asserting his independent and apostolic authority are clearly stated in verses 3–5, and the problem that has called forth Paul's drastic assertion of his divine right appears in verses 6–9. What is crucial here is not Paul's self-esteem or status but, rather, the validity of the gospel as he has preached it in Galatia and elsewhere. It is the one true and saving message, beside which there cannot be rival or competing versions. Paul calls down the sternest *anathema* (the Greek term for *curse*) upon anyone who preaches a gospel contrary to his own—not because it is his gospel, but because it is God's. Paul sounds inflexible and dogmatic. Yet his defense is not the dogmatic expression of an opinion, but the confession of one who feels himself moved by a God who has called and directed him. Thus Paul's understanding of his commissioning as an apostle and his insistence upon the validity of his message go hand in hand. Each apart from the other becomes untenable. Paul's claim of apostolic authority would be empty apart from the power and truth of his message. Conversely, the truth of the message is guaranteed by Paul's apostolic commission, which comes directly from the Lord.

Apparently Paul's vigorous assertion of his authority and his gospel was evoked by intruders in the Galatian church who sought to discredit his preaching as something less than the whole truth by calling in question his apostolic legitimacy, and therefore his God-given authorization. In 3:1–5:12 Paul argues against the version of the gospel preached by these people. From this central section of the letter it is clear that the intruders sought to introduce circumcision and obedience to the Jewish law as requirements for membership in the Christian community. To them Paul's gospel must have seemed the broad and easy path that leads to destruction rather than the hard and narrow one that leads to life (cf. Matt. 7:13 f.). Very likely they suspected Paul of making the gospel easy by dispensing with circumcision and the law. They called him a man-pleaser (1:10), one who has softened the requirements of the gospel. In attempting to institute what they regarded as their correct version, they must have claimed that Paul's preaching and status were inferior because he had received his gospel from men. That is, his gospel of grace and freedom was a human idea rather than divine revelation. Paul does not tell us directly, but his violent and repeated rejection of the idea that he is dependent on some human authority (1:1, 10, 11 ff.) makes it highly probable that such charges were brought against him.

Paul justifies the contention that his gospel was from God and was received by revelation with a recitation of his own history, into which this revelation had broken. Thus in 1:13–17 he strikingly combines personal reminiscence with the confession of God's initiative and activity in his life. This passage is the only description of his so-called conversion that comes directly from Paul. Actually, he does not call it his "conversion" at all, although it might be so understood from the standpoint of the psychology of religion. He speaks instead of God's foreordination and call (vs. 15) and of the revelation of the Son of God to him in order that he might preach the gospel to the Gentiles. Paul does not focus upon his "religious experience" but upon the revelation of God which he discerns in his own personal history (cf. Jeremiah 1). He regards the decisive moment of this history to be the manifestation of the risen Lord to him (cf. I Cor. 15:8).

The scope of God's action and purpose is not, however, limited to the single event of this revelation and call. The remainder of the narrative (1:18–2:10) is principally intended to show that none of Paul's subsequent actions calls in question the certainty or adequacy of the commission that he received in the first instance directly from God. He does not immediately thereafter seek human confirmation or assurance. Only after three years does he first go to Jerusalem, the seat of the original Christian community (vs. 18), to see Cephas (Peter). When after fourteen years he makes another trip, he is guided by revelation. Let no one think he has been summoned by his superiors! Did he circumcise Titus (2:4) to placate anyone? He did not consider the possibility for an instant (2:5).[5] Moreover, he showed no special deference to the reputed pillars of the Jerusalem church (2:6, 9), and on good theological grounds (vs. 6).[6] Indeed, he did not hesitate to reproach Peter himself, when the latter was not straightforward about the truth of the gospel (vss. 11 ff.).

---

[5] Paul here denies that Titus was circumcised at all (not that his circumcision took place because of outside pressure), as has been shown by E. D. Burton, *A Critical and Exegetical Commentary on the Epistle to the Galatians* (Edinburgh: Clark, 1921), pp. 75 ff. Cf. Hans Dieter Betz, *Galatians: A Commentary on Paul's Letter to the Churches in Galatia* (Philadelphia: Fortress, 1979), pp. 91–92, for the same view.

[6] The pillars are, of course, James, Cephas, and John (2:9). John is presumably the Son of Zebedee, who also appears in the stories of Acts 3–5. James is not the brother of John, but the brother of Jesus himself (1:19). Cephas (literally, "Rock") is the original Aramaic name of Peter. The fact that in Galatians 2:9 James is mentioned first (cf. 1:18 f.) may be an indication of the pre-eminence that by this time he already enjoyed in the Jerusalem church.

Yet, although Paul strongly asserts his apostolic commission and independence of human authorization, he also believes that the gospel did not originate with him, but with God, and that it is not given to him alone but to the church. Thus, although he insists upon his independence of those who were apostles before him (1:17), he is eager to show that these same apostles approved his preaching of the gospel (2:7–10). In fact, he candidly says that he put his gospel before them for their approval, as if everything depended upon that (2:2).

At first glance, Paul's assertion of his independence and his concern for apostolic approval may seem contradictory. Paul is not, however, concerned to say that his gospel is novel or unique, but to affirm God's initiative in revealing it to him and commissioning him to preach it to the uncircumcised (2:7), that is, to Gentiles (cf. 1:16). He does not, in other words, put himself forward as the second founder of Christianity, the one and only man to whom the true meaning of Christ's coming has been revealed. For despite the claims for his own commission and authority, which he is not in the least embarrassed to make, Paul wishes to show that his gospel is the same gospel with which the church has been entrusted. The uniqueness of his commissioning lies in the fact that God has made him apostle to the Gentiles. Paul does not even put forward his central doctrine of justification by grace through faith as an original insight, but as an elementary deduction from the gospel itself, and one that anyone should have been able to make. Thus he can upbraid Peter for his dissimulation (2:11 ff.) rather than his ignorance.

Paul was a charismatic figure and an original thinker; yet he did not wish to set himself above, but only alongside, those who were apostles before him. Although not dependent on them, he actively sought their approval. For Paul was a churchman and was concerned for the unity of the church. He enthusiastically agreed to make a collection in his mission field for the poor in the Jerusalem church (2:10; cf. I Cor. 16:1–4; II Cor. 8, 9; Rom. 15:25–29). This act was more than charity. It was a visible and tangible expression of the oneness of the churches he had founded with the church at Jerusalem and, by implication, of the unity of the gospel.

THE RECEIVED TRADITION (I Cor. 15:1–8)

Does the tradition that Paul has received count as revelation?

Paul claims to have received the gospel and the commission to preach it to the Gentiles by divine revelation. Does this mean that the content of the gospel, the facts about Jesus' life, and especially his crucifixion and resurrection, were given to him quite apart from any human action or agent? Such a claim would present obvious

difficulties, and Paul apparently does not mean that the content of
Christian tradition came to him as a sudden revelation. In Galatians, Paul stated that he had been a persecutor of the Christian
church (cf. Acts 9). Doubtless he did not persecute a movement
about which he knew nothing. Moreover, in II Corinthians 5:16 he
speaks of having once regarded Christ from a human point of view
(Greek, *kata sarka*, literally, "according to the flesh"). This phrase
probably refers to Paul's distorted perception of Christ prior to his
conversion.

Paul was baptized (Acts 9:18). At that time he presumably made
a confession of faith in Jesus as the Messiah, a confession that had
perhaps already attained the status of a traditional liturgical formula. We may also assume that he received some further instruction in faith, although we can say little or nothing about its exact
nature. But we know that Paul at some time had received a traditional interpretation of the gospel. In I Corinthians he writes: "For
I delivered to you as of first importance, what I also received" (15:3).
He then proceeds to repeat the essential elements of the early Christian preaching.[7] Most certainly traditional are the affirmations that
Christ died for our sins and that this happened according to the Hebrew scriptures, that he was buried, that he was raised on the third
day according to the scriptures, and that he appeared to Cephas
(Luke 24:34) and to the twelve (Luke 24:36 ff.; Matt. 28:16 ff.; John
20:19, cf. vs. 24). Also, when Paul refers to what he has received and
what the Corinthians have received, he seems to be using terminology associated with the passing on of tradition. ("Tradition" itself
means a process of passing on from one person or generation to another.) How much of the remaining material in I Corinthians 15:3–
8 is traditional is a matter of debate. Clearly Paul adds his own experience to the list of resurrection appearances.

If Paul received and used such traditional material, does this be-
lie his claim in Galatians that he did not receive the gospel from
human hands? The Greek word for *receive* (Gal. 1:12) is the same
word Paul uses in I Corinthians 15:1, 3 of what he has received from
tradition, which he significantly describes as "of first importance"
(cf. 11:23). In the light of I Corinthians, how can Paul baldly claim
that the gospel came to him through no human mediation, but
through a revelation of Jesus Christ (Gal. 1:12)? The answer may be
that Paul is simply inconsistent, but inconsistency on such a crucial
point would have been a serious matter. More likely Paul distinguished between the initial revelation of the gospel to himself and
his later appropriation of common kerygmatic or creedal formula-

[7] At least this much can now be said in the wake of C. H. Dodd's important
study of *The Apostolic Preaching and Its Developments* (New York: Harper & Row,
1951) and the discussion of the questions it raised. Cf. Hunter, *Paul and His Predecessors*, pp. 15–23, and M. Dibelius, *From Tradition to Gospel*, trans. B. L. Woolf
(New York: Scribner, 1934), pp. 16–22.

tions. The use of such formulations does not call in question Paul's claim that he first was confronted by and believed the gospel not because of human preaching, but because of a revelation of Jesus Christ (I Cor. 9:1, 15:8). Paul is interested in affirming not the uniqueness of his gospel but the uniqueness of God's revelation of it to him. Paul's willingness to submit his gospel to the pillars in Jerusalem and his desire to demonstrate his essential agreement and unity with the Jerusalem church show that he does not espouse an individualism independent of tradition. The crucial point for Paul is that apart from the divine initiative in his life he would have had no gospel and no apostolic status. For both he owes everything to God. By the canons of human behavior and expectation he should have gone on disbelieving the gospel and persecuting the church. But by God's action toward him, an action ordained from before his birth (Gal. 1:15), he was turned around and set upon a new course. He was made an apostle of the gospel that he had once persecuted. This astounding reversal of his life Paul can attribute only to God.

The revelation of God's Son (Gal. 1:16) was given to Paul as an appearance of the risen Christ. Paul's belief that he had seen the risen Lord (cf. I Cor. 9:1; 15:8) was the ground of his claim to be an apostle independent of any human authority. The apostles of the primitive church were apparently those who could claim a commission from the Lord himself, and such a commission was usually tied to a resurrection appearance (cf. John 20:21; Acts 1:8; Matt. 28:16 ff.). Thus, through God's action in Jesus Christ, and specifically through Christ's appearance to him, Paul has "received grace and apostleship to bring about obedience to the faith for the sake of his name among all the nations" (Rom. 1:5). Nevertheless, Paul stands within, not above, the church. To prove his claim to divine revelation he shows that his gospel is the same as that of the other apostles. Furthermore, he is quite willing to concede that the specific content of this gospel is something given him by tradition.

THE WORD OF THE LORD (I Cor. 7:10 f.; 9:14; and 11:23–26)

Did Paul know the words of Jesus found in the Gospels?

The fact that Paul speaks of his relationship to Jesus Christ raises the question of how he knew Jesus. The answer is, first of all, through the manifestation of the risen Lord at Damascus, and, second, through tradition.[8] That much is already clear. In admonishing

---

[8]Relatively negative conclusions to which the investigation of Paul's knowledge of Jesus has come are emphasized by V. P. Furnish, "The Jesus-Paul Debate: From Baur to Bultmann," *Bulletin of the John Rylands Library*, 47 (1964–1965), 342–381. More positive views on Paul's knowledge and use of Jesus traditions are espoused by C. F. D. Moule, "Jesus in the New Testament Kerygma," in *Verbum Veritas: Festschrift für Gustav Stählin*, ed. O. Böcher and K. Haacker (Wuppertal: Brockhaus,

"The Last Supper" by Emil Nolde (1909). (Courtesy of Alinari Art Reference Bureau.)

the Corinthians about their table fellowship (I Cor. 11:17–34), however, Paul again invokes what he has received (*paralambanō*) from the Lord and delivered (*paradidōmi*) to them (I Cor. 11:23–26). The terminology of verse 23 is exactly the same as that of 15:3. In addition, the words of the Lord that Paul gives are substantially the same as Jesus' words of institution found in Matthew 26:26–28; Mark 14:22–24; and Luke 22:19–20. As it is unlikely that Paul received these words directly from the Lord either on the Damascus road or elsewhere, we must suppose that he is here giving a tradition about Jesus that he has received in the church, but a tradition that the church traces back to the Lord himself. Moreover, the close parallel with the Synoptic accounts demonstrates conclusively the traditional character of this material. The life situation that preserved such words of the Lord as in 11:23–26 is clear: the continuing worship of the church, which in celebrating the Lord's Supper looked back to the earthly ministry and death of Jesus, and forward to his return (II Cor. 11:26).

1970), and David Dungan, *The Sayings of Jesus in the Churches of Paul* (Philadelphia: Fortress, 1971). Dungan deals extensively with the passages from I Corinthians chaps. 7 and 9, which we discuss subsequently.

In at least two other instances (I Cor. 7:10 f. and 9:14) Paul draws directly upon a traditional word of Jesus, and in a way calculated to define the limits of the discussion. In both cases Paul applies Jesus' saying to a specific situation and need. Thus in 7:10 f. he adduces a saying of the Lord forbidding divorce that appears in another form in Mark 10:11 f. (Matt. 5:32). It is applied directly to an actual situation in the Corinthian church, where some believers are apparently considering separation from unbelieving spouses. Couples consisting of a believer and an unbeliever should remain united, unless the unbelieving partner wants to separate. In that case the marriage can be dissolved. Of course, the situation to which Paul applies Jesus' command and the way in which he qualifies it were neither anticipated nor intended by Jesus. But Paul was probably not the first to fit the meaning of Jesus' commands to a new setting or problem. In 9:14 Paul refers to another command of Jesus, and perhaps Luke 10:7 and Matthew 10:10 afford a parallel in sense if not in wording to the decree that the person who preaches the gospel should make a living by it. Paul has in mind the right of the missionary preacher to receive pay from his churches, a right which he himself foregoes. Again Paul makes a saying of Jesus speak to a new situation.

Paul reveals certain other knowledge of Jesus' ministry (Gal. 1:19; 2:9; 3:1; 4:4; I Cor. 2:2; 15:4 ff.; Rom. 1:3). Yet his letters contain disappointingly little information about the life and teaching of Jesus. We find him preoccupied with the question of the meaning of the crucifixion and resurrection of Jesus Christ, with eschatology, and with the history of salvation. When Paul is read in and for himself and not from the standpoint of the Gospels, it is apparent that he does not seek to expound the meaning of the event of Christ by reference to the specific historical details of Jesus' life. It is easy to forget this fact, because it is customary and natural to read the Gospels before Paul and, so to speak, assume them as we read his letters. The canonical Gospels, as we have them, developed only after Paul and thus cannot form the background and source of Paul's theological reflections. Although the oral tradition of Jesus was both preserved and valued in some quarters, there is no longer any sure way of knowing how much Paul knew of it. Aside from the allusions to Jesus' life and the rare instances where he explicitly cites a word of the Lord, there are several places in which Paul seems to hark back to such a saying (Rom. 12:14; 13:9; 14:14; II Cor. 13:1). But one can rarely be certain whether Paul actually had a saying of Jesus in mind or was only drawing upon a common Jewish or Christian ethical tradition. Living when he did, having visited Jerusalem many times, if indeed he was not educated there (Acts 22:3),[9] Paul

---

[9] W. C. Van Unnik, *Tarsus or Jerusalem? The City of Paul's Youth*, trans. G. Ogg (London: Epworth, 1962), argues that Paul was reared and grew up in Jerusalem.

had ample opportunity to become acquainted with those who had known Jesus. In fact, in Galatians he mentions his personal acquaintance with James, the brother of the Lord, as well as with Peter and John. Why did he not take the trouble to learn more about Jesus? Or, if he did, why does he not refer more clearly and explicitly to this tradition in his letters? It can always be argued that, after all, we have no specimens of the apostle's actual preaching and that perhaps in his oral delivery of the gospel he spoke more extensively of the ministry of Jesus. Yet we have in Romans an extensive presentation of his theological thought which is strangely silent on this score.

On the other hand, before it was discovered that the Gospels were composed later than Paul's letters and cannot be presupposed in the interpretation of them, the letters were read against the background of the Gospels and little or no incongruity was discerned. In fact, most people continue to read them in that way today. The shape of the canon, with the Gospels first, invites such a reading. Despite many differences of terminology, conceptuality, and emphasis, it is clear that they both have to do with the same person.

The Freedom of the Gospel

Paul has with good reason been called the founder of Christian theology.[10] His thought arises out of real, concrete situations and is expressed in letters addressed to such situations. A Paul separated from his world or church is inconceivable. So one must study Paul in the context that was important to him. Paul had a keen sensitivity for important and profound issues underlying specific human situations and the relevance of the gospel to them. In such questions as whether Thessalonian Christians should continue to work, whether Galatian Christians should allow themselves to be circumcised, or Corinthian Christians should eat meat that had been offered to idols, Paul discerned theological and ethical issues that he deemed to be of great importance, and the history of Christianity has confirmed his judgment.

NOTES ON THE THESSALONIAN LETTERS

The two Thessalonian letters are probably the earliest surviving letters of the apostle Paul, here joined in writing by Silvanus and Timothy. Emphasis falls on the necessity for a sober, moral life. The Christian should continue to work hard while awaiting the imminent return of Jesus. Anxiety about his failure to return before the death of some brethren (I Thess. 4:13)

---

[10]R. Bultmann, *Theology of the New Testament,* I, trans. K. Grobel (New York: Scribner, 1951), p. 187.

as well as overzealous willingness to believe that he had already come back (II Thess. 2:1 ff.) played a role in prompting Paul to write.

The immediate occasion of I Thessalonians is described in 2:17–3:10 (cf. Acts 17:10–15; 18:5). I Thessalonians 3:1 ff. seems to contradict Acts 17:14 f., but 3:6 corresponds to Acts 18:5, which would point to Corinth as the point of origin for the letters. If so, they would have been written during the second missionary journey, probably in A.D. 50 or 51.

Pauline authorship of II Thessalonians is subject to some doubt. Its relationship to I Thessalonians is unclear and the apocalyptic mythology of 2:1–12 is unlike anything else we find in Paul. The emphasis upon the genuineness and authority of the letter (cf. 2:1; 3:14 f., 17) suggests that the author protests too much and thus arouses suspicion. Yet the supposition of pseudonymity (i.e., that the author only writes under Paul's name) does not immediately and completely clarify the situation and interpretation of the letter.

OUTLINE OF I THESSALONIANS

Salutation (1:1)
Personal and Related Matters (1:2–3:13)
    Thanksgiving (1:2–10)
    Paul's Missionary Work (2:1–16)
    Timothy's Mission (2:17–3:10)
    Prayer (3:11–13)

Exhortation and Encouragement (4:1–5:27)
    General Instructions (4:11–12)
    The Return of Jesus (4:13–5:11)
    Final Instructions and Prayers (5:12–27)
Concluding Benediction (5:28)

HOPE (I Thess. 4:13–5:11)

How does Paul relate his apocalyptic view to the Thessalonians' situation?

Beginning his letter with his usual greeting (1:1) and an extended thanksgiving to God for the Thessalonian Christians (1:2–10), Paul proceeds to recount his visit to Thessalonica, in which he preached the gospel and founded the church (2:16). Although not strident, this section appears to be an apology. Paul defends himself by reminding his readers of his conduct in Thessalonica. He then expresses his great desire to see them again (2:17–20) and refers to the dispatch of Timothy to visit them and his return (3:1–10). Obviously, Timothy is the source of Paul's most recent information about that church.

After a brief prayer (3:11–13), Paul turns his attention to their situation and problems. He adopts an entirely positive tone in exhorting his readers (4:1). What they have been doing they are to continue doing, only more so. Sexual immorality is to be avoided. Marriage is a matter of holiness, not heat (4:4 f.)! Mutual love should abound (4:9 f.), and by their good conduct the Thessalonians should command the respect of others (4:11 f.). The letter concludes with a series of general exhortations (5:12–22) followed by a benediction.

In the midst of this lengthy exhortation, consisting of rather brief general admonitions and reminders only loosely tied together, we find a sustained discussion of the return of Jesus (4:13–5:11). Its purpose is similarly hortatory. Paul intends to bolster and encourage (5:11) the Thessalonians by reminding them of a central aspect of his teaching, namely, hope.

In Thessalonica there is not only discouragement, but anxiety over Christians who have already died. Apparently in the earliest days of the new faith, many thought that believers would not die until the Lord returned. As time passed, more and more Christians died, and it became increasingly difficult to attribute their deaths to a fall from faith (cf. I Cor. 11:30). In this passage (esp. vss. 13–18) Paul reassures his readers that those members of the community who have died in faith are not lost. When the Lord (i.e., Jesus) returns, the "dead in Christ" (4:16) will rise and together with those who are left alive will ascend to meet the descending Lord in the air (4:17). Thus the dead in Christ, the believers who have died, suffer no disadvantage. With these words the readers may comfort one another (4:18).

If Paul is not quoting directly from Jesus himself (vs. 15: "by the word of the Lord"), he nevertheless intended to give the substance of what Jesus had said. The early Christians believed that Jesus had spoken of his return in glory and preserved sayings that expressed this intention (e.g., Mark 8:38; cf. Matt. 10:33; Luke 12:9). Moreover, collections of such sayings, attributed to Jesus, grew up among Christians (Mark 13 parr.). In these discourses Jesus described in detail his coming and the events leading up to it. Probably the brief word of the Lord to which Paul refers is an early form of this apocalyptic tradition, which, although it flowered quickly and luxuriantly, had roots in the authentic sayings of Jesus.[11] In I Corinthians 15:20–28 and II Thessalonians 2:1–11 we find other descriptions of the end time. Although neither of these is traced back to Jesus, in each case Paul seems to be drawing upon common Christian beliefs and perhaps traditions about the events leading up to the end.

The present passage is intended as a source of encouragement and hope for the Thessalonians. For unbelievers the day of the Lord may be wrath (1:10; 5:2 f.), but for those in Christ it is joy and vindication. In the second part of this rather long discussion of the coming of Jesus (5:1–11), Paul discusses the way in which Jesus' imminent coming should affect not the dead, but the Thessalonians who are alive. The day of the Lord will come suddenly, as a thief in the night (5:2; cf. Matt. 24:43; Luke 12:39; Rev. 3:3; 16:15; II Peter 3:10), and its coming will clearly be a cause of dismay for those who

[11] See pp. 468 f. of this book.

have not believed or are not prepared (5:2–4).[12] But the Thessalonians, like all those who believe in Christ, will understand that they already belong to that day.

Paul plays upon the technical, eschatological term "day of the Lord." The day will not surprise the believers, for they are not in darkness as others are. Because they are sons of the light, they are also sons of the day (5:5), not sons of daytime generally, however, but sons of that particular day, the day of the Lord. Needless to say, the imagery of day and night is quite appropriate to Paul's hortatory purpose. Night is the time of sleep or drunkenness (5:6 ff.). Day is the time of wakefulness and sobriety. But Paul's exhortation turns upon the point that Christians already have the day of the Lord, at least in anticipation. That is, God has destined them for salvation, not for wrath (5:9). Therefore, their conduct should reflect who and what they are before God. "Belonging to the day" (5:8) is more than general metaphorical language. It has a specific reference in Paul's own thought: the day of the Lord's coming. This day is for his Christian readers an occasion for hope and therefore for encouragement. Such hope frees a person from despair, whether for himself or for his loved ones who have already died.

NOTES ON GALATIANS

The Galatian letter was written to combat the influence in the Galatian churches of so-called Judaizers—that is, people who insisted that Christians be circumcised and keep the law. The exact location of these churches is in doubt. According to the South Galatia theory, they were to be found in the region of Pisidian Antioch, Lystra, and Derbe, which Paul evangelized on his first missionary journey (Acts 13 and 14). According to the North Galatia theory, they were located farther north in the ethnic region called Galatia after its inhabitants; this is probably the area referred to in Acts 16:6 and 18:23. Supporters of the North Galatia theory stress the fact that Paul repeatedly refers to his readers as Galatians, which he would scarcely have done had he been addressing merely the inhabitants of the Roman province.

Apparently because he was angry about the course of events in the Galatian churches, Paul omitted the usual formal thanksgiving immediately following the salutation at the beginning of the letter (cf. Rom. 1:8–15; I Cor. 1:4–9). Galatians is the only extant Pauline letter in which such an omission occurs.

Galatians has sometimes been considered the earliest of Paul's letters. This is just possible if the South Galatia theory is accepted, in which case Galatians could have been written from Antioch after the first missionary journey. Galatians 2:1–10 seems to deal with the same Jerusalem Council

---

[12]The Day of the Lord is, of course, the eschatological day or the day of judgment. The use of the term goes back to the pre-exilic prophets; see Amos 5:18–20.

described in Acts 15 and could have been written soon thereafter. But the Greek of Galatians 4:13 probably means "the first time" (RSV, "at first"), implying not one, but two previous visits. This would necessarily date Galatians after Acts 16:6, and we would thus already be in the second missionary journey and the period of the Thessalonian correspondence. However, if the North Galatia theory is accepted and two previous visits to Galatia must be posited, then the letter cannot be earlier than the third missionary journey, for the two visits would be those noted in Acts 16:6 and 18:23. This would put the writing of the letter in the period of Paul's Ephesian ministry (Acts 19), as indicated on the chronological table, probably about A.D. 54. Moreover, such a dating is supported by the many affinities with I and II Corinthians and Romans, which are more striking than any similarities to the early Thessalonian letters.

OUTLINE OF GALATIANS

Introduction or Salutation (1:1–5)
Paul's Defense (1:6–2:21)
  Paul's Charge Against the Galatians (1:6–9)
  Autobiographical Section (1:10–2:10)
  Justification by Faith (2:11–21)
Law and Faith (3:1–4:31)
  Appeal to the Galatians (3:1–5)
  The History of Salvation (3:6–4:11)

Personal Reminiscences and Appeal (4:12–20)
The Allegory of the Two Women (4:21–31)
Freedom and Spirit (5:1–6:10)
  Freedom Versus Circumcision (5:1–12)
  Living by the Spirit (5:13–6:10)
Conclusion (6:11–18)

FAITH (Gal. 2:11–21)

Why is circumcision a crucial point of controversy?

With scarcely a break Paul moves from the autobiographical section of Galatians (see pp. 313–317) to a discussion of the principal problem facing the Galatian church. The two are, of course, intimately related. Paul's long apology is not merely self-justification, much less self-glorification, for he must establish his apostolic authority as given by God and approved by his fellow apostles to defend the validity of the gospel he preaches. He therefore attacks those who call it in question, add to it, or subtract from it, because they undercut the work that God intends to do through Jesus Christ. At the same time Paul reiterates his own view of the essence of the gospel.

That Paul had already been vigorously defending his own preaching and probably had to do so recurrently becomes apparent in 2:11 ff. Presumably the incident with Peter had occurred some time before. Obviously Peter, Paul, Barnabas, and other Jewish

Christians had been enjoying table fellowship among the Gentile Christians until some representatives from James appeared on the scene (2:11–13). They, and perhaps James also, represented the "circumcision party," a powerful group of Jewish Christians, probably based in Jerusalem, who regarded circumcision as a necessity for Christians as well as Jews. Apparently for them, as for Paul, "circumcision" implied the obligation to keep the Jewish law and therefore entailed far more than the rite itself. They seem to have regarded themselves as Jews who had recognized Jesus as the Jewish Messiah. Perhaps they looked for his imminent return (as did Paul, see pp. 323 ff.) and the establishment of the kingdom or reign of God in a radically transformed world (cf. Rev. 21:1–8).

This same circumcision party had evidently made inroads into the Galatian church, occasioning Paul's letter. As one begins reading the letter it is not entirely obvious that this is what has happened, although Paul immediately denounces those who preach "another gospel" (1:6–9). Paul argues at first in a more general manner about the place of the law. Yet it is clear from such passages as 5:1 ff. and 6:11 ff. that the controversy in Galatia focused on the question of circumcision, and appropriately so. As Paul says (5:3), the whole Jewish legal system was bound up with this rite. It had become the fitting symbol of the problem of whether Christians must be held accountable to the Jewish law.

The appearance of the circumcision party in Antioch doubtless intimidated the Jewish Christians who had previously been exercising their freedom in Christ in disregard of Jewish restrictions against eating with Gentiles.[13] By eating with Gentiles the Jew inevitably exposed himself to the possibility of contamination by violating the Jewish laws concerning food and drink (cf. Leviticus 11). We know that Peter was not immune to intimidation (recall his threefold denial of Jesus in the courtyard of the high priest). When he succumbed, Barnabas and the rest understandably followed suit. Possibly the separation of Paul and Barnabas recounted in Acts 15:36–41 really resulted from Barnabas' behavior on this occasion. Paul's reproach to Peter (2:14 ff.) has understandably been something of an embarrassment to later Christian interpreters. It surely shows Peter in a bad light vis-à-vis Paul, although admittedly we have only Paul's version of the story.

Paul's reproach to Peter is based not on his own interpretation of the gospel, but on what he plainly believes is the understanding of the gospel which Peter also accepts. The right understanding of the gospel is at stake. The simple statement that Peter and the others "were not straightforward about the truth of the gospel" (vs. 14)

---

[13]On the historical background of this situation in the early church, see the excellent brief discussion of Betz, *Galatians*, pp. 81–83.

and the use of "we" (vss. 15–17) show that Paul was not trying to convince Peter of the truth of his own position, but recalling him to an agreement about the gospel which they had shared. That this was more than merely intellectual assent is borne out by the fact (vs. 14) that Peter himself had been living like a Gentile. Whether Peter and company later began trying to force Gentiles to live like Jews or only made this a prerequisite of continued table fellowship is uncertain. In any event the net result was apparently the same. Gentiles were forced to submit to Jewish regulations to participate in the life of the church on an equal footing. For Paul this development was unthinkable, despite the fact that he and Peter were by birth Jews (vs. 15), and not "Gentile sinners." It was unthinkable not because it was unnecessary or impolite but, rather, because Paul and Peter knew that a person is not justified (i.e., judged acceptable to God) on the basis of "works of the law" but by faith in Christ. At least Paul knew it, and he felt that Peter should.

From verse 16 on it is clear that Paul does not entertain the possibility of two modes of salvation—one by the law, the other by faith in Christ. He is not just saying that one must choose one way or the other, although that is indeed necessary. In actuality there is only one way, since no one will be justified by works of the law. The important thing for Paul is that a new and viable access to God has been opened by his Son just when other avenues had shown themselves to be blind alleys. This conviction lies at the heart of the gospel.

If for the moment we use the somewhat anachronistic term *Christianity,* which Paul never uses, we may say that for Paul Christianity is faith in Christ. On the other hand, faith in Christ makes possible the concept of Christianity as something new and distinct. For apart from the insistence that faith alone, not works of the law, justifies (i.e., makes one righteous before God), Christianity does not clearly distinguish itself from Judaism—as the Jewish Christians apparently did not. To believe that a particular person was the Messiah (Greek, *Christos*) was possible *within* Judaism. The Messiah, or Christ, would then be understood within the framework of Jewish messianism and eschatology. Paul's understanding of the essential meaning of the gospel of Jesus Christ goes beyond this confession, however. For to say, as he does, that Jesus Christ alone is the crucial factor in the determination of a person's destiny breaks through the categories of Jewish messianic expectation and makes the Jewish legal requirements of no avail in the quest for salvation. Individuals cannot make themselves righteous before God by their obedience to the many specific injunctions of the law. They can only accept this righteousness as something given to them (cf. Rom. 3:21 ff.). This view was certainly radical doctrine, and it is no wonder that some Christians with a Jewish background found it intolerable. Yet Paul insists (Gal. 2:21) that it is an either-or matter. Either Christ is sufficient or he is not, and if one sets up other criteria for participation in the Christian church instead of, or alongside, faith in Christ he is undercutting the Christian conviction and confession. In effect, Paul not only points unerringly to the distinctively Christian confession, but at the same time lays down the fundamental criterion for Christian community. Thus he can say in relation to Jew and Greek, slave and free, male and female: "You are all one in Christ Jesus" (3:28). There is no room for invidious human distinctions or discrimination within the church of Christ.

In verse 17 an objection is met. It had probably been raised by the circumcision party against the doctrine of justification by faith and its corollaries of freedom from the law and uninhibited free association among Jewish and uncircumcised Gentile Christians. In endeavoring to be justified by Christ and giving up adherence to the Jewish law, have the Antiochene Jewish Christians become sinners like Gentiles (cf. 2:15) and made Christ an agent of sin? Certainly not, says Paul. But does Paul deny that they have become sinners, or that Christ has become an agent of sin? Certainly the latter, and probably only the latter. In the opening chapters of Romans Paul argues that all people, whether they claim to keep the law or not, are really sinners apart from the grace of God in Christ. Thus it should not surprise us here if he should concede that people "become sinners" in seeking to be justified by Christ. Of course, it may by no means be inferred that those who seek to be justified by the law thereby escape the onus of sin. They simply do not understand their condition.

The real sin or transgression would be to go backward, to submit again to the law after having escaped its grasp. This is the meaning of verse 18, as verse 19 shows. Paul has died to the law that he might live to God. Paul's dying to the law and his dying with Christ seem to be the same thing. He necessarily dies to the law that he may live to God and that Christ may live in him. And Paul can now describe his own life as Christ's living in him. Christ's living in him is not, however, an esoteric mystical experience, but faith: "The life I now live in the flesh I live by faith in the Son of God, who loved me and gave himself for me" (vs. 20). Paul ends this description of his encounter with Peter—somewhere along the way his focus seems to have shifted from the debate with Peter to the problem of the Galatian churches—with a succinct statement of his tight theological logic. Justification does not come through the law, or else Christ died to no purpose (2:21). If one insists on observance of the law as a prerequisite to salvation, he implies that faith in Christ is not enough and that the law supplies what is lacking. For Paul, who understands the gospel to be absolutely Christocentric, this suggestion is intolerable.

We have been using the word *justification* up to this point as if its meaning were obvious, but it is not. Justification means, in the first place, righteousness. With respect to God, "righteousness" refers to a quality of relationship in dealings with the world and especially his people. Concretely, the righteousness of God manifests itself in the Old Testament covenant relationship between God and Israel, through which in fulfilling his part of the covenant God shows himself to be righteous. With respect to humanity, righteousness means primarily standing in the right before God. This idea too takes concrete shape in the Bible in relation to the Old Testament idea of the covenant. In fulfilling the appropriate role in the covenant relationship human beings may expect to be accounted righteous before God. Thus for the Jew the fulfilling of the covenant is obedience to the law, the obligation the forefathers accepted at Mt. Sinai (see pp. 363 f.).

Paul's concept of righteousness lies within the sphere of Israelite and Jewish thought. Thus he understands that in Judaism righteousness is sought through "the works of the law." His new faith, however, revolves about the conviction that in Jesus Christ God offers people the status of being righteous, prior to and apart from their own efforts to justify themselves. In fact, God puts them in the right—pronounces them righteous—before him. This is what Paul means by grace. Righteousness before God cannot be earned; it can only be accepted in faith. To attempt to earn it is both impossible in and of itself and a rejection of the good news (gospel) that God has given freely. This is what the heated discussion of Galatians is all about. Paul sees in the effort of the Judaizers to impose circumcision and the law upon the newly formed church the rejection of the very thing that distinguishes and is essential to the gospel. Chapters 3 and 4 are devoted to explaining in some detail, and in language and concepts that are not always clear to the modern reader, why this is so. Chapters 5 and 6 draw the practical consequences.

In chapter 3 Paul sets about to show the secondary role of the law, not only in the light of the coming of the Messiah, but also in the history of Israel, and therefore in the plan and purpose of God. Abraham, the father of Israel, is not a man under law, but a man under promise and the prime example of faith (3:6–18; cf. Rom. 4). The law was given by God and fulfills a real, if secondary and temporary, role in the history of salvation (3:16–19). Yet there is no justification, no righteousness, no salvation by the law (3:21). Its role is a negative and restraining one. In turning to the law after faith has already come (3:23), the Galatians are falling out of the realm of the Spirit and back into that of the flesh (3:3). Now that they have been brought out from under the confinement of the law (cf. 3:23) and come into their own as heirs of Abraham, why should they remain in bondage? Paul's obvious chagrin and perplexity (4:12–20) stem from his fear that the Galatians are reversing the direction of the history of salvation in moving from grace to law after already having come all the way in the other direction. The allegorical scriptural interpretation (4:21–31) is therefore intended to underscore the status of the person of faith as already a child of the promise and therefore free.

This new status is made plain in 5:1 ff.: "For freedom Christ has set us free; stand fast therefore, and do not submit again to a yoke of slavery." Paul now lays out the practical implications of his theological position, and at the same time comes to terms with the specific and immediate problem in the church of Galatia. Should Christians accept circumcision? Paul reiterates in 5:2 the principle already enunciated in 2:21. Here circumcision stands in place of law, for, as we noted previously, the rite of circumcision as the expression of membership in the Jewish community already implies the law. Paul makes clear that to accept circumcision means to obligate oneself to the keeping of the whole law and to cut oneself off from the grace of Christ (vss. 3 f.). Yet circumcision is not in itself bad (vs. 6; cf. 6:11–16, esp. 15). Those who are already circumcised have nothing to fear (cf. I Cor. 7:18 f.). Rather, the desire to have circumcision or any mark of religious accomplishment after one has already been baptized into Christ (3:26 ff.), is blameworthy, for it is a movement away from grace to the law and away from the Spirit to the flesh (3:3; 5:4; 6:12). Paul regards such a retrogression as incredible and perverse. It is a negation of one's freedom in Christ.

Yet this freedom is not freedom without responsibility. But the person of faith no longer experiences responsibility as a burden and no longer lives under the law to earn salvation. The believer is not a slave to the law or to anything else. At the same time the law continues to be the valid expression of the will of God (Gal. 5:14) and gives ethical content and direction for the new life in Christ under God. The freedom for which Christ sets humanity free is not anarchy or freedom to do as one pleases. Paul can, in fact, describe this freedom as faith working through love (5:6). He states the character and purpose of freedom most aptly and succinctly: "For you were called to freedom, brethren; only do not use your freedom as an opportunity for the flesh, but through love be servants of one another" (5:13).

NOTES ON THE CORINTHIAN LETTERS

The letters to the church Paul founded in the Greek city of Corinth were written from Ephesus in Asia (I Corinthians) and perhaps from Macedonia (II Corinthians) in the mid-fifties of the first century, probably during Paul's third missionary journey (see the time chart, p. xix). I Corinthians was written before II Corinthians. This is clear not only from their order

*in the New Testament, but from their content. II Corinthians presupposes
a much deteriorated relationship between the Corinthian church and Paul,
whose once-acknowledged status as apostle is now being challenged. In I
Corinthians Paul was able to speak authoritatively; the church's acknowledgment of his apostolic authority was not yet the major question (although the problem does emerge in chap. 9). A date of 54 for the one and
55 for the other is likely.*

*I Corinthians was at least the third letter in the correspondence be-
tween Paul and Corinth. Paul had already written the Corinthians previously (cf. 5:9), and they him (7:1). Neither of these letters survive. Much of
the latter part of I Corinthians (from 7:1 on) is devoted to answering questions raised by the Corinthians. Chapters 1–4 deal with problems in the
Corinthian church reported by Chloe's people (1:11). Chapters 5 and 6 are
concerned with moral problems Paul has learned about from some undes-
ignated source. It is sometimes suggested that I Corinthians is a composite
of several letters, but the original unity of the document is defended by
most scholars.[14] For further notes on the Corinthian correspondence, see
pp. 339 f.*

OUTLINE OF I CORINTHIANS

Introduction: Salutation and
   Thanksgiving (1:1–9)
Division in the Church (1:10–4:21)
   The Corinthian Situation (1:10–
      17)
   Paul's Own Practice and Exam-
      ple (1:18–3:4)
   Paul and Apollos as Servants
      (3:5–4:7)
   Admonition to the Corinthians
      (4:8–21)
Immorality in the Church (5:1–
   6:20)

Sexual Immorality (5:1–13)
Christians in Court Against One
   Another (6:1–11)
Uses of the Body (6:12–20)
The Corinthians' Questions (7:1–
   15:58)
   Church Discipline (7:1–10:33;
      esp. 8:1–13)
   Church Worship and Order
      (11:1–14:39)
   The Resurrection (15:1–58)
Conclusion: The Collection and
   Other Church Business
   (16:1–24)

LOVE (I Cor. 8:1–13)

Why is any restriction put upon eating meat offered to idols?

In Corinth Paul faced a situation quite different from that in
Galatia. The Corinthian problem was not legalism but, if anything,
just the opposite—freedom has become license.

In I Corinthians 1–4 Paul is concerned with divisions or parties
in the church. Behind this problem, however, lurks the question of

---

[14] For scholars espousing this position, see John Hurd, *The Origin of I Corinthians* (New York: Seabury, 1965), p. 45.

the very character of Christian faith and life. Paul argues passionately that the Christian gospel is different from any worldly wisdom (chaps. 1, 2). At its heart is the word of the cross, the crucified Lord, folly to the Greeks and scandal to the Jews. This word shakes old confidences and offers new possibilities of life. Throughout this letter, however, there are indications that the Corinthians, or some people in the Corinthian church, take a different view of the matter. Some of them think that Christian faith centers in a privileged knowledge (Greek *gnōsis*), beside which questions of ethics are of strictly secondary importance (cf. chap. 8). Therefore, various practical ethical problems have arisen that demand resolution, at least in Paul's view. A man is living with his father's wife, though presumably not his own mother (chap. 5); Christians are involved in lawsuits against one another (6:1–8); apparently some have not given up sexual intercourse with prostitutes (6:12–20). The existence of what Paul considers immorality in the church is understandable, because at least some of the Corinthian Christians had led immoral lives before their conversion (6:9–11). Their backgrounds would not predispose them to understand the Christian faith in ethical terms.

Over and above these morally dubious situations, of which Paul had evidently been informed by Chloe's people (cf. 1:11; 16:17), the Corinthians raised in a letter to Paul (cf. 7:1) a number of knotty problems. The first concerns marriage and relations between men and women. In chapter 7 Paul offers his wisdom on the subject. From the Lord, Paul has the prohibition against divorce, which we find also in the Synoptic Gospels (7:10 f.; cf. Mark 10:2–9 parr.). Beyond that he is more or less on his own (I Cor. 7:12), and he obviously exercises some freedom in interpreting Jesus' words (7:15 f.). Paul's advice in this chapter will not commend itself to modern men and women, inside the church or out. The contemporary minister or priest will scarcely counsel a couple contemplating engagement that, although total continence is preferable, it is better to marry than to burn (7:9). Yet though Paul has a definite preference for the ascetic life (7:1, 6 f.), he grants the legitimacy of the married state and discourages celibacy within marriage (7:1–5) as well as undue suppression of strong sexual instincts (7:9). One very important factor in understanding Paul's attitude toward marriage is his anticipation of an imminent crisis culminating in the return of Jesus and the end of world history as we know it (7:29–31, cf. 16:22; I Thess. 4:13–18; Rom. 13:11 f.). In view of such times, marriage and the assumption of family responsibility were scarcely things to be sought. Paul does not, however, oppose marriage, even under these conditions. Yet it is perhaps true that Paul's own ascetic bent has contributed to the high premium placed upon celibacy in Christianity, which has so often manifested itself in the denigration of the physical, especially the sexual, dimension of life, and which has often prevented the church from assigning a thoroughly positive role to sexual relations. But we should not too quickly blame Paul for this attitude. There is in the history of religion considerable evidence of people's uneasiness about what to do with their sexual instincts, an uneasiness that manifests itself, on the one hand, in religious asceticism and celibacy and, on the other, in cultic prostitution.

The subsequent brief chapter (8) dealing with the question of what to do about meat offered to idols is even more useful than the interesting chapter on women in revealing the fundamental character of Paul's problems at Corinth. On the face of it this question may seem an unlikely choice, inasmuch as the problem of sex is very much alive in Western culture, whereas the number of persons who either offer meat to idols or worry about the problem of whether to eat such meat is microscopic. A sympathetic reading, however, reveals that far more is involved than the resolution of a practical problem faced by Christians in the ancient world. A fundamental theological and ethical question is raised. (See also Rom. 14:1–15:6.)

We should begin by attempting to understand the specific problem. Christians living in a pagan world, among associates, relatives, and friends who were not Christian, were frequently placed in the position of having to eat or refuse to eat meat that had been offered to idols. Even if Christians avoided feasts in the temples of pagan gods, as Paul sternly admonishes them to do (I Cor. 10:14–22), they could not entirely escape the problem. For in the ancient world, much of the meat sold in the markets had also been offered to idols, even if in a most perfunctory way. The slaughtering of animals was frequently accompanied by a quasi-religious rite or token sacrifice. So closely related were slaughter and sacrifice that the same verb (*hiereuein*) could be used not only to mean "offer a sacrifice" but also simply "to slaughter."[15] So the Greek stem *hier-*, which basically denotes the holy, becomes itself associated with the slaughter of animals for eating. Thus although Paul, in instructing the Corinthians, seems to assume that some meat had not been offered to idols, it is at the same time clear that Christians could scarcely have avoided the problem of whether to eat meat that had been so offered. It would sooner or later have been thrust upon them unless they withdrew from the world, an alternative that Paul does not recommend (I Cor. 5:9 f.).

If we compare the way in which Paul approaches this problem

[15] Cf. J. Weiss, *Der erste Korintherbrief*, 9. Aufl. (Göttingen: Vandenhoeck & Ruprecht, 1910), pp. 210 ff.

Hades carrying off Persephone, the daughter of Zeus and queen of the underworld. From a fourth-century B.C. Apulian vase. (Courtesy of Metropolitan Museum of Art. Gift of Miss Matilda W. Bruce, 1907.)

with the way in which he approached the question of table fellowship in Galatians 2, he seems at first glance to be taking an inconsistent position. In Galatians Paul attacked Peter for withdrawing from table fellowship with Gentile Christians because of the arrival of Jewish Christians from Jerusalem to whom this was offensive (see pp. 327 f.). There Paul seems to regard the matter of clean and unclean foods, so important to the Jew, as of no significance. More important, he is not concerned to avoid offending the Jew or Jewish Christians. Therefore we are surprised to discover that in I Corinthians 8 Paul admonishes Christians *not* to eat meat known to have been offered to idols. This admonition, however, has an entirely different basis. The Christian refuses to eat meat offered to idols out of respect for the weaker brother (i.e., another Christian; cf. 8:7, 11), who may follow him in eating the meat and think that it really has some special potency or sanctity because it has been offered to idols. Or the weaker brother may believe that he has incurred real guilt before God for eating the idol meat because he would not know that the idol has no real existence (vs. 4) and that there is only one God, the Father, and one Lord Jesus Christ. Interestingly enough, Paul

Ruins of the ancient Temple of Apollo (sixth century B.C.) at Corinth, capital of the Roman province of Achaia. (Courtesy of Greek Press and Information Service.)

does not deny that other gods and lords exist (vs. 5), but only that they have any significance for the Christian.[16]

Paul grants that the Christian who has such knowledge may buy and eat meat without raising the question of whether it has been offered to an idol or to a pagan god—indeed, he defends his own right to do so (10:29b–30)—but he does not consider this an unrestricted privilege. It must be exercised with due regard toward one's Christian brother. Thus knowledge must be restricted by love. Love takes precedence over knowledge whenever the two come into conflict. The person with knowledge has no inalienable right to exercise that knowledge at the expense of the other. At the same time, however, one does not have to submit to needless scruples except in a

---

[16]Paul, of course, would have denied that there were other gods and lords of equal power and authority with the one God and Father of Jesus Christ. That otherworldly and supernatural powers hold sway over the heathen Paul need not deny. Indeed, he seems to assume their existence (cf. our discussion of Colossians, pp. 348 ff.).

concrete instance in which one's eating meat offered to idols might
defile the conscience of another Christian (vs. 7). In this connection
it is important to observe that Paul has transcended the belief that
cultic food per se has the power to condemn (or save; cf. 10:1–13).
Sin is no longer the violation of ritual observance or taboo, but
breaking faith, betrayal of one's convictions. The concept of sin is
interiorized in this respect, which is not to say that it is spiritualized
so as to have nothing to do with one's actions. Sin is still offense
against God (I Cor. 6:12–20) and neighbor (8; 10:23 ff.). Eating or
drinking things offered to idols may be of no significance to the person who knows this to be so, but it may be disastrous for one who
does not. The former therefore must care for the ignorance of the
latter. Moreover, knowledge is not to be flaunted. So, an act itself no
longer defines sin but, rather, the effect it has on one's neighbor.

Paul was aware of the potential danger of knowledge in a way
that the Corinthians were not. He therefore makes it clear at the
outset (8:1–3) that knowledge alone is a questionable gift. Some Corinthians were evidently so smitten with their newly found knowledge and consequent freedom that they identified knowledge and
freedom with the essence of Christian existence. Paul found this
intolerable.

At the beginning of this discussion Paul puts love and knowledge in proper perspective (8:1 f.). Paul will go so far as to agree with
the Corinthians that "all of us possess knowledge." But he immediately issues a warning: Knowledge, especially that knowledge that
knows that it knows, and by implication takes pride in the fact, is
a potential menace. The contrast between such knowledge and love
is graphically put. Knowledge puffs up; love builds up. To be puffed
up is bad. (The same word meaning literally "to be puffed up" is
translated "arrogant" in 5:2 in the RSV—an accurate translation,
which unfortunately loses the connection with chap. 8.) To be built
up on the other hand is highly desirable. The term implies inner and
outer strengthening of the church and the individual (cf. 3:10–15).
The priority of love over knowledge is driven home most memorably in I Corinthians 13, the famous chapter on love. At the beginning of this hymn in praise of love Paul accords it a place above
prophecy, knowledge, and faith (13:2). Again in 13:8, 9 he comes
back to the theme of the superiority of love over knowledge. There
is nothing wrong with knowledge per se, but in this world and this
life it must give place to faith, hope, and love. Perfect knowledge
will characterize the life to come, but in the present age the Christian must not make knowledge a primary concern (13:12 f.). The key
to I Corinthians 8 is the supremacy of love over knowledge, not the
impropriety of giving offense.

There is, then, no real inconsistency between Paul's attack upon
Peter for withdrawing from table fellowship with Gentiles and what

Jesus and the disciples at the Last Supper by an unidentified Indian painter. (Courtesy of Spartaco Appetiti.)

he writes the Corinthians. In Galatians the gospel is being called in question by the behavior of Peter and his followers; therefore, right understanding of the gospel takes precedence over any possible offense caused to "Judaizers" by continuing in table fellowship with Gentile Christians. The deeper offense against the Gentile Christians was no mere breach of social amenities, but a breach of faith against the gospel. There could be no question of the Gentile Christians meeting Jewish standards in order not to offend the circumcision party. In both cases (I Cor. 8 and Gal. 2), a vital dimension of the gospel is at stake. In Galatians the gospel is threatened by the reimposition of legalism implied by Peter's action; in Corinth the gospel is threatened by those who understand it as a special knowledge and freedom rather than a new relation to God and to their fellow human beings. The tendency of the Corinthians to interpret their new freedom as freedom to do as they pleased without respect to their relations to others, which are inseparable from their relation to Jesus Christ (I Cor. 6:12–20), verges in the direction of genuine lawlessness—that is, anarchy. Paul stands as firmly against this as against the reintroduction of the law as the means of justification.

The character of the problems Paul faced in Corinth and his attitude toward them may be accurately assessed on the basis of I Corinthians 8. Thereafter, as before, Paul deals for the most part with specific problems. Chapter 9 is a defense of his apostleship and his conduct. In chapter 10 he returns to the question of food offered to idols in the light of the danger of a return to idolatry. In chapter 11 there begins a discussion of matters pertaining to the church, which continues through chapter 14. Chapters 11 and 14 deal with worship and the Spirit; 12 is the well-known description of the church as the Body of Christ; 13 is the chapter on love. In chapter 15 Paul takes up the defense of the bodily resurrection of the dead, a doctrine that has at least been questioned, and perhaps denied, in Corinth. This view would accord with the attitude of the Corinthians, who fancied that they possessed superior knowledge. Against them Paul contends that to deny the bodily resurrection is to deny the resurrection of Jesus as well. Yet in the face of incredulity about the concept of the resurrection as the resuscitation of so many corpses (a concept hardly more acceptable today than it was then), Paul maintains a distinction between the present physical body and the future resurrection body, which is a spiritual body. Chapter 16, devoted to personal and business matters, includes Paul's plans for a collection for the Jerusalem church and his intention of visiting Corinth from Ephesus, where I Corinthians was doubtless written (vs. 8).

The Struggle of the Gospel

For Paul life in faith was more than the appropriation of the tradition and the application of theological principles to life. It was also a struggle. No adequate interpretation of Paul can leave out of account his consciousness of the reality and significance of decisions and actions in everyday life. Whether in personal duress, conflict with opponents, or the tasks of ministry, Paul was continually engaged in struggle. Although he found this state of affairs sometimes painful and even perplexing, he was nevertheless able to interpret it to himself and others as a positive aspect of Christian life in which God's grace and power were available to faith.

FURTHER NOTES ON THE CORINTHIAN LETTERS

Whether the letters or letter under the name II Corinthians were written to combat the same problems found in I Corinthians is doubtful. In II Corinthians the question of Paul's own apostolic authority predominates. Some interlopers have challenged Paul personally and gained the allegiance of a part of the Corinthian church. It has often been suspected that the opponents who entered the Corinthian church were the same Judaizers whom Paul opposed in Galatia, and there is some reason for this view (see esp. II Cor. 11:22). Yet circumcision and the law are not discussed in II Corinthians, so the grounds of the opposition—whoever the opponents may have been—was somewhat different. Apparently the specific questions and problems that engaged Paul in I Corinthians had, by the time of II Corinthians, paled into insignificance as new threats appeared. But there is probably some continuity between the two situations. For it is altogether likely that the intruders in the Corinthian church, with their pretensions and claims and their attack upon Paul (chaps. 10, 11), would have had considerable appeal for these Corinthian Christians who were already puffed up with knowledge. Whatever their doctrine, they seem to have taken delight in just the sort of self-glorification that Paul attacked in I Corinthians. If this was the case, the rather irritated and injured attitude of Paul in II Corinthians becomes all the more understandable.

There is more evidence for the composite character of II than of I Corinthians. In its present position, 6:14–7:1 interrupts the flow of thought. Perhaps it is a fragment of a previous letter (cf. I Cor. 5:9). Also, chapters 10–13 introduce a harsh and jarring note at the end of II Corinthians which does not seem appropriate and does not fit well with what precedes. This section may be a separate letter, or a fragment thereof, perhaps that letter referred to by Paul in II Corinthians 7:8 as one that had grieved the Corinthians. In addition, both chapters 8 and 9 deal with the collection Paul was making for the Jerusalem church, but from somewhat different perspectives. In 9:1 Paul appears to be introducing the subject anew. This may indicate that they are separate notes or belong to different letters. If one accepts this critical analysis of the Corinthian letters, the correspondence between Paul and Corinth may be reconstructed as follows:

1. Paul's "previous letter" (cf. I Cor. 5:9).
2. A letter from the Corinthian church to Paul raising certain questions (cf. I Cor. 7:1).
3. This letter and the visit of Chloe's people (I Cor. 1:11) evoke a response from Paul—namely, the writing of I Corinthians.
4. Paul learns of continued opposition in Corinth.
5. Paul's second visit to Corinth, which evidently was neither pleasant nor successful. (Cf. I Cor. 16:5 f., which indicates that Paul planned another visit to Corinth; II Cor. 12:14 and 13:1, in which he anticipates a third, thus implying that he had made a second; II Cor. 1:23 and 2:1, in which he refers to a previous painful visit and his cancellation of a subsequent visit for fear it would likewise be unpleasant.)
6. Paul's "angry letter," written as an aftermath of that visit (cf. II Cor. 7:8): II Corinthians 10–13.
7. Paul's meeting in Macedonia with Titus (cf. II Cor. 7:6 f.), who brings news of developments in Corinth favoring Paul.
8. Resulting "joyful letter" of Paul: II Corinthians 1–8.
9. Subsequent collection note: II Corinthians 9.
10. Eventual third visit to Corinth (cf. Rom. 15:25–29; Acts 20:2 ff.).

The preceding reconstruction is hypothetical, although not without substantial supporting evidence. Nevertheless, some scholars still regard II Corinthians as a single letter and reject the separation of stages 6–9.[17]

COURAGE IN MINISTRY (II Cor. 4:1–15)

In what respects is Paul's ministry an imitation of Jesus?

In II Corinthians 3 (see pp. 311 ff.) Paul has described his own task as a ministry of the Spirit, in contrast to the letter. In 4:1–15 he elaborates on the nature of that ministry.

[17]Most recently, W. G. Kümmel, *Introduction to the New Testament*, trans. H. C. Kee, rev. ed. (Nashville, Tenn.: Abingdon, 1975), pp. 290–293.

As a minister of Christ Paul is not relieved of the limitations and weaknesses of his human condition. Indeed, he is plunged farther into them. His work is a trial as well as a joy to him, as he plainly reveals. Yet in spite of this he is not discouraged (vs. 1). His conduct is appropriate to his ministry (vs. 2). If in some cases his preaching of the gospel does not meet with approval and acceptance, the reasons lie outside his control (vss. 3 f.). Paul says the gospel is veiled (or concealed) to those who are perishing, picking up the imagery of chapter 3. The meaning of the veiling is then explained (vs. 4), but the explanation may raise more questions than it resolves. Who is the God of this world? Presumably Paul does not mean that there are two gods, the God of heaven revealed in Christ and another, equal God of this world, although we know that Gnostic Christians later interpreted his words in this way. Paul elsewhere speaks of many so-called gods in heaven and on earth (I Cor. 8:4–6), and of the "elemental spirits of the universe" (Col. 2:8; Gal. 4:3). Probably by these he means supernatural beings, powers, or forces that influence human life. After all, for him Satan is a person, even as God is (II Cor. 2:11).

Paul is himself free from these powers because of Christ, whom he here calls the likeness or image (Greek, *eikon;* cf. English icon) of God. Into the dark world controlled by the "god of this world" who is darkness, who blinds the eyes of those who do not believe so that they must live in darkness, the light of the gospel of the glory of Christ shines (vs. 4). In chapter 3 the word *doxa,* here rendered as "glory," is translated as "splendor." The latter term implies a shining of light and underscores the strong polarity or tension between light and darkness which Paul has set up (see esp. vs. 6). This polarity tends to replace that of spirit and flesh with which Paul had worked in Chapter 3.

Not surprisingly, Paul emphasized that he, as a minister, preaches Jesus Christ as Lord (vs. 5). This is the center and substance of the Christian message. But why does he say that he does not preach himself, stressing his servant role? Perhaps his rivals or opponents, who are apparently trying to seize the leadership of the church from him, extol themselves. This at least is Paul's opinion of them (see chap. 11 esp.). In contrast to apostles or ministers who think they must impress the Corinthians by their letters of recommendations, mighty works, or spiritual virtuosity, Paul effaces himself to present Jesus Christ more adequately. In so doing Paul becomes, so to speak, transparent to the gospel he preaches (vs. 6).

Yet it is not only a matter of a successful missionary technique. Paul's conduct and attitude are both realistic and right. The fact that Paul is an apostle makes him no less subject to human limitations: "We have this treasure in earthen vessels" (vs. 7). Paul's own afflictions demonstrate this (vs. 8). But such afflictions (vss. 8 f.) do more than show that Paul is human; they recapitulate the death and resurrection of Jesus (vss. 10 f.). To suffer as Paul does is to carry in the body the death of Jesus, through which the life of Jesus becomes manifest (vs. 11). Probably Paul means by the life of Jesus not his earthly life, but the resurrection from the dead (cf. vs. 14). Because of Paul's dying the Corinthians experience life, even as through Christ's death human beings gain life. Paul's offering is therefore vicarious, on behalf of others.

Paul, however, is not a stand-in for Jesus who makes his work unnecessary. His affliction is significant only because of Jesus' death and to the extent that it conforms to it. This discussion doubtless has some connection with Paul's own situation and relation to the Corinthians. The superlative apostles (11:5; 12:11) have boasted of their credentials and powers, and Paul is not without comparable reason for boasting, as he informs the Corinthians (chaps. 10–12). Yet all boasting comes to nothing. If he boasts, he will boast only of his weakness (12:5). God's power, and Christ's, is perfected in weakness rather than in spectacular accomplishments (12:9). Paul's understanding of his own ministry of the gospel as a treasure in earthen vessels is, of course, based on Christ and his ministry, particularly his death. Yet it is also informed by a consideration of his own style of apostolic ministry in the light of the contrast afforded by his rivals. Paul's ministry does not exalt his own role. Rather, it is marked by humility. "What we preach is not ourselves, but Jesus Christ as Lord, with ourselves as your servants for Jesus' sake" (4:5).

Paul concludes this characterization of his ministry by referring to the scriptures (vs. 13), calling to mind his earlier discussion of Christ's crucial role in the proper interpretation of the Bible (3:16). Paul has the same spirit of faith as the psalmist who wrote: "I believed, and so I spoke" (Ps. 116:10). While the coming of Christ marks the decisive turning point of history for Paul, the faith it calls forth is not different from the true faith of Israel. Paul's faith, however, focuses primarily upon Jesus and here upon his hope in Jesus. Typically, Christian hope has found its basis and warrant in the resurrection of Jesus, and Paul is a pioneer in reflecting this fundamental pattern (vs. 14). The section is rounded off by the declaration, "For it is all for your sake" (vs. 15). Apparently, the "all" includes God's raising of Jesus, the gospel message, and Paul's affliction in his apostolic ministry. Its ultimate end is the glory of God himself, as God is extolled in thanksgiving by ever-increasing numbers of believers (vs. 15).

NOTES ON THE "CAPTIVITY EPISTLES" AND PHILIPPIANS

Both Philippians and Colossians, along with the brief personal letter to Philemon, were written from prison (Phil. 1:12–18; Col. 4:10; Philem. 1, 23). Ephesians also purports to be a prison epistle (3:1; 4:1), but probably this is part of a garb of pseudonymity by which apostolic authorship is claimed for the work of a second-generation Paulinist. Philemon and Co-lossians are closely related by many personal references (e.g., the slave Onesimus in Philem. 10 and Col. 4:9; Epaphras in Philem. 23 and Col. 1:7; 4:12) and by common destination (Colossae). They were apparently dis-patched at the same time, possibly by the same bearers (Col. 4:7–9). Philip-pians, on the other hand, stands somewhat apart.

Although the evidence of the so-called prison epistles is not unambig-uous, tradition has it that they were written from Rome during the two-year imprisonment of Paul recounted in Acts 28—that is, about A.D. 59–61. We know, however, that Paul was in prison at other times in other places (cf. II Cor. 11:23): in Caesarea (Acts 24–26), Philippi (Acts 16:19–40), and possibly Ephesus (I Cor. 15:32; cf. Acts 19:28–41). It is, therefore, not im-possible that one or more of the captivity epistles was written from else-where. This position has been argued with vigor and some cogency by sev-eral scholars. Still, there is no compelling alternative to the long-standing view that the captivity letters were written in Rome toward the end of Paul's ministry. As a matter of fact, such general considerations as the character of the Colossian heresy and Paul's reminiscent frame of mind in Philippians suggest a late date for these letters and therefore point in the direction of a Roman origin. We shall proceed on the assumption that these are the last extant letters of Paul, probably written from Rome. (The Pas-toral Epistles and Ephesians will be dealt with in Chapter 10.)

The captivity or prison epistles bring out aspects of Paul's character and work which we see only intermittently in his other letters. In Philip-pians he looks back over a long and arduous ministry with at least the intuition that it is now drawing to a close. Such resentment as he has toward his enemies and the enemies of the gospel—Paul never distin-guished between them—is now overshadowed by his feelings of apprecia-tion for the church that has supported him in bad times as well as in good.

In Philemon, Paul writes briefly on behalf of Onesimus, a Christian slave, to his Christian master Philemon, urging compassion and forebear-ance upon him. The same conciliatory spirit that pervades the greater part of Philippians is found also in Philemon.

In Colossians Paul seems to be writing to exhort, encourage, and warn a church that is endangered by the encroachment of a heretical teaching. The exact nature of this heresy is obscure, but it involved the incorporation of Christ into an already established hierarchy of heavenly powers or di-vine beings. Paul's response is not to deny their existence, but to say that Christ ranks far above them. Although Paul obviously felt that important matters were at stake, he did not respond to the Colossian challenge with the almost bitter invective that we find in Galatians and II Corinthians. To this extent Colossians shares something of a common stance or attitude with the other prison letters.

Moreover, Colossians, like Philippians and Philemon, reflects both Paul's concentration upon his own task as an apostle and his reliance upon the grace of God. With the end perhaps in view (cf. Phil. 1:21 ff.), Paul never ceases to take seriously the task of caring for the churches which falls to him as an apostle of Christ, whether this task requires an expres-sion of gratitude, a plea for personal reconciliation, or a sustained theolog-ical argument, as in Colossians. At the same time, we find in Paul, para-

doxically perhaps, an utter reliance upon God's grace. This can be seen in his theological argument in Colossians, as well as in his quiet reflection upon his own lot in Philippians.

Perhaps the question of the place and date of origin of Philippians needs to be stated in the plural, because that loosely structured document (see outline) may be a composite of three Pauline letters or fragments.[18] If so, the segments would be (1) 1:1–3:1; (2) 3:2–4:1; (3) 4:10–20, with the distribution of 4:2–9 and 21–3 uncertain. One commentator suggests Rome as the place of origin of the first and third letters or fragments (during the captivity described in Acts 28) and leaves the time and place of origin of the second undecided.[19] Although this partitioning of Philippians is commended by breaks in the structure and flow of thought, it is not impossible that these irregularities stem from Paul himself and that the letter was an original unity. In any event, our text (1:12–26) was probably written from Rome during Paul's imprisonment there. By contrast, there is no uncertainty about the Philippian destination of the letter (1:1; 4:15), unless perhaps chapter 3 as a separate letter or fragment was not originally intended for Philippi. According to the Acts account (16:11–40), with which Philippians 4:15 seems to agree, Philippi was Paul's first mission stop on his initial journey into Macedonia and Greece.

OUTLINE OF PHILIPPIANS

Introduction: Salutation and Thanksgiving (1:1–11)
Personal and Theological Communication (1:12–3:1)
Personal Reminiscences and Reflection (1:12–26)
Exhortation and Encouragement to the Philippians (1:27–2:18)
Plans to Dispatch Emissaries (2:19–3:1)
A Warning (3:2–21)
Paul's Own Life as an Example Against the Evil-Workers (3:2–17)
Denunciation of the Evil-Workers (3:18–21)
General Exhortation and Personal Matters (4:1–20)
Conclusion (4:21–23)

JOY IN HARDSHIP (Phil. 1:12–26)

How does Paul's attitude toward his own misfortune show his understanding of the gospel?

The most striking thing about this passage is Paul's own buoyant spirit and enthusiasm. He is in prison (vss. 7, 13) in Rome on account of his preaching of the gospel (vs. 13). (An account of his

[18]H. Köster, "The Purpose of the Polemic of a Pauline Fragment (Philippians iii)," *New Testament Studies*, 8 (1962), 317, especially n. 1 for the relevant literature.
[19]Cf. F. W. Beare, *A Commentary on the Epistle to the Philippians* (New York: Harper & Row, 1959), pp. 4 f., 101.

arrest and imprisonment is found in Acts 21–28.) Despite his unfortunate circumstances, Paul is despondent neither over himself nor his cause. Far from having impeded his work and the advance of the gospel, his opponents have done just the opposite (vs. 12), for by his very imprisonment Paul bears witness to Christ (vs. 13). In addition, and contrary to what might have been expected, Paul's coworkers have been emboldened rather than intimidated by the treatment accorded the apostle. Do these attitudes merely bespeak the foolhardiness, if not the foolishness, of these Christians? Are they so far removed from reality that even misfortune seems to be fortunate, and genuine threats to their existence are not taken with due seriousness? Such an assessment is always possible, and doubtless many of Paul's contemporaries would have agreed with it.

Yet the attitude which Paul expresses is at least no casual or passing foolishness, but a fundamental tenet of his faith. It is an aspect of the foolishness of God, which is the gospel of the crucified Messiah (I Cor. 1:18–25). "My grace is sufficient for you," the Lord, the exalted Christ, had said to Paul, "for my power is made perfect in weakness" (II Cor. 12:9). Paul actually believed that "God chose what is foolish in the world to shame the wise . . . what is weak in the world to shame the strong . . . what is low and despised in the world, even things that are not, to bring to nothing things that are, so that no human being might boast in the presence of God" (I Cor. 1:27–29). His ultimate ground for believing this was the cross of Jesus, in which the humiliation of God's Son becomes the demonstration not only of his love, but of his power. Likewise for the apostle and the whole church, humiliation and even suffering may be expected to redound to God's glory in the spreading of the gospel. For through such unlikely means the church bears unmistakable and effective witness to its crucified Lord. Paul not only can confess this as a matter of faith; he sees it actually coming about: through the suffering and hardship of the disciple, the cause of the gospel is being advanced. This is a token of God's grace.

That Paul was not engaged in daydreaming is underscored by his realistic assessment of the motivations of his colleagues in preaching (1:15–18). We know that Paul was not everywhere welcome, even among Christians in his own churches. Therefore it should not be surprising that his appearance among Roman Christians aroused not only love but also envy and rivalry. Paul was not modest about the importance of his own role in the apostolic preaching and suffered from no sense of personal inadequacy in comparison with his colleagues (Rom. 15:17; I Cor. 15:10; II Cor. 11:5, 21 ff.). He was doubtless capable of arousing antagonisms. In all probability, therefore, he is presenting a true picture in verses 15–18.

Paul was able to rise above petty jealousies not merely because of superior personal or moral character, but on the basis of theological insight. The proclamation of the word of the gospel, not the personalities (cf. I Cor. 3) or even the motivations of the preachers, was for him primary. The gospel had a validity and an effect independent of the one who conveyed it. Paul did not think the motivation and moral character of the preacher was unimportant, but he would not grant that the validity and effectiveness of the gospel was dependent upon them. Thus, in spite of the intention of some rivals to harass him, presumably by making more converts than he could while he languished in jail, Paul was able to rejoice, for "whether in pretense or in truth, Christ is proclaimed" (vs. 18).

His present rejoicing was, however, only a harbinger of what was to come: "and I shall rejoice." Paul had confidence in the community and the Spirit. Therefore he had hope. The interdependence of one member of the community with another, so graphically portrayed in Paul's image of the Body of Christ (I Cor. 12; Rom. 12:3–8), finds practical expression in verse 19. The prayers of the church and the Spirit of Jesus work together for Paul's deliverance. Deliverance from what? It is by no means certain that Paul means deliverance from the Roman executioner or from prison. That Paul contemplates the possibility of release is already implied by the last clause of verse 19. Yet the word translated "deliverance" in our English text also means "salvation," and Paul's use of this and related terms usually has a future, eschatological reference. Paul can regard death as well as life as the fulfillment of his hope for deliverance (vs. 20). He does not, however, allow himself to yearn for death—a not uncommon attitude in the ancient world. From verse 20 he desires only to face either life or death with courage, so that Christ will be honored in his body (vs. 21). Here, moreover, is a good example of Paul's distinctive use of the Greek term *sōma*, "body." In this context it surely does not mean merely the physical shape and substance, but Paul's individual and personal presence in the world.

In verses 22–25 Paul lays out the relative advantages of living or dying and indicates what he means by "to die is gain." Life means labor (vs. 22), whereas death means being with Christ (vs. 23). Because of the continuing needs of the Philippians, Paul regards it as more urgent at the moment that he continue to live (vs. 24). This necessity is apparently the basis of his confidence that his life will now be spared so that he may visit the Philippians again (1:25 f.). Whether events proved him right in this expectation is a debatable question. If he was writing from Roman imprisonment, in all probability they did not. But the point is that Paul's eager expectation and hope of deliverance or salvation could by no means be disappointed, whatever the outcome of his situation, for he hoped in the God who raised Jesus Christ from the dead. This same Jesus Christ, in his humiliation, death, and resurrection life, was for Paul the pattern of Christian existence and the ground of Christian hope. So at what was very likely the end of his ministry, with the possibility of his own death facing him, Paul had confidence, and not only confidence but joy (1:4, 18, 19). This was not, however, the first time that Paul had faced death or mortal danger (cf. I Cor. 15:32; II Cor. 11:23 ff.).

In 1:27 ff. Paul makes an easy transition from encouragement to exhortation and in 2:1–11 (esp. 5–11) offers a Christological model for Christian ethics. The pattern of humiliation, death, and exaltation found here is derived explicitly from Christ and is applied to the Christian. Paul may employ an earlier Christ-hymn in verses 6–11, but at least the ethical application is his own. This confession and its application are to be understood in conjunction with Romans 6. There Paul discusses Christian baptism as the analogue of Christ's death and resurrection and interprets it in terms of its ethical implications. In both cases Paul assumes that there is, or must be, an integral relation between Christ and the Christian. The characteristic Pauline phrase *in Christ* also implies such a relationship, as do the concepts *body* and *body of Christ*.

After 2:1–11 the remainder, and thus the greater part, of the letter to the Philippians consists of words of encouragement, a warning against heretics (especially in chap. 3), exhortation, personal reflections, and an expression of thanks. This last (4:14–20) may have provided the occasion for the entire letter. The tone of the whole letter, with the possible exception of chapter 3, is consonant with this expression of thanks. Indeed, Philippians shows an ease and familiarity not found in Paul's other letters. Even chapter 3 implies no division between Paul and the church, but warns against outsiders and intruders, who quite possibly had not yet appeared in Philippi. More is implied in 4:14 ff. than perfunctory thanks; there exists a mutual sympathy and understanding between Paul and the first church he founded on the European continent.

After the problems of Galatians and the Corinthian letters, it is a refreshing change to find Paul in a calmer state of mind. Possibly the preservation of his more controversial and polemical correspondence has produced a distorted picture of Paul as a man constantly agonized and agonizing. There is no question of his readiness to defend his understanding of the gospel and to attack those who endanger it; that is abundantly clear in the extant documents. What may be lacking is proportionate evidence of the Paul of Philippians, a man capable of genuine human affections and motivated by a profound faith and confidence that enable him to face the possibility of death with tranquility and to overlook the machinations of his rivals when they do not affect the truth and advancement of the gospel.

NOTES ON COLOSSIANS

Whereas the Pauline authorship of Philippians is generally accepted, the same cannot be said of Colossians. The chief arguments against its authenticity are (1) differences in style from the undoubtedly Pauline epistle, (2) differences in development of theological thought, (3) the complex character of the "heresy" that Paul combats (Could it have developed in Paul's lifetime?), and (4) the close relation both in style and in thought to Ephesians, which is probably the work of a later Paulinist rather than of Paul himself. The facts are undeniable; the problem is how to interpret them.

In the discussion that follows, the tradition of Pauline authorship is maintained, because (1) there are variances in style among the uncontested Pauline epistles; (2) changes or developments in theological thought on the part of the same author are not inconceivable; (3) earliest Christianity was characterized by considerable doctrinal variety; and (4) if, in fact, Ephesians is a pseudonymous work based on Colossians the author of Ephesians apparently took Colossians to be Pauline. Like Philippians, Colossians and Philemon were probably written during Paul's Roman imprisonment, which was of at least two years' duration (Acts 28:30). Assuming that Paul was the author of Colossians, the date and occasion of writing must have coincided very closely with Philemon, Paul's brief personal note on behalf of the slave Onesimus. The writing of Colossians was probably occasioned by the return of Epaphras from Colossae to Paul bearing news of the condition and problems of the church in that city (1:7; 4:12 f.).

OUTLINE OF COLOSSIANS

Introduction: Salutation and Extended Thanksgiving (1:1–14)
Doctrine of Christ (1:15–2:7)
  Christ's Status (1:15–20)
  Christ's Saving Work (1:21–23)
  Christ's Ministry—Paul's Service (1:24–2:7)
Warning Against Erroneous Teaching (2:8–23; esp. 2:8–15)
Exhortation to Good Conduct (3:1–4:6)

Death and Resurrection the Basis for Christian Conduct (3:1–11)
General Advice (3:12–17)
Advice to Families (3:18–4:1)
Further General Admonitions (4:2–6)
Conclusion: Instructions and Personal Matters (4:7–18)

STEADFASTNESS AGAINST HERESY (Col. 2:8–15)

Why is the heresy that Paul attacks harmful?

Colossians is a difficult book. Moreover, knowledge of the original language only multiplies the difficulties. The RSV translators have made sense of a number of quite obscure sentences whose meaning may never be surely known. Colossians appears to have been written to warn the church of Colossae against the dangers inherent in a certain aberrant form of Christianity, which, for want of a better term, we shall call the Colossian heresy.[20] Our knowledge of this heresy has to be gleaned from Paul's own statements. So the task of understanding it, and of fully understanding Colossians, is a difficult one. But in 2:8–15 Paul gives some hints about its nature.[21] He characterizes it as "philosophy and empty deceit" having to do with "human tradition" and the "elemental spirits of the universe" and not with Christ (vs. 8.). There is a fundamental opposition between this teaching, as Paul sees it, and the Christian gospel.

The key phrase (vss. 8, 20) seems to be "elemental spirits of the universe" (Greek, *kosmos*). Paul uses the term elsewhere only in Galatians 4:3, 8 ff., where he apparently regards the observance of Jewish ceremonial law as submission to such spirits. This may also be the case in Colossians (2:20 ff.). But in Colossians such observance is also an expression of a philosophy or world view in which Christ has a subordinate place. In it the elemental spirits of the universe may have been natural phenomena that were thought to sustain or determine life and therefore were endowed with a semireligious aura—for example, the heavenly bodies, which, like the sun, sustain life, or, like the stars, determine it. Within these natural phenomena the divine influences that work upon humanity were deemed to be active and accessible. Ritual demands and taboos and calendar observances accompanied this "philosophy" (2:16 ff., 20 ff.). For as the universe was filled with such numinous powers, it behooved people to propitiate them through the appropriate ritual.

What seems most to have disturbed Paul was not ritual observance per se, although he would have rejected any legalistic insistence upon that, but the heretics' apparent willingness to subsume Christ under the system of elemental spirits. Such religious syncretism was in the habit of absorbing strange deities, and Christ presented no special problem. The statement of verse 9 may counter the Colossian heretics' claim that the deity dwelt or subsisted in the elemental spirits of the universe. For Paul the whole fullness of deity dwells in Jesus Christ. The term *bodily* in this connection probably does not refer to the earthly body of Jesus but to the dwelling

[20]*Heresy* and *heretic* are somewhat anachronistic terms, since they presuppose a creedal orthodoxy that did not, in fact, exist at the beginning of the development of Christian thought. Nevertheless, they are useful in describing Paul's Colossian opponents.

[21]Although verses 16–23 enlarge upon the description of the Colossian heresy, we shall, for the sake of brevity, concentrate upon 2:8–15. In his recently translated commentary E. Lohse treats Colossians 2:6–15 as a unit; cf. *Colossians and Philemon*, trans. W. R. Poehlmann and R. J. Karris and ed. H. Koester (Philadelphia: Fortress, 1971), pp. 92–113. Verses 6 f. are, however, general introductory exhortation.

of the deity in Christ, understood as the body of the church or universe. For in Colossians both church (1:18) and the universe (1:15–
17; 2:10) are described as the body of Christ, or the body of which
Christ is the head.

"Fullness of life" (vs. 10) may have been offered by the heretics
through subservience to the elemental spirits of the universe.
Against this contention Paul argues that fullness of life comes only
from Jesus Christ. Far from being subordinate to these elemental
spirits, he is the head of all rule and authority (vs. 10). Paul does not
directly deny the existence of such beings, but only insists that they
have been subordinated to Christ. Therefore there is no reason for
the Christian to have any regard for them. In a different context
Paul has already stated the same basic idea: "For although there are
many so-called gods in heaven or on earth—as indeed there are
many 'gods' and many 'lords'—yet for us there is one God, the Father, from whom are all things and for whom we exist, and one
Lord, Jesus Christ, through whom are all things and through whom
we exist" (I Cor. 8:5 f.).

Paul reminds the Colossians, who may be about to succumb to
this misleading teaching, of the real ground of their hope and confidence (vss. 11 ff.). The reference to "circumcision made without
hands" (vs. 11) may imply that the Colossian heretics, like the so-
called Judaizers of Galatia, demanded that Christians submit to circumcision in the flesh. Christian circumcision, replies Paul, is not
"in the flesh" but has the effect of "putting off the body of flesh"
(vs. 11). This does not mean leaving this mortal life, of course, but
putting off the life that is determined by the flesh. (See the discussion of flesh and spirit, pp. 380 ff. and the reference to the "sensuous
mind," literally "mind of the flesh" in 2:18.) The death of the body
(and mind) of the flesh occurs in baptism, where the new believer is
buried and rises with Christ in a recapitulation of Christ's death and
resurrection (vs. 12; cf. Rom. 6). Typically, Paul does not claim that
this dying and rising is an automatic or magical occurrence; rather
it takes place through faith. Notice the close relation between sin
and death, forgiveness and life (vs. 13), a pattern typical of Paul, who
nevertheless usually speaks of righteousness or justification rather
than forgiveness.

Although Paul suggests his familiar interpretation of Christ as
God's justifying grace, in verse 15 he introduces another interpretation of Christ's work, one better adapted to the situation in Colossae. Christ, he says, has decisively triumphed over the "principali-
ties and powers." These are doubtless included among the elemental
spirits of the universe, if not identical with them. His redemptive
work means not only freedom from flesh, sin, death (vs. 13), and the
law (vs. 14) but freedom from the oppressive powers of the universe

that have held humanity under their dominion (cf. Galatians 4:1 ff.). For the baptized believer subjection to such worldly spirits, powers, or authorities was a thing of the past. As an individual, he had been freed from bondage to them. Yet this deliverance was not the ultimate extent of Christ's work, for the release that the believer enjoyed had its basis in the triumph of Christ over these powers. The Christian was free because they had been conquered and rendered harmless or "disarmed."

Thus in the theology of Colossians the event of Christ has its objective as well as its subjective side. There are cosmological implications to be derived from the historical event of the life and death of Jesus. Christ is the universal or *cosmic* redeemer.

Paul now draws the ethical implications of his theological argument, and most of the remainder of the epistle (2:16–4:6) is concerned with them. In 2:16–23 he rejects the spurious asceticism of the Colossian heretics, which does not take account of Christ's lordship over the world, but is simply subservience to the things that Christ has already overcome (2:20). Such religiosity, ascetic though it may be, does not finally escape the lordship of the flesh (2:23; note esp. the RSV's alternative reading). The believer is not, however, subject to the elemental spirits of the universe. He is instead in the realm of the resurrected Christ (3:1 ff.). With Christ and the believer now portrayed as sitting at the right hand of God, Paul seems on the verge of speculative fancy. But such resurrection life is interpreted as this-worldly existence free from the power of sin, death, and "earthly things" (vs. 2; Paul probably has in mind those elemental world spirits of which he has already spoken). To all these the believer has died. Life is now secure with God (vs. 3), and the believer hopes to share in the eschatological glory of Christ (vs. 4).

Such statements might be taken as encouraging moral complacency. Paul will not, however, allow this interpretation. Beginning in 3:5 and continuing throughout this long central section (3:1–4:6), he encourages the Colossians to greater and greater ethical sensitivity and effort. This characteristic paradox lies close to the heart of Pauline theology. What the believer in Christ has as a gift, what is assured by God's grace, what is guarded and preserved through the Holy Spirit—this must be continually received by faith and made real in life. The gospel of grace that Paul preaches could mean ethical complacency and has in fact been reduced to that by some of Paul's successors. But for the apostle such complacency is entirely impossible. God's grace is not based on righteous works and is not their reward. Something like the opposite relationship holds: God's grace is the basis for righteous works. Because the Colossians have received God's grace they may be encouraged to obey him. This is what Paul elsewhere calls the obedience of faith (Rom. 1:5). It is the only valid obedience, because it is based on a God-given freedom, and not upon a legalism or a philosophy that is already under the sway of powers that predispose humanity toward evil.

In this chapter we have studied ten representative passages and six letters from the apostle Paul. By any standard and in several respects Paul was a truly remarkable man. After having vigorously, if not brutally, persecuted the church, he overnight became one of its staunchest advocates and defenders. He had not, of course, been a disciple of Jesus himself; probably he never knew or saw Jesus. Paul was not only a Jew, but had been a Pharisee (Phil. 3:5). The Pharisees appear throughout the Gospels as opponents of Jesus, and had Paul known Jesus he doubtless would have opposed him. Paul's entire career and life swing on the axis of his conversion to faith in Jesus the Messiah of Israel. Probably there was no less likely prospect for so radical a change than Saul, who became known as Paul after his conversion (Acts 13:9). But after Paul became an adherent of the new faith, he surpassed virtually everyone in dedication and accomplishment (I Cor. 15:10).

Other church people and apostles may have raised questions about the genuineness of Paul's conversion (Acts 9:26; cf. Gal. 1:22–24). It is perhaps not surprising that in the churches of Galatia and Corinth, as well as elsewhere, serious questions were raised about his credentials as an apostle. When Paul writes (I Cor. 9:1) "Am I not an apostle? Have I not seen Jesus our Lord?" he is referring to his vision of the Risen Lord that turned him to faith in Jesus. That was not enough for some people, who insisted that it was necessary to have been a companion of Jesus of Nazareth before his crucifixion to be an apostle (cf. Acts 1:21–22). Yet Paul obviously knew, and relied upon, earlier Christian tradition which he shared with other apostles and missionaries. Because Paul raised fundamental questions about the necessity, and even the propriety, of keeping the law, he antagonized not only Jews, but Jewish Christians (i.e., Christians who did not wish to surrender their status as Jews). Antagonism to Paul's mission and apostleship went hand in hand with opposition to his views.

Paul was a convert, a missionary preacher, an organizer of churches, an author and theologian, and, in a sense, a teacher and administrator for the churches he founded. His life was filled with hard work, travel, controversy, even physical punishment and imprisonment. Rarely, however, does any hint of what Paul endured, the fatigue he must have experienced, appear in his letters (but cf. II Cor. 11:23–29). Obviously, Paul's dedication was matched by a strong physical constitution. Not many people have the sheer energy to do what Paul did. When one considers that he did it in the

"The Apostle Paul" by Rembrandt (1606–1669). (Courtesy of National Gallery of Art, Washington, D.C. Widener Collection.)

face of hardship and opposition, his accomplishment becomes even more remarkable.

Ironically, the one activity through which he is best known to us, letter writing, is not even mentioned in the extensive depiction of Paul in the Book of Acts. Luke probably did not know that Paul wrote letters, although conceivably he knew but did not consider it worth mentioning. Almost certainly Luke had not read the letters themselves. Paul's justifiable reputation as a theologian, and in some sense the father of Christian theology, is based mainly on letters which occupied him for only a fraction of his time and for which he was evidently not remembered in the immediately succeeding generation. (Yet the fact that according to II Cor. 10:10 Paul's opponents attest the significance of his letters means he had in his own lifetime gained some reputation as a letter writer.) This remarkable fact underscores the breadth and extent of Paul's work. He was a man for all seasons and tasks, a person of practical insight, who possessed skills of leadership and organization. At the same time Paul had a remarkable capacity to think. He was capable of theological reflection at a very sophisticated level. Instances of such reflection have already been observed.

In every case Paul's theological thinking arose out of a practical situation. In I Thessalonians (4:13–5:11) Paul expresses hope for the return of Jesus to encourage believers whose zeal is waning. He admonishes the Thessalonians not to become discouraged and to maintain their faith and discipline. The appearance of Jesus will be the realization of the hope by which the church has lived from the beginning. Paul's sharpest insights about faith come in response to a severe challenge (Gal. 2:11–21). Those who have questioned Paul's own apostolic credentials claim that Christians must undergo circumcision, the mark of membership in the Jewish community. Sharply rejecting their claims, Paul argues that acceptance by faith of Jesus as God's salvation is the heart and soul of the gospel. Faith is negated if one insists on circumcision, for circumcision implies acceptance of the law as the way of salvation. For Paul, the expression of faith in human relationships is love (I Cor. 8:1–13). Love takes precedence over knowledge. Knowledge leads to the sort of confidence in one's own power that can defeat faith. Love honors the other person, whom God also loves. In one place Paul even gives love precedence over faith and hope (I Cor. 13:13). By this he cannot mean that faith and hope are dispensable, but that they fail the test of genuineness apart from love.

Suggestions for Further Reading

The suggestions for Further Reading at the end of the following chapter (9) include works on Paul's theology. General treatments of his letters and his career are to be found in the standard New Testament introductions and histories mentioned in the General Bibliography, IV.

A simple book by a reputable scholar is F. W. Beare, *St. Paul and His Letters* (Nashville, Tenn.: Abingdon, 1962). More recently there is an excellent brief treatment by C. J. Roetzel, *The Letters of Paul* (Richmond, Va.: John Knox, 1975). The subject of Pauline chronology, which involves the relationship of the data of Acts to that of the Letters is now much discussed (see p. 310, n. 2). The most recent work in English is R. Jewett, *A Chronology of Paul's Life* (Philadelphia: Fortress, 1979).

A comprehensive treatment of Paul's career and thought is G. Born-kamm's *Paul*, trans. D. M. G. Stalker (London: Hodder & Stoughton, 1971), which takes account of trends in continental Pauline research. More recently there is a full-scale historically oriented treatment in F. F. Bruce, *Paul: Apostle of the Heart Set Free* (Grand Rapids, Mich.: Eerdmans, 1978). An informed Jewish interpretation of Paul may be found in S. Sandmel, *The Genius of Paul: A Study in History*, 2nd ed. (New York: Schocken, 1970). W. A. Meeks, *The Writings of St. Paul* (New York: Norton, 1972), contains a valuable anthology of essays, ancient and modern, on Paul.

Paul's debt to his predecessors and to the earlier Christian tradition is the subject of a helpful book by A. M. Hunter, *Paul and His Predecessors*, rev. ed. (Philadelphia: Westminster, 1961). His relation to Jesus and the Synoptic tradition has received fresh treatment in D. L. Dungan's *The Sayings of Jesus in the Churches of Paul: The Use of the Synoptic Tradition in the Regulation of Early Church Life* (Philadelphia: Fortress, 1971), which represents a move toward seeing considerable knowledge of the Jesus tradition on the part of Paul and his churches. An eschatologically oriented interpretation of Paul's self-understanding and career is offered by J. Munck, *Paul and the Salvation of Mankind*, trans. F. Clarke (Richmond, Va.: John Knox, 1959). The collection that Paul made among his Gentile churches for the Jerusalem church has been studied by K. F. Nickle, *The Collection: A Study in Paul's Strategy* (Naperville, Ill.: Allenson, 1966). Paul's apostleship is set in the context of modern social theory in J. H. Schütz, *Paul and the Anatomy of Apostolic Authority* (New York: Cambridge University Press, 1975).

The Corinthian Letters. J. C. Hurd, *The Origins of I Corinthians* (New York: Seabury, 1965), thinks that the Corinthian controversies were in large measure the result of Paul's own changing position. The stimulating, if controversial, work of W. Schmithals, *Gnosticism in Corinth*, trans. J. E. Steely (Nashville, Tenn.: Abingdon, 1971), contains significant discussions of Gnosticism, literary problems of the Corinthian letters, and the situation that Paul faced in Corinth.

The Harper commentaries of C. K. Barrett, *A Commentary on the First Epistle to the Corinthians* (New York: Harper & Row, 1968), and *A Commentary on the Second Epistle to the Corinthians* (1973), are first rate. Hans Conzelmann, *I Corinthians*, trans. J. W. Leitch (Philadelphia: Fortress, 1975), is based on the Greek text; but the editors of the Hermeneia series of which it is a part supply English translations of Greek terms so that the reader who knows no Greek can use this commentary.

Galatians. Hans Dieter Betz, *Galatians* (Philadelphia: Fortress, 1979), in the Hermeneia series, is now the standard commentary. Like the Conzelmann commentary, it can be used by the student who reads English only. See also George Howard, *Paul: Crisis in Galatia* (New York: Cambridge University Press, 1979).

Philippians. The work of F. W. Beare, *A Commentary on the Epistle to the Philippians* (New York: Harper & Row, 1959), is still worthwhile. There is a valuable monograph on Philippians 2:5–11 and its interpretation: R. P. Martin, *Carmen Christi* (New York: Cambridge University Press, 1967).

I and II Thessalonians. Ernest Best, *A Commentary on the First and Second Epistles to the Thessalonians* (New York: Harper & Row, 1972), is a good and reliable guide. Best accepts II Thessalonians as Pauline.

Colossians and Philemon. Edward Lohse, *Colossians and Philemon* (Philadelphia: Fortress, 1971), in the Hermeneia series, is the standard commentary. Lohse concludes (p. 181) that Paul is not the author of Colossians. (The Pauline authorship of Philemon is not contested.) For a judicious espousal of Pauline authorship, see the commentary of J. L. Houlden, *Paul's Letters from Prison: Philippians, Colossians, Philemon, and Ephesians* (Philadelphia: Westminster, 1970, 1977), pp. 134–139. While accepting the authenticity of Colossians Houlden regards Ephesians as non-Pauline, just as we do.

CHAPTER NINE

Romans:
The Gospel
of Grace

This most profoundly theological of all Paul's letters was probably written during, or shortly after, Paul's last visit to Corinth. It followed the resolution of the problems of the Galatian and Corinthian churches and the completion of the collection for Jerusalem (cf. Rom. 15:17–29; II Cor. 1:16; 8; 9; Acts 20:2 f.). Paul was clearly heading for Jerusalem when he wrote this letter (Rom. 15:25, 28, 30 f.). Romans was thus written in the mid- to late fifties of the first century, probably in A.D. 56. Paul regarded his work in the eastern part of the Mediterranean world as complete and was looking forward to a subsequent journey to Spain. Little did he realize that his plans were to be foreclosed by his arrest and imprisonment (cf. Rom. 15:23–29 and Acts 20:25, 38). Romans is not addressed to a church lying within what had heretofore been Paul's missionary orbit. It is sent rather to a church that Paul expected to visit. For some reason Paul wished to present himself to the church or Christians at Rome. Perhaps he hoped to use Rome as the center for his future missionary endeavors in Spain. In any event, Romans is the fullest presentation of Paul's theological views that we possess.

Galatians, especially the account of Paul's earlier conversation with Peter (Gal. 2:11–21), indicates that the seeds of Romans had already been planted in Paul's thought long before. Yet Paul was likely driven by experiences with his churches in Galatia and Corinth to formulate more carefully his understanding of the gospel. The basic theological themes set forth in Galatians receive more extensive and considered treatment in Romans, whereas some of the theological themes as well as the practical counsel of the Corinthian correspondence also appear here (e.g., the Body of Christ in Rom. 12:3–8; love in 12:9 ff.; 13:8 ff., and elsewhere; conscience and the weaker brother in chap. 14). One has the distinct impression that Romans *embodies Paul's relatively later and more considered reflection, a judgment borne out by other evidence for dating the letters.*

OUTLINE OF ROMANS

Introduction: Righteousness by
Faith (1:1–17)
God's Wrath: The Problem of Sin
(1:18–3:20)
God's Righteousness and the Response of Faith (3:21–4:25)
Justification by Faith (3:21–31)
Abraham and the Promise to
Faith (4:1–25)

God's Grace and Human Freedom
(5:1–8:39)
The New Situation (5:1–21)
Freedom from Sin (6:1–23)
Freedom from the Law (7:1–25)
Life in the Spirit (8:1–39)
God's Faithfulness (9:1–11:36)
The Obedience of Faith (12:1–
15:13)
Conclusion (15:14–16:27)

Introduction: Righteousness by Faith (1:1–17)

How does the introduction of Romans embody its message?

Romans opens with a long, formal salutation (1:1–7), containing a confessional statement (vss. 2–4) as well as Paul's description of his apostolic office. The reference to the Davidic sonship of Jesus and such terms as "Spirit of holiness," both rare in Paul, suggest that the confessional statement may represent an earlier tradition. On the other hand, the equally rare phrase "obedience of faith" (vs. 5) sets out an important emphasis of Romans.[1] By it Paul means the obedience to, or acknowledgment of, God accomplished through faith.

The customary thanksgiving extends from verses 8 through 15, perhaps through verse 17. Although verses 16 f. introduce the theme of the letter, they are integrally related to what precedes. Paul praises the Romans' faith and gives elaborate assurances about his own prayers for them. Although such expressions were conventional in Hellenistic correspondence of the time,[2] Paul is not merely engaging in conventionalities, as is shown by the specific content of his prayers (vs. 10) and by the appropriateness of his praise for the Roman Christians.

The full meaning and import of verses 16 f. can only be seen in the light of the entire letter. Yet several points stand out. Paul's disavowal of any shame (vs. 16) can be understood against the background of attacks upon him and his interpretation of the Christian

[1] The exact phrase occurs again only in 16:26 in the probably secondary doxology, but there is no reason to suspect its genuineness here.
[2] Cf. A. S. Hunt and C. C. Edgar, eds. and trans., *Select Papyri, I* (London: Heinemann, 1932–1934), pp. 339, 369, for examples of conventional thanksgivings.

The Colosseum at Rome with the Arch of Constantine in the left foreground. Built by Vespasian and Titus about A.D. 80 as an outdoor theater, it was used before Constantine for persecution of Christians. (Courtesy of Lufthansa German Airlines.)

gospel, which he sums up here in a kind of theological shorthand: "the power of God for salvation." This means God's grace, something freely given rather than earned. The pairing off of Jew and Greek is a further extension of the same line of thought. God gives his grace without regard for merit or national origin, without regard even for special religious distinction. It is bestowed universally. Although *Jew* means for Paul "an Israelite according to the flesh," *Greek* is virtually a synonym for Gentile. The substance of Paul's gospel is spelled out more fully in verse 17. It is the revelation of the righteousness (*dikaiosynē*; see pp. 328 ff. and 368 ff.) of God. By this Paul might mean a doctrine or fact about God, that he is righteous rather than unrighteous, which Paul would have by no means denied. But for Paul the term *righteousness of God* has a specific, dynamic meaning (cf. Rom. 3:26). It refers primarily to how God acts and relates to human history.

The gospel shows forth and interprets God's righteousness, and it is this theme that Paul develops in Romans. His righteousness is made known to, and appropriated by faith; faith has now become a universal possibility. As we have already noticed in Galatians, emphasis on the importance and indispensability of faith is characteristic of Paul.[3] The theme of the righteousness of faith will be developed and refined in Romans.

God's Wrath: The Problem of Sin (1:18–3:20)

What is the state of humanity in the light of God's revelation?

Paul speaks of the revelation of God's righteousness in 1:17; in 1:18 he turns to the revelation of God's wrath. Both terms, *righteousness* and *wrath*, are here eschatological. That is, they refer to revelations expected in the last days of this world as signs that God is bringing human history to a climactic and perhaps catastrophic conclusion. Paul places God's righteousness and his wrath over against one another as if he believed that their presence already marked the final turning point of world history. Indeed, Paul can refer to Christians as those upon whom the end of the ages has come (I Cor. 10:11) and can advise against marriage or any other too close attachment to this world on the grounds that it is passing away (I Cor. 7:31). We may also recall the dramatic description of the return of Jesus in I Thessalonians 4:14 ff., which Paul evidently thought at one time that he might live to see.

Although the main tension in 1:17 f. is between God's righteousness and his wrath, Paul introduces a secondary tension between the righteousness of God and the wickedness of humanity. This tension is somewhat obscured in the RSV translation, which does not represent the Pauline play upon the *dikaiosynē* ("righteousness") of God and the *adikia* ("wickedness") of humanity. With the setting up of these tensions or polarities the problem of Romans is posed, and the fundamental theological questions are raised. What is the relation between God's wrath and his righteousness? Moreover, how is it possible for humanity, characterized by *adikia*, lack of righteousness, to stand before a holy God, whose very essence is his righteousness?

Paul does not yet deal fully with these questions. He will first characterize humankind as the object and occasion of God's wrath (Rom. 1:18–3:20). At the outset (vs. 18) Paul makes clear that the characterization will not be favorable, even though he does not yet indicate the extent of wickedness. Paul speaks of a present outpouring of God's wrath, parallel with the revelation of his righteousness just mentioned. Actually he describes the condition of humankind

---

[3] Probably the RSV's alternative translation of the quotation from Habakkuk 2:4 in Romans 1:17 is preferable: "The righteous shall live *by faith.*" This seems to be the meaning of the passage in the Hebrew text, the LXX, and the Targum (Aramaic translation), as well as the Habakkuk commentary of the Qumran sect. Moreover, this is surely what Paul intends in Galatians 3:11, where he quotes the same passage.

from the standpoint of the revelation of God's righteousness and wrath in and through the gospel. He does not present the human condition from the perspective of the neutral and strictly objective onlooker. Thus Paul could scarcely have expected everyone to subscribe to his description. The wrath of God against human wickedness accompanies the revelation of his righteousness, and only against the background of this norm—the righteousness of God as revealed in Jesus Christ—does human wickedness stand out in bold relief.

This wickedness is first said to be suppression of the truth (vs. 18), that is, failure to recognize the truth about the creator implicit in the creation (vss. 19–20). It is not as if the world had no access to knowledge of God. In fact, precisely the opposite is true. Therefore Paul can say, "They are without excuse" (vs. 20). Not only do people have the possibility of knowing God and fail to exercise it; Paul goes so far as to attribute to them an actual knowledge of God (vs. 21). They lack, however, a proper *acknowledgment:* "They did not honor him as God or give thanks to him." Instead they became senseless and practiced disobedience—namely, idolatry (vss. 22 f.)— with the resulting defilement or dishonoring of their bodies (vs. 24). The grounds for the existing state of affairs lies in the fact that the values and loyalties of people have become perverted, even inverted, since they "exchanged the truth of God for a lie and worshiped and served the creature rather than the creator" (vs. 25).

Three important points now emerge. First, Paul speaks of wickedness, or unrighteousness, without yet saying that it is universal. Paul leaves open the option of extending the condemnation of human wickedness to include all people but does not yet explicitly do so. Second, although Paul speaks initially of the present revelation of the wrath of God (vs. 18), he changes over to the past tense in describing the course of sin in the human race. Thus he indicates that the present situation, against which God's wrath is directed, did not come about in a day, but has a long and significant past. Third, Paul asserts that God gives people up to their lusts, an idea that occurs first in verse 24 and recurs in verses 26 and 28. He does not mean that God is the cause of sin but, rather, that God allows people to fall prey to the overt sinning that is already implicit in their misdirected loyalty and worship.

This inversion of the "natural order" (worship of the creator) concludes the first stage in the development of Paul's description of the human situation (vs. 25). The remainder of chapter 1 really elaborates and reiterates what has already been said. Nevertheless, verses 26–27 are especially interesting. Paul makes more explicit the nature of the impurity and dishonoring of the body already mentioned (vs. 24). As a Jew, Paul could scarcely have considered sexual relations within marriage dishonorable, even though he himself was unmarried. He evidently had in mind in verse 24 the homosexuality he describes in verses 26 f.

Paul's singling out of homosexuality is not accidental. The Bible condemns homosexuality in the strictest terms (cf. Leviticus 18:22; 20:13), which in itself indicates it was not unheard of in Old Testament times (Genesis 19:4–8; Judges 19:22–26). Apparently, this practice was fairly prevalent in the Greco-Roman world as, for example, Plato's *Symposium* implies. But Paul does not speak simply as a pious Jew enraged at what he regards as a most heinous violation of law and nature. Paul has already argued that people's lack of righteousness results from their lack of a proper knowledge of God— a failing that bears its expected fruit in idolatry. For him idolatry, as a worshiping and serving of the creature rather than the creator (vs. 25), is literally a perversion or, as we have already suggested, a glaring manifestation of the inversion of the natural order of things. The result of this reversal of the natural order—or, better, the created order—is the disordering and confusion of human life in general. Homosexual practices reverse the order in which sexual relations were obviously intended. Therefore not a puritanical disposition but Paul's understanding of a fundamental wickedness (idolatry) suggests homosexuality as the best outward example of the depravity of human sinfulness. Sin is not merely the breaking of commandments or laws, although it certainly involves that; rather, sin is a complete disorientation of life such that human existence and behavior become completely divorced and estranged from the ground of their being, the God who creates and orders all things.

Such disorientation does not stop with sexual aberrations, but extends to all life. "Improper conduct" (vs. 28) translates a Stoic expression meaning what is out of accord with the proper nature of humanity. Moreover, "a base mind" translates *adokimon noun*, which plays upon the preceding assertion that men did not *edokimasan* ("see fit to acknowledge") God. One commentator aptly translates: "And as they did not see fit to take cognizance of God, God handed them over to an unfit mind."[4] Human perversity in refusing to acknowledge God is thus manifest in homosexuality and no less strikingly in the general disordering of life, most especially of human relationships, for most of the catalogue of vices (vss. 29– 31) pertains to human relationships. Paul describes people turned toward one another in animosity and suspicion rather than love. This is unnatural. It is a violation of the intended order of creation.

Paul has not yet explicitly extended his condemnations to include all of humanity. From the prominence given to homosexuality

---

[4]C. K. Barrett, *A Commentary on the Epistle to the Romans* (New York: Harper & Row, 1957), p. 32. *Adokimon* seems to mean "unfit" in the sense of "unapproved" or "disapproved," therefore "base" (RSV).

and the subsequent catalogue of vices, the Jewish reader would be justified in suspecting that Paul has in mind the Gentile and is making an exception of the Jew. After all, Paul was not above referring disparagingly to "Gentile sinners" (Gal. 2:15), as if the terms were practically synonymous. Probably Paul does have in mind here the sinful conduct of the Gentile. For the Jewish or Jewish-Christian reader, what he has to say might seem quite convincing. In fact, in the apocryphal book of the Wisdom of Solomon one can find ideas akin to those that Paul sets forth here. For example, the author, in agreement with Paul, seems to assume that knowledge of God should be attainable from creation, although people by and large do not attain it (13:6–9). He gives a similar assessment of the relation between idolatry and immorality (14:12) and presents a catalogue of specific sins (14:22 ff.) not unlike that of Romans 1:29 ff.[5] So far in Romans there is little to make the Jewish reader uneasy. What Paul has written could pass as an eloquent condemnation of Gentile sin.

That Paul intends something more than this, however, is already clear from the first few verses of chapter 2. As Paul has the Gentile in the back of his mind in 1:18–32, so he seems here to be thinking of the Jew. That Paul would apply his hard words in 2:1–5 to any presumptuous and self-righteous human being need scarcely be denied, but that he specifically intends them for the Jew as well as the Greek soon becomes apparent (2:6 ff.). The idea that God shows no partiality (2:11) means that the Jew is brought to judgment on the same basis as the Gentile, as Paul in fact makes quite explicit (vss. 9–10). This naming of the Jew alongside the Gentile probably indicates that the Jew has been in mind from the beginning of chapter 2.

What Paul has already stated in verses 9–11, he develops now by setting forth the basis for God's impartial judgment of Jew and Gentile (vss. 12–16). Interestingly, the law—and apparently Paul means here the Jewish law—is accepted as the definitive expression of the will of God, according to which he will judge all people on the last day (vss. 12 ff.; but cf. vs. 16). Mere possession of the law has, however, no particular value. Therefore, if any Gentile fulfills the requirements of the law, even without knowing it in its concrete form (vss. 14–15), that obedience is perfectly acceptable. The idea that God's election of Israel constitutes a special privilege and advantage even if Israel does not respond appropriately is already rejected (vss. 12 f.). In the two closing paragraphs (vss. 17–24 and 25–29) this point is driven home with the clear implication (esp. in vss. 17–24) that the Jews by and large stand condemned. Despite their advantage as

[5] The New Testament, and especially Paul's epistles, are full of these catalogues of vices (e.g., Rom. 13:13; I Cor. 5:10 f.; 6:9 f.; II Cor. 12:20 f.; Gal. 5:19 ff.; Eph. 4:31; 5:3 ff.; Col. 3:5, 8; I Tim. 1:9 f.; II Tim. 3:2–5).

the recipients and bearers of God's law, they do not in fact do what the law commands. Thus their desire to instruct or reprove others is sheer presumption. Really to be a Jew is to obey God. Such obedience is not a matter of outward show, but "a matter of the heart, spiritual and not literal" (vs. 29). This, of course, does not mean that obedience has no visible form or tangible expression. The true Judaism of which Paul speaks can be nothing less than obedience to God in the real world. It is not a specious and amorphous spirituality without concrete manifestations. Yet quite clearly being a real Jew is not to be identified with belonging to an institution or nation, or with fleshly marks of the same, such as circumcision.

Paul's questions (3:1) are now well motivated, and from what has so far been said, we might expect negative replies. In a sense this would be fitting, since the Jew has no advantage just because he is a Jew, and circumcision has no merit in and of itself.[6] Yet the Jewish possession of the scriptures (the "oracles of God," vs. 2) is in and of itself a great advantage. Paul mentions this as the first of what was apparently intended to be a series of items. But he immediately becomes sidetracked and does not mention the remaining advantages in this context (graphic proof of the more or less occasional character of even Romans). For the moment (vss. 3–8), Paul is obviously concerned with matters about which he has probably been challenged or attacked. We thus encounter a series of embarrassing questions (vss. 3, 5, 7), which Paul was probably not the first, or the last, to ponder. (1) The unfaithfulness of the Jews constitutes a problem, because they do not now receive the promises vouchsafed to them (vs. 3): "Does their faithlessness nullify the faithfulness of God?" (2) To resolve this problem by blaming Israel rather than God so that God's righteousness is not impugned but rather established (vs. 4) raises the further problem of how God can justly condemn the transgressor when his wickedness really serves to vindicate God's righteousness (vs. 5). (3) In other words, "if through my falsehood God's truth abounds to his glory, why am I still being condemned as a sinner?" (vs. 7). Paul hardly answers these questions at this point. Indeed, he dismisses the questioner rather rudely (vs. 8). Yet, as we shall see, these questions are pivotal points in Paul's argument in Romans, and at length he returns to them in chapters 9–11.

In the next paragraph (3:9–20) the argument concerning the universality of sin which Paul has been developing since the introductory part of the letter is concluded. Uncertainty about the meaning of the particular form of a Greek verb makes it unclear whether in

[6]Paul seems to use the term *circumcision* in interesting ways. It may refer to the act or fact of removing the foreskin. It may also, however, imply belonging to the community of the circumcised as a whole—that is, Israel. Thus it can refer to the community of the circumcised.

verse 9 Paul is asking whether the Jews are better or worse off than others. Whatever the question, however, Paul's basic contention is unaltered, as his positive statement shows (vs. 9). The Jews are actually no better off. To clinch his demonstration Paul characteristically calls upon the scriptures (vss. 10–18). If there has been any doubt about what Paul is trying to prove, these verses should dispel it. Old Testament quotations from many different books (see the notes on the RSV text) have been skillfully woven together by Paul—if he did not find them already conjoined in an early Christian collection of Old Testament texts—to describe the general state of mankind (vss. 10–12) and to specify the details of that condition (vss. 13–18). Next comes an interpretative clarification (vs. 19) to remove any uncertainty as to the application of these Old Testament texts. They apply not only to Gentiles, but particularly to those under the law—that is, Jews. Finally, Paul makes his own theological statement about what the law can and cannot do (vs. 20; see also 4:15; 5:20; 7:8, 10 f.). Clearly this long section extending from 1:18 to 3:20 is intended to show the universal sinfulness of humanity as the backdrop for the proclamation of the gospel (cf. 3:23), which reveals God's righteousness and also his wrath.

Is this lengthy prolegomenon a frightening diagnosis intended to induce the patient to accept the radical new cure? At first glance it may appear so. Yet Paul has already referred to the present, rather than the past, revelation of the wrath of God (1:18) precisely as proof that the revelation of God's righteousness is also taking place. For Paul sinfulness becomes apparent only now with the revelation of the righteousness of God in Christ (see 3:26). Paul did not understand his own pre-Christian life as a period of disappointment over sinful humanity and disillusionment with his own sin.[7] His darker view of the predicament of humanity and his own past situation apparently arose only after his conversion to the Christian faith. Thus Paul does not think the hearer of the Christian preaching could be convinced of the seriousness of his plight apart from the message that the crucified one was the Christ.

On the other hand, we cannot maintain that nothing in this section (Rom. 1:18–3:20) could have been said by Paul except in the light of the Christian revelation and on the basis of Christian faith. His condemnation of the universal fact of Gentile sinfulness and his admission of the theoretical possibility of Gentile righteousness apart from the law are not unique to Paul the Christian. Probably he could have said as much before his conversion. Jewish condemnation of Gentile sin was not uncommon in New Testament times,

---

[7] Cf. Gal. 1:14 and Phil. 3:4–6. Romans 7 is the crucial text usually cited in support of Paul's alleged pre-Christian depression and discouragement, but it cannot be taken at its face value as either autobiographical or necessarily describing the pre-faith state (see pp. 379 ff.).

and in the New Testament itself (cf. Matt. 5:47; 6:7; Gal. 2:15). More unusual are Paul's inclusion of the Jew and Gentile under the same standard of judgment and his view that, when the Jew and Gentile are judged on the same basis before God, the Jew will have no particular advantage. And even this might not have seemed so offensive to his fellow Jew had Paul not gone on to say that the Jew actually falls short of fulfillment of the will of God and consequently stands condemned with the Gentile. In the light of the revelation of God's righteousness in the gospel of his Son, all are sinners. Paul's affirmative answer to the question about the advantage of the Jews (3:1) scarcely seems convincing in the light of his wholesale condemnation of Jew and Gentile.

But is this condemnation really intelligible? Paul could scarcely argue that the unvarnished facts of human life support his position, unless he viewed all peoples, Jew and Gentile, from a particular perspective, that of the revelation of God's righteousness and judgment in Jesus Christ. For even if we grant that Paul's condemnation (or, as he understands it, God's condemnation) of human sinfulness is just, given his unique perspective, the origin of sin remains a mystery. Paul could have maintained that human nature in and of itself is evil. If so, what Paul calls wickedness, unrighteousness, or sin would be not a human possibility but a necessity. There would then be no such thing as meaningful human responsibility. Such a position with respect to a part of humanity may have been possible for some of Paul's contemporaries, but this sort of determinism does not explain Paul's thought. On the one hand, the corruption of which he speaks extends to all humanity, not just a portion. On the other, Paul goes to great pains to maintain that the plight of humanity is the result not of a corrupt nature but of concrete sinning. Thus the point of verse 1:19 is, as we have seen, the establishment of mankind's responsibility for the human condition. God's giving people over to certain forms of wickedness (1:24, 26, 28) does not mean that God causes them to be evil, but that he allows them to be. Therefore Paul proclaims that humanity stands in a state of universal sinfulness because of actual sinning. That specific acts of sinning carried with them ominous consequences for the future and future generations is implied by verses 1:24, 26, 28, where Paul doubtless has more than one generation in view. Is sin some disease, perhaps, that has infected the human race at the outset and been passed on from one generation to the next? If so, then every person would be born with an inclination toward sin. Perhaps Paul would have agreed that this is the case. But he does not set out that venerable conception of original sin, according to which a sinful nature is inherited by each generation from its predecessor. That is a later development in the history of Christian doctrine.

Yet Paul clearly does not regard sin as personal wickedness or individual transgression resulting from the ill will of single persons.

"The Fall of Man" by Albrecht Altdorfer (1480–1538). (Courtesy of National Gallery of Art, Washington, D.C. Samuel H. Kress Collection.)

Although he indicates that individuals are responsible for their sin and do not sin inevitably or by nature, he is quite aware of the suprapersonal character of evil among the human race. Specifically, he traces the origin of this evil or sin to Adam (Rom. 5:12–21; cf. I Cor. 15:45 ff.). Elsewhere he can refer to the bondage of the creation to decay (8:21) or to the present evil age (Gal. 1:4) without every mentioning Adam. Also without mentioning him, Paul speaks of sin as an external power that can enslave humanity (chap. 6) and describes how it insidiously attacks through the law (chap. 7). Yet in the light of his specific references to Adam we may maintan that his understanding of the corporate character of sin owes much to that strand of Jewish thought which laid responsibility for the corrupt state of humanity at Adam's doorstep (cf. esp. IV Ezra 7:116—126 and II Baruch 54:15—19).

In summary, Paul's conception of sin has two foci, which remain in paradoxical and unresolved tension with one another. People sin willingly, but inevitably. Paul can never speak of sin in such a way as to relieve all of humanity, and indeed the individual, of responsibility for it. Yet he would by no means subscribe to a purely personal or individualist concept of sin. Like his predecessors among the ancient prophets of Israel, Paul was fully aware of both its individual and corporate dimensions.

Admittedly, Paul's conceptual categories are foreign to us. We like to "explain" human evil in terms of historical cause and effect and environmental influence. Generally we do not describe our own situation, no matter how evil or dangerous, in terms of oppression by mythological demonic powers (Rom. 8:38). Yet awareness of the awful depth and mystery of human evil, illumined but by no means exhausted by historical and sociological explanation, comes to

Christ acts as judge. Detail from the sixteenth-century Italian artist Michelangelo's "Last Judgment," in the ceiling of the Sistine Chapel at the Vatican in Rome. (Courtesy of Alinari Art Reference Bureau.)

expression in works of art, literature, and the theater. Rational efforts, significant as they may be, do not suffice to exorcise or even comprehend the demonic dimensions of our society and our world. Paul's awareness of being beset by mysterious, supernatural forces outside our control, far from being utterly strange, corresponds to the character of contemporary existence. Moreover, his refusal to release humanity from responsibility for sin, paradoxical as it may appear, also characterizes our apprehension of life. We know that injustice, violence, and racism are our heritage, but also our responsibility.

God's Righteousness and the Response of Faith (3:21–4:25)

God's wrath is not his last word. Although God has every reason to display righteous wrath against human rebelliousness and perversity, he does not leave humankind to its deserved condemnation. Instead, he turns toward humanity in mercy and compassion, and, according to Paul, the evidence of this grace is Jesus Christ. The historic and public crucifixion of the expected Jewish Messiah reveals God's righteousness and his power for salvation (1:16). At a pivotal point of Romans, Paul announces this manifestation of God's righteousness in terms drawn largely from the Jewish sacrificial system (3:21–31).

JUSTIFICATION BY FAITH (3:21–31)

Does Jesus Christ offer himself as a sacrifice to God for human sin?

Paul now spells out his concept of God's righteousness and how it is effected through Jesus Christ. In this discussion the bleak picture of humankind held captive under the power of sin set forth in the preceding chapters is presupposed. Although knowledge of God is given to everyone in creation (1:19 ff.), and despite the fact that knowledge of God's will is accessible to both Jew and Gentile (2:12 ff., 17 ff.), their plight is a dire one (3:19 f.). Paul challenges fundamentally those who consider themselves righteous by virtue of their own accomplishments. That righteousness is shown to be unrighteousness. For "now the righteousness of God has been manifested apart from the law, although the law and the prophets bear witness to it" (Rom. 3:21).

Paul is intrigued by paradox. The revelation of God's righteousness is attested in advance by the law and the prophets (the Old Testament), although the revelation does not come through the law. Neither is this righteousness gained through works of the law. Rather, it is contingent upon faith in Christ (vs. 22). Human wisdom, power, and righteousness all stand in opposition to the cross of Christ, because they represent the attempt to establish life as secure apart from God (cf. 1:25). Faith is the means by which one may receive God's righteousness. That this is the only possibility of righteousness and life is clearly spelled out by Paul in verses 22b–23, a summation of Paul's argument of 1:18–3:20. In verse 24, Paul specifies how God makes his righteousness accessible as a gift. This is in essence what "by his grace" means. Only in the last half of verse 24 and the first part of 25 does Paul refer to the historic event of the cross of Christ in which according to his gospel, this grace is bestowed.

The brief series of assertions in verses 24–26 is as difficult as it is important, for here, and especially in verse 25, Paul introduces unfamiliar terminology taken largely from Jewish sacrificial practice. The word *redemption* (vs. 24), however, means literally a buying back from slavery, although the specific meaning in this context is not certain. Redemption may simply have the general meaning of deliverance, for in the next verse Paul drops this legal term and changes back to a sacrificial vocabulary. Thus in verse 25, he says that God put Christ forth as an expiation by his blood. The term *expiation* means a doing away with sin. The conviction that sin must be expiated is deeply imbedded in Old Testament religion and doubtless in the consciousness of Paul and the earliest Christian community. Paul's reference to blood makes clear that the expiation of the altar is in view. The model for conceiving the significance of Christ's death is the sacrifice of the animal on the altar and the sprinkling of his blood. Paul, however, qualifies this idea of ritual sacrifice with the phrase *to be received by faith,* showing that for him the effect of the sacrifice is dependent upon the manner of its reception. Christ is an expiation—but for faith alone.

Yet the power of the sacrifice itself is not thereby dissipated. The event of Christ's death, understood as a sacrifice, shows God's righteousness (vs. 25). This righteousness needed to be demonstrated or vindicated, because God had not dealt with sin in the past (vs. 25b). This is apparently what is meant by his divine forbearance in passing over former sins. God exercises patience with sin, but not tolerance. In the face of human sin and evil, which has been allowed to go unchecked and unpunished, God must act to demonstrate his righteousness (vs. 26). This could not have been done by a thunderbolt from the heavens, so to speak, but only by an event within human history. It is done in the cross of Christ, which God set forth as an expiation, literally, a means of dealing with sin.

Although Christ is cast in the sacrificial role, he does not offer himself to appease an angry God, nor is he offered by humankind in its own behalf. Rather, God himself sets Christ forth as an expiation and, in so offering his own Son, contradicts ordinary notions of wisdom and power. The meaning of expiation in this context is ambiguous. The Greek word here translated "expiation," can be used of the "mercy seat," or the covering of the Ark of the Covenant, which was kept in the holy of holies of the pre-exile temple in Jerusalem (cf. Heb. 9:5). No one was allowed to enter the holy of holies except once a year, when the high priest entered on the Day of Atonement (Yom Kippur; the Hebrew word *kippur* is based on the same stem as the term *kapporeth,* which is translated into Greek as *hilastērion).* Once inside he sprinkled the covering of the Ark once and the Ark itself seven times with the blood of the sacrificial bull (Leviticus 16) to cover the pollution of the sins of the priests. This so-called mercy seat came to be thought of as a place of revelation, where God appeared to pronounce forgiveness upon his people. Paul seems to suggest that Christ, especially in his death, is the new mercy seat, the new place of forgiveness. Such a meaning would make good sense in the present context. The actual Ark, and with it the mercy seat, had, of course, long since disappeared; it was probably destroyed in the conquest of Jerusalem by the Babylonians six centuries earlier. The way was thus open for the establishment of a new one, and the death of Christ would have provided the occasion for announcing the existence of a new place where God deals with sin.

Sacrifice of a bull. To the left is Nike and in the center stands a beardless figure, probably Heracles. Pre-350 B.C. (Courtesy of the British Museum.)

Not only *expiation*, but a number of other words and expressions found in verse 24 are rare in Paul. Even the term *redemption* (vs. 24) is not common in his letters. Moreover, Paul does not often speak of the blood of Christ, but of the cross, death, or body of Christ. The Greek word translated "show" (vs. 25) and "prove" (vs. 26) is otherwise rare in Paul, as is the term meaning "forbearance" and the Greek noun translated "he had passed over" (vs. 25). Also the word translated "put forward" (vs. 25) appears nowhere else in the Pauline corpus with this sense. Paul has probably drawn upon traditional terms and concepts in this definitive statement of the nature and effect of the work of Christ. The source of his language may be the words of institution of the Lord's Supper (I Cor. 11:23–26; Matt. 26:26–28; Mark 14:22–24; Luke 22:17–19), where Jesus interpreted his own coming death as a sacrifice, or the primitive liturgy connected with it. Indeed, the belief that Christ's death was a sacrifice for sin is quite common in the New Testament (cf. I Cor. 15:3; John 1:29; I Peter 2:24; I John 2:2; and the theme of the entire Epistle to the Hebrews). Paul here identifies his own view of the work of Christ with commonly accepted ideas about it (cf. also II Cor. 5:21; Gal. 3:13), if he is not drawing directly upon earlier creedal or liturgical formulations. There is, of course, no reason to believe that he in any way questioned such traditional affirmations. In fact, Paul used sacrificial terminology elsewhere in Romans to describe the character of the Christian life (12:1 f.). Nevertheless, he was able to develop other interpretations of the significance of Christ's death independent of the sacrificial imagery (cf. I Cor. 1:18–25; II Cor. 5:16 ff.). Already in the passage under consideration he places emphasis on faith (vs. 25). Although the first clause of verse 26 only reiterates what has been said in the previous verse, the second and concluding clause takes the thought further and in a decidedly Pauline direction. God shows himself to be righteous in justifying the person of faith.

The Greek verb translated "justify" (*dikaioō*) has exactly the same stem as the Greek noun translated "righteousness" (*dikaiosynē*). Therefore, according to the literal sense of the Greek word, to justify means "to make righteous." In Paul's thought, however, this process is not simply an infusing or a miraculous re-creation or transformation, but in the first instance a reckoning. As one can see (chap. 4), God reckons faith as righteousness and thus puts the believer in the right before him. To use the archaic English term, God *rightwises.*[8] The model that Paul has in mind is the law court, with God the righteous judge. Thus it is a *forensic* righteousness, the verdict of righteousness pronounced over a person on trial. Quite clearly then, this righteousness is less an ethical quality than a relationship. A person who is righteous in this sense is one who is vindicated in the court of law, or acquitted. His righteousness takes its meaning from that legal context.[9]

[8]This term was first suggested by Kendrick Grobel in his translation of Rudolf Bultmann's *Theology of the New Testament,* 2 vols., trans. K. Grobel (New York: Scribner, 1951–1955). In public lectures Leander E. Keck has proposed the use of the terms *righteousness, rectify,* and *rectification* to maintain the same stem in all forms, as in biblical Greek.

[9]Ibid., I, p. 272: "When it denotes the condition for (or the essence of) salvation, *dikaiosynē is a forensic term.* It does not mean the ethical quality of a person. It does

That *righteousness* has this forensic meaning in Paul is plain in such passages as Romans 3:4, where Paul quotes Psalm 51:4 (here we find the verbal form translated "justified"), and 8:34, where the act of justifying or rightwising is set over against that of condemning in the context of a court scene when the judge pronounces a verdict. (Cf. Gal. 3:11 and Rom. 3:20, where the forensic meaning is also clear, and I Cor. 4:4, where the verb *dikaioun* is translated "acquitted.") The Old Testament precedent for this understanding of righteousness in the sense of "to pronounce righteous" can be seen in Isaiah 43:9:

> Let all the nations gather together, and let the peoples
>   assemble . . .
> Let them bring their witnesses to *justify them*
>   [that is, show them righteous],
> and let them hear and say, It is true.[10]

Although this quotation shows a certain agreement between the Pauline and Old Testament understanding of righteousness, there is also an important difference with respect to the righteousness of God. For the Old Testament and Judaism generally it is self-evident that the *sinner* is not to be acquitted ("justified"), but the *righteous man* (Exodus 23:7; Proverbs 10:27 ff.; Psalm 1). Paul, on the other hand, maintains that God pronounces precisely the ungodly as righteous (Rom. 4:5; 5:7 f.) and this is the marvel of the gospel.

Paul does not, however, envision God merely as a judge, much less as one who sits somewhere in heaven, aloof from human affairs, holding court and pronouncing verdicts. The righteous God is a saving God, and his righteousness and salvation are closely related. The background of this relationship can be seen in the Hebrew literary construction called synonymous parallelism found in the Old Testament:

> The lord has made known his victory, he has revealed his vindication [Septuagint *dikaiosynē* = righteousness] in the sight of the nations. [Psalm 98:2]
>
> I bring near my deliverance [righteousness], it is not far off, and my salvation will not tarry. [Isaiah 46:13]
>
> My deliverance [righteousness] draws near speedily, my salvation has gone forth. . . . [Isaiah 51:5]

---

not mean any quality at all, but a relationship. That is, *dikaiosynē* is not something a person has on his own; rather it is something he has in the verdict of the 'forum' (= law-court—the sense of *forum* from which *forensic* as here used is derived) to which he is accountable. He has it in the opinion adjudicated to him by another. . . . Specifically, the 'righteous' one is that one in a legal action (. . . Rom. 3:4) who wins his case or is acquitted."

[10] Cf. Isaiah 50:8 f.; 58:2. The terms used in the Septuagint are exactly those which Paul employs. This is particularly significant in view of the fact that when Paul quotes the Hebrew scriptures (Old Testament) he usually uses the Septuagint.

In such passages God's righteousness is understood as a saving act or event. Similarly, God *reveals* his righteousness in the gospel (Rom. 1:17), while at the same time manifesting his wrath against sin (1:18). Thus, for Paul God's righteousness is not primarily an abstract quality. Although a judgment, it is not a disinterested judicial pronouncement. It is an event in which God goes forth to judge and save—indeed, the climactic deed of salvation in the history of God's dealing with humanity.

The Christ event does not, of course, transport believers into heavenly bliss. Yet it radically alters their status in the present world. That verdict of righteousness that the Jew expected or hoped for in the final judgment (cf. Rom. 2:12) has already been spoken in favor of humankind through Jesus Christ. Thus God does not simply sit back and wait until the end of history to pass judgment, but in the manner known to the Old Testament goes forth to judge in favor of, and to save, humanity. Although Paul believes that this salvation is only consummated at the day on which the Lord returns in judgment (Rom. 13:11; cf. II Cor. 5:10), he nevertheless maintains that those who trust in what God has done already find themselves in a decisively new situation. Thus they live in a creative tension characterized by past assurances and hope for the future.

ABRAHAM AND THE PROMISE TO FAITH (4:1–25)

Why does Paul use Abraham rather than Jesus as an example?

God's saving act in Jesus Christ is appropriated by faith rather than by works of the law (3:27 ff. and chap. 4). That this is no novel idea is shown by the example of Abraham, the father of Israel (chap. 4; cf. Gal. 3). Long before the law was given or even the requirement of circumcision established, Abraham "believed God and it was reckoned to him as righteousness" (Genesis 15:6). As Paul has already argued in the letter to the Galatians (see pp. 326–331), a person is accounted righteous before God by faith, not works. One is pronounced righteous before God not on the basis of the character or quantity of his deeds—much less the accident of birth—but on the basis of that fundamental conviction or allegiance which determines life. Now in view of Christ's crucifixion and resurrection this allegiance must focus upon a specific historical person and event. Paul sees Abraham's faith as a general prototype of specifically Christian faith and the righteousness reckoned to him as the model of that which the Christian receives by faith—that is, apart from works. Abraham, the father of Israel, shows that faith in God's promise has from the beginning of the story of salvation been the proper attitude before God.

God's Grace and Human Freedom (5:1–8:39)

Faith for Paul is not just believing a set of facts, much less adhering to a theory. Faith is trust in God's faithfulness. It is living in the new situation that God has created. After having shown the appropriateness and indispensability of faith by his argument based upon Abraham (chap. 4), Paul affirms the reality of this new situation (chap. 5). In fact, chapters 5–8 can profitably be viewed as Paul's effort to show that such a new situation actually exists, despite indications to the contrary.

THE NEW SITUATION (5:1–21)

What has actually been changed by the coming of Christ?

As he speaks of this new reality (5:1–5), Paul's style suddenly changes. To this point he has set forth the revelation of God's wrath and righteousness to argue that the latter can be apprehended only in faith. Now he speaks from the standpoint of the community of faith and in the first person plural. What he has previously sought to establish now becomes his working assumption. "Therefore, since we are justified by faith. . . ." On the basis of the new reality Paul can now speak of "this grace in which we stand." Having been put in the right through God's act in Christ, the person of faith has peace with God and enjoys his grace. For Paul "grace" encompasses the entire Christ event and its effects. Grace is the mode of God's working and the resulting state in which believing humanity is placed. Grace is God's benevolent disposition and action on humanity's behalf, prior to and apart from any human effort and accomplishment, the framework, so to speak, for the response of faith.

The nature of grace is then spelled out (vss. 6–11). It is not an abstraction, but has to do with a real and specific event in human history, and recent history at that. Moreover, this event, the death of Christ, took place for the sake of sinful people (vss. 6–8). The pathos of this death is deeply felt by Paul himself, and reflected especially in verse 7. Significantly, Paul does not reckon Christ's death as showing his own love for us, but God's (vs. 8). Paul thus emphasizes, not the personal motivation of the man Jesus as he went to the cross, but the underlying purpose and disposition of God. For God, even the cross is not wanton and meaningless violence; it is rather the means by which judgment and salvation are made known to and for sinners.

That God justifies precisely the ungodly and unrighteous has already been said in 4:3–8. There Paul first quotes Genesis 15:6— "Abraham believed God, and it was reckoned to him as righteousness." Then he interprets Genesis in the light of Psalm 32:1–2—

"Blessed are those whose iniquities are forgiven . . . blessed is the man against whom the Lord will not reckon his sin." The one reckoned righteous by faith is the one whose iniquities are forgiven; God justifies the ungodly person who believes.

The distinction between salvation as future fulfillment and justification as the present assurance of this future reality comes to light in verse 9. "Blood" refers to the death of Christ, again alluding to the sacrificial system. Paul uses a form of the argument from the less to the greater in both verses 9 and 10. If *a* be true, then how much more is *b* also true. In both cases the point is that if God freely justifies even the ungodly, then we may safely infer that he will also preserve them from the wrath of judgment and grant them eternal life (cf. 2:7 for the Pauline use of "eternal life" as the destiny of the just). Because the future is no longer in jeopardy, but secure by virtue of the accomplished work of Christ, the believer already has grounds for rejoicing in God through the Lord Jesus Christ (vs. 11).

Between verses 9 and 10 a subtle shift of terminology occurs. Paul first speaks of being justified (vs. 9), the term used in the key statement of 3:21–23 and in the discussion of Abraham in chapter 4. Now, however, the key word for the same state of affairs becomes "reconciled" and "reconciliation" (vss. 1 and 11). The work of Christ is no longer described in terms of the sacrificial cultus, but of the reorientation of the person. The one who was at odds with God is rightwised ("justified"), thereby at peace with God (5:1), and no longer under the dire threat of his wrath (1:18; 5:9). Paul thus maintains that the death of Christ directly affects the individual, who is transformed from a state of hostility to one of reconciliation and peace. In a previous letter Paul described the result of Christ's coming as reconciliation and his own mission, or that of the Christian, as the ministry of reconciliation (II Cor. 5:18 ff.). Indeed, so radical was the transformation of the human situation that Paul declared the person in Christ to be a "new creature" or "new creation" (II Cor. 5:17).

In Romans 5:12–21 Paul completes the transition from the discussion of the righteousness of faith (3:21–4:25) to the exposition of the new life which results from God's power and grace. The passage is, however, perplexing. The sentence structure and train of thought break off abruptly at the end of verse 12, but the basic idea is picked up again in verses 15–18. The digression of verses 13 f. is puzzling, because Paul's relatively simple earlier statements about Christ and Adam (I Cor. 15:21 f. and 45 ff.) seem needlessly complicated by the introduction of the ideas of sin and the law. Yet Paul introduces the complication because he is not satisfied to see the human problem as one of mortality and its solution as resurrection or the assurance of eternal life. The intrusion of sin and the law, which are integrally related to death (I Cor. 15:56), render the human problem more complex. Death is not simply the termination of all vital bodily functions. Instead death follows from sinfulness and ultimately negates and condemns human life. In turn, sin is accentuated rather than removed by the law (Rom. 3:20). Over against this hopeless plight in oppression and bondage Paul places the assurance of God's all-sufficient grace in Jesus Christ. This power, effective for humanity in the righteous obedience of Jesus, frees people from the oppressive and enslaving bondage of sin, death, and law. Against the triumvirate of sin, death, and law are arrayed righteousness, life, and grace. As through one man, Adam, humanity was bound, so in one man, Jesus, humanity is set free. If condemnation and death could follow from one man's disobedience, then freedom and life can follow from one man's obedience.

Paul sees death as the ultimate threat to human life, and sin as the ultimate problem, and knows that the two are interrelated. The human predicament is not just death, but that death occurs in a state of rebellion against the creator and in alienation from one's fellow human beings. Thus dying is death indeed. This plight is not helped, but worsened, by the law, which says what to do, but cannot give the power to do it. Thus not only death but sin and dying in sin become the human fate, without God's ceasing to hold people responsible for their waywardness. One is at the same time responsible for existence and trapped in it. Paul may have thought that physical death was the result of Adam's sin, an idea that was current in his day. In any event that death which enters human life through Adam's sin represents condemnation before God. Similarly, for Paul life is more than conscious existence; life is that final blessedness whose essence is righteousness, that is, being accounted as righteous before God.

Paul has testified that those who are accounted righteous by faith can live in grace with confidence about their ultimate destiny (5:1–11). Now he declares that those powers that oppressed humanity are overcome (5:12–21). Thus the rejoicing and reigning of the justified (see 5:2, 3, 11; 5:17) are not a fancy but a genuine, palpable reality. Whether this assertion can be maintained in the face of life's hard facts and whether conditions have actually changed so that the power of sin, law, and death are overcome are the fundamental questions to which Paul next addresses himself (chaps. 6, 7, and 8).

This entire section (chaps. 5–8) is the center and heart of Romans, for here Paul sets forth and describes "this grace in which we stand" (5:2). Chapter 5 dealt with this new state in a more or less general way. Now chapters 6–8 take up specific problems and objections, phrased by Paul in the form of a battery of questions that punctuate these chapters: "Are we to continue in sin that grace may abound?" (6:1). "Are we to sin because we are not under the law but under grace?" (6:15). "Do you not know . . . that the law is binding on a person only during his life?" (7:1). "What then shall we say? That the law is sin?" (7:7). "Did that which is good, then, bring death to me?" (7:13). "Wretched man that I am, who will deliver me from this body of death?" (7:24). "What shall we say to this? If God is for us, who is against us?" (8:31). "Who shall separate us from the love of Christ?" (8:35). From these questions the reader may correctly infer that chapter 6 deals with the new life under grace and the problem of sin; chapter 7 with the newly found freedom from the oppression of the law; and chapter 8 with the role of the Spirit and the ground of the believer's hope.

FREEDOM FROM SIN (6:1–23)

Why not sin to increase God's outpouring of grace?

In chapter 6 Paul poses a problem that probably had already been raised by others. If the believer receives grace in proportion to the sin that must be overcome (5:20 f.), why should one not go on sinning to increase the supply of grace? Paul understands the question, but not the motivation of the questioner (6:2 f.). The grace of God in Jesus Christ is indeed freedom (6:15 ff.; cf. Gal. 4–5), but freedom *from* sin, not freedom *for* sin. Paul understands sin as an oppressive and finally fatal enemy of mankind, a bondage and a burden. Therefore, he declares that baptism, understood as dying and rising with Christ, is a dying to sin and a rising to "newness of life." Paul assumes that all believers have been baptized and that baptism is the event through which the new believer is united with Christ, particularly with his death and resurrection. He evidently feels that he can presuppose this understanding of baptism among his readers (vss. 3, 6). Taking this concept of baptism as dying and rising with Christ, he gives it his own, ethical, interpretation. For Paul it is most important that baptism not be an end, but a beginning. Anyone who has in baptism died to sin is henceforth freed from it. Life is no longer under sin's dominion. Of course, sin continues to exist as a power and a reality. But to return to it after having been freed from it in Christian baptism would be a contradiction of the new basis of one's existence. Such a reversal is for Paul unthinkable (vs. 2).

"Newness of life" is already a reality, but it calls forth a personal human response. Paul does not believe that this response is automatic; an automatic response would nullify human freedom and genuine responsibility. He therefore exhorts his readers not to let sin reign over them (vs. 12), not to yield themselves to sin (vs. 13) but, rather, to yield themselves to God as instruments of righteousness, and not to allow sin to have dominion over them (vs. 14). For

Paul there is no question of obtaining newness of life through right behavior, as a reward. What God gives in Christ he gives freely. But the acceptance of that free gift takes the form of yielding one's own life to the power and reality to which one has been joined in baptism, that is, to God's redemptive act in Jesus Christ.

FREEDOM FROM THE LAW (7:1–25)

If the law is from God, why does it not save humanity?

A question repeatedly implied, if not explicitly stated (3:31), in Paul's discussion so far concerns the place of the law. Paul's statements about the law seem to contradict one another. On the one hand, he obviously takes the law (i.e., the law as contained in the Old Testament) to be the definitive expression of God's will for the ordering of human life (Rom. 2; 3:31). On the other, he maintains that the law does not enable one to escape the sinful and death-oriented existence which is now the human lot (cf. 3:20; 4:15; 5:13, 20). Moreover, as we shall see, the law itself becomes an oppressive factor in mankind's plight.

Paul begins his extended discussion of the law by describing how death sets aside a former legal obligation (7:1–6). The marriage analogy that Paul introduces in verses 1–3 is not completely appropriate for the point he wants to make and, therefore, must not be pressed. What Paul says here makes sense when we see that his argument is simply that a legal obligation is set aside by means of a death. Therefore, as the law binding a woman to a man is set aside by his death, so the law to which men formerly owned allegiance is set aside through dying with Christ (7:4).

The subsequent discussion of the law (vss. 7–25) ought to be understood in the light of the basic contention that death sets aside the law. Why should this fact be so important to Paul? This long excursus answering the question of whether the law is sin implies the prior question of why one must die to the law, or, conversely, why one may not be saved by it. Why does not life, in the pregnant sense of the word, result from keeping the law? The Jew believed that it did, and Paul himself had once believed it. Because his own view of law had been reversed so radically, however, he has a great deal at stake in showing that death cancels law. After having shown this (vss. 1–6), he proceeds to explain why the law cannot bring about the life it intends (7–25). Paul's question (7:7) introduces this explanation. To maintain his position and avoid the charge of antinomianism, he must answer in such a way as to maintain the integrity of the law (3:31), but at the same time refuse to concede that the law in the present situation can rescue mankind from its predicament. Whether he successfully does this is a matter that the reader

will have to decide, but in this connection a few points need eluci-
dation.

The example of how the law makes sin known and stimulates
it to action (7:7) is taken from the tenth commandment, "You shall
not covet" (Exodus 20:17; Deuteronomy 5:21). In the Greek translation, which Paul quotes, the word *covet* also has the broader
meaning of desire. So Paul's use of this commandment as an example is probably not accidental. He implies that the law inflames desire, a root cause of sin, rather than conquering it. Nevertheless, this
is not the fault of the law, but of sin (7:8 ff.). Here again is the concept of sin as a power working upon and even in the human race
from without. The medium and victim of sin's pernicious working
is the flesh (vss. 14 ff.). One might think that by "flesh" Paul refers
to the material side of human nature as contrasted with the spiritual
(cf. 8:1–11 for the explicit contrast of flesh and spirit). Therefore, a
person would sin because of the body, with all its instincts and
urges. Yet this is not what Paul means. The matter is much more
complex. Paul can speak of the mind or mind-set of the flesh (literal
translation of 8:7; in Col. 2:18 "sensuous mind" is really "mind of
the flesh") and living according to the flesh (8:12). Moreover, he
baldly asserts that those who are in the flesh cannot please God
(8:8). On the basis of the preceding interpretation this would suggest
that one must die, and thus forsake this fleshly life, to please God.
Yet on the heels of this Paul can tell his readers, who presumably
are not ghosts, that they are not in the flesh (8:9) but in the Spirit.
In the distinctive Pauline usage, flesh and Spirit are not two parts of
a person, but two possibilities of existence. They are two realms,
two dominions; a person may live in one or the other.[11] There is a
sense in which one must "die" and thus forsake the flesh to please
God. This dying is not, however, a physical death, but a dying with
Christ to the enslavement of sin.

Looking back now to Paul's discussion of the law (7:7–25), we
see that sin's perversion of the law takes place because people are
under the power of sin which works in their flesh (7:14). Yet this
flesh is not simply to be equated with the physical side of being
human any more than is the body of death from which one yearns
to be free (7:24). Sin has laid claim upon the intangible as well as
the tangible aspects of life. When Paul says that "nothing good

---

[11] Paul can also relegate religious acts and attitudes to the realm of the flesh, as
in Philippians 3:4–6, where he refers to his own Jewish background as "reason for
confidence in the flesh" (vs. 4). Moreover, the Judaizers' demand that the Galatian
Christians accept circumcision is to be traced to their desire to make a show in the
flesh (6:12 f.). Here the two fold connotation of *flesh* is apparent: on the one hand,
the physical substance of the body (II Cor. 12:7), on the other, a way of life (Gal. 3:3).
"Flesh" can also be a way of referring to mankind, in the style of the Old Testament
(cf. Rom. 3:20, where RSV's "no human being" translates what is literally "no flesh").

dwells within me, that is, in my flesh" (7:18), he is not qualifying the first assertion by the second (". . . that is, in my flesh"), but defining it. The "me" he speaks of here is the fleshly person in Adam, as contrasted to the person in Christ. This individual knows that the law is good, but cannot keep it. Life is a conflict between what is intended and what is actually accomplished (7:13 ff., 21 ff.). Entrapped under sin and flesh, the law only adds to the torment, because in the very hearing of the law one disobeys it and is led further into sin. So, although the law continues to be holy and just and good (7:12), for the person "under the law" in the specifically Pauline sense it is fatal (vss. 11, 13).

But how does this perversion of the law by sin come about? In this regard 7:7–12 is of some help, especially if we are right in suggesting that Paul chose his example from the law (7:7) with deliberate forethought. Yet one aspect of Paul's thought regarding the relation of sin and the law is not made explicit here—the law, when misappropriated by sinful humanity, becomes the occasion for boasting. Faith in Christ, or what Paul calls the obedience of faith (literal translation of 1:5), is the antithesis of works of the law and boasting (3:27 ff. and chap. 4; cf. Rom. 9:30 ff.; 10:3 ff.; Phil. 3:4–11). The intrinsic character of the righteousness that seeks to establish itself by works is self-defeating. Such righteousness contradicts that submission to God that is the indispensable prerequisite to obedience, because, as Paul understands the matter, it is fundamentally self-seeking and therefore still rebellious. Paul never questions the goodness of the law itself. He does inveigh against "works of the law"—that is, the misuse of the law to the end of self-righteousness and boasting.

It may seem that one central problem of 7:7–25 has so far been ignored. What about the fact that Paul everywhere speaks in the first person singular and even in the present tense? Is he, as at first we might think, recounting his own present experience, or does 7:9 indicate that he is speaking of his earlier life as a Jew under the law? Or is it possible that by *I* Paul does not really refer to himself at all? In the language of Paul's time *I* did not necessarily mean the speaker or writer personally, but could mean humanity generally ("one," the German *man;* or the French *on*). Paul uses the first-person pronoun in some such sense in I Corinthians 13, where the *I* includes himself but is not necessarily limited to Paul personally. Moreover, in spite of a long history of interpretation that sees Paul grappling with his own inadequacy and sin in 7:7–25, nothing in the context or in Paul's letters generally indicates that he had such a pessimistic view of his own possibilities *in Christ.* Quite the contrary. And it is far from clear that this is even a passing moment or phase of his consciousness. That the passage refers back to his conscious experience as a Jew is not borne out by Philippians 3:4 ff. and other passages (esp. Gal. 1:14) where Paul talks about his earlier life. At those points at which Paul is clearly talking about his past he does not indicate that he was anxious or depressed. Probably the correct explanation of this difficult passage is that Paul writes of his own, or any person's, experience under the law, but that he now sees it from a new, Christian perspective. Thus, Paul speaks of this experience as he could not have before his conversion. In a certain sense this passage may then be autobiographical, but it reflects a present consciousness of a past experience, not the consciousness of that experience when it was actually taking place.[12] Although the passage cannot apply to Paul's Christian awareness, many Christians have since found their own experience echoed in it. This is not surprising, for although it is a Christian reflection upon life lived under law rather than grace, to retreat into a life under law, rather than under grace, remains a possibility, even for the believer.

LIFE IN THE SPIRIT (8:1–39)

What are the functions of the Spirit?

If we understand Romans 7:7–25 as a description of the way in which sin works through the law, rather than an autobiographical confession or reminiscence, the problem of how to fit it (esp. 7:14) into Paul's personal experience disappears. It is not about something he has felt. Paul is analyzing law, sin, and existence under their dominion, rather than portraying his own state of mind. The opening verses of chapter 8 bear out this interpretation, for there the reverse of the situation described in chapter 7 is presented as typical of Paul and those in Christ. For them a great revolution has occurred.

> For the law of the spirit of life in Christ Jesus has set me free from the law of sin and death. For God has done what the law, weakened by the flesh, could not do: sending his own son in the likeness of sinful flesh and for sin, he condemned sin in the flesh, in order that the just requirement of the law might be fulfilled in us, who walk, not according to the flesh but according to the Spirit. [8:2–4]

Life is no longer dominated and defined by flesh, sin, law, and death—that is, by the old Adam—but by Spirit, righteousness, grace,

---

[12] Actually, verse 15a translated literally makes clear that Paul is not describing a conscious state of affairs in the past. "I do not know what I am bringing about." the *RSV* translation of verse 15a, however, can be taken to mean that the subject does know what he is bringing about, but cannot understand why he is doing it. Cf. R. Bultmann, "Romans 7 and the Anthropology of Paul," *Existence and Faith: Shorter Writings of Rudolf Bultmann*, trans. S. M. Ogden (New York: Meridian, 1960), pp. 147–157, especially p. 155.

and life—that is, by the new Christ. God himself has brought about this revolution in the human estate. The Spirit is God's Spirit. (Paul also speaks of the Spirit of Christ, and he does not distinguish carefully between them; in verse 9 he refers in the same breath to the Spirit of God and the Spirit of Christ.) The conviction that God has acted decisively on mankind's behalf in the historical appearance of Jesus as the Christ leads Paul to encourage his fellow Christians. He speaks of the Spirit and its assuring role (vss. 16, 23, 26 f.), of the hope that lies ahead (vss. 18–25), and of the invincible plan and purpose of God (vss. 28–30), grounded in God's love (vss. 28, 35, 37, 39). With the magnificent peroration of verses 35–39, Paul ends this central section of his letter, having shown how the revelation of God's grace as righteousness in Christ has brought about a truly new situation in which the bondage of the old age has been broken and the promise of a new age is finding fulfillment.

Paul thinks it important that the knowledge of this new reality is given in and by the Spirit. He speaks frequently of the work of the Spirit, especially in Romans 8. The term itself translates the Greek *pneuma*, which like the Hebrew *ruach*, can also mean "wind" or "breath." Accordingly, in the Old Testament and earliest Christianity the appearance of the Spirit implied the advent of extraordinary divine power (cf. Acts 2 and the discussion in Chapter 6; also I Cor. 14). Usually Paul means by "spirit" the Spirit of God or Christ, although he also uses the word in a somewhat more general sense of the human faculty (body, soul, and spirit), and it is sometimes difficult to know whether one should speak of spirit with a small or capital letter. For Paul the Lord is the Spirit (II Cor. 3:17); that is, he does not differentiate precisely between the risen Lord Jesus Christ and his Spirit. The Spirit is his and God's active and supporting presence in the individual believer and the whole community. As such, the Spirit is also the first fruits (Rom. 8:23) and guarantee (II Cor. 1:22; 5:5) of the salvation that lies just ahead. In the interim between the earthly appearance of Jesus the Messiah and his coming in glory, the Spirit is given.

Probably Paul's chief contribution to Christian thinking about the Spirit is his belief that the Spirit is both the life-giving power and the ethical guide for the believer's life (Gal. 5:25). Those who live in or by the Spirit live out of God's resources rather than their own and are able to break free from the power of the flesh, that is, the fate of human existence estranged from God ("the law of sin and death" of Rom. 8:2), and to attain life (Rom. 8:9–11). Paul's comprehensive view of the functioning of the Spirit allows him to understand the believer's whole life in terms of the Spirit (Rom. 8:3–8) and its gifts (I Cor. 12–14, esp. 12:4–11; cf. Gal. 5:22 f.). Thus, he can also think of human spirits as attuned to God's Spirit (Rom. 8:16) and of Christians as "spiritual" in this sense (Gal. 6:1). Nevertheless, Paul does not succumb to the temptation of portraying life in the Spirit as invulnerable to sin. One's willing and doing must be in accord with the Spirit in its particular character as the Spirit of God and Christ. Spirit is not merely God's power in the eschatological age. The presence of the Spirit is marked by such qualities as love, joy, peace, and patience (Gal. 5:22) in human relationships. Whatever may be said or claimed, the opposite qualities in human relationships are a sign of the dominance of the flesh (Gal. 5:19 ff.). Paul exhorts his readers not to live according to the flesh (Rom. 8:12 f.). The Spirit is given in the new age for a new obedience (see 12:1 ff.).

God's Faithfulness (9:1–11:36)
What will be the destiny of the Jews?

With the coming of the new age in Christ (cf. II Cor. 5:16–21) and the consequent fulfillment of God's promises in the new Christian community a serious question is raised about the promises of God to the old community, Israel (see 3:1 ff.). Paul never understands the Christian faith as a new religion founded by Jesus of Nazareth. Rather he sees the event of Christ's coming within the framework of a larger history of interaction between God and people which centers in Israel and is recorded in the Hebrew scriptures (Old Testament). For him the question now revolves about that history and those promises. Were they meaningless and are they now null and void?

Before Paul seriously tackles this question he makes clear by way of introduction (9:1–5) his abiding kinship with the Jewish people. He assumes, however, that the Jews have not, for the most part, accepted Jesus as the Messiah, thus they remain outside the circle of the new community (vss. 1–3). This situation is the crux of the problem with which Paul wrestles in Romans 9–11. Paul will not write off his kinsfolk, nor will he concede that God has written them off. Although Paul discounts his own Jewish religious pedigree and accomplishments because of Christ (Phil. 3:7), he is unwilling to discount the distinctive position of Israel as a people before God (9:4 f.; cf. 3:1 ff.). Apart from other considerations, Christ himself was by birth a Jew (9:5). Moreover, the very concept of Christ or Messiah is unintelligible outside the context of Israel's history and hope.

Yet not Paul's own feelings, nor his high esteem for the gifts God bestowed on Israel, nor even the fact that Jesus was a Jew are the primary considerations for Paul. His fundamental reason for regarding the given situation as a problem has to do with God, not

Israel. For if the word of God has in fact failed, if God has simply canceled out his promises, then everything that has been said by Paul up to this point is called into question, for God's righteousness is then jeopardized by his unfaithfulness (9:6). Paul will not countenance such blasphemy (cf. 3:3 ff.). If God were unjust (9:14), the note of supreme confidence struck in chapter 8 would be undermined. To put it bluntly, if God had reneged on his promises to Israel, how could the Christian be certain that God would not change his mind again? At stake is nothing less than the validity of the promises of God and by implication the character of God as righteous deliverer. For if the promises of God are revocable, then how can one have faith in his righteous judgment on humanity's behalf in Jesus Christ? Paul now turns to the questions of the faithfulness and righteousness of God in history (cf. Rom. 3:1–8). Romans 9–11 is not an appendix dealing with a peripheral question. Rather, for the gospel to make sense, Paul must show that God's faithfulness vindicates itself in history.

Paul meets in four different ways the implied charge that the word of God has failed. In the first place, he argues that God's promise is based on the principle of election (9:5–26). Moreover, this promise is not automatically passed down from one generation to the next, but is a dynamic process in history by which God continues to call and to choose (9:6b–13). From verse 18 it might appear that Paul thought God somewhat capricious in this respect. Indeed, in verses 19 ff. he seems to defend that capriciousness. Yet here Paul grounds election in a prior faith in God as Creator and Lord of creation (vss. 20 ff.), for what Paul ultimately has in view is not God's arbitrary rigor, but his mercy (vss. 22 ff.). Moreover, the rejection of large numbers of the sons of Israel is predicted by the prophets Hosea and Isaiah (vss. 25–29). Thus God himself has declared that it must occur.

In the second place, sufficient grounds for the rejection of Israel can be found in her own misguided effort to please God. In 9:30–10:4 Paul clarifies the concept of the righteousness of God. Because Israel has not understood that God's righteousness is to be received by faith (9:30 ff.), she has sought to establish her own by works (10:3). But Paul insists that God's righteousness is just that, God's. It cannot be earned. God pronounces people righteous and thus brings them into the right before himself through the cross of Jesus. Christ becomes "our righteousness" (I Cor. 1:30), and in the apostles' preaching the cross of Jesus is said to be the revelation of God's righteousness (1:16 f.; cf. I Cor. 1:18 ff.). The effort to establish your own righteousness means that you refuse the gift of God and seek to promote your own piety or morality.

Israel thus brings reprobation upon herself (9:30–10:4; cf. 3:3 f.). To make clear that the responsibility rests fully upon Israel, not

God, Paul contends that Israel has in fact heard the preaching of the gospel and rejected it (10:5–21, esp. 14–21). He drives home this point, not by making specific references to the preaching of good news to the Jews, as he certainly could have, but by once again referring to scripture (10:18–20).

So far Paul has assumed the unbelief of Israel as the state of affairs calling for an explanation. Beginning with chapter 11, however, Paul's argument takes a new tack as he makes his third point. To the question of whether God has rejected his people Paul now says no. He himself is an Israelite (11:1). The example of Elijah (vss. 2–4) serves to show that Paul is not alone: "So too at the present time there is a remnant, chosen by grace" (vs. 5). Paul combines Isaiah's concept of the remnant with the idea of election already set forth in chapter 9 and his own understanding of the gospel as God's grace. Actually what Paul says here fits very well with the election doctrine of chapter 9. God's grace in Jesus Christ becomes the point at which the process of election in history takes another step forward, while the remnant from Israel provides continuity with the Old Testament people of God. So far, Paul's exposition of the way in which God works in history does not differ in principle from the Old Testament and Jewish understanding, or at least his interpretation of it. God elects not according to national, ethnic, or familial principles, however, but according to his own free choice. The only unhappy aspect of this doctrine is that God's election seems to work through a process of elimination, whereby the number of the elect becomes progressively fewer—not exactly a happy outcome except in view of the consideration that God could have elected to save no one at all.

But then the discussion takes another decisive and surprising turn as Paul makes his fourth point (11:11). The prospect is not pessimistic, as we might have been led to expect. Paul now expounds his expectation of God's continuing work in history for the salvation of mankind, Jew as well as Greek (vss. 11–32). The salvation of the Gentiles is to make the Jews jealous and thus to bring them back into the fold.

How seriously one can take this as a view of history is at least a legitimate question. For one thing, Paul did not anticipate an indefinite continuation of world history even as late as the time of the composition of Romans (see 13:11 f.). He thought history was coming rapidly to a close, and that Christ would soon return. Of course, the sequence of eschatological events that Paul anticipated has not occurred. The conversion of the Gentiles does not seem to be complete—although "the full number of the Gentiles" (vs. 25) may not mean every Gentile. Moreover, there is not yet any indication of the conversion of Israel. Paul's image of the olive tree (vss. 17–24; cf. Jeremiah 11:16) nevertheless provides a graphic picture of his under-

This wall is part of the original wall of Herod that enclosed the temple area. Known as the "Wailing Wall," it has become sacred to adherents of Judaism. (Courtesy of Israel Information Services.)

standing of Gentile Christianity's relationship to contemporary Judaism and to the true Israel of God represented by the root of the tree. Gentile Christians are branches grafted in only because some original branches were broken off. The olive tree itself is the new universal people of God intended to comprise both Jew and Greek. This imagery ought not to be interpreted as Paul's attempt to predict the future; instead we have here an affirmation of faith in the ultimate fulfillment of God's purposes.

In concluding his argument, Paul here neatly summarizes an important paradox of Christian faith: "For God has consigned all men to disobedience, that he may have mercy upon all" (11:32). This astounding statement is neither a passing thought nor a means of easing a difficult predicament into which Paul's argument has led him (cf. the occurrence of the same basic idea elsewhere, notably in 5:20 and Gal. 3:22). Even in the extremity of his severity, God's purpose, the end and goal of his activity, is mercy. In the history of peoples, as of individuals, God's saving activity is grace, surpassing and contradicting human expectation and hopes, appearing where least expected and on behalf of the ungodly (4:5). For Paul, the ungodly are

in the end all mankind, "for God has consigned all men to disobedience, that he might have mercy upon all."

The final paragraph of this chapter and of this section of Romans
is a confession in almost hymnic form (vss. 33–36). Paul wishes to
emphasize the continuing mystery, which his elaboration has only
partly exhausted. Nevertheless, verse 32 implies Paul's conviction
that he has received the key to God's dealing with humanity, not
only in his own times but in all times. The seeming triumph of
iniquity in the human race is deceptive. The complete revelation,
which is God's to give, is not yet completely disclosed. Because Paul
understands the fundamental character, intention, and goal of God's
working in history, he boldly suggests the theological significance of
the acceptance of the gospel by the Gentiles while it is being rejected by the majority of his fellow Jews. God works in history to
the end that he has mercy upon all. Yet Paul's faith is not in his
own theological exposition of history, but in the God who makes
his mercy known in Christ: "For from him and through him and to
him are all things. To him be glory forever. Amen."

The Obedience of Faith (12:1—15:13); Conclusion (15:14—16:27)

What are the practical, ethical implications of accepting God's grace?

The final major division in the structure of Romans occurs after
the hymn of praise (11:33–36) which concludes Paul's discussion of
the destiny of Israel. With a general exhortation (12:1–2) Paul then
introduces a series of ethical instructions which concludes at 15:13.
The character of this long section and its relation to what precedes
can best be grasped by looking closely at the introductory exhortation.

Addressing the Roman Christians as brethren, Paul bases his appeal on the "mercies of God." The most likely clue to the meaning
of this term is to be found in the word "therefore," which suggests
that Paul grounds what he now proposes to say in what has gone
before. The extended theological discussion of chapters 1–11 might
then be understood as an exposition of "the mercies of God," in the
sense of the merciful activity of God on behalf of sinful and wayward humanity.[13] Paul is basing his ethical exhortations on the prior
claim that God has on believers by virtue of the grace shown them
in Jesus Christ. The theological indicative ("what God has done for
you") becomes the ground for the ethical imperative ("what you
must do for your fellow human being"), and this is altogether char-

[13] Barrett, *A Commentary on the Epistle to the Romans,* p. 230.

acteristic of Paul's thought (cf. esp. Rom. 6). This interpretation of the mercies of God also suggests that Paul is picking up in 12:1 the theme of mercy from 11:32: "For God has consigned all men to disobedience, that he may have mercy upon all." Admittedly, the Greek term in 12:1 is not identical with that in 11:32 (despite the English translation); nevertheless, the basic idea is the same.

The problem of the relation of 12:1–2 to what precedes is not as difficult as the interpretation of the text itself. "To present your bodies as a living sacrifice" and "spiritual worship" are perplexing phrases. Here as previously (cf. 3:21 ff.), Paul appropriates the language of the sacrificial cult at a crucial point of his exposition. Obviously, the sacrificial language cannot be taken literally, for it is quite clear that Paul is not talking about a material sacrifice when he speaks of "spiritual worship." Paul means a bodily commitment or offering to God in response to his mercy in Jesus Christ. By the sacrifice of the body Paul means the surrender of the self, most particularly that self that has heretofore been subjected to sin, flesh, and death (cf. 8:9–11; 7:21–25). Thus the sacrificial language is quite appropriate when understood in terms of "spiritual worship."

In verse 2 Paul introduces that tension between present and future which is characteristic of early Christian eschatology. The RSV's alternative translation, "Do not be conformed to this *age,*" is almost surely more accurate than "this *world.*" As we have already seen, the coming of Christ has inaugurated a new age, even though the old age continues. Believers must no longer conform to the old age as the regulative principle of life, but to the new. "*In Christ* they have entered the new age; already they have received the first-fruits of the Spirit (8:23), and are under obligation not to the flesh but to the Spirit (8:12)."[14]

Paul warns his readers not to be schematized (the English cognate of the Greek word which Paul actually uses) according to the pattern of this old age, but to be metamorphosed (literally, changed in form or shape; again the English derivative of Paul's Greek) by the *renewal* of the mind. The mind here evidently means both the knowing and willing faculties, but the importance of the mind as the seat of intelligence and common sense should not be understated. Paul does not believe that anyone can come to God through rational means alone. Nevertheless he deems it possible and necessary for the one who has come to God in faith to exercise his mind in God's service.[15] "Prove" is to be understood in the sense of "try and approve." (Cf. Paul's use of the same term in 2:18 and 14:22, where it is translated "approve" and in I Cor. 3:13, where it is ren-

---

[14] Ibid., p. 232.
[15] See G. Bornkamm, "Faith and Reason in Paul," *Early Christian Experience,* trans. P. L. Hammer (New York: Harper & Row, 1969), pp. 29–46.

dered "test."} "What is the will of God . . . good, acceptable and perfect" is to be tested and proved in the doing of the deed as well as in contemplating it. What is the will of God, of course, agrees perfectly with what is good and acceptable and perfect. For Paul, that goes without saying.

Thus 12:1–2 forms the connecting link between Paul's long theological discourse in chapters 1–11 and the ethical exhortations of chapters 12–15. These exhortations are of a general and more or less stereotyped nature and may not reflect Paul's own firsthand knowledge of the situation among the Christians in Rome.[16] Doubtless they indicate the state of Paul's own thinking and perhaps to a considerable degree the problems that he encountered in other churches. Probably also they contain certain pre-Pauline traditional materials.

The use of the image of the body to illumine the relation of Christians to one another and to Christ (12:3–8) recalls its earlier and more extensive elaboration in I Corinthians 12. The paragraph 12:9–13 is simply a continuation of the preceding section. The general ethical injunctions of 12:14–21 recall the Old Testament, and verse 20 the words of Jesus (Matt. 5:44 and Luke 6:27). Yet in verse 20 Paul seems actually to be quoting directly from Proverbs 25:21 f. rather than giving Jesus' own words. This accounts for the inclusion of the "burning coals" clause, which is not found in Jesus' saying. The discussion of the governing authorities in 13:1–7 is strikingly similar to I Peter 2:13–17 and, if I Peter is not dependent upon Romans, probably indicates the existence of a common viewpoint and tradition regarding the relation of the church to worldly authority (cf. II Thess. 2:6, which may refer to the Roman government or the emperor; I Tim. 2:1–2; Tit. 3:1). In 13:7 we may see a dim reflection of the word of Jesus of Mark 12:17. Although this verse seems to summarize the teaching of the famous pericope of Mark 12:13–17, it is by no means certain that Paul had this story before him, or even in mind, when he wrote. Similarly, 13:8–10 evokes Mark 10:19 and especially 12:31, but without conforming closely enough to suggest any direct dependence. The eschatology of 13:11 ff. is quite Pauline (cf. I Cor. 7:31; I Thess. 4:13–18), as is the manner in which eschatology and ethics are combined (cf. 12:2). Chapter 14 continues the ethical reflections about the Christian's responsibility to his brother which we have already studied in I Corinthians 8 and 10. In 15:1–3, as he is bringing his exhortations to a close, Paul introduces the example of Christ himself (Phil. 2:5–11; cf. I Pet. 2:21; Mark 8:34, 10:38 ff.). The principle of Old Testament

---

[16] But Paul S. Minear, *The Obedience of Faith: The Purposes of Paul in the Epistle to the Romans* (London: SCM Press, 1971), argues that there is a definite correlation between Paul's exhortations and distinct groups within the Roman church.

interpretation enunciated in verse 4 is stated more extensively in I Corinthians 9:8–10; 10:6, 11; and II Corinthians 3. In verses 5, 6, and 13 Paul's exhortation becomes almost a benediction or prayer. Paul introduces the subject of the Gentile mission by means of Old Testament quotations in 15:7–13, and is thus preparing the way for the exposition of his own missionary accomplishments and plan in 15:14–33. Chapter 16 is an appendix containing personal greetings.[17]

The hortatory chapters of Romans may seem somewhat anticlimactic after the theological and rhetorical pinnacle reached by Paul at the end of chapter 11. Yet these chapters are not merely perfunctory admonitions, notwithstanding the fact that a concluding hortatory section is a stylistic characteristic of Paul's letters. Faith for Paul is not abandonment of moral responsibility, but the way to come to obedience to God (Rom. 1:5; 15:18). As he stresses again and again in Romans, faith in Christ does not overthrow the law but, rather, upholds it. Paul has absolutely no tolerance for a Christianity that is morally lax or indifferent. That would be as much "another gospel" or "no gospel" as the legalism of the Judaizers in Galatia. Thus the concrete ethical exhortations and advice in Romans 12:1–15:13 are entirely in accord with—in fact, the outgrowth of—Paul's fundamental theological stance. The gospel must elicit a faithful response that is obedience to God. Yet obedience in some vague or general sense is not enough. The obedience of faith must have specific relevance for the actual situations of life; otherwise it is vain and empty.

Throughout this chapter we have been endeavoring to understand Romans; now let us attempt to draw some threads together. The specific *historical occasion* of Romans can no longer be known with exactitude, although clearly it was written after the resolution of the Corinthian crisis—quite possibly in Corinth—and before Paul's subsequent arrest in Jerusalem. Paul himself indicates that he had in mind further missionary work in the West, beyond Rome (15:22 ff.). Evidently he sought at least the good wishes of the Roman church in this endeavor. To this end he wrote the letter to the Romans, preparing them for his forthcoming visit and further travels. The letter serves as a kind of theological introduction to Paul, and this is probably the purpose for which it was originally intended.

In Romans more than in any other letter, Paul is in conversation

[17]That chapter 16 (but not the doxology of 16:25–27) was an authentic part of the original letter to Rome has been convincingly argued by Harry Gamble, Jr., *The Textual History of the Letter to the Romans: A Study in Textual and Literary Criticism* (Grand Rapids, Mich.: Eerdmans, 1977).

and debate with his Jewish heritage and theological background. Not surprisingly then, Paul makes a concerted effort to do justice to his traditional roots, both Jewish and Jewish Christian. Thus Romans contains a considerable amount of traditional material of which 1:2–4 and 3:24–26, as well as much of the hortatory material of chapters 13–15, afford good examples. Yet one cannot make much headway in distinguishing *tradition* from *redaction* in Romans, for Paul is more likely to pick up traditional language and concepts than to use extended sources. Moreover, such traditional materials or concepts as he adopts have been well assimilated to his thought. It is more profitable simply to ask what Paul was thinking or what he intended. Although there are real difficulties of interpretation, the broad outline of his thought are clearly discernible from the structure and emphases of Romans.

The *structure* of Romans is more like a theological argument than is that of any other book in the New Testament. It really has to be studied in its entirety to be understood, for one part relates to or is built upon another. After a long introduction, in which the themes of the letter are set forth, Paul gives an extensive account of the human condition. He concludes that sin has pervaded the entire human race and has left all Jews as well as Gentiles in need of redemption (1:18–3:20). Paul then turns to the sacrificial and saving death of Jesus (3:21–26) and to the necessity of faith as the only way the benefits of that death can be gained. Abraham is brought forth as the prime example and the confirmation of the saving efficacy of faith: "Abraham believed God, and it was reckoned to him as righteousness" (Rom. 4:3; cf. Genesis 15:6).

The beginning of chapter 5 marks a turning point in the letter. Paul shifts from an argumentative to a confessional style and from the second and third persons to the first. Chapters 5 through 8 are concerned with the question of whether and how the conditions of human existence have been changed by Christ's coming. According to Paul, because of God's love in Christ (chap. 5), believers live a new life in this old world, even before salvation has fully arrived, and while the world continues to decay. They are able to overcome sin (chap. 6); they are no longer under the law they cannot fulfill (chap. 7); and they are full of the Spirit of life and free from death (chap. 8). Thus in chapters 5 through 8 Paul spells out the nature and effects of "this grace in which we stand" (5:2).

Chapters 9 through 11 are concerned with the question of God's faithfulness to his promises to Israel, a question lurking in the background since 3:3 f. This is an urgent matter because on Paul's own terms Israel does not seem to be inheriting the promise. If God has been faithless with Israel, can he be counted on to be faithful to the Christian church? Yet it is not God, but Israel, who has defected on the terms of the promise. Moreover, Paul maintains that at length even a wayward Israel will return to God's favor and be saved.

The final major section of the letter spells out the meaning of Christian faith for life's various circumstances (12:1–15:13). Paul scarcely strives for comprehensiveness; rather, he lays down guidelines and directions, often relying on earlier and traditional formulations to specify what the obedience of faith (1:5) demands in concrete situations. Here as elsewhere the imperative, what the person in Christ is to do, flows from the indicative, what God in Christ has done. Thereafter, Paul gives an insight into his view of his own ground-breaking apostolic work, sketches out his plans to visit Rome and eventually to go to Spain (15:14–33), and ends with sundry words of personal greeting and a final general exhortation (chap. 16).

What are the principal *emphases* of Romans? These should already be apparent from our study of the text and its structure, but perhaps they can now be stated more succinctly. Romans concerns the meaning of the event of the Messiah's coming, particularly the fact of his death and the faith that he is risen. The Christ event sheds light backward, so to speak, to show the enormity of human sin, and forward to show the possible boundlessness of human freedom and life under grace. Paul carries on his discussion against the background of problems and assumptions arising out of his Jewish heritage. Thus the meaning of Christ is not discussed in abstraction, nor over against the problems of human existence in general, but with the history of Judaism and her understanding of God and humanity in view. The principal question arising out of that heritage in the light of the revelation of God's righteousness and wrath in Christ is how sinners can be accounted righteous before God. Paul accepts this question as fundamental, but answers it in a new way. For Judaism the righteousness of God is to be attained or fulfilled by works of the law, good works. For Paul, the righteousness of God is revealed in Jesus Christ; it is an action and pronouncement of God. God bestows his righteousness freely. Thus he shows himself to be a righteous and gracious God. Faith is the proper response to God's graciousness. This means, first of all, that one must believe in what God has done—that is, believe in Jesus Christ. But this belief is not intellectual assent in the abstract. It must find expression in a new life. The possibility and power of the new life are already given. Still, it must be received and lived out. Paul not only speaks to his hearers in the indicative mood to tell them what God has done, he also appeals to them in the imperative mood to make their lives conform with this new reality.

Paul seems relatively little interested in the historical dimensions of Jesus' ministry as we see them in the Gospels. Many reasons for this neglect have been suggested and need not be discussed here. The most obvious, and perhaps the most important, reason, however, is that Paul was concerned principally with the *meaning* of Christ's appearance, death, and resurrection. Thus Romans is a thoroughly theological book, not uninvolved with Jesus' history in principle, but not much concerned with its details. More particularly, Paul was interested in the significance of Christ for the proper understanding of God, humanity, and their relation, especially in view of the Jewish theological heritage, which was his own personal background.

Suggestions for Further Reading

An historically important treatment of Paul's theology is to be found in R. Bultmann, *Theology of the New Testament*, vol. I, trans. K. Grobel (New York: Scribner, 1951–1955), pp. 185–352. V. P. Furnish, *Theology and Ethics in Paul* (Nashville, Tenn.: Abingdon, 1968), makes a useful contribution; a survey of modern interpretations of Paul's ethic is included. Two full-scale treatments of Paul's theology have appeared recently: H. Ridderbos, *Paul: An Outline of His Theology*, trans. J. R. deWitt (Grand Rapids, Mich.: Eerdmans, 1975), and J. C. Beker, *Paul the Apostle* (Philadelphia: Fortress, 1980). J. A. Fitzmyer offers a concise interpretation of Paul's theology in *Pauline Theology: A Brief Sketch* (Englewood Cliffs, N.J.: Prentice-Hall, 1967); see also L. E. Keck, *Paul and His Letters*, Proclamation Commentaries (Philadelphia: Fortress, 1979). Interpretative essays by a distinguished German scholar are collected in E. Käsemann, *Perspectives on Paul*, trans. M. Kohl (Philadelphia: Fortress, 1971). Important scholarly works that view Paul against a contemporary Jewish background are A. Schweitzer, *The Mysticism of Paul the Apostle*, trans. W. Montgomery (New York: Holt, 1931); W. D. Davies, *Paul and Rabbinic Judaism*, 4th rev. ed. (Philadelphia: Fortress, 1980); H. J. Schoeps, *Paul: The Theology of the Apostle in the Light of Jewish Religious History*, trans. H. Knight (Philadelphia: Westminster, 1961); R. Scroggs, *The Last Adam: A Study in Pauline Anthropology* (Oxford: Blackwell, 1966); and E. P. Sanders, *Paul and Palestinian Judaism* (Philadelphia: Fortress, 1977), who enters into dialogue with Schweitzer, Bultmann, and Davies.

On Romans, C. K. Barrett, *A Commentary on the Epistle to the Romans* (New York: Harper & Row, 1957), is especially useful. Also worth noting are F. J. Leenhardt, *The Epistle to the Romans: A Commentary*, trans. H. Knight (London: Lutterworth, 1961); F. F. Bruce, *The Epistle of Paul to the Romans* (Grand Rapids, Mich.: Eerdmans, 1963); and M. Black, *Romans* (London: Oliphants, 1973). E. Käsemann, *Commentary on Romans*, trans. G. W. Bromiley (Grand Rapids, Mich.: Eerdmans, 1980), is a major exegetical-theological work, but will be of limited use to the student who does not know Greek. For a collection of recent, significant essays, see K. P. Donfried (ed.), *The Romans Debate* (Minneapolis: Augsburg, 1977).

CHAPTER TEN

Post-Pauline Writings: The Development of the Church

The Community as Institution
The Unity of the Church (Ephe-
sians 2:11–22)
Church Organization (I Timothy
4:1–16)
A Community of Discipline and
Doctrine
Faith and Action (James 2:14–
26)
Christ and Christians

The Suffering Servant (I Peter
2:11–25)
The Superior High Priest (He-
brews 4:14–5:10)
A Community of Love and Hope
The Spirit of Jesus as Love (I
John 4:1–21)
The Vision of the Prophet on
Patmos (Revelation 1:1–
20)

Literary activity in the Christian church did not come to an end with the passing of the first generation of apostles, witnesses, and converts. Indeed, it increased. The second and later generations were, as far as we can tell, more productive than the first. Indeed, the Gospels in the form in which we have them are not products of the first generation of Christians, although Mark may stand on the boundary, so to speak. They were written in light of, or in anticipation of, the passing of the first generation from the scene. As close examination has revealed, they bear the marks and express the interests of the times and places in which they were written. The Gospels bear witness to the life of the church as well as the life of Jesus.

In the outpouring of literature in the last third of the first century, the Gospels occupy a unique position. While they may have some precedent in the religious biography of antiquity, they are the closest thing we have to a distinctly Christian literary form. The other New Testament books adapt the forms and conventions of the day. The historical narrative (Acts) has Jewish and Hellenistic precedents. The apocalypse (Revelation) is a mainly Jewish phenomenon. The letter, in that day as in ours, was universally popular and necessary. Of the twenty-seven New Testament books, twenty-one are called letters. A number of these are not actually letters, but in whole or in part have been cast in that form. Not only do we have the Pauline and later New Testament letters but also the seven letters of the first three chapters of the book of Revelation, and, outside the New Testament, a first-century letter from Rome to Corinth and a whole collection of letters from Ignatius, bishop of Antioch, which were written near the beginning of the second century. There are additionally a number of later noncanonical letters, some of them obviously spurious documents attributed to Paul and even to Jesus.[1]

In this chapter a representative selection of passages from the post-Pauline writings of the New Testament other than the Gospels is treated. Our aim is to introduce this literature and to display its character. In doing so we must take account of its purpose. That means relating the individual writings to the church situations from which they came and to which they were addressed. The similarity of churchly interest and purpose which to a very large degree characterizes these documents confirms the judgment that they should be taken together as representative of a later stage in the growth of the church. As we examine them we shall find ourselves dealing again and again with problems and concerns of a church now a generation or more removed from its origins.

It is customary and convenient to divide the letters into two groups: (1) the deutero-Pauline—those ascribed to Paul—and (2) the Catholic (general) Epistles—those ascribed to various persons and directed to wide areas of Christendom or to the church in general.[2] The later pseudonymous letters of the New Testament which are explicitly or traditionally attributed to Paul are Hebrews, I and II Timothy, and Titus. Probably Ephesians, possibly Colossians and II Thessalonians, also belong in this category. (Ephesians is still regarded as genuine by some scholars, and Colossians and II Thessalonians by many.) The Catholic Epistles or letters are James, I and II Peter, I, II, and III John, and Jude. These last letters differ widely in character and literary relationships. Thus the Johannine letters stand much closer in style and content to the Fourth Gospel than to the other Catholics, whereas II Peter is in some ways more closely

---

[1] William G. Doty, *Letters in Primitive Christianity* (Philadelphia: Fortress, 1973), has set the Pauline and later letters in the context of ancient forms and practices of letter writing.

[2] Cf. the work of A. E. Barnett, *Paul Becomes a Literary Influence* (Chicago: University of Chicago Press, 1941), who shows the extent of the literary dependence of the later New Testament and other early Christian writings on Paul.

related to Jude than to I Peter. The Book of Revelation is, of course, in a class by itself. It has some affinities with the other Johannine writings, but it is the only apocalypse in the New Testament. That genre is, however, found elsewhere in early Christianity and Judaism.

The Community as Institution

After the initial expansion and enthusiasm of the apostolic age, the interest and attention of Christians underwent a certain transformation. Contrary to the expectations of many, the disciples died away, although Jesus had not returned (cf. Mark 9:1; John 21:23). Consequently, Christians prepared to live in the present world for an indefinite period of time. Under such circumstances, it was natural that they turned their attention increasingly to reflection upon the nature of the church and to its establishment as an institution.

NOTES ON EPHESIANS

Although Ephesians certainly purports to be a letter of Paul (1:1; 3:1; 4:1), it is probably the work of a disciple of the next generation. Several considerations point in this direction: (1) style and language differ from the other Paulines; (2) Ephesians seems to be directly dependent upon Colossians; (3) there are certain theological divergences from the other Pauline letters.[3] *The style and language of Ephesians are markedly ceremonial and even formal in comparison with the rest of Paul. Yet Ephesians appears also to draw upon words and phrases of the other letters, especially Colossians.*[4] *This is hard to understand if Ephesians was written by Paul, but not if it is the work of a disciple or imitator. At the same time, the theological perspective of Ephesians differs in ways we shall observe. The fact that Ephesians seems to presuppose no specific situation or audience also has some bearing upon the question of authorship. (Note that the RSV text, following the better manuscripts, does not have "at Ephesus" in 1:1.) The genuine letters seem to be addressed to specific churches and concrete problems.*

If Ephesians was not written by Paul, why was it written in his name? It has been suggested that Ephesians was written by a disciple of Paul as a covering letters for the Pauline corpus, which he himself had collected

---

[3] See W. G. Kümmel, *Introduction to the New Testament*, trans. H. C. Kee, rev. ed. (Nashville, Tenn.: Abingdon, 1975), pp. 360–362.

[4] The dependence of Ephesians upon Colossians has been shown by E. J. Goodspeed, *The Key to Ephesians* (Chicago: University of Chicago Press, 1956), and C. L. Mitton, *The Epistle to the Ephesians: Its Authorship, Origin and Purpose* (Oxford: Clarendon, 1951), pp. 55–97. Cf. also John Knox, *Philemon Among the Letters of Paul: A New View of Its Place and Importance*, rev. ed. (Nashville, Tenn.: Abingdon, 1959).

from the various churches to which Paul had written.[5] *We note that, although more than half of Acts is devoted to Paul's career, the author does not mention his writing letters. This may well mean that Acts was written before the Pauline letters were collected and circulated. A second-generation disciple of Paul could have used Acts to trace down these letters, however, because the major churches that Paul founded are indicated there. Remarkably, all the churches to which Paul's extant letters are addressed are mentioned in Acts, with one notable exception, Colossae, and Colossians is the one document upon which the author of Ephesians seems to have relied.*

Perhaps then the hypothetical second-generation disciple of Paul who composed Ephesians was already familiar with Colossians, as well as the book of Acts. Perhaps he himself was from Colossae, about one hundred miles from Ephesus. If with the help of Acts he set about to collect and publish the Pauline letters, then to write a covering letter, he would likely have recovered the letters from the churches mentioned in Acts and in his own composition made the greatest use of the one additional letter with which he had long been familiar. It would then be natural for his own letter to be regarded in later times as intended for the one great Pauline church (Ephesus) from which no genuine letter actually survives. This would explain the existence of manuscripts with "at Ephesus" in the salutation. Although hypothetical, this is a plausible account of the circumstance under which Ephesians came to be written. It takes into consideration the probability that Paul was not the author together with the fact that, as far as we know, the genuine letters never circulated as a group without Ephesians. The same cannot be said for the Pastorals or Hebrews.

Ephesians does not possess a structure that stands out. Unlike Romans, it is not a theological argument that falls into several well-defined stages. Unlike I Corinthians it does not divide itself according to a series of specific problems and questions. Ephesians seems to alternate between the rehearsal of God's saving work in Jesus and its practical outworking in the situation of Christians and the church.[6] *At best three major parts of the letter, apart from the address (1:1–2) and conclusion (6:21–24), may be discerned.*

OUTLINE OF EPHESIANS

Address (1:1–2)
Thanksgiving and Praise of God
    and Christ (1:3–23)

Christ's Work and Its Results (2:1–
    3:21)
Christ's Saving Work (2:1–10)

[5] Goodspeed sets forth this proposal in *The Meaning of Ephesians* (Chicago: University of Chicago Press, 1933). The following discussion of the origin of Ephesians takes up principal elements of his position. For a criticism of Goodspeed's, and particularly J. Knox's, position see C. F. D. Moule, *The Epistles of Paul the Apostle to the Colossians and to Philemon* (New York: Cambridge University Press, 1957), pp. 14–18.

[6] J. P. Sampley, *"And the Two Shall Become One Flesh": A Study of Traditions in Ephesians 5:21–33* (New York: Cambridge University Press, 1971), p. 11, attributes this helpful insight to Professor N. A. Dahl.

The Unity of the Church (2:11–22)

Paul's Ministry (3:1–13)

Prayer for the Church (3:14–21)

Ethical Instructions and Exhortations (4:1–6:20)

Basis for Ethics in Christ and the Church (4:1–16)

General Instructions for Christians (4:17–5:20)

Instructions for Families (5:21–6:9)

Final Summary Exhortation (6:10–20)

Conclusion and Benediction (6:21–24)

THE UNITY OF THE CHURCH (Eph. 2:11–22)

How are the themes Jew, Gentile, and Church related?

The hymn of praise (1:3–23) takes up and elaborates the characteristic Pauline thanksgiving. Whereas the typical thanksgiving makes contact with the concrete situation of the church Paul is addressing, the Ephesian thanksgiving does not. It is long, solemn, and liturgical. The thanksgiving ends with chapter 1, and the second major phase of the letter begins. It is a kind of declaration or address to the readers. The author starts in the second person, but more than once slips over into the confessional first person plural (cf. 2:3–7, 10).

The section 2:1–10 relates God's saving act in Jesus Christ, already set forth in Old Testament imagery (1:15–23; cf. Psalm 110), to believers. The Pauline language and conceptuality are clearly visible. No single passage from Paul's epistles is the source or model of this passage, but many familiar Pauline themes appear. The relationship to Romans 6 or Colossians 2:11–15 is perhaps clearest. For obvious reasons, 2:8 f. is often quoted as a succinct statement of Pauline theology in the New Testament, and it is, even though it was probably not written by Paul. This whole section is to be placed alongside others (Rom. 3:21–31; 5:1–11; I Cor. 1:18–25; II Cor. 5:16–21; and Gal. 2:14–21) as a classical summation of Pauline theology.

The same solemn tone that has so far dominated the letter continues into 2:11–22, but a subtle shift of emphasis occurs. Whereas 2:1–10 deals with the work of Christ on behalf of individuals, 2:11–22 has to do with the church. Of course, in 2:1–10 the church is already in view (cf. 1:22 f.), and the individual is not lost sight of in 2:11–22. Nevertheless, in a special sense the passage in question (2:11–22) focuses upon the church. Although the word *church* does not appear, emphasis falls upon the idea of community and the creation of this community through the death of Jesus.

From 2:11 we infer that the author envisions the church as composed primarily of Gentiles rather than Jews (see also 3:1; cf. 4:17). Inasmuch as he speaks for Paul, he naturally takes the position of the Jew. Already in this verse we read of the existence of two groups, distinguished by their circumcision or lack of circumcision in the flesh. They are both communities in and of the flesh, which at best means that they are ethnic communities. As far as the author is concerned, the circumcision made in the flesh by hands does not give the circumcised any particular advantage. Yet this does not mean that Israel as God's people has no theological significance. Here the author remains quite close to Paul's own thought. Israel as an ethnic group, as the circumcision, has no particular advantage, but the same may not be said of Israel as the inheritor of God's promises. The advantage of the Jew or of Israel in the latter sense (cf. Rom. 3:1, 9, and 9:1 ff.) is apparent in the statement that follows immediately (vs. 12). Even the phrase "separated from Christ" implies the advantage of the Jew over the Gentile, because the Messiah is promised to Israel. To be "alienated from the commonwealth of Israel" is also to be separated from the messianic hope, as is indicated by the phrase "strangers to the covenants of promise." Obviously what is meant are the covenant promises to Israel. Notice the way in which Gentiles are characterized: "separated," "alienated," "strangers." Their situation is one of being alone, cut off, lost in the most profound and far-reaching sense of the word. Moreover, they are hopeless and godless. Although the author does not grant any particular advantage or significance to fleshly circumcision per se, he ascribes the greatest significance to Israel as the object of God's redemption and the community of God's people. To be apart from Israel is to be without hope and without God in the world.[7]

In verse 13 the work of Christ is interpreted as the recovery of the estranged. "In the blood of Christ" could as well be translated "*by* the blood of Christ." The reference is, of course, to Christ's death understood as a sacrifice on behalf of humanity. The concept of being "far off" can be understood in the light of what immediately precedes (vss. 11–12). But what is meant by "have been brought near"? Naturally, one would suspect that, since the estrangement was defined in terms of separation from Israel, reconciliation and salvation would be described as union or reunion with Israel. Thus "being brought near" would mean the Gentiles' association, or incorporation into, the covenant people. This is partly what is meant; however, Christ is peace for both Jew and Gentile (vs. 14). He effects reconciliation (vs. 16) between them, making them one (vs. 14) by breaking down the "dividing wall of hostility."[8] More-

---

[7] Cf. Sampley, *"And the Two Shall Become One Flesh,"* pp. 161 f.

[8] The translation of this passage is difficult. In the Greek "hostility" is actually a noun in the accusative case, which could stand in apposition to the law as well as to the dividing wall (as in RSV). Thus KJV translates: "Having abolished in his flesh the enmity (hostility), even the law of commandments. . . ."

The breaking down of the middle wall of hostility (2:14), if indeed that is the correct translation, is often taken to be an allusion to the destruction of the wall of

over, he sets aside the Jewish law, the commandments and ordinances (2:15). Jesus' abolishing them in his flesh refers to his death. The author doubtless has in mind other similar Pauline statements (cf. Gal. 3:13; Rom. 7:4 and 8:3). His death marks the end of the period in which the law holds sway. Thus Christ is the end of the law (Rom. 10:4). By bringing the law to naught Christ does away with the thing that separates Jew from Gentile, and thus becomes their peace. It is not simply a matter of Gentiles becoming Jews, for the fundamental status of the Jew is also changed. Notice the author's careful qualification of the law as the "law of commandments and ordinances." This implies that Christ sets aside the particular Jewish formulation of the law of God, not that he annuls every concrete expression of God's will and introduces an era of lawlessness. (But what is said here does not square with Paul's positive statements about the law in Romans 6.) The result of the abolition of the distinction between Jew and Gentile is the creation of the "one man" (vs. 15), the new humanity in Christ. The Greek word translated "man" is the generic term for the human species (*anthrōpos*, whence the English *anthropology*), not the word for an individual male (*anēr*). The creation of the "new man" is the prerequisite for peace among all peoples (vs. 15), as well as with God (vs. 16).

At least three things stand out as important in verses 11–16. First, the recovery and reintegration of the Gentile is not by conversion to Judaism. For Christ does away with the law, the hallmark of Judaism as a religion. Furthermore, the "new man," or humanity, is neither Jewish nor Gentile. As the new man he replaces the old (cf. 4:22 f.; "nature" is a free translation of *anthrōpos*). The Jew, as much as the Gentile, is in need of, and therefore the recipient of, reconciliation (vs. 16). Second, peace or reconciliation is not a purely human matter. There can be reconciliation among people only as they are reconciled to God. Here again the author sets forth a genuine and fundamental theological conviction of Paul. Verse 16 recalls Paul's definitive statement of the work of Christ as reconciliation in II Corinthians 5:16–21. Indeed, the idea of the *creation* (vs. 15) of the "new" man in place of the "old" man probably intentionally recalls II Corinthians 5:17: "If anyone is in Christ, he is a new creation; the old has passed away, behold, the new has come." Third, while peace with God is necessary before there can be peace among people, reconciliation to God and peace with him necessarily mean reconciliation and peace at the human level (2:14–16).

The idea that reconciliation comes through the cross of Christ

---

the Jerusalem temple which separated the court of the Gentiles from the inner court open only to Jews. This would allow those who were far off (the Gentiles) to be brought near (2:13). The destruction of Jerusalem in A.D. 70 and the consequent demolition of the temple walls may have suggested this way of describing the work of Christ. That this allusion to the temple is intended is suggested by the extensive use of temple imagery in verses 20–22.

is what we might have expected from a Paulinist (vs. 16). The term *body* (Greek *soma*) is thoroughly Pauline. In fact, Ephesians here combines different Pauline uses. Obviously the primary reference is to the crucified body of Jesus, who becomes a curse for us (Gal. 3:13), who becomes sin, or a sin offering, for our sake (II Cor. 5:21), who died for our sins (I Cor. 15:3), whose death is our reconciliation: "while we were enemies we were reconciled to God by the death of his Son" (Rom. 5:10). In addition, the peculiar wording of Ephesians 2:16, "in one body," implies an identification of those being reconciled with the reconciler. Again the union of the believer with the crucified is a typical Pauline motif: "I have been crucified with Christ" (Gal. 2:20); "you have died to the law through the body of Christ" (Rom. 7:4). Moreover, the body is an important Pauline image signifying the unity of Christians in Christ—that is, the church (Eph. 1:22; I Cor. 12; Rom. 12:3–8). The initial theme of this passage was community, and the recitation of Christ's work has focused upon its effect in reconstituting unity or community between God and humanity and, especially, among peoples.

This emphasis on restored community is reiterated (vss. 17 f.). Those who are far off are doubtless Gentiles, and those who are near, Jews (vs. 17). Verse 18 describes the present unified status before God of both Jew and Gentile. Once again, the thought is a legitimate echo of Pauline theology. The idea of a new access to God through Jesus has appeared already (Rom. 5:2). That the mode of this access to God is the Spirit is a thought that pervades Paul's writings (cf., for example, I Cor. 12; Rom. 8). The Spirit assures the reality of the new condition enjoyed by the believer. The Spirit and Christ are not to be identified, but the Spirit is the means or mode of Christ's presence, and therefore of access to God.

Mention of the one Spirit leads to the theme of the unity of the new community (vss. 20–22) constituted by the new humanity. Again we have a Pauline web of ideas. For the new community is characterized by the possession of the Spirit, and the Spirit-possessed community is the body of Christ (cf. vs. 16 and I Cor. 12:12 f.). The idea of Spirit and body is not developed immediately, however. Instead, another typical Pauline image, that of the house or temple, is invoked, but with some uncharacteristic variations, as we shall soon see.

Verse 19 solemnly declares that the situation of separation (vss. 11 f.) is no more. The Gentiles have been incorporated into the reconstituted humanity which is the church. They are now "fellow citizens with the saints"—that is, Israel. Yet as we have seen, "Israel" herself has been thoroughly redefined through Christ, who puts an end to the law and by implication to the "circumcision which is made in the flesh by hands" (2:11). "Saints" (vs. 19) now simply means "those consecrated to God," a common Pauline designation of Christians (I Cor. 1:2).

"Household of God" (vs. 19; literally "householders of God") evokes the temple imagery, which is developed in verses 20–22. The foundation of the building that is to be the temple is first described (vs. 20). The description given here may be contrasted to I Corinthians 3:11, where Paul emphatically maintains that Jesus Christ alone is the foundation of the building which is the church. Although the sharpness of the disagreement is softened by the designation of Christ as the chief cornerstone (probably the keystone that holds the entire structure together, as in an arch; cf. vs. 21), there is still a considerable and important difference. This difference is heightened when the prophets and apostles are called "holy" (3:5). In contrast to Paul for whom every true member of the church is holy or a saint (the two words are the same in Greek), the word is here used to set apart the apostles and prophets as a special and superior group within the church—much in the manner in which the words are used in medieval and modern ecclesiastical parlance. The prophets and apostles appear to be elevated as a special group (vs. 20). Even though in Paul's own thought the apostle plays a key role and the prophet is second only to him (I Cor. 12:28), Paul goes out of his way to maintain that there are no fundamental distinctions among the members of Christ's body (I Cor. 12, esp. 12:13). Probably the author of Ephesians would not have denied this. Yet the idea of a special status of the apostolate slips into his understanding of the structure of the church.

Ephesians does not, however, consciously downgrade the role of Jesus Christ in favor of the apostles (cf. vs. 21). The church holds together in Christ and grows in him. Although being in Christ is a Pauline concept, there is a new twist here in that the church grows in Christ (vs. 21; 4:13, 15). Again, the Pauline imagery is developed further in Ephesians, moreover, in this passage, by a process of combining motifs. For actually the temple, not the body, is the explicit subject. Yet obviously the concept of growth relates to the body, as is made plain at other points in this letter (cf. esp. 4:12, 16, where the building imagery also appears). Apparently the image of the body is in the background (cf. 1:22 f.; 2:16) and enriches the temple image.

The Gentiles, who at one time were alienated and then were brought near and made fellow citizens, are now actually built into a new building or structure, which is to be a dwelling place of God in the Spirit (vs. 22). That God or his glory dwells in his temple is an Old Testament and Jewish idea that was applied to the Jerusalem temple until its destruction. Although that temple had probably been destroyed by the time Ephesians was written,[9] making way for the designation of the church of Christ as the new temple, Paul had

---

[9] See note 8, pp. 400 f. If, as we suggest, Ephesians is pseudonymous and not the work of Paul, a date before the destruction of the temple becomes highly unlikely.

already anticipated this event by his use of the temple imagery in relation to the new community and its members (I Cor. 3:16 f.; 6:19 ff.; II Cor. 6:16). That God dwells in the church through his Spirit is an integral part of this complex of ideas, and of Paul's thought in general. Whereas the older view of God's dwelling in his temple envisoned his abiding in a building, in the new conception the "building" is the community of persons, the church. In I Peter 2:4 ff., the figure of the building or temple is taken yet a step farther, and the individual Christians are described as "living stones."

The passage we have considered (2:11–22) marks the culmination of the theological themes that the author has been developing. Formally, the theological section of the epistle continues to the benediction at the end of chapter 3. But that chapter, with the possible exception of verses 9 and 10 (but cf. 1:22 f.), is basically a recapitulation of what has gone before, but with special reference to the ministry of Paul.

Significantly, the drama of salvation narrated in 2:11–22 is in 3:4, 6 described as Paul's insight into the mystery of Christ, "that is, how the Gentiles are fellow heirs, members of the same body, and partakers of the promise in Christ Jesus through the gospel." Clearly the author regards this as the peculiarly Pauline understanding of the gospel. It is true that for Paul the gospel implies the church, and the church abolishes the distinctions of an age that is already passing away. Moreover, the Old Testament prophecies are directed to persons of faith, not to Israel according to the flesh. But Paul does not regard the incorporation of the Gentiles into the body of Christ as his *central* insight into the mystery of the gospel. The elements of the thought are Pauline, but somehow the focus has shifted. There has been a subtle change in the center of interest and emphasis in Ephesians from Christ to the church. This does not mean that the importance of Christ is lessened, but that the church as the result of Christ's work and the historical embodiment of Christ increasingly becomes the main subject of the author's theological concern.[10] Hence he takes Paul's central insight to be an ecclesiological one. He returns to the theme of the church again and again (1:22 f.; 2:11–22; 3:6, 10; 4:1–16; 5:21–33; 6:10–20). After chapter 2 what is not explicit discussion of the church is exhortation to the church. This exhortation, unlike Paul's, seems not to be directed to specific, individual problems and situations but to the church in general, "for the equipment of the saints, for the work of ministry, for building up the body of Christ, until we all attain to the unity of the faith and of the knowledge of the Son of God, to mature manhood, to the measure of the stature of the fullness of

[10] Cf. E. Käsemann, "Ephesians and Acts," *Studies in Luke-Acts*, ed. L. E. Keck and J. L. Martyn (Nashville, Tenn.: Abingdon, 1966), p. 290.

The "Pieta" by the Italian sculptor Michelangelo (1475–1564). (Courtesy of Alinari Art Reference Bureau.)

Christ" (4:12 f.). Even the practical instructions regarding the relationship of husband and wife are to be seen as expressing the exemplary relation of Christ and the church—"the two shall become one" (5:31 f.).

Ephesians is apparently an exposition or re-exposition of Paul's thought in the light of a new situation, such a document as Paul himself might have written had he lived into the following generation. Its concentration of interest upon the church is not un-Pauline so much as it is a development on the basis of Paul. It is moreover, a development in the light of a peculiar state of affairs that Paul did not anticipate and that, in a certain sense, makes us and the author of Ephesians closer to each other than to Paul. Paul anticipated the imminent return of Christ and the end of the age. No such urgent anticipation is reflected in Ephesians. The church will have to exist as an institution in this world for quite a while. The solemn injunction to put on the whole armor of God indicates that the author expects a long fight. The author manifests no weakening of conviction or zeal, however, no attenuation of the faith. Rather, he goes enthusiastically into battle, not knowing when the end will be, but knowing that the victory belongs to Christ and his church.

NOTES ON I TIMOTHY AND THE PASTORALS

I Timothy, II Timothy, and Titus constitute the Pastoral letters traditionally attributed to the apostle Paul. They are called "Pastoral" because they contain instructions for carrying out the pastoral or ministerial office of the church. These instructions are directed to two of Paul's associates, known from Paul's letters. Timothy is also mentioned in Acts. According to the Pastorals Timothy is at Ephesus (I Tim. 1:3; II Tim. 1:15–18), Titus in Crete (1:5).

The Pastorals as a group present a number of distinct peculiarities, and problems:

1. The first collection of Pauline letters for which we have concrete evidence, that of Marcion in the middle of the second century, did not contain the Pastorals. Although Marcion was condemned as a heretic, and his orthodox foe Tertullian accused him of rejecting the Pastorals, the charge is probably inaccurate, because later Marcionite Christians seem to have included the Pastorals in their canon.[11] Probably he did not know them. An early (ca. A.D. 200) papyrus manuscript of the Greek New Testament (p46) does not have, and perhaps never contained, the Pastorals. There seems to be no incontestable attestation of the Pastorals as Pauline letters until the latter part of the second century.

2. The style and especially the language of the Pastorals differ from that of the acknowledged letters as a whole by a factor of about two to three times the variation found in any one, or in any group, of the other letters. The Pastorals do not, however, differ from each other. They represent a single stylistic and linguistic group over against the other letters. Significantly, the Pastorals diverge from Pauline language in the direction of common Greek speech and, particularly, the vocabulary of the Apostolic Fathers and Apologists of the second Christian century.[12]

[11] J. C. Beker, "The Pastoral Letters," *IDB*, III, p. 670.
[12] The linguistic and stylistic evidence has been set forth by P. N. Harrison, *The Problem of the Pastoral Epistles* (Oxford: Humphrey Milford, 1921), pp. 18–86.

3. *The Pastorals presuppose an historical setting found neither in Acts nor in the other letters.*[13] *They seem to envision a situation in which Paul had been released from his Roman imprisonment (Acts 28; cf. II Tim. 4:16 f.) for further work in the East. Apparently he was then arrested and imprisoned again, and it is implied that a second release was not to be expected (II Tim. 4:6–18). The only tangible early evidence for this historical reconstruction, however, is the Pastorals themselves.*

4. *The church situation is distinctive in two respects. First, the danger of heresy is now acute. Second, a regular ministry and system of ordination seems to exist (I Tim. 3:1–13; 4:14). Ministry and laity are now distinguished within the church. Both these situations represent a development beyond what is found in the other letters of Paul.*

5. *A certain theological distance from the genuine Pauline letters is implied by the different use of Pauline words. For example "faith" has now generally become "the faith" (I Tim. 3:9; 4:1; II Tim. 4:7); it is not primarily a relationship, but a body of doctrine.*

It may be argued that all these facts taken individually mean nothing more than that Paul faced changing situations and times. But taken together, as they must be, they raise difficulties for the tradition of Pauline authorship. In fact, they suggest that the letters were written fifty or so years after Paul by a man attempting to speak for Paul in his own day. Evidence that is difficult to reconcile with the tradition of Pauline authorship illumines and supports the hypothesis of a later and different author. It is therefore not surprising that the weight of critical scholarly opinion now falls on the side of this hypothesis.

I Timothy and Titus are concerned with ecclesiastical organization, order, and doctrine, and somewhat secondarily with heresy, although the threat of false teaching may be a major motivation of the letters. II Timothy, on the other hand, is primarily concerned with the threat of false doctrine. In I Timothy injunction is piled on injunction and exhortation on exhortation, with much traditional instruction and admonition having to do with the conduct of church business and the behavior of church functionaries.

OUTLINE OF I TIMOTHY

Address (1:1–2)
Warning Against Heresy and Heretics (1:3–20)
Manual of Church Order (2:1–4:5)
  Worship (2:1–15)
  Qualifications and Duties of the Clergy (3:1–16)
  Appearance of Heresy (4:1–5)
Manual for Ministers (4:6–6:19)

Teaching in the Church (4:6–16)
Dealing with Elders and Widows (5:1–22)
Personal Advice (5:23–24)
Advice to Slaves (6:1–2)
Dangers of False Teachers and Teachings (6:3–10)
Exhortation to Ministers (6:11–19)
Conclusion (6:20–21)

[13] A good brief statement of the difficulties may be found in Kümmel, *Introduction to the New Testament*, pp. 264–268.

CHURCH ORGANIZATION (I Tim. 4:1–16)

Why has ordained ministry become important?

Although the fourth chapter of I Timothy may not be a particularly noteworthy piece of prose, it is a good cross section of the letter revealing most of the distinguishing features of the Pastorals. The first five verses deal with heresy, false teaching, that has arisen within the Christian community. The remainder of the chapter is the opening of the section designated in the outline as a manual for ministers.

When the author says of the heretics against whom he struggles that they were to be anticipated (4:1), the edge is taken off the hard and discouraging fact that even within the community of faith error persists. This unhappy circumstance occurs with the foreknowledge of God; the Spirit predicts it. The same motif appears elsewhere in the New Testament (Acts 20:28–30; Mark 13:5 f.; Jude 18; II Pet. 3:3; and I John 2:18). The common element in these texts is the fact that the church has been duly warned of the appearance of evil persons within her midst. At an earlier period Paul recognized the existence and danger of such persons (Phil. 3:1 ff.) but said nothing about their having been predicted.

The attitude of our author is intolerant because the heretics have "departed from the faith" by attending to "deceitful spirits" and "demonic doctrines." Those responsible for this state of affairs, perhaps heretical teachers, are referred to in verse 2. There is no hesitancy in calling a spade a spade. The luxury of allowing each his or her own view in religious matters is impossible for the author. The writer is a churchman concerned about the truth of the Christian message, the church's proper preservation of it, and the obedient ordering of church life in the light of the gospel. The false doctrine that he denounces and deplores has immediate practical ramifications; for the beliefs of the heretics lead inevitably to the wrong ordering of life (vss. 3–5).

The ascetic, world-denying character of their heresy is apparent (vs. 3). Their asceticism—avoidance of sex and certain food—suggests that the opponents are closely related to, if not identical with, the Gnostics denounced by the Christian Fathers in the second century. The earlier description of the false teachers (1:3–7) corresponds rather well with this aberrant form of Christianity. Confirmation is also found in 6:20, where Timothy is advised to "avoid the godless chatter and contradictions of what is falsely called knowledge." The Greek word translated *knowledge* is *gnōsis*, whence the name of this heresy, Gnosticism. The widespread appearance of this heretical version of the Christian gospel, which defined the Christian message as a program of escape from this evil world to a better one above, was one of the most important developments in the history of second-century Christianity. At this time it was by no means certain that Christian thought would move in the direction indicated in the New Testament books and the later creeds. The Gnostics, so numerous that in many places they constituted the majority of Christians, did not, of course, consider themselves heretics. Consequently, the history of Christian thought in the second and early third centuries is very largely the story of the exclusion of their point of view from the area of permissible Christian beliefs. Indeed, it was either Gnosticism or the "orthodox" form of Christianity that eventually had to emerge victorious, for Gnosticism was not a few doctrines added to or subtracted from Christianity, but a comprehensive, alternative understanding of it. I Timothy probably represents an early stage in the emergence, identification, and rejection of the Gnostic viewpoint. Perhaps an even earlier stage of the heresy is resisted in Paul's own writings, possibly in the Corinthian correspondence and very likely in Colossians. We cannot assume, however, that Gnosticism is the only heresy attacked in the Pastoral letters.[14]

In opposition to this specious and harmful asceticism, the author lays out the Christian position (vss. 4 f). His view had already been adumbrated in verse 3 ("received with thanksgiving"; cf. the same phrase in vs. 4), where the phrase "by those who believe and *know the truth*" may be consciously formulated in opposition to the claims of the Gnostics. I Timothy (4:4 f.) vigorously reasserts the claim of the Old Testament (Gen. 1:29), Judaism, and Jesus himself that God's creation is fundamentally good. This belief, though not denied by the earliest generation of Christians, was relegated to the periphery because of eager expectation of further revelations from the Lord and a correspondingly low estimate of this world.[15] I Timothy clearly formulates what has become the classical Christian position. "Everything created by God is good, and nothing is to be rejected if it is received with thanksgiving." "Thanksgiving" involves consecration by the word of God and prayer (vss. 4 f.). What the "word of God" means in this context is not obvious. Possibly it is a reference to prayer in biblical terminology. It could mean scrip-

---

[14] For further discussion of the "false teachers," see M. Dibelius and H. Conzelmann, *The Pastoral Epistles*, trans. P. Buttolph and A. Yarbro (Philadelphia: Fortress, 1972), p. 65 f.

[15] The apocryphal Acts of Paul presents a contrary view of the apostle, for "in practically every episode the motif of sexual continence plays a dominant role. . . . The basis of this attitude is the conviction that the goods of this world are worthless and unprofitable, that salvation lies in the world to come, and that all depends on the securing of this other-wordly salvation," according to E. Hennecke, *New Testament Apocrypha*, II, ed. W. Schneemelcher and trans. R. McL. Wilson (Philadelphia, Pa.: Westminster, 1965), p. 350.

ture, although the New Testament per se had not yet been formed.

The author does not mean that "anything goes" because everything is created by God. No one could read the rest of his writings and imagine that. But he does express the fundamental conviction that there is nothing wrong with the well-ordered use and enjoyment of the things God has created. Probably he would have agreed with the more extensive statement of this position found in a document composed a couple of hundred years later:

> If any bishop, elder, or deacon or anyone of the clergy abstains from marriage, meat, or wine, not through self-discipline, but through abhorrence of them as evil in themselves, forgetting that "all things are very good" and that "God made man male and female," and thus blasphemously repudiating creation, either let him amend or be deposed and cast out of the church; likewise for a layman also.[16]

The next two paragraphs (vss. 6–10 and 11–16) instruct Timothy, and therefore the clergy, about the ministry and administration of the church. The section extending from 5:1 to 6:2 contains specific guidance for dealing with various groups in the church, especially widows, who were considered the responsibility of the community. We have then a kind of manual for the minister.

"These instructions" (vs. 6) may refer to all that has preceded in the letter or to what follows. Either makes good sense. The term *minister* (literally, "one who serves") here designates an office or class of offices in the church. In chapter 3 the qualifications for the ministry, the offices of bishop and deacon, have been outlined. "Timothy" is himself such a "minister" in the official clerical sense. He has been ordained to this ministry through the laying on of hands (vs. 14). The investment of the historical Timothy by a board of elders seems unlikely and does not agree with the account of Paul's enlistment of Timothy in Acts 16:1–3. This section of the letter is more intelligible on the assumption that it was written for the benefit of the nascent official ministry of the church a generation or two after Paul.

The emphasis on right doctrine (vs. 6b) supports this view. "The words of the faith," an un-Pauline expression, refers to the right formulation of the confession of faith, as the immediately succeeding mention of "good doctrine" shows. For Paul, faith is belief, trust, obedience, an orientation of life, a relationship. Of course, faith for Paul has an object toward which it is directed and about which intelligible things can be said. In fact, Paul becomes quite exercised over dangerous and erroneous teaching. Thus much of his extant correspondence, especially the Corinthian and Galatian letters, is

---

[16]*Apostolic Constitutions*, VIII, 47, 51. Quoted by F. D. Gealy, "The Pastoral Epistles: Introduction and Exegesis," *IB*, 11 (1955), 428.

A portion of the Isaiah Scroll of the Dead Sea Scrolls, housed in the Shrine of the Book in Jerusalem. (Courtesy of Israel Information Services.)

devoted to polemic, argument, and persuasion. Yet Paul does not emphasize the correct doctrinal formulation in the way in which the Pastorals do. Much less does he understand faith in the sense of "the faith"—the correct doctrinal formula.

A major reason for the difference between Paul and the Pastorals appears in the reference to godless and silly myths (vs. 7). Doubtless the rise of strange teachings leads to the emphasis upon right doctrine that we find in the Pastorals. The appearance of contradictory beliefs necessitates the definition of the true teaching. Now we may use the term *heresy* in its proper sense (cf. pp. 481 ff.). The false teachers are considered beyond the pale (cf. 4:1–5; 6:3 ff.); indeed, there is no question of discussion with them, much less of winning them back. They must be prevented from contaminating the church and pulling others down with them. It is a good question whether

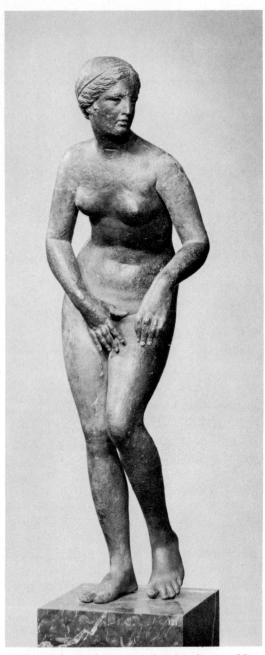

A classical Greek statue of Aphrodite, goddess of love and beauty (*ca.* fourth century B.C.). (Courtesy of Metropolitan Museum of Art. Rogers Fund, 1912.)

the difference between the Pastorals and their opponents and Paul and his foes is more than one of degree. In any event the gulf that separates them is wider and the lines of separation are more sharply drawn.

The author's attention next focuses (vss. 7b–10) upon the relative merits of physical training and training in godliness. The rather vague reference of verse 9 is apparently to verse 8. The Pastorals regularly underscore an important saying with some such assertion as "the saying is sure" (cf. 1:15; 3:1; II Tim. 2:11; Tit. 3:8). Probably this formula indicates a traditional saying. The KJV's "bodily exercise profiteth little" is closer to the Greek original than is the RSV; I Timothy wishes to contrast the little profit of bodily training with the great values of training in godliness—instead of wild speculations (vs. 7a), right doctrine, and godliness. "Godliness" is a word found not at all in Paul, and quite rarely in the New Testament outside the Pastorals and II Peter. It is, in fact, a term at home in ancient Hellenistic piety rather than in specifically Biblical or Christian faith. "Piety" might be an equally good translation of the Greek word in question. The high value that the Pastorals plainly ascribe to this quality is significant. More light may be shed on the thought of the Pastorals by comparing further their outlook with Paul's at this point. For Paul the mode of Christian existence is faith, life in Christ or in the Spirit, and the term godliness or piety does not occur. In the Pastorals the mode of Christian existence is godliness and piety, and faith is the body of right doctrine. The concepts of "in Christ" and "in the Spirit" play little or no role in the Pastorals. We seem to have a contrast between Paul's vital faith, expressed in terms that convey the intimate relation of the believer to Christ and the Spirit, on the one hand, and an understanding of Christianity as institution, doctrine, and religious living, on the other. Thus it is typical of the Pastorals that the promise for the present life and the life to come is not related directly to Christ and the Spirit but instead to "godliness" (vs. 8b).

To disparage the Pastorals as documents reflecting the degeneration of faith into institutionalism, dogmatism, and the practice of piety is unfair. The continuing vitality of the tradition that the author seeks to guard comes to light in verse 10. The toiling and striving of those whose exercise is godliness has as its end and goal the believers' hope in the living God and Savior. The anti-Gnostic character of the Pastorals' polemic appears again in this affirmation of God as the Savior of all. Commonly in Gnosticism only an elect group with a disposition for and capability of possessing knowledge could attain salvation. Here God in intention is the Savior of all, not a special class. That God actually saves only those who believe is the probable meaning of the last clause (cf. 2:1–6). But I Timothy declares quite clearly that no one stands *a priori* outside the potential realm of God's redemption.

The specific referent of "these things" in the following exhortation is again unclear (vs. 11, cf. vs. 6). Does it refer to what precedes or what follows, or is it a general exhortation without any specific point of reference? The latter is more likely. At any rate, what immediately follows (vss. 12–16) is not material that Timothy would command and teach, but advice to him personally. The injunction to Timothy to let no one despise his youth (vs. 12) and the indication that Paul plans a visit (vs. 13) lend a note of genuineness to the correspondence, but they are probably a part of the cloak of pseudonymity in which the letter is clad. The rest is general instruction to the pastor, like much of the Pastorals. We have already noted that verse 14 presupposes the existence of an ordained ministry. The word here translated *gift* is the Greek *charisma*, which implies a special spiritual endowment. Paul held that the *charismata*, "spiritual gifts," were distributed among all the members of the community, so that, although there are varieties of gifts and services, all Christians are, so to speak, gifted (I Cor. 12). Here, however, the charismatic gift is limited, whether consciously or not, to the particular power and authority of ministerial office. It is granted by the laying on of hands as well as by prophetic utterance. *Prophetic utterance* is probably an allusion to the Spirit-inspired designation of people for certain tasks, which was characteristic of earliest Christianity (Acts 13:2). But in spite of the continuation of prophetic utterance, the dispensation of the Spirit is apparently tied to institutional office, and ordination. What then of the free movement and authority of the Spirit in the community? Is spontaneity being sacrificed to the need for unity and order in the community? If so, is this necessary, or is the price too great to pay? The Pastorals do not represent the last period in the history of the church which has entertained such questions as these.

The other injunctions (vss. 12 f. and 15 f.) mirror the continuing life of the community, now a religious institution. The official leaders are to set the example in faith, conduct, and related matters (vs. 12), seeing after their duties of conducting public worship (vs. 13) and supervising the education of the people in sound doctrine (vss. 13–16), to the end that the ship of the church will safely make harbor, that both minister and people will be saved (vs. 16). The model of the church as a continuing community composed of leaders and followers, clergy and laity, making its way through the world toward greater things that God has in store, is the legitimate legacy of the Pastoral epistles.

A Community of Discipline and Doctrine

James, I Peter, and Hebrews, though in some ways similar to Ephesians and the Pastorals, also show significant differences in their focus and form of presentation. While the latter explicitly stand within the Pauline tradition, James, I Peter, and Hebrews do not. Although each of the latter books was probably influenced in some way by Paul, none is ascribed to him, not even Hebrews.[17] All are traditionally regarded as letters, but they do not possess the carefully worked out epistolary form of Ephesians and the Pastorals. James has only a salutation with no conclusion; I Peter has both, but there is some suspicion that they are later additions to an original tract or homily; Hebrews has an epistolary conclusion but no salutation. Moreover, there is a perceptible difference of emphasis. Ephesians is concerned with the theological understanding of the church and the Pastorals with its practical organization and administration, whereas James, I Peter, and Hebrews are more concerned with the inner life of the church, that is, the conduct and conviction of its members.

NOTES ON THE LETTER OF JAMES

The very first verse of the letter of James presents problems. Who is James? There are several possibilities: The brother of Jesus himself; one of the two disciples of Jesus bearing that name; or someone else. Who or what are the twelve tribes of the dispersion (1:1)? The reference is obviously to the twelve tribes of Israel dispersed around the Greco-Roman world, but James is not a letter to Jews (cf. 1:1; 2:1; 2:14–26). Apparently Christians could be referred to as the "dispersion" also (I Pet. 1:1). The letter is addressed to Christians but to no single Christian congregation. The conditions existing in a single congregation or in specific congregations are no more reflected in the letter as a whole than in the salutation. The conclusion tells us nothing; the "letter" stops quite abruptly.

Although tradition has ascribed the book to James, the brother of the Lord, it does not seem to have been known and quoted by other Christian writers until the early third century. The fourth-century church historian Eusebius of Caesarea indicates that some Christians of his day doubted that it belonged in the New Testament at all. Martin Luther criticized the letter, calling it an epistle of straw, and apparently did not regard it as the work of Jesus' brother. In fact, the letter itself nowhere makes this claim. Nor is the ascription of James to Jesus' brother supported by considerations of language and style. The style is that of the Greek diatribe, and the quality of the Greek is reasonably good, probably better than that which an Aramaic-speaking Galilean would produce. The content is nevertheless Jewish—so Jewish, in fact, that some scholars have proposed that James is really the product of a Christian editing and augmenting of a Jewish

[17]Although KJV gives the title of the document as the Epistle of St. Paul to the Hebrews, all reference to St. Paul has been dropped in RSV.

tract.[18] *Whatever may be said for or against this thesis, it corresponds to the essentially Jewish, and especially Hellenistic Jewish, character of the book, its ethical emphasis, and content.*

Plainly, little is known about the origin of James. Probably James represents a form of Jewish Christianity at the end of the first century or the beginning of the second. Its ethical exhortations reflect a knowledge and use of what had by then become an extensive ethical tradition—much of it drawn from Jewish and even pagan sources—in the expanding and consolidating Christian community. The best known section (2:14–26) probably betrays a knowledge of the Pauline letters, especially Galatians and Romans.[19] *If so, then the author very likely knew the collected Pauline corpus, which would date his writing no earlier than toward the end of the first century. On the other hand, Paul or the views of Paulinists are not above criticism (contrast II Pet. 3:15–17), making a much later date unlikely. Because the kind of Judaism that formed the background of James existed in many parts of the Hellenistic world, it is futile to try to locate the book's place of origin.*

Despite the Jewish cast of James, references and quotations from the Old Testament are not frequent. There are a number of possible references or allusions to Jesus' sayings and teachings, however, especially in 5:1–6, 12. Whether these indicate a knowledge of any of our Gospels, or only of an independent tradition, is uncertain.

OUTLINE OF JAMES

Address (1:1)
Exhortation to Christian Practice (1:2–27)
Faith and Ethics (2:1–26)
  Faith and the Poor (2:1–7)
  The Importance of the Law (2:8–13)
  Faith and Works (2:14–26)
Teaching and Wisdom (3:1–18)

Condemnation of Pride and Passion (4:1–12)
Concluding Exhortation (4:13–5:20)
  Warning Against Boasting and Riches (4:13–5:6)
  Exhortation to Patience, Prayer, and the Restoration of the Sinner (5:7–20)

FAITH AND ACTION (Jas. 2:14–26)

Why are works emphasized by James? Is he opposed to Paul?

The letter of James seems to have arisen out of the actual needs of the expanding and consolidating Christian church, even though it is addressed to no specific congregation. Members of the newly

[18]For this view, B. S. Easton, "The Epistle of James: Introduction and Exegesis," *IB*, 12 (1957), 3–74, esp. pp. 9–14. Easton cites the ground-breaking work of Spitta, Massebieau, and especially Arnold Meyer.

[19]A full collection of possible parallels between James and the Pauline letters may be found in Barnett, *Paul Becomes a Literary Influence*, pp. 186–196. Possible allusions to Paul are numerous, but there are no direct quotations. Barnett is cautious in drawing conclusions, but seems to agree with Goodspeed that the author knew Romans, I Corinthians, Galatians, and probably Ephesians (p. 196).

St. James on a plaque of a French altar frontal—second half of thirteenth century. (Courtesy of Metropolitan Museum of Art. Gift of J. Pierpont Morgan, 1917.)

formed churches needed concrete guidance about what to do in actual life situations in which ethical decisions were required. For the Christian converted from Judaism, the problem was less acute, because such a person possessed the powerful and comprehensive tradition of the Jewish law. Even Paul, who emphatically rejected the law as a way of salvation, still appreciated and used the law as a way of life, although he himself probably did not continue to adhere to it in strict Pharisaic fashion. In addition, in certain circles of the early Christian church, the teachings of Jesus were widely circulated and used for moral and spiritual guidance.[20] The existence of a substantial tradition of Jesus' teaching in the Gospels, especially Matthew and Luke, is ample testimony to this fact. The appropriation of the Jesus tradition in the Gospels and the incorporation of all four Gospels into the canon of the church naturally resulted in the increasing availability and use of the tradition of Jesus' ethical teaching as a norm and guide for Christian life. Already in James we may see this development in those passages that are similar to sayings of Jesus known from the Synoptic Gospels.

But why was this ethical instruction necessary? From Paul's letters we can already see that there were various ideas about what it meant to be Christian. The character of Christian existence had to be defined, and for the individual this definition by and large took place after, not before, the experience of conversion. "The apostles went out into the highways and hedges and compelled men to come in—and the post-apostolic church had to contend with the result. . . . Great numbers of men and women had not learned the first elements of morality and were in pressing need of instruction and discipline."[21]

James helps to define Christian life by concrete advice and admonition. The contact with the tradition of Jesus' sayings has just been observed. Even more impressive is the prevalent hortatory style, the stringing together of one injunction after another, which was a common early Christian literary and traditional form, with roots in the pagan and Jewish culture of the day. The ethical exhortations of James have much in common with those of other Christian documents, such as the Pauline epistles (cf. I Thess. 4:1–12; Col. 3:5–4:5): Ephesians (4:25–6:20); I John (3:11–18); Hebrews (13:1–8); the postapostolic Letter of Barnabas; and the Didache.

Perhaps the ethical interest and character of James is portrayed most graphically at the point at which the author evidently combats what he considers to be a dangerous form of Christianity, which holds that a person is justified before God by faith alone (2:14–26). The initial hypothetical situation (described in vss. 14–17) and the moral lesson drawn from it appeal immediately to pious, practical Christian people. For the person, ancient or modern, for whom theological subtleties are either incomprehensible or irrelevant, James' point of view seems refreshingly plain and obviously right. No doubt his point well deserves making, especially against all forms of ortho-

---

[20] The literature on this subject is immense. Perhaps most illuminating is M. Dibelius, *From Traditional to Gospel*, trans. B. L. Woolf (New York: Scribner, 1934), esp. pp. 9–132.

[21] B. S. Easton, quoting B. W. Bacon, in *The Pastoral Epistles: Introduction, Translation, Commentary and Word Studies* (New York: Scribner, 1947), pp. 3 f.

doxy or piety that exclude moral considerations or push them to the periphery. On the other hand, a quite narrow understanding of faith is presupposed; for James, faith equals belief (vs. 19). This view of faith, similar to that of the Pastorals, takes faith to be primarily assent to certain propositions. It is different from Paul, for whom faith is the *act of believing* and the *relationship* between the believer and the one believed.

The contrast between faith and works reminds the reader of Paul's intense theological discussion of this very subject. Possibly James' arguments are directed against the position of Paul. Paul would have surely agreed with the intention of verses 18 and 20. Yet the use of the example of Abraham (vss. 21 ff.) and the citation of the same Old Testament passage (Genesis 15:6) that Paul used to prove a quite different point (Rom. 4 and Gal. 3) suggest some sort of contact and disagreement with Paul or an interpretation of him. The disagreement, of course, concerns the relationship of faith and works and the place of works in the economy of salvation (vss. 21–24).

We have already noted the discrepancy between James' and Paul's view of faith. We must now ask how James understands works and whether he regards them as necessary for salvation. Paul, of course, espouses justification by faith alone and excludes "works of the law." James, on the other hand, does not oppose justification by works to justification by faith. He does not accept Paul's posing of the alternatives. Rather, he regards the performance of "works of the law," along with faith, as indispensable for justification (2:24). Yet he does not intend to espouse the kind of legalism that Paul condemned. He refers to the law more than once as the "law of liberty" and in 2:8 brings forth the Old Testament passage (Leviticus 19:18) with which both Jesus (Matt. 22:34–40; Mark 12:28–31; Luke 10:25–28) and Paul (Rom. 13:8–10; Gal. 5:14) sum up the law. That he opposes a crass legalism may be inferred also from 2:12 f. Still, Paul and James really differ on the question of justification. Whether James would have expressed himself in this fashion had he understood Paul's view of faith or faced Paul's situation in the controversy with Jewish Christians is a moot question. There is, however, a kind of practical agreement between them. James says (vs. 24) that belief alone is not enough, that pure religion, as he styles it (1:27), involves faith and ethics. Paul would have quite agreed: "For in Christ Jesus neither circumcision nor uncircumcision is of any avail, but faith working through love" (Gal. 5:6). James insists on works as the proof of faith (vs. 18); faith without works is dead. Paul would prefer to say that faith without obedience is not genuine faith.

We cannot determine whether James intends to oppose Paul directly. He seems to be fighting a misunderstood Paulinism that separates faith from life. Quite possibly this is his own misunderstanding. Or such a misunderstanding of Paul's thought may have been prevalent in the church of his day (cf. II Pet. 3:15–17). Paul encountered in Corinth among his own converts those who thought that their knowledge and possession of the Spirit put them beyond any paltry considerations of right and wrong, sin and righteousness. They separated faith or piety from this-worldly ethical questions. Thus Paul had to exhort the Corinthian Christians to abstain from, or give up, immoral practices. It would therefore not be surprising if the subtletes of Paul's theological and ethical reflection, his relating of the indicative and the imperative, of grace, faith and obedience, were lost on later generatons of Christians. After all, Paul is not widely understood in church circles today, which is why some people prefer the less demanding, and less profound, commonsense view of James.

Whether the simple paralleling of faith and works in James is adequate depends on how one understands the human situation and what one takes to be the essential problem in human life. If one is free to do and to believe according to one's own choice and without any predisposition to good or evil, then James certainly does make more sense than Paul. On the other hand, if present existence in the world is to be understood in terms of oppressive bondage to sin, as alienation and rebellion, then the simple gospel of James does not suffice, at least not as a theological analysis of the state of humanity in the world and the manner of redemption. In the final analysis, however, James is a manual for Christian behavior, not a fundamental theological treatise. James may display a certain theological shallowness alongside a Paul or John, but in its own way his book had, and has, its usefulness and function within the Christian community.

CHRIST AND CHRISTIANS

The theme of the relation of Jesus Christ and the Christian is developed most extensively, if indirectly, in the Gospels and the pre-Gospel tradition. In addressing his disciples in the Gospel narratives, Jesus also addresses his church. In fact, even in Paul, the crucified and resurrected Christ, if not Jesus as an historical individual, is used as a model for the ethical behavior of the Christian (Phil. 2:6–11; Rom. 6). Moreover, Paul's metaphor of the body of Christ also reflects a consciousness of the close relationship. I Peter and Hebrews mark a significant stage in the use of the figure of the earthly Jesus in theological and ethical reflection. Here we find for the first time outside the Gospels the explicit recognition of the conviction that the life of Christians has an indispensable connection with the historic life of Jesus. In I Peter this relationship is expounded for the sake of its ethical implications, whereas in Hebrews the theological significance of the relationship is primary.

NOTES ON I PETER

I Peter presents itself as the work of the great apostle; no grounds for doubting this claim were advanced until modern times. Yet there are at least three reasons for questioning this tradition:

1. The Greek of I Peter is very good. Could a Galilean fisherman have written it? Aramaic, Peter's native tongue, differs from Greek more than Greek differs from English.

2. I Peter contains many Pauline motifs and ideas, especially the concept of Jesus' death atoning for sin and effecting righteousness (1:18 f.; 2:24). The Pauline expression "in Christ" also occurs in I Peter (3:16; 5:10, 14), and there is a striking similarity between the view expressed in 2:14 ff. and the attitude toward the state commended by Paul in Romans 13:1– 7. Did the author of I Peter know Romans? The Pauline letters? If he knew the collected Pauline letters, this would imply that I Peter was written perhaps a generation later and could not be the work of Peter, who is reported to have died in the sixties in Rome. Still the possibility that Peter could have known only Romans cannot be excluded.

3. I Peter contains no indication of acquaintanceship with the historical Jesus of the sort we would expect from the man who in many ways was closest to him. The claim to be a witness of the suffering of Christ (5:1) does not necessarily mean an eyewitness. According to the Gospels, Peter fled Jesus on the night he was betrayed and presumably did not see the crucifixion. Moreover, the passage that deals with Christ's suffering and death (2:22 ff.) seems to be based on the suffering servant passages of Isaiah rather than on historical observation. Although this does not disprove Peter's authorship, the text can scarcely be taken as evidence for it.

Modern defenders of Petrine authorship acknowledge the weight of at least the first and second arguments and offer the explanation that these factors are due to Silvanus (5:12), a coworker of Paul (I and II Thess. 1:1), who as secretary actually composed the letter in its present form. But if Silvanus is the same as the Silas of Acts, as is usually supposed, he too was originally an Aramaic-speaking Palestinian (Acts 15:22, 27); therefore the first difficulty would not be removed.

If the letter is by Peter, it must date from about A.D. 60, give or take a few years. The suffering of Christians to which the letter refers would be the persecution of the Emperior Nero. In that case the warnings and admonitions would seem misdirected, for Nero's persecution took place in Rome (the probable place of origin; "Babylon," 5:13; cf. Rev. 18), not in Asia Minor, to which the letter is addressed. If the letter is not Petrine, the period of the Emperor Domitian's persecution would be the probable time of composition. This would date I Peter in the last decade of the first century and also make knowledge of the Pauline letters a possibility. Whatever the conclusion concerning the origin of I Peter, the purpose of the author was to encourage early Christians in their faith.

Structurally, I Peter presents some peculiarities. Salutation (1:1–2) and epistolary conclusion (5:12–14) fall easily away. At 4:11 there is a conclusion of sorts and 4:12 makes a new beginning. The fact that in 4:12 ff. persecution seems an imminent possibility, whereas in the preceding part of the letter it is more remote, has led to speculation that the different parts were written at different times. The hortatory and even homiletical *character of much of the letter suggests that its basis may be a baptismal sermon (cf. 3:21), with the epistolary form a later editorial addition.*

OUTLINE OF I PETER

Address (1:1–2)
The Hope of Salvation (1:3–12)
The Holiness of Christians (1:13–2:10)
Instructions and Appeal for Good Conduct (2:11–4:11)
  Honoring Public Opinion and Institutions (2:11–17)
  Proper Household Relationships (2:18–3:7)
    Servants (2:18–25)
    Wives and Husbands (3:1–7)

Christian Conduct Before the World (3:8–4:6)
  In the Face of Hostility (3:8–22)
  In the Face of Immorality (4:1–6)
  Concluding Exhortation (4:7–11)
Conduct in the Face of Persecution (4:12–5:11)
Conclusion (5:12–14)

THE SUFFERING SERVANT (I PET. 2:11–25)
Why should Christians accept persecution?

I Peter is one of the choice writings of the early Christian period and of the New Testament, whether or not one reckons it to be the work of the apostle Peter. It is written with good taste and restraint, and it bespeaks a wholesome, if critical, understanding of the world. I Peter calls the Christian to obedient work and witness in the world without surrendering to the world's standards and demands.

The interests of I Peter are primarily ethical and secondarily theological. The main body of the document falls into four sections, the last three having to do with Christian conduct. The first of these (1:13–2:10) is more explicitly theological, dealing with the basis of the ethical demand of the gospel, and culminating in the hortatory use of the image of building or temple (2:4–10), an image already noted in Ephesians and I Corinthians. The second (2:11–4:11) is specific and practical, without losing contact with its theological roots or becoming banal or trivial. Throughout this section the theme of submissiveness recurs (2:13, 18; 3:1). Yet quite obviously this submission is no cowardly groveling before worldly power, but an acceptance of the divinely ordained structures of order and authority in the world. Christians submit without capitulating and without surrendering their conscience. That they may have to suffer is a real possibility reflected throughout the letter. The final section (4:12–5:11) deals specifically with conduct in the face of persecution. The central point is that Christians should be obedient to God, conducting themselves in a manner beyond reproach and enduring with patience and courage the evil that unrighteous people may inflict.

The author expresses himself clearly and impressively in 2:11–

25. The first paragraph (vss. 11–12) is a general introductory exhortation. "Aliens and exiles" alludes possibly to Genesis 23:4 (LXX), where Abraham calls himself an alien and exile (cf. also Heb. 11:13 and Psalms 39:12). The Christian church is a pilgrim people, as was the Old Testament people of God. The language and conceptuality applied to Israel in the Old Testament are adopted for the Christian community, which regards itself as heir to the ancient promises of God. The urgent appeal to abstain from the passions of the flesh which war against the soul probably owes something, but not everything, to Pauline usage. Uncharacteristic of Paul is the flesh-soul dualism, which is typically Greek. Yet despite the adoption of this conceptuality Peter apparently does not mean to condemn the physical aspect of human nature and exalt the psychic. For insofar as we can discern the nature of these fleshly passions, they are not primarily sexual or related lusts, but the "natural" desires of the unredeemed life. Thus although the playing off of flesh against soul is not Pauline, the actual understanding of the term *fleshly* seems to be.

The author's main interest (cf. vs. 12) is that the Christians' behavior before the world should be above reproach. Obviously he anticipates that Christians will be denounced by the Gentiles. "Gentiles" here seems to mean non-Christian rather than non-Jew, an indication that the church regards itself either as a "third race" distinguishable from both Jew and Gentile or as the true Israel. In any case, the church sees itself against the background of a largely Gentile culture. This viewpoint bespeaks a second- rather than first-generation origin for I Peter. "The day of visitation" refers to the Last Judgment, an event anticipated in the near future (4:7). It is implied that there may be some hope for those Gentiles who have previously maligned Christians if in the end they are led by their good works to an acknowledgment of God (which seems to be the meaning of "glorify"). Such a humane and hopeful view would accord with I Peter's doctrine of Christ's preaching to the dead (i.e., "the spirits in prison"; cf. 3:19; 4:6).

In line with the kind of conduct expected of Christians in this world, the author urges subjection to and support of civil authority (2:13–17). This passage finds a close parallel in Romans (13:1–7). If the author of I Peter did not know Romans, the similarity may rest on a common tradition concerning church and state reflected also in I Timothy (2:1 f.) and perhaps going back to Jesus himself (Mark 12:17). In any event, I Peter declares that Christianity is not a politically revolutionary movement. The government is ordained by God for the enforcement of order and justice (2:14; cf. Rom. 13:1–5). Whereas Paul assumed that the civil authority would carry out this function, this is not quite so clear in I Peter. Nevertheless, fundamental confidence in the emperor is affirmed (vss. 13, 17).

Obedience is not urged for the sake of sheer conformity, how-

424 The Apostles and the Early Church

ever, and is therefore not fundamentally self-serving. It is intended to silence the calumnies against the church and against Christians that must already have broken out. Moreover, its ultimate end is not that Christians should be docile and enslaved to whatever worldly order exists at any given time or place. The twofold injunction of verse 16, "Live as free men . . . live as servants of God," makes this very clear. I Peter intends to prepare Christians for blameless behavior in the world so that charges brought against them from any quarter may be shown to be palpably false. The author does not blandly assume that all will be well in this world for Christians whose conduct is unexceptionable. The prospect of unmerited punishment and suffering is for him and for his church already a real one (1:6; 4:12 ff.; 5:9 f.). The Christian is to *respect* the secular ruler, along with all people and to *fear* only God and to *love* the brotherhood, meaning fellow Christians in the church (2:17).

The following paragraph (vss. 18–25) is directed specifically to servants, but has far-reaching implications for other Christians. The term translated "servants" (vs. 18) is literally "house servants," almost surely to be understood in the sense of "slaves of the household" (cf. vs. 20). Verse 19 expresses a fundamental conviction, a point that the author makes in various ways and with respect to various situations. Within the established order Christians conform to the legitimate demands that are placed upon them. Even in the face of illegitimate demands and punishment they accept their lot without rebelling. The person who has done wrong and suffers has nothing of which to boast. Rather, the righteous one who suffers unjustly has God's special approval (vss. 19, 20). The warrant for such an assertion is the example of Jesus Christ (vss. 21–25). Because Christ has suffered for them, believers follow in his steps by suffering willingly also.

The mention of Christ's suffering leads into a series of descriptive and theological statements about the suffering of Jesus (vss. 22 ff.). These are probably constructed out of the Septuagint version of the servant songs of Isaiah. Their intrinsic appropriateness should not disguise the fact that they are not primarily historical descriptions. If they seem appropriate when applied to the suffering and death of Jesus, it is partly because from I Peter on—and perhaps earlier—these Isaiah passages have been used in describing and interpreting Jesus' death. We have in I Peter the *locus classicus* for the interpretation of the death of Jesus in terms of suffering. Indeed, in relating Christ and Christians this passage marks an important point in the development of Christological thought and its ethical implications—the recognition that Jesus' death is the norm and model for the Christian's own conduct.

The author's immediate purpose, to speak a redeeming and comforting word, a word of encouragement, is accomplished by pointing to the real and meaningful relation between the slave who is unjustly beaten and Christ, who was also unjustly punished, but by whose wounds the same slaves are healed. As they are united with him in suffering, so they will be united in his glory (1:3–9; 5:10). The relevance of the suffering of Christ is not, however, limited to slaves who are being unjustly punished. Any person of faith who suffers evil unjustly for righteousness' sake will be blessed (3:14), for it is better to suffer for doing right than for doing wrong (3:17). Such a one, who suffers according to God's will, is comparable to Christ himself (3:18). Indeed, that person may be said to share in the sufferings of Christ (4:13).

The question of what historical circumstance evoked this emphasis on suffering (cf. also 1:6) has been touched upon in the notes. In all probability I Peter anticipates the harassment, if not the systematic persecution, of the readers *as Christians*. It is uncertain, however, whether the author expects a general state-sponsored persecution of Christians. The references to suffering as a Christian (4:14, 16) and the coming "fiery ordeal" (4:12) suggest as much. Yet the positive attitude to Roman authority expressed in 2:13–17 implies that the authority of the state is not behind the persecution of Christians, or at least is not recognized as hostile. The tenor of I Peter suggests a time or place in which the state's hostility to the church had not yet been unequivocally manifested but was anticipated.[22]

Although the possible persecution, punishment, and harassment of Christians were very much on the author's mind, the situation was apparently not so acute that he was preoccupied with this problem. Most of the letter concerns the normal day-to-day business and behavior of individuals and church congregations. Thus we find in I Peter something already seen in James, Ephesians, and Colossians: the more or less stereotyped and probably traditional ethical exhortation directed to various persons or groups. In fact, despite its originality in appealing to the suffering of Christ, 2:18–25 is just such an exhortation addressed specifically to slaves. Similar exhortations

---

[22] Possibly I Peter reflects a situation similar to that described in the correspondence between Pliny and the Roman Emperor Trajan (ca. A.D. 112). Pliny writes Trajan asking for instructions on handling the problem presented by Christians, and especially accusations made against Christians, and Trajan responds. Although Pliny and Trajan are not disposed to let Christians go unpunished, neither do they want to hunt them out. The motivating force in the persecution is apparently not Roman officialdom, but the hostility of citizens who denounce Christians to the government. Yet though Pliny and Trajan display an admirable desire to act fairly, it must also be noted that they preside over the execution of Christians who refuse to recant. Does this policy and procedure admit of the kind of approbation found in I Peter 2:13–17? [The correspondence between Pliny and Trajan is available in English translation in Henry Bettenson, *Documents of the Christian Church* (New York: Oxford University Press, 1947), pp. 5–7.]

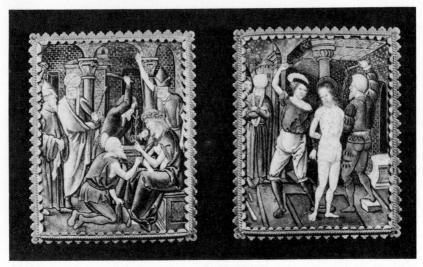

Mocking and flagellation of Christ from French painted enamels by Pierre Reymond (sixteenth century). (Courtesy of Metropolitan Museum of Art. Fletcher Fund, 1945.)

to wives (3:1–6), husbands (3:7), and the whole congregation (3:8–12) follow. Possibly also the exhortations to patience, courage, and steadfastness in the face of suffering are of a traditional nature.[23] The author may be an original thinker or writer, but he is also a churchman steeped in what has already become a significant body of Christian tradition. In and by tradition the church is guided and maintains countinuity with its past.

NOTES ON THE LETTER TO THE HEBREWS

Traditionally Hebrews has been ascribed to the apostle Paul, but as some theologians and scholars of the ancient church suspected, it is not his work. The letter itself does not claim Pauline authorship. Even less than the Pastorals, and far less than Ephesians, does it express typically Pauline ideas and interests. For example, in the Pastorals faith has become belief in doctrine about Jesus instead of a relationship to Christ; in Hebrews faith is simply steadfastness. Neither expresses Paul's view of the relationship of Christians to Christ.

Hebrews' literary character is also subject to question. Is it a letter at all? Despite the lack of an epistolary salutation, Hebrews concludes as if it were a letter (cf. 13:22–25). Yet without chapter 13 Hebrews would probably be taken for a tract or perhaps a sermon. Extensive hortatory passages or exhortations are scattered throughout the book. Hebrews differs from many other New Testament books, however, in that such passages are in-

[23] So E. G. Selwyn, *The First Epistle of Peter: The Greek Text with Introduction, Notes and Essays*, 2nd ed. (New York: Macmillan, 1947), pp. 439–458.

tegrally related to the author's theological thought. They do not appear to be traditional or conventional bits of ethical wisdom and admonition joined, so to speak, end to end.

The thought of Hebrews is complex, subtle, and sophisticated. The author, whoever he may have been, was no amateur in the use of the Greek language and the methods of biblical interpretation of his day. We should not expect to grasp the full range and complexity of Hebrews on first reading. A few questions might well be borne in mind at the outset lest the reading of the book lose direction. What was the character of the life of the church (or churches) to which Hebrews was addressed? Were its problems similar to those Paul encountered in Galatia or Corinth? Does the character of the church and its people—for example, their seeming lassitude—indicate anything about the times in which Hebrews was written? Is any practical purpose or goal reflected in the author's subtle treatment of Old Testament themes?

The exact date, author, intended readers, place of origin, and geographic destination of Hebrews are uncertain. The situation and mood of the intended readers and the kind of ethical exhortations suggest second-generation Christianity, perhaps ca. A.D. 80–90. Yet the author does not mention the destruction of the Jerusalem temple (A.D. 70) in the course of his argument concerning the new priesthood in Jesus Christ, and an earlier date is therefore sometimes proposed. He is concerned with the Old Testament tabernacle and not with the contemporary temple, however, and this fact alone may explain his silence.

The identity of the author remains unknown. Apollos, co-worker with Paul (Acts 18:24; I Cor. 1:12, 3:4 ff.), has been suggested by some, including Martin Luther in the sixteenth century. The suggestion is reasonable but can' scarcely be either proven or disproven. The readers suggested by the title would be Jewish Christians, not Jews. The title is probably a later addition, however, and the author's argument does not necessarily demand a Jewish background for his readers, only a Christian one. The reference to those from Italy sending greetings (13:24) suggests that Rome may have been the destination of Hebrews, as does its use in the late first-century letter of Clement of Rome. Because of the similarities in biblical exegesis and thought patterns between Hebrews and Philo of Alexandria, it is often conjectured that the document was composed in or near Alexandria in Egypt.

OUTLINE OF HEBREWS

Prologue: God's Final Word to Man (1:1–2)
Argument: Jesus as Son and High Priest (1:3–10:18)
  The Person of the Son (1:3–4:13)
    His Superiority to Angels (1:3–2:18)
    His Superiority to Moses (3:1–6)
    Warning and Admonition (3:7–4:13)

The Son as High Priest (4:14–10:18)
  Jesus' Qualifications as High Priest (4:14–5:10)
  Exhortation to Maturity (5:11–6:20)
  The Superiority of Christ's Priesthood (7:1–28)
  The High Priestly Work of Jesus (8:1–10:18)

Application: the Necessity of
Faithfulness (10:19–12:29)
The Response of Faith (10:19–
39)
Forerunners in Faithfulness
(11:1–12:11)
The Examples of Israel (11:1–
40)

The Example of Jesus (12:1–
11)
Exhortation and Warning
(12:12–29)
Conclusion: Final Exhortation,
Personal Matters, and Benediction (13:1–25)

THE SUPERIOR HIGH PRIEST (HEB. 4:14–5:10)
Why is Jesus presented as the high priest?

The author of Hebrews has been described as one of the three
theologians of the New Testament, the others being Paul and John.[24]
But Paul, by virtue of his incisiveness and insight into the human
situation, and John, because of his mystical appeal and masterly portrayal of Jesus as the Christ, make contact more readily with the
interests of later generations than does the author of Hebrews,
whose central image is Jesus the great High Priest. Nevertheless,
Hebrews is an important example of the depth and range of early
Christian thought.

The Christological statement of the first two chapters deals with
the exaltation of Jesus to heaven (cf. 1:3 f.). There as the Son of God
he reigns above all the angels (1:4 ff), that is, above all heavenly and
earthly powers. The exaltation of Christ is grounded in his pre-existence and role in creation (1:2; cf. I Cor. 8:6; John 1:1 ff.). Already
the Christological confession contains a word of warning and admonition to the reader (2:1–4). Moreover, not just the heavenly exaltation of the Son, but also his earthly ministry comes into view
(2:5–9), and the essential aspects of that ministry are emphasized.
The example of Christ's faithfulness (3:16) leads to an extended exhortation to the readers about their own faithfulness (3:6–4:13). But
this section is not just a series of exhortations; Hebrews represents
a careful and elaborate argument in which the church's situation is
compared with that of Israel in its forty years of wandering in the
wilderness. On the basis of the Old Testament scriptures, the author
strenuously contends that there is a "sabbath rest for the people of
God," toward which his readers, or the church, must strive. They,
like ancient Israel, are a people on the way, although their goal is
not the attainment of an earthly territory or kingdom, but one that
is future and heavenly. The author views the church as the wandering people of God.[25] Although this conception is based upon an

---

[24]Edwyn Hoskyns and Noel Davey, *The Riddle of the New Testament* (London:
Faber & Faber, 1947), pp. 146 ff.

[25]E. Käsemann, *Das wandernde Gottesvolk: Eine Untersuchung zum Hebräer-
brief,* 2. Aufl. (Göttingen: Vandenhoeck & Ruprecht, 1957).

interpretation of the Old Testament, it is also related to the actual situation of the church to which the author wrote. Plainly in need of challenge, in danger of losing faith and never reaching the promised rest (already in 2:3 and 2:12–14; but note especially 5:11–6:12 and 10:19–12:29), the church faced the danger of weariness after the enthusiasm and hope of the earliest days had faded—perhaps when the first apostles had died. (Compare the problem found here with the excess of enthusiasm that Paul faced in Corinth, or the zeal for the observance of the law which became a problem in the Galatian churches.) The road ahead was long, and many were tempted to abandon the journey. There was a danger that they would fall back into Judaism or perhaps simply into conventional, lifeless piety.

The author's method of paralleling the Christian church with the Old Testament is typological, that is, an Old Testament figure or institution is understood as the type or prototype of some aspect of Christian revelation. Still the moving force of his appeal is not the Old Testament, but hope and faith in Jesus. Faith is mentioned quite apart from Jesus (cf. chap. 11), and in the long section 3:6–4:3 faith is not related to Jesus in the way we would expect in the light of Acts, Paul, the Gospels, and even James. For Hebrews faith is steadfastness or persistence in hope; this is clear here as well as in chapter 11 where faith is not specifically faith in Jesus Christ. Indeed, Jesus is himself the prime example of faith.

Yet ultimately the ground of faith is Jesus Christ, for the "holding fast" of faith (4:14 ff.) would be pointless apart from him. Central to the author's presentation of Jesus is the concept of the "great high priest who has passed through the heavens." He is the guarantor of the salvation that is promised. The description of the heavenly enthronement of Jesus as the Son (chaps. 1 and 2) precedes an extended discussion of the high priestly activity of the heavenly Christ. The explanation and exposition of his high priestly ministry is the subject of much of the remainder of the letter, especially chapters 7–10.[26] Hebrews thus seeks to show in detail how Jesus' heavenly high priesthood directly affects the church and the Christian. It is the surety supporting the Christians' life in the world and sustaining their hope. With such encouragement they can "hold fast our confession" (4:14), which is the church's expression of faith and hope in God through Jesus Christ.

[26] The author could assume his readers' familiarity with the concept of a priest as a mediator between God and humanity, especially in matters of sin and purification, if only from the Old Testament. Until its destruction sacrifices were, of course, made at the Jerusalem temple, over which the priesthood, headed by the high priest, presided. The function of the priest was to maintain an open channel of communication with the divine and, by offering sacrifice for sin and abolishing impurity, to ensure the divine favor. Ordinary priests had to offer sacrifice continually to ensure this favor. Thus the effectiveness of their work was always temporary. According to Hebrews, however, Jesus sacrificed himself in obedience to God and became the eternal sacrifice and High Priest, a sure and permanent mediator of divine favor.

That the high priestly ministry of Jesus is the basis for renewal of confidence and hope is succinctly stated in verses 4:15 f. The Christology of Hebrews is well summarized in 4:14–16, especially in the two very different assertions about Jesus in verses 14 and 15— namely, that he is the great heavenly high priest (vs. 14) and at the same time the "one who in every respect has been tempted as we are, yet without sinning" (vs. 15). It is not sufficient to ground the church's confidence in the heavenly ministry of Jesus. This alone could have no effect, no relevance for people on earth. Already the author's logic impresses itself upon the reader. Christ could not act for others unless he sympathized with them and he could not sympathize unless he had really shared human nature and experience (cf. 2:14). The heavenly, high priesthood of Jesus is relevant to mankind because it is the high priesthood of a real human being. Hebrews contains perhaps the earliest clear, straightforward New Testament statement of what in later years came to be called the classical Christian understanding of the incarnation—that is, God's human presence in Jesus of Nazareth. God is present in Jesus, in his earthly and in his heavenly ministry, but not in such a way that Jesus ceases to be a man and becomes by this fact a heavenly supernatural being, unbelievable or irrelevant to ordinary mortals.

In spite of Jesus' full participation in human life, he is not overcome by its temptation; he does not sin. It would be a mistake to think that the author of Hebrews had such intimate historical knowledge as to know that at every moment of his earthly existence Jesus was free from sin. On the other hand, it would be equally wrong to suppose that by sin the author meant some kind of personal impurity. "Without sinning" means that Jesus did not succumb to the fundamental temptation to abandon God in faithlessness—that is, in weakness, cowardice, lack of persistent steadfastness—the sin against which the author warns his readers.

The twofold Christological assertion of verses 14 f. lays the basis for the following exhortation and invitation (vs. 16). The term *throne of grace* implies the presence of Christ the high priest at the right hand of God (1:3). The understanding of the gospel as God's grace is, of course, thoroughly and typically Pauline. The fact that the concept of grace was from the first recognized as Pauline is shown by its presence not only in the genuine Pauline letters, but also in the Pastorals, Ephesians, and Acts, especially the chapters dealing with Paul. The use of *grace* in I Peter and Hebrews may indicate that these documents also belong within the Pauline sphere of influence, for elsewhere in the New Testament the term is surprisingly infrequent.[27] Although in Hebrews *grace* is not the object

[27] The Greek *charis*, grace, occurs not at all in Matthew and Mark, a few times in Luke (but more often than not without theological meaning), only in the prologue

of theological discussion, it seems to have Pauline roots. It is God's graciousness, his love freely given. As in the case of faith, however, in Hebrews grace does not appear to be tied explicitly to the event of Christ's coming. Yet the concept of grace is important to the author in that he wishes to emphasize the God-givenness as well as the dependability of the ground of the Christian hope. For all his urgings, he does not ask that the church become what it is not, but only that it be what it already is—a people whose status and assurance is grounded in a merciful God (vs. 16; 6:13–20). Confidence is expected to lead not to complacency but, rather, to further striving. No one is asked to act, to get busy and do something, because of desperate circumstances. On the contrary, one's welfare is assured, if only one will persist in faith and not grow weary.

The people of God must not lose its will or its way; therefore, they must be reminded of the sure hope of reaching the goal. Although the general theme of the wandering people of God gives continuity to the entire book, the climactic theological moments have to do with Christ himself, the heavenly high priest.[28] An extensive statement of Jesus' qualifications for the high priesthood appears in 5:1–10. It falls into two distinct parts—first, a general statement of the qualifications for the high priesthood (5:1–4) and, second, a declaration of the way in which Jesus corresponds to these qualifications (5:5–10).

The model of the high priestly ministry (5:1–4) is the Jewish priesthood, which administered the temple cult in Jerusalem according to the mandates of the Old Testament until the siege and ultimate destruction of the city and the temple in the Roman war.[29] No other priesthood comes into consideration except insofar as the Jewish priesthood bore certain resemblances to that of other religions. This priesthood provides the pattern for Jesus' own ministry. The succinct, clear definition of the high priest's office and function (vs. 1) could equally apply to the entire Levitical priesthood. Although the high priest had a special office, he could effectively exercise this office only because of his common lot with the people (vs. 2). This is, in effect, the first qualification of the high priest. But because what he shared with the people led him to sin, He had to offer sacrifice on his own behalf (vs. 3). Christ, on the other hand, although subject to human temptation, was without sin (4:15). The second qualification of the high priest (vs. 4) was the divine calling.

In showing that Christ fulfills both qualifications for the high

---

of John, twice in one verse and nowhere else in James, twice each in II and III John and Jude, but not at all in I John. By contrast *charis* occurs in every Pauline and deutero-Pauline letter, including the brief note to Philemon, and is quite frequent—for example, twenty-two occurrences in Romans and eighteen in II Corinthians.

[28] Käsemann, *Das wandernde Gottesvolk*, p. 156.

[29] On the meaning of sacrifice see the discussion of Romans 3:21 ff., pp. 369 f.

priesthood (vss. 5–10), the author begins with the second. He affirms with the New Testament generally that the significance, honor, and glory of Christ are not things he claims for himself. They are based neither upon fantastic egoism nor self-esteem. Quite the contrary, Jesus' own life is one of self-giving service, not arrogance. His peculiar dignity has no human basis, but stems from the call and appointment of God. As proof the author turns once again to the Old Testament, which he regards as the definitive expression of the will and purpose of God, when rightly understood and interpreted. Psalm 2:7, quoted in 5:5, appears also in 1:5 and in Acts 13:33 and seems to have been an important Christian proof-text. However,, the quotation from Psalm 110:4 (Heb. 5:6) is even more important for the author's argument. For the theological exposition from this point through chapter 10 (as distinguished from the exhortation) will be devoted to the theme of Jesus as high priest after the order of Melchizedek.

The larger part of the next paragraph (vss. 7–9) deals with Jesus' fulfillment of the first qualification of the high priest (cf. vs. 2), his shared humanity. Here the author takes up and develops ideas already set forth (2:9, 11, 14, 17 f.). There is little doubt that verse 7 is an intentional reference to the agony of Jesus in the Garden of Gethsemane (Mark 14:32–42 parr.), although the details do not correspond to the Synoptics. The meaning of the last clause of verse 7 is not clear for Jesus apparently was not heard. God did not save him from death, unless we suppose that the author has the resurrection in view. This is a possible conclusion, although the more appropriate understanding of the text may be that such prayer does not necessarily remove suffering, even when God hears it. God heard Jesus, but did not spare him from the cross. The author of Hebrews emphasizes the real humanity of the Son, so that he can claim Jesus' own experience as a relevant example for the church of his day. That church, like Jesus, must learn obedience through suffering (vs. 8); its obedience may be the willing acceptance of suffering.

The perfection of Jesus (vs. 9) comes about then through suffering. It is stated explicitly in 2:10 that Jesus, the "pioneer of salvation," was made perfect through suffering. This does not mean that one who was morally imperfect was made perfect, for Jesus was already without sin. Rather, perfecting here means completing and fulfilling the qualifications of the great high priest, who as one of the people leads them before God. The term *pioneer* in 2:10 is well chosen, for the author looks upon Jesus not only as the heavenly high priest above and beyond the people, but as the one who leads them to salvation, undergoing the same experience as they (cf. again 2:10; also 2:14 ff.). The wandering people of God have Jesus as their pioneer. Through suffering he has been made perfect. Thus he has already arrived at the heavenly goal. His people follow, enabled to do so because he has both led them and arrived ahead of them. He now lives and works at God's right hand as the superior high priest after the order of Melchizedek (5:10). So the author can affirm:

> We have this as a sure and steadfast anchor of the soul, a hope that enters into the inner shrine behind the curtain, where Jesus has gone as a forerunner on our behalf, having become a high priest forever after the order of Melchizedek. [6:19–20]

To say that Jesus is the great Melchizedekian high priest does not seem to be a very helpful way of explaining who he is. Yet about four chapters of Hebrews (7–10) are devoted to this theme. Why should the author attempt to explain the relatively better known Jesus by means of the lesser known Melchizedek (cf. Genesis 14:17–20; Psalm 110:4)?

The author proposes to demonstrate that the Old Testament Jewish priesthood is but a prototype and a shadow of the true priesthood and that this true priesthood is to be found in Jesus Christ. The key to his procedure is concealed in the quotation from Psalm 110:4 in Hebrews 5:6. When this Psalm is read in its entirety, the reason for the author's preoccupation with Melchizedek comes to light.[30] The Psalm is addressed to the king, the Lord's anointed (the Messiah), and he is called a priest forever after the order of Melchizedek in verse 4. Since Jesus was the Messiah, the Christ, what is said of the Messiah in Psalm 110 is said of him. Thus the Melchizedek title is taken to be a messianic designation applying to Jesus. Genesis 14:17–20, the brief Old Testament story of Melchizedek, then serves to demonstrate that the Melchizedekian (i.e., messianic) high priesthood is superior to the Levitical (cf. Heb. 7:1–10). It is the true, real, and effective priesthood. This point is elaborated and supported by additional Old Testament evidence and other arguments, which comprise the greater part of chapters 7–10. The author does not wish to say anything about Melchizedek per se, but the concept of his priesthood provides a means of showing from scripture that the Levitical priesthood and sanctuary are only a shadow and prototype of the one great High Priest in his heavenly sanctuary (9:24).

The central fact is the eternal validity and effectiveness of the ministry of Jesus, the exalted Lord, as heavenly High Priest (8:1 ff.). The discussion of the nature of the Old Testament Levitical high priesthood serves indirectly to illumine it. That high priesthood was not fraudulent or unnecessary, but it was, nevertheless, ultimately ineffectual. It was only a shadow and a copy (8:5) of Jesus' heavenly

---

[30] Traditions about Melchizedek were current in his day. See Fred L. Horton, *The Melchizedek Tradition: A Critical Examination of the Sources to the Fifth Century A.D. and in the Epistle to the Hebrews* (New York: Cambridge University Press, 1976).

Seven-branched Menorah found on the northern entryway to synagogue at Khirbet Shema, Galilee—one of the largest candelabra ever recovered from an ancient Jewish site. (Courtesy of Eric M. Meyers.)

high priesthood, and it had to be replaced by him. The author seeks to make the death and heavenly ministry of Christ intelligible through the biblical descriptions of the purpose and practice of the Levitical high priesthood. The sacrificial system then becomes a means of understanding and interpreting what Christ accomplished and accomplishes. What other priests did over and over again in a vain attempt to deal with sin, Christ has done once and for all (9:25–10:10).

The assertion of the sufficiency of Christ's work, in contrast to the work of other priests, leads to an exhortation to those who have benefited from his priestly offering (10:19 ff.). Here again there is the alternation between Christology and exhortation typical of Hebrews. In this case the exhortation includes a threat of judgment (vss. 26–31), followed by a recollection of the readers' earlier courage and confidence (vss. 32–39). The latter passage amounts to an encouragement to keep the faith, and leads into the classic chapter (Heb. 11), in which numerous examples of faith are brought forward from the Old Testament. The rehearsal of the faithful worthies of biblical history, culminating in Jesus the pioneer and perfecter of faith (12:2 f.), leads to yet a further exhortation to the readers (chap. 12).

The final section of Hebrews (chap. 13) evokes Paul's epistolary style. In it there is a rather long hortatory section (vss. 1–18), which differs from the exhortations found earlier in the epistle. These instructions are diverse and disconnected and are not directly related to Hebrews' theological themes. After a benediction (vss. 20 f.) comes an epistolary closing (vss. 22–25). This final chapter sounds more like Paul than the rest of Hebrews and tends to support the traditional view that the letter was Paul's own work.

The essential message of Hebrews is summed up in the call to follow, to be steadfast, to have faith, in the reality of this true High Priest, qualified by virtue of his human experience, validated by Old Testament prophecy, and now at the right hand of God. Having successfully run the course himself, he is not only the great example but, as heavenly High Priest, the source of encouragement and consolation for those who have grown weak or faithless along the way.

A Community of Love and Hope

Along with the Gospel of John, the three letters of John and the Revelation to John have become known as the Johannine literature. (Only Revelation is ascribed in the body of the text to someone named John.) This group of writings embraces the major types of literature found in the New Testament—narrative, letter, and apocalypse. A recurring motif is the tension between the Christian and the world. This dualism, already noted in our study of the Gospel of John, receives further distinct expression in the letters and Revelation.

NOTES ON THE JOHANNINE LETTERS

Although II and III John seems to be genuine letters, it is not clear that I John was conceived originally as a letter. It lacks the customary epistolary introduction as well as a conclusion. In fact I John seems to end in midair with no conclusion at all. Nevertheless, the text more than once indicates that the author is writing to someone (2:12 ff., 26; 5:13); thus at least in this respect the document has the appearance of a letter.

Significant similarities of I John to the Gospel of John will be pointed out in the discussion of the text. They are both formal and substantial, stylistic and theological. Although there are also some differences, the close relation of the Gospel and letters cannot be denied.

The place and date of origin of the Johannine letters are uncertain. According to ancient church tradition, like the Gospel, they were written in Ephesus by the apostle John. But most of the same reservations cited in connection with the tradition of the Gospel's origin and authorship apply also to the letters. There was a noted Asian churchman called the Elder John who flourished at the end of the first century or the beginning of the second and was actually confused with the apostle John in ancient times (Eusebius, EH, III, xxxix). It is tempting to suggest that he is the "John" who wrote the Gospel and letters, as the author of the brief second and third letters identifies himself as "the Elder." Perhaps, but this is slim evidence for identifying the author of II and III John with this ancient and largely unknown man. "Elder" was a common ecclesiastical title and "John" a common name.

II and III John are so brief as to yield little data about their origin. Their obvious theological and stylistic similarities to I John strongly suggest that they were written by the same author. Although II John seems to pre-

*suppose and resist the same heretical views opposed by I John, this prob-
lem is not discussed in III John. Rather, some question of ecclesiastical
politics seems to be the center of attention. Possibly Diotrephes (vs. 9) is
trying to establish himself as a sort of ruling bishop in a particular church
in order to resist the spiritual authority of the Elder.*[31] *Unlike the Gospel
and Revelation, I John has little distinct structure or pattern. The identification of the following major thematic units may assist the reader in
understanding the book.*

OUTLINE OF I JOHN

Prologue: Christian Fellowship (1:1–4)

The Nature and Essence of Christianity (1:5–2:29)

The Marks of True Life in the Community (3:1–24)

Criteria for Certainty and Assurance Among the Faithful (4:1–5:12)

The Spirit of Jesus as Love (4:1–21)

Obeying the Commandments (5:1–5)

The Three Witnesses (5:6–12)

Postscript: Sin and Forgiveness (5:13–21)

THE SPIRIT OF JESUS AS LOVE (I John 4:1–21)

How does one tell a good spirit from a bad one?

There is no logical progression of thought in I John. After the introductory prologue, which is strikingly similar to that of the Fourth Gospel, the author treats two basic themes, the Christian life and the Christian faith. He defines the Christian faith so as to exclude certain erroneous views, including the notion that it is possible to have faith without its taking concrete form in a distinct manner of life.

The passage selected for more intensive examination (chap. 4) is actually not a complete literary unit according to most analyses of I John, including our own. But because the structure of the document is at best indefinite, and at any rate indecisive for interpretation, this is of little consequence. In fact, by taking a segment of this length from virtually any point in the book, one could obtain a fair idea of its nature and content, because the major themes are intertwined and repeated throughout.

Chapter 4 begins with a warning to test the spirits (vss. 1–6). The spirits are ultimately only two, the spirit of truth and the spirit of error (vs. 6). The spirit of error manifests itself in false prophets (vs. 1). This is the spirit of the antichrist, whose coming was pre-

[31] E. Käsemann, "Ketzer und Zeuge," *Exegetische Versuche und Besinnungen,* I (Göttingen: Vandenhoeck & Ruprecht, 1960), pp. 168–187.

dicted (vs. 3; cf. I Tim. 4:1 and pp. 408 f.). It is now in the world, and those who obey it are of the world (vss. 4 f.), whereas the intended readers are of God (vs. 6). The opposition of world and God in I John is well-nigh irreconcilable (cf. 2:15–17).

A fuller understanding of this passage entails some knowledge of the phenomenon of prophecy in the early church. The role of the Christian prophet has probably been underestimated, because none of the New Testament books except Revelation seems to have been written by a person who was primarily a prophet. Yet Paul ranks prophets immediately after apostles in importance (I Cor. 12:28). When the author of Ephesians speaks of the church's being built upon the foundation of the prophets and the apostles, he probably means not Old Testament but Christian prophets (2:20). Although prophets were doubtless important figures (cf. also Acts 11:27 ff.; 21:10 ff.), they constituted a potential problem. Their claim to speak inspired words of Christ or the Spirit (cf. Rev. 1:1–3; 22:18 f.) might result in confusion, especially if divinely inspired prophets disagreed. Thus, the early Christians saw the necessity of distinguishing among the spirits—"test the spirits" (4:1). The idea of discerning among the spirits, or among the prophets claiming to speak in the Spirit, is already present in Paul (I Thess. 5:19–22), who laid down some fundamental rules for distinguishing the inspiration of the Holy Spirit in I Corinthians 12:3 and went on to outline procedures for regulating Spirit-inspired prophecy (I Cor. 14). A half-century or so later the author of the Didache was to suggest that prophets who stayed in one place for longer than a brief period, sponging off the community, were very likely false prophets—not to mention those who, while purporting to speak in prophetic ecstasy, ordered a meal or demanded money.[32]

John's criterion for distinguishing the Spirit of God from that of the antichrist (4:2 f.) reveals a great deal about the understanding of Christianity which he opposed. His own positive affirmation or confession comes to light in verse 2: the person inspired by the Spirit of God confesses that Jesus Christ has come in the flesh. The contrary confession would then deny that Jesus had come in the flesh and would presumably maintain that he was actually a spirit or matterless manifestation that had only appeared to take on an actual human body. In the apocryphal New Testament literature of the second century one may clearly see the burgeoning of this docetic view (*docetic* from the Greek word meaning "to seem or appear"; that is, Christ only seems to be human). It was characteristic of Gnostic Christianity and went hand in hand with the abhorrence of this world and all things material (cf. I Tim. 4:3–5; pp. 408 ff.).

---

[32]*Didache* xi, 7–12; xii–xiii. Yet, "Every true prophet who wishes to settle among you is worthy of his food" (xiii, 1).

John rejects this docetic Christology as the work of the antichrist. Not confessing Jesus means to deny the genuinely human dimension of the Christ event. An important textual variant (vs. 3) reads "divides Jesus" instead of "does not confess Jesus." It was understood by the interpreters of the ancient church to refer to the Gnosticizing division between Jesus and the Christ. Although this reading is probably not original, it would be an accurate commentary on our text, if the heretics distinguished ("divided") between "Jesus" and "the Christ" and denied that God had really revealed himself in Jesus that "the Word had become flesh" (John 1:14).[33]

The antichrist (vs. 3), whose spirit speaks through the false prophets, is the antithesis of God's revelation in Christ. Therefore the typically Johannine dualism or polarity of God and world can be used in describing him and his adherents (vss. 4 ff.). The world in this sense is not the good creation of God but the bad creation of human beings. The world represents human society organized and operating without reference to, or concern for, the existence and will of God. World and Christ, world and church, are placed sharply over against one another. We have observed that in the Fourth Gospel this world is nevertheless described as the object of God's love (3:16 ff.); I John is not so explicit, yet even here Jesus is called "the Savior of the world" (4:14).

The antichrist is an apocalyptic figure, whose traces appear elsewhere in the New Testament. Although the actual term *antichrist* is found only in the Johannine letters, the idea of an individual or collective opponent of God's purposes, especially of his Messiah, appearing as a prelude to the winding up of world history, is not uncommon in Jewish and early Christian apocalyptic (cf. Mark 13; II Thess. 2; and Revelation). I and II John (cf. I John 2:18–25; II John 7) apparently presuppose a tradition concerning the appearance of the antichrist at the last hour. This concept, however, is significantly altered. Instead of seeing the antichrist as a purely supernatural, apocalyptic being, the author now equates him with the emergence of false teachers (2:18) or false teaching—that is, with an historical event. That teaching which denies the humanity of the Son of God, and in effect denies Jesus, is the spirit of the antichrist.

In the face of this powerful movement, represented by the antichrist, which is "of the world" (vs. 5) the Christian can be of good courage. The Christian has overcome the false spirits (vs. 4), for as the author elsewhere says, "the darkness is passing away, and the

[33] It is interesting, and perhaps indicative of the Fourth Evangelist's interest in the historical Jesus, that he uses the name Jesus 237 times, as against 150 times in Matthew, 81 in Mark, 89 in Luke. At the same time he uses the name Christ only 19 times, whereas Paul uses it 65 times in Romans alone. See R. Morgenthaler, *Statistik des neutestamentlichen Wortschatzes* (Zurich: Gotthelf-Verlag, 1958), pp. 107, 156.

true light is already shining" (2:8). The effective power of the new life which God gives through Christ is already present and available to the Christian. With Christ the believer has already overcome the power of the world (cf. John 16:33). Notice how the concept of the world develops in verses 3 ff. From the simple statement that the antichrist is in the world, and a neutral concept of world, we move to an idea of the indwelling of the antichrist, or perhaps of Satan, in the world analogous to God's dwelling in the believer (vs. 4). Now the world becomes the hostile entity of which we have already spoken. Thus it can be said that those heretics who have the spirit of the antichrist are "of the world" in the negative sense so characteristic of John's understanding of the term. As they are of the world, so the Christian is of God (vs. 6). Those who do not "listen to us," but presumably listen to the heretics instead (that is, those who do not accept the orthodox teaching about Christ), thereby show themselves to be not of God, but of the world.

The next section (4:7–12) introduces a major new motif. Being born of God is joined to the exhortation to love. The act of love determines one's relationship to God. Who is born of God and knows God? He who loves. The possibility of knowing God in lovelessness is absolutely excluded (vs. 8): "God is love." The very character of love is to be understood with reference to the way in which God has loved by sending his Son as the expiation for sin (vs. 9; cf. John 3:16 ff. and Rom. 3:25). Love is not a quality by which God is to be defined. Rather, God is the active subject by which love is to be defined. Therefore, the question of human love toward God is secondary (vs. 10). Yet human love is certainly not a matter of indifference. Because God loves, Christians ought to love one another (vs. 11). The primary responses to God's love are faith in Jesus, as God's revelation in the flesh, and love for the other. The real Christian, as distinguished from the pretender, is the one who believes in Jesus and practices love. Through such human love God and his love becomes real and accessible, despite the fact that no one sees God (vs. 12; cf. John 1:18).

The assurance that God abides in the believer and the believer in God is the Spirit (vs. 13). Obviously, one cannot possess the Spirit without love. What is more, neither love nor Spirit are abstract qualities or concepts. They are based upon a particular confession of Jesus Christ, restated in verses 14 and 15. The confession of Jesus, and of God's action toward the world in Jesus (vss. 15 and 14, respectively), is the basis for the Christian's understanding of both love and the Spirit. Of course, no one can truly claim the Spirit who does not believe in Jesus and live in love. The Spirit gives the Christian assurance (vs. 13), but not in abstraction from faith and love. Those who lack faith and love can only be possessed of the spirit of the antichrist (4:1, 3).

The meaning of verse 17 is not entirely clear. John refers again to the ground of the Christian's confidence, which is ultimately confidence before God in the day of judgment. Presumably, the perfecting of love of which he speaks is based upon a relation to Jesus (*he* translates the Greek *ekeinos*, "that one," a common designation of Jesus in John). Therefore, as Jesus is in this world, so is the Christian; one's pattern of life is modeled after Christ's (cf. John 13:12–17). In verse 18 the thought of confidence is carried a step forward by the introduction of a new idea, the incompatibility of love and fear. The perfecting of love means confidence in the day of judgment, because love excludes fear. One could, of course, think that perfect love casts out fear because it does away with the danger of judgment. Yet the author's initial statement, "there is no fear in love," indicates that he wished to assert an intrinsic incompatibility between fear and love. "Perfect love casts out fear," because the one who loves is born of God and knows him (vs. 7), and because love is the negation of that concern for self that breeds anxiety. Therefore, the presence of fear means that one is not perfected in love. Here the terms *perfect* and *perfected* are based on a Greek stem meaning "complete" in the sense of finished. In the person who is perfected, love has reached its desired fulfillment: it determines life.

John returns to the theme of God's prior love and the way in which it motivates people to love in verse 19. The chapter ends with a simple but pointed statement on the relationship of love of God and love of brother (vss. 20 f.); the author puts it succinctly and pungently. The commandment (vs. 21) cannot be exactly identified as to origin. One thinks also of Jesus' "new commandment" of John 13:34 or his "great commandment" of Mark 12:28–21 and parallels. In either case the commandment concisely conveys the burden of Jesus' teaching. At the same time it effectively reiterates a central conviction of our author, that faith and obedience, religion and ethics, the vertical and horizontal dimensions of human existence, can on no account be separated from one another, but always belong together.

The similarities of I John 4 to the Gospel of John are numerous. Some have already been noted, but in conclusion it will be helpful to call attention to the most prominent. The concept of the Spirit (I John 4:1 ff.) plays a prominent role in the Gospel. "Spirit of Truth" (I John 4:6) occurs several times in the farewell discourses (John 14–16), although it is not set over against the spirit of error or the antichrist as in I John. The idea of Jesus' coming in the flesh (I John 4:2) is reminiscent of John 1:14. The negative valuation of the world (I John 4:5) is typical of the Fourth Gospel (John 4:6; cf. esp. John 17). The idea of birth (1 John 4:7) as regeneration also appears in John (esp. chap. 3). We have already noted the importance of the theme of love (I John 4:7 ff.) in the Fourth Gospel. Most remarkably, I John 4:9 reflects the basic motifs and even the language of John 3:16. That no one has ever seen God (I John 4:12) is also an affirmation of the prologue of the Gospel (1:18). The concept of abiding in Christ (I John 4:13, 15 f.) and the themes of seeing and testifying or witnessing (4:14) are commonplace in John, and the possible connection of "this commandment" (I John 4:21) and the "new commandment" of the Fourth Gospel has already been noted. Furthermore, the Greek text reveals many common stylistic traits that cannot be reproduced easily in English.[34]

Still, the Fourth Gospel does point to the past, that is, to the glory of the crucified and resurrected Jesus, whereas I John stresses the present necessity of love among the brethren. The final Johannine writing, the book of Revelation, looks to the future.

NOTES ON REVELATION

Revelation was written during a period of crisis in the church brought about by the active opposition of the Roman government. It is a message of resistance and hope in times of hardship and persecution. As to the place and conditions of writing and the identification of those addressed, there is no reason to doubt the statements of 1:9. Nor is there any reason to doubt what the author says about himself in the same chapter. He is clearly an important church figure of Asia, a prophet, whose name is John. The traditional identification with John, the son of Zebedee, is not impossible, but nothing in the book itself either demands or indicates this. This John does not call himself an apostle, and he refers to the apostles as revered figures of the past (18:20; 21:14). He gives no indication of having accompanied Jesus or having known those who did. The suggestion that the author is the churchman known from second-century sources as the Elder John is plausible, but sufficient evidence is lacking either to confirm or deny it.

A problem arises when we attempt to identify the Roman emperors alluded to in chapters 13 and 17 and by so doing date the book. The beast is presumably the empire and the seven heads seven emperors (cf. 17:9 ff.). Which emperors are represented? Julius Caesar was the first emperor, so Claudius would be the fifth and Nero the sixth. The sixth, according to 17:10, is currently reigning. It is true that Nero (A.D. 57–69) put to death a number of Christians in Rome after the burning of that city, but he conducted no systematic persecution of Christians throughout the empire such as Revelation presupposes (1:9; 2:10; 2:13; 6:9–11; 14:12 f.; 17:6; and so on). Nero also did not attempt to force Christians to worship him as a god.

---

[34]Nevertheless, I John, and the Johannine letters generally, seem to embody a perspective and interests different from the Gospel. H. Conzelmann has pointed to the interest in guarding the tradition that pervades I John and distinguishes it from the Gospel; see " 'Was von Anfang war'," in *Neutestamentliche Studien für Rudolf Bultmann* (Berlin: Töpelmann, 1957), pp. 194–201.

The emperor Domitian (A.D. 81–96), on a Roman coin. (Courtesy of American Numismatic Society.)

Domitian (A.D. 81–96), however, demanded divine honors for himself and put to death Christians who refused to worship him (cf. 13:4–10, 12, 15). A date during Domitian's reign also corresponds to the earliest Christian tradition and to the postapostolic character of the book. The problem of identifying the emperors represented by the horns if the composition of the book is placed in Domitian's reign may be resolved by regarding the statement of 17:10 (and perhaps much related material) as coming from a source dating from the time of Nero.

As the only thoroughly apocalyptic book in the New Testament, Revelation is unique. Of course, apocalyptic materials and themes appear also in the letters of Paul and in the Gospels. The Apocalypse, as it is sometimes called, deals with "what must soon take place" (1:1; 22:6)—that is, the winding up of worldly history and the events leading thereto. This series of cataclysmic events is described with a wealth of symbols and images, many of which are quite strange to us. Understanding Revelation is further complicated by the fact that John purports to be relating things he has seen in visions. To what extent the visions are simply a literary device is unclear, for visions were a stock in trade of the authors of Old Testament, Jewish, and Christian apocalyptic. The visionary material contains numerous Old Testament allusions, references, and quotations. Even if the visions are to some extent literary devices, this does not necessarily mean that the book that lies before us does not have its origin and roots in the visionary experiences of the author. Such an origin of the material in Revelation may account for some of the many obscurities. To become more familiar with the nature of apocalyptic literature, the student should read in the Old Testament Ezekiel 37–39; Isaiah 24–27; Joel; Zechariah; Zephaniah; Obadiah 15 ff.; and Daniel 7–12. The intertestamental books and the literature of Qumran also illustrate the flourishing of apocalyptic writing in the period before, during, and after the time of Jesus and the earliest Christian church.

The structure of Revelation is complex, and there is some reason to suspect that the original order has at points been disrupted or augmented. The following outline is developed in terms of a simple time scheme.

Testament. The uniqueness of Revelation, however, is that in one way or the other this theme is constantly in the foreground and is always presented in apocalyptic imagery.

The remainder of the Christological confession (vss. 5b–7) appears to be traditional (cf. vs. 5b with Rom 3:23 ff.; 8:35 ff.; Gal. 2:20; and vs. 6 to I Pet. 2:9). That Christians in some sense already possess the good things promised is typical of the realized or partially realized eschatology of other parts of the New Testament. Yet the future-oriented apocalyptic point of view, more characteristic of our author, appears again in verse 7. Jesus' return to earth as conqueror "coming with the clouds" is not a new idea (cf. Daniel 7:13; Mark 13:26; 14:62; Matt. 24:30; 25:31). That every eye shall see him forecasts the future universal recognition of the lordship of Christ (cf. I Cor. 15:25 ff. and Phil. 2:10 f.). The references to piercing and wailing allude to the crucifixion (cf. Zechariah 12:10 and John 19:37) and the judgment of the nations which it implies.

The end of the epistolary salutation is indicated by the "Even so. Amen," a liturgical formula. The prophetic word of verse 8 has no obvious connection with what precedes or follows. In a sense the verse is related to the prediction of the coming of Jesus in verse 7, because it affirms that God is the sure ground of this hope. The first and last parts of the statement, the word of the Lord God ("I am the Alpha and the Omega") and the description of him in terms of past, present, and future, are more closely related than may initially appear. Alpha and omega are the first and last letters of the Greek alphabet, the equivalent of the English expression "from A to Z." God is the first and last (cf. 22:13, where this explanation is given), the one who was and is and is to come. Thus he is the Lord of history at the beginning, at its end, and in the interim. The apocalyptic character of the book and its abuse by ancient and modern enthusiasts have obscured the indispensable link with the past and the significance of the present as real and important aspects of the author's thought. In connection with verses 4–7 we have already observed the significance of the past: church tradition, the historical Jesus, and the Old Testament. As for the present, the author's message for the contemporary churches of Asia appears in chapters 2–3. Although chapters 19 ff. plainly have to do with the future return of Christ and the end of world history, the long central section (chaps. 4–18) does not deal solely with the end time. Although the end is constantly in view, the author is also concerned with his own period. For example, the material of chapters 11, 12, and 13 is almost surely to be understood as John's apocalyptic interpretation of past and present historical events—that is, the destruction of Jerusalem (chap. 11), the destiny of the Messiah and the church in the world (chap. 12), and the depredations of the Roman Empire (chap. 13). All history is under the sign of the alpha and the omega, the lordship of the God who was and is and is to come; nothing falls outside the scope of his revelation.

John's own involvement in that history becomes clearer in the following paragraph (1:9–11), and the reader learns that this involvement includes participation in the events of the world as well as in the life of the church. This section marks the beginning of the book proper, for it serves to introduce the visions, which comprise chapters 2 and 3 as well as the rest of his work. The so-called letters to the seven churches are no less visions (1:11–20) than the sighting of New Jerusalem (chap. 21). Yet the naming of the locations of the churches (vs. 11) makes graphic and concrete the this-worldly dimension of Revelation.

Verse 9 is crucial for grasping John's situation as he writes, and therefore for understanding his book. John's statement that he was on Patmos "on account of the word of God and the testimony of Jesus" is subject to several interpretations. Probably, however, he means that he is on Patmos as punishment for preaching the word of God and testifying to Jesus; this is especially likely in view of his use of these same terms in connection with martyrdom (cf. 6:9 and 20:4). John speaks of sharing not only the kingdom, but the tribulation and the patient endurance. *Tribulation* is perhaps a technical eschatological term referring to the woes just preceding the last days (7:14). The persecutions perpetrated against God's people are a part of these woes. They call for "steadfast endurance." Hebrews also mentioned the need for endurance with the possibility of persecution already in view (10:34 f.; 12:4). In Revelation persecution is the predominant reality. Moreover, we know that Patmos was used as a penal colony, a place of banishment, by the Romans. Ancient church tradition also understood John to have been in prison because of his Christian preaching.[36] We are justified in accepting this tradition as an accurate interpretation of Revelation 1:9.

John receives his revelations "in the Spirit" (vs. 10); the association of the Spirit with visions and ecstatic utterances is common to primitive Christianity. The speaking in tongues that Paul discusses in I Corinthians 14 is called the utterance of mysteries in the Spirit (cf. Acts 2:1 ff.). By "the Lord's day" John evidently means Sunday. He was in the Spirit on Sunday. If so, this is one of the earliest references to Sunday, the Lord's day, as the distinctly Christian holy day. "The sabbath" in the New Testament as in the Old always means the Jewish sabbath, that is, Saturday. Now, however, Sunday has appropriately replaced Saturday as the Christian day of celebration, for according to tradition it was on Sunday (the third day after, and including, Friday) that Jesus rose from the dead. The

---

[36] Charles, *The Revelation of St. John,* I, 23, cites the relevant passages from Pliny, Tertullian, Clement of Alexandria, and Origen.

"Saint John the Evangelist on Patmos" by Titian (1490–1576). (Courtesy of National Gallery of Art, Washington, D.C. Samuel H. Kress Collection.)

voice like a trumpet which John hears is probably that of the Son of Man (vs.13), the heavenly Christ.

John writes not of his own accord but by command (vs. 11) and by command sends what he writes to the seven churches of Asia. The command is to "write what you see" rather than what you hear. The mode of the communication of revelation is not verbal, as is usual in the earlier Old Testament prophets, but visual, as in the tradition of Ezekiel, the later, postexilic prophets, and, above all, the Jewish apocalyptic writers. Despite the bizarre character of what John sees and writes, this vision is not meant to remain his own personal experience or the property of certain esoteric circles. The whole book, visions, predictions, warnings, condemnations, and commendations, is a communication to the church. During this time of crisis John delivers to the church a revelation containing dire warnings along with profound encouragement.

With verse 12 the visionary scenes begin and we encounter for the first time the problem of how to understand them. On the one hand, the narrations of the visions are carefully constructed literary works, replete with allusions to and quotations from the Old Testament. On the other hand, we cannot exclude ecstatic or visionary experience as the real basis for what the author has written. Evidence of the genuineness of the attested experiences is the absence of certain conventionalities of literary form that appear in most late Jewish apocalyptic. As we have observed, John is not pseudonymous and does not utilize the fiction of prophecy written in an earlier era. In other words, he does not find it necessary to accredit his message by concealing himself, nor does he attempt to gain credence for his prophecy of things to come by dressing out as predictions the recitation of generally known historical facts.

Verse 12 means only that John turned to see who was speaking to him, not that he expected to *see* a voice. The seven lampstands recall the seven-branched candelabrum (Hebrew, *menorah*) that was said to stand outside the second veil of the Israelite tabernacle (Exodus 25:31–40; cf. Zechariah 4). In all probability the allusion is intentional despite the fact we here seem to be dealing with seven separate stands, not one. The presence of the lampstands indicates an approach to the holy place.[37] However, the explicit interpretation of John is that the seven lampstands represent the seven churches to be addressed in chapters 2 and 3. The appearance of the Christ (vs. 13) evokes Daniel 7:13, "one like a son of man." We are not told that this figure is the Christ, and John does not favor Son of Man as a messianic title (but cf. 14:14); yet 1:17 ff. makes this identification with Christ certain. The clothing of this still mysterious figure (vs. 13) may have been suggested by Ezekiel 9:2 and 11 and Daniel 10:5. The remainder of the description is for the most part derived from the appearance of the one that was Ancient of Days (Daniel 7:9), although the comparison of his voice to the sound of many waters probably comes from Ezekiel 1:24 and 43:2.

Obviously John's mind was steeped in the language and imagery of the Old Testament. He regards the words of the Old Testament and its prophecies as applying to the coming of Jesus Christ, to the church and the times in which it lives, and to the course of world history up to and including its completion. This view of the Old Testament fits perfectly with the author's understanding of the lordship of God over history. God directs history and makes known its secrets to his prophets, principally through the gift of rightly understanding the Old Testament.

The seven stars (vs. 16) are interpreted in verse 20. The sharp two-edged sword recalls Genesis 3:24 (cf. Ezekiel 21:9–10) and es-

---

[37] Furthermore, the connection of the *menorah* with the appearance of the Christ may have been suggested to the author by the *menorah* in Zechariah 4, a passage dealing with the messianic hope of Israel.

Ancient tomb at Beth Shearim with the seven-branched menorah. (Courtesy of Israel Government Tourist Office.)

pecially Hebrews 4:12. In the latter passage, as apparently here, the sword symbolizes the word of God. Christ's shining face indicates nearness to, if not possession of, the glory of God himself (cf. II Cor. 3:7–18; 4:6). With verse 16 the description of the vision of the Son of Man is complete. John's reaction and Christ's response in identifying himself and explaining the vision to John follow (vss. 17–20).

John's physical reaction to his vision (vs. 17) is not only understandable, but also liturgically appropriate. Daniel 10:7–10 is evidently the immediate background if not the direct inspiration of this verse. Christ reaches out, restores John (vs. 17), and identifies himself to him (vss. 17b–18). That Christ is the first and the last implies that like God, and with him, he exercises lordship over history from beginning to end. From verse 18 it is apparent that the speaker is Christ. "Living one" and "alive forevermore" in conjunction with the statement "I died" refer unmistakably to the crucifixion and resurrection. The power of the keys, in Matthew 16:19 given to Peter, is here reserved for Christ. This means that as a result of his own death and resurrection Christ assumes power over death and Hades. "Death no longer has dominion over him" (Rom. 6:9 f.). Rather Christ has dominion over death and Hades. His resurrection is no mere resuscitation, but exaltation to supreme power and authority. The divine ascriptions and prerogatives applied to Christ mean that humanity's ultimate destiny depends upon and is assured by him. The statement of 1:18 may also be related to the primitive Christian concept of Christ's descent into hell and his freeing of the captives there (I Pet. 3:18–22; 4:6; cf. Eph. 4:8–10).

Attention turns once again to the prophet's task (vs. 19). The Book of Revelation is written in response to command. It concerns not only the unfolding of the future, but also the interpretation of present events: "what is" as well as "what is to take place hereafter." Christ interprets the seven stars and seven lampstands (vs. 20). The notion that nations, communities, or even individuals had guardian angels was not uncommon in the ancient world (cf. Tobit 5:21); so each church has its angel, who serves it as a medium of revelation or communication with the divine. The letters to the seven churches (chaps. 2 and 3) are then directed to them through these guardian angels.

The seven letters are no ordinary letters at all, but are as much supernatural in their source and delivery as the rest of the book. Nevertheless, they again show the author's concern, not only with heavenly things and things to come, but with the this-worldly life and problems of the churches. This concern is directed both toward the inner life of the church and toward its witness to a hostile world. Naturally, the two are related, for no church with chinks in its moral armor would be strong enough to stand before such a world and resist the demand that it worship the gods of that world.

The remainder of Revelation presents a jarring juxtaposition of the heavenly and the earthly, the historical or worldly and the eschatological. Chapters 4 and 5 picture the heavenly court. The seer describes the throne of God himself and the momentous events taking place there, particularly the designation of the Lamb who had been slain to open the scroll. The Lamb is, of course, Christ. The opening of six of these seals is described in chapter 6. Heavenly events and realities have their earthly counterparts and consequences. With the opening of the seals catastrophes break out across the earth. Then there follows an interlude (chap. 7). The first part (7:1–8) shows the gathering of the elect from the four corners of the earth and the latter (vss. 9–17) their appearance in heaven. At the beginning of chapter 8 we have the opening of the seventh seal—and silence. After about half an hour of silence, the sounding of the seven trumpets begins (chaps. 8 and 9; 11:15–19) with disasters erupting upon the earth.

Chapters 10–13 deal with contemporary events or those of the recent past. The prophet's own experience (chap. 10) is like that of the prophet Ezekiel (Ezekiel 2:8–3:3). Since Ezekiel's word of the Lord had to do with lamentations and woes, especially against Jerusalem (cf., e.g., Ezekiel 4:1 ff.), not surprisingly Revelation 11 reflects the devastation of that same city. The birth and persecution of the Messiah and of his church are envisioned in chapters 12 and 13. In chapter 12 the heavenly dimension of the conflict is paramount, whereas in 13 attention focuses on Rome, described under the apocalyptic symbol of the beast. The sounding of the seventh trumpet is delayed by intervening scenes, just as the opening of the seventh seal was delayed. The seventh and final stage of each sequence has a peculiar significance, for apparently it stands symbolically at the borderline between the apocalyptic and catastrophic dissolution of this world and the coming of God's kingdom. The events following upon the sounding of the trumpets recapitulate those following the opening of the seven seals. Yet there may also be a progression. After the seventh seal there is only silence, but after the seventh trumpet we get a preview of the glory that is to come (11:15–19).

From chapter 14 onward we no longer have apocalyptic interpretations of the immediate past or present. Again the seer has a vision of heaven (14:1–5), this time followed by a series of warnings from angels flying in heaven and the command that the heavenly Christ reap the harvest of the earth (14:14–20). Chapters 15 through 18 describe in appropriately symbolic terms the final upheavals to be wrought on earth by the outpouring of the bowls of divine wrath.

The seer's prophecy about the remainder of world history is completed with the outpouring of the seventh bowl of wrath and the destruction of Babylon, which is, of course, Rome (chaps. 17 and 18). Yet we can actually discern no clear distinction between world history as we understand it and the last days. John understands his own time to be the last days. He does not conceive the present as a period of secular history where everything is governed by natural, social, or psychological laws of cause and effect. There is for him no secular history, for all time is ultimately under the lordship of God.

Nevertheless, immense powers of evil, with otherworldly origins and dimensions (e.g., the beast, the dragon or serpent, who is called the Devil and Satan, 12:9), presently hold sway in the world. Their lordship is, however, ephemeral. God's wrath is directed against them and they are overthrown. But victory does not occur easily or without vast repercussions. Chaos and disaster break out upon earth as the power of God overwhelms the forces of evil. Even the advent of Christ, traditionally called the second coming, does not put an end to the struggle once and for all (chap. 19). After the thousand-year reign of Christ, the millennium (after the Latin word for thousand), there is still another outbreak of evil, led by Satan himself (chap. 20), before God finally brings everything into subjection (21:1–22:5). Yet the substance of the seer's message is not that the end is a long way off, but that the night is already far spent, the day is at hand (Rom. 13:12). The apocalyptic drama is underway and moves inexorably toward its conclusion. "Surely I am coming soon. Amen. Come, Lord Jesus!" (22:20).

Christians of John's day were willing to resist at the risk of their lives the demand that they worship the Roman emperor (13:1–15; cf. 18:24), the incarnation of worldly order and power, the epitome of a man's deification of himself. Why did they dare to do so? Such worship seems little more than a perfunctory gesture, although it was a significant token of subjection to the power and authority of this world. These Christians resisted because they believed in an authority that transcends this world, an authority revealed in the death of a man upon the cross and in his exaltation from the dead to God's own right hand. They refused to worship the deities of this world, preferring to obey God rather than men. The Book of Revelation shows that for many, if not most, of them this conviction and the refusal to fall down and worship the beast were set in the context of a lively future hope, not primarily for their own personal survival of physical death, but for the manifestation of God's authority and rule before all humanity. God's Christ and his saints were to be vindicated before the eyes of a skeptical and evil world.

Thus Revelation gives testimony to faith in the lordship of God over history. The author is convinced that the apparent confusion of events does in fact lead somewhere. It is not meaningless. Yet this meaning is not apparent in individual events, for it can only be grasped when history is viewed in its entirety—that is, from the standpoint of its expected end. Christ is the light by which all history is illuminated for John. The Old Testament provides the imagery by means of which he portrays the end. Of course, Revelation is not unprecedented in the New Testament in its interest in the final days. Already Paul's correspondence testifies to his conviction that the projected end provides the key to understanding the present. The various apocalyptic discourses of the Gospels (Mark 13

"The Vision of St. John the Divine" by the Spanish artist El Greco (1541–1614). (Courtesy of Metropolitan Museum of Art. Rogers Fund, 1956.)

parr.) disclose the existence of widespread early Christian concern about the end time, its signs and warnings. For the early church and the writers of the New Testament, faith meant not only looking upward to God and Christ, but backward to the manifestations of God's reality in the past and forward in expectation to his further and final revelations in the future. The look backward fixed first and foremost upon Jesus of Nazareth, a real historical person whose mission and message inaugurated the expected kingdom of God. The look forward anticipated the end of history as it was known and the completion of God's kingdom with the return of Christ. All the while the Christian lived by faith in the reality of God's presence through the Spirit in the church.

In this chapter we have studied texts from seven different books. Two (Eph. 2:11–22; I Tim. 4:1–16) are attributed to the Apostle Paul. The Pauline authorship of Ephesians is still defended by a number of scholars, but few would any longer regard the Pastorals as coming directly from Paul himself. Both Ephesians and Timothy, however, represent typically Pauline concerns about the church. The passage from Ephesians deals with the problem and the theological reality of the unity of the church. That from I Timothy grapples with the presence of erroneous teaching and with the means of combatting it and keeping it in check, namely, an ordained ministry commissioned with the responsibility for right teaching and good order. Paul himself does not know an ordained ministry, but recognizes the necessity of strong leadership. Moreover, he exercises such leadership as an apostle. There is a sense in which I Timothy and the other Pastorals conceive of that Pauline leadership as having now been passed on to a succeeding generation.

The Book of James (2:14–26) treats another Pauline issue, the relationship of faith and works. Referring to the same Genesis passage which Paul quotes (15:6), James argues that both faith and works, not faith alone, make a person acceptable to God. James' position can be understood as a rejection of Paul, although it is uncertain that the author knew the Pauline letters. Certainly he must have somehow been acquainted with Paulinism, if only in an attenuated form. However that may be, James faces a genuine question of church life, the relationship between belief and action, faith and works. How does one's religious conviction affect one's conduct? Christianity is fundamentally committed to the view that it does, or should. Yet discrepancy between profession and performance was evident from the beginning as Paul's own letters make clear. In I Peter (2:11–25) the problem is attacked by holding before the believers' eyes the example of Jesus himself, particularly his acceptance of suffering and death. This sort of exhortation and appeal to Jesus apparently anticipates persecution from without, that is the prospect of Christians facing suffering on account of their faith.

Persecution and the possibility of further suffering seems also to be reflected in Hebrews (10:32–39; 12:4). In the text we examined (4:14–5:10) Jesus is presented as the Son of God, the "great high priest who has passed through the heavens." At the outset nothing could seem further removed from the situation of the readers. Yet this Jesus has "learned obedience through what he suffered" (5:8), a clear reference to his agony in Gethsemane. Perhaps more than any epistle in the New Testament, Hebrews explicitly and directly relates the experience, origin, and especially the suffering of Jesus to the life of the believer.

Throughout most of these books we have observed, either in the foreground or the background, a sense of the importance of right teaching and an abhorrence of heresy or error. Emphasis on right teaching, whether doctrinal or ethical, dominates I John. In Chapter 4 there is a noticeable alternation between exhortations to test the spirits and to adhere to the right confession and admonitions to love. Clearly those who adhere to the confession that Jesus is the Christ (i.e., the Christ is that real human being) will also love their fellow Christians. In the view of ancient Christian writers orthodoxy in confession is accompanied by ethical uprightness and love, and those who fall into error become morally corrupt.

Most of the books we have treated are concerned with the faith, community life, and witness of the church in the world, the maintenance of the church as institution. That is perfectly normal and what we might expect at this point in the history of early Christianity. There is one book, however, that cannot be accurately or fully described in such terms. It is, of course, the Revelation to John. While the author of Revelation was certainly not unmindful of contemporary issues facing the church, his eye was steadfastly fixed upon the future, particularly that day when God would make all things new (21:5). Although only Revelation in the New Testament is a thoroughly apocalyptic book, the apocalyptic perspective and the orientation toward the future that characterizes it are found throughout the New Testament, and especially in the Synoptic Gospels and in Paul. Christianity began in an atmosphere of apocalyptic excitement, to which it contributed, and throughout the New Testament period was characterized by an attitude of expectancy and hope. Indeed, as we saw already in Paul's earliest letters, nurturing such hopes and maintaining discipline and a semblance of normal life in the midst of those hopes was a problem for the early church (I Thess. 4:13–5:22). Toward the end of the century Christians still lived between the limitations and grim necessities of today and the hope of glory tomorrow. Such tension gave their life its distinctive, urgent character.

Suggestions for Further Reading

The development of the church, particularly its ministry, during the period of the later letters is dealt with by B. H. Streeter, *The Primitive Church* (London: Macmillan, 1929). E. Schweizer has analyzed the understanding of the structure of the church explicit or implicit in the various New Testament books; his *Church Order in the New Testament* (Naperville, Ill.: Allenson, 1961) will be particularly helpful for the later New Testament books. A good summary of these books and their meaning is found in J. C. Beker, *The Church Faces the World* (Philadelphia: Westminster, 1960).

Ephesians. Perhaps the best commentary on the English text is C. L. Mitton, *Ephesians* (London: Oliphants, 1976), who adopts in general the theory of E. J. Goodspeed, *The Meaning of Ephesians* (Chicago: University of Chicago Press, 1933), regarding the letter's post-Pauline origin; cf. Mitton, *The Epistle to the Ephesians: Its Authorship, Origin, and Purpose* (Oxford: Clarendon, 1951). The position of Goodspeed on the origin of Ephesians is developed by J. Knox, *Philemon Among the Letters of Paul,* rev. ed. (Nashville, Tenn.: Abingdon, 1959). A reliable shorter commentary is found in J. L. Houlden, *Paul's Letters from Prison* (Philadelphia: Westminster, 1970), pp. 233–341.

Pastorals. The most recent and thorough commentary is M. Dibelius, rev. by H. Conzelmann, *The Pastoral Epistles,* trans. P. Buttolph and A. Yarbro (Philadelphia: Fortress, 1972); technical, but as in all Hermeneia series commentaries the Greek is translated. A shorter and less technical commentary is C. K. Barrett, *The Pastoral Epistles* (Oxford: Clarendon, 1963). P. N. Harrison, *The Problem of the Pastoral Epistles* (Oxford: Humphrey Milford, 1921), demonstrates why the Pastorals in their present form can scarcely be considered the writings of Paul.

James. Martin Dibelius, rev. by H. Greeven, *James,* trans. M. A. Williams (Philadelphia: Fortress, 1976), is a classic commentary dating from 1920 but revised as recently as 1964 before being translated for the Hermeneia series. A shorter, less technical commentary is now available: S. Laws, *The Epistle of James* (San Francisco: Harper & Row, 1981).

I Peter, II Peter, Jude. E. Best, *I Peter* (London: Oliphants, 1971), is a helpful and reliable commentary, as is J. N. D. Kelly, *A Commentary on the Epistles of Peter and Jude* (New York: Harper & Row, 1969). On Peter himself, see R. E. Brown, K. P. Donfried, and J. Reumann, *Peter in the New Testament* (Minneapolis and New York: Augsburg and Paulist Press, 1973).

Hebrews. F. F. Bruce, *The Epistle to the Hebrews* (Grand Rapids, Mich.: Eerdmans, 1964) is perhaps the most extensive recent commentary on the English text of Hebrews. Note also the commentaries of H. Montefiore, *A Commentary on the Epistle to the Hebrews* (New York: Harper & Row, 1964), and of J. Héring, *The Epistle to the Hebrews,* trans. A. W. Heathcote and P. J. Allcock (London: Epworth, 1970). G. Hughes, *Hebrews and Hermeneutics* (New York: Cambridge University Press, 1979), sets Hebrews in the context of a discussion of significant theological issues.

The Johannine Letters. Representative recent commentaries are those of R. Bultmann, *The Johannine Epistles,* trans. R. Funk et al. (Philadelphia: Fortress, 1973), and J. L. Houlden, *The Johannine Epistles* (New York: Harper & Row, 1973). The commentary of C. H. Dodd, *The Johannine Epistles* (London: Hodder & Stoughton, 1946), still merits attention. R. E. Brown will soon publish a commentary in the Anchor Bible series.

The Revelation to John. Old, but extensive and useful, is the commentary of I. T. Beckwith, *The Apocalypse of John* (New York: Macmillan, 1922; reissued by Baker Book House). More recent commentaries include G. B. Caird, *A Commentary on the Revelation of St. John the Divine* (New York: Harper & Row, 1966), and G. R. Beasley-Murray, *The Book of Revelation* (London: Oliphants, 1974). Note also P. S. Minear, *I Saw a New Earth: An Introduction to the Visions of the Apocalypse* (Washington: Corpus Books, 1968). On apocalyptic literature see D. S. Russell, *The Method and Message of Jewish Apocalyptic: 200* B.C.–A.D. *100* (Philadelphia: Westminster, 1964).

CHAPTER ELEVEN

Literature and Community: The New Testament and Early Christianity

The Emergence of Early Christianity
  The Primitive Church and Jesus
    The Crucifixion of Jesus
    The Expectation of His Return
    The Preservation of Jesus' Teaching
    The Recounting of His Miracles
  The Mission and Expansion of Christianity

The Preaching of the Gospel
The Success of the Gospel
Christianity's Identity
  The Distinction of Orthodoxy and Heresy
  Ordination, Creeds, Scripture
  The Significance and Shape of the Canon

The New Testament is a book, or a collection of books. To study the New Testament is, as we have seen, to endeavor to understand these books individually and as a whole. New Testament study is then the study of literature, a body of ancient religious literature. Therefore, such study has certain significant similarities, or analogies, to the study of any such material.

The study of literature is usually impoverished if history is ignored. One may watch or study Shakespeare without knowledge of Elizabethan England and be fascinated, amused, and moved. Yet

"Christ in Glory," a tapestry in the Coventry Cathedral, England, designed by Graham Sutherland. It is 78 feet long, 38 feet wide, and weighs nearly a ton. (Courtesy of Thompson Art Reference Bureau.)

one's understanding and appreciation will be greatly enhanced by knowledge of the period from which the plays stem. The same is true for the Bible in general and the New Testament in particular. Thus, this book began with a chapter about the world, the historical circumstances, of the New Testament. It seems fitting to end with some description of the relatively small world of the early Christian community in which the New Testament writings and, ultimately, the collection of New Testament books took shape. In the middle there is another historical chapter, on Jesus. The necessity of such a chapter signifies something distinctive about New Testament study.

The desire to know about Jesus is inspired by something other than sheer antiquarian interest. Although historical knowledge may illumine Shakespeare's plays, it makes little difference for the appreciation of Shakespeare whether or not his characters ever actually existed, though many of them did. For vitally interested readers of the New Testament, however, that sort of historical question is more than a matter of academic interest. The New Testament writers believe and claim that in Jesus and among the events and disciples clustered about him God was active and making himself known. Moreover, they invite and in some cases seem even to compel the reader to decide about their claim. It should be emphasized that this claim extends to the history following the active ministry of Jesus as well as to that ministry itself. If we had reason to ask what really happened with Jesus, we have equal reason to ask about what happened with the early church.

Although the claims of the New Testament itself motivate historical investigation of Jesus and the early Christian church, such an investigation can scarcely do justice to the Christian claims, to prove or disprove them. One could at most show with a high degree of probability that the Gospels deal with real events, such as the crucifixion of a messianic pretender—a man at least believed by his disciples to be the Messiah of Israel. Similarly, one could show from the Book of Acts and Paul's letters that there existed after his death communities of believers convinced that he had risen from the dead and would soon return to earth. Indeed, the last book of the New Testament—Revelation—is pervaded by the hope and expectation that Jesus would soon return and the kingdoms of this world would become the kingdoms of our Lord and of his Christ (Rev. 11:15).

Manifestly, that expectation was directed to Jesus' imminent return (Rev. 22:10, 12, 20; cf. I Thess. 4:15; I Cor. 16:22; Rom. 13:11–12; Mark 9:1; Matt. 10:23), not an eventual return after two or three thousand years. Needless to say, the expectation of a vindication of Jesus before the entire world (Rev. 1:7) has not occurred. Indeed, the fact that it was perceived to be delayed became a problem for the early church (II Pet. 3:3–10; cf. John 21:20–23). But Paul had already laid the groundwork for addressing it with his conviction that the event decisive for salvation had already occurred. John built upon that conviction (see, e.g. 11:24–25; 14:22). Probably neither expected the world to continue for long, just as many today look for some imminent apocalypse, whether nuclear, environmental, or purely religious. Yet they and others established the theological basis for the continuation of Christianity through history, whether for a century or millennia.

The apocalyptic scaffolding of that early Christian and New Testament depiction of the world and of history as the arena of God's activity has long since proven itself treacherously unstable, as many times as it has been shored up. Nevertheless, the conviction that it expresses, namely, that God gives history meaning and purpose, is not necessarily tied to the scaffolding. That conviction outlived the disappointment of early apocalyptic expectation and has continued to outlive subsequent delays and disillusionments. Other factors and other modes of expectation, as well as a sense of fulfillment, nourished the church.

We turn now to examine the early church to understand better the realities or forces that undergirded and enhanced its life. As we shall see, it is difficult to give a continuous and coherent account of that history. The sources do not permit it. Certainly to know the history would not necessarily convince the disinterested observer that God was active in it. One could always conclude that the early Christians were mistaken or deluded. Yet it belongs to the nature of the New Testament, as well as to the character of Christian faith, that the serious student should be concerned with its history.

The Emergence of Early Christianity

Basically, the order of the New Testament books does not mislead us about early Christian history, which was much more complex than at first appears. But the earliest Christians had little interest in recording history, in part because of the expectation of its early end. The Book of Acts, for example, was in all probability written a half-century or more after the crucifixion of Jesus and a quarter of a century after the death of Paul. Likewise, the Gospels were not written down until the original eyewitnesses and apostles had virtually died out. This is certainly true of Luke (1:1–3), and in all probability also of Matthew. John is explicitly traced to one of the last remaining disciples of Jesus (21:23–24), but whether he wrote the Gospel in its present form remains questionable. Mark, the earliest Gospel, was not written by one of the twelve, although ancient church tradition links the evangelist with Peter and implies that it was written either toward the end of his career or soon after his death. The earliest Christian writings of which we have any knowledge were letters written out of the pressing demands of the moment. Indeed, when the Gospels appeared, they were written primarily for religious, theological, inspirational, and instructional purposes. That they were about a real, historical person was certainly important, and they are valuable as historical sources. Nevertheless, they were not written to record history for the sake of history. Perhaps Luke comes closest to matching the purpose or intention of an ancient, if not a modern, historian. Significantly, it was Luke who in Acts first wrote for posterity about the life of the early church. It is quite clear, as we have seen, that Luke intended to describe an historical movement, namely, the progress of the gospel across the known world, from Jerusalem to Rome. His purpose, while historical, was charged with a theological motivation.

Having read Acts, we know Luke's version of the history of the early church. As we have already noticed, however, some things were occurring that Luke does not describe or even mention, and some things that he does mention create as many problems for the historian as they solve. Luke's portrayal of the gospel's progress fixes primarily upon the missionary work of Paul. Where Paul goes the gospel goes. We do not learn, however, how Christianity reached Rome or Egypt, although it got there prior to and apart from Paul's efforts. We do not learn from Acts about the transmission and preservation of tradition about Jesus, although his Gospel attests to its existence. (Luke does, however, portray the apostles as referring to Jesus' ministry in their missionary preaching.) We gain from Acts little sense of the lively expectation of Jesus' return and the coming of God's kingdom that we find in the Gospels and Paul's letters.

Luke gives in Acts a great deal of data about Paul's missionary work that makes contact with what we can glean from Paul's letters. Obviously, the information found in Acts is not fabricated. For example, with the exception of Colossae, all the churches to which Paul's extant letters are addressed figure in the Acts narrative, and Paul himself indicates that he has not visited Colossae (2:1). Positive correlations can sometimes be made between the Acts narrative and Paul's letters (see pp. 275–277). On the other hand, there are also difficulties. Although much of what Paul says in Galatians 1 and 2 about his second visit to Jerusalem corresponds to the narrative of the Jerusalem Council in Acts 15, there are also differences. For example, the Jerusalem Council is Paul's *third* visit to Jerusalem according to Acts, not his second (Gal. 1:20). That complete tranquility on the issue of Gentile Christians did not, as Acts implies, result from the council is already clear in Galatians 2:11–21. Despite these problems, in Acts as well as the Pauline letters we have important sources for understanding earliest Christianity, but they must be used with critical care.

For the latter part of the first century, or of the New Testament period, valuable information can be gleaned from Ephesians, the Pastoral and Catholic Epistles and from Revelation, as well as from I Clement of the so-called Apostolic Fathers (see the Glossary). Of course, it is still arguable that certain of these letters, namely, Ephesians, James, and I Peter are the work of the apostolic authors to whom they are ascribed. Hebrews is sometimes taken to be earlier than the Roman war (66–70), although it cannot any longer be ascribed to Paul. But at the least, the Pastorals, the Johannine Epistles,

II Peter, Jude, and Revelation, along with I Clement, inform us about conditions in the churches as the first century drew to a close. They are second-generation, or later, documents. As we have seen (Chapter 10), they reflect just such situations and problems as are known to have existed. They are concerned with church order, organization, discipline, and leadership, and also with the appearance of what seems to them to be obviously erroneous and dangerous teaching— often accompanied by moral degradation. Strong church leadership and strict adherence to firm doctrinal and moral standards are enjoined in the face of such aberrations.

The question of whether Christians must observe the Jewish ceremonial law and males be circumcised is apparently settled: they need not. Yet the Old Testament and its Decalogue continue to carry authority. The relationship of Christianity to Judaism is still an issue, but the separation of church and synagogue (cf. John 9:22; 12:42) seems to have taken place. The danger of persecution by the Roman state is by now increasing. I Peter, Hebrews, and Revelation, especially, are concerned with this problem and what the Christians' attitude toward it should be. Both persecution and the problem of heresy continued to occupy the church far beyond the New Testament period, as did the question of the relationship of Christianity and Judaism.

Just such problems or situations as these are not foreign to the Gospels, most of which were written nearer the end than the middle of the first century. That the Gospels are primary sources for the history of the church of their times and only secondary sources for Jesus' own ministry may be an overstatement. Yet the very existence of the Gospels is unthinkable apart from the interests of the churches that produced them. Their interests were not completely different from those of Jesus and the earliest apostles, but neither were they identical. The impact of Jesus upon subsequent generations has been filtered mainly through the New Testament, especially the Gospels. It was transmitted initially through those followers who recalled his words and ministry and spoke of them to others. In doing so they exercised a significant and selective role in shaping the tradition and, ultimately, the Gospels. Of course, in selecting, editing, and arranging such tradition the evangelists further influenced and directed the historic impact of Jesus.

Having studied the Gospels and other documents of the developing Christian movement, it will now be useful to consider how in the life of the church the impact of Jesus himself maintained itself and grew, even before the Gospels were written. We shall then examine the reasons for the missionary thrust and success of early Christianity and the ways in which it established its own identity in the New Testament period and thereafter. The continuing need for self-definition was an important factor in the development of the New Testament as we know it.

A Byzantine medallion with Christ enamelled on gold (eleventh century). (Courtesy of Metropolitan Museum of Art. Gift of J. Pierpont Morgan, 1917.)

THE PRIMITIVE CHURCH AND JESUS [1]

The execution of Jesus was the pivotal point in the transition from the movement he led among Palestinian Jews to the community we know as the Christian church. Whether or in what sense Jesus founded the church is a difficult and debated question. We do know that the church came into being in the aftermath of his ministry and death, and in some sense as its result. Closely related to his death was the conviction that he had risen from the dead and would soon return to reign in power. Probably belief in Jesus' resurrection and his glorious return and rule were at first closely related, although they soon became separate articles of belief, as they are in the historic Apostles' Creed. This relationship explains the question of the disciples to the risen Jesus: "Will you at this time restore the kingdom to Israel?" (Acts 1:6). Apparently the early Christians also did not clearly distinguish between Christ's resurrection and exaltation to heaven, as the very early confessions and hymns of the New Testament show (e.g., Acts 2:24 ff.; Rom. 1:4; I Tim. 3:16; I Pet. 3:18 ff.). Be that as it may, the importance attached to Jesus' death and the consequent belief in his resurrection, exaltation and return are unmistakable in the New Testament. Of course, Jesus himself was a memorable and impressive person. He obviously said and did things that elicited both a following and an opposition. At least this much is clear from the Gospel accounts. Nevertheless, Christianity as a movement, as a gospel (i.e. a message of good news), began with the death of Jesus rather than his historic life.

Before undertaking a more careful examination of the missionary expansion of the early church, we shall consider briefly the various aspects of Jesus' career and their impact upon the people who

---

[1] For the typology followed in this section we are indebted to H. Koester, "One Jesus and Four Primitive Gospels," in *Trajectories Through Early Christianity*, by James M. Robinson and Helmut Koester (Philadelphia: Fortress, 1971), pp. 114–158.

believed in him. The point is to develop a conception of the various ways in which a community grew up around the figure of the crucified and risen Jesus, a community originally consisting of Jesus' disciples, but very quickly expanding to include others. For it was out of this community and its perceptions of Jesus that the church developed.

THE CRUCIFIXION OF JESUS

Jesus was executed by the Romans during or just before the annual Jewish Passover feast. The exact date is uncertain, although it was probably A.D. 30 or before.[2] Jewish authorities probably played a role in the arrest and trial of Jesus, as the Gospels allege, although the Christian sources show a tendency, which must be viewed critically, to shift responsibility from the Romans to the Jews. Even though the Gospels state that Jesus had foreknowledge of his impending death and Christian belief takes it for granted that he willingly consented to die, the execution of their leader obviously took his disciples by surprise and left them in disarray (Mark 14:27). The famed inscription on the cross ("The King of the Jews," Mark 15:26) indicates that Jesus was condemned and died as a messianic pretender. Yet his fate contrasted sharply to normal expectations concerning a king (I Cor. 1:23). Other messianic pretenders met similar fates (Acts 5:35–39; cf. 21:38) and did not gain the recognition to which they aspired. Why should Jesus differ from them? Why should his followers continue—or begin—to insist that he was the Messiah or Christ? The most obvious answer, right as far as it goes, is that they believed him to have been raised by God from the dead and set at his own right hand (Acts 2:24 ff.; I Cor. 15:4). Once this is granted, however, further problems arise. Why should belief in a resurrection mean that the resurrected one was the Messiah? Probably because that claim had previously been made, or at least entertained by the disciples. Moreover, even a report of his resurrection, which certainly was not universally believed, did not explain the tragic fate of Jesus as the Messiah, the one destined to rule over an earthly kingdom of Israel.

For those followers who believed in Jesus' resurrection the tragic implications of the crucifixion were overcome. But there remained the task of convincing others that the ignominious fate that he had suffered did not really contradict the traditions and expectations of Israel's Messiah. To accomplish this task believers in Jesus turned

[2]The actual dates of the life of Jesus do not correspond to the B.C.–A.D. scheme of dating that we commonly use. This scheme, according to which our era begins with the year of Jesus' birth, was introduced in the sixth century by a monk named Dionysius Exiguus. Unfortunately, the date of Jesus' birth was incorrectly calculated, if as both Matthew (2:1) and Luke (1:5) indicate, Jesus was born before Herod's death (4 B.C.).

to the scriptures. Thus the earliest references to Jesus' death were often accompanied not only by the proclamation of his resurrection but also by the assertion (I Cor. 15:3) and a demonstration (Luke 24:25–27; Acts 2:24 ff.) that he had died "according to the Scriptures." That is, his death was in accord with the will of God as revealed in the Bible.[3] Thus the earliest Christians doubtless had to explain Jesus' crucifixion because it was a problem, a "stumbling block," as Paul says, to other Jews. Even the proclamation of the resurrection could not be made credible until the stigma of the cross was removed or explained (Gal. 3:13; II Cor. 5:21). It is surely significant that the passion narratives of the Gospels are studded with Old Testament quotations and allusions. Their fundamental purpose was to expound, to whatever audience, the importance and necessity of Jesus' death as the accomplishment of God's will. Doubtless such references were found already in the preaching, teaching, and controversies of the primitive church.

For many of the earliest believers, however, the cross was not only a liability to be explained. It was seen as the very focal point and event of salvation, the vehicle of God's redemption. This understanding of the cross as in some important way a redemptive event was a part of the confessional tradition that Paul had received ("He died for our sins according to the scriptures," I Cor. 15:3; cf. Rom. 4:25 and Heb. 13:20), and it lies at the heart of the ancient words of institution of the Lord's Supper (I Cor. 11:23–26; cf. Mark 14:22–25). From the beginning, or very near it, Jesus' death on the cross has been an important element of Christian preaching and liturgy, as, for example, in Paul's view of baptism (Rom. 6:3–11) and the Lord's Supper (I Cor. 11:17–34). It is therefore a recurring motif in the New Testament, in the Pauline letters particularly, but also in the Gospels, where the relative length of the narration of Jesus' final week in Jerusalem indicates its importance.[4]

For at least the last half-century many New Testament scholars have regarded it as virtually certain that the Gospels' passion narratives were based upon earlier traditions or sources. The discipline of form criticism was founded on the conviction that the shape and nature of the Gospel materials were related directly to the interests, social functions, and character of the Christian communities. Inasmuch as the prominence of Jesus' death in early Christian preaching and liturgy was apparent from other sources, it was deemed nat-

---

[3] On the early use of the scriptures to explain Jesus' death, see Barnabas Lindars, *New Testament Apologetic: The Doctrinal Significance of the Old Testament Quotations* (Philadelphia: Westminster, 1961), pp. 75–137.

[4] The centrality of the crucifixion and resurrection in the development of early Christian preaching and literature was emphasized by C. H. Dodd, *The Apostolic Preaching and Its Developments* (New York: Harper & Row, 1951), who popularized the word *kerygma* as a technical term for the proclamation of the gospel.

ural to suppose that some recitation of the narrative of Jesus' death
became fixed in the tradition long before the evangelists wrote. This
would have been, in effect, a narrative of God's saving act, a necessary prolegomenon to the announcement of the resurrection. Probably one or more accounts of the passion were, in fact, put in writing
prior to the composition of the Gospels. If so, this would explain the
existence of two parallel narratives of the passion in Mark and John,
which often differ unaccountably, but are in the main similar. Otherwise, it must be maintained that John knew Mark, a view which,
although oftentimes held by scholars, has become difficult to defend.

THE EXPECTATION OF HIS RETURN

Both Paul (e.g., I Cor. 15) and the Synoptic Gospels (e.g., Mark
13), as well as the Book of Revelation, mirror the early Christians'
expectation that the risen Jesus would soon return in glory to reveal
his true identity, hold judgment, and inaugurate the kingdom of
God. This return is often spoken of as the *parousia* (Greek for "appearance"). Understandably, therefore, many Christians regarded the
present as only an interim, a time of waiting or preparation for the
consummation. This expectation is expressed in the phrase, apparently common in early Christian worship, "Our Lord, come!" (I Cor.
16:22; cf. Rev. 22:20).

Although this apocalyptic expectation was clearly important to
many, if not most, of the first generation of Christians, remarkably
it did not become a part of the earliest Christian confessions, as far
as can be judged from the New Testament.[5] Still, apocalyptic traditions began to grow, perhaps as soon as it was apparent that the end
was somewhat delayed in coming, and perhaps in part to explain the
delay. Embryonic forms of such traditions are found in I Thessalonians 4:15–18; I Corinthians 15:23 ff.; and II Thessalonians 2:3–12.
A more developed example is Mark 13,[6] called the Little Apocalypse
because of its similarity to the Apocalypse of John (Revelation) and
the parallel material in Matthew and Luke.

Doubtless Jesus himself spoke of impending events, but the
growth of apocalyptic tradition in early Christianity was largely the
work of Christian prophets or seers. Paul speaks of prophets and
ranks them second only to apostles (I Cor. 12:28). The best known
Christian prophet is John of Patmos, the author of the Book of Rev-

[5]H. Conzelmann, "On the Analysis of the Confessional Formula in I Corinthians 15:3–5," *Interpretation*, 20 (1966), 23, states flatly, "No old confessional formula
speaks of the parousia."

[6]See Lars Hartman, *Prophecy Interpreted: The Formation of Some Jewish Apocalyptic Texts and of the Eschatological Discourse Mark 13 par.* (Lund: Gleerup,
1966), esp. pp. 181 ff. on the relation of I Thess. 4:13–18 to Mark 13, and pp. 195 ff.
on the relation of II Thess. 2:1–17 to the Markan apocalypse.

elation. It is noteworthy that he sometimes speaks in the name of Jesus himself (esp. in chap. 1–3). Probably prophets regularly spoke in the name of Jesus, *ex ore Christi* ("out of the mouth of Christ"). The synoptic apocalypses, although they are based upon some genuine words of Jesus, are largely the work of such prophets, and the warnings against false prophets in these very discourses (Mark 13:22; Matt. 24:11) attest their origin among the "true" prophets. The necessity for criteria to test early Christian prophets is recognized in I John 4:1–3, as well as in the writings of the Apostolic Fathers (see the Didache XI, 7–XIII, 7). The work of Christian prophets was not limited to apocalyptic utterances, but they originated and thrived in the atmosphere of eager expectancy that pervaded early Christianity.

That Paul also expected the consummation of history in the near future can scarcely be doubted in view of his positive statements and the way he takes up apocalyptic materials or traditions. Moreover, scattered throughout the Gospels are sayings of Jesus which anticipate the end, including a distinct group in which he speaks of the coming of the Son of Man (e.g., Mark 8:38), by which Christians have assumed he meant his own return. To what extent the latter sayings express Jesus' own viewpoint is debatable. It is clear, however, that they would have never been preserved (or formulated) by Christians had they not themselves lived in a state of eschatological expectation. More likely than not this expectancy was rooted in Jesus' own attitude.

The antiquity of the apocalyptic, eschatological material is confirmed by the fact that it is to a considerable extent preserved in documents for which the expectation of the imminent return of Jesus had already become a problem. Of course, Christians could at once believe in the saving efficacy of the cross of Jesus and in his imminent return, as the example of Paul shows. Yet faith in the crucifixion as salvation event tends to locate deliverance initially in the past, or perhaps the present, whereas the eschatological expectation located final deliverance in the future. We are at least dealing with two separate moments of early Christian experience which found different modes of expression and tended to be characteristic of different groups of Christians in the earliest period.

THE PRESERVATION OF JESUS' TEACHING

The earliest extant documents of Christianity, Paul's letters, contain surprisingly little teaching which Paul attributes to Jesus himself. From this it might be inferred that Paul worked at a time, or in places, where no extensive tradition or body of Jesus' sayings was known or used. Yet Paul does on occasion cite a word of Jesus (I Cor. 7:10; 9:14; 11:23–26), so the practice of preserving and referring to Jesus' own words cannot have been unknown to him. Still, as we have seen, the focus of Paul's preaching and teaching seems to be elsewhere, pre-eminently upon the meaning of the crucifixion and resurrection.

Aside from Paul's own occasional example, there are stronger indications that Jesus' sayings, his teachings, were preserved and transmitted among his followers. All the Gospels, including John, portray Jesus as a teacher, a portrayal that is scarcely a fabrication. Moreover, they contain evidence of the existence of the teaching material in earlier, pre-Gospel, forms. The Gospel of Matthew's famous Sermon on the Mount (chaps. 5–7) is paralleled in Luke by a Sermon on the Plain (6:20–49), which, although much shorter, is obviously an alternative, probably earlier, recension of much of the same material. Therefore, the Sermon on the Mount seems to be neither a single utterance of Jesus nor a composition of Matthew. Rather, it is based upon a traditional collection of Jesus' sayings, which Matthew has doubtless augmented. Traces of similar sayings of Jesus may be found, for example, in the letter of James. But the most impressive evidence for collections of Jesus' sayings is the parallel materials of Matthew and Luke, of which the Sermon on the Mount (or Plain) is only a small part. This parallel material was scarcely copied from one Gospel by the author of the other,[7] but was drawn by both from the same or a similar source, which was in all likelihood a collection of Jesus' sayings without any narrative structure or framework, called by scholars the Q source. A similar collection of Jesus' sayings, the apocryphal Gospel of Thomas, has now been found among the Coptic Gnostic manuscripts uncovered at Nag Hammadi in upper Egypt.[8]

Moreover, the shape of certain narratives in the Gospels suggests that they functioned primarily to preserve a saying of Jesus. Also, smaller complexes (groups) of sayings in the Gospels may have once circulated as separate units before having been incorporated into the Gospel. Probably some ancient and genuine materials found their way into Gospels, such as the Gospel of the Hebrews or the Gospel of the Egyptians, which are known to us from early Christian writers but otherwise lost. Perhaps eventually copies of some of these long-lost Gospels will, like the Gospel of Thomas, become known again.

The evidence of the collection, preservation, and transmission of Jesus' sayings, whether in oral or written form, shows that some

---

[7]For the commonly accepted solution of the problem of Synoptic relationships, see pp. 62–64 of this book.

[8]On the formal type or *Gattung* of the sayings collection, see James M. Robinson, "Logoi Sophon: On the Gattung of Q," in *Trajectories Through Early Christianity*, pp. 71–113. A full-scale treatment of the theology of Q is now available in English: Richard A. Edwards, *A Theology of Q: Eschatology, Prophesy, and Wisdom* (Philadelphia: Fortress, 1976).

The Roman Forum with the Arch of Titus and the Colosseum in the background. Just to the left of this picture is the site of Mamertine Prison where tradition asserts that Paul and Peter were prisoners. (Courtesy of Robert Spivey.)

common sense. Yet it can be shown to be factual, at least in some cases. Furthermore, it bears a relationship to what obviously occurred among early Christians.[10] The continuing failure of the parousia did not lead to the dissolution of early Christianity, as might have been expected. Instead, the churches continued to make converts, indeed more and more converts the longer the parousia was delayed. Probably the belief of Luke (Acts 1:7–8) and even Paul (cf. Rom. 11:25), that the parousia was delayed in order for converts to be made, was widely held. Yet it does not necessarily cancel out or contradict the dissonance theory; rather it tends to confirm it.

THE SUCCESS OF THE GOSPEL

As we have seen, the New Testament contains the documents of a movement that is obviously succeeding. Of the religions of that period and place, only Judaism and Christianity survive. In view of the Roman persecution which the church faced until the fourth century, and which Judaism has endured both before and since, it is remarkable that either has survived from antiquity. Even before

---

[10] See John C. Gager, *Kingdom and Community: The Social World of Early Christianity* (Englewood Cliffs, N.J.: Prentice-Hall, 1975), pp. 34–49.

Christianity became the official and dominant religion of the Roman Empire under the Emperor Constantine, it flourished and grew rapidly. Can the reasons for this advance be understood and described? Most Christians have believed that the real reason was the providence and purpose of God, the work of the Holy Spirit, a factor that lies beyond the purview and grasp of a study such as this. But there are other causes that are easier to isolate and measure.

Exclusiveness. Quite possibly the exclusiveness and seeming intolerance with which Christianity (and Judaism) insisted upon total and individual allegiance was a factor that abetted survival and health. To many people, modern and ancient, this attitude seems unnecessarily harsh. It is entirely clear from later as well as New Testament sources, however, that Christians were anything but tolerant of pagan religion, which they regarded as pernicious, standing in the way of the truth, and immoral.

In an age when people tended to divide or combine religious allegiance and when religions themselves were syncretistic (i.e., tending to borrow from one another), Christianity and Judaism testified to their seriousness and self-confidence by expecting the complete and undivided devotion of their followers. To be sure, there were defections from both, and strong influences from surrounding culture and religions left neither unaffected, but neither religion had any doubts about its identity and distinctiveness vis-à-vis a pagan[11] world. The only point at which this sense of identity became blurred was in their interrelation. The question of whether Christianity and Judaism were mutually incompatible was debated during the first Christian century and for some time thereafter.

Hope. Along with its sense of exclusiveness early Christianity embodied and offered to men and women a profound and pervasive hope. Alongside the hope for Jesus' return and the establishment of God's kingdom there was a trust and confidence in the individual's destiny with which each Christian seems to have been imbued. The prospect of death is depressing, particularly when death implies isolation, meaninglessness, nothingness, or futility. For the early Christians the consciousness of having overcome the prospect and present oppressive power of death was strong, and it is reflected particularly in Paul's letters and the Gospel of John. The idea that a person survives death in some manner was widely held by pagans as well as Jews. But Christians were distinguished by their belief that Jesus had already conquered death, as living witnesses to his resurrection

---

[11] The word *pagan* is not used in any pejorative sense, but with its proper meaning as a designation of anything lying outside the Jewish, Christian, or Islamic religious traditions.

could testify, and that by faith in him or through unity with him they too could overcome its power. Although the resurrection of Jesus in the New Testament meant more than that the believer would also conquer death, it meant at least that to most Christians.

Community Life. The early Christian hope was not simply a hope for individual survival after death, but was tied to the hope for the Kingdom of God, a corporate or collective concept. Moreover, it was a hope held in the context of a community of hope. The Protestant ethos, which stresses the individual's significance, fails to emphasize the corporate, societal aspects of Christian existence embedded in the New Testament. Modern Old Testament scholarship has emphasized the fact that in ancient Israel the community as well as the individual was thought of as having characteristics of personhood.[12] The same is true of the early church. Paul uses the image of the body, an organic unity, to describe the Christian community (I Cor. 12). All the members are interrelated. This interrelationship or community was an extremely important element of the strength of primitive Christianity. Not coincidentally it found adherents among the lower classes and outcasts of society (I Cor. 1:25–31), who gained from their faith and participation in the church a sense of identity and belonging (cf. I Pet. 2:9 f.). Primitive Christianity, particularly in the Gentile world, was an urban religion. Doubtless countryfolk were not excluded, but the missionary preaching seems to have had its most notable success in cities. The Christian gospel and community met a fundamental, and in a sense, this-worldly need of people who felt alone and rejected among masses of their fellow human beings. There was more to be gained than hope for a better world tomorrow.

The existence of the church, of concrete communities, meant that some organization and regulation of life was necessary. Except for the early Jerusalem church, described in the first chapters of the Book of Acts, we do not hear of Christians living together in communes, although perhaps they sometimes did. Christians gathered at least weekly for worship, usually on Sunday (I Cor. 16:2; Col. 3:16) as is still the custom, although Jewish Christians probably continued to observe the sabbath. Doubtless they had considerable contact with one another and showed concern for each other during the week.

Although rules for communal living were usually not necessary,

[12] The classical exposition of this view may be found in H. Wheeler Robinson, *Corporate Personality in Ancient Israel* (Philadelphia: Fortress, 1964), a booklet containing two of Robinson's important articles. As many reservations as may have been entered against Robinson's concept of "corporate personality," his emphasis is a valid corrective of modern Western individualism as a presupposition of biblical interpretation.

the church had to be organized for worship, instruction, and the care of its ill or impoverished members (cf. James 5:13–18; I Tim. 5:3–5). Moreover, matters of conduct could not be left to chance or private taste. Jesus was an Israelite, recognizing the full authority of the law of God, as radically as he may have interpreted it. So were the first apostles, and so was Paul. From the beginning the people associated with Jesus had been attracted and directed by the moral attitude and demand which suffused his teaching and conduct. Whatever may be said of the relation of Jesus and the church, this attitude clearly carried over into the community which stemmed from him. This is nowhere clearer than in Paul, the apostle of Christian freedom. Although Paul stoutly maintained that the Jewish law by itself could not save a person from sin and death, he also insisted that freedom is not license (Gal. 5:13). Freedom cannot contradict the nature of the gospel itself. For the gospel is not the negation of God's law, but its fulfillment. Doubtless Paul goes out of his way to portray the sad state of pagan and Jewish morality in his own day (Rom. chaps. 1–3). We may doubt that he gives an entirely fair picture, yet in all probability a part of Christianity's attractiveness lay in the fact that it offered a refreshing alternative in a world where sordidness and degradation had grown tiresome to many people.

The intrinsically moral character of primitive Christianity manifests itself in a variety of ways in the New Testament. Unlike Paul's letters, the Gospels spell out the new life in Christ primarily by remembering and repeating the teaching of Jesus, which becomes a source book of Christian ethics, if not a new law. Paul, as well as later letter writers, sometimes resorts to stereotyped or set forms of moral exhortation, principally the expression of commonsense wisdom. The Pastoral Epistles (I and II Tim. and Titus) are full of this sort of ethical exhortation, which the author is intent on applying to the establishment of suitable standards for the Christian ministry.

That the early Christian churches worshiped as congregations is evident from the New Testament.[13] According to the opening chapters of the book of Acts the followers of Jesus worship in the Jerusalem temple as well as in private homes (2:46). Although this portrayal appears in a summary passage which Luke himself composed at a much later date, it is probably not inaccurate. Paul discusses the conduct of the Lord's Supper (I Cor. 11:17 ff.) and other aspects of worship (I Cor. 14) with his fellow Christians. The prominence of the Lord's Supper in Paul, as well as in the Synoptic Gospels, indicates that it was an important part of worship. Baptism was also practiced by the early Christians (Gal. 3:27; Rom. 6:1 ff.). In the

---

[13] The importance of worship for the development of the New Testament writings is underlined by C. F. D. Moule, *The Birth of the New Testament* (New York: Harper & Row, 1962), esp. pp. 11–32.

view of early Christians its practice was rooted in Jesus' own example and command, as was the Lord's Supper. It appears that these two were the most widespread and significant cultic acts performed among Christians. (Perhaps significantly, they are not called sacraments in the New Testament, nor are they grouped together as though they belonged in the same category.) From I Corinthians 14 and other New Testament passages it appears that worship also included prayer, prophecy or a sermon, speaking in tongues, the reading of scripture, and the singing of hymns. If Christian worship to some extent paralleled synagogue worship, this should not be surprising. In many instances Christian groups developed in or from a synagogue.

The Contribution of the Synagogue. It may seem unfair to Judaism to describe the Hellenistic synagogue as the conduit through which Christianity passed into the wider Greco-Roman world, for the synagogue existed in its own right and for its own purposes. But as we have already observed (pp. 51 ff.), the rapid spread of Christianity across the Roman Empire—and it was within the Roman Empire that it gained its most significant and permanent foothold—would hardly have been possible without the synagogue. The earliest Christians were Jews who claimed that Jesus was the Jewish Messiah, and the synagogue would have been the obvious place for them to expound their views. If Paul's habit of first going to the synagogue upon entering a new city corresponds to the theological program of Luke-Acts, as it does, it probably also conforms to the apostle's actual practice. John's Gospel seems to reflect an intense struggle between Christians and Jews over the messiahship of Jesus which originated in the synagogue as a controversy between Jews who believed Jesus was the Messiah and the majority who did not. The Epistle to the Hebrews contains the sort of exegetical skill that likely originated in Judaism. We do not know how the church of Rome began, but in all probability it developed from the Jewish community of that city. A similar origin for Alexandrian Christianity is not unlikely. However much the presence of the synagogue contributed to the growth of the church, the two nonetheless became a problem for one another. Doubtless the synagogue viewed the activity of the followers of Jesus with alarm, whereas Christians looked upon the rejection of their message by most Jews (cf. Rom. 9:1–5; 10:1–4) as a token of their obduracy, if not of divine displeasure. Thus the split that had been a possibility from the beginning became a reality within a very short time. The New Testament is for the most part the product of a church that has already separated from the synagogue, as deep as its roots may lie in it. But the imprint of that painful divorce is clearly discernible in many of the New Testament writings.

Christianity's Identity

Christianity's greatest difficulty in securing an identity naturally lay in its relation with Judaism. In some ways this relation is yet to reach a mutually satisfactory solution. Study of the New Testament leads to this problem time and again, and not only in the Pauline letters. For it was only partly—not entirely—the problem of whether Christians had to obey the law. The second century saw the relationship of Christianity to forms of pagan piety, particularly Gnosticism, also become an important issue. Doubtless the roots of this problem lay in the first century, although they are hard to trace with certainty. Already Paul faced a kind of religious enthusiasm among the Corinthians which he regarded as foreign and harmful to Christian faith and community. Other, perhaps related, phenomena appear in Colossians, the Pastorals, and the Johannine Epistles, whereas in the letters to the seven churches (Rev. 1:1–3:21) specious forms of Christianity are again denounced. In the Gospels the appearance of "deceivers" within the church is predicted (Mark 13:21–23, for example).

The Apostle Paul very early found it necessary to set forth and defend his understanding of the gospel against competing versions (Gal. 1.1–2:21). Various forms of Christian perspective, which to some extent were correlated with literary genres, (e.g., apocalyptic tracts, collections of Jesus' sayings) invited developments leading to really diverse or incompatible understandings of Christianity. But such opposing developments often failed to materialize fully, for it was characteristic of the early church to comprehend competing, or potentially competitive, positions within a larger perspective. We see this happening in the combination of miracle tradition, apocalyptic discourse, and passion narrative, together with some sayings, parables, and other stories in the Gospel of Mark. An analogous combination of miracles, discourse, and passion occurred in the Gospel of John. The composition of the longer Gospels of Matthew and Luke involved the combination of Mark's Gospel with a large tradition of Jesus' teaching that had heretofore existed independently. The result was an even more comprehensive definition of Christianity. The Book of Acts shows an effort to link Paul and the earlier apostles with each other and ultimately with Jesus. From Paul's own letters, however, it is clear that relations among them were somewhat less cordial than Luke portrays.

Thus the New Testament contains evidence of the importance of the recurring and ever-pressing task of attempting to say what Christianity is and what it is not. In the controversies of the Galatian and Corinthian letters Paul has begun to attack this problem. He asserts the authority of his gospel, backed by his own status as an apostle. In his own way the author of the Epistle of James addresses this question when he argues against an important Pauline saying and insists that both faith and works—not faith alone—are necessary for salvation. Mark may well have been moved to write his Gospel because of what he regarded as inadequate ways of understanding Christianity in the church or churches that he knew. Matthew and Luke apparently felt the need of improving upon Mark, or at least of speaking to different situations. Luke plainly implies that he believes he can produce a more adequate account than his predecessors (Luke 1:1–4). Matthew is less explicit on this point, but his intention to embody the proper understanding of Christianity within the framework of a Gospel is clear enough. In fact, in Matthew's Gospel Jesus goes out of his way to reiterate that his real disciples are not those who just call upon his name and hear his words, but those who keep them and do them (7:21–27; cf. 25:31–46; 28:16–20). Clearly he has in view those who say "Lord, Lord" but do not obey Jesus. Whereas for Paul the word of the apostle himself seems to have had a special authority, for Matthew the word of Jesus—hearing and doing it—is all important. Something essential is thereby said about what is Christianity and what is not. By the same token, the hallmark of Christian community is established. The church of Jesus' true disciples is the community in which his words are heard and obeyed.

THE DISTINCTION OF ORTHODOXY AND HERESY

The period of the writing of the New Testament books began about A.D. 50 or before and extended down past the year 100. To speak of orthodoxy and heresy during this period is anachronistic, because strict canons of orthodoxy had not yet been laid down. But, as we have seen, there existed diverse views and perspectives,[14] and some fundamental conflicts such as the one between Paul and certain Jewish Christians over whether Gentile Christians had to obey the Jewish law. Such conflicts demanded a decision one way or the other. But at the time of Paul, and for a long while thereafter, there was no machinery for adjudicating such disputes. Divisions and antinomies sometimes resulted. In the case of this particular dispute Paul's position was eventually vindicated, but without Paul's theology being well understood. Paul's opponents, who doubtless considered themselves the conservers of God's truth and therefore orthodox, were themselves eventually considered heretics.

[14] For more extensive discussions of this matter, see H. Koester, *"Gnomai Diaphoroi:* The Origin and Nature of Diversification in the History of Early Christianity," in *Trajectories Through Early Christianity*, pp. 114–157. The pioneering work, now available in English, is W. Bauer, *Orthodoxy and Heresy in Earliest Christianity*, trans. and ed. R. A. Kraft and G. Krodel et al., 2nd ed. (Philadelphia: Fortress, 1971).

The author of the Pastoral Epistles, probably not Paul but some-one endeavoring to follow in Paul's footsteps, appears certain enough of his own orthodoxy that he can denounce those whom he regards as corrupters of the faith and place a ban of excommunica-tion upon them. Similarly, the Johannine Epistles face a crisis in which wrong doctrine is being taught in the name of Christ by some, and the author, like the author of the Pastorals, wants to put those who persist in their error or blindness beyond the pale. Those whom Matthew deprecates for saying "Lord, Lord," but not doing God's will as Jesus taught it, can be called heretics only by stretch-ing the usual meaning of the term, but it is obvious enough that Matthew regards their state as quite deplorable.

Although a clear distinction between orthodoxy and heresy did not arise, and could not have arisen, during the time when most New Testament books were being composed, the basis of that dis-tinction was already being laid. It only remained to be seen which of the emerging views of Christianity would endure, how they might combine and survive, and which would pass from the scene.

ORDINATION, CREEDS, SCRIPTURE

During the course of the second century and thereafter, standards of orthodoxy in faith were established. These developed as the var-ious churches, which had from the beginning a sense of their unity of origin and purpose, began to express that sense by establishing or-ganizational structures with clearly designated positions of author-ity. The resulting distinction between church leaders, ordained and set aside for their tasks, and the rest of the congregations proved to be a momentous one. Already the Pastoral Letters show an explicit awareness of this distinction between clergy and laity, and they im-ply that the authority of the Apostle Paul is exercised through Tim-othy and Titus, who in turn delegate it to ordained bishops and eld-ers. Not without reason the language of the Pastorals appears in liturgies and certificates of ordination in some denominations.

It is interesting to contrast the situation envisioned in the Pas-torals with that of the Johannine Epistles. In the Pastorals, when doctrinal or moral lassitude appear, appeal can be made to minister-ial authorities, who are charged with guarding the purity of the church's confession, as well as the uprightness of its members' con-duct. In the Johannine Epistles, on the other hand, no such recog-nized ministerial office is evident. The exact status of the author, the "Elder," is unclear. He may be an episcopal claimant attempting to assert his authority, but he never appeals to his ordination or ecclesiastical rank. Rather he appeals to the "old commandment" (of love) and the "right confession" (that Jesus is the Christ). But who is to say what party is obeying the commandment or what is

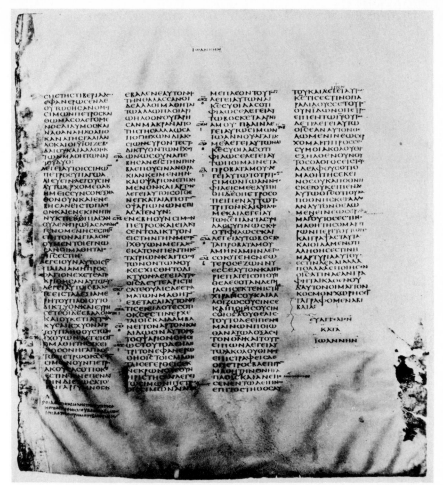

Codex Sinaiticus, one of the great fourth-century manuscripts of the New Testament, discovered by C. Tischendorf at the monastery of St. Catherine on Mt. Sinai in 1859. (Courtesy of American Bible Society and British Museum.)

As for the Gospels, we again know little about the circumstances of their collection. Ignatius seems to have known Matthew and perhaps John, but possibly he was principally familiar with oral traditions that have been incorporated into those Gospels. Marcion at mid-second century knew at least Luke. At the same time Justin Martyr appears to have known the Synoptic Gospels. He probably knew the Gospel of John also, but he betrays a curious reticence in referring to it. His disciple Tatian somewhat later in the second century combined the four canonical Gospels into one unified account of Jesus' ministry called the *Diatessaron* (the Greek name indicates that it has been composed out of four other documents). In the last quarter of the second century, Irenaeus wrote at some length about the four Gospels and made a point of the appropriateness and the necessity of four, as if he were addressing himself to people who did not think that four were needed. And, in fact, there were those in the early church who questioned the right of the Fourth Gospel to be regarded as apostolic and authoritative. In all probability, Marcion, whose canon contained only one Gospel, reflects the earlier practice. For in the beginning an individual church, or even a geographical area, would have used only one Gospel. A multigospel canon would have come into use only as the Gospels of various churches were combined. In the process of combination some Gospels doubtless fell by the wayside. In the early Christian writers we catch glimpses of some of these other Gospels, which for one reason or another were rejected in the process of sifting and choosing that led to the formation of what we know as the New Testament.[16]

THE SIGNIFICANCE AND SHAPE OF THE CANON

The New Testament as a collection of authoritative books, a canon of holy scripture, was born out of a coming together of theological interests and practical needs. But these interests and needs were not simply imposed from without upon the New Testament books. Doubtless the apostle Paul, for example, did not think that he was writing holy scripture when he wrote to the Corinthians or even to the Romans. Yet he was quite consciously asserting his apostolic authority to say what distinctively Christian faith was and what it implied for the life of believers under certain specific circumstances. Similarly, those who preserved the sayings of Jesus may not have thought of themselves as setting up a rival to Moses. Nevertheless, they believed in the sayings of Jesus as faithful guides to the will of God and applied them like holy scripture to the situations that arose in the life of the church. The impulses to establish a canon and thus to provide resources for the guidance and enrichment of the church did not begin long after the writing of the last New Testament book, but in some form actually preceded and motivated the writing of many of those books.

Of course, the various New Testament books do not all say the same thing. In fact, there are real differences and even some disagreements among them. For the most part, however, the New Testament books show an interest in what is apostolic, authoritative, and original. They attach importance to the earthly life and ministry of Jesus, even if, as in the case of Paul, that interest concentrates

[16] Portions of these Gospels that survive have been conveniently collected and analyzed in E. Hennecke, *New Testament Apocrypha*, Vol. I, ed. W. Scheemelcher and trans. R. McL. Wilson (Philadelphia: Westminster, 1963).

mainly upon his death. They regard the death and resurrection of Jesus as the central saving event. They look upon Christ and the church as the fulfillment of Old Testament prophecy, and they look forward to the final revelation of God's power and glory. Moreover, they agree in attaching fundamental importance to the moral life. It is by no means a safe assumption, however, that all early Christians or their literature agreed on these points. Increasing evidence that they did not continually comes to the fore. We have discovered that Paul encountered Christians who thought the gospel was a new legalism and others who found in it a license to do as they pleased. The Pastoral Epistles, II Peter, and Revelation all lash out at supposedly wrongheaded and dangerous ideas held by Christians. The Christian Gnostic texts recently discovered in Egypt reveal an aberrant form of Christianity with ancient roots. Significantly, some words of Jesus in the Synoptic Gospels, especially Matthew, are applied against misguided Christians.

The New Testament as a whole is an effort on the part of the early Christian church to define the faith and indicate its consequences for life. Intended to lay down certain directions and set boundaries, it is not simply a random or even a representative specimen of opinion. It goes beyond, but does not contradict, the purposes of the individual authors in writing. When we think of the meaning of the New Testament, therefore, we concern ourselves not only with what the authors intended but with the meaning of the canon as a whole.

Suggestions for Further Reading

Recently several important works in this field have appeared or been translated. A survey reflecting the perspectives and results of much recent research is H. Conzelmann, *History of Primitive Christianity*, trans. J. E. Steely (Nashville, Tenn.: Abingdon, 1973). On the diversity of early Christianity as it developed in various places, one should consult W. Bauer, *Orthodoxy and Heresy in Earliest Christianity*, trans. and ed. R. A. Kraft and G. Krodel et al., 2nd ed. (Philadelphia: Fortress, 1971). There is a collection of noteworthy essays by J. M. Robinson and H. Koester entitled *Trajectories through Early Christianity* (Philadelphia: Fortress, 1971). A more conservative approach to the history of Christian origins is represented by F. F. Bruce, *New Testament History*, rev. ed. (London: Oliphants, 1971).

On questions of church-state relations, persecution, and martyrdom, note O. Cullmann, *The State in the New Testament* (London: SCM, 1963); R. M. Grant, *The Sword and the Cross* (New York: Macmillan, 1955); and W. H. C. Frend, *Martyrdom and Persecution in the Early Church* (Oxford: Blackwell, 1965; paperback, Anchor), an extensive scholarly work.

The development of the Christian canon of scripture is comprehensively treated by H. von Campenhausen, *The Formation of the Christian*

Bible, trans. J. A. Baker (London: Black, 1972). For an excellent brief survey, see R. E. Brown and J. C. Turro, "Canonicity," in *The Jerome Biblical Commentary,* ed. R. E. Brown et al. (Englewood Cliffs: Prentice-Hall, 1968), pp. 515–534.

Important older works are H. Lietzmann, *The Beginnings of the Christian Church,* trans. B. L. Woolf, 3rd ed. (London: Lutterworth, 1953; paperback, Meridian); J. Weiss, *Earliest Christianity,* 2 vols., trans. F. C. Grant et al. (New York: Harper Torchbook, 1959); and W. Bousset, *Kyrios Christos: A History of the Belief in Christ from the Beginnings of Christianity to Irenaeus,* trans. J. E. Steely (Nashville, Tenn.: Abingdon, 1970), all of which were written in German in the earlier part of this century. F. E. Peters, *The Harvest of Hellenism* (New York: Simon & Schuster, 1970), integrates the political and spiritual history of the world of early Christianity from Alexander to Constantine.

Primary sources pertinent to the New Testament period are mentioned at the end of Chapter 1, pp. 54–56. Early Christian writings not found in the New Testament or Apostolic Fathers, but in many cases ascribed to apostolic figures, have been collected and discussed in E. Hennecke (ed.), *New Testament Apocrypha,* trans. R. McL. Wilson, 2 vols. (Philadelphia: Westminster, 1963, 1965). See also J. Stevenson (ed.), *A New Eusebius: Documents Illustrative of the History of the Church to* A.D. *337* (London: SPCK, 1957).

Epilogue:
The Anatomy
of the New Testament

A T THE END of each major treatment of a New Testament book we have summarized the results by reviewing them under four aspects: (1) *structure,* (2) *tradition* and *redaction,* (3) the principal *emphases,* and (4) the *historical situation* from which the book appeared. In conclusion, it will be useful to attempt to see the entire New Testament in relation to each of these aspects.

The *structure* of the New Testament is simple. The twenty-seven books are divided into four Gospels, the Book of Acts, twenty-one Epistles, and the Revelation to John. Ancient canonical lists give different orders within the Gospels and Epistles, but the integrity of the groupings is generally observed. As we have noticed already, the canonical order makes a certain sense and is therefore helpful to the reader. Although the genuine Pauline letters were written first, the Gospels stand at the head of the canon. From an historical perspective on the beginnings of Christianity this may be misleading, but for the Christian churches which over a period of many years brought the New Testament to its present shape this order makes sense. Jesus is primary, theologically as well as chronologically, for Christian faith.

Within the fourfold Gospel canon Matthew stands first. Despite tradition and occasional scholarly theories supporting the priority of Matthew, Mark was likely the first Gospel written. Yet Matthew's primacy in the Gospel canon and in the New Testament is understandable, and, from the standpoint of the church that formulated the New Testament, quite proper. Matthew presents Jesus as the founder and teacher of the church. The final Gospel, John, may well have been the last of the four to have been written, although one cannot be certain. Yet whatever its date of composition, the Fourth Gospel's character as a theological reflection in narrative form suits it admirably for the final position in the Gospel canon. For most of the church's history John has provided the theological and Christological perspective for understanding Jesus.

Although Acts was written after at least two of the Gospels, and at least a generation after the genuine Pauline letters, it appropriately bridges the gap between Gospels and Epistles. As historical sources the Pauline letters are to be preferred to Acts. Yet those letters provide only bits and fragments of history. The Book of Acts is the first attempt to write a continuous account of the earliest church. As such it provides a rudimentary basis and background for reading and understanding the Epistles. Its emphasis upon the missionary work of Paul, to whom fourteen of the New Testament Epistles have been traditionally ascribed, is quite appropriate.

Among the Epistles Romans stands first in the order that has become standard among Christian churches. Again, it was not written first, but it has valid claim to that position as the most thorough exposition of Paul's theology. After Romans the Pauline letters tend to group themselves in descending order of length or importance. Not coincidentally the Pastorals, written a generation or so after Paul, come near the end, and Hebrews, whose ascription to Paul was seriously doubted in antiquity, is last of all. The Pauline corpus is then followed by the Catholic Epistles, all of which are in fact later than Paul and represent the interests of emerging, institutional Christianity.

But as though the claims and interests of the institution should not have the last word, the New Testament concludes with Revelation. In all probability its position in the canon is related to the fact that in antiquity serious doubts were raised about its apostolicity, and therefore its right to be included. But apart from such considerations, its position at the end is quite appropriate. It points toward the future, toward the end of history, and expresses in terms of apocalyptic imagery the fundamental Christian conviction that God rules, appearances to the contrary notwithstanding.

It is not customary to speak of the *redaction* of the entire New Testament, or of the distinction between *redaction* and *tradition* in the canon as a whole. That sort of distinction is applied to the individual documents. Tradition is generally considered to be the work of the community, redaction the work of an individual editor or author. With respect to the canon as a whole, any distinction between community and individual is, of course, inapplicable. Although it is sometimes suggested that some of the New Testament books underwent redaction in the process of being incorporated into the canon (e.g., the Gospel of John, II Corinthians), it is impossible to isolate or identify the results of such a redactional process with certainty. We do know that late in the second century a church leader named Tatian attempted to combine all four canonical Gospels, and perhaps other material, into one "super-Gospel" called the *Diatessaron*. His effort was, however, eventually rejected in favor of the fourfold canon. Therefore, one cannot speak of tradition and redaction of the canon as a whole in a way analogous to the individual books.

On the other hand, the incorporation of the various documents into the framework or *structure* which we have just described may be thought of as a redactional process. Materials given by tradition and "traditioned" (i.e., passed down), namely, the finished books, were incorporated, albeit gradually, into larger structures: first into the collections of Gospels and Epistles separately, then into the

New Testament as a whole. Moreover, this entire collection was then put alongside another and more ancient collection of sacred scriptures, the Old Testament. (Of course, the Old Testament could not be known as the "Old Testament," even by Christians, until there was a New Testament.) The result was quite analogous with what occurred in the case of individual books, especially Gospels. Older and more or less fragmentary parts were incorporated into a larger whole. The whole then becomes more than the sum of its parts; it becomes a new entity. At the same time each part loses something, even as it gains something, in being taken up into the new whole.

Thus, for example, when the Gospel of John, which presents a picture of Jesus in many ways different from and even contradictory to the picture which emerges from the Synoptics (despite the latters' individual differences), is taken up into the fourfold canon along with the other Gospels, the perspective of the reader on this Gospel is changed. It requires great effort on the part of the student to imagine the view of Jesus he would have had he read no other Gospel but John's. (Mark would afford a similar, if less extreme, example of the same state of affairs.) As it is, John is read alongside the other Gospels, and the sharp edges of his portrayal of Jesus are tempered by their portraits. With the other Gospels alongside, John can be read without losing touch with the humanity of Jesus. Whether it would be possible to read John alone and gain an impression of this humanity is doubtful.

In the same way, the letters of Paul are placed alongside and after the Gospels. If one wishes to understand Paul historically, one cannot presume the Gospels as a background for interpreting his letters. The Gospels were written later, as we have seen, and it is by no means certain or even likely that he was familiar with most of the material that they contain. Yet it is difficult to read Paul without being influenced by the portrayal of Jesus in the Gospels. The fundamental intention of the redactional process that put Paul into the canon alongside and after the Gospels was, of course, that we should not read Paul apart from them. So successful was the redactional process in fulfilling this intention that even trained scholars have difficulty in isolating any longer the historical Paul. Even within the traditional Pauline canon the sharp polemic of Galatians or of II Corinthians is tempered by the inclusion of the Pastorals, and nascent Pauline ideas and images are developed further. In Ephesians, for example, the idea of church as body of Christ attains a development lacking in I Corinthians or Romans. Moreover, these "Pauline" letters check the development of Paulinism, evident in such literature as the Acts of Paul and Marcion's canon, toward a Gnostic dualism.

From a perspective governed by historical interests this history of redaction may seem unfortunate because it obscures the pristine clarity of Pauline or Johannine ideas. From a theological perspective governed by the insights of a Paul or a John, the process can also be viewed as a degeneration, though perhaps necessary under the circumstances and for the time in which it occurred. We need not, however, pass judgment upon what happened. It is sufficient to observe the phenomenon and to place it within the context of a process that had been going on from the beginning in the production and transmission of traditions and in the composition of individual books (cf. pp. 480 ff.).

That the New Testament as a whole embodies certain *emphases* which to some extent determined the process of canonical development is clear. That we have in the New Testament no letters from Paul's opponents in Corinth is not coincidental. Certain viewpoints were put beyond the pale in the course of the doctrinal development that produced our New Testament, the great ancient creeds of the church, and the carefully articulated sacramental and clerical organization. Nevertheless, theological viewpoints that were at one time at odds with one another gained representation within the canon. Thus the Epistle of James, which in fact and perhaps intentionally contradicts Paul, stands in the same New Testament with Romans and Galatians. If the opponents of Paul in II Corinthians were miracle-working charismatics, their opposition to him did not prevent a similar point of view from finding expression in the miracle traditions of Mark and John, though even there the tradition is modified and redirected. The New Testament represents no strict doctrinal unity. Be that as it may, there is nevertheless a remarkable continuity of perspective and emphasis in most of the canonical writings.

Not only was Jesus a Jew, but Christianity began as a Jewish sect. From this origin it rather quickly branched off into a separate religious group. Yet fundamental Jewish assumptions, drawn from the Old Testament, continued to inform the new religion and were, in fact, fundamental to its development and shape. For one thing, the Old Testament itself was retained in the Christian canon, despite the efforts of some early Christians to set it aside or overthrow it. Retention of the Old Testament signified Christianity's continuing commitment to what it represents and embodies: law, prophecy, history, and eschatology.

Although Paul's controversy with Jewish Christians over the observance of the law resulted in his vindication, early Christianity did not lose touch with the fundamental moral emphasis of the law. Ritual law was quickly allegorized, forgotten, or replaced by the new liturgical life of the church, but the basic moral commandments of the Hebrew Bible, epitomized in the Ten Commandments, continued to be honored. In this respect early Christianity was perhaps a bit more conservative than either Jesus or Paul, but neither of them denied the validity of the law as an expression of God's will, much less the general thrust or intention of the law.

Although the character of the scriptures as law was not denied by Christians, they tended to read them primarily as prophecy of Christ. Thus from the beginning the revelation in Christ was seen and interpreted as the fulfillment of scripture (I Cor. 15:33 ff.). The scriptures provided the conceptual categories for the gospel. This is nowhere clearer than in the title Christ itself, which is simply the Greek translation of Messiah, the Hebrew word meaning "[the Lord's] anointed."

Precisely the Jewish heritage and scriptural foundation of earliest Christianity explains the tenacity with which it clung to and emphasized the importance of history and eschatology. This was by no means a happenstance. As the new faith broke with Judaism and spread across the Hellenistic world, becoming mostly Gentile in constituency, many saw no real point in this insistence upon God's revelation in a historically real past and future. In some areas many, if not most, Christians were Gnostic. The Gnostic Christians characteristically rejected the Old Testament (except insofar as they might interpret it in an idiosyncratic or esoteric way), had little interest in Jesus as an historical and human figure and looked above for salvation rather than to any meaningful future. In response to and rejection of such a theological stance, the early church harked back to writings and traditions that emphasized fulfillment of (Old Testament) scripture in Jesus, his historical and human reality, his return and the coming of God's kingdom. The Gnostic idea that this world was not the creation of the true God and Father of Jesus Christ was also rejected, despite the troubles and adversity that Christians encountered in this world. Thus the most Gnostic-sounding of the major New Testament books, the Gospel of John, insists that the God of Jesus Christ is the Creator (1:3). Even the miracles of the Gospels indicate the seriousness with which Jesus and his followers in the first and second centuries took this world and its conditions.

At no point in this study has the *historical situation* of the New Testament been far from view. Chapter 11 described the circumstances that led to the establishment of the canon of the New Testament, and we have touched upon them again here. It will be useful, moreover, to reflect upon the fact that the historical situation of early Christianity in the formative period of the New Testament was twofold. In a real sense the development of Christianty was determined from within, first by the historical fact of Jesus, then by the preaching of the gospel about him and the effort to keep that preaching in touch with his historical person and the struggle against forms of piety that denied or diluted it.

Nevertheless, Christianity was never at any point sealed off from the secular and religious world of its time. Its language, cultic practices, and ethics were influenced and determined by the surrounding culture. Because from earliest times this cultural environment was increasingly Hellenistic and Gentile, it is not surprising that early Christianity began to absorb its coloration. This fact is clearly discernible in the great Christian creedal statements of the fourth and fifth centuries, which presuppose and are set forth in terms drawn from Greek philosophy rather than the Hebrew scriptures. In the New Testament period the transition from Jewish to Gentile environment was greatly facilitated by Judaism's own accommodation to the surrounding world. Most Jews no longer lived in Palestine or spoke Hebrew as the language of ordinary intercourse. In making the transition the gospel did not always break new ground, but often followed well-established paths.

The influence of the broader Hellenistic world made itself felt in the cult, in worship, where familiar practices were Christianized. In I Corinthians Paul struggles against the profanation of Christian worship by its intermingling with pagan elements (I Cor. 10:14 ff.). Yet the worship which he approved, with sacraments of baptism and Lord's Supper, was understood by Gentile converts in ways that Paul the Jew did not anticipate (I Cor. 10:1–13). The sorts of people attracted to the church were not unlike those drawn to the mystery cults, and if the bases of these religions were different, in the practice and understanding of common people they could easily be assimilated. If the earliest New Testament understanding of baptism and the Lord's Supper is not to be seen as an outgrowth of the mysteries, the later development of Christian sacramentalism could not ignore and remain unaffected by its rivals. For scholars who study the New Testament and Christian origins as an intellectual pursuit, there is always the danger of over-intellectualizing the object of study. Christianity grew not in a scholar's cloister, nor even in the rabbi's study, but in the excitement and despair of late antiquity. Its center of focus was its worship, and there the ordinary Christian gained and sustained his understanding of what it was all about.

This milieu also affected the development of Christology, the categories of which were given by Judaism and the Jewish scriptures. Although the Jewish basis was not forgotten, other factors came to play a large role. In all probability the intense concentration upon the person of Jesus Christ in Christianity is related to the role he played in worship. For Paul, his churches, and even his Christian opponents (cf. II Cor. 13:3a), Jesus Christ is a living reality, not just a figure of the past. Christians call upon his name (I Cor. 1:2). In effect, they worship him, not to the exclusion of the God of Israel, but alongside him as God incarnate. The seeds of an irrevocable split with the parent religion were thus planted, as in a Gentile environment Christianity becomes liturgically, as well as theologically, increasingly Christ-centered.

The world's influence was not always felt in benign or contributive ways. The Roman Empire's initial reaction to Christianity was to ignore it in the hope that it, like other excesses and superstitions, would go away. When it did not, Rome often took a harsh line against Christians and the church in an effort to stamp out the new religion. This hostility is already manifest in the New Testament, particularly in Revelation. Roman persecution was by no means universal and sustained, but it was at certain times and places brutal and intensive. In the face of such opposition some Christians saw their hope of salvation to lie only in another world. Some denied their faith on the presumption that they could later take it up again. Remarkably, however, the church's ultimate response was to deny neither the world nor its own faith. The world continued to be viewed as the object of God's love and his salvation. Despite the fact that a small lie in denial of Christ might seem inconsequential in comparison with the great suffering that might result from confessing allegiance to Christ, a good and true confession before the world and its rulers was required of Christians. Thus in a painful way the faith was honored, but the world and its reality were honored too. In this as well as other ways this honoring of the faith and the world is characteristic of early Christianity and the New Testament. Indeed, the refusal to surrender either the reality of the faith or the reality of the world is one of the fundamental structures which characterizes the anatomy of the New Testament.

Glossary

Abba: the intimate, familiar Aramaic word for father. In the normal piety of first-century Judaism this form of address was too intimate to be used of God. But Jesus (Mark 14:36) and the early Christians (Rom. 8:15; Gal. 4:6) used it in this way.

A.D.: abbreviation of the Latin *Anno Domini*, which means "in the year of our Lord." In the Western world the birth of Christ is customarily the point of reference for dating events. Events occurring before the birth of Jesus are indicated by the abbreviation B.C., "before Christ." Alternatively, one may speak of C.E. (current era) or B.C.E. (before current era).

Agrapha: literally, unwritten words or sayings. The term refers to words and sayings of Jesus not contained in the canonical Gospels.

Allegory: a story whose details or actions illustrate or tell about something quite different. Each element of an allegory possesses its own distinct meaning, which is determined by something outside the story, for example, the Christian faith in the case of Bunyan's *Pilgrim's Progress*.

Amen: the transliteration of a Greek word that in turn transliterates a Hebrew word. In common usage *amen* is either a solemn confirmation of what has been said or a response of assent to words of another.

Antichrist: an apocalyptic figure, the archenemy of Christ, who will appear shortly before the parousia to wage war against the friends of Christ. (*See* Parousia.)

Antinomianism: the belief that the Christian who has been freed by Christ has no ethical or moral obligations at all.

Antitheses: the six contrasts with ancient teaching that Jesus proclaims in the Sermon on the Mount (Matt. 5:21–48) in the antithetical form, "You have heard. . . . But I say to you. . . ."

Apocalyptic: an uncovering or a revelation. The term is applied to a type of literature that is pessimistic about humanity's possibilities and hence discloses God's plan for the last days (e.g., the Apocalypse or Revelation to John). Although related to prophecy and eschatology, apocalyptic thought stresses more precisely and forcefully the future intervention of God in the end time. (*See* Eschatology; Revelation.)

Apocrypha: the fourteen books of the Septuagint Bible not found in the Hebrew Bible; usually it is a part of the Catholic Bible but not the Protestant Bible. More generally the adjectival form, *apocryphal,* means "hidden or spurious" and is also applied to early Christian writings not admitted to the New Testament.

Apostle: a term meaning "one who is sent" specifically applied to the twelve disciples who were close to Jesus (see Mark 3:14 ff.). Paul also appropriates this designation for himself because of the risen Christ's appearance to him (see I Cor. 15:1 ff.).

Apostolic Fathers: a collection of second-century noncanonical writings supposedly written by personal followers of the apostles.

Aramaic: the language of Palestine during the time of Jesus and the early church. A Semitic tongue, it is closely related to Hebrew.

Archaeology: the scientific study of ancient cultures on the basis of their remains, such as fossil relics, artifacts, monuments, pottery, and buildings.

Aristeas, Epistle of: a pre-Christian, Jewish pseudepigraphical writing which presents a legendary account of the translation of the Hebrew Bible into Greek in Alexandria, Egypt.

Ascension: traditionally the visible departure of Jesus into heaven forty days after his resurrection (see Acts 1:9).

Baptism: the act or sacrament by which a person was received into the early Christian church. The Greek term means "to dip" or "immerse."

B.C.: the abbreviation of "before Christ." (*See* A.D.)

Beatitudes: the nine blessings that stand at the beginning of Jesus' Sermon on the Mount (see Matt. 5:3–12).

Canon: a term originally applied to a reed used for measuring. It was later used of those books or writings that became standard or authoritative for the early Christians. By the close of the fourth century the Christian canon was largely fixed. (*See* Apocrypha; Pseudepigrapha.)

Catholic: universal, affecting mankind as a whole; an adjective used by the early church to refer to whatever was universally shared among the various churches.

Catholic Epistles: James; I and II Peter; I, II, and III John; and Jude. These seven letters are supposedly "general" in destination and in character and hence Catholic.

Charisma: "free gift." The term came to be used in the early church for the various gifts of the Spirit, such as wisdom, knowledge, faith, healing, and speaking in tongues (see I Cor. 12).

Christ: *See* Messiah.

Christology: that aspect of Christian thought concerned specifically with the revelation of God in Jesus the Christ.

Church: the community of believers in Jesus Christ. The term is used of individual congregations and of the entire fellowship of Christians.

Council of Jamnia: the group of rabbinical scholars who settled in Jamnia shortly before the fall of Jerusalem in A.D. 70 and helped to standardize the Jewish religion. They are usually credited with having fixed the Hebrew canon of the Old Testament, now followed by Protestants as well as Jews.

Covenant: a solemn agreement that binds two parties together. The Old Testament (Covenant) depicts the agreement by which God and the people of Israel were bound together, and the New Testament (Covenant) tells the story of the new agreement effected by God with the new Israel through Jesus the Christ. Ordinarily in biblical usage a covenant is sealed in blood.

Crucifixion: a Roman form of execution in which the victim was nailed or bound to a wooden cross and left to die.

Dead Sea Scrolls: ancient Jewish documents from the period of Christian origins, found near the Dead Sea. (*See* Essenes; Qumran.)

Decalogue or Ten Commandments: the name given to the words Moses received, according to tradition, from God on Mt. Sinai. (See Exodus 20:1–17 and Deuteronomy 5:6–21).

Diaspora or dispersion: the Jewish community scattered (dispersed) outside the holy land of Palestine. This dispersion originated in the Babylonian exile of 587 B.C.

Didache or "Teaching of the Twelve Apostles": an anonymous second-century Christian manual for church life.

Docetism (derived from the Greek meaning "to seem"): an early Christian heresy according to which Jesus Christ only seemed to suffer and die. A divine being, it was thought, could not suffer.

Epistle: a letter of a formal or didactic nature; the term used to be regularly applied to the New Testament letters.

Eschatology: discourse about the last things or the end of the age (Greek *eschatos,* meaning "last"). Traditionally the term is used of Christian thought concerning all the events and actions associated with both the end of history and the end of human life. (*See* Apocalyptic; Parousia.)

Essenes: an ascetic, Jewish religious group existing at the time of the New Testament. They stressed radical obedience to the Jewish law. (*See* Qumran.)

Ethics: a broad term applied to such related matters as moral codes and practices, theories of value, and the imperatives of Christian faith as they pertain to relations of one person to another (not God and humanity).

Eucharist: the sacrament of the Lord's Supper in which bread and wine are consecrated and distributed to the faithful Christians. (*See* Lord's Supper; Sacrament.)

Exegesis: the critical interpretation of a text. Literally the term means "to lead out" the meaning from the text.

Exile: specifically the removal of defeated Israelites by the Babylonians in 587 B.C.

Exodus: a going out; used specifically of Israel's departure from Egypt under the leadership of Moses about the thirteenth century B.C.

Expiation: "making right" by means of some act or rite the offense done by one party to another, especially expiation for sin before God. (*See* Propitiation; Sacrifice.)

Form Criticism: the classification of the "forms" in which the tradition, especially the Gospel tradition, circulated before being written down and the attempt to determine the "setting in life" of the church which they reflect. (*See* Pericope; Redaction Criticism.)

Gentile: a non-Jew. The original Greek term translated "Gentiles" means "Nations."

Gnosticism: a religious movement or attitude widespread about the time of the emergence of the Christian faith. Believers possessed a secret knowledge (*gnōsis*) and sought to escape the ephemeral earthly world for the eternal heavenly world.

Gospel: originally the message of good news that God has revealed Himself as gracious in the event of Jesus Christ. The term later came to designate also the literary form in which the good news of Jesus' life, death, and resurrection is narrated; for example, the Gospel according to Matthew.

Hasmonean: another name for the Maccabees, leaders of the Jewish revolt against Syria. (*See* Maccabees.)

Hellenization: the process or result of the spread of Greek language and culture in the Mediterranean world after Alexander the Great (died 323 B.C.).

Holy: that which has to do with God or the divine power and majesty.

Immanence: the nearness or involvement of God in the world. (*See* Transcendence.)

Incarnation: literally means "becoming flesh"; the embodiment of God in Jesus of Nazareth.

Justification: the act or process by which God brings people into proper relationship with himself. In Paul the justification or righteousness of God is to be received by faith, not works. (*See* Righteousness.)

Kerygma (literally "proclamation"): the early Christian preaching about Jesus as the Christ intended to elicit the decision of faith.

Kingdom of God or rule of God: God's Lordship over humankind and the world. The kingdom is the center of Jesus' message in the Synoptic Gospels.

Koinē ("common" in Greek): the everyday Greek speech used throughout the Hellenistic world during the period of early Christianity. The New Testament books are written in *koinē* Greek.

Law: in the New Testament generally the revelation of God through Moses to the people of Israel embodied in the cultic, ritual, and moral commandments of the Old Testament. (*See* Gospel; Torah.)

Lord's Supper: the church's continuing re-enactment of the last supper of Jesus with his disciples. (*See* Eucharist.)

Maccabees: the priestly family who successfully led a revolt against Hellenistic Syrian rule beginning in 167 B.C. They ruled over Palestine from 142 B.C. to 63 B.C. (*See* Hasmonean.)

Manuscripts: handwritten documents, especially the ancient New Testament documents from which our present text is determined. The earliest complete New Testament manuscripts come from the fourth century, although there are sizable fragments of earlier date.

Messiah: from the Hebrew term meaning "annointed one." It was used of the Davidic king, whose restoration was expected in Jesus' day. Its Greek equivalent is *Christos* (Christ), the basic designation of Jesus in the New Testament. He was believed to be the expected Messiah of Israel.

Midrash: the form, activity, or product of biblical interpretation, particularly as carried out in rabbinic Judaism. *Midrashim* (pl.) may be legal (halakic) or illustrative and even narrative (haggadic) in character.

Miracle: an extraordinary event, contrary to normal expectations, a manifestation of the activity of God.

Mishnah: the authoritative Jewish legal traditions which developed in rabbinic and Pharisaic Judaism (cf. Mark 10:5–13) and were codified in the early third century. The term is usually applied to the written form. The Mishnah and the learned commentary upon it (*Gemara*) constitute the Talmud. (*See* Talmud.)

Myth: the result of people's efforts to communicate their faith in transcendent reality by means of story and symbol. This technical use of the term should be distinguished from the popular meaning of a fantastic or untrue story.

Oral Tradition: any teaching or similar material transmitted from person to person or generation to generation by word of mouth rather than by use of writing; also the process of such transmission.

Parable: a brief story that makes its point by the unusual development or imagery of the narrative. The various details do not function as allegory but are significant for the story itself. Although the parable was already known to the Jewish religious tradition, Jesus made especial use of it. (*See* Allegory.)

Paraclete: helper, comforter, or mediator. The term is used in the Fourth Gospel of the Holy Spirit as the Christian community's helper after the death of Jesus (see John 14:16, 15:26; 16:7).

Parousia (literally "coming" or "presence"): the early Christian belief in the second coming of Christ, a glorious advent in power and judgment at the end of the age. (*See* Eschatology; Son of Man.)

Passion: suffering, particularly the suffering of Jesus during the last week of his life in Jerusalem and especially the suffering leading to his death.

Passover: the annual Jewish celebration of the deliverance from slavery in Egypt under the leadership of Moses. Jesus was crucified at the time of the Passover. (*See* Exodus.)

Pastoral Epistles: I and II Timothy and Titus. These letters give advice to the church leader or pastor concerning matters of church government and discipline.

Patriarch: the father of a people, especially the three great ancestors of the people of Israel (Abraham, Isaac, and Jacob). The period of Israel's history before the Exodus from Egypt is frequently called the patriarchal period.

Pentecost: the Jewish Feast of Weeks, beginning on the fiftieth day after Passover. According to the Book of Acts it was the occasion of the descent of the Holy Spirit upon the disciples of Jesus, and thus it is looked upon as the beginning of the church.

Pericope: a "cutting around" or section. The term is used of the individual, complete units of tradition about Jesus that circulated separately in the early church and were ultimately joined together to form the Gospels. (*See* Form Criticism; Redaction Criticism.)

Pharisees: the dominant Jewish religious group at the time of Jesus, who practiced strict observance of both the written and oral law of Judaism. The name probably comes from a Semitic term meaning "separated." (*See* Sadducees.)

Pre-existence: the term used to designate the New Testament belief that Jesus of Nazareth in some way existed with God before his earthly advent. (*See* John 1:1–18.)

Priest: a holy man authorized to perform ritual and cultic acts whereby man and God are enabled to commune with another. (*See* Holy; Sacrifice.)

Procurator: an official of the Roman Empire, responsible to the emperor, exercising administrative authority in a province or district.

Prophet: someone who speaks or acts for the divine, transcendent reality. In general, the prophet not only predicted God's action but also pled with the people to respond to God's will. Prophets existed in the early church as well as in ancient Israel.

Propitiation: a placating or pacifying of the diety; a sacrifice that induces God to be favorable or beneficent to the sacrificer. (*See* Expiation.)

Pseudepigrapha: literally "false writings," particularly a group of late Jewish writings claiming Old Testament figures as their authors. They reflect Jewish religious thought in the intertestamental period. (*See* Apocrypha.)

Q Source: the hypothetical source, consisting primarily of sayings of Jesus, used by both Matthew and Luke in the writing of their respective Gospels.

Qumran: the site on the northwest shore of the Dead Sea where a Jewish sect lived in strict obedience to the law of its covenant community until approximately A.D. 70. Near this site the library of the community or the Dead Sea Scrolls was discovered. (*See* Essenes.)

Rabbi: "master," a Jewish religious leader especially trained and qualified to expound and apply the law of Moses.

Redaction Criticism: the separating of tradition from redaction, especially in the Gospels. One who edits, revises, or shapes the literary sources that he has at hand is called a redactor. (*See* Form Criticism; Pericope.)

Redemption: literally "to buy" or "take back," particularly the act or process of God's taking back sinful or rebellious humanity by means of the event of Jesus Christ.

Resurrection or rising from the dead: a central hope in the New Testament based upon the early Christians' belief that Jesus was raised from the dead by God. In general the New Testament view of resurrection of the body or person should be distinguished from the widely held notion of the immortality of the soul.

Revelation (translated from the Greek word *apokalypsis*): an uncovering, revealing, or laying bare. It refers to the uncovering of the transcendent God in human events, particularly the event of Christ in the Christian tradition. (*See* Apocalyptic.)

Righteousness: primarily the quality and action of God; hence human righteousness proceeds from God's initiative in Christ and is based upon a relation with God as revealed in Christ. Righteousness and justification translate the same Greek noun in the New Testament. (*See* Justification.)

Sacrament: a sacred rite, "an outward and visible sign of an inward and spiritual grace," namely, the presence of the transcendent God. The term *sacrament* per se does not occur in the New Testament, but it is commonly used to refer to the acts of baptism and the Lord's Supper, which are reported there. (*See* Baptism; Eucharist.)

Sacrifice: the act of offering something held valuable to the deity. By the act of sacrifice communion with the divine is initiated, re-established, or continued. (*See* Priest.)

Sadducees: a religious group of the intertestamental period who represented the priestly aristocracy of Jewish life. In distinction from the Pharisees, they held only to the written Mosaic law and did not believe in the resurrection.

Salvation: the state of complete liberation from sin, brokenness, and estrangement between humanity and God. In general, the New Testament locates salvation in the future, although its inauguration is already effected in Christ.

Sanctification: the process of being made holy. The term refers to the life of the Christian under the guidance of the Spirit as the effects of Christ's work, especially the love of God and of others, become more and more manifest.

Scribes: a title applied to learned men in postexilic Judaism who studied and copied the law and exercised judgment in matters pertaining to the law. (*See* Pharisees.)

Second Coming: *See* Parousia.

Septuagint (usually designated LXX): the Greek translation of the Hebrew Old Testament for diaspora Jews which originated before the rise of Christianity. (*See* Apocrypha.)

Sin: generally any act, whether in thought or deed, which violates the law or will of God. In the New Testament particularly, it denotes the broken or estranged relation between the human race and God. (*See* Righteousness.)

Sitz im Leben ("setting in life"): the term is employed widely by form critics to refer to the community setting and, implicitly, the function of traditions.

Son of God: in Hebraic thought someone especially selected or anointed by God for a task, such as the king of Israel, a prophet, or the people of Israel. In Hellenistic religious thought the term refers frequently to a male offspring of the gods. In the New Testament Jesus functions as the Son of God primarily in the Hebraic sense.

Son of Man: an apocalyptic Jewish figure who was to come at the end of the ages to serve as judge between the righteous and the wicked. In the Gospels the use of the title Son of Man is confined almost entirely to Jesus. (*See* Apocalyptic; Parousia.)

Soteriology: discourse about salvation. Soteriology refers to the New Testament understanding of the righteousness of God, sin, the work of Christ, the response of faith, and the work of the Spirit in sanctification.

Soul: a spiritual entity within each person that survives death. This concept of the soul plays little role in Hebraic or New Testament thought. Its prominence in Christian thought derives from later Greek influence.

Source Criticism: the work of identifying the written sources that were used in the composition of any given document, such as one of the Gospels.

Spirit: the dynamic power and activity of God directed toward the world, especially active in the history of Israel, the life of Jesus, and the early church; in the Christian tradition usually referred to as the Holy Spirit.

Synoptic Problem: the problem of understanding the relationship between the Synoptic Gospels (Matthew, Mark, and Luke), taking account of their great similarities as well as their distinct differences. The generally accepted solution is that both Matthew and Luke used Mark, the Q source consisting largely of Jesus' sayings, and distinct material to which each had access separately.

Talmud (meaning instruction or study): the authoritative body of Jewish tradition consisting of Mishnah (q.v.) and Gemara (commentary upon it) that developed in the several centuries immediately preceding and following the beginning of the Christian era. It exists in Palestinian (early fifth century) and Babylonian (late fifth century) forms. (*See* Mishnah.)

Theology: discourse on God; the study of or reflection upon the nature of God and the nature of God's relationship to humanity.

Torah: the Hebrew term meaning law or teaching, especially law as divine revelation. (*See* Law.)

Transcendence: in theology God's distance from the world; alternatively, God's holiness or "otherness" as distinct from the secular or profane. (*See* Immanence.)

Trinity: the Christian doctrine that God exists in three persons: the Father, Jesus Christ as the Son, and the Holy Spirit. The developed doctrine is not found in the New Testament although Father, Son, and Spirit are spoken of frequently.

Virgin Birth: the miraculous birth of Jesus to Mary, his mother, without the participation of a human father in the conception.

Witness: in the New Testament includes both observation and testimony, especially to the life, death, and resurrection of Jesus. In one sense, martyrdom is an especially appropriate witness to Jesus. The English term *martyr* is a transliteration of the Greek word for "a witness."

Word: a technical, literary designation of a complete saying, especially a saying of Jesus. In the Johannine literature Jesus himself is called the Word (John 1:1–18).

Word of God: frequently a designation for the Holy Bible. In the New Testament, however, it is used in close connection with the event of Jesus Christ, especially the preaching about that event. (*See* Kerygma.)

Works or works of the law: the attempt to earn righteousness before God instead of acknowledging sin and relying on His grace. (*See* Justification.)

Zealots: members of a Jewish sect who sought to overthrow Roman rule of Palestine by means of violent revolution.

General Bibliography

Subtitles and series have been omitted to conserve space.

I. Biblical Texts in English Translation

The Revised Standard Version has become the English version most widely used in America, and justly so, for it is a good and reliable translation. A comparable, but freer, official translation made in Great Britain, *The New English Bible* (Oxford University Press and Cambridge University Press, 1970), has now appeared. Two excellent modern translations by Roman Catholic scholars are *The Jerusalem Bible*, eds. A. Jones et al. (Garden City, N.Y.: Doubleday, 1966), and *The New American Bible*, trans. members of the Catholic Biblical Association of America (New York: P. J. Kenedy, 1970). The Authorized, or King James, Version is a monument of the English language, but it contains numerous archaic expressions and it is based on late and unreliable Hebrew and Greek originals. Earlier revisions of this most famous English Bible, the English Revised Version and the related American Standard Version, are accurate literal translations, but not very readable. L. R. Bailey has edited a collection of critical essays on recent translations to be published in 1981 by John Knox Press. Most of them appeared originally as an issue of *The Duke Divinity School Review*, 44 (Spring 1979). Needless to say, not all modern translations are equally reliable.

A good and accessible edition of the Synoptic Gospels arranged in parallel columns for easy study and comparison is B. Throckmorton, Jr. (ed.), *Gospel Parallels: A Synopsis of the First Three Gospels*, 4th ed. (Nashville, Tenn.: Nelson, 1979), which is based on the RSV. For close comparisons, however, H. F. D. Sparks, *A Synopsis of the Gospels: The Synoptic Gospels with the Johannine Parallels* (Philadelphia: Fortress, 1964), has the very literal and consistent Revised Version.

A good treatment of the history of the English Bible has been written by I. M. Price, *The Ancestry of Our English Bible*, 3rd rev. ed. by W. A. Irwin and A. P. Wikgren (New York: Harper & Row, 1956). *The Cambridge History of the Bible*, eds. P. R. Ackroyd et al., 3 vols. (New York: Cambridge University Press, 1963–70), is more comprehensive.

II. Tools for New Testament Study

Because relatively few students will likely know or learn New Testament Greek, we shall include under II and III such aids as may be employed by the student who uses only English.

Concordances, which cite the occurrences of every significant word in the Bible, are often very helpful in determining what that word means in the New Testament or in a particular book or author. For absolute accuracy a Greek concordance must be used, for one Greek word may be translated by several English words, whereas a single English word may translate more than one Greek term. In C. Morrison, *An Analytical Concordance to the Revised Standard Version of the New Testament* (Philadelphia: Westminster, 1979), we now have a reliable guide to the original Greek upon which the RSV is based. For the serious student without a command of Greek, it will prove most useful.

The most up-to-date dictionary of biblical terms, names, places, and the like is G. A. Buttrick (ed.), *The Interpreter's Dictionary of the Bible*, 4 vols. (Nashville, Tenn.: Abingdon, 1962); a *Supplementary Volume*, ed. K. Crim, L. R. Bailey, and V. P. Furnish, was published in 1976. There are several one-volume Bible dictionaries of quality, such as J. Hastings (ed.), *Dictionary of the Bible*, rev. ed. by F. C. Grant and H. H. Rowley (New York: Scribner, 1963), and M. S. and J. L. Miller, *Harper's Bible Dictionary*, 8th ed. (New York: Harper & Row, 1973), and idem, *Harper's Encyclopedia of Bible Life*, rev. ed. by B. M. Bennett and D. H. Scott (New York: Harper & Row, 1978). For the meaning of theological terms, there is the compact work of A. Richardson, *A Theological Word Book of the Bible* (New York: Macmillan, 1950). More extensive is X. Leon-DuFour (ed.), *Dictionary of Biblical Theology*, trans. J. P. Cahill (New York: Desclee, 1967). Even those without Hebrew and Greek may be helped by G. Kittel et al., *Theological Dictionary of the New Testament*, trans. G. W. Bromiley (Grand Rapids, Mich.: Eerdmans, 1964), all volumes of which are now available in English translation, with the exception of the comprehensive bibliography (Bd. 10, t. 2 in German).

There are several good Bible atlases. G. E. Wright, *The Westminster Historical Atlas to the Bible,* rev. ed. (Philadelphia: Westminster, 1956), is widely used; also see H. G. May (ed.), *The Oxford Bible Atlas.* 2nd ed. (New York: Oxford University Press, 1974). F. van der Meer and C. Mohrman, *Atlas of the Early Christian World,* ed. and trans. M. F. Hedlund and H. H. Rowley (New York: Nelson, 1958), provides detailed maps and information of New Testament and later times. A valuable atlas is that of Y. Aharoni and M. Avi-Yonah, *The Macmillan Bible Atlas* (New York: Macmillan, 1968). Note also G. E. Wright, *Biblical Archaeology,* rev. ed. (Philadelphia: Westminster, 1962), and Jack Finegan, *The Archaeology of the New Testament: The Life of Jesus and the Beginning of the Early Church* (Princeton, N.J.: Princeton University Press, 1969).

III. *Commentaries*

Among the tools for New Testament study none is more important than a reliable commentary on the text. Several good commentary series should be noted. *Harper's* (in England *Black's*) *New Testament Commentaries* (New York: Harper & Row) is a serious but nontechnical series, as is *The New Century Bible* (London: Oliphants). The Gospel commentaries of the latter are, for the most part, more recent. *The Cambridge Bible Commentary* (New York: Cambridge University Press), another recent series, is based on the *New English Bible* and provides guidance for the general reader. New volumes in the comparable *New Clarendon Bible* (Oxford: Clarendon) are also based on this translation. A new technical series based on the Greek text, *Hermeneia—A Critical and Historical Commentary on the Bible* (Philadelphia: Fortress), is generally excellent. Since all Greek and other foreign language citations are translated, it can be used by the student who lacks command of Greek. *The New International Commentary on the New Testament* (Grand Rapids, Mich.: Eerdmans) is a series of thorough commentaries written from a more conservative perspective. *The Anchor Bible* (Garden City, N.Y.: Doubleday) is a very ambitious commentary series on both Testaments. In the nature of the case, commentaries in a series are not all of the same quality. An excellent one-volume commentary on the Bible is *Peake's Commentary on the Bible,* eds. M. Black and H. H. Rowley (New York: Nelson, 1962). Also noteworthy are C. M. Laymon (ed.), *The Interpreter's One-volume Commentary on the Bible* (Nashville, Tenn.: Abingdon, 1971), and *The Jerome Biblical Commentary,* ed. R. E. Brown, J. A. Fitzmyer, and R. E. Murphy (Englewood Cliffs, N.J.: Prentice-Hall, 1968). There are modern editions of the Bible which provide brief, but useful, introductory articles and notes on the text: *The Jerusalem Bible,* eds. A. Jones et al. (Garden City, N.Y.: Doubleday, 1966), and *The New Oxford Annotated Bible,* eds. H. G. May and B. M. Metzger (New York: Oxford University Press, 1977).

IV. Introductions

There are a number of introductions to the New Testament and similar general books intended for various purposes and readers. Many are quite good. The standard technical introduction is W. G. Kümmel, *Introduction to the New Testament*, rev. ed. trans. H. C. Kee (Nashville, Tenn.: Abingdon, 1975). Also to be noted is the extensive *Introduction to the New Testament*, ed. A. Robert and A. Feuillet and trans. P. W. Skehan et al. (New York: Desclee, 1965). The Kümmel book is a work of Protestant scholarship, whereas the Robert and Feuillet volume was compiled by Roman Catholic scholars.

Among recent less technical introductions, two are particularly worth noting: R. H. Fuller, *A Critical Introduction to the New Testament* (London: Duckworth, 1966), and W. Marxsen, *Introduction to the New Testament: An Approach to its Problems*, trans. G. Buswell (Oxford: Blackwell, 1968). Marxsen's book is designed to point up questions crucial for interpretation. C. F. D. Moule, *The Birth of the New Testament* (New York: Harper & Row, 1962), helpfully explains the origins of the New Testament by displaying the church situations and needs which led to the composition of the various books and the formation of the canon. B. E. Beck, *Reading the New Testament Today: An Introduction to New Testament Study* (Atlanta: John Knox, 1978), makes a cogent and convincing case for the necessity of the discipline. H. Koester, *Einführung in das Neue Testament* (Berlin: de Gruyter, 1980), is an introduction oriented around the religious and cultural history of the Mediterranean world; an English translation is expected from Fortress Press, probably in 1983. R. N. Soulen, *A Handbook of Biblical Criticism* (Atlanta: John Knox, 1976), provides a mine of interesting and useful information.

On the text and canon of the New Testament, the best compact treatment is probably A. Souter, *The Text and Canon of the New Testament*, rev. C. S. C. Williams (London: Duckworth, 1954). A longer treatment of textual history and criticism is provided by B. M. Metzger, *The Text of the New Testament*, 2nd ed. (New York: Oxford University Press, 1968).

V. New Testament Theology

After a generation, R. Bultmann, *Theology of the New Testament*, trans. K. Grobel, 2 vols. (New York: Scribner, 1951–1955), has not yet been displaced as the most important single work, although it virtually ignores the Synoptics and deals principally with John and Paul. Shorter, but more recent, treatments of the subject are H. Conzelmann, *An Outline of the Theology of the New Testament*, trans. J. Bowden (New York: Harper & Row, 1969); and W. G. Kümmel, *The Theology of the New Testament According to its Major Witnesses: Jesus–Paul–John*, trans. J. E. Steely (Nashville, Tenn.: Abingdon, 1973). More conservative, but not fundamentalist, is G. E. Ladd, *A Theology of the New Testament* (Grand Rapids, Mich.: Eerdmans, 1974). There are two recent contributions to the discussion of the nature of the field: R. Morgan, *The Nature of New Testament Theology* (London: SCM, 1973), which contains translations of seminal essays of W. Wrede and A.

Schlatter, and G. F. Hasel, *New Testament Theology: Basic Issues in the Current Debate* (Grand Rapids, Mich.: Eerdmans, 1978).

Of more limited scope is O. Cullmann, *The Christology of the New Testament,* trans. S. C. Guthrie and C. A. M. Hall, rev. ed. (Philadelphia: Westminster, 1964). The definitive statement of Cullmann's position concerning the theological significance of history in the New Testament is his *Salvation in History,* trans. S. G. Sowers (New York: Harper & Row, 1967). C. H. Dodd's brief but important treatment of *The Apostolic Preaching and Its Developments* (New York: Harper & Row, 1951; orig. 1936) has not lost its significance as an investigation of the earliest stages of Christian proclamation. More up-to-date and complex is R. H. Fuller, *The Foundations of New Testament Christology* (New York: Scribner, 1965), which also deals with the earliest period. Somewhat similar to Fuller in scope and perspective is F. Hahn, *The Titles of Jesus in Christology: Their History in Early Christianity,* trans. H. Knight and G. Ogg (New York: World, 1969). M. Hengel, *The Son of God,* trans. J. Bowden (Philadelphia: Fortress, 1976), makes the case for the Jewish antecedents of this crucially important title.

Recent efforts to deal with ethics in the New Testament include R. Schnackenburg, *The Moral Teaching of the New Testament,* trans. J. Holland-Smith and W. J. O'Hara (New York: Herder & Herder, 1967), and V. P. Furnish, *The Love Commandment in the New Testament* (Nashville, Tenn.: Abingdon, 1972). J. L. Houlden, *Ethics and the New Testament* (New York: Oxford University Press, 1977), is well-informed and insightful. The question of applicability is raised in such a way as to enhance historical understanding, as is the case with his other slim volume, *Patterns of Faith: A Study in the Relationship between the New Testament and Christian Doctrine* (Philadelphia: Fortress, 1977). Serious unresolved problems in dealing with the theological dimensions of scripture are described and discussed by B. S. Childs, *Biblical Theology in Crisis* (Philadelphia: Westminster, 1970).

VI. History of Criticism and Interpretation

Probably the most important work on the modern period is W. G. Kümmel, *The New Testament: The History of the Investigation of Its Problems,* trans. S. M. Gilmour and H. C. Kee (Nashville, Tenn.: Abingdon, 1972). A very readable and useful book, written by a British churchman who is not a New Testament scholar, is Stephen Neill's *The Interpretation of the New Testament: 1861–1961* (London: Oxford University Press, 1964). A survey of the history of Biblical interpretation from earliest times is provided by R. M. Grant, *The Bible in the Church: A Short History of Interpretation* (New York: Macmillan, 1958; paperback title, *Short History of the Interpretation of the Bible*). The three-volume *Cambridge History of the Bible* (see Section I) is also relevant here.

VII. Bibliography

Since the resources for biblical study are immense, there is a problem in selecting worthwhile and helpful works. The introductions of Robert and Feuillet and Kümmel provide extensive and reliable guidance. The journal *New Testament Abstracts,* published at Weston College, Weston, Massachusetts, catalogues and summarizes articles and important books in New Testament as they appear. J. C. Hurd, Jr., has published *A Bibliography of New Testament Bibliographies* (New York: Seabury, 1966), which will be of great value for the student doing a thorough piece of research. Probably more relevant to the needs of the majority of students is F. W. Danker, *Multipurpose Tools for Bible Study* (Saint Louis: Concordia, 1960), some of which is intended to aid the student who knows the biblical languages. Much of the discussion, however, should be helpful to the student limited to English. More recent bibliography is included in D. M. Scholer, *A Basic Bibliographic Guide for New Testament Exegesis,* 2nd ed. (Grand Rapids, Mich.: Eerdmans, 1973); cf. S. B. Marrow, *Basic Tools of Biblical Exegesis,* 2nd ed. (Rome: Biblical Institute Press, 1978). Also excellent for bibliography is the second part of Vol. 10 of Kittel's *Theologisches Wörterbuch zum Neuen Testament,* ed. G. Friedrich (Stuttgart: Kohlhammer, 1979), in which articles are grouped under the appropriate Greek words.

NAME AND SUBJECT INDEX

Abraham, 33f., 99, 144; as man of faith, 374ff.

Achtemeier, Paul J., *Mark*, 96

Acts of the Apostles, The, 3, 273, 275–308, 396, 493, authorship, 275f.; emphases, 305f.; historical character, 276f.; 286f., 306; historical situation, 307f., 462; literary composition and structure, 275, 286f., 305, 307f.; outline, 277; purpose, 285, 290f.; relation to Paul, 275f., 290f., 480; *See also Luke, Gospel According to*; Luke

Acts of Paul, 306, 409

Adam, in genealogy of *Luke*, 144, 163, 303; in Paul's thought, 367, 376f.

Aharoni, V., et al., *The Macmillan Bible Atlas*, 512

Alexander the Great, 17, 35f., 38

Allegory, allegorical interpretation, 41f., 52, 500; of parables, 226ff.

Anchor Bible, The, 512

Anderson, Hugh, *Jesus and Christian Origins*, 260, 267, *The Gospel of Mark*, 96

Anna, a prophetess, 139–141

Antichrist, 438, 500

Antioch, Pisidian, 295, 325

Antioch, in Syria, 295ff., 325

Antiochus IV (Epiphanes), 18

Apocalyptic, apocalypticism, 29–34, 120ff., 461f., 468f., 501; in Jesus' teaching, 224ff.; *I John*, 438; *Mark*, 88; *Matthew*, 113; *Paul*, 322ff., *Revelation*, 441ff.

Apocrypha, The, 501

Apollonius of Tyana, 210f.

Apostle, concept of, 280f., 501; in *Ephesians*, 403; *Luke–Acts*, 159, 279ff.; Paul's understanding, 280f., 313ff.

Apostles' Creed, 484

Apostolic Constitutions, 410

Apostolic Fathers, 463, 501

Apuleius, *The Golden Ass*, 46

Areopagus (Mars Hill), 299; Paul's address, 298–303

Aristeas, Epistle of, 501

Ark of the Covenant, 370

Ascension of Jesus, 277–280, 282, 284f., 501

Asclepius, 51

Astrology, 51

Athens, Paul's speech in, 298–303

Atonement, Day of, 26, 370

Augustus Caesar, 39, 43, 45, 139

Avi-Yonah, M., et al., *The Macmillan Bible Atlas*, 512

Babylonian exile of the Jews, 15, 17, 33, 35, 99

Bacon, B. W., 418, *Studies in Matthew*, 104

Bailey, L. R., 510; *The Interpreter's Dictionary of the Bible: Supplementary Volume*, 511

Bammel, E., *The Trial of Jesus*, 268

Baptism, Christian, 467, 478f., 484f., 501; Cornelius' household, 294; origin of, 127f., 285, in Paul, 378f., 467; *See also* Jesus; Baptism

Bar Kochba, Simon, 22f.

Barabbas, 89, 156, 251, 257

Barbour, R. S., *Traditio-Historical Criticism of the Gospels*, 269

Barnabas, 293, 326f.; as companion of Paul, 295, 297f., 303

Barnabas, The Letter of, 418, 485

Barnett, A. E., *Paul Becomes a Literary Influence*, 396, 416

Baron, S. W., et al., *Judaism: Post-Biblical and Talmudic Period*, 55

Barrett, C. K., *A Commentary on the Epistle to the Romans*, 362, 388f., 394; *A Commentary on the First Epistle to the Corinthians*, 355; *The Gospel According to John*, 167f., 200, 203; *Luke the Historian in Recent Study*, 164; *The New Testament Background: Selected Documents*, 42f., 46, 49, 55, 73, 211; *New Testament Essays*, 171; *A Commentary on the Second Epistle to the Corinthians*, 355; *The Pastoral Epistles*, 458

Barth, G., et al., *Tradition and Interpretation in Matthew*, 107, 109, 119, 121, 124, 125, 132

Bartimaeus, 82

Baruch, II, 367, 444

Bauer, W., *Orthodoxy and Heresy in Earliest Christianity*, 481, 489

Bea, Augustin Cardinal, *The Study of the Synoptic Gospels*, 95

Beare, F. W., 129; *A Commentary on the Epistle to the Philippians*, 344, 355; *The Earliest Records of Jesus*, 96, 117, 214, 216; *St. Paul and His Letters*, 354

Beasley-Murray, G. R., *Baptism in the New Testament*, 285; *The Book of Revelation*, 458

Beck, B. E., *Reading the New Testament Today*, 513

Beckwith, I. T., *The Apocalypse of John,* 458
Beker, J. C., 406; *The Church Faces the World,* 457; *Paul the Apostle,* 394
Beloved Disciple, 168; as symbolic figure, 189
Best, E., *The Temptation and the Passion: The Markan Soteriology,* 96; *A Commentary on the First and Second Epistles to the Thessalonians,* 355; *I Peter,* 458
Bethlehem, 102
Bettenson, H., *Documents of the Christian Church,* 44, 425
Betz, H. D., *Christology and a Modern Pilgrimage,* 96; *Galatians,* 316, 327, 355
Bickerman, E., 262
Bishop, 410, 436, 482ff.
Black, M., et al., (eds.), *Peake's Commentary on the Bible,* 512; *The Scrolls and Christian Origins,* 56, 285; *An Aramaic Approach to the Gospels and Acts,* 238; *Romans,* 394
Black's New Testament Commentaries, See Harper's New Testament Commentaries
Blau, J. L., et al., *Judaism: Postbiblical and Talmudic Period,* 55
Blinzler, J., *The Trial of Jesus,* 268
Body of Christ, 357; in Ephesians, 402f., 404f.; in Paul, 349f., 389f., 420
Bornkamm, G., 119, 127f.; *Early Christian Experience,* 389; *Jesus of Nazareth,* 249, 252f., 259, 267; *Paul,* 355; *Tradition and Interpretation in Matthew,* 132
Borsch, Frederick, *The Son of Man in Myth and History,* 240, 243, 268
Bortin, Virginia, 264
Bousset, W., *Kyrios Christos,* 490
Bowker, J., *Jesus and the Pharisees,* 267
Bowman, J. W., *The Intention of Jesus,* 241
Brandon, S. G. F., *Jesus and the Zealots,* 230, 236, 251, 268; *The Trial of Jesus,* 268
Brown, R. E., 458; *The Gospel According to John,* 167f., 171, 185, 200; *The Birth of the Messiah,* 99, 208, 269; *Peter in the New Testament,* 118, 458; *The Community of the Beloved Disciple,* 201; *The Jerome Biblical Commentary,* 490, 512
Bruce, F. F., *Commentary on the Book of Acts,* 308; *The Epistle to the Hebrews,* 458; *The Epistle to the Romans, a Commentary,* 394; *New Testament History,* 489; *Jesus and Christian Origins Outside the New Testament,* 266; *Paul: Apostle of the Heart Set Free,* 355
Buber, Martin, *Two Types of Faith,* 34
Bultmann, Rudolf, 177, 311; *Existence and Faith,* 382; *The Gospel of John,* 167, 194, 200; *History of the Synoptic Tradition,* 78, 86, 90, 95, 214ff., 243; *Jesus and the Word,* 267; *Primitive Christianity in Its Comtemporary Setting,* 55; *The Johannine Epistles,* 458; *Theology of the New Testament,* 205, 268, 322, 372, 394, 513
Burkill, T. A., *Mysterious Revelation,* 96, 268
Burkitt, F. C., 225
Burrows, Millar, *The Dead Sea Scrolls,* 28f.; *More Light on the Dead Sea Scrolls,* 28
Burton, E. D., *A Critical and Exegetical Commentary on the Epistle to the Galatians,* 316
Buttrick, G. A. (ed), *The Interpreter's Dictionary of the Bible,* 511
Cadbury, H. J., *The Book of Acts in History,* 276, 308; *The Making of Luke–Acts,* 165, 286, 308; *The Beginnings of Christianity,* 279
Caesarea, 292ff., 343; Paul's imprisonment in, 304, 343
Caesarea Philippi, Peter's confession at, 83f.; centrality in Mark, 94; as turning point of Jesus' ministry, 294; *See also* Peter, Simon
Caiaphas, 21, 188
Caird, G. B., *A Commentary on the Revelation of St. John,* 458; *The Gospel of St. Luke,* 164
Cambridge Ancient History, The, 56
Cambridge Bible Commentary, The, 512
Cambridge History of the Bible, 511, 514
Cambridge History of Judaism, The, 55
Campenhausen, H. von, 262; *The Formation of the Christian Bible,* 489f.
Canon, New Testament, 485ff., 493ff., 502; formation of, 485ff., 493ff.; collections within, 486ff., significance of, 488f.
Capernaum, 146
Cartlidge, David P., et al. (eds.), *Documents for the Study of the Gospels,* 96, 204, 211
Case, S. J., *Experience with the Supernatural in Early Christian Times,* 268
Catchpole, D. R., *The Trial of Jesus,* 268f.
Catholic Epistles, 396, 463, 494, 502
Cephas (Peter), 316; *See also* Peter, Simon
Charles, R. H., *The Apocrypha and Pseudepigrapha of the Old Testament,* 32, 54; *A Critical and Exegetical Commentary on the Revelation of St. John,* 36, 448
Charlesworth, J. H. (ed.), *John and Qumran,* 197; *The Old Testament Pseudepigrapha,* 54
Childs, B. S., *Biblical Theology in Crisis,* 514
Christ, Jesus, cosmic or creative role, 172ff., 394ff.; description in *Revelation,* 450f.; in *Ephesians,* 400ff.; as example, 347, 420ff., 439f.; as God's grace (q.v.), 375; importance in Fourth Gospel, 200; *See also* Jesus
Christianity, early, 273, 462ff.; background in Judaism, 13ff., 51ff., 472, 480; community life in, 477ff.; exclusiveness of, 476; nonsubversive character, 162f., 307; *See also* Church, early
Church, early, 116f., 131f., 149f., 462ff., 273–490 *passim*; authority of, 118f.; background of New Testament, 462ff.; discipline, 119f., 273, 415–435; as institution, 273, 382–414; in Jerusalem, 276f., 287, 477; mission, 113, 127f., 288ff., 472ff.; organization, 408–414; orthodoxy in, 408ff., 481f.; cf. 496f.; world, 194, 196f., 422ff.; *See also* Christianity, early
Circumcision, 327ff., 354, 400; party of, 294, 327, 329; in Paul's usage, 364
Cleanthes, *Hymn to Zeus,* 42f., 300
Clement (of Rome), I, 306, 484
Clement of Alexandria, evidence of New Testament canon, 486
Colossians, The Letter to the, 342ff., 348ff., 396ff.; authorship of, 310, 348; circumstances of origin, 342ff., 480; and *Ephesians,* 342f., 396ff.; heresy refuted, 348f., 409; outline, 348
Conzelmann, H., 441, 468; *History of Primitive Christianity,* 489; *Jesus,* 84; *An Outline of the Theology of the New Testament,* 513; *The Theology of St. Luke,* 65, 134, 144, 154, 164; *I Corinthians,* 355; *The Pastoral Epistles,* 409, 458

Corinth, 298, 309ff., 496; problems of church, 332ff., 339ff., 480f.
Corinthians, The First Letter of Paul to the, 310f., 317ff., 331ff.; circumstances of writing, 332ff., 480; date, 332; Ephesian origin, 331; outline, 332
Corinthians, The Second Letter of Paul to the, 310ff., 331f., 339ff.
Cornelius, conversion of, 291ff.
Creeds, development of, 484f.
Crim, K., *The Interpreter's Dictionary of the Bible: Supplementary Volume,* 511
Cross, F. M., *The Ancient Library of Qumran and Modern Biblical Studies,* 56
Crucifixion (Passion) of Jesus, 88–92, 124, 154–158, 247–258, 466ff., 469, 471f., 502; foreshadowed, 79ff., 84ff., 150, 157; as glorification of Jesus in Fourth Gospel, 177, 179, 190ff., 199; necessity of, 90, 158; as outcome of Jesus' life and mission, 258; in Paul, 368ff.; in preaching, 205f., 465; in the tradition, 254–258; witnesses, 92, 158f.; words from the cross, 90f., 156
Cullman, O., *Baptism in the New Testament,* 285; *Christ and Time,* 205; *The Christology of the New Testament,* 235, 238, 241, 243, 514; *The Johannine Circle,* 200f.; *Peter: Disciple–Apostle–Martyr,* 117, 276; *Salvation in History,* 514; *The State in the New Testament,* 489
Dahl, N. A., 207, 398
Danby, H. (trans.), *The Mishnah,* 25, 55
Danker, F. W., *Multipurpose Tools for Bible Study,* 515; *Luke,* 164
Davey, Noel, et al., *The Riddle of the New Testament,* 428
David, 15, 78, 85, 99, 236, 358
Davies, W. D., *Christian Origins and Judaism,* 32; *Paul and Rabbinic Judaism,* 394; *The Sermon on the Mount,* 98, 132; *The Setting of the Sermon on the Mount,* 104, 121, 132, 232; *Torah in the Messianic Age and/or the Age to Come,* 234; *The Gospel and the Land,* 15; *The Cambridge History of Judaism,* 55
Deacon, 288, 410
Dead Sea Scrolls, 28ff., 411, 502; and Johannine origins, 168f., 197f.; *See also* Qumran
Demon exorcisms, 71ff., 82, 212ff.
Devil, 149; *See also* Satan
Diaspora Judaism, 51ff., 479
Diatessaron of Tatian, 487
Dibelius, Martin, *From Tradition to Gospel,* 95, 318, 418; *Jesus,* 252, 267; *The Pastoral Epistles,* 409, 458; *Studies in the Acts of the Apostles,* 286, 308; *James,* 458
Docetism, 437f., 502f.
Dodd, C. H., 213; *The Apostolic Preaching and Its Developments,* 205, 318, 467, 514; *Historical Tradition in the Fourth Gospel,* 200; *The Interpretation of the Fourth Gospel,* 175, 200; *The Johannine Epistles,* 458; *Parables of the Kingdom,* 213
Domitian, Emperor, 421, 442

Donahue, John R., *Are You the Christ?,* 253
Donfried, Karl P., *Peter in the New Testament,* 118, 458; *The Romans Debate,* 394
Doty, William G., *Letters in Primitive Christianity,* 396
Dualism, apocalyptic, 29f., 33, 225; Gnostic, 49; Johannine, 191, 197, 435
Dungan, David S., *The Sayings of Jesus in the Churches of Paul,* 320, 355; et al. (eds.), *Documents for the Study of the Gospels,* 96, 204, 211
Easton, B. S., 416; *The Pastoral Epistles,* 418
Edgar, C. C., et al. (ed.), *Select Papyri,* 358
Edwards, Richard A., *A Theology of Q,* 470
Elder, 410f., 482
Elder John, 435f., 441, 482
Elijah, 70, 85, 90, 146, 386
Ellis, E. E., *The Gospel of Luke,* 164
Emmaus, road to, 158ff., 260f.
Emperor worship, 43f.; in *Revelation,* 454
Enoch, I, 238
Ephesians, The Letter of Paul to the, 397–406; authorship, 310, 342f., 396, 397f., 463; Gentile audience, 399f.; historical circumstances of, 397f.; literary style, 397f.; outline, 398f.; relation to *Colossians,* 348, 397f.; relation to Paul, 404ff., 456; role in collection of Pauline corpus, 397f.
Ephesus, 298, 343, 397f.; traditional place of origin of Johannine literature, 167f., 197, 435.
Epstein, I. (trans.), *The Babylonian Talmud,* 25f.
Eschatology, 31ff., 191ff., 199f., 324f., 468f., 474f.; and ethics in Jesus' teaching, 220–234; Luke's revision, cf. 144, 278f.; in *Matthew,* 131; and Messianism, 235ff.: parousia of Jesus in Paul, 323ff.; in *Revelation,* 443ff.; *See also* Apocalyptic; Kingdom of God
Essenes, 28ff., 184, 204, 503; *See also* Dead Sea Scrolls; Qumran
Eternal life, 191f.
Eucharist, 215, 503; *See also* Lord's Supper
Eusebius, *Ecclesiastical History,* 54, 62, 66, 97, 306, 415, 435
Exorcisms, *See* Demon exorcisms
Expiation, 370f., 503
Ezekiel, 449f., 453
Ezra, IV, 238, 367
Faith, and action, 416ff.; in Fourth Gospel, 175f., 200; and healings, 86ff., 217f.; in *Hebrews,* 426, 429, 434; in *James* and Paul, 418f.; in *Mark,* 75, 88, 92ff.; in *Paul,* 328ff., 354, 369ff.; in Paul and the *Pastorals,* 410ff.
Farmer, W. R., *The Synoptic Problem,* 63
Feeding of multitude, 116f.
Fenton, J. C., *The Gospel of St. Matthew,* 132
Ferguson, J., *The Religions of the Roman Empire,* 56
Festus, 304
Feuillet, A., et al., *Introduction to the New Testament,* 118, 513, 515
Finegan, Jack, *The Archeology of the New Testament,* 512
Finklestein, L., et al., *The Cambridge History of Judaism,* 55
Fitzmeyer, J. A., *Pauline Theology,* 394; *The Jerome Biblical Commentary,* 512
Flender, H., *St. Luke: Theologian of Redemptive History,* 137

Flesh, in *Ephesians*, 400; in Fourth Gospel, 176, 191; in *I Peter*, 423f.; in Paul, 380ff.
Foakes-Jackson, F. J., *The Beginnings of Christianity*, 308
Foerster, W., *Gnosis: A Selection of Gnostic Texts*, 55
Forgiveness, in church, 116f., importance in *Luke–Acts*, 147f., 151ff., 163, 285f.; through Jesus, 101, 156, 246; in Paul, 350, 375f.
Form criticism, 64, 503
Fortna, R. T., *The Gospel of Signs*, 167, 200
Fourth Gospel, See John, the Gospel According to
Franklin, E., *Christ the Lord*, 164
Frend, W. H. C., *Martyrdom and Persecution in the Early Church*, 489
Fridrichsen, A., *The Problem of Miracle in Primitive Christianity*, 212, 268
Fuller, R. H., *The Mission and Achievement of Jesus*, 243; *The Formation of the Resurrection Narratives*, 260, 269; *Interpreting the Miracles*, 268; *A Critical Introduction to the New Testament*, 513; *The Foundations of New Testament Christology*, 514
Furnish, V. P., 319; *Theology and Ethics in Paul*, 394; *The Interpreter's Dictionary of the Bible: Supplementary Volume*, 511; *The Love Commandment in the New Testament*, 514
Gager, John C., *Kingdom and Community*, 475
Galatians, The Letter of Paul to the, 313–317, 325–331, 480; addresses, 325f.; opponents of Paul, 315f., 325, 326ff.; outline, 326
Galilee, 20f., 159; as beginning point of Gospel, 163; in Fourth Gospel, 166; in *John* and Synoptics, 198; resurrection appearances in, 93, 125, 159, 260ff.; significance in *Luke*, 143–149
Gamaliel, 22
Gamble, Harry, Jr., *The Textual History of the Letter to the Romans*, 391
Gärtner, B., *The Areopagus Speech and Natural Revelation*, 302
Gasque, W. W., *A History of the Criticism of the Acts of the Apostles*, 308
Gaster, T. H., *The Dead Sea Scriptures*, 225
Gealy, F. D., 410
Gentiles, 277f., 290, 294f., 327, 472ff., 497ff., 503; conversion confirmed by Jerusalem council, 295, 297; in *Ephesians*, 399f.; in *Luke–Acts*, 146, 157f., 163, 277f., 291–295, 298ff., 304f.; in *Mark*, 93; *Matthew* 113; in Paul, 386ff.; in *I Peter*, 423; sinfulness of, 362ff.
Georgi, Dieter, *Die Gegner des Paulus in 2. Korintherbrief*, 53
Gerhardson, B., 226
Gethsemane, 190f.; 218, 251, 253; Jesus' prayer in, 109, 190f., 218, 245, 257; missing in Fourth Gospel, 166; reflected in *Hebrews*, 432
Gilmour, S. M., 145
Glossolalia, in *Acts* and Paul, 282
Gnosticism, 47–51, 173, 497, 503; in Fourth Gospel, 50, 194; Gospels, 51, 204; in *I John*, 437f.; Mandaeism, 50; Manichaeism, 50; Nag Hammadi, 50, 204; 470; in Pastorals, 408f.; redeemer myth, 49f., 51; salvation in, 49f.
God, as Creator, 385; faithfulness of, 384–388;

impartiality of, 363f., 366; Jesus as, 178f.; as love, 439; righteousness of, 330, 369–374, 384ff., 393
Goguel, Maurice, *Jesus and the Origins of Christianity*, 204, 256, 267
Goldin, J., *The Living Talmud*, 55
Goldstein, Morris, *Jesus in the Jewish Tradition*, 204, 266
Goodspeed, E. J., *The Key to Ephesians*, 397f.; *The Meaning of Ephesians*, 457
Gospel, in *Mark*, 70f.; meaning of Greek term, 61, 465; in Paul, 326ff.; spread of, 463, 472–480
Gospel of Truth, The, 49f.
Gospels, 3, 6, 61f., 206, 464ff., 478, 480, 493ff., 503; historical interest in Jesus, 206, 461; and kerygma, 205f.; oral tradition in, 61f.; reason for composition, 395, 462, 481; *See also* Synoptic Gospels, *Matthew, Mark, Luke, John*
Gospels, noncanonical, 50, 204, 211; *Ebionites*, 107; *Egyptians*, 470; *Hebrews*, 107, 470; *James*, 211; *Peter*, 204, 471; *Philip*, 204; *Thomas*, 50, 204, 470; *Thomas, Infancy Gospel of*, 76, 204, 211, 471; *Truth*, 49f.
Grace (of God), 176, 178; in *Hebrews*, 430f.; in Paul, 330f., 375ff., 387
Grant, F. C., 79; *Hellenistic Religions*, 55; *Roman Hellenism and the New Testament*, 56; *Form Criticism*, 95
Grant, R. M., *Miracle and Natural Law in Greeco–Roman and Early Christian Thought*, 268; *The Sword and the Cross*, 489; *The Bible in the Church*, 514; *Short History of the Interpretation of the Bible*, 514
Greco–Roman world, 34–54
Greek culture, 35ff.
Greek language, 3, 35ff.; *Koine*, 36; importance for Judaism, 51f.
Greek religion, 40ff.
Grobel, Kendrick, 372
Haenchen, E., *The Acts of the Apostles*, 298, 308
Hahn, F., *The Titles of Jesus in Christology*, 514
Harnack, A. von, *What Is Christianity?*, 221
Harper's New Testament Commentaries, 512
Harrison, P. N., *The Problem of the Pastoral Epistles*, 406, 458
Hartman, Lars, *Prophecy Interpreted*, 468
Hasel, G. F., *New Testament Theology*, 514
Hasmonean, *See* Maccabeans
Hastings, J. (ed.), *Dictionary of the Bible*, 511
Heaven, Kingdom of (in *Matthew*), 106, 114ff.; *See also* Eschatology; Kingdom of God
Hebrews, The Letter to the, 396, 426–435, 456, 479, 494; authorship, 310, 396, 426f., 434; date, 427; high priesthood of Jesus, 428ff.; historical origin, 426f.; literary character, 426f.; Old Testament in, 428ff.; outline, 427f.; relation to Paul, 396, 398, 426, 434
Held, H. J., et al., *Tradition and Interpretation in Matthew*, 100, 112, 132
Hellenistic religions, 40ff.
Hellenists, in early church, 288; persecution of, 297
Hellenization, Hellenistic civilization, 11, 17, 20, 35ff., 504; importance for Judaism and Christianity, 35ff., cf. 51ff., 497ff.
Hengel, M., *Judaism and Hellenism*, 18, 25, 28,

51f., 55; *Victory over Violence*, 230, 268; *Was Jesus a Revolutionist?*, 230, 268; *The Son of God*, 514

Hennecke, E., et al., *New Testament Apocrypha*, 76, 107, 133, 142, 204, 211, 266, 409, 488, 490

Heresy, incipient, 273, 343, 347, 348–354, 407ff., 496; in *I John*, 436ff.; in *Pastorals*, 407ff.

Hering, J., *The Epistle to the Hebrews*, 458

Hermeneia, 355, 356, 458, 512

Herod Agrippa I, 20, 307

Herod Antipas, 20, 21, 79, 156

Herod the Great, 20, 99, 102, 104, 139, 466

Herodians, 79

Hiers, R. H., *The Kingdom of God in the Synoptic Tradition*, 222, 224

Hill, D., *The Gospel of Matthew*, 132

History, and apocalyptic, 224f.; lordship of God, 447f., 454f.; in the New Testament and today, 454ff.; and revelation, 13f., 454f.; of salvation, 162

Holladay, Carl H., *Theios Aner in Hellenistic Judaism*, 76

Holy Spirit, *See* Spirit

Hooker, M. D., *Jesus and the Servant*, 241

Hope, Christian, 323ff., 476f.; *See also* Eschatology; Resurrection

Horton, Fred L., *The Melchizedek Tradition*, 433

Hoskyns, E., *The Fourth Gospel: The Riddle of the New Testament*, 428

Houlden, J. L., *Paul's Letters from Prison*, 356, 458; *The Johannine Epistles*, 458; *Ethics and the New Testament*, 514; *Patterns of Faith*, 514

Howard, George, *Paul: Crisis in Galatia*, 355

Hughes, G., *Hebrews and Hermeneutics*, 458

Hunt, A. S., et al. (ed.), *Select Papyri*, 358

Hunter, Archibald M., *Paul and His Predecessors*, 309, 318, 355

Hurd, John, *The Origin of I Corinthians*, 332, 355; *A Bibliography of New Testament Bibliographies*, 515

Idols, meat sacrificed to, 334ff.

Ignatius of Antioch, 396; on importance of church offices, 484; silence on John's residence in Ephesus, 167; witness to New Testament canon, 486f.

Incarnation, 504; in Fourth Gospel, 174ff.; in *Hebrews*, 430; in *I John*, 437f.

Irenaeus, and the canon of the New Testament, 486, 488; and development of creeds, 484

Isaiah, 385, 424

Israel, 13–15, 29, 32f.; and church in *Luke–Acts*, 157f., 162f., 305ff.; in *Ephesians*, 400ff.; in Fourth Gospel, 175; in *Hebrews*, 428f.; hopes fulfilled in Jesus, 99ff., 305f.; in Paul's thought, 384–388, 392; *See also* Judaism

Jairus' daughter, 216

James, Jesus' brother, 316, 322, 415; mentioned by Josephus, 204

James, The Letter of, 415–420, 456; authorship, 415f., 463; ethical character, 416ff.; historical origin of, 415f.; outline, 416; relation to Paul, 415, 418ff., 456, 480f., 496; style of, 415

James, son of Zebedee, death of, 156, 276

Jamnia, Council of, 14; as background of Fourth Gospel, 185

Jeremias, Joachim, *The Eucharistic Words of Jesus*, 252, 267; *The Parables of Jesus*, 157, 226ff., 267; *The Unknown Sayings of Jesus*, 205; *The Servant of God*, 241; *Jerusalem in the Time of Jesus*, 267; *New Testament Theology*, 267; *Rediscovering the Parables*, 267

Jerusalem, 14f., 19f., 102, 162f., 248ff., 401, 477; in Ascension narrative, 279; in Fourth Gospel, 166, 198; importance in *Luke–Acts*, 137, 139, 150ff., 159, 162f., 278f., 288ff., 305; Jesus' entry, 83, 250f.; Paul's arrest in, 304; in resurrection tradition, 159, 260ff., in *Revelation*, 453; role in *Acts*, 297; site of Jesus' death, 248ff.; Paul's visits to, 357, 391

Jerusalem Council, The, 295, 297, 316f., 319, 325f., 463

Jervell, J., *Luke and the People of God*, 308

Jesus, 59–266 *passim*, 273, 465ff.; ascension, 279; authority, 245ff.; baptism by John, 67–71, 106ff.; birth and infancy, 99–105, 137–142; date of birth, 39, 466; death, 88–92, 124, 154–156, 248–254, 466–468; debates with opponents, 76–80; demon exorcisms, 73–76, 82; disciples, call of, 244f.; entry into Jerusalem, 83, 250f.; eschatology, 221–231, 231f., 468; as ethical teacher, 220f., 231ff.; exaltation of, 465; feeding of multitudes, 215; granting forgiveness, 245ff.; importance of his sayings in early Christianity, 418, 469, 471; Law, interpretation of, 109–112, 233f., 246, 478; Messianic consciousness, 235–244; Messianic secret, 83f.; miracles, 71ff., 112f., 146f., 166, 180–189, 209–220, 247f., 471f., 505; mother, *See* Mary; non-Christian sources, 203f.; parables, 84, 505; political question, 236, 251f.; at prayer, 74f., 86, 190–197; *See also* Gethsemane; preaching, 74, 108, 145–148; and Qumran, 28ff.; resurrection, 205f., 258–266; Sabbath question, 78f.; with sinners, 77; suffering, 240f., 247–258; teaching of, 109ff., 220–247, 469ff.; temptation, *See* Temptation of Jesus; tradition about, 202–209, 319–322, 418, cf. 465–472; transfiguration, 82, 85; trial of, 243, 253; *See also* Disciples; Son of Man, etc.

Jewett, Robert, *A Chronology of Paul's Life*, 310, 354

Jewish Christians, 352, 477, 479, 327, 496ff.

Jews, advantages of, 363ff.; in Fourth Gospel, 175, 185ff.; in Paul, 384–388; reconciliation in *Ephesians*, 400ff.; role in crucifixion, 253; sinfulness of, 363ff.; *See also* Israel

Johannine letters, 396, 435–441, 482ff.; historical circumstances of, 435f., 463f., 480ff.; relation to Gospel, 167, 396, 435f., 440f.; *See also John, The First Letter of*

Johannine Literature, 6, 166–201, 435–458; authorship problem, 167f., 435f.; *See also John, The First Letter of; John, The Gospel According to; Johannine Letters*

John the Baptist, 30, 68ff., 106ff., 144, 209; baptism of Jesus, 68–71, 106ff., 144; birth of, 137; and Christian baptism, 285; disciples of, 77, 244, 175; eschatology, 33, 225; in Fourth Gospel, 169, 171f., 174f.; identified with Law and prophets, 110; and Jesus, 114; mentioned by Josephus, 204; preaching of, 106ff.; prophetic character, 69

John the Elder, *See* Elder John
John, The First Letter of, 435–441; Antichrist in, 437ff.; Christology, 437ff.; heresy combatted, 436–439, 457, 482ff.; outline, 436; Spirit and spirits, 436ff., 483; *See also* Johannine letters
John, The Gospel According to, 6, 166–201, 202f., 479, 487, 493ff.; anti-Gnostic character, 194; authorship problem, 166ff., 462; background, 168f., and *passim,* 479; Christology in, 173ff., cf. 192, 199; composition and order, 166f.; date, 168; death of Jesus in, 177, 179, 181, 190ff., 197, 198, 254; dualism, 173, 197f.; eschatology, 191f., 461, cf. 198, 230; faith in, 175f., 200; farewell discourses, 192–197; Galilee and Judea in, 166, 248; historical origin of, 166ff., 197f., 479; historicity of, 202f., cf. 6, 168; "I am" sayings, 181f.; intended readers, 168f.; and Judaism, 169, 172f., 175f., 185, 197f.; Last Supper, 183, 190, 193; love in, 196; man born blind, 180–189; miracles in, 166, 177, 180–189, 471; outline of, 169; prologue of, 169–179, 198; and Qumran, 168f., 197f.; resurrection in, 183, 197, 199; Spirit in, 282; and Synoptics, 166ff., 180ff., 190, 198, 235f., 480; structure, 198f., cf. 169; tradition and redaction, 166ff., 171–189 *passim,* 198; theological development of miracles, 181ff.; world in, 175, 191f., 194, 195, 435; *See also* Johannine Literature
John Mark, 62, 298
John the Son of Zebedee, 167f., 189, 276, 316, 322, 435, 441
Johnson, Sherman, 100
Jonas, H., *The Gnostic Religion,* 56
Jones, A., et al., *The Jerusalem Bible,* 510, 512
Joppa, 292f.
Joseph, 100ff.; recognized as father of Jesus, 146
Joseph of Arimathea, 92, 254
Josephus, 17, 28, 53; *Against Apion,* 153; *Jewish Antiquities,* 17, 53, 204; *The Jewish War,* 31
Judaism, 13–34, 472, 476; diaspora, 51ff., 479ff.; eschatology, 31ff.; Hellenization of, 17ff., 51ff.; history, 13–34, esp. 17–23; land, 15; law, 14f., 24–31; proselytism, 53; worship, 14f., 52f.; *See also* Jews
Judaizing Christians, 288f.; in Corinth, 339f.; in Galatia, 330f.; *See also* Jewish Christians
Judas the Galilean, 22, 244
Judas Iscariot, 190, 253, 256, 279f.
Judas Maccabeus, 19
Jude, The Letter of, 396, 464
Judea, 17ff.; in *Acts,* 278, 290; in Fourth Gospel, 166
Judgment, in Fourth Gospel, 186; God's impartiality, 363ff.; in *I John,* 440; in Judaism, 32f.; in parables, 228f.; by the Son of Man, 122f.; *See also* Eschatology; Kingdom of God; Son of Man
Jülicher, A., 227
Justification, 330, 369–372, 419, 504; *See also* Righteousness; Paul, theology and teachings
Justin, Martyr, 50; evidence of New Testament canon, 486f.; evidence of development of creeds, 484
Kähler, Martin, *The So-Called Historical Jesus and the Historic Biblical Christ,* 81

Käsemann, E., 207, 404, 436; *The Testament of Jesus,* 200; *Essays on New Testament Themes,* 232, 245; *Perspectives on Paul,* 394; *Commentary on Romans,* 394; *Das wanderende Gottesvolk,* 428, 431
Keck, Leander, 70, 267, 372; *Studies in Luke–Acts,* 137, 164f., 277, 404; *A Future for the Historical Jesus,* 269; *Paul and His Letters,* 394
Kee, H. C., *Jesus in History,* 96, 266; *Community of the New Age,* 96
Kelly, J. N. D., *A Commentary on the Epistles of Peter and Jude,* 458
Kerygma, early Christian, 205f., 293, 504; cf. 462ff., 472, 473ff., 484f.
Kilpatrick, G. D., *The Origins of the Gospel According to St. Matthew,* 98, 132
Kingdom of God, 33, 70f., 468, 504; inaugurated by Jesus, 234; in Jesus' teaching, 221–234, 247, 251ff.; Luke's understanding of, 154, 278; and miracles, 212f.; *See also* Eschatology; Heaven, Kingdom of; Son of Man
Kingsbury, Jack Dean, *Matthew: Structure, Christology, Kingdom,* 104, 114, 116, 132; *Matthew,* 132
Kittel, G., *Theological Dictionary of the New Testament,* 157, 177, 245, 511, 515
Klausner, Joseph, *Jesus of Nazareth,* 204, 209, 221, 267
Knox, John, 310; *Philemon Among the Letters of Paul,* 397, 458
Koester, H., 344; *Trajectories through Earliest Christianity,* 465, 470, 481, 489; *Einführung in das Neue Testament,* 513
Kümmel, W. G., *Introduction to the New Testament,* 63, 84, 97, 297, 340, 397, 407, 513, 515; *Promise and Fulfillment,* 223; *The Theology of the New Testament According to Its Major Witnesses,* 513; *The New Testament: The History of the Investigation of Its Problems,* 514
Kysar, R., *The Fourth Evangelist and His Gospel,* 200
Ladd, G. E., *A Theology of the New Testament,* 513
Lake, K., *The Beginnings of Christianity,* 279, 308
Lampe, G. W. H., 212
Lane, W. L., *The Gospel According to Mark,* 96
Last Supper, 160, 223f., 287; eschatological overtones, 252; in Fourth Gospel, 183, 190, 193; as Passover, 252; and table fellowship, 287; *See also* Lord's Supper
Law (Jewish Torah), 24–31, 34, 496f., 504; in early Christianity, 417f., 464; in *Ephesians,* 400f.; Jesus' understanding of, 233ff., 246; Matthew's interpretation, 120ff.; and Moses in Fourth Gospel, 178; Paul's position, 312f., 326ff., 363f., 369ff., 379ff.; and sin, 379ff.
Laws, S., *The Epistle of James,* 458
Laymon, C. M. (ed.), *The Interpreter's One-Volume Commentary on the Bible,* 512
Lazarus, 180, 188f., 217
Leaney, A. R. C., *A Commentary on the Gospel According to St. Luke,* 164
Leenhardt, F. J., *The Epistle to the Romans,* 394
Leon-DuFour, X. (ed.), *Dictionary of Biblical Theology,* 511
Letter, as literary form in New Testament, 396

Levi (Matthew), 77
Lietzmann, H., *The Beginnings of Christianity*, 490
Lievestad, R., 240, 242
Lindars, B., *The Gospel of John*, 200; *New Testament Apologetic*, 467
Loewe, H., et al., *A Rabbinic Anthology*, 26
Lohse, E., *Colossians and Philemon*, 349, 356
Lord's Prayer, 222
Lord's Supper, 215, 467, 478, 484f., 498, 504; missing in Fourth Gospel, 166; in Paul, 319f., 372; *See also* Last Supper
Lord, as title of Jesus, 116, 186, 235, 473
Love, in Jesus' teaching, 110; importance in Johannine Literature, 196, 199, 438, 439f.; in Paul, 336f., 354
Lüdemann, Gerd, *Paulus der Heidenapostel*, 310
Luke, Gospel According to, 133–165, 480; apologetic character, 164; authorship, 133, 462; date, 134; historical situation of origin, 133f., 136, 163f., 307; journey motif, 150–154; literary character and style, 133f.; outline, 134; plan and structure, 135ff., 150, 161f.; purpose, 136f., 161; redaction of tradition, 163, cf. 134ff.; relation to Mark and Q, 62ff., 134, 470, 480; relation to Paul, 133; universal motifs, 137–142 (*See also* Acts, Luke)
Luke, historical sensibility, 135ff., 161, 275ff., 305, 462f.; productivity, 310
Lundström, Gösta, *The Kingdom of God in the Teaching of Jesus*, 222
Maccabeans, 18f., 504
Maccabees, The First Book of, 18
Machovec, Milan, *A Marxist Looks at Jesus*, 243, 269
MacRae, George, 49
Mandaeans, 50, 175
Manichaeism, 50
Manson, T. W., *The Teaching of Jesus*, 221, 267; *Jesus the Messiah*, 241, 268
Marcion, Evidence of New Testament canon, 406, 487
Mark, The Gospel According to, 61–96, 207, 480; authorship, connection with Peter, 62, 462; apocalypse of, 88, 454f., 468; emphases, 94f.; as first Gospel, 62f., 395; Gentile audience, 66; historical origins, 62ff., 95; messianic secret, 83f., 94f.; miracles, 71ff., 471; original ending lost, 92; outline, 67; parables, 227f.; redaction, 95; Roman origin, 66; structure, 94
Marrow, S. B., *Basic Tools of Biblical Exegesis*, 515
Marshall, I. H., *Luke: Historian and Theologian*, 164
Martin, R. P., *Carmen Christi*, 355
Martyn, J. L., *Studies in Luke–Acts*, 137, 164f., 277, 404; *History and Theology in the Fourth Gospel*, 185, 200
Marxsen, Willi, *Introduction to the New Testament*, 311, 513; *Mark the Evangelist*, 65, 93, 96
Mary Magdalene, 260f.
Mary and Martha, 188
Mary, mother of Jesus, 100f., 137ff.
Massebieau, 416
Matthew, The Gospel According to, 97–132,

470, 480f., 493; antinomian character, 110, cf. 131; authorship, 97, 462; background in Judaism, 97f., 99ff., 131; date, 98; emphases, 130; eschatology, 131; historical setting, 98f., 131f.; outline, 99; and Paul, 131, 285; purpose, 98f., cf. 128ff.; redaction in, 113, 130f., cf. 124; relation to *Mark* and Q, 62ff., 98, 128, 480; structure, 98, 104, 129f.
Matthias, selection of, 279f., 305
Mauser, U. W., *Christ in the Wilderness*, 69
May, H. G. (ed.), *The Oxford Bible Atlas*, 512; *The New Oxford Annotated Bible*, 512
Mays, J. L., *Interpreting the Gospels*, 96
McConnell, R. S., *Law and Prophecy in Matthew's Gospel*, 111
Meeks, W. A., *The Prophet-King*, 178; *The Writings of St. Paul*, 355
Meier, John P., *The Vision of Matthew*, 104, 132
Messiah, Messiahship, 466f., 504; apocalyptic overtones, 32, 236, 238ff.; in Jewish Christianity and Paul, 328f.; political implications, 21ff., 236; title of historical Jesus, 202ff. *passim*, esp. 235f.
Metzger, B. M., *The New Oxford Annotated Bible*, 512; *The Text of the New Testament*, 513
Meyer, Arnold, 416
Meyer, Paul, 208
Meyers, E. M., et al., *Archaeology, Rabbis, and Early Christianity*, 55
Midrash, 504
Miller, M. S. and J. L., *Harper's Bible Dictionary*, 511; *Harper's Encyclopedia of Bible Life*, 511
Minear, P. S., 137, 142; *Commands of Christ*, 267; *The Obedience of Faith*, 390; *I Saw a New Earth*, 458
Ministry of the Church (Pastorals), 480ff., esp. 410, 414
Miracles, 209–220, 471f., 505; in apocryphal Gospels, 211; in early church, 286, 472; eschatological context, 212f., 220; and faith, 86ff., 217f.; in the first century, 210f.; in Fourth Gospel, 166, 177, 180–189, 199, 217f., 471; healings, 213ff.; of Jesus, 209–220, 472; in *Mark*, 71ff., 82; in *Matthew*, 129ff.; nature miracles, 215f.; and Old Testament, 209, 215f.; scientific laws, 211, 218ff.; and Spirit of God, 212; in Synoptic Gospels, 211–218
Mishnah, 18, 25f., 55, 505, 508
Mission, in early Christianity, 288ff., 472–479; to Gentiles, 291ff.; Matthean discourse, 113
Mithraism, 48
Mitton, C. L., *The Epistle to the Ephesians*, 397, 458; *Ephesians*, 457
Mohrman, C., et al., *Atlas of the Early Christian World*, 512
Montefiore, C. G., et al., *A Rabbinic Anthology*, 26
Montefiore, H., *A Commentary on the Epistle to the Hebrews*, 458
Moore, G. F., *Judaism*, 24, 55, 69
Morgan, R., *The Nature of New Testament Theology*, 513
Morgenthaler, R., *Statistik des neutestamentlichen Wortschatzes*, 438
Morrison, C., *An Analytical Concordance to the Revised Standard Version of the New Testament*, 511

Moses, 24, 70, 85, 102, 104, 311ff.; compared with Jesus, 109f., 233f., 246, 311ff.; in the Fourth Gospel, 178, 185

Moule, C. F. D., 319; *Miracles*, 268; *The Significance of the Message of the Resurrection for Faith in Jesus Christ*, 269; *The Epistles of Paul the Apostle to the Colossians and to Philemon*, 398; *The Birth of the New Testament*, 478, 513

Munck, J., *Paul and the Salvation of Mankind*, 355

Muratorian Canon, 133, 486

Murphy, R. E., et al., *The Jerome Biblical Commentary*, 512

Mystery religions, 44–47, 498

Naphtali, Testament of, 70

Nathanael, 180, 188f.

Nazareth, 102, 104f., 145ff.

Neill, Stephen, *The Interpretation of the New Testament: 1861–1961*, 514

Nero, Emperor, 66f., 203f., 275, 421, 441f.

Neusner, Jacob, *From Politics to Piety*, 25, 56; *First Century Judaism in Crisis*, 56

New American Bible, The, 510

New Century Bible, The, 512

New Clarendon Bible, 512

New English Bible, The, 510, 512

New International Commentary on the New Testament, The, 512

New Testament Abstracts, 515

Nickle, K. F., *The Collection*, 355

Nicodemus, 183, 188

Nineham, D. E., *The Gospel of St. Mark*, 96

Nock, A. D., *Conversion*, 472

Obedience, of faith in Paul, 358, 388–391; to Jesus, 232ff.; theme of *Matthew*, 99–105, 110, 122

Old Testament, 3f., 14f., 464, 495ff.; in Passion tradition, 87, 90, 254ff., 467f., 474; prophecy of resurrection, 260, 474, in Sermon on the Mount, 109ff.; in Transfiguration scene, 85; use in *Ephesians*, 399; use in Fourth Gospel, 172f., 192; use in *Hebrews*, 427ff.; use in *Luke–Acts*, 145f., 158ff., 280f., 283f., 297, 299, 305; use in *James*, 419; use in *Mark*, 67f., 78, 87; use in *Matthew*, 99ff., 106, 112; use in Paul, 297, 299, 311ff., 342, 365, 368–388; use in *I Peter*, 423f.; use in *Revelation*, 442; *See also* Law

O'Neill, J. C., *The Theology of Acts in Its Historical Setting*, 308

Onesimus, 343, 348

Orthodoxy (and heresy), 273, 481f.

Otto, R., *India's Religion of Grace and Christianity*, 152

Pagels, Elaine, *The Gnostic Gospels*, 204

Palestine, 15, 17ff., 51; *See also* Judaism, history of

Pantheon, Greco–Roman, 40ff.

Papias, testimony of, 62, 97

Parables, 226–231, 505; catch of fish, 230; disciples' understanding, 115; great judgment, 123; harvest, 229; of the kingdom, 226–231; leaven, 229; lost coin, 152; lost sheep, 151f.; in *Luke*, 151f.; in *Mark*, 227f.; in *Matthew*, 114f., 226; and messianic secret; mustard seed, 229; pearl, 229f.; pounds, 154; prodigal son, 152; redaction of, 226ff.; rich man and Lazarus, 153; sower, 148f., 226, 228;

ten maidens, 122f.; talents, 123; two sons, 122; treasure, 229f.; weeds in the field, 226, 228f.; wicked servant, 120; wicked tenants, 122, 157f.

Parousia, of Jesus, 447, 468f., 505; cf. 324, 354; in Galilee, 93

Passover, 252, 282, 505

Pastorals, 406–414, 463f., 478, 480, 482, 505; authorship, 310, 396, 406f.; differences from Paul, 406f., 411ff., 456; Gnostic heresy in, 408f., 410ff.; ministry of the church in, 407, 410, 414, 482, 484; piety in, 413; relation to Pauline corpus, 398, 456; right doctrine emphasized, 410ff.; Spirit and office in, 414; style, 406

Paul, life and career, 309–394; apostolic career, 309–356, 479; apostolic commission for Gentile mission, 315ff.; authority as an apostle, 313ff., 352, 480f.; collection for Jerusalem Church, 317, 340, 357; chronology, 309f., 313; conversion of, 290, 304, 352; conversion as resurrection appearance, 318f.; corpus of letters, 353f., 396, 397ff., 406f., 416, 486, 494; disputes with Peter, 316, 327f., 337f.; Galatian opponents, 315, 339, 480; imprisonment (Caesarea), 304f.; imprisonment (Rome), 304f., 343, 348, 407; at Jerusalem Council, 297, 313, 316, 463; Jerusalem to Rome, 304f.; knowledge of Jesus, 319ff; literary influence, 486; martyrdom, 306; mission according to *Acts*, 295–303, 479; persecution of church, 352; preaching of, 295ff., 298ff.; predecessors of, 311–322; relation to Gospels, 321f., 472, 495; relation to Jerusalem Church, 316f., 319; role in *Acts*, 275f., 289f.; role in Stephen's death, 289; theology of Areopagus speech, 298ff.; use of tradition, 311ff.; 317ff., 299ff.; as wonder-worker, 210; *See also* Paul, theology and teachings

Paul, theology and teachings, Adam's role in human sin, 367, 376f., 381f.; apocalyptic, *See* Eschatology; apostleship, 281, 290f., 313ff., 339ff.; baptism, 285, 378, 467; Body of Christ, 338, 349f., 390, 402f., 420; Christ as ethical model, 347, 420ff.; Church, *See* Body of Christ; 309–356 *passim*; circumcision, 315f.; 327ff.; death of Christ, 329, 341f., 368ff., 379ff.; election, 385f.; eschatology, 322., 386ff., 389, 454, 461, 468f.; ethics, 351f., 388ff., 477f.; faith, 328ff., 337ff., 369–374, 375ff., 381, 393; faithfulness of God, 384–388, 393; flesh, 350, 382ff., 423; freedom, 331, 332ff., 377.; grace of God, 328ff., 343f., 351ff., 375.; his gospel, 313ff., 326ff.; historical Jesus, 319ff., 352, 393f.; Israel and Christ, 374, 384–388, 392; Jewish background, 330, 391f.; justification, *See* Righteousness of faith; knowledge, 333ff.; Law (*Torah*), 312ff., 315ff., 327 ff., 350, 363f., 369ff., 358–382, 478; Lord's Supper, 320; meat offered to idols, 334ff.; obedience of faith, 358n 388ff.; Old Testament, 297, 299, 311ff., 365, 369–388 *passim*; reconciliation, 376, 400f.; resurrection, 259f., 338f.; righteousness of faith, 328ff., 337ff., 369–374, 384ff.; sacrificial terminology, 369ff., 376, 389; salvation as future, 376; sex and marriage, 333f.; sin, 329, 360–368, 369ff., 378f., 392f.; Spriit, 312, 330, 338, 346,

382ff.; tradition, 285, 317ff., 318, 319ff., 390; universality of gospel, 359; wrath of God, 360ff.; *See also* Paul, life and career
Pauline corpus, 396, 397f., 406f., 416
Pentateuch, *See* Law
Pentecost, 281ff., 294f., 505
People of the Land *(am haaretz)*, 34; and Jesus, 34
Perrin, N., 84, 96; *The Kingdom of God in the Teaching of Jesus*, 213, 222ff., 225, 266; *Jesus and the Language of the Kingdom*, 222; *Rediscovering the Teaching of Jesus*, 240, 267f.
Persecution of Christians, 43f., 499; in *Hebrews*, 448; in *Mark*, 62, 66f., 87; in *I Peter*, 421, 425f.; in *Revelation*, 441, 448, cf. 446
Peter, The First Letter of, 396f., 420–426; authorship, 421, 463; Church and world, 423ff.; civil authority in, 423f.; date of, 421; outline, 422; and Paul, 421, 423; quality of Greek, 421; structure, 421f.; use of Old Testament in, 423f.
Peter, The Second Letter of, 396f., 464
Peter, Simon, 210, 276, 305, 322; authorship of *I Peter*, 421; confession at Caesarea Philippi, 82, 83–86, 166, 243; confession of sin, 147; connection with *Mark*, 62; conversion of Cornelius, 291–295; in Gentile mission, 291; martyrdom in Rome, 276, 306; Paul's dispute with, 316, 327f., 337f.; Pentecost sermon, 281ff., 294; in resurrection tradition, 260ff.; as the Rock of the Church, 117f.; speech at election of Matthias, 280f.
Peters, F. E., *The Harvest of Hellenism*, 56, 490
Pharisees, 24–26, 28, 31ff., 98, 105, 223, 506; criticized by Jesus, 82, 110; debate with Jesus, 76–80; in Fourth Gospel, 184f.; opposition to Jesus, 87, 253, 352
Philemon, The Letter of Paul to, circumstances of origin, 342ff.
Philip, 289
Philippi, 298, 343; Paul's relation to Church of, 347
Philippians, The Letter of Paul to, 310, 342–347; circumstances of origin, 342ff.; composition of, 344; outline, 344
Philo of Alexandria, 28, 52f.
Pilate, Pontius, 20, 88, 92, 156, 163, 183, 188, 236, 257
Pliny and Trajan, correspondence between, 43f.
Polycarp of Smyrna, 486
Pontifical Biblical Commission, *Instruction Concerning the Historical Truth of the Gospels*, 95
Price, I. M., *The Ancestry of Our English Bible*, 511
Price, J. L., *Interpreting the New Testament*, 224
Priests (Jewish), 26–28, 370, 428ff., 506
Prophet, 468f., 506; Christian, 403, 437; as title of Jesus, 185, 235f.
Psalms of Solomon, 32
Pseudepigrapha, 32, 506
Ptolemies, 17f.
Q-source, 63f., 207, 470f., 506; use in *Luke*, 134, 136, 143; use in *Matthew*, 97
Qumran, community, 28–31; dualism, 29f., 173; and early Christianity, 30f., 98f.; Messiah, 236; parallels to Christian baptism, 285;

Johannine origins, 169, 173, 197; scrolls, 28–31, 56, 411, 506
Rabbinic literature, 32, 55
Ramsey, I. T., *Religious Language*, 218, 259
Reconciliation, in *Ephesians*, 401ff.; in Paul's thought, 376f.
Redaction criticism, 64f., 493ff., 506
Redemption, 506; in Paul, 369ff.
Reicke, B., *The New Testament Era*, 55
Renan, E., *The Life of Jesus*, 220
Repentance, in early Christian preaching, 271; and John's baptism, 67, 123; in *Luke–Acts*, 147f., 151–154, 163, 285
Resurrection, 24, 27, 33, 506; of believer with Christ, 350f., 376f.; of Jesus and general resurrection, 339; in mystery religions, 46f.
Resurrection of Jesus, 258–265, 465ff., 471 473f., 476f.; appearances, 259ff.; in Areopagus speech, 300; centrality in New Testament, 205f., 258f.; effect on disciples, 263ff.; empty tomb, 110f., 259–263; and historical criticism, 259, 263ff.; in *John's* account, 183, 197, 199, 259ff.; in *Luke*, 158–160, 259ff.; in *Mark*, 92–94, 259ff.; in *Matthew*, 124–128, 259ff.; meaning for earliest Christians, 264f.; nature of, 263–265; in Paul's letters, 259ff.; relation to kingdom proclamation, 264; reported theft of body, 262; in *Revelation*, 446; "third day," 260; tradition, nature of, 259–263; women as witnesses, 260ff.
Reumann, John, et al., *Peter in the New Testament*, 118, 458
Revelation to John, The, 3, 441–455, 457, 468ff., 494; apocalyptic character of, 225, 442, 443f., 461f.; authorship, 167, 441; circumstances of writing, 441f.; date of writing, 441f.; letters to seven churches, 396, 444ff., 480; Old Testament in, 442; outline of, 443
Revised Standard Version (Bible) or RSV, 510
Rhoads, David M., *Israel in Revolution: 6-74 C.E.*, 21, 55
Richardson, A., *A Theological Word Book of the Bible*, 511
Ridderbos, H., *Paul: An Outline of His Theology*, 394
Riddle, D. W., 310
Rivkin, E., *A Hidden Revolution*, 56
Robert, A., et al., *Introduction to the New Testament*, 118, 513, 515
Robinson, H. Wheeler, *Corporate Personality in Ancient Israel*, 477
Robinson, J. A. T., *Redating the New Testament*, 168
Robinson, J. M., 76; *The Nag Hammadi Library in English*, 49, 204; *The Problem of History in Mark*, 69, 96; *A New Quest of the Historical Jesus*, 267; *Trajectories Through Earliest Christianity*, 465, 470, 481, 489
Roetzel, C. J., *The Letters of Paul*, 354
Rohde, J., *Rediscovering the Teaching of the Evangelists*, 95
Roman Empire, 11, 38ff., 162f., 497; conquest of Palestine, 15, 17, 19; government, 38–40; importance for early Christianity, 39, 307; Jewish war with, 22; law, 39; roads, 39; Paul's imprisonment in, 342ff.; pax romanum, 38f.; in *Revelation*, 447f.; taxes, 77; role in crucifixion, 251, 257, 307; rule of Palestine,

Roman Empire (*continued*)
19ff.; use of Greek in, 38; *See also* Persecution

Roman religion, 41ff., 476

Romans, The Letter of Paul to, 357–394, 494; circumstances of origin, 357f.; emphases of, 393f.; historical occasion, 391; outline of, 358; relation to Corinthians and Galatians, 357; structure of, 392f.; traditional material in, 358, 371f., 390f., 392; *See also* Paul, theology and teaching

Rome, 203f., 427; burned by Nero, 441; Christianity in, 66f., 276, 357; goal of Christian mission in *Luke–Acts*, 163f., 278, 304ff.; *See also* Romans; Nero

Rose, H. R., *Religion in Greece and Rome*, 56

Rostortzeff, M., *A History of the Ancient World*, 38, 56

Rowley, H. H., et al. (ed.), *Peake's Commentary on the Bible*, 512

Russell, D. S., *The Method and Message of Jewish Apocalyptic*, 55, 458

Sacrament, 478f., 498, 507; *See also* Baptism; Lord's Supper

Sacrifice, 507; in *Hebrews*, 428ff.; in Paul, 370ff., 389

Sadducees, 26–28, 31f., 184, 507

Samaria, 20, 150, 278, 289f.

Samaritan woman, 180, 188

Sampley, J. P., *"And the Two Shall Become One Flesh,"* 398, 400

Sanders, E. P., *Paul and Palestinian Judaism*, 394

Sanders, Jack T., *The New Testament Christological Hymns*, 171

Sandmel, S., *Judaism and Christian Beginnings*, 55, 204; *The Genius of Paul*, 355

Sanhedrin, 20, 32, 253

Satan, 341; in apocalyptic thought, 225; his defeat, 223; and miracles, 212f.; in *Revelation*, 454; role in demon possession, 73; role in Jesus' temptation, 70f.; struggle with Spirit, 75; *See also* Devil

Schille, Gottfried, 98

Schillebeeckx, E., *Jesus*, 269

Schlatter, A., 513f.

Schmidt, K. L., 117

Schmithals, W., *Gnosticism in Corinth*, 355

Schnackenburg, R., *The Gospel According to St. John*, 200; *The Moral Teaching of the New Testament*, 514

Schneemelcher, W., et al., *New Testament Apocrypha*, 76, 107, 133, 142, 204, 211, 266, 409, 481, 490

Schoeps, H. J., *Paul*, 394

Scholer, D. M., *A Basic Bibliographic Guide for New Testament Exegesis*, 515

Schubert, Paul, 165

Schürer, E., *The History of the Jewish People in the Age of Jesus Christ*, 55

Schütz, J. H., *Paul and the Anatomy of Apostolic Authority*, 355

Schweitzer, A., *The Mysticism of Paul the Apostle*, 394; *The Quest for the Historical Jesus*, 220, 249, 266

Schweizer, E., 119; *The Good News According to Mark*, 96; *The Good News According to Matthew*, 132; *Lordship and Discipleship*, 241, 244; *Church Order in the New Testament*, 457

Scribes, 25, 507; interpretation of Scripture, 246; linked with Pharisees, 24f., 110

Scroggs, R., *The Last Adam*, 394

Seleucids, 17f.

Selwyn, E. G., *The First Epistle of Peter*, 426

Septuagint, 507; cf. 35, 52

Sermon on the Mount, 105, 109ff., 124, 231–233, 470

Shepherd of Hermas, The, 485

Shroud of Turin, 264f.

Silas, 298, 421, cf. Silvanus, 322, 421

Simeon, 139–141, 163

Simon Peter, *See* Peter, Simon

Sin, 329, 360–368, 507; freedom from, 378f.; God's dealing with, 370ff.

Sinaiticus, Codex, 485, 487

Sinners, Jesus' association with, 152, Jesus calls, 246

Slaves, in *I Peter*, 424f.

Sloyan, G. S., *Jesus on Trial*, 269

Smallwood, E. Mary, *The Jews Under Roman Rule*; 20ff., 55

Smith, D. M., *John*, 201

Socrates, 37, 298

Son of David, 116

Son of God, as title of Jesus, 235f., 507f.; in Fourth Gospel, 179; in *Hebrews*, 428f.; in *Mark*, 67ff., 85f., 91f.; in *Matthew*, 108, 116

Son of Man, as title of Jesus, 84, 116, 235–243, 508; apocalyptic figure, 469, 471, 238–240; earthly activity, 240, 242; in Fourth Gospel, 186; as judge, 118, 121, 125; as lord of the sabbath, 78; in relation to kingdom, 224; in *Revelation*, 450f.; as suffering servant, 240f.; use of title by Jesus, 238

Soulen, R. N., *A Handbook of Biblical Criticism*, 513

Source criticism, 62ff.

Souter, A., *The Text and Canon of the New Testament*, 513

Spain, Paul's plan to visit, 357, 393

Sparks, H. F. D., *A Synopsis of the Gospels*, 511

Spirit, 508; in church, 265, 403f.; descent in *Acts*, 281ff., 294f.; in *Ephesians*, 402, 403f.; in Fourth Gospel, 282; at Jesus' baptism, 69f., 107; and Jesus' miracles, 212; in *I John*, 437ff.; in *Luke–Acts*, 142, 144, 163, 281ff., 294f.; in Paul's thought, 312f., 331, 338, 346, 382–384; in *Revelation*, 444–446, cf. 452; role in Christian mission, 278; spiritual gifts and office, 414; in struggle with Satan, 75

Spitta, F., 416

Stendahl, Krister, 102; *The School of St. Matthew*, 98f., 132

Stephen, 156; speech, 289, 295; stoning of, 289

Stevenson, J. (ed.), *A New Eusebius*, 490

Stinespring, William, 141

Stoicism, 41–43; allegorical interpretation of myths, 41ff.; concept of God, 41–43; in Paul's Areopagus speech, 299f.; in Paul's thought, 362

Strange, J. F., et al., *Archaeology, Rabbis, and Early Christianity*, 55

Streeter, B. H., *The Four Gospels*, 95; *The Primitive Church*, 457

Suffering servant, Jesus as, 241; Jesus and Christian as, 424; relation to Son of Man, 240f.

Suggs, M. J., *Wisdom, Christology, and Law in Matthew's Gospel*, 128, 132

Swanson, Reuben J. (ed.), *The Horizontal Line Synopsis of the Gospels,* 63

Synagogue, 52f., 479; origin, 52; role in Paul's mission, 297; worship, 15, 52, 145

Synoptic Gospels, 61–165, cf. 480f.; 202–269 *passim;* form and redaction criticism, 64f., 213; miracles in, 211–218; problem of, 62–66, 508; sources for Jesus, 205; *See also* Gospels

Tacitus, *Annals,* 66f., 203f.

Talbert, C. H., 154; *Literary Patterns, Theological Themes, and the Genre of Luke–Acts,* 164; *What Is a Gospel?,* 206

Talmud, 25f., 209, 262, 508

Tannehill, R. C., *The Sword of His Mouth,* 267

Tarn, W. W., *Hellenistic Civilization,* 41, 56

Tatian, *Diatessaron,* 487, 494

Tatum, W. B., 137

Taylor, Vincent, *The Gospel According to St. Mark,* 86, 90, 92; *The Formation of the Gospel Tradition,* 95; *Jesus and His Sacrifice,* 241

Tcherikover, V., *Hellenistic Civilization and the Jews,* 55

Teacher of righteousness, 28, 30; *See also* Qumran

Temple, Jerusalem, 14f., 18f., 26f., 162, 370, 400f.; cleansing of, 251, 255; earliest Christians in, 287; Herod's rebuilding, 20; as image of church, 403f.; importance to Luke, 137, 142, 154f.; in Johannine Christology, 177; in Stephen's speech, 289; worship in, 52

Temptation of Jesus, 70, 108, 166, 218

Ten Commandments, 14

Tertullian, evidence for New Testament canon, 486

Theissen, G., *A Sociology of Early Palestinian Christianity,* 268

Theology, 508; in the Fourth Gospel, 199f.; in *Paul, John,* and *Hebrews,* 428

Theophilus, 136, 277

Thessalonian letters, 310f., 322–325

Thessalonians, The First Letter of Paul to the, 310f., 322–325

Thessalonians, The Second Letter of Paul to the, 322f.; authorship problem, 310, 323, 396

Thessalonica, 298

Theudas, 22, 244

Thomas, disciple, 176, 178, 188f., 265

Thomas, Gospel of, 50, 204, 470

Throckmorton, Burton H. (ed.), *Gospel Parallels,* 63, 96, 511

Tiede, D. L., *The Charismatic Figure as Miracle Worker,* 76

Timothy, joins Paul in writing, 322f.

Timothy, The First Letter of Paul to, 396, 406–414, 456; outline of, 407; *See also* Pastorals

Timothy, The Second Letter of Paul to, 396, 406f.

Titus, circumcision of, 295

Titus, The Letter of Paul to, 396, 406f., 482; *See also* Pastorals

Tobit, 452

Tödt, H. E., *The Son of Man in the Synoptic Tradition,* 240, 242, 268

Torah, 508; *See also* Law

Tradition, Christological confession, 447; ethi-

cal exhortations in *I Peter,* 425f.; of Jesus, 202–209; oral, 505; in Paul, 317ff., 392

Transfiguration of Jesus, 85

Turro, J. C., 490

Twelve (apostles), importance in *Luke,* 144, 148, 276, 279ff.; in *John,* 190; Paul's understanding of, 281; role in resurrection appearances, 260ff., 318

Van Buren, P. M., *The Secular Meaning of the Gospels,* 259

Van der Meer, F., et al., *Atlas of the Early Christian World,* 512

Van Unnik, W. C., *Tarsus or Jerusalem?,* 321

Vermes, G., *The Dead Sea Scrolls,* 56; *The Dead Sea Scrolls in English,* 28, 30, 55; *Jesus the Jew,* 267

Via, D. O., Jr., *The Parables,* 226, 267

Vielhauer, Ph., 240, 277

Von Campenhausen, H., 241; *The Formation of the Christian Bible,* 512

Wagner, Günter, *Pauline Baptism and the Pagan Mysteries,* 46

Weiss, J., *Jesus' Proclamation of the Kingdom of God,* 266; *Der erste Korintherbrief,* 334; *Earliest Christianity,* 490

Wilckens, Ulrich, *Die Missionsrede der Apostelgeschichte,* 302

Wilcox, Max, *The Semitisms of Acts,* 286

Wilder, Amos, *The Language of the Gospel,* 267

Wilkinson, J., *Jerusalem as Jesus Knew It,* 267

Williams, C. S. C., *A Commentary on the Acts of the Apostles,* 308

Willoughby, H. R., *Pagan Regeneration,* 56

Wilson, R. McL., *Gnosis and the New Testament,* 56; *New Testament Apocrypha,* 76, 107, 133, 142, 204, 211, 266, 409, 481, 490

Wilson, W. R., *The Execution of Jesus,* 268

Winter, Paul, *On the Trial of Jesus,* 253, 268

Wisdom of Solomon, 52, 363

Wise men, 102

Witness, witnessing, 509; importance in *Luke–Acts,* 139ff., 143ff., 148, 158f., 160ff., 279ff., 288ff., 306; as martyrdom in *Revelation,* 443, 446

Women, role in *Luke,* 144, 163; in *Mark,* 93; in *Matthew,* 100f.

Word, in Johannine prologue, 172ff., 509

World, concept of in the Johannine literature, 175f., 191, 194ff., 435, 438ff.; in *I Peter,* 422ff.

Worship, in Judaism, 14f., 26; in the New Testament, 171, 478f., 498; in the synagogue, 52f., 145, 479; *See also* Lord's Supper; Priests; Sacrifice; Temple

Wrede, William, 513; *The Messianic Secret,* 84, 96, 268

Wright, G. E., *The Westminster Historical Atlas to the Bible,* 512; *Biblical Archeology,* 512

Yamauchi, Edwin M., *Pre-Christian Gnosticism,* 51, 56

Zealots, 22, 31f., 184, 509

Zechariah, a priest, 137, 142, 162

Zehnle, R. F., *Peter's Pentecost Discourse,* 286

Zeus, 41, 42f.

Zimmerli, W., *The Servant of God,* 241

Zoroastrianism, 32, 173

BIBLICAL INDEX

Old Testament

Genesis
1 172
1:3 172
1:3–5 173
1:29 409
3:24 450
11:1–9 282
12:1–3 99
14:17–20 433
15:6 374, 375, 392, 419, 456
18:6 229
19:4–8 362
23:4 423
32:29 73
38 100
50:20 181

Exodus
1:15–2:10 102
3:8 68
3:13 73
4:22 69, 102
10:4 68
19 109
19:2f. 102
19:16ff. 85
20:1–17 502
20:2–3 14
20:17 380
23:7 373
23:20 68
25:31–40 450
34:28 70, 102
34:29–35 312
34:33 312
34:35 312

Leviticus
11 327
12:2–8 140
13:45 214
16 370
18:22 362
19:18 419
20:13 362

Deuteronomy
5:6–21 502
5:21 380
6:3 68

Joshua
2 100
6 100

Judges
19:22–26 362

Ruth
3 100

I Samuel
21:1–6 78

II Samuel
7:12–17 100
11–12 100

I Kings
19:8 70
19:9ff. 85

II Kings
1:8 68
4:42–44 215

Psalms
1 373
2:7 69, 85, 236, 432
8:4 238
16:8–11 284
22 90, 254
22:1 14, 89, 254
22:7 254
22:18 254
22:27f. 90
32:1–2 375
39:12 423
51 286
51:4 373
65:7 216
69:21 254
69:25 280
80:17 238
89:9 216
98:2 373
105:34 68
106:9 216

107:23–32 216
109:8 280
110 399, 433
110:1 284
110:4 432, 433
116:10 342
118:22f. 158, 257
126:6 228

Proverbs
10:27ff. 373
24:13 68
25:21f. 390

Isaiah
6:9–10 306
7:14 101
8:14f. 158
9:1f. 106
9:3 228
24–27 442
26:19 33
29:18f. 209, 212
33:4 68
35:5f. 209, 212
40–66 474
40:3 30, 68, 106
40:9 61
42:1 69
42:6 141
43:9 373
46:13 373
49:6 141, 297
50:6 254
50:8f. 373
51:5 373
52:7 61, 474
52:10 141
53 241, 249
53:4 101, 112, 209
53:9 254
53:12 160, 254
56:7 255
58:2 373
58:6 145
61:1 61, 209, 212, 474
61:1–2 145

Jeremiah
1 316
7:11 255

11:16 386
31:9 69

Ezekiel
1:24 450
2:1 238
2:8–3:3 453
3:3 68
4:1ff. 453
9:2 450
9:11 450
21:9–10 450
37–39 442
43:2 450

Daniel
4:17 229
7 33, 186
7–12 442
7:2–8 225
7:9 450
7:13 78, 447, 450
7:13f. 238
10:5 450
10:7–10 452
12:2 33

Hosea
6:6 115
11:1 69, 102

Joel
2:28–32 69, 212, 283
3:1 283

Amos
5:18–20 325

Obadiah
15ff. 442

Habakkuk
2:4 360

Zechariah
4 450
9:9 255

Zechariah (cont.)
11:12–13   280
12:10   447
13:7   257

Malachi
3:1   68, 251

New Testament

Matthew
1–2   102
1:1   144
1:1ff.   99
1:1   100
1:1–17   67
1:1–18   102
1:1–2:23   98, 99, 129
1:3   100
1:5   100
1:6   100
1:13–15   102
1:14   102
1:15   102
1:16   100
1:17   99
1:18   100, 107
1:18–25   99, 100
1:19   101
1:20   100, 101
1:21   101
1:22f.   101
1:23   100, 101, 107, 128
1:24   101, 128
1:25   100, 101
2   102
2:1   466
2:1ff.   113
2:2   102, 120, 125
2:8   102, 120
2:11   102, 104, 120
2:16ff.   104
2:16–19   102
2:23   104
3–7   112
3:1–12   225
3:1–4:25   105
3:1–7:29   105, 129
3:2   106
3:3   106
3:7   131
3:7–10   105, 107
3:9   99, 127
3:9f.   105
3:10   106
3:11f.   107
3:13   106
3:13–17   106, 107
3:13ff.   144
3:14   106
3:15   101, 106, 107, 110, 124, 128
3:17   107, 108
4:1–11   70, 108, 155, 213, 245
4:2   102
4:3   108
4:4   108
4:6   108
4:7   108
4:7–10   22
4:8–10   236
4:10   108
4:11   149
4:12–16   108
4:16   106

4:17   106, 108, 131, 223
4:17–16:20   104
4:18–22   108
4:19   244
4:20   108
4:22   108
4:23–25   108
5–7   109, 145, 231, 232, 470
5:1   125
5:1–7:29   105
5:1–12   112
5:2   109
5:3   222
5:3–5   109, 119
5:3–12   109, 501
5:6   107, 128
5:6–12   119
5:10   107
5:10–12   118
5:17   14, 107, 232
5:17–19   110
5:17–20   101, 109, 110
5:18   245
5:18f.   131
5:19b   110, 131, 224
5:19   110
5:20   101, 106, 107, 110, 111, 128, 131, 224, 230
5:21–48   102, 111, 232, 233, 246, 501
5:22   105, 232
5:28   232
5:32   121, 232, 321
5:33   101
5:33–37   124
5:34   109, 232
5:39   109, 232
5:44   105, 232, 390
5:47   366
5:48   111, 121, 232, 233
6   233
6:5   105
6:5–15   111
6:7   366
6:10   109, 222, 223
6:14f.   120
6:16–18   78
6:20   124
6:25–34   111
6:25   232
6:33   107, 111, 128
7:1   105, 229, 232, 233
7:1–5   111
7:7   233
7:11f.   111
7:12   25
7:13f.   315
7:14   125
7:15f.   105
7:15–27   101
7:15–29   110
7:16   106, 110
7:17   105
7:18–20   105
7:19   233

7:21   110, 128, 224, 232
7:21–23   105, 123, 127
7:21–27   481
7:24   106, 110, 124
7:24–27   112, 233
7:28f.   98, 125
8–9   112
8–10   113
8:1ff.   101
8:1   113
8:1–4   213
8:1–11:1   112, 129
8:2   120
8:2–17   112
8:5–10   180
8:5–18   113
8:9   125
8:11f.   225
8:12   115, 230
8:16f.   114
8:16–17   113
8:17   101, 112, 209, 241, 247
8:18–22   112
8:18–27   215
8:18–9:17   112
8:20   240
8:22   245
8:23–27   112, 119
8:28–34   112
9:1–7   101
9:1–8   112
9:1–13   101
9:6   125
9:8   125
9:9   97, 244
9:9–13   112
9:13   115
9:14–17   112
9:18   120
9:18–38   112
9:18–26   112, 216
9:27–31   112
9:32–34   112
9:34   112, 131
10   112, 113, 114
10:1   113
10:1–11:1   127, 245
10:3   97
10:5f.   473, 474
10:5   113
10:6   131
10:10   321
10:14f.   113
10:17–25   113
10:18   113
10:23   113, 461, 473, 474
10:32f.   239, 242
10:33   324
10:40   115
10:40–42   123, 128
10:42   112, 114
10:51   214
11:1   98, 113
11:2–6   212, 226, 243
11:2–13:52   114, 129

11:2–19   114
11:3   114
11:4–6   209
11:5   61, 115
11:6   243
11:9   238
11:11   114, 222
11:11–15   110
11:18f.   240
11:20–24   114, 115
11:25–29   115
11:25–30   114
11:28–30   115
12   114
12:7f.   115
12:12b   115
12:18   241
12:18ff.   241
12:18–21   113, 118
12:20   125
12:28   114, 212, 218, 222, 223
12:33–37   115
12:39   210, 213
12:40   240, 242
12:45   115
12:49   115
12:50   115
13   114, 222, 226
13:3–8   115, 228
13:8   228
13:10–17   115
13:11   114
13:16   151
13:18–23   226, 228
13:21   228
13:24–30   228, 230
13:29   229
13:30   229
13:31f.   229
13:33   229
13:36–43   226, 229
13:36ff.   240
13:41–43   239
13:42   115, 230
13:44f.   229
13:44   229
13:45f.   229
13:47–50   230
13:47–48   230
13:49–50   230
13:50   115
13:51   115
13:52   98, 115, 128
13:53   98
13:53–17:21   116
13:53–19:2   116, 129
13:58   217
14.5   238
14:13–21   116, 215
14:17   116
14:18   116
14:19b   116
14:22–33   116
14:30   116
14:31   119

14:33   102, 116, 120
15:1–20   119, 234
15:10   110
15:22–28   113
15:29   125
15:32–39   116
15:33   117
15:36   117
16:1   225
16:1–2   119
16:8   119
16:9–20   127, 128
16:13   242
16:13–23   117
16:13–20   128
16:17   117
16:17–19   116, 117
16:19   117, 120, 452
16:21   118
16:21–28:20   104
16:22   118
16:22f.   118
16:23   118
16:24–27   128
16:24–28   118
16:27   118, 239, 245
16:28   223
17:1   125
17:1ff.   109
17:4   116
17:20   119
17:22   119
17:22–19:1   116
17:22–19:2   119
17:22f.   240
17:24–27   119
17:26   119
17:26f.   131
18:1–6   128
18:3   119, 224
18:5   119
18:5–9   119
18:10   119
18:10–14   119
18:12–14   151
18:14   119
18:15f.   119
18:15–22   119
18:17–18   117
18:17b   119
18:18   117, 119, 120
18:20   101, 120, 128
18:21f.   101, 119, 120
18:23–35   120
18:26   125
19:1   121
19:1f.   98
19:3–12   120, 246
19:3–23:39   121
19:3–26:1   120, 130
19:9   121
19:16–30   120
19:21   121
19:23   224
19:26   121
19:27–30   121
19:28   239, 281
20:1–16   121
20:15   121
20:17   249
20:20   120
20:26–28   128
20:28   241
21   121
21:1   121, 250
21:9   251
21:10   121
21:11   238
21:19   121, 122

21:21   217
21:23–27   122
21:25   122
21:28–32   101, 122, 128
21:28–46   122
21:30   122
21:32   122
21:33–43   127
21:33–44   121
21:33–46   122
21:33   157
21:34   122
21:41   122
21:42   122
21:43   122, 157
21:45   122
21:45f.   122
22   121
22:7   98
22:11–14   128
22:13   115, 230
22:15–22   120
22:16   244
22:23–33   120
22:32   99
22:34–40   110, 120, 419
22:40   110
23   98, 110, 120, 131
23:2f.   24
23:3   110
23:8   128
23:13   110
23:23   110
23:23f.   120, 234
23:25   110
24   120, 122, 131, 224
24:1ff.   155
24:1   121
24:6   131
24:11   469
24:14   113, 224
24:26f.   242
24:29–44   239
24:30   447
24:34f.   127
24:36–51   120
24:36ff.   131
24:37–39   242
24:42ff.   131
24:43   324
24:44   242
25   120, 122
25:1–13   123
25:14–30   123, 154
25:31   447
25:31ff.   121, 239
25:31f.   474
25:31–46   122, 123, 128,
   239, 244
25:34   224, 481
25:35f.   123
25:37ff.   123
25:40   123
25:41–46   121
25:46   474
26:1f.   98
26:2   124
26:2–28:20   98, 124, 130
26:6–13   124
26:18   124
26:26–28   320, 372
26:28   101, 131, 247
26:29   224
26:32   125
26:39   121, 124
26:42   109, 124
26:45   240
26:52   109
26:54   124

26:56   124
26:63   109, 124
26:68–75   124
27:3–10   280
27:4   109
27:9f.   193
27:11   124
27:19   109
27:24   109
27:29   124
27:37   124
27:40   124
27:42   124
27:43   124
27:46   254
27:51–54   124
27:54   156
27:57   128
27:60   254
27:62–66   125, 261
28:1–20   259, 261
28:7   125
28:9f.   125
28:9   120, 125, 261
28:11–15   125, 261, 262
28:13–15   92
28:16   159
28:16ff.   109, 130, 318,
   319
28:16–20   125, 131, 224,
   261, 262, 473, 481
28:17   102, 104, 120, 125
28:18   125
28:18–20   129
28:19f.   111, 113
28:19   102, 113, 127, 484
28:20   101, 102, 115, 125,
   261
28:20a   127

Mark
1:1   70, 85, 91, 95, 473
1:1–15   67, 94
1:2–3   68, 69
1:2–8   68, 70, 238
1:7   69
1:8   69
1:9–11   70, 106
1:9   106
1:9f.   144
1:9–13   69
1:11   65, 85, 91, 95, 108
1:12   70
1:12–13   70, 75
1:13   149
1:14   68, 70, 74
1:14f.   221, 223
1:15   68, 70, 71, 75, 106,
   144, 218, 225, 244
1:16–8:21   71
1:16–20   62, 75, 77, 147,
   244
1:17   92, 244
1:21   74
1:21–3:11   108
1:21–45   73
1:21ff.   109
1:21–28   73, 78, 145
1:22   74, 77
1:24   73, 75
1:25   78, 215
1:27f.   79
1:27   74, 93, 218
1:28   75
1:29–31   62, 74
1:32–34   74
1:34   73, 75, 84
1:35f.   62

1:35–39   74
1:35   86
1:39f.   113
1:39   73, 74
1:40–45   73, 74, 75, 213
1:41   213
1:43   213
1:43f.   72
1:44   84
2:1–3:6   76
2:1–12   77
2:4f.   214
2:5   246
2:7   77, 101, 246
2:10   78, 85, 240
2:12   218
2:13f.   77
2:14   97, 244
2:15–3:6   80
2:15–17   77
2:17   78, 246, 257
2:18   244
2:18–22   77
2:18f.   229
2:19   77
2:19b–20   78
2:20   78
2:21f.   78
2:22   78
2:23–28   78
2:25   85
2:27f.   240
2:27   78
2:28   85
3:1–6   78
3:6   79
3:7–12   79
3:11   73
3:12   72, 84
3:13f.   136
3:13–19   62, 79
3:14   73, 144, 501
3:15   73
3:16–19   77
3:18   97
3:20–30   73
3:21f.   210
3:22   73, 218
3:23–29   70
3:27   70, 73
3:28   245
3:28–30   79
3:30   73
3:31–35   79, 148
3:34   115
4:1–9   148
4:1–20   79
4:1–34   148
4:2   148
4:3–8   228
4:8   79
4:10ff.   84
4:10–13   227
4:13   115, 149
4:13f.   148
4:15   149
4:20   79, 149
4:30–33   229
4:33f.   79, 84
4:35–41   73, 79, 215
4:39   215
4:40   86, 91, 93
4:40f.   215
4:41   79
5:1–13   73, 79
5:1–20   80
5:7   73
5:9   73
5:14–20   79

Mark (cont.)
5:15 86
5:21–43 80, 216
5:25–34 216
5:28–30 216
5:30 217
5:31 80
5:34 80, 217
5:35f. 217
5:35–43 73
5:36 216, 217
5?37 80
5:39 217
5:40 80
5:41 66, 73, 80
5?43 72, 84
6:1–6 80, 145, 146
6:3 68, 146
6:4 238
6:5f. 217
6:7–13 80, 113, 245
6:12f. 113
6:13 73
6:14ff. 79
6:14f. 83
6:14–9:32 117
6:14–29 79, 80
6:29 79
6:30–44 73, 80, 116, 215
6:32–44 180
6:37 116
6:41 116, 215
6:45–51 180
6:45–52 73, 74, 116
6:46 75, 86
6:50 91
6:51f. 116
7:1–23 82, 246
7:3f. 66
7:11 66
7:14f. 110, 234
7:17f. 84
7:34 66, 73
7:36 84
8 80, 84
8:1–10 73, 116
8:4 117
8:6 117
8:7 117
8:11 78
8:11f. 213
8:12 76, 210, 225
8:15 79
8:21 80
8:22ff. 94
8:22–9:9 83
8:22–10:52 82, 83
8:22–15:47 71, 80
8:22–26 82, 83
8:23 182
8:27 242
8:27–30 82, 84
8:27–33 83, 117, 243
8:29 85
8:30 83
8:31 66, 80, 82, 84, 85, 240, 249
8:31–38 82
8:32 83
8:32f. 84
8:34 80, 390
8:34ff. 83
8:34–9:1 84, 85, 118
8:34–38 66, 218
8:35 70, 95, 253
8:38 85, 239, 242, 244, 245, 324, 469
9 84
9:1 85, 86, 223, 397, 461

9:2–8 82
9:2–9 85
9:6 85, 86, 93
9:7 85, 91, 92, 95
9:8 85
9:9 84, 240
9:9–13 85
9:12 85
9:13 85
9:14–32 86
9:15 93, 218
9:17 86
9:20 86
9:21f. 86
9:23 86, 87, 88
9:24 86
9:26 86, 87
9:29 75, 86, 91
9:30–32 86
9:31 66, 82, 87, 240
9:32 86, 93
9:33–37 82
9:33–41 86
9:33–50 66
9:34 87
9:35 74, 92
9:38 87
9:39f. 84
9:40 149
9:41 85, 87
9:47 224
9:50 87
10–13 120
10 84
10:1 87
10:1–12 120
10:2 78
10:2–9 333
10:2–12 87, 246
10:10 84
10:10–12 121
10:11f. 321
10:12 66
10:13–16 88
10:15 224
10:17 191
10:17–22 87
10:17–31 245
10:19 390
10:21 121
10:23–31 86, 87, 88
10:24 93
10:29 70
10:30 192
10:32 87, 91, 93, 249
10:32–34 80
10:32–45 84, 88, 245
10:33f. 66, 82, 240, 256
10:35–45 74, 82, 92
10:38 70
10:38–45 66
10:38ff. 390
10:39 168
10:42–44 236
10:43–45 83
10:45 74, 92, 240, 241, 249, 257
10:46–52 88
10:47f. 85
10:52 93
11:1 87, 250
11:1–10 236, 251, 255
11:1–11 83
11:1–14:72 80
11:1–19 87
11:9 87
11:10 251
11:11–19 236
11:11–18 255

11:15–19 251
11:18 93, 252
11:20–26 88
11:22 93
11:22f. 217
11:22–26 86
11:24 86, 91
11:27–33 251
11:28 252
12:1 157
12:1–11 74
12:1–12 87, 122, 157, 251
12:6 157
12:9 122
12:10f. 158, 257
12:11 122
12:13–17 22, 87, 251, 252, 390
12:13 78, 79
12:15 78
12:17 93, 252, 390, 423
12:18–27 87, 251, 252
12:26f. 33
12:27 252
12:28–31 419, 440
12:28–34 110, 251, 252
12:31 390
12:34 222, 252
12:35 236
12:35ff. 85
12:35–37 85, 87
12:41–44 88, 252
13 87, 88, 93, 122, 190, 224, 239, 251, 324, 438, 468
13:1ff. 86, 155
13:2 66, 251, 252, 289
13:5f. 408
13:6–8 88
13:7 88
13:9 88, 113, 256, 474
13:9–13 66, 79, 113
13:10 70, 157, 159, 474
13:11 256
13:12 256
13:14 66, 88
13:19 88
13:21 88
13:21f. 85
13:21–27 88
13:21–23 480
13:22 469
13:24–26 252
13:24–37 85
13:26 77, 85, 88, 239, 447
13:29 88, 224
13:30 88
13:32 88, 226, 278
13:32f. 252
13:35 88
14 66
14–15 88
14:1–9 88
14:3–9 148, 251, 253
14:9 70
14:10f. 88, 257
14:10 256
14:10–21 253
14:12–25 88, 190, 251
14:12–28 88
14:17 159
14:18 257
14:21 240, 257
14:22–24 320, 372, 484
14:22–25 467
14:24 241
14:25 224, 252
14:26 159
14:26–31 88, 190

14:27 466
14:27f. 257
14:28 93
14:31 256
14:32 86, 103
14:32–42 75, 86, 88, 190, 251, 432
14:34f. 91
14:36 90, 124, 190, 191, 218, 245, 253, 257, 500
14:37 159, 253
14:38 75, 86
14:38–41 82
14:40 253
14:41 240, 257
14:41f. 257
14:43–65 251
14:48f. 236
14:48–50 124
14:50 82, 87, 92, 159, 217, 263
14:51–52 87
14:53–65 88
14:57f. 252
14:58 251, 289
14:61 85
14:62 85, 243, 447
14:66–72 82, 87, 253
15 66
15:1 256, 257
15:1–5 88, 156
15:1–15 88
15:1–47 80
15:2 236
15:6–15 89, 251, 257
15:7 156
15:10 256, 257
15:14 257
15:15 255, 256, 257
15:16–20 89
15:16–32 88
15:16–47 251
15:18 236
15:19 254, 255
15:21–32 89
15:22 66
15:23 255
15:24 254
15:26 466, 236
15:28 254
15:29 251, 254, 289
15:29f. 90, 257
15:29–32 90
15:31 257
15:32 85, 236
15:33 89
15:33–47 88
15:34 14, 89, 90, 254, 255
15:36 254
15:37 90, 253, 255
15:38 90
15:38f. 124
15:39 86, 90, 91, 217
15:40f. 91, 159
15:41 92
15:42–47 91
15:43 92, 224, 254
15:43ff. 254
15:44 92, 253
16:1–4 93
16:1–8 92, 159, 259, 260
16:5 159, 261
16:6 93
16:6 261
16:7 93, 159, 474
16:8 87, 92, 93, 94
16:9–20 92, 94, 127
16:14 125

Luke
1–2 142
1:1 159
1:1–3 462
1:1–4 67, 133, 134, 135, 159, 481
1:2 136, 148, 163, 206
1:3 136
1:4 136, 159, 281
1:5ff. 137
1:5 139, 466
1:5–2:51 305
1:5–2:52 137
1:14 151
1:15 142
1:26 139
1:32 137
1:32ff. 140
1:35 142
1:37 142
1:39–45 137
1:41 142
1:44 151
1:45 137
1:53 139
1:67 142
1:76 137
1:80 137
2:1 139, 143, 163
2:8ff. 139
2:10 151, 163
2:13ff. 140
2:21 139
2:22ff. 139
2:22–35 139
2:22–40 139
2:25 142
2:26 142
2:27 140
2:29–32 140
2:32 140, 157, 163
2:33 140
2:34f. 140
2:34 142
2:36ff. 139
2:36–38 141
2:37 141
2:38 141
2:39 139
2:40 137, 142
2:41–52 142, 155
2:48 142
2:49 142
2:51 142
2:52 137, 142
3:1 139, 143, 163
3:1–9:50 143, 162
3:2ff. 144
3:3 144, 148
3:4ff. 137
3:7–9 105
3:16 144
3:18 163
3:18–21 144
3:20f. 144
3:21 144
3:38 144, 163
4:1–13 70, 155, 213, 245
4:5–8 22
4:13 149
4:15 144
4:16–30 145, 306
4:16 145
4:16ff. 162
4:16–21 212
4:18 163
4:21 145, 152, 163
4:22 146

4:23 146
4:24–29 163
4:29f. 146
4:31ff. 147
4:31f. 147
4:41 147
4:42 144
4:43 144, 147
5:1 144
5:1–11 144, 147
5:8 147
5:10 244
5:12–16 213
5:15 144
5:16 144
5:27f. 244
5:30 144, 147
5:32 147
6:2 144
6:12f. 136
6:12 144
6:13 144
6:14–16 279
6:17 144
6:17–49 109
6:20 139, 222
6:20–49 470
6:22 185
6:23 151
6:27 390
6:31 25
7:11 144
7:11–17 216
7:18–23 212, 226
7:18–35 175
7:22 115, 139, 163
7:22f. 209, 212
7:23 243
7:28 144, 222
7:33f. 240
7:36–50 148, 246
7:43 148
7:47f. 148
7:48 163, 246
8:1–3 148
8:1–21 148
8:1 144
8:2f. 144
8:4 148
8:4–8 148
8:4–21 163
8:5–8 228
8:11 148, 149, 163
8:12b 149
8:15 148, 149
8:16 149
8:19ff. 142
8:21 148
8:22–25 149, 215
8:26–39 149
8:40–42 149
8:40–56 216
8:43–48 149
8:49–56 149
9:1–2 149
9:1–6 245
9:7–9 149
9:10–17 149, 215
9:18 144
9:18–22 118
9:18–20 149
9:21–27 149
9:26 239, 242, 245
9:27 144, 223
9:28f. 144
9:43b–45 149
9:44 240
9:50 149
9:51 137, 150, 162

9:51–19:27 150, 151, 152, 249
9:51–56 150
9:53 150
9:57–62 150
9:58 240
9:59–62 244
9:62 224
10:1 150
10:1–17 150
10:1–12 245
10:7 321
10:9 152, 212
10:11 152
10:18 149, 154, 223
10:23 151
10:25–28 419
10:33 151
10:38 150
10:38–42 151
11:1 151, 175
11:1ff. 151
11:2 191, 222, 223
11:20 149, 151, 152, 154, 212, 222, 223
11:27f. 142, 151
11:29 225
11:29f. 240
11:30 242
11:37–12:3 151
12:1 151
12:7 158
12:8 239, 242
12:8f. 242
12:9 324
12:13–34 151
12:22 151
12:22–34 109
12:32 224
12:39 324
12:40 239, 242
12:41 151
12:41–49 151
13:1–9 151
13:1–5 181
13:10–35 151
13:18f. 229
13:20f. 229
13:22 150
13:33 150, 162, 238, 249
14:13 151
14:21 98
14:23 151
14:25–35 151
14:33 151
14:35 151
15 144, 163, 229
15:1 151
15:1–32 151
15:2 151, 152
15:7 151, 151
15:7f. 152
15:10 151, 152
15:14 156
15:17 152
15:24 152
15:25–32 152
15:32 151, 152
15:39 156
16:1 151
16:11 151
16:14 151
16:16 144, 163
16:19–31 151
16:19ff. 153
17:1 151
17:5 151
17:11 150
17:11–21 153

17:12–15 182
17:18 151
17:20ff. 151
17:20f. 154, 223, 226
17:20 152, 154
17:22 151
17:22f. 154, 242
17:22–30 239
17:26f. 242
18:1ff. 153
18:8 239
18:9ff. 153
18:9–14 246
18:17 224
18:18–23 153
18:22–30 151
18:30 152
18:31 249
18:35–43 153
18:43 157
19:1–10 151, 153, 163
19:9 152, 153
19:10 240
19:11–27 151, 154
19:11 150, 154
19:12–27 123
19:27 154
19:28 250
19:28–24:53 141, 154, 162
19:28–40 151
19:38 251
19:43f. 134
19:47f. 162
19:47 137, 155
19:47–20:8 157
19:48 157
20:1 155
20:9 157, 163
20:9–19 157
20:9–18 163
20:16 157
20:16b 157
20:17f. 157
20:18 158
20:19 157
20:19–26 156, 163
20:26 157
21 224
21:5–28 155
21:8 154
21:12 158
21:13 158
21:18 158
21:20 134
21:22 158
21:31 224
21:36 239
21:37f. 137
21:37ff. 155
21:38 157
22:3 149
22:14–27 287
22:14–19 160
22:14 159
22:15f. 158, 160
22:17–19 372
22:18 224
22:19–20 320
22:22 156
22:27 240
22:28 159
22:30 281
22:31 149
22:37 158, 160
22:39 159
22:45 159
22:48 240
22:53 155
23:1–5 156

Luke (cont.)
23:4 156, 163
23:6ff. 156
23:14–16 156
23:14ff. 163
23:19 156
23:22 156, 163
23:25 156
23:34 152, 156, 246, 254
23:35 157
23:39–43 152, 156
23:41 156, 163
23:43 163
23:47 156, 163, 307
23:49 145, 150, 159
23:55f. 145
24 160, 278
24:1–12 159
24:1–53 259, 261
24:4 263
24:6 137, 159
24:11 159, 261
24:13ff. 159
24:13 137
24:13–35 158, 261
24:14 159
24:16 159
24:18 137, 159
24:19 159
24:19–21 159
24:21 31, 141, 278
24:25–27 158, 467
24:26 158, 259
24:26f. 159, 160
24:27 156, 162
24:30 160
24:31 160, 261
24:32 158, 160
24:33 137
24:34 260, 262, 318
24:35 160, 261, 287
24:36–43 160, 261
24:36 261
24:36ff. 277, 318
24:41 125, 160
24:42f. 160, 287
24:44 162
24:44–49 160
24:44ff. 278
24:45–49 473
24:45f. 160
24:47 144, 152, 154, 156, 159, 160, 163, 261, 278
24:48 159
24:48f. 160
24:49 278
24:50f. 279
24:50–53 160, 261
24:51 279
24:52f. 162
24:53 137, 155, 156

John
1:1–18 169, 506, 509
1:1–51 169
1:1 173, 192, 428
1:1–5 171, 172
1:1–4 173
1:1–14 174
1:1ff. 428
1:2 173
1:3 174, 497
1:4 174
1:4ff. 187
1:5 174, 175
1:6–8 171, 172, 174, 175
1:8 175
1:9ff. 174

1:9 175
1:9–12 171
1:9–13 172, 175
1:10–12 198
1:10 174, 175
1:10–13 174
1:11 174, 175
1:12f. 176
1:13 171
1:14–18 171, 172
1:14 176, 177, 178, 179, 191, 438, 440, 442
1:14–17 179
1:15 171, 175, 178
1:16 178
1:16–18 179
1:17–18 171
1:17 173, 178
1:18 178, 179, 439, 441
1:29 372
1:30 175
1:35 244
1:45f. 176
1:45–51 180
1:46 186
1:47ff. 188
2–12 175, 177, 185, 192, 199
2:1–12 180
2:1–12:50 180
2:4 189
2:9 316
2:11 177
2:13–22 180, 183
2:19 289
2:19–22 177
2:19ff. 191
2:22 179, 181, 193
2:23–25 218
3 176, 181, 183, 191, 440
3:16ff. 186, 191, 196, 438, 439
3:16 176, 247, 257, 441
3:16f. 197
3:17 183
3:17f. 186
3:19ff. 186
3:21
3:30 274
3:31ff. 186
4 180, 181, 183
4:6 400
4:7ff. 188
4:20ff. 191
4:43ff. 169
4:46–54 180, 188
4:48–50 218
5 169, 180, 181, 183, 184, 188
5:6f. 214
5:6 218
5:18 181
5:19–24 192
5:21 181
5:22ff. 186
5:27 239
5:30–46 192
5:36 199
5:45–47 185
6 169, 181, 183
6:1 169
6:1–14 180, 215
6:15 22
6:15ff. 215
6:16–21 180
6:26ff. 180
6:35 181
6:42 186
6:66f. 190

7 187
7:2–10 189
7:3 190
7:15 34, 176, 186
7:27 186
7:39 179, 181, 193
7:41 176
7:41f. 186
7:49 34
7:50 188
7:52 176, 186
8 187
8:12 187
8:17 178
8:23 186
8:37 181
8:40 181
8:41f. 186
8:48 176
8:57f. 186
8:59 181
9 178, 180, 181, 188, 218
9:1–41 180
9:1–12 181
9:2f. 181
9:3 181
9:3f. 183
9:4f. 181, 183
9:4 199
9:5 181, 187
9:6f. 182
9:8ff. 184
9:8–12 184
9:8f. 183, 184
9:9–13 187
9:13–17 184
9:14 184
9:15 184
9:16 184
9:18–23 184, 185
9:18 185
9:20 185
9:21 185
9:22 464
9:22f. 185, 186
9:24–34 184
9:24ff. 185
9:24 185
9:25 185
9:26 185
9:27 185
9:28f. 185
9:29 185
9:30 186
9:31–33 186
9:34 181
9:35ff. 186
9:35 186
9:36 186
9:37 186
9:38 186
9:39ff. 186, 187
9:39 187
9:41 187
10:11 181
10:11–18 196
10:34 195
11 180, 181, 183, 187, 188
11:1–44 276
11:4 181
11:6 189
11:9f. 181
11:24–25 461
11:25 181
11:38–44 183
11:47–50 236
12 175, 190, 198
12:1–11 180

12:1–8 148
12:12–19 180
12:16 179, 193
12:23 191, 199
12:23ff. 177
12:27f. 190
12:37–43 179, 191
12:42 185, 464
12:46 187
12:47 186, 191
13–17 183, 199
13 190
13–16 193
13:1–17 196
13:1–21:25 190
13:7 193
13:12–17 440
13:21–30 180
13:34f. 196, 199
13:34 262, 440
13:36–38 190
14 178
14–16 190, 193, 440
14:1–7 192
14:5 188
14:6 176, 181
14:9 179
14:13f. 218
14:16 505
14:22 461
14:27 194
15:1 181
15:1ff. 196
15:6–17 196
15:11 194
15:13 196
15:26 505
16:2 185
16:7–15 193
16:7 505
16:20 194
16:24 194
16:29f. 193
16:31f. 193
16:32 190, 263
16:33 176, 194, 439, 446
17:1–5 192
17:1–8 192
17 179, 190, 440
17:1 191, 192, 193
17:2 191, 192
17:3 191, 192, 194
17:4 192, 199
17:5 191, 192, 196
17:6–19 192, 195
17:6 191, 192, 197
17:6–8 192
17:7 192
17:8 192
17:9–19 195
17:10 193
17:11 193, 195
17:12 192, 193, 197
17:13 193, 194
17:14 192, 194
17:15 194
17:16 194
17:17 194, 195
17:18 195
17:19 195
17:20ff. 191, 193, 195
17:20–23 192
17:21 195
17:22 195
17:23 196
17:24 192, 196
17:24–26 192, 196
17:25f. 196

17:25 197
17:26 197
18–19 250
18:1ff. 190
18:28ff. 188
18:36 230
19:30 199, 254
19:37 447
19:39 188
20 183
20:1–21:25 259, 261
20:17 261
20:19 318
20:21–23 282
20:21 319, 473
20:22 261
20:24 318
20:25 125
20:26–29 265
20:29 178, 183, 195, 199
20:30f. 180, 473
20:31 206
21 168, 169, 183, 260, 262
21:1–14 287
21:3 262
21:20–24 206
21:20–23 461
21:23–24 462
21:23 397
21:24 168

Acts
1–13 301, 303
1 278, 281, 306
1–2 142, 275
1:1 133, 275
1:1–2:47 277
1:1–3 275
1:1–11 277
1:3 277, 278, 282
1:4 137, 278
1:4f. 278
1:5 278, 294
1:6 465
1:6ff. 154
1:6–11 278
1:6–8 278
1:7–8 475
1:8 137, 160, 278, 319, 473
1:9 501
1:9–11 149, 261, 279, 289
1:11 144
1:12–26 279
1:12–14 279
1:13 276
1:15–26 193
1:16–22 280
1:18–19 280
1:18–23 302
1:20 280
1:21–22 280, 352
1:21f. 145
1:21–26 136, 159
1:22 69, 281
1:23–26 280
2 259, 286, 294, 383
2:1ff. 448
2:1–4 282
2:1–13 281
2:1–47 281
2:6–8 282
2:8–11 283
2:11 282
2:12 283
2:13 283
2:14–16 283

2:14 283
2:14–41 472, 474
2:14–42 283
2:14–43 281
2:17–21 212, 283
2:17–22 69
2:17–18 283
2:19–20 283
2:21 283
2:22 158, 284, 471
2:22–24 283
2:23 156, 284
2:24ff. 465, 466, 467
2:24 284
2:25–28 284
2:29–31 284
2:32 284
2:33 284
2:34f. 284
2:36 285
2:37–42 285, 294
2:38 163, 286
2:38f. 163
2:39 285
2:42–47 287
2:42 160
2:43–47 275, 281
2:43 286
2:44f. 286
2:46 155, 160, 478
2:46–3:1 141
2:47 286
3–5 288, 316
3–12 288, 305
3 286
3:1ff. 155
3:1–10 275, 286, 287
3:1–12:25 288
3:1–16 471
3:12 158
3:13 241
3:18 156
3:26 241
4:1 26
4:10 157
4:19 288
4:21 286
4:25–30 241
4:36f. 286
5:1–6 286
5:1–11 275
5:3 149
5:12 210
5:17f. 26
5:20 155
5:26 253
5:29 288
5:33–39 286
5:35ff. 22
5:35–39 466
6:1–7:60 288
6–7 288
6:1 288
6:1–7 148
6:5 288
6:8ff. 474
6:8–15 288
6:11 288
6:13 289
6:13f. 288
6:14 289
7:1–53 289
7:1 289
7:47ff. 289
7:53 289
7:54–8:3 156
7:58f. 253
7:58ff. 289
8:4 289

8:9–24 210
8:32ff. 156
9 290, 304, 318
9:1 156
9:1–9 263
9:15 304
9:18 318
9:26 352
9:32–35 286
9:36–43 286
10:1–8 292
10:1–11:18 163, 291, 297
10:2 292
10:3–6 294
10:9–16 292
10:17 292
10:17–19 292
10:25 293
10:28 293
10:28f. 293
10:30–33 292, 293
10:33 293, 294
10:34–43 293
10:34f. 293
10:37 69
10:38 149, 209, 471, 472
10:39ff. 294
10:42 294
10:44 294
10:45 294
10:46 294
10:47f. 294
11 277
11:1ff. 294
11:1–18 292
11:3 294
11:4–10 294
11:9 276
11:13–15 294
11:14 294
11:15 294
11:16 294
11:17 295
11:18 146, 294
11:19–20 295
11:19–21 289
11:27ff. 437
12 276
12:1ff. 156
12:2 167
13–21 305
13–28 275
13 295, 297, 325
13:1–3 297
13:1–14:28 295
13:1–21:14 295
13:2 414
13:9 352
13:10 149
13:16 158, 297
13:17–41 295, 297
13:33 432
13:43 297
13:44–47 297
13:45 297
13:46–48 158
13 295, 297, 325
14:12f. 43
14:15f. 303
14:15 293, 303
14:15–18 297, 301, 302, 303
14:17 303
15 277, 291, 297, 298, 326, 463
15:1–35 295
15:7–9 295
15:22 421
15:27 421

15:36–18:21 309
15:36–18:22 295
15:36–41 298, 327
16 298
16:1–3 410
16:6 325, 326
16:9 298
16:11–40 344
16:19–40 343
17:1–9 298
17:10–15 323
17:14f. 323
17:16 298
17:16–34 298
17:17 298
17:18 298, 299
17:19 299
17:20f. 299
17:22 40, 299
17:23 299
17:24 300
17:24f. 299
17:24ff. 299
17:25 300
17:26ff. 299
17:26–28 300
17:26 299, 300
17:27 299, 300
17:27f. 300
17:28 299, 300
17:29 300
17:30f. 303
17:30 156, 300, 302
17:31 300, 302
17:32 300
17:33 300
17:34 300
18 298
18:5 323
18:12ff. 309
18:23–21:14 295
18:23 325, 326
18:24 427
18:25 175
19 298, 326
19:1–7 175, 285
19:23ff. 43
19:28–41 343
20:2ff. 340
20:2f. 357
20:22–25 275, 304
20:25 357
20:28–30 408
20:35 205
20:38 275, 304, 357
21–28 304, 345
21 277, 291, 297
21:10ff. 437
21:15–28:31 304
21:17–26 287
21:28 304
21:33 304
21:38 466
22 290, 304
22–28 304, 305
22:3 321
22:4–11 263
22:21 146
23:6 24, 33
23:29 304
24–26 304, 343
24:27 163
25:25 163, 304
26 290, 304
26:9–18 263
26:17 157
26:18 149
26:23 157
26:31f. 163, 304

Acts (cont.)
26:32 307
27 304
27–28 304
27:24 304
28 306, 343, 344, 407
28:14ff. 276
28:25–28 305
28:26f. 157
28:26–28 158
28:28 146
28:30 348
28:30f. 275, 306
28:31 163, 304

Romans
1–3 478
1–11 388, 390
1:1
1:1–7 358
1:1–17 358
1:2–4 358, 392
1:3 236, 321
1:4 465
1:5 319, 351, 358, 381, 391, 393
1:8 67
1:8–15 325, 358
1:10 358
1:16 358, 369
1:16f. 358, 385
1:17 358, 359, 360, 374
1:17f. 360
1:18 303, 360, 361, 365, 374, 376
1:18–3:20 360, 365, 369, 392
1:18–32 363
1:19 366
1:19ff. 369
1:19–20 361
1:20 361
1:21 361
1:22f. 361
1:24 361, 362, 366
1:25 361, 362, 369
1:26 361, 366
1:26–37 361
1:26f. 362
1:26 361, 362, 366
1:29–31 362
1:29ff. 363
2 363, 379
2:1–5 363
2:6ff. 363
2:7 376
2:9–10 363
2:9–11 363
2:11 363
2:12 374
2:12f. 363
2:12–16 363
2:12ff. 363, 369
2:14–15 363
2:16 363
2:17–24 363
2:17ff. 369
2:18 389
2:25–29 363
2:29 364
3:1–8 385
3:1ff. 384
3:1 364, 366, 400
3:2 364
3:3–8 364
3:3f. 385, 392
3:3ff. 385
3:3 364

3:4 364, 373
3:5 364
3:7 364
3:8 364
3:9–20 364
3:9 364, 365, 400
3:10–12 365
3:10–18 365
3:13–18 365
3:19 365
3:19f. 369
3:20 365, 373, 377, 379, 380
3:21ff. 302, 328, 389, 431
3:21–4:25 368, 376
3:21–23 376
3:21–26 392
3:21–31 369, 399
3:21 369
3:22 369
3:22b–23 369
3:23 365
3:23ff. 447
3:24 369, 371
3:24–26 369, 392
3:25 369, 370, 371, 372, 439
3:25b 370
3:26 359, 365, 370, 371, 372
3:27ff. 374, 381
3:31 312, 379
4 330, 372, 374, 375, 376, 381, 419
4:1–25 374
4:3–8 375
4:3 392
4:5 373, 387
4:15 365, 379
4:25 241, 467
5–8 375, 377, 392
5 375, 377, 392
5:1 376
5:1–11 377, 399
5:1–8:39 375
5:1–21 375
5:1–5 375
5:2 377, 392, 402
5:3 377
5:6ff. 256
5:6–11 375
5:6–8 375
5:7 375
5:7f. 373
5:8 247, 257, 375
5:9 376
5:10 376, 402
5:11 376, 377
5:12–21 367, 376, 377
5:12 376
5:13f. 376
5:13 379
5:15–18 376
5:17 377
5:20 365, 379, 387
5:20f. 378
6–8 377
6 264, 350, 367, 377, 378, 383, 389, 392, 399, 401, 420
6:1–23 378
6:1ff. 478
6:1–11 46
6:1 377
6:2 378
6:2f. 378
6:3 378
6:3–11 467
6:6 378

6:9f. 452
6:12 378
6:13 378
6:14 378
6:15 378
6:15ff. 378
7 365, 367, 377, 378, 382, 392
7:1 378
7:1–25 379
7:1–6 379
7:1–3 379
7:4 379, 401, 402
7:7 378, 379, 380, 381
7:7–12 312, 381
7:7–11 312
7:7–25 379, 380, 381, 382
7:8ff. 380
7:8 365
7:9 381
7:10f. 365
7:11 381
7:12 381
7:13ff. 381
7:13 378, 381
7:14ff. 380
7:14 380, 382
7:15a 382
7:18 381
7:21ff. 381
7:21–25 389
7:24 378, 380
8 377, 378, 382, 383, 385, 392, 402
8:1–11 380
8:1–39 382
8:2 383
8:2–4 382
8:3–8 383
8:3 401
8:7 380
8:8 380
8:9 380, 383
8:9–11 383, 389
8:12 380, 389
8:12f. 384
8:15 245, 500
8:16 383
8:18–25 383
8:21 367
8:23 383, 389
8:26f. 383
8:28–30 383
8:28 383
8:31 378
8:34 373
8:35 378, 383
8:35ff. 447
8:35–39 383
8:37 383
8:38 367
8:39 383
9 386
9–11 364, 384, 385, 392
9:1–5 384, 479
9:1–11:36 384
9:1–3 384
9:1ff. 400
9:4f. 384
9:5–26 385
9:5 384
9:6 385
9:6b–13 385
9:14 385
9:18 385
9:19ff. 385
9:20ff. 385
9:22ff. 385
9:25–29 385

9:30ff. 381, 385
9:30–10:4 385
10:1–4 479
10:3ff. 381
10:3 385
10:4 401
10:5–21 386
10:11ff. 474
10:11–21 472
10:14–21 386
10:18–20 386
11 386, 391
11:1 386
11:2–4 386
11:5 386
11:11 386
11:11–32 386
11:17–24 386
11:25–32 474
11:25 386, 475
11:32 387, 388, 389
11:33–36 388
12–15 390
12:1–2 388, 389, 390
12:1–15:13 388, 391, 393
12:1ff. 384
12:1f. 372
12:1 389
12:2 389, 390
12:3–8 346, 357, 390, 402
12:9ff. 357
12:9–13 390
12:14 321
12:14–21 390
12:20 390
13–15 392
13:1–7 390, 421, 423
13:1–5 423
13:8–10 419
13:7 390
13:8ff. 357
13:8–10 390, 419
13:9 321
13:11ff. 390
13:11f. 333, 386
13:11 374
13:11–12 461
13:12 454
13:13 363
14 357, 390
14:1–15:6 334
14:14 321
14:22 389
15:1–3 390
15:4 391
15:5 391
15:6 391
15:7–13 391
15:13 388, 391
15:14–33 391, 393
15:14–16:27 388
15:17 345
15:17–19 357, 474
15:17–29 357
15:18 391
15:22ff. 391
15:23–29 357
15:25 357
15:25–29 317, 340
15:28 357
15:30f. 357
16 391, 393
16:25–27 391
16:26 358

I Corinthians
1–4 332
1 333

1:2 402, 498
1:4–9 325
1:11 332, 333, 340
1:12 427
1:18–25 345, 372, 399
1:18ff. 385
1:22 210
1:23 466
1:23ff. 256
1:24 210
1:25–31 477
1:26–29 54
1:27–29 345
1:30 385
2 333
2:2 321
3 346
3:4ff. 427
3:10–15 337
3:11 403
3:13 389
3:16ff. 404
4:4 373
5 332, 333
5:2 337
5:9 332, 340
5:9f. 334
5:9ff. 194
5:10f. 363
6 332
6:1–8 333
6:8 317
6:9f. 363
6:9–11 333
6:12 131
6:12–20 333, 337, 338
6:19f. 404
7 299, 333
7:1 332, 333, 340
7:1–5 333
7:6f. 333
7:9 333
7:10f. 309, 319, 321, 333
7:10 205, 469
7:12 205, 333
7:15f. 333
7:18f. 331
7:25 205
7:29–31 333
7:31 360, 390
8 333, 334, 335, 337, 338, 390
8:1f. 337
8:1–3 337
8:1–13 309, 332, 354
8:4 335
8:4–6 341
8:5 44, 336
8:5f. 350
8:6 174, 428
8:7 335
8:11 335
9 299, 332, 338
9:1 281, 290, 319, 352
9:8–10 391
9:14 309, 319, 321, 469
10 338, 390
10:1–13 337, 498
10:6 391
10:7 337
10:11 360, 391
10:14–22 334, 336
10:14ff. 498
10:23 131
10:23f. 119
10:23ff. 337
10:29b–30 336
11 338
11:17–34 320, 467

11:17ff. 478
11:23ff. 234
11:23 64, 318, 320
11:23–26 205, 309, 319, 320, 372, 467, 469, 484
11:30 324
12 338, 346, 390, 402, 403, 414, 477, 502
12:3 437
12–14 383
12:4–11 383
12:10 471
12:12f. 402
12:13 403
12:28 403, 437, 468, 471
12:29 471
13 337, 338, 381
13:2 217, 337
13:8 337
13:9 337
13:12f. 337
13:13 310, 354
14 282, 338, 383, 437, 448, 478
15 338, 446, 468
15:1–8 309, 317
15:1 61, 318, 501
15:3f. 205
15:3–5 318, 468, 484
15:3 205, 256, 260, 318, 320, 372, 402, 467
15:3–8 259, 260, 318
15:4 466, 260
15:4ff. 321
15:5 281
15:7 281
15:8 260, 281, 290, 316, 319
15:10 345, 352
15:14 258
15:17 258
15:20–28 324
15:21f. 376
15:23ff. 468
15:25ff. 447
15:32 343, 347
15:33ff. 497
15:35–58 263
15:45ff. 367, 376
15:50 263
15:56 377
15:57 263
16 339
16:1–4 317
16:2 477
16:5f. 340
16:8 339
16:17 333
16:22 333, 461, 468

II Corinthians
1–8 340
1:16 357
1:22 383
1:23 340
2:1 340
2:11 341
2:13 311
2:14–7:4 311
3 311, 340, 341, 391
3:1 311
3:2 312
3:3 312, 313
3:4–6 312
3:6 312
3:7–11 312
3:7 312
3:7–18 451

3:12–18 309, 311
3:14 312, 313
3:15 312
3:16 312, 342
3:17 313, 383
3:17f. 313
3:18 313
4:1–15 309, 340
4:1 341
4:2 341
4:3f. 341
4:4 341
4:5 341, 342
4:6 341, 451
4:7 341
4:8 341
4:8f. 341
4:10f. 342
4:11 342
4:13 342
4:14 342
4:15 342
5:5 383
5:10 374
5:16 318
5:16ff. 372
5:16–21 384, 399, 401
5:17 376, 401
5:18ff. 376
5:21 467, 372, 402
6:14–7:1 340
6:16 404
7:5 311
7:6f. 340
7:8 340
8 317, 340, 357
8:9 256
9 317, 340, 357
9:1 340
10 339
10–12 342
10–13 340
10:10 354
11 339, 341
11:5 311, 342, 345
11:15–29 127
11:21ff. 345
11:22 339
11:23 343
11:23f. 347
11:23–29 352
11:26 320
12:1ff. 127
12:5 342
12:7 380
12:9 342, 345
12:11 342
12:12 210, 471
12:14 340
12:20f. 363
13:1 321, 340
13:3a 498

Galatians
1 463
1:1–2:10 309, 313
1:1–2:21 480
1:1 315, 316
1:3–5 315
1:4 367
1:6–9 315, 327
1:10 315, 316
1:11ff. 316
1:11–17 290
1:11–24 289
1:12 318
1:13 474
1:13–17 316

1:14 365, 382
1:15ff. 304
1:15 316, 319
1:16 317, 319
1:17 310, 317
1:18–2:10 316
1:18f. 316
1:18 313, 316
1:19 316, 321
1:20 463
1:22–24 352
2 335, 338, 463
2:1–10 325
2:1 313
2:2 317
2:4 316
2:5 316
2:6 316
2:7 317
2:7–10 317
2:9 316, 321
2:10 317
2:11ff. 291, 316, 317, 326
2:11–13 327
2:11–21 309, 354, 357, 463
2:14–21 399
2:14ff. 327
2:14 327, 328
2:15–17 328
2:15 328, 329, 363, 366
2:16 328
2:17 329
2:18 329
2:19 329
2:20 329, 402, 447
2:21 329, 331
3 330, 374, 419
3:1 321, 384
3:1–5:12 315
3:3 330, 331, 380
3:6–18 330
3:11 360, 373
3:13 372, 401, 402, 467
3:16–19 330
3:21 330
3:22 387
3:23 330
3:26ff. 331
3:27 478
3:28 329
3:29 33
4–5 378
4 330
4:1ff. 351
4:3 341, 349
4:4 321
4:6 245, 500
4:8 349
4:9
4:12–20 331
4:13 326
4:21–31 331
5 330
5:1
5:1ff. 327, 331
5:2 331
5:3 327
5:3f. 331
5:4 331
5:5
5:6 331, 419
5:13 331, 478
5:14 331, 419
5:19ff. 363, 384
5:22 384
5:22f. 383
5:25 383
6 330

Galatians (cont.)
6:1   383
6:11ff.   327
6:11–16   331
6:12   331
6:12f.   380
6:15   331

Ephesians
1   399
1:1   397
1:1–2   398
1:3–23   399
1:15–23   399
1:22   402
1:22f.   399, 403, 404
2   404
2:1–10   399
2:3–7   399
2:8f.   399
2:10   399
2:11–16   401
2:11–12   400
2:11–22   395, 399, 404, 456
2:11   399, 402
2:11f.   402
2:12   400
2:13   400, 401
2:14–16   401
2:14   400
2:15   401
2:16   400, 401, 402, 403
2:17f.   402
2:17   402
2:18   402
2:19   402, 403
2:20–22   401, 402, 403
2:20   403, 437
2:21   403
2:22   403
3   404
3:1   342, 397, 399
3:4   404
3:5   403
3:6   404
3:9   404
3:10   404
4:1   342, 397
4:1–16   404
4:8–10   452
4:12f.   405
4:12   403
4:13   403
4:15   403
4:16   403
4:17   399
4:22f.   401
4:25–6:20   418
4:31   363
5:3ff.   363
5:21–33   398, 404
5:31f.   405
6:10–20   404
6:21–24   398

Philippians
1:1   344
1:1–3:1   344
1:4   347
1:7   344
1:12–18   342
1:12–26   309, 344
1:12   345
1:13   344, 345
1:15–18   345
1:18   346, 347

1:19   346, 347
1:20   346
1:21ff.   343
1:21   346
1:22–25   346
1:22   346
1:23   346
1:24   346
1:25f.   346
1:27ff.   347
2:1–11   347
2:5–11   347, 390
2:6–11   171, 347, 420
2:6f.   174
2:8   256
2:10f.   447
3   344, 347
3:1ff.   408
3:2–4:1   344
3:4–6   365, 380
3:4   380
3:4–11   381
3:4ff.   381
3:5   362
3:7   384
4:2–9   344
4:10–20   344
4:14ff.   347
4:14–20   347
4:15   344
4:21–23   344

Colossians
1:7   343, 348
1:15f.   174
1:15–20   171
1:15–17   350
1:18   350, 446
2:1   463
2:6–15   349
2:8   341, 349
2:8–15   309, 348, 349
2:10   350
2:11   350
2:11ff.   350
2:11–15   399
2:12   350
2:13   350
2:14   340
2:15   350
2:16–4:6   351
2:16–23   249, 351
2:16ff.   349
2:18   350, 380
2:20   349, 351
2:20ff.   349
2:23   351
3:1–4:6   351
3:1ff.   351
3:2   351
3:3   351
3:4   351
3:5   351, 363
3:5–4:5   418
3:8   363
3:16   477
4:7–9   343
4:9   343
4:10   62, 342
4:12   343
4:12f.   348
4:14   133
4:16   486

I Thessalonians
1:1   323, 421
1:2–10   323

1:9–10   302
1:10   324
2:16   323
2:17–3:10   323
2:17–20   323
3:1   303
3:1ff.   323
3:1–10   323
3:6   323
3:11–13   323
4:1–12   418
4:1   323
4:4f.   323
4:9f.   323
4:11f.   323
4:13   322
4:13–5:11   309, 323, 324, 354
4:13–18   324, 333, 390, 468
4:13–5:22   457
4:14ff.   360
4:15–18   468
4:15   324, 461
4:16   324
4:17   324
4:18   324
5:1–11   324
5:2f.   324
5:2   324
5:2–4   325
5:5   325
5:6ff.   325
5:8   325
5:9   325
5:11   324
5:12–12   323
5:19–22   437

II Thessalonians
1:1   421
2   438
2:1   323
2:1ff.   323
2:1–11   324
2:1–12   323
2:1–17   468
2:3–12   468
2:6   390
3:14f.   323
3:17   323

I Timothy
1:3   406
1:3–7   408
1:9f.   363
1:15   413
2:1–2   390
2:1–6   413
2:1f.   423
3   410
3:1   413
3:1–13   407
3:9   407, 484
3:16   171, 465, 484
4:1–5   411
4:1–16   395, 408, 456
4:1   407, 408, 437
4:2   408
4:3–5   408, 437
4:3   408, 409
4:4   409
4:4f.   409
4:6–10   410
4:6   410, 414, 484
4:6b   410
4:7a   413

4:7   411
4:7b–10   413
4:8   413
4:8b   413
4:9   413
4:10   413
4:11–16   410
4:11   414
4:12–16   414
4:12f.   414
4:12   414
4:13   414
4:13–16   414
4:14   407, 410, 414
4:15f.   414
4:16   414
5:1–6:2   410
5:3–5   478
6:3ff.   411
6:20   408

II Timothy
1:15–18   406
2:11   413
3:2–5   363
4:6–18   407
4:7   407
4:11   62, 133
4:16f.   407

Titus
1:5   406
3:1   390
3:8   413

Philemon
1   342
10   343
23   342, 343
24   62, 133

Hebrews
1   429
1:2f.   174
1:2   428
1:3   430
1:3f.   428
1:4ff.   428
1:5   432
2   429
2:1–4   428
2:3   429
2:5–9   428
2:9   432
2:10   432
2:11   432
2:12–14   428
2:14   430, 432
2:14ff.   432
2:17f.   432
3:6–4:3   429
3:6–4:13   428
3:16   428
4:12   451
4:14f.   430
4:14   429, 430
4:14–5:10   395, 428, 456
4:14ff.   429
4:14–16   430
4:15f.   430
4:15   430, 431
4:16   430, 431
5:1   431
5:1–10   431
5:1–4   431

5:2 431, 432
5:3 431
5:4 431, 433
5:5–10 431, 432
5:5 432
5:6 432, 433
5:7–9 432
5:7 432
5:8 432, 456
5:9 432
5:10 433
5:11–6:2 302
5:11–6:12 429
6:13–20 431
6:19–20 433
7–10 429, 433
7:1–10 433
8:1ff. 433
8:5 433
9:5 370
9:24 433
9:25–10:10 434
10 432
10:19ff. 434
10:19–12:29 429
10:26–31 434
10:32–39 434, 456
11 429, 434
11:13 423
12 434
12:2f. 434
12:4 456
13 421, 426, 434
13:1–8 418
13:1–18 434
13:20f. 421, 434
13:20 467
13:22–25 426, 434
13:24 427

James
1:1 415
1:27 419
2:1 415
2:8 419
2:12f. 419
2:14–26 395, 415, 416, 418, 456
2:14–17 418
2:18 419
2:19 419
2:20 419
2:21ff. 419
2:21–24 419
2:24 419
5:1–6 416
5:12 416
5:13–18 478

I Peter
1:1 415
1:1–2 421
1:3–9 425
1:6 424, 425
1:13–2:10 422
1:18f. 421
2:4ff. 404
2:4–10 422
2:9 447
2:9f. 477
2:11–4:11 422
2:11–12 423

2:11–25 395, 422, 456
2:12 423
2:13–17 390, 423, 425
2:13 422, 423
2:14 423
2:14ff. 421
2:16 424
2:17 423, 424
2:18 422, 424
2:18–25 424, 425
2:19 424
2:20 424
2:21 390
2:21–25 241, 424
2:22ff. 421, 424
2:24 372, 421
3:1 422
3:1–6 426
3:7 426
3:8–12 426
3:14 425
3:16 421
3:17 425
3:18–22 452
3:18 257, 425
3:18ff. 465
3:19 423
3:21 422
4:6 423, 452
4:7 423
4:11 421
4:12 421, 425
4:12f. 421
4:12–5:11 422
4:12ff. 424
4:13 425
4:14 425
4:16 425
5:1 421
5:9f. 424
5:10 421, 425
5:12–14 421
5:12 421
5:13 62, 421
5:14 421

II Peter
3:3 408
3:3–10 461
3:10 324
3:15–17 416, 420
3:16 486

I John
1:1ff. 178
2:2 372
2:8 439
2:12ff. 435
2:15–17 437
2:18 408, 438
2:18–25 438
2:21–23 484
2:26 435
3:11–18 418
3:11ff. 196
3:15–18 196
4 436, 440, 457
4:1ff. 440
4:1–3 469, 484
4:1–6 436
4:1–21 395, 436
4:1 436, 437, 439

4:2 437, 440
4:2f. 437
4:3ff. 439
4:3 437, 438, 439
4:4 438, 439
4:4f. 437
4:4ff. 438
4:5 438, 440
4:6 436, 437, 439, 440
4:7 440
4:7ff. 441
4:7–12 439
4:7–21 196
4:8 196, 439
4:9f. 196
4:9 439, 441
4:10 439
4:11 439
4:12 439, 441
4:13 439, 441
4:14 438, 439, 441
4:15 439, 484
4:15f. 441
4:16 196
4:17 440
4:18 440
4:19 440
4:20f. 440
4:21 440, 441
5:4 446
5:13 435

II John
7 438

III John
9 436

Jude
3 484
18 408

Revelation
1:1–20 395, 443
1:1 442, 443, 444
1:1–3 437, 443
1:1–3:21 480
1–3 469
1 441, 443
1:2 443, 446
1:3 443
1:4 444
1:4ff. 444
1:4–7 447
1:5 446
1:5b–7 447
1:5b 447
1:6 447
1:7 447, 461
1:8 447
1:9 441, 448
1:9–11 448
1:10 448
1:11 444, 448, 449
1:11–20 448
1:12ff. 444
1:12 449, 450
1:13 449, 450
1:16 450, 451
1:17ff. 450

1:17–20 451
1:17 451, 452
1:17b–18 452
1:18 452
1:19 452
1:20 450, 452
2–3 446, 447, 448, 450, 452
2:10 441
2:13 441, 446
2:26 446
3:3 324
4–18 447
4 452
5 452
5:6 446
6 453
6:9 448
6:9–11 441
7 453
7:1–8 453
7:9–17 453
7:14 448
8 453
9 453
10–13 453
10 453
10:34f. 448
11 447, 453
11:3–7 446
11:15 461
11:15–19 453
12 447, 453
12:4 448
12:9 454
13 441, 447, 453
13:1–15 454
13:4–10 442
13:12 442
13:15 442
14ff. 453
14:1–5 453
14:12f. 441
14:14 450
14:14–20 453
15–18 453
16:15 324
17 441, 453
17:6 441, 446
17:9ff. 441
17:10 442
18 421, 453
18:20 441
18:24 454
19ff. 447
19 454
19:6 446
20 454
20:1–3 223
20:4 448
21 448
21:1–8 225, 327
21:1–22:5 454
21:5 457
21:14 441
22:6 442, 443
22:6ff. 443
22:8 443
22:10 461
22:12 461
22:13 447
22:16 443
22:18f. 437
22:20 444, 461, 468

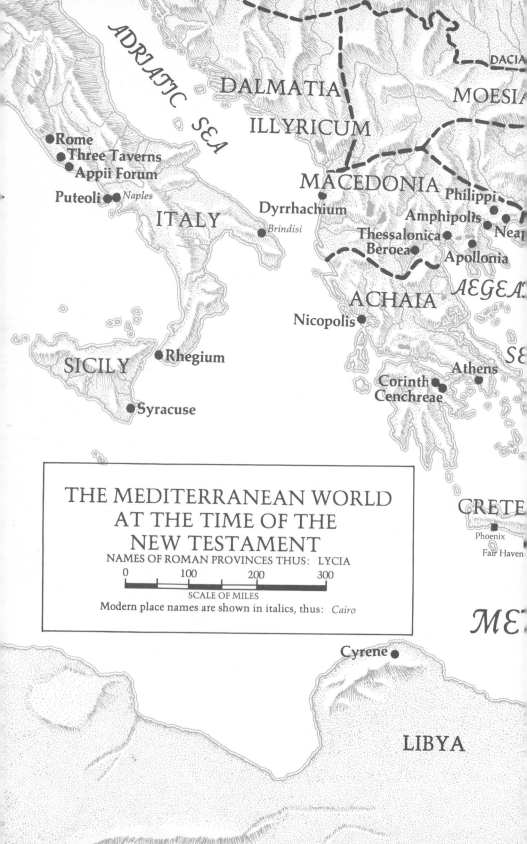

THE MEDITERRANEAN WORLD
AT THE TIME OF THE
NEW TESTAMENT

NAMES OF ROMAN PROVINCES THUS: LYCIA

0   100   200   300

SCALE OF MILES

Modern place names are shown in italics, thus: *Cairo*